Management Accounting

Wayne J. Morse
Clarkson College

James R. Davis
Clemson University

Al L. Hartgraves
Emory University

Addison-Wesley Publishing Company
Reading, Massachusetts · Menlo Park, California
London · Amsterdam · Don Mills, Ontario · Sydney

Management Accounting

Sponsoring Editor:	*Frank Burns*
Production Manager:	*Karen M. Guardino*
Production Editor:	*Doris L. Machado*
Text Designer:	*Marie E. McAdam*
Illustrator:	*Jay's Publishing Service, Inc.*
Cover Designer:	*Hannus Design Associates, Richard Hannus*
Cover Photographer:	*Al Giese*
Art Coordinator:	*Susanah H. Michener*
Copy Editor:	*Robert E. Fiske*
Manufacturing Supervisor:	*Hugh J. Crawford*

Material from the *Certificate in Management Accounting Examinations,* copyright © 1972 through 1981 by the National Association of Accountants, is reprinted (or adapted) with permission.

Material from *Uniform CPA Examination Questions and Answers,* copyright © 1964 through 1982 by the American Institute of Certified Public Accountants, Inc., is reprinted (or adapted) with permission.

Material from the *1978 Certified Internal Auditor Examination,* by The Institute of Internal Auditors, Inc., Altamonte Springs, Florida, is reprinted with permission.

Library of Congress Cataloging in Publication Data

Morse, Wayne J.
   Management accounting.

   Includes index.
   1. Managerial accounting. I. Davis, James
Richard, 1947–   . II. Hartgraves, Al L.
III. Title.
HF5635.M864   1984   658.1'511   83–6397
ISBN 0–201–15870–1

ABCDEFGHIJ-HA-8987654

Preface

This book is concerned with the development and use of accounting information within specific organizations for the purposes of planning, control, and the analysis of special decisions. The topics discussed are important to all students of business and management regardless of their career objectives. While *Management Accounting* is intended for use by students who have had previous exposure to financial accounting, the amount of financial accounting background required is a function of the material selected from this text. In the typical situation, where students have completed a course in financial accounting, any or all material may be used. Even if students in a professional development program or in an accelerated survey course have not been exposed to journal entries, all but Chapters 11 and 12 on product costing and cost allocation may be used. The flow of product costs are introduced and illustrated in Chapter 2 with the aid of diagrams rather than journal entries.

GOALS OF THE TEXT

The authors and Addison-Wesley Publishing Company have attempted to make this book **relevant, flexible, clear,** and **accurate.** The text is relevant to the educational objectives of students of business and management. The book is flexible so that it may be compatible with the backgrounds of different students, the curricula of different institutions, and the course objectives of different instructors. Extensive efforts have been made to make the text clear and accurate in order to maximize the student's knowledge and understanding of management accounting while minimizing the time required of the instructor to explain material contained in the text. The instructor is thereby freed to provide additional enrichment or assistance, depending on the needs of individual students. Actions taken to meet these four goals are outlined below:

Relevant

- Emphasis is on accounting information as a management tool rather than as an end. Topics in management accounting are related to the functions of management.
- The book deals with the use of management accounting in merchandising, service, manufacturing, not-for-profit, and government organizations.
- Considerable attention is given to how standards are developed and to the interpretation of standard cost variances.
- The text includes a major, optional, appendix on budgeting in not-for-profit organizations.
- The use of quantitative models as decision aids and the need to develop relevant cost data for use in such models are clearly illustrated, in a nontechnical manner, in an optional chapter.
- The impact of taxes on a wide variety of management decisions is clearly illustrated and discussed in an optional chapter. This chapter may be of particular value to students not planning to enroll in a tax course.
- Financial statement analysis and the statement of changes in financial position are presented in a manner that emphasizes their relevance to internal planning and control.
- The impact of changing prices on the use of managerial accounting data for internal planning and control is thoroughly discussed in an optional chapter. This chapter includes a thorough presentation of capital budgeting in an inflationary environment.

Flexible

- Once the first three chapters are covered, the remaining material can be sequenced in a variety of ways.

- The material can be packaged into a concise short course or a full semester, with the instructor still being able to select from an abundance of material.
- A wide variety of assignment material allows the instructor to adopt the text to a variety of teaching styles, program emphasis, and time constraints.
- The text contains nearly 700 questions, exercises, and problems for class use or homework assignment.
- Numerous representative problems have been adapted from professional examinations.
- Redundant assignment material makes it possible for the instructor to vary similar assignments between sections and subsequent course offerings.
- Numerous appendixes lend flexibility to coverage of material allowing the instructor to select the most appropriate depth of coverage.
- The mechanics of product costing are placed in optional chapters, which may be emphasized, surveyed, or omitted.
- Alternative sequencing of material can provide a product-costing emphasis, a planning-and-control-emphasis, or a broad survey.
- Case type problem material can be used to promote a discussion of issues raised in other chapters, or even other courses, at the discretion of the instructor.

Clear

- An outline presented at the start of each chapter provides an orientation to the chapter material and its structure.
- The purpose or primary learning objective of each chapter is clearly stated and highlighted in the introduction to each chapter.
- The writing style is direct and important relationships are always expressed in words.
- A two-color format with wide margins in which to write notes and the generous use of topical headings and subheadings promote readability and learning.
- Multicolor illustrations emphasize key points.
- Key terms are highlighted when first introduced, listed at the end of each chapter, and defined in a glossary at the back of the book.
- A summary at the end of each chapter reiterates key points contained in the chapter.
- Review questions at the end of each chapter ask the student to recall basic concepts presented in the chapter. The questions are sequenced in the order in which topics are introduced in the chapter.

- The end-of-chapter exercises reinforce the student's knowledge of technical material contained in the accompanying chapter. Exercises are generally short and sequenced in the order in which topics are introduced in the accompanying chapter.

- The end-of-chapter problems provide detailed assignments related to the material presented in the accompanying chapter. However, there are some case problems and technical problems that may raise several issues or reinforce subjects covered in previous chapters. These problems frequently come from professional examinations and they often contain hints to point the student in the right direction.

- The topical coverage of each exercise and problem is clearly identified in a boldfaced heading.

- Assignment materials based on chapter appendixes are clearly identified with boldfaced headings.

Accurate

- All text and instructor's manual materials, including the questions, exercises, and problems, have been prepared, reviewed, revised, and proofread by the authors.

- Developmental and marketing reviews by instructors at other institutions guided the authors in the preparation and revision of the text, and helped fine tune the finished product.

- Text and assignment materials have been classroom tested.

- The accuracy of examples, exercises, problems, and solutions have been verified by instructors at other institutions who reviewed all calculations contained in the textbook and independently solved all assignment material.

SUPPLEMENTS

A variety of supplementary materials accompany the text.

- The instructor's manual contains alternative course outlines, suggested problem assignments, check figures, solutions to all assignment material, and an evaluation of all assignment material as to level of difficulty and estimated completion time.

- A separate student study guide, prepared by Al Hartgraves, reemphasizes and reinforces basic concepts.

- A separate test bank, prepared by Al Hartgraves, is available in hardcopy or from Addison-Wesley's computerized testing service.

- Transparencies for the solutions of selected exercises and problems are available.

- Check list of key figures for solutions are available in quantity.

ORGANIZATION AND COURSE OUTLINES

The text is divided into four parts. It is likely that most instructors will cover most or all of the material in Part I, Essential Elements of Management Accounting, and Part II, Planning and Control. Part III, Product Costing and Cost Allocation, focuses on a set of topics some instructors may wish to emphasize while others may desire to omit or defer to a subsequent cost accounting course. Part IV, Selected Topics for Further Study, contains a variety of topics which may be chosen by the instructor to achieve particular course objectives. The following course outlines are intended to illustrate some of the alternative ways of sequencing text material. Detailed outlines are contained in the instructor's manual.

Alternative Assignment Schedules: Product Costing Emphasis

Chapter	Title
1.	Accounting and Management
2.	Cost Concepts
3.	Cost Behavior
11.	Product Costing
*11	Appendix A: Normal Factory Overhead Accounting
12.	The Assignment of Common Costs
*12	Appendix: Joint Products and By-products
4.	Cost-Volume-Profit Analysis
*5.	Relevant Costs for Management Action
6.	Operating Budgets
7.	Responsibility Accounting and Flexible Budgets
8.	Performance Evaluation of Standard Cost Centers
8	Appendix: A Closer Look at Fixed Overhead Variances
*11	Appendix B: Product Costing Using Standard Costs
*9.	Control of Decentralized Operations
*10.	Inventory Valuation and Approaches to Segment Reporting†
*14.	Capital Expenditures

* May be deleted on the basis of time constraints.

† Coverage of Chapter 10 may be limited to Absorption and Variable Costing.

Alternative Assignment Schedules: Planning and Control Emphasis	Chapter	Title
	1.	Accounting and Management
	2.	Cost Concepts
	3.	Cost Behavior
	4.	Cost-Volume-Profit Analysis
	5.	Relevant Costs for Management Action
	*13.	Relevant Costs for Quantitative Models
	6.	Operating Budgets
	*6	Appendix: Budgeting in Not-for-Profit Organizations
	7.	Responsibility Accounting and Flexible Budgets
	8.	Performance Evaluation of Standard Cost Centers
	9.	Control of Decentralized Operations
	10.	Inventory Valuation and Approaches to Segment Reporting
	*14.	Capital Budgeting
	*15.	The Impact of Taxes on Capital Budgeting and Management Decisions†
	*16.	Financial Statement Analysis and the Statement of Changes in Financial Position§
	*17.	The Impact of Changing Prices

ACKNOWLEDGMENTS

Management Accounting could not have been completed without the generous cooperation, assistance, and support of numerous individuals and organizations. We are especially grateful to the following professors whose insight, comments, and suggestions made a significant contribution to the quality of this text:

Ronnie J. Burrows (University of Dayton)
Charles Caldwell (University of South Carolina)
Richard Chesley (Dalhousie University)
Charles Davis (University of Wisconsin, Madison)

---

* May be deleted on the basis of time constraints.

† The coverage of Chapter 15 may be limited to the impact of taxes on capital budgeting.

§ The coverage of Chapter 16 may be limited to Financial Statement Analysis.

Ray Dillon (Georgia State University)
James B. Edwards (University of South Carolina)
Jeff Gillespie (University of Delaware)
Douglas A. Johnson (Arizona State University)
Arthur L. LaPorte (Salem State College)
Daren Lewis (St. Bonaventure University)
John Marquardt (University of Michigan, Flint)
Harold Roth (University of Tennessee, Knoxville)
Larzette Hale (Utah State University)
John Waterhouse (University of Alberta)

Appreciation is extended to the Institute of Management Accounting of the National Association of Accountants for permission to use adaptations of problem materials from past Certificate in Management Accounting (CMA) examinations, these materials are identified as "CMA adapted." We are also greatful to the American Institute of Certified Public Accountants and the Institute for Internal Auditors for permission to use adaptations of materials from their professional examinations, these materials are identified as "CPA adapted" or "IIA adapted."

Comments or suggestions from users are most welcome.

Potsdam, NY   W.J.M.
Clemson, SC   J.R.D.
Atlanta, GA   A.L.H.
November 1983

Contents

7 *Responsibility Accounting and Flexible Budgets*   **251**

8 *Performance Evaluation of Standard Cost Centers*   **291**

14 *Capital Expenditures* **567**

15 *Impact of Taxes on Capital Budgeting and Other Management Decisions* **597**

Management Accounting

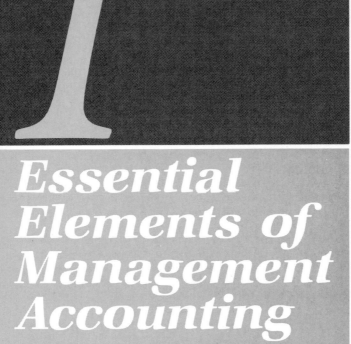

I

Essential Elements of Management Accounting

1

Accounting and Management

An **organization** is a group of people united to achieve a common goal. As students, instructors, employees, citizens, relatives, sports players, and, perhaps, volunteers, we are members of a variety of organizations. The members who direct the affairs of an organization are identified as managers. In the process of performing their duties, managers utilize many kinds of information, including that provided by management accounting.

The purpose of this chapter is to provide an overview of **management accounting,** which is concerned with providing accounting information to managers and other persons inside specific organizations. Because management accounting is concerned with providing information to managers, we begin by discussing some important characteristics of organizations and the functions of management. We then describe how managers use accounting terms, relationships, and information in performing their duties. We will also consider the duties of accountants and the relationships that exist among managers, accountants, and other information specialists.

Accounting is broadly classified into financial accounting and management accounting. This classification is based on differences in the relationship between the organization and the person or persons to whom information is supplied. To provide an orientation to the study of management accounting, we will carefully distinguish between these two types of accounting. We conclude this chapter by summarizing why managers and management accountants must have a thorough understanding of management accounting.

ORGANIZATIONS AND THEIR GOALS

Organizations vary widely in their goals. Whereas the goal of a college or university is to provide educational services, the goal of a department store or a steel company is to earn a profit by providing customers with goods, and the goal of the Red Cross is to provide humanitarian service. An organization is likely to have several goals. The local department store, for example, which has profit and providing customers with consumer goods as goals, may also support cultural activities and local charities with the goal of being regarded as good community citizens.

We frequently distinguish between organizations on the basis of profit motive. **For-profit organizations** have profit as a primary goal, and **not-for-profit organizations** do not have profit as a goal. Clearly, the General Electric Company is a for-profit organization, whereas the City of New York and the Red Cross are not-for-profit organizations.[1] Regardless of the

---

[1] The term *nonprofit* is frequently used to refer to what we have identified as *not-for-profit* organizations. We avoid this term because it can be confused with a *non-profit* (i.e., zero or negative profit) situation.

presence or absence of a profit motive, an organization should use resources efficiently in accomplishing its goals. Every dollar that the Salvation Army spends on fuel is a dollar that cannot be used to feed the indigent. Private not-for-profit organizations (such as colleges) and government units (such as cities) can go bankrupt if they are unable to meet their financial obligations. The common need to utilize resources efficiently indicates the existence of a common need for a good accounting system that will help management plan, organize, and control the use of the organization's limited resources.

FUNCTIONS OF MANAGEMENT

Smooth functioning organizations do not just happen. They are a result of the actions of the managers who are responsible for their operation. Management entails planning, organizing, and controlling. In all but the smallest organizations, the manager's job is to get things done through people. The manager of the local department store does not order goods, stock shelves, place advertising, operate the cash register, drive the delivery truck, or record accounting transactions. The manager assigns these tasks to other people (organizing) and ensures that they are properly completed (controlling). More fundamental, the manager has to decide what tasks are needed and how they should be accomplished (planning).

Planning

Planning, which is the formulation of a scheme or program for the accomplishment of a specific purpose or goal, consists of two basic activities: (1) setting goals and (2) selecting a way to accomplish these goals. A distinction is often made between long-range planning and short-range planning. Long-range planning emphasizes the selection of goals the organization hopes to achieve over several years and the selection of programs that will enable the organization to achieve these goals. Short-range planning is based on the organization's long-range plan as well as its current situation and focuses on specific activities to be taken in the near term to move the organization from its current situation to its long-range goals. Short-range planning involves both the interpretation of long-range goals into performance objectives for the coming year and the selection of specific actions to achieve these objectives. The following example illustrates the difference between long-range and short-range plans.

Good Department Stores currently operates three stores in the suburbs of a large metropolitan area. Professional people, such as engineers, scientists, doctors, lawyers, and managers, live in this market area. Good's long-range plans are to achieve the highest annual dollar sales volume of all suburban department stores in the market area and to provide their investors with an acceptable level of earnings. Important elements of this plan include: the opening of one new store during each of the next five years, a reorientation of merchandise lines toward goods likely to be purchased by professional people, and increased support of cultural activities. Good's short-range plans for the coming year call for the hiring of personnel and the acquisition of merchandise for one new store currently under construction. Discontinuing the sale of hardware, expanding the offerings of furniture and women's business apparel, adding an art department, and starting a Good Summer Concert Series are also among management's plans. Management believes these activities will produce a 40 percent increase in sales revenue and a 35 percent increase in after-tax profits during the coming year.

Good's short-range plans are made in the light of its long-range plans. Care is taken to ensure that the short-range plans support the long-range goals. Short-range goals are more specific than long-range goals; they have to be, since they are statements of what management hopes to accomplish next year.

Organizing

Through **organizing,** the process of making the organization into a well-ordered whole, management attempts to structure and divide the tasks that need to be done. Specific people are assigned specific tasks. Within a formal structure established to show the relationships between organization members, authority is delegated to managers and other employees who are subsequently held accountable for the activities they control.

An **organization chart** illustrates the formal set of relationships that exists among the elements of an organization. An organization chart for Good Department Stores is shown in Exhibit 1–1. The blocks represent organizational units, and the lines represent the relationships between organizational units. Top management delegates authority, which flows down the organization, to use resources for limited purposes to subordinate managers who, in turn, delegate more limited authority to accomplish more structured tasks to their subordinates. Responsibility increases as one moves up the organization. People at the bottom of the chart are responsible for specific tasks, but the president (chairman, agency head) is responsible for the operation of the entire organization.

Following the formal sequence of authority and responsibility (sometimes referred to as the chain of command), a problem in the Appliance Department of the Eastside Store is first brought to the attention of the Store Manager and then to the Vice President of Operations by the Store Manager. Normally, the head of the Appliance Department does not take the problem directly to the attention of a manager two or more levels above him or her, since this action violates the chain of command.

A distinction is made between line and staff managers. Line managers are directly responsible for the activities that create and distribute the goods and services of the organization. They exercise authority over all

EXHIBIT 1–1   Good Department Stores Organization Chart

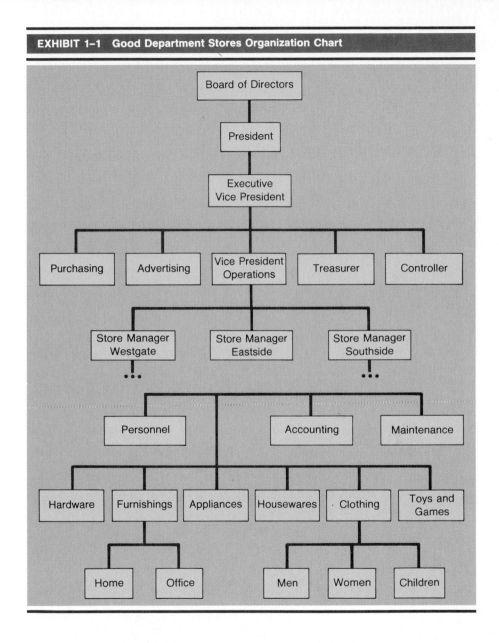

the other managers and employees below them on the organization chart. Staff managers, on the other hand, exercise authority over only the employees in their own departments. Staff departments exist to help facilitate line activities. Although staff members often advise line managers, they do not exercise authority over them. In Exhibit 1–1 we see that Good Department Stores has two levels of staff organizations, corporate and store. The corporate staff units are Purchasing, Advertising, Treasurer, and Controller. Staff departments at the store level are Personnel, Accounting, and Maintenance. All other units are line departments. Note that a change in plans can necessitate a change in the organization. For example, Good's plan to discontinue the sale of hardware and add an art department during the coming year will necessitate an organizational change.

In addition to the formal relationships specified in the organization chart, many informal relationships develop between individuals and organizational units. Such relationships can become so important that the organization cannot function without them. Many times knowledgeable and persuasive individuals exert an influence on the organization far in excess of what their formal position would suggest; this is especially true in the case of staff members who are experts in a specialized area and offer advice concerning that area to line managers.

Controlling

Controlling is the process of ensuring that results agree with plans. In the process of controlling operations, management compares actual performance with plans. If actual results deviate significantly from plans, manage-

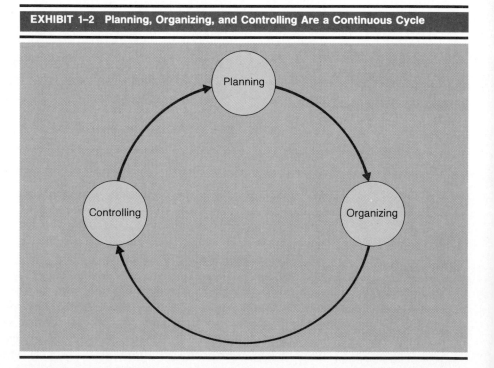

EXHIBIT 1–2   Planning, Organizing, and Controlling Are a Continuous Cycle

ment either will attempt to bring operations into line with the original plan or will adjust the plan. The original plan will be adjusted if management determines that it is no longer appropriate because of changed circumstances. Hence, the process of controlling feeds back into the process of planning to form a continuous cycle. This cycle is best illustrated in Exhibit 1–2.

ACCOUNTING AS A MANAGEMENT TOOL

Managers make extensive use of accounting in the performance of their functions. This is true regardless of the nature of their business. Accounting information is important in managing a volunteer fire department, a religious organization, the city of Chicago, and General Motors. There are two basic reasons for this: (1) accounting terms are the language of business, and (2) accounting relationships serve as a model of the firm.

Accounting Terms Are the Language of Business

Accounting terms are an important part of every manager's vocabulary. Because financial data provide a common denominator for measuring and summarizing widely diverse activities, accounting terms are a basic means of communication within and between organizations. The need to summarize widely diverse activities becomes increasingly important as we move up the organization chart. Good's President would be overwhelmed by detailed information on the unit sales of specific items in individual stores, but the sales of Good Department Stores are easily understood when they are summarized in terms of dollars of sales revenue. Note, however, that the manager of the Home Furnishing Department in a particular store would want detailed unit sales information. Dollars also provide a convenient measure of effectiveness in for-profit organizations. By looking at the bottom line of the income statement, a manager can immediately determine if the organization met its profit goal for the period.

Accounting Relationships Serve as a Model

A **model** is a simplified representation of some real-world phenomenon. Managers study models to obtain an understanding of the related real-world phenomenon, and they use models to predict the impact of a proposed action. A proper understanding and use of models leads to better decisions. Because the accounting system used to classify and summarize data reported in general purpose financial statements touches every area of activity within an organization, accounting relationships serve as a model of the organization.

An understanding of the organization's accounting system helps the manager understand the organization and the interrelationships that exist within it. The statement of financial position (balance sheet) serves as an economic picture of the organization at a particular moment. The income statement summarizes the economic activity of the organization during a period of time. An understanding of these and other accounting reports also helps the manager understand the organization. These statements are particularly valuable in planning; for example, a manager who is familiar with the income statement can use it to quickly predict the probable impact of a proposed action on net income.

Accounting Information Assists in Planning, Organizing, and Controlling

Accounting relationships are used extensively in planning, organizing, and controlling activities. These relationships provide the framework used to develop the budget for the coming year. A **budget** is a formal plan of action expressed in monetary terms. An organization's budget for the coming year includes projected financial statements and detailed schedules indicating the financial consequences of all expected activities. In budgeting the same accounting relationships that are used to report the financial implications of transactions after they have occurred are also used to predict the financial consequences of transactions before they occur. By analyzing the financial consequences of alternative actions, management is better able to select those transactions that lead to the most desirable outcome(s).

The budgeting process also assists management in its organizing function. Detailed supporting schedules for revenues, expenditures, costs, and activities are drawn up for all units of the organization. Because all these pieces must fit together in the overall budget, flaws in organizational design become apparent as the budgeting process is nearing completion.

Accounting information also assists management in controlling operations subsequent to the adoption of a budget. During and after the budget period management is provided with **performance reports** that compare actual results with plans. A performance report for the Maintenance Department of the Eastside Good Department Store is presented in Exhibit 1–3. The differences between actual and allowed costs are identified as **variances.** Expenditures of less than the allowed amounts are **favorable variances** (F), and expenditures of more than the allowed amounts are **unfavorable variances** (U).

Copies of this performance report are provided to the Maintenance Department supervisor and to the store manager. The maintenance supervisor, who uses the report as a *scorecard,* can determine from it how well he or she is doing. The store manager, who uses the report as an *attention director,* can determine from it whether or not he or she should inquire further or take some action regarding the performance of the Maintenance Department. This is consistent with the concept of **management by exception,** whereby managers focus their attention on those aspects of operations that are not operating as planned, rather than constantly inquiring about all aspects of performance. If the store manager deemed any of the variances in Exhibit 1–3 to be significant, the manager would inquire further about

EXHIBIT 1–3   Typical Performance Report

Good Department Stores: Eastside
Maintenance Department Performance Report
For the month of September, 19x2

	Actual Costs	Allowed Costs	Variance*
Salaries and wages	$14,000	$12,000	$2,000 U
Utilities	800	850	50 F
Supplies	300	210	90 U
Equipment rentals	1,000	1,000	—
Totals	$16,100	$14,060	$2,040 U

* F = Favorable
  U = Unfavorable

their cause. If the unfavorable variance for salaries and wages was caused by an increase in wage rates, management might revise the budget (change its plans) for this item. If the variance was caused by excessive labor hours due to poor supervision, management would attempt to bring operations into conformity with the original plans.

Performance reports are developed for all units and subunits in the organization, and all costs incurred by the organization during a period should appear in at least one of these performance reports. Furthermore, some manager, or group of managers, should be held responsible for the incurrence of each cost. The process of developing a system to assign costs to responsible managers assists management in its organizing and controlling functions. If problems are encountered in assigning responsibility for costs, the most likely cause is either a weakness in organization structure or a failure to communicate areas of authority and responsibility to organization members. The resolution of responsibility for accounting problems is accompanied by the development of a clearer organizational structure.

Though we are particularly concerned with the role of monetary data, nonmonetary data are an important part of planning and control systems. Nonmonetary data increase in importance as we move down the organization chart. Performance reports stated in terms of units of production, pounds of materials, and hours of labor are more useful to clerks, factory workers, and first level production supervisors who work with physical units rather than with monetary symbols. First level managers must be able to speak to their subordinates in terms of units of activity and to their supervisors in accounting terms.

Nonmonetary measures of performance are also important in organizations where units of output cannot be related to revenue generation and profit. This is likely to be the case in the research and development department of a for-profit organization as well as for many activities of not-for-profit organizations, especially government agencies. It is difficult, for example, to determine the bottom-line impact of a good fire department. A budgeting and performance evaluation technique known as management by objectives is widely used in organizations where activities cannot be related to profit.

Under a program of **management by objectives** the head of an agency or department and the head's immediate superior agree to a set of short-run nonmonetary objectives. Care is taken to ensure that the short-run objectives are in agreement with the overall objectives of the organization. The short-run objectives are subsequently used as a performance measure for the agency or department head. One possible objective for a fire department might be to reduce the average response time to a fire alarm from five to four minutes.

Accounting Information Assists in Problem Solving

Accounting information is useful in evaluating unusual problems or opportunities. For example, a supplier might offer to provide a major component that goes into a manufactured product. The manufacturer must determine whether it is better to continue to manufacture the component or to purchase it from the supplier. A detailed analysis of cost data will assist in determining the costs to manufacture the component, which are then compared to the costs to buy the component. Another example might involve a government agency contracting with a university to provide educational services on the basis of the costs of those services. In this case both the government agency and the university must have a clear agreement on exactly how costs are to be determined. As a final example, consider the case of a bank that is trying to determine whether to continue or discontinue the operations of a particular branch. Before this decision is made, a careful analysis should be performed of how revenues and expenses will differ if the branch is closed. In these and many other examples discussed in later chapters, the proper accounting information will focus on how costs or revenues, or both, will differ under each alternative.

External Forces Increase the Importance of Accounting

A number of forces outside business organizations have increased the importance of accounting information as a basis for management decisions. Large insurance companies often require hospitals to justify their rates by using prescribed accounting procedures for cost assignments. Several government agencies award contracts on the basis of cost plus a specified allowance for profit. The U.S. Government has occasionally imposed controls limiting price increases to amounts that can be justified by documented increases in costs. Numerous lawsuits are initiated in an attempt to recover damages caused by the alleged failure of persons or organizations to complete their contractual obligations. The damage claims are based upon cost data, and the success of the suit, or the defense, often centers on how well the parties demonstrate an understanding of cost concepts and develop and explain cost data supporting their position. In this type of environment, all managers should have a basic understanding of cost concepts.

ACCOUNTANTS IN THE ORGANIZATION

All accounting activities within an organization are under the overall supervision of the **controller,** who is the organization's chief accountant.[2] The organization chart illustrated in Exhibit 1–1 shows that the controller is a member of top management's staff. As a staff member, the controller does not have any formal authority to direct the activities of anyone outside the controller's department but does, however, exert a strong influence on other members of the organization. This influence comes about because the controller frequently gives directions on behalf of top management and because the position provides the controller with an in-depth understanding and detailed knowledge of the organization.

Duties of the Controller

As the organization's chief accountant, the controller is responsible for a widely diverse set of activities. Although they vary from organization to organization, the duties most frequently assigned to the controller's office include:

- Designing, installing, and maintaining the accounting system.
- Preparing financial statements for external users.
- Coordinating the development of the budget.
- Accumulating and analyzing cost data.
- Preparing and analyzing performance reports.
- Providing information for problem solving and special decisions.
- Consulting with management about the meaning of accounting information.
- Planning and administrating taxes.
- Internal auditing.

---

[2] The word controller is occasionally spelled "comptroller." The pronunciation remains the same as the first spelling, and both refer to the same position.

- Designing, installing, and maintaining computer based information systems.

Somewhat related to the controller's function is that of the treasurer. The **treasurer** is the officer responsible for money management and serves chiefly as the custodian of the organization's funds. Typical duties of the treasurer include:

- Receiving, maintaining custody of, and disbursing monies and securities.
- Investing the organization's funds.
- Directing the granting of credit.
- Maintaining sources of short-term borrowing.
- Establishing and maintaining a market for the organization's debt and equity securities.

The positions of the controller and the treasurer are sometimes combined into the single position of **chief financial executive.** Other titles of this combined position include "chief financial officer" and "vice president of finance."

Organization of the Controller's Department

As a member of top management, the controller personally performs few of the above duties. Rather, the actual execution of these tasks is delegated to members of the controller's department. The organization chart for a typical controller's department is illustrated in Exhibit 1–4. By studying this exhibit from left to right, you should be able to determine where each of the duties listed above would be performed in the controller's department. The first two duties are part of General Accounting, and the next three are part of Cost Planning and Analysis.

The actual structure of a controller's department varies between organizations. The duties assigned Special Studies, Internal Auditing, and Electronic Data Processing in Exhibit 1–4 are likely to be performed elsewhere. The Special Studies section is assigned the task of providing information for problem solving and special decisions. This unit will also spend considerable time consulting with management about the meaning of accounting information.[3] Establishing a separate accounting unit for special studies was one of the major recommendations of a research effort conducted by Herbert A. Simon and others more than thirty years ago. They believed

---

[3] Many other persons within the Controller's Department would also provide such consultations in conjunction with their other duties.

EXHIBIT 1–4   Organization Chart of a Controller's Department

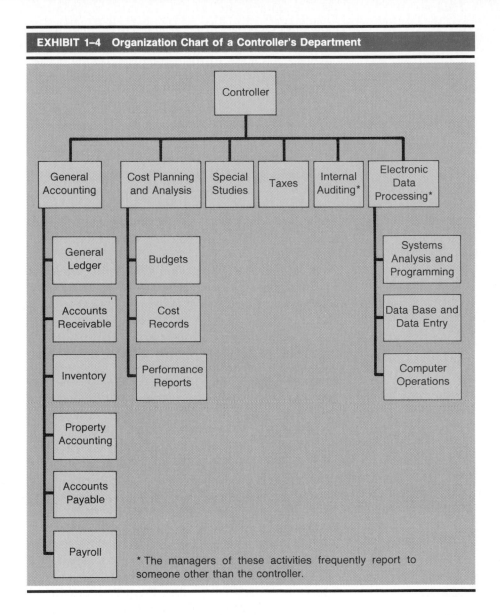

* The managers of these activities frequently report to someone other than the controller.

that the unstructured, analytic tasks of providing information for problem solving and special studies could not be performed effectively by the persons who were responsible for record keeping.[4] The required, day-to-day record

---

[4] Herbert A. Simon et al., *Centralization Vs Decentralization In Organizing the Controller's Department* (New York: Controllership Foundation, 1954).

keeping activities that have near-term due dates would always be done first, and frequently to the exclusion of unstructured tasks. Although our experiences support this conclusion, many organizations request accountants, who are performing more structured tasks, to complete special studies as staff time is available.

Internal auditing is intended to ensure that management's operating policies are being followed and that the organization's assets are not being subjected to fraud or waste. A significant portion of the internal auditor's time is devoted to ensuring that the accounting system is accurate and adequate. Since 1977, when the Foreign Corrupt Practices Act was passed by the U.S. Congress, all publicly held American companies have been *required* to maintain an adequate system of internal accounting controls. Even though the Internal Auditing section is part of the Controller's Department in Exhibit 1–4, there is a trend toward having the internal auditors report to the president or board of directors. Many persons believe that reporting to the board strengthens the internal auditor's independence. The U.S. Securities and Exchange Commission requires the internal auditing staff of many public corporations to report to the outside directors[5] regardless of where the internal audit staff is placed in the organization chart.

Electronic data processing (EDP) involves the storage, manipulation, retrieval, and communication of data by electronic means. Electronic data processing systems almost always involve the use of computers. Because the first large-scale applications of EDP systems were in accounting (payroll, receivables, payables), the responsibility for EDP operations has traditionally been placed under the overall direction of the controller. Today, however, an ever-increasing amount of computer time in large organizations is devoted to nonaccounting applications: engineering, scientific, personnel management, word processing, and so forth. To recognize and encourage applications of electronic data processing across functional areas, many firms have now established EDP as an independent staff department reporting directly to top management. In many organizations electronic data processing activities are placed within a department that has the more inclusive title of management information systems (MIS). The title of management information systems is broad enough to include all aspects of management accounting, but MIS activities are usually related to electronic data storage and processing. Regardless of where EDP activities are placed in the organization, the controller has a vital interest in the availability, accuracy, timeliness, and security of accounting information.

---

[5] Outside directors are members of the organization's board of directors who are independent of management. That is, they are neither officers nor employees of the organization.

FINANCIAL ACCOUNTING AND
MANAGEMENT ACCOUNTING

Accounting is an information system.[6] We previously indicated that accounting is broadly classified into financial accounting and management accounting and that this classification is based on the difference in the relationship that exists between the organization and the person or persons to whom information is supplied. **Financial accounting** is concerned with providing financial information to persons outside the firm, especially investors, creditors, labor unions, and the general public. **Management accounting** is concerned with providing financial information to persons inside the organization, especially managers. This difference in orientation results in significant differences between these two types of accounting.

Financial Accounting Has an External Orientation

Financial accounting is concerned with the development of *general purpose* financial statements (such as the statement of financial position and the income statement) that are intended for the primary use of persons *external* to the organization. These statements, which are *highly aggregated* and, therefore, provide little detail, are summaries of the financial affairs of all the organization's subunits and activities and are typically issued quarterly and annually. Compared to the frequency with which management accounting reports are issued (daily, weekly, monthly), financial accounting reports cover *relatively long time periods.*

Financial accounting statements report on management's handling of the affairs of the organization in the *past.* The U.S. Securities and Exchange Commission *requires* publicly held corporations to issue financial statements. To ensure conformity, understandability, and fairness, general purpose financial statements are prepared in accordance with *external standards* imposed by the public accounting profession (in the form of generally accepted accounting principles) and by regulatory agencies (such as the U.S. Securities and Exchange Commission). A significant feature of these external standards is their emphasis on *objectivity.* General purpose financial statements should not be influenced by emotion, surmise, or personal prejudice. They should be based on observable phenomena, such as the historical cost actually paid for a product or service.

You should not interpret the preceding comments on external reporting as implying that management has little interest in financial accounting.

---

[6] *Information* is something that contributes to knowledge. Data taken alone do not contribute to knowledge. The number 500 is a datum, but, taken by itself, it is not knowledge. An advertisement stating that a local discount store is selling color television sets for $500 is information. It does contribute to our knowledge.

Managers can benefit greatly from financial accounting information. Management often uses financial statements as a starting point in evaluating and planning the overall affairs of the firm. Because of the wide availability of financial accounting data, managers can learn a great deal about the operation of their firm by a comparative financial analysis of their own and competing firms. Financial accounting numbers, such as net income, or ratios, such as earnings per share of common stock, are often used as goals. Furthermore, financial accounting statements are a major means of communication with persons outside the firm. Obviously, management is most interested in the content of this message. Finally, employees, who have a personal interest in the economic health of the organization for which they work, can gain an understanding of this economic health by studying their firm's financial statements.

Management Accounting Has an Internal Orientation

Management accounting is concerned with providing information to managers and other persons *inside* the organization. Management accounting reports are *special purpose*. Designed to fit the specific needs of individual or group decision makers, they emphasize factors under the decision makers' control. In this regard management accounting might be called a decision support system. At lower levels of management, planning and control decisions must be made quite frequently. To serve the needs of these decision makers, management accounting provides information for *relatively short periods of time*—a month, a week, a day, or even some portion of a day. Because managers are primarily concerned with the impact of their decisions on the future performance of the organization, management accounting reports are *future oriented*. Past and current activities are reported

EXHIBIT 1–5 Differences between Financial and Management Accounting	
Financial Accounting	*Management Accounting*
Provides information to external users	Provides information to internal users
Generates general purpose financial statements	Generates special purpose financial statements and reports
Statements highly aggregated; provide little detail	Statements and reports may be disaggregated; provide much detail
Relatively long time period	May be relatively short time period
Reports on past	Reports on past or outlines future plans
Required by law	Not required by law
Must conform to externally imposed standards	Has no externally imposed standards
Emphasizes objective data	Allows subjective data

to the extent that this information helps management plan for the future or ensure future conformance with current plans. Management accounting reports exist to serve the needs of management. Because they are *not required* by law, the development and use of these reports are subject to a cost-benefit analysis. Management accounting reports should only be provided if the perceived benefits of their development and use exceed the related costs.

No external standards are imposed on information provided to internal users. Consequently, management accounting reports may be quite *subjective.* In developing a budget, management is more interested in a subjective estimate of next year's sales volume than in an objective report on last year's sales. The significant differences between management accounting and financial accounting are summarized in Exhibit 1–5.

Professional Accountants

Public corporations are required by law to have outside auditors perform an independent evaluation of their general purpose financial statements. This audit is performed in order to determine whether or not the statements are prepared in accordance with generally accepted accounting principles. In the United States the persons who perform these independent evaluations are designated as **Certified Public Accountants** (CPAs). In Canada and several other countries they are designated as **Chartered Accountants** (CAs). All CPAs have passed an examination and meet the education and experience requirements of the state in which they are certified. The CPA is widely recognized as a professional designation. Indeed, until recent years, U.S. business executives often cited the CPA as the only available guide to the professional competence of American accountants. This situation has changed since the National Association of Accountants (NAA) established a program to recognize professional competence and educational attainment in the field of management accounting. The NAA's program leads to the **Certificate in Management Accounting** (CMA). According to a booklet distributed by the NAA:

> *The CMA program requires candidates to pass a series of uniform examinations and meet specific educational and professional standards to qualify for and maintain the Certificate in Management Accounting. NAA has established the Institute of Management Accounting to administer the program, conduct the examinations and grant certificates to those who qualify.*[7]

A significant aspect of the CMA examination is its interdisciplinary nature. This is reflected in the five major parts of the exam:

---

[7] *Certificate In Management Accounting: 1982–1983 Announcement,* Institute of Management Accountants of the National Association of Accountants, p. 2.

1. Economics and business finance.
2. Organization and behavior, including ethical considerations.
3. Public reporting standards, auditing, and taxes.
4. Periodic reporting for internal and external purposes.
5. Decision analysis, including modeling and information systems.[8]

The interdisciplinary nature of the CMA examination is intended to reflect the dual role of the management accountant as both an accountant and a member of the management team. Robert Shultis, the Executive Director of the National Association of Accountants, has even expressed the view that "the management accountant needs to be a businessman *first* and an accountant *second.*"[9]

SUMMARY

Accounting is an information system that is classified into financial accounting and management accounting. Financial accounting is concerned primarily with providing information to persons outside the organization. Management accounting is concerned primarily with providing information to persons inside the organization.

A manager is someone who directs the affairs of an organization. In planning, organizing, and controlling the activities of an organization, managers use many types of information, including that provided by management accounting. To perform their jobs, managers need to have a thorough understanding of accounting in general and management accounting in particular. Managers use accounting terms to communicate with employees, other managers, and persons in other organizations. They use accounting information as a basis for decision making and are very much involved in budgeting. Accounting reports are used to evaluate their performance and the performance of others. Accountants must also have a thorough understanding of management accounting concepts in order to ensure that the accounting information system supplies the information management needs for planning and controlling ongoing operations and for solving special problems.

KEY TERMS

Organization

Management accounting

For-profit organization

Not-for-profit organization

Planning

Organizing

---

[8] Additional information about the CMA program is available from the Institute of Management Accounting, 570 City Center Building, Ann Arbor, Michigan 48104.

[9] Robert Shultis, "Management and Management Accountants," *Survey of Business*, Fall, 1981, p. 6.

Organization chart

Controlling

Budget

Performance report

Variance

Favorable variance

Unfavorable variance

Management by exception

Management by objectives

Controller

Treasurer

Chief financial executive

Internal auditing

Electronic data processing

Financial accounting

Certified Public Accountant (CPA)

Chartered Accountant (CA)

Certificate in Management Accounting (CMA)

REVIEW QUESTIONS

The review questions at the end of each chapter are intended to assist in reviewing conceptual material. These questions are arranged in the same order that material is covered in the chapter.

1–1 Why do not-for-profit organizations need a good accounting system?

1–2 Identify and briefly describe the three functions of management.

1–3 What is the proper relationship between short-range and long-range planning?

1–4 Distinguish between the authority of staff and line managers. Why do staff departments exist?

1–5 What characteristic of accounting data is largely responsible for top management's wide use of accounting?

1–6 Why is a model useful to management?

1–7 How does the accounting model of the firm assist in planning?

1–8 How does accounting assist in controlling?

1–9 How does budgeting and the development of a system of responsibility accounting assist in organizing?

1–10 The controller frequently exerts a stronger influence on the affairs of line managers than one would expect from a staff officer. Why?

1–11 Identify several duties frequently assigned the controller.

1–12 Identify several duties frequently assigned the treasurer.

1–13 Why should the responsibility for special studies be assigned to a separate unit within the controller's department?

1–14 Why is electronic data processing frequently under the overall direction of the controller? Why are many large organizations establishing separate departments for electronic data processing?

1–15 Distinguish between financial and management accounting on the basis of the following: specificity of reports, users who receive reports, level of aggregation in reports, relative time period between reports, time orientation of reports (past, future), legal requirements for reporting, external pressures specifying content and form of reports, and emphasis on objective data.

Basic Cost
Concepts

Cost is generally defined as a monetary measure of the economic sacrifice made to obtain some product or service. The economic sacrifice can be a cash expenditure, the giving up of another valuable asset, the forgoing of an economically desirable opportunity, or the incurrence of an obligation to pay cash in the future. Cost measurement is a significant aspect of financial and management accounting. However, although the general definition of cost is adequate for most external purposes, a variety of cost concepts and related measurements are needed for internal planning and control.

The purpose of this chapter is to introduce cost concepts and measurements that are widely used in management accounting. In the course of our study, we will determine how costs are best measured for different purposes. Much of the material presented here is an overview with in-depth coverage contained in subsequent chapters.

Managers, in order to communicate with one another and with accountants, must be familiar with cost concepts. Accountants must be equally familiar with cost concepts to ensure that the accounting information system provides management with the information it needs. Both managers and accountants should understand the basic cost measurements that comprise a significant part of the accounting model of the organization, which is used to plan and control organizational activities.

DIFFERENT COSTS FOR DIFFERENT PURPOSES

Accountants and managers employ many different cost concepts, such as historical costs, budgeted costs, future costs, allowed costs, relevant costs, opportunity costs, and sunk costs, to name just a few. These cost concepts are not used randomly; instead, *different costs are used for different purposes*. Consider, for example, some of the alternative inventory costs that might be used in a department store. For the purpose of external reporting, the cost of goods sold is based on the historical cost actually paid for inventory. In developing a budget for next year, the store's management predicts the future cost of inventory purchases. The performance of the store's purchasing agent is evaluated by comparing the actual cost of purchases to the allowed cost of purchases.

Cost Measurement Systems

Though purpose is the primary consideration in selecting a cost concept, a system of cost measurement also needs one or more cost objectives, a determination of the cost elements assignable to each objective, and one or more techniques for assigning cost elements to cost objectives. The **costing purpose** is the basic reason a cost concept is used and a cost measurement is made, the **cost objectives** are the objects or activities to which costs are assigned, the **cost elements** are the detailed categories of costs assignable to a cost objective, and the **costing techniques** are the procedures used to assign cost elements to cost objectives.

One purpose of a public corporation's accounting system is to provide general purpose financial statements to persons outside the organization. For this purpose each major type of asset, such as buildings, is a cost objective. The cost elements assignable to buildings include the amount paid to purchase them and the cost of major improvements. Alternative costing techniques for measuring the adjusted cost of buildings include straight-line, sum-of-the-years'-digits, and double-declining-balance depreciation.

Costs and Benefits of Cost Measurement

Cost measurement is intended to provide useful information. In general, information should not be developed unless the benefits derived from its use exceed its acquisition cost. Exceptions to this generalization occur when forces outside the organization (such as government agencies) require the disclosure of certain information.

Many corporations are legally required to maintain an accounting system capable of providing cost data for inclusion in general purpose financial statements. It is possible to estimate the cost of installing and operating this system, but the related benefits are difficult to quantify. To a large extent the benefits accrue to shareholders, creditors, and other persons outside the organization.

Even with a system primarily designed for external reporting, many cost reducing measures are taken that do not significantly reduce the accuracy of cost measurement. One example is the treatment of transportation-in on goods purchased for resale. Theoretically, these costs should be assigned to inventory items at the time of purchase and included in the valuation of ending inventory and cost of sales. In practice, however, the less costly and slightly less accurate treatment of immediately assigning transportation-in to a separate expense account is widely used.

Because management accounting information is not required by law, it should be provided only if the benefits obtained from the information exceed the costs of its measurement and processing. To reduce costs, wherever the information needs of management can be satisfied with data accumulated for external reporting, the data used for external reporting may be rearranged in a format suitable for management. Consider, for example, the cost of merchandise in a department store. For external reporting purposes, the financial accounting system must account for the actual cost of merchandise purchased either as merchandise inventory or as cost of goods sold. For the purpose of evaluating the performance of the purchasing department, the management accounting system compares the actual cost of purchases to the allowed cost of purchases. Although actual cost data are contained in both the external financial statements and the internal reports, they are configured differently.

Because much management accounting information is derived from the financial accounting information system, much of this chapter is devoted to the study of costing objectives, elements, and techniques developed for external reporting. This study will provide an understanding of the accounting data base used in both financial and management accounting.

INVENTORY COSTS IN DIFFERENT ORGANIZATIONS

The importance and complexity of inventory cost measurement varies widely among organizations. The importance of inventory costing is a function of the dollar size of inventories, whereas the complexity of inventory costing is a function of the number of major inventory categories and the number of cost elements assigned to each category. Using inventory as a basis, we can distinguish between service, merchandising, and manufacturing organizations. **Service organizations** perform work for others. Included in this category are banks, barber shops, hospitals, restaurants, movie theaters, electric utilities, schools, most government agencies, railroads, bus companies, and accounting firms. **Merchandising organizations** buy and sell goods. Included in this category are department stores, grocery stores, wholesale distributors, shoe stores, and discount stores. **Manufacturing organizations** process raw materials into finished products. Included in this category are automobile companies, steel mills, computer manufacturers, and furniture makers.

In general, service organizations have a low percentage of their total assets invested in inventory, which usually consists only of the supplies needed to facilitate their operations. Merchandising organizations usually have a high percentage of their total assets invested in inventory. Their most significant inventory is merchandise purchased for resale, but they also have supplies inventories.

Manufacturing organizations convert raw materials into finished products that are sold to other organizations and, like merchandisers, usually have a high percentage of their total assets invested in inventories. However, rather than just one inventory category, manufacturing organizations have three major categories: raw materials, work-in-process, and finished goods. **Raw materials inventories** contain the physically existing items that are to be converted into a finished product. **Work-in-process inventories** contain the raw materials that are in the process of being converted into a finished product. **Finished goods inventories** contain the manufactured products that are intended for sale to other organizations.

Manufacturing organizations also have minor investments in supplies inventories. Some of these supplies are used to facilitate production. Others are used in selling and administrative activities. The cost of supplies that are used in production, such as lubricating oils and small tools, are a cost element of the finished product.

Exhibit 2–1 illustrates the flow of inventory costs in service, merchandising, and manufacturing organizations. Notice that in all three types of orga-

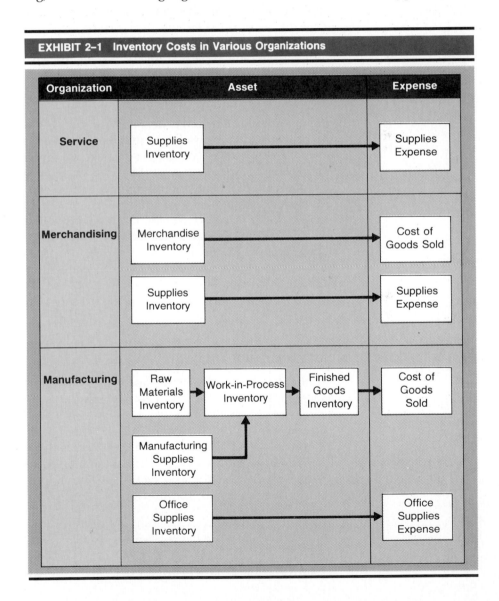

EXHIBIT 2–1   Inventory Costs in Various Organizations

nizations all inventories are eventually consumed or sold and become expenses.[1]

PRODUCT COSTING AND SERVICE COSTING

The process of assigning costs to inventories as they are converted from raw materials to finished goods is called **product costing.** Product costs must be determined for the purposes of inventory valuation and expense measurement in required general purpose financial statements. Product cost information is also used by management to plan and control firm activities.

The process of assigning costs to services is called **service costing.** Examples of service costing include measuring the cost of check processing (for a bank), instructional hours (for a college), operating room minutes (for a hospital), and passenger miles (for an airline). Though costs are seldom accumulated by service categories in external financial statements, service cost information is used internally to plan and control firm activities. The management of a bank, for example, might like to know the cost of processing a check drawn on a customer's account or the cost of processing an application for a personal loan. This information would assist in budgeting, pricing, and performance evaluation.

The focus of this chapter is mainly on product costing, rather than service costing because product costing concepts are more fully developed and easier to generalize and understand. Please note, however, that most product costing concepts are applicable to service costing.

PRODUCT COSTS FOR EXTERNAL REPORTING

In financial accounting it is important to differentiate between unexpired costs and expired costs. **Unexpired costs** are recorded as assets on the statement of financial position, and **expired costs** are deducted from revenues on the income statement. A cost is classified as an asset, or an unexpired cost, to the extent that the cost objective it is related to has a future service potential. This service potential can be either future revenues to be generated from the sale or use of the asset, or future costs that can be avoided because of the previous acquisition of the asset. For instance,

---

[1] For the purposes of this classification, agriculture might be included in the category of manufacturing organizations. A cattle ranch, for example, has a high percentage of its total assets invested in cattle (work-in-process). The cattle are raised from calves (raw material) and sold to slaughterhouses or feed lots when they obtain sufficient size (finished goods).

the cost of merchandise inventory is an asset to a retail store because future revenues can be generated from the sale of merchandise; the cost of an apartment building is an asset to its owners because future revenues can be generated from apartment rentals; and the cost of prepaid insurance is an asset to a dentist because the dentist can avoid the cost of buying additional insurance for the coverage period.

As a cost objective loses its service potential, the costs assigned to that objective are reclassified as expired costs. The loss of service potential may be sudden or gradual. Thus, the cost of merchandise inventory is reclassified as the costs of goods sold when the merchandise is sold, the cost of an apartment building is depreciated over the building's life, and the cost of prepaid insurance is reclassified as insurance expense with the passage of the coverage period.

The difference between expired and unexpired costs is often difficult to discern. Consider the case of a newly constructed office building. Because the building presumably has a future service potential, the cost of the building is initially recorded as an asset. As this service potential is realized, the cost of the building is systematically reclassified as an expense. The accounting problem is how and when to properly record the expiration of the cost of the building. To meet this problem several alternative depreciation procedures are used. Even though these procedures may not accurately depict the decline in the value of the building, they do assign its costs, in an understandable manner, to the periods that benefit from the use of the building.

Depreciation procedures are complex, but they are not so complex as the techniques used to differentiate expired from unexpired product costs. Because manufactured products can be sold, they have a future service potential. Consequently, *the cost of raw materials and other costs incurred to transform raw materials into finished goods become part of the cost of the finished goods.* These costs are recorded as assets, since they are unexpired costs, until the finished goods are sold, when they become an expense, that is, the cost of goods sold.

Product Costs and Period Costs

In manufacturing organizations, an important distinction is made between costs assigned to products and nonproduct costs that expire during the period. **Product costs** are costs assigned to products. They are expensed when the products are sold. **Period costs** are expired nonproduct costs. They are always recorded as an expense.

For external reporting purposes, product costs include the costs of raw materials and all other factors necessary to transform raw materials into finished products. Because all manufacturing costs "attach to" or are "absorbed by" the units produced, external reports are often said to state manufacturing inventories on an *absorption cost* basis. *According to the*

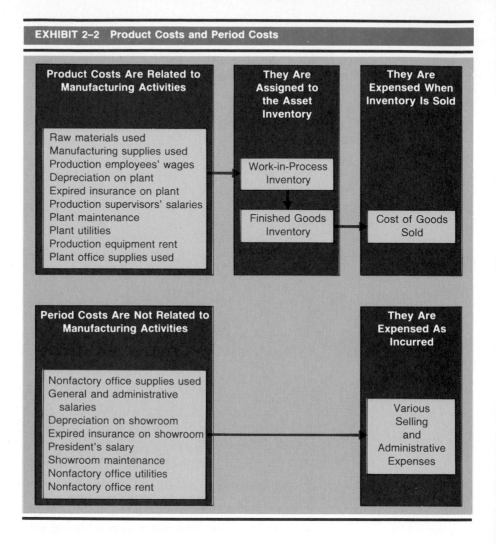

EXHIBIT 2–2   Product Costs and Period Costs

absorption cost basis of external reporting, *all manufacturing costs are product costs, and all selling and administrative costs are period costs.*

The proper treatment of several product and period costs is illustrated in Exhibit 2–2. Note in particular that depreciation, expired insurance, the cost of utilities, and so forth are not automatically classified as period costs. When these costs are incurred in connection with manufacturing activities, they are product costs; when they are incurred in connection with other activities, they are period costs. The future service potential of factory buildings and equipment is transformed into the future service potential of manufactured products. Depreciation on manufacturing buildings and equipment is absorbed by the product; hence, this depreciation is a product cost. The future service potential of office buildings and equipment expires with the passage of time. Depreciation on office buildings and equipment is not absorbed by products; hence, this depreciation is a period cost.

Three Product Costs   The manufacture of even a simple product, such as a wooden rowboat, requires three basic ingredients: materials (such as wood), labor (such as that of a boat craftsman), and production facilities (such as a building to work in, a saw, and a hammer). Corresponding to these three basic ingredients, product costs are classified into three categories: direct materials, direct labor, and factory overhead. Just as materials, labor, and production facilities are combined to produce a finished product, the costs of direct materials, direct labor, and factory overhead are accumulated to obtain the cost of finished goods. Exhibit 2–3 illustrates that these costs are accumu-

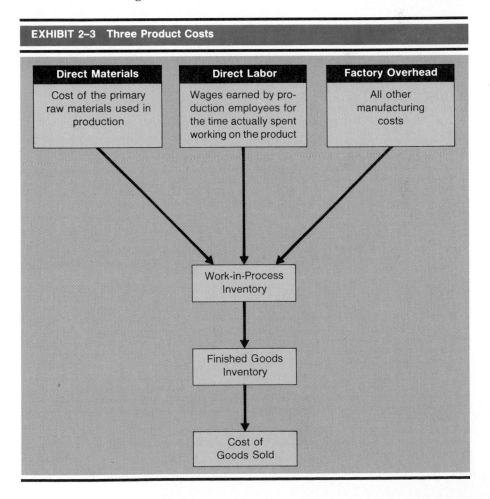

EXHIBIT 2–3   Three Product Costs

Direct Materials	Direct Labor	Factory Overhead
Cost of the primary raw materials used in production	Wages earned by production employees for the time actually spent working on the product	All other manufacturing costs

Work-in-Process Inventory

Finished Goods Inventory

Cost of Goods Sold

lated in Work-in-Process[2] as production takes place and transferred to Finished Goods Inventory when production is completed. Product costs are finally assigned to Cost of Goods Sold when the finished goods are sold.

The costs of the primary raw materials converted into finished goods are called **direct materials.** Examples of primary raw materials include iron ore to a steel mill, coiled aluminum to a manufacturer of aluminum siding, cow's milk to a dairy, logs to a sawmill, and lumber to a builder. Note that the finished product of one firm may be the raw materials of another. Two-by-fours are the finished product of a sawmill but the raw material of a carpenter.

At the time of purchase, the costs of primary raw materials are assigned to the account Raw Materials Inventory. As raw materials are placed in production, their costs are removed from Raw Materials Inventory and assigned to Work-in-Process Inventory as direct materials. Direct materials costs are computed as the number of units of raw materials placed in production times their related cost per unit.

Wages earned by production employees *for the time they actually spend working on a product* are identified as **direct labor.** Direct labor costs are computed as the number of hours employees work on production times their hourly wage rate.

All manufacturing costs other than direct materials and direct labor are collectively identified as **factory overhead.**[3] Examples of factory overhead include manufacturing supplies; depreciation on manufacturing buildings and equipment; and the costs of plant taxes, insurance, maintenance, and utilities. Also included are production supervisors' salaries and all other manufacturing labor costs not specifically classified as direct labor. The assignment of factory overhead costs to Work-in-Process Inventory is discussed later in this chapter.

Analyzing Activity in Inventory Accounts

An understanding of account activity and account interrelationships is extremely important for product costing and for internal planning and control. During any time period, the activity in any account can be broken down into four parts:

Beginning balance + Increases − Decreases = Ending balance.

---

[2] Account titles are capitalized to make it easier to determine when reference is being made to a physically existing item, such as work-in-process inventory, and the account Work-in-Process, which discloses the costs assigned to work-in-process inventory.

[3] Factory overhead is also called "manufacturing overhead," "burden," "manufacturing burden," and "overhead." All but the last of these terms are acceptable. The word "overhead" by itself does not indicate the type of overhead. Merchandising organizations occasionally refer to administrative costs as overhead.

Knowing any three of these items, we can always find the fourth. Typical accounts and their activity include:

Cash	Merchandise Inventory	Accounts Payable
Beginning balance	Beginning balance	Beginning balance
+ Cash receipts	+ Purchases	+ Purchases on account
= Total cash available	= Total available	= Total payable
− Cash disbursements	− Cost of goods sold	− Payments on account
= Ending balance	= Ending balance	= Ending balance

The totals are inserted for computational ease. Assume that the management of a department store is trying to budget purchases for the coming year. The beginning merchandise inventory costs $50,000, and management desires to have an inventory of $45,000 at the end of the year. If the cost of goods sold is budgeted to be $350,000, knowledge of account activity can be used to budget purchases:

Activity	Given Information	Solution
Beginning balance	$ 50,000	$ 50,000
+ Purchases	+ ?	+345,000
= Total available	$?	$395,000
− Cost of goods sold	−350,000	−350,000
= Ending balance	$ 45,000	$ 45,000

Purchases should be budgeted at $345,000.

Activity in one account always affects at least one other account. Inventory purchased on account in a merchandising organization increases Merchandise Inventory and Accounts Payable. Payments on account reduce Cash and Accounts Payable. Inventory issued to the factory in a manufacturing organization decreases Raw Materials Inventory and increases Work-in-Process Inventory. A complete analysis of a manufacturing organization's inventory account relationships is presented in Exhibit 2–4.

In Exhibit 2–4 the cost of raw materials placed in production reduces Raw Materials Inventory and increases Work-in-Process Inventory. The total additions to Work-in-Process Inventory are collectively identified as **current manufacturing costs,** and the total costs assigned to products completed are collectively identified as the **cost of goods manufactured.** The cost of goods manufactured is deducted from Work-in-Process Inventory and added to Finished Goods Inventory. Once the relationships between inven-

EXHIBIT 2–4   Analysis of Activity in Manufacturing Inventory Accounts

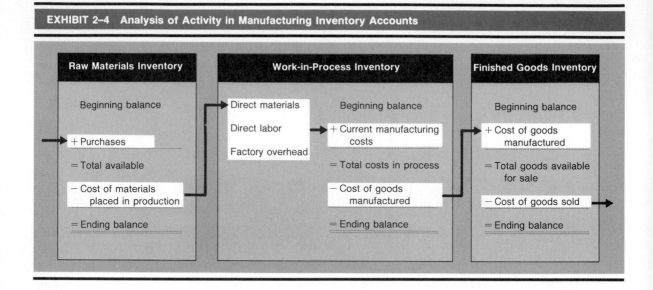

tory accounts are known, items of interest (such as the cost of materials placed in production, the cost of goods manufactured, or the cost of goods sold) are readily determined. Consider the following example.

On September 1, 19x4, the beginning inventory balances of the Harmon Manufacturing Company were

Raw Materials Inventory	$ 5,000
Work-in-Process Inventory	8,000
Finished Goods Inventory	11,000

During the month of September, raw materials costing $12,000 were purchased. Direct labor and factory overhead costs were $20,000 and $15,000, respectively.

The September 30 inventory account balances were

Raw Materials Inventory	$ 7,000
Work-in-Process Inventory	14,000
Finished Goods Inventory	6,000

An analysis of activity in inventory accounts is presented in Exhibit 2–5. For computational ease the ending balance in each account is subtracted from the total to determine the items of interest:

Cost of materials placed in production	$10,000
Cost of goods manufactured	39,000
Cost of goods sold	44,000

This example focused on inventory account activity. Cost of goods sold is, of course, just one item on the income statement. Harmon's September income statement would also include revenues and other expenses. Harmon's September 30 statement of financial position would include inventory and many other assets, as well as liability and shareholders' equity accounts.

Because activity in one account always affects at least one other account, the analysis here is incomplete. The acquisition of raw materials and direct labor and the incurrence of factory overhead costs affect many other accounts. We have ignored these accounts for the moment in order to emphasize the essential inventory relationships found in product costing.

EXHIBIT 2–5　Analysis of Harmon's Inventory Accounts

Raw Materials Inventory

Beginning balance		$ 5,000
Purchases		12,000
Total available		$17,000
Ending balance		− 7,000
Cost of materials placed in production (direct materials)		$10,000

Work-in-Process Inventory

Beginning balance		$ 8,000
Current manufacturing costs:		
Direct materials	$10,000	
Direct labor	20,000	
Factory overhead	15,000	45,000
Total costs in process		$53,000
Ending balance		−14,000
Cost of goods manufactured		$39,000

Finished Goods Inventory

Beginning balance		$11,000
Cost of goods manufactured		39,000
Total goods available for sale		$50,000
Ending balance		− 6,000
Cost of goods sold		$44,000

Statement of Cost of Goods Manufactured

The activity in raw materials and work-in-process inventory accounts is formally summarized in a **statement of cost of goods manufactured.** Harmon Manufacturing Company's September 19x4 Statement of Cost of Goods Manufactured is presented in Exhibit 2–6. To show the relationship between this statement and the income statement, Harmon's September 19x4 Income Statement is also presented in the exhibit. For this example assume September sales of $90,000 and selling and administrative expenses of $30,000.

The activity in all major inventory accounts can be summarized in a single **statement of cost of goods manufactured and sold,** such as the one presented in Exhibit 2–7, along with an accompanying income statement. These statements, like all formal accounting statements, begin with

---

EXHIBIT 2–6   Statement of Cost of Goods Manufactured

Harmon Manufacturing Company
Statement of Cost of Goods Manufactured
For the month ending September 30, 19x4

Current manufacturing costs:			
Cost of materials placed in production:			
Raw materials, 9/1/x4	$ 5,000		
Purchases	12,000		
Total available	$17,000		
Raw materials, 9/30/x4	−7,000	$10,000	
Direct labor		20,000	
Factory overhead		15,000	$45,000
Work-in-process, 9/1/x4			8,000
Total costs in process			$53,000
Work-in-process, 9/30/x4			−14,000
Cost of goods manufactured			$39,000

Harmon Manufacturing Company
Income Statement
For the month ending September 30, 19x4

Sales		$90,000
Cost of goods sold:		
Finished goods inventory, 9/1/x4	$11,000	
Cost of goods manufactured	39,000	
Total goods available for sale	$50,000	
Finished goods inventory, 9/30/x4	−6,000	−44,000
Gross profit		$46,000
Selling and administrative expenses		−30,000
Net income		$16,000

EXHIBIT 2–7   Statement of Cost of Goods Manufactured and Sold

Harmon Manufacturing Company
Statement of Cost of Goods Manufactured and Sold
For the month ending September 30, 19x4

Current manufacturing costs:			
Cost of materials placed in production:			
Raw materials, 9/1/x4	$ 5,000		
Purchases	12,000		
Total available	$17,000		
Raw materials, 9/30/x4	− 7,000	$10,000	
Direct labor		20,000	
Factory overhead		15,000	$45,000
Work-in-process, 9/1/x4			8,000
Total costs in process			$53,000
Work-in-process, 9/30/x4			−14,000
Cost of goods manufactured			$39,000
Finished goods inventory, 9/1/x4			11,000
Total goods available for sale			$50,000
Finished goods inventory, 9/30/x4			− 6,000
Cost of goods sold			$44,000

Harmon Manufacturing Company
Income Statement
For the month ending September 30, 19x4

Sales	$90,000
Cost of goods sold	−44,000
Gross profit	$46,000
Selling and administrative expenses	−30,000
Net income	$16,000

a heading that indicates the name of the organization, the name of the statement, and the statement date or time period. Statement formats and details vary. Factory overhead may, for example, be itemized rather than be presented as a single amount.

Combined Product Costs

A clear association exists between the physical product and the direct materials and direct labor costs. Direct materials and direct labor costs are easily traced to finished goods. The number of units of raw materials that enter into each finished unit can be counted, and the time production employees work to produce a finished unit can be measured. Because of this direct association with the finished product, direct materials and direct labor costs are jointly identified as **direct product costs** or **prime product costs.**

All product costs other than direct materials and direct labor are classified as factory overhead. It is difficult to associate factory overhead costs with specific units of product. Factory overhead costs (such as depreciation on plant, insurance on plant, production supervisors' salaries, plant maintenance, and plant utilities) are incurred to facilitate the production of all products. Because it is difficult to establish an immediate association between these costs and individual units of product, factory overhead costs are often identified as **indirect product costs.**

Direct labor and factory overhead costs, which are incurred to convert raw materials into finished goods, are jointly identified as **conversion costs.** The relationships between these new cost terms are illustrated in Exhibit 2–8. The September 19x4 amounts for the Harmon Manufacturing Company are as follows:

Direct product costs:		
Direct materials	$10,000	
Direct labor	20,000	$30,000
Prime product costs:		
Direct materials	$10,000	
Direct labor	20,000	$30,000
Indirect product costs		
(factory overhead)		$15,000
Conversion costs:		
Direct labor	$20,000	
Factory overhead	15,000	$35,000

Notice that direct materials refers to the cost of materials placed in production rather than the cost of materials purchased.

EXHIBIT 2–8   Product Costing Terminology

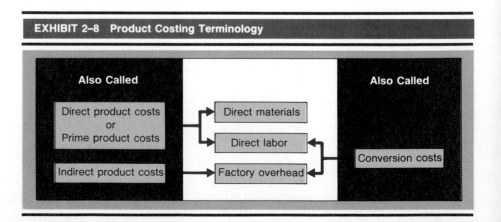

A Closer Look at Factory Overhead

As production occurs, it is easy to transfer direct materials costs from Raw Materials Inventory to Work-in-Process Inventory. Direct materials costs are the number of units of raw materials transferred to the factory multiplied by the related cost per unit. It is also easy to assign direct labor costs to Work-in-Process Inventory. Direct labor costs are the number of direct labor hours worked times the appropriate rate per direct labor hour. But what about overhead?

Factory overhead is the most generally defined and difficult to measure product cost. It includes all production costs other than those specifically identified as direct materials and direct labor. If there is a company subsidized cafeteria in the plant, factory overhead will even include depreciation on the kitchen sink.

Selecting a Basis for Overhead Application. The costs and benefits of alternative measurement techniques are important considerations in the accumulation and assignment of factory overhead. As a cost reducing measure, all factory overhead costs may be grouped together into a single collection of related costs, called a **cost pool.** These costs are then assigned to Work-in-Process Inventory on the basis of some factor that has a high correlation with the incurrence of overhead, is common to all products, and is easy to measure. Frequently used bases of overhead application include direct labor dollars, direct labor hours, and machine hours.

The variety and different natures of factory overhead costs make it difficult to accurately apply them using a single application basis. Some factory overhead costs are related to people, others are related to the existence of buildings and equipment, and still others are related to the use of buildings and equipment. Accuracy could be improved by grouping overhead costs into two or more cost pools that have common characteristics and applying each on a separate basis. For example, labor related costs might be pooled and applied on the basis of labor hours, whereas equipment related costs might be placed in another cost pool and applied on the basis of machine hours. This should be done only if the management accountant believes the increased accuracy is worth the added cost of operating the more complex cost measurement system.[4]

Using Predetermined Overhead Rates. The timely assignment of actual factory overhead costs is difficult because the amount of many overhead costs cannot be determined until after the end of the period. September's electric utility and water bills, for example, may not be received until mid-October. Waiting until September's actual overhead costs are known would necessitate an undesirable delay in product costing. September's statement

---

[4] Cost systems that use two or more factory overhead cost pools are discussed in Chapter 12.

of cost of goods manufactured could not be prepared until mid- to late October.

To overcome this timing problem, and other problems such as smoothing the work load of the bookkeepers, most firms use a predetermined rate to assign factory overhead costs. A **predetermined factory overhead rate** is determined at the start of the year by dividing the predicted overhead costs for the year by the predicted activity for the year. A predetermined overhead rate per direct labor hour is computed as

$$\frac{\text{Predetermined overhead rate}}{\text{per direct labor hour}} = \frac{\text{Predicted total overhead for the year}}{\text{Predicted total direct labor hours for the year}}.$$

Using a predetermined overhead rate based on direct labor hours, we compute the assignment of overhead to Work-in-Process Inventory as

$$\frac{\text{Factory overhead}}{\text{assigned to}} = \frac{\text{Actual direct labor hours}}{\text{hours}} \times \frac{\text{Predetermined overhead rate per}}{\text{direct labor hour.}}$$

Late in 19x3 Harmon Manufacturing Company predicted a 19x4 activity level of 25,000 direct labor hours with 19x4 factory overhead totaling $187,500. Using this information, we find that their 19x4 predetermined overhead rate per direct labor hour was computed as

$$\frac{\text{Predetermined}}{\text{overhead rate}} = \frac{\$187,500}{25,000}$$

$$= \$7.50 \text{ per direct labor hour.}$$

If 2000 direct labor hours were used in September 19x4, the applied overhead would equal $15,000:

$$2000 \times \$7.50 = \$15,000.$$

When a predetermined overhead rate is used, small monthly variations between actual and applied factory overhead are expected. In some months actual overhead is less than applied overhead; in some months it can be more. If the difference between cumulative actual and cumulative applied overhead builds up in a single direction over a period of time, it will be necessary to change the predetermined overhead rate. Underapplied and overapplied overhead costs are considered further in Chapter 11.

Materials and Labor Costs in Factory Overhead. As discussed earlier, direct materials costs include only the costs of primary raw materials clearly identified with the finished product, and direct labor costs include only the wages earned by production employees for time spent working on products. All other materials and labor costs are elements of factory overhead. Materials and labor costs normally in factory overhead include: indirect materials, indirect labor, idle time, overtime premiums, and employee fringe benefits.

Indirect materials are relatively low cost materials that are difficult to associate with specific units of final product. Wood is a primary raw material in the manufacture of wooden bookcases; its cost is a direct materials cost. Nails, screws, glue, and varnish are indirect materials whose costs are assigned to Manufacturing Supplies Inventory at the time of purchase and transferred to the factory overhead cost pool as they are used.

Indirect labor includes the salaries and wages earned by production employees for the time they spend performing all production related tasks, except physically working on the product. These production related tasks include receiving instructions, oiling machinery, and cleaning the work area. Salaries earned by production supervisors and wages earned by maintenance personnel may also be classified as indirect labor.

Idle time is time employees are not working on the product or performing other production related tasks. Included in this category are the time employees wait for instructions, materials, or repairs. Unless idle time becomes excessive, the salaries and wages paid employees for idle time are regarded as a normal operating cost and included in the factory overhead cost pool. In most organizations it is difficult to structure activities so that employees have no unassigned time. Some employers also pay idle time wages to employees who report for work when no work is available.

Overtime premiums are bonus wages in excess of the regular hourly rate that are paid to production employees for working more than the regular number of hours. Employees who regularly work 40 hours per week will receive an overtime premium for working more than 40 hours. Assume an employee whose regular wage rate is $12 per hour is entitled to a 50 percent overtime premium. If the employee works 45 hours in a given week, the employee's total wages will be $570.

Regular hourly wages (45 × $12)	$540
Overtime premium (5 × $6)	30
Total wages	$570

Overtime premiums are usually treated as factory overhead even if the overtime hours are identified with particular units of product. Overtime is the result of the overall level of activity. If there were less activity, products worked on during overtime hours would be worked on during regular hours. Accordingly, overtime premiums are spread over all production as part of factory overhead. In the above example, $540 is classified as direct labor, and $30 is classified as factory overhead.

Employee fringe benefits are additional labor costs paid by the employer on behalf of the employees. Employee fringe benefits are not included in the computation of employees' salary or wage rates, nor are they disclosed on employees' pay stubs as part of gross earnings or as a deduction in arriving at net earnings. Typical employee fringe benefits include: the employer's share of social security (FICA) taxes, federal and state unemployment taxes, workmen's compensation insurance, medical insurance premiums, employer paid pension plans, and vacation pay.

In the past, employee fringe benefits were a small percentage of total labor costs. Because of their relatively small size, management accountants believed that the increased accuracy that would result from separately accounting for them was not worth the additional bookkeeping cost. Consequently, the cost of employee fringe benefits has traditionally been assigned to the factory overhead cost pool.

However, a recent U.S. Chamber of Commerce survey reported that, in many organizations, employee fringe benefits now exceed 35 percent of the total labor bill. This has led some management accountants to question the propriety of the traditional method of accounting for them. There is a concern that employee fringe benefits will dominate the factory overhead cost pool and cause an inaccurate allocation of either the employee fringe benefits or the other overhead costs. Rather than mixing the cost of fringe benefits with other overhead costs, many firms now place employee fringe benefits in a separate cost pool and assign them to products on the basis of direct labor costs.

COST CONCEPTS FOR MANAGEMENT ACTION

The product costing concepts and techniques introduced above are used to develop the historical cost information presented in general purpose financial statements. Management is interested in historical cost information primarily because it is useful in controlling current operations and planning future operations.

Historical Costs for Prediction and Control

To plan a trip you need to know your current location, your destination, and alternative ways of traveling between them. Likewise, to plan for the future a manager must understand the organization's current situation, its goals, and alternative ways of traveling between them. A manager can obtain an understanding of where the organization is (its current economic situation) by studying historical cost data and reports. A detailed analysis of historical cost data also assists in determining whether the organization has the capabilities needed to achieve its goals. If, for example, an organization's plant is old and its production costs exceed competitor's selling prices, the organization cannot currently compete in the market for its final product.

Management is often interested in how costs respond to changes in the volume of activity. Some costs increase in direct proportion to increases in activity, whereas others do not change at all. An analysis of historical cost data provides an excellent starting point in determining cost behavior. Furthermore, predictions of future costs are often based on historical cost relationships, adjusted for changes in prices and technology. Cost behavior is studied in Chapter 3, and predicted cost relationships are used for profit planning in Chapters 4 through 6.

Subsequent to planning, actual (historical) costs are accumulated and analyzed for the purpose of controlling operations and improving future plans. In Chapters 7 through 10, performance reports are developed that compare allowed and actual costs. Special attention is given to the problem of determining who is responsible for each cost.

Sunk Costs and Relevant Costs

Although an analysis of historical cost information is a useful starting point in predicting future costs, historical costs, in and of themselves, are irrelevant to decisions about the future. In the context of decision making, historical costs are called sunk costs.

Sunk costs result from past decisions that management no longer has control over. Because sunk costs cannot be changed, they are irrelevant to decisions about the future and should be omitted from any analysis prepared to assist in decision making. Including sunk costs makes it difficult for management to focus on important decision variables; furthermore, management may be misled into making bad decisions on the basis of sunk costs that cannot be changed.

Relevant costs are future costs that differ among competing alternatives. Because relevant costs can be changed by management decisions (selecting one alternative rather than another), they should be included in any analysis prepared to assist in decision making. Assume management is evaluating the desirability of replacing a four-function calculator with a new ten-function calculator that has several memory units. The old calculator was purchased yesterday for $25 and has a used sales value of $15. The new calculator costs $90. Using the new calculator rather than the old one will save three labor hours per week at a cost of $15 per hour. For simplicity assume a planning period is 10 weeks, at the end of which both calculators will cease to operate and have a zero salvage value.

The cost of the calculator purchased yesterday is irrelevant to a decision to keep it or replace it with a new calculator. The relevant factors for this decision are the cost of the new calculator, the disposal value of the old calculator, and the cost savings derived from using the new, rather than the old, calculator. The net benefit of acquiring the new calculator is $375.

Labor cost reduction (10 wk. × 3 hr. per wk. × $15 per hr.)		$450
Additional investment:		
Cost of new calculator	$90	
Less disposal value of old calculator	−15	−75
Net benefit		$375

The $25 cost of the old calculator was not included in the analysis because it is a sunk cost.

Sunk costs are not relevant to an economic analysis of decisions about the future, but they do have behavioral implications. Even though it is economically advantageous to acquire the new calculator, a manager might be reluctant to do so lest this new decision should reflect poorly on the decision to acquire the old calculator. Sometimes accounting procedures increase this fear when, for example, it is necessary to compute and disclose a "loss" on the disposal of an old asset. This is a situation where good decisions will be made only if managers and management accountants have a clear understanding of the proper uses and limits of accounting data.

Opportunity Cost

An **opportunity cost** is the net cash inflow that could be obtained if the resources committed to one action were used in the most desirable other alternative. An opportunity cost results from a forgone opportunity. By selecting one opportunity, management forgoes an alternative. Other things equal, management desires to select the alternative with the smallest total cost, including any opportunity cost. Consequently, opportunity costs are relevant costs and, as such, should always be considered in decision making. Note, however, that because there are no cash receipts or cash expenditures incurred in connection with a forgone opportunity, opportunity costs are not recorded in the accounting records.

Opportunity costs are a significant part of the cost of your education. How much more could you earn this year, at your current education and skill level, if you were not enrolled in college? $10,000? If so, $10,000 is the opportunity cost of your college education this year. This opportunity cost should be added to tuition, room, board, books, and so forth in computing your total educational investment.[5]

---

[5] The benefits of this investment will accrue in the future. Ways to equate monetary future benefits with current investments are considered in Chapter 14. There are, of course, many nonmonetary benefits associated with a college education.

What, then, is the opportunity cost of acquiring the new calculator? The answer depends on the best other alternative use of the $75 additional investment. If the money were to remain in a noninterest bearing checking account or earn $6 interest in a short-term savings certificate, the best other alternative action would be to invest in the savings certificate, so the opportunity cost would be $6. In this case, the $6 opportunity cost should be compared to the net benefits of the new calculator to determine the net advantage or disadvantage of purchasing the calculator. The net economic advantage of purchasing the calculator would, therefore, be $369 ($375 net benefit − $6 opportunity cost).

It is important to understand that the opportunity cost of an action is a function of the *other* alternative actions. Investing in the savings certificate has an opportunity cost of $375 because this is the net cash inflow from the most desirable other action, namely, buying the calculator. Likewise, the opportunity cost of leaving the $75 in a noninterest bearing checking account is $375.

SUMMARY

Though cost is generally defined as a monetary measure of the economic sacrifice made to obtain some product or service, different cost concepts and measurements are required for different purposes. A system for cost measurement includes a costing purpose, cost objectives, cost elements, and costing techniques. For the purpose of external reporting, products are important cost objectives in manufacturing organizations. The cost of a product contains three major cost elements: direct materials, direct labor, and factory overhead. The pooling of all product costs other than direct materials and direct labor into a single factory overhead cost pool and the application of factory overhead to products using a predetermined overhead rate are important product costing techniques.

In manufacturing organizations a distinction is made between product costs and period costs. Product costs are assigned to products and accounted for as assets until the product is sold. At that time they become an expense, that is, the cost of goods sold. Period costs are nonproduct costs that are accounted for as expenses in the period their service potential expires.

Product costing is emphasized in this chapter because product costing is well developed, easily generalized and understood, and required for external reporting. Many of the concepts discussed here are also applicable to service costing. The accounting system used for product costing also provides the data used for many management accounting purposes.

In and of themselves, historical costs are not relevant to an economic analysis of the future. They are sunk costs that management can no longer control. An economic analysis prepared to assist management in making decisions should focus on relevant costs, that is, on future costs that differ among competing alternatives.

KEY TERMS

Cost

Costing purpose

Cost objective

Cost element

Costing technique

Service organizations

Merchandising organizations

Manufacturing organizations

Raw materials inventory

Work-in-process inventory

Finished goods inventory

Product costing

Service costing

Unexpired cost

Expired cost

Product cost

Period cost

Absorption cost basis of external
reporting

Direct materials

Direct labor

Factory overhead

Current manufacturing costs

Cost of goods manufactured

Statement of cost of goods
manufactured

Statement of cost of goods
manufactured and sold

Direct product costs

Prime product costs

Indirect product costs

Conversion costs

Cost pool

Predetermined factory overhead rate

Indirect materials

Indirect labor

Idle time

Overtime premium

Employee fringe benefits

Sunk cost

Relevant cost

Opportunity cost

**REVIEW
QUESTIONS**

2–1   What relationships exist between costing purpose, cost objectives, cost elements, and costing techniques?

2–2   Why is management accounting information subject to more stringent cost-benefit analysis than financial accounting information?

2–3   Distinguish between service, merchandising, and manufacturing organizations on the basis of the importance and complexity of inventory cost measurement.

2–4   Distinguish between raw materials, work-in-process, and finished goods inventories.

2–5   Distinguish between product costing and service costing. Why do we emphasize product costing rather than service costing in this chapter?

2–6   In general, how do we determine whether a cost is an expired cost or an unexpired cost?

2–7   When is depreciation a product cost? When is depreciation a period cost?

2–8   What are the three major product cost elements?

2–9 How can you determine when a manufacturing cost should be classified as factory overhead?

2–10 Which product cost element is both a prime cost and a conversion cost?

2–11 What are the characteristics of a good basis of overhead application?

2–12 How are predetermined overhead rates developed? Why are they widely used?

2–13 What labor costs are often elements of factory overhead?

2–14 Of what use are historical costs in planning for the future?

2–15 Are opportunity costs relevant costs? Why or why not?

EXERCISES

2–1 Cost Terms: Matching

For each of the numbered phrases or statements, select the *most appropriate* cost term. Each term is used only once.

1. Objects or activities costs are assigned to
2. Has three inventory categories
3. Sold to other organizations
4. Benefit forgone
5. Performs work for others
6. Cannot be changed
7. Manufacturing costs except direct materials and labor
8. Future costs that differ
9. Total additions to Work-in-Process
10. These costs are assigned to inventories

a. Product costs
b. Service organization
c. Sunk cost
d. Relevant costs
e. Opportunity cost
f. Cost objectives
g. Manufacturing organization
h. Current manufacturing costs
i. Finished goods
j. Factory overhead

2–2 Cost Terms: Matching

For each of the numbered phrases or statements, select the *most appropriate* cost term. Each term is used only once.

1. Direct materials and direct labor
2. Direct labor and factory overhead
3. Used to assign cost elements to cost objectives
4. Selling and administrative expenses
5. Buys and sells goods
6. Being converted to a finished product
7. All manufacturing costs are product costs
8. A collection of related costs
9. A measure of economic sacrifice
10. Transferred to Finished Goods Inventory

a. Costing technique
b. Merchandising organization
c. Work-in-process
d. Absorption cost basis of external reporting
e. Cost of goods manufactured
f. Cost pool
g. Cost
h. Direct product costs
i. Period costs
j. Conversion costs

2–3 Classification of Product and Period Costs

Classify the following costs incurred by a furniture manufacturer as product costs or period costs. Further classify the product costs as direct or indirect product costs.

1. Depreciation on factory
2. Rent on cars used by salespersons
3. Power and water consumed in the factory
4. Advertising in national magazines
5. Broken saw blades
6. Vacation pay of production workers
7. Carpenters' wages
8. Depreciation on table saws
9. Glue used in furniture assembly
10. Supervisors' salaries
11. Materials used in packing finished goods prior to shipment
12. Participation in regional trade shows
13. Management training seminar
14. Depreciation on corporate headquarters
15. Prime lumber

2–4 Classification of Product and Period Costs

Classify the following costs incurred by an automobile manufacturer as product costs or period costs. Further classify the product costs as direct materials or conversion.

1. Automobile window glass
2. Salaries of legal staff
3. Depreciation on word processor in president's office
4. Plant fire department
5. Automobile tires
6. Automobile bumpers
7. Wages paid assembly line maintenance workers
8. Salary of corporate controller
9. Automobile engines
10. Subsidy of plant cafeteria
11. Wages paid assembly line production workers
12. National sales meeting in Detroit
13. Overtime premium paid assembly line workers
14. Advertising on national television
15. Depreciation on assembly line

2–5 Account Activity and Interrelationships

For each of the following independent cases find the required information.

1. *Cash*

Beginning balance	$ 20,000
Ending balance	25,000
Cash receipts	130,000

Find: Cash disbursements

2. *Merchandise Inventory*

Purchases	$104,000
Cost of goods sold	80,000
Ending balance	70,000

Find: Beginning balance

3. *Accounts Payable* (to suppliers)

Ending balance	$ 56,000
Payments on account	302,000
Beginning balance	88,000

Find: Purchases on account

4. *Accounts Receivable*

Sales on account	$260,000
Collections on account	291,000
Beginning balance	57,000

Find: Ending balance

5. *Merchandise Inventory*

Beginning balance	$15,000
Ending balance	40,000
Cost of goods sold	95,000

Accounts Payable (to suppliers)

Beginning balance	$ 5,000
Ending balance	6,000

Find: Payments on account when all purchases are on account

6. *Merchandise Inventory*

Beginning balance	$ 39,000
Ending balance	29,000
Purchases	110,000

Accounts Receivable

Beginning balance	$ 23,000
Ending balance	120,000

Find: Collections on account when all sales are on account and the selling price is 150 percent of cost

2–6 Account Activity and Interrelationships

For each of the following independent cases find the required information.

1. *Raw Materials*

Beginning balance	$ 5,000
Ending balance	14,000
Purchases	48,000

Find: Direct materials

2. *Work-in-Process*

Ending balance	$22,000
Cost of goods manufactured	21,000
Beginning balance	8,000

Find: Current manufacturing costs

3. *Finished Goods Inventory*

Cost of goods manufactured	$62,000
Ending balance	15,000
Cost of goods sold	61,000

Find: Beginning balance

4. *Merchandise Inventory*

Purchases	$210,000
Cost of goods sold	223,000
Beginning balance	41,000

Find: Ending balance

5. *Raw Materials*

Beginning balance	$ 9,000
Ending balance	12,000
Direct materials	42,000

6. *Finished Goods Inventory*

Beginning balance	$ 22,000
Cost of goods manufactured	100,000
Ending balance	30,000

Accounts Payable (to suppliers)		*Accounts Receivable*	
Ending balance	$11,000	Beginning balance	$ 16,000
Beginning balance	6,000	Ending balance	50,000
Find: Payments on account		*Find:* Collections on account	
when all purchases are on		when all sales are on account	
account		and the selling price is 200	
		percent of cost	

2–7 Analyzing Activity in Inventory Accounts

Selected data concerning the past fiscal year's operations of the Televans Manufacturing Company are presented below.

	Beginning	Ending
Raw materials used		$326,000
Total manufacturing costs charged to production during the year (includes raw materials, direct labor, and factory overhead applied at a rate of 60 percent of direct labor cost)		686,000
Cost of goods available for sale		826,000
Selling and general expenses		25,000
	Inventories	
Raw materials	$75,000	$ 85,000
Work-in-process	80,000	30,000
Finished goods	90,000	110,000

Required: Determine each of the following:

1. The cost of raw materials purchased.
2. The direct labor costs charged to production.
3. The cost of goods manufactured.
4. The cost of goods sold.

(CMA Adapted)

2–8 Statements: Cost of Goods Manufactured, Income

Information from the records of the Roanoke Manufacturing Company is given below for the month of August, 19x4.

	August 1	August 31
Sales		$205,000
Selling and administrative expenses		63,000
Purchases of raw materials		20,000
Direct labor		30,000
Factory overhead		32,000
	Inventories	
Raw materials	$ 7,000	$ 5,000
Work-in-process	14,000	11,000
Finished goods	15,000	19,000

Requirements

a) Prepare a statement of cost of goods manufactured and an income statement for the month of August.

b) Determine each of the following:

Direct product costs.
Prime product costs.
Indirect product costs.
Conversion costs.

2–9 Statements: Cost of Goods Manufactured and Sold, Income

Information from the records of Flint Products is given below for the month of January, 19x7.

Sales			$350,000
Selling and administrative expenses			55,000
Purchases of raw materials			90,000
Direct labor			120,000
Overhead is applied using a predetermined overhead rate of 130 percent of direct labor.			
		Inventories	
	January 1		*January 31*
Raw materials	$12,000		$ 5,000
Work-in-process	50,000		25,000
Finished goods	30,000		40,000

Requirements

a) Prepare a statement of cost of goods manufactured and sold and an income statement for the month of January.

b) Determine each of the following:

Direct product costs.
Prime product costs.
Indirect product costs.
Conversion costs.

2–10 Developing and Using a Predetermined Overhead Rate

The following predictions were made for 19x9:

Total factory overhead for the year	$1,125,000
Total direct labor hours for the year	125,000

Actual results for January, 19x9 were as follows:

Factory overhead	$ 73,000
Direct labor hours	8,000

Requirements

a) Determine the 19x9 predetermined overhead rate per direct labor hour.

b) Using the 19x9 predetermined overhead rate, determine the factory overhead applied to Work-in-Process during January.

c) Determine the amount of any overapplied or underapplied overhead at the end of January.

2–11 Developing and Using a Predetermined Overhead Rate

The following predictions were made for 19x2:

Total factory overhead for the year	$360,000
Total machine hours for the year	20,000

Actual results for February, 19x2 were as follows:

Factory overhead	$ 55,200
Machine hours	3,100

Requirements

a) Determine the 19x2 predetermined overhead rate per machine hour.

b) Using the 19x2 predetermined overhead rate per machine hour, determine the factory overhead applied to Work-in-Process during February.

c) As of February 1, actual overhead was underapplied by $500. Determine the cumulative amount of any overapplied or underapplied overhead at the end of February.

2–12 Assignment of Overtime Premium

Susan Dove is a telephone installer in a college-oriented community. During the last week of August she spent 25 hours installing telephones in Riverview Apartments, 23 hours installing telephones in Sam's Luxury Apartments, and 3 hours on general tasks. Mrs. Dove has a regular 40-hour workweek with scheduled daily hours from 8 A.M. to 12 P.M. and from 1 P.M. to 5 P.M., Monday through Friday. Of the 23 hours at Sam's Luxury Apartments, 11 were after 5 P.M. Mrs. Dove's wage rate is $9 per hour with time-and-a-half for overtime.

Required: Determine the amount of Mrs. Dove's labor cost that should be assigned to each apartment complex. Explain why some of Mrs. Dove's labor costs should be assigned to overhead.

2–13 Determining and Classifying Labor Related Costs

Joan Keller works on the assembly line of the National Computer Company. She installs cathode ray picture tubes in personal computers. Because of the high demand for the company's products, Joan often works overtime hours. During a recent week her total reported time was 48 hours with 42 hours spent working on the assembly line.

The base wage rate for assembly line workers is $12 per hour. Employee fringe benefits amount to 40 percent of the base wage rate. Employees are paid time-and-a-half for overtime. The regular workweek is 40 hours.

Requirements

a) Determine the total wages and benefits earned by Joan Keller.

b) If all earnings other than the base wages paid for working on products are classified as factory overhead, classify Keller's total earnings as direct labor and factory overhead.

c) If base wages paid for working on products and related fringe benefits are classified as direct labor, with all other earnings classified as factory overhead, classify Keller's total earnings as direct labor and factory overhead.

2–14 Determining and Classifying Labo Related Costs

Gary Dicer is a teller at the Big Bucks National Bank. During a recent week he worked a total of 52 hours with 38 hours spent at a drive-up banking window and 14 hours spent on breaks and miscellaneous tasks.

The base wage rate for tellers is $6 per hour. Employee fringe benefits amount to 30 percent of the base wage rate. Employees are paid time-and-a-half for overtime. The regular workweek is 40 hours.

Requirements

a) Determine the total wages and benefits earned by Gary Dicer.

b) To determine the cost of bank activities, Big Bucks classifies the earnings of tellers as direct labor and operating overhead. If all earnings other than the base wages paid for working at the teller's window are classified as operating overhead, classify Dicer's total earnings as direct labor and operating overhead.

c) If base wages paid for working at the teller's window and related fringe benefits are classified as direct labor, with all other earnings classified as operating overhead, classify Dicer's total earnings as direct labor and operating overhead.

2–15 Establishing Overhead Cost Pools

A cost pool is a collection of related costs. Presented are a number of factory overhead costs. Classify these costs into one of three cost pools:

Pool 1: The existence of buildings and equipment.
Pool 2: The use of buildings and equipment.
Pool 3: The availability and use of direct labor.

Factory overhead costs:

Depreciation on buildings and machinery.
Power.
Water.

Fringe benefits.
Idle time wages.
Property taxes.
Supervisors' salaries.
Property insurance on buildings and equipment.
Overtime premiums.
Lubricants for machines.
Safety hats and shoes.
Night and weekend security.
Subsidy of employee cafeteria.

2–16 Relevant Costs

Sally Byte is a computer science major just starting her senior year. To complete her extensive programming assignments, Sally goes to the computer lab every Saturday and Sunday. Because she lives off-campus and does not have a car, she takes the bus to and from campus at a round trip cost of $1.20.

A local Computer Shack store has offered to rent Sally a computer terminal and modem (a telephone connection) so that she can complete her programming assignments at home by dialing the college computer. The rental fee is $300 for the academic year, payable in advance. The academic year is 30 weeks long.

If Sally rents the modem, she will be able to work four additional hours each week at a part-time job that pays $4 per hour.

Required: Determine the net benefit of renting the computer terminal and modem for the 30-week academic year.

2–17 Relevant Costs

John Bright recently spent $5 to purchase a regular flashlight that operates on two size D batteries. While walking through a discount store, John came upon a rechargeable flashlight that was on sale for $20. The promotional literature indicated that the rechargeable flashlight could be plugged into an electric outlet and recharged for only $0.25.

Additional information:

- Size D batteries cost $0.50 each.
- John will replace batteries or recharge the flashlight an average of four times a year.
- The expected life of both flashlights is 5 years.
- A friend has offered to pay John $2.00 for the regular flashlight.

Required: Determine the net benefit (or cost) of replacing the regular flashlight with a rechargeable flashlight.

2–18 Sunk Costs Versus Relevant Costs

A medium size consulting firm has a number of portable computers for the use of its professional staff. The firm's bookkeeper, Mr. Eyeshade, is responsible for issuing the computers to authorized persons and seeing that they are returned in good condition.

A recently hired employee checked out a computer and was crossing the street on her way to her first assignment when she slipped and fell on the ice, breaking a leg. The computer crashed to the ground and slid under the wheels of a speeding taxicab. Bystanders called an ambulance and the sound of the ambulance siren brought Mr. Eyeshade to the window. After surveying the scene, the employee with a broken leg, the damaged computer, and the angry taxi driver, Mr. Eyeshade observed, "I'm glad the computer was fully depreciated."

Required: Comment. Be sure to distinguish between relevant and irrelevant costs. What would Mr. Eyeshade's reaction have been if the computer were not fully depreciated?

2–19 Opportunity Costs

Specialty Products paid $10,000 for a specialized machine and then discovered that the market for the product the machine was intended to produce had completely disappeared. Specialty Products has two offers for the machine:

1. A machine shop has offered to buy the machine for $3000 with the intention of disassembling it and reselling the machine's parts.
2. A promotional firm has offered to rent the machine for one year. They would pay a rental fee of $5000; however, Specialty Products would have to spend $1500 modifying the machine. At the end of the year the machine would be worthless.

Required: Determine the opportunity cost associated with each alternative. Which offer should Specialty Products accept?

2–20 Opportunity Costs

Mr. Fury purchased an antique Plymouth for $4000 and spent another $16,000 reconditioning it. Mr. Fury is currently considering three alternative uses for the car:

1. DeSoto's Auto Museum has offered Mr. Fury a lease-purchase agreement that involves leasing the car to the museum for one year with the museum purchasing the car at the end of the year. The lease payment of $3000 and the purchase price of $20,000 are both payable at the end of the year.
2. A local car buff has offered Mr. Fury $20,000 in cash for the car. If Mr. Fury accepts this offer, he will invest the money in a one year bank certificate that pays 10 percent interest.
3. He can keep the car in a local warehouse for one year, and then sell it for $25,000. The storage costs of $1000 are payable at the end of the year.

Required: Determine the opportunity cost of each action.

PROBLEMS

2–21 Statements: Cost of Goods Manufactured, Income

Presented is information from the records of the Rocking Horse Craft Shop for the month of June, 19x2.

Purchases:	
Lumber	$ 4,500
Glue, paint, sandpaper, and small tools	100
Office supplies	210
Sales	15,000
Salaries: Selling and administrative (including	
fringe benefits of $250)	2,000
Wages: Production (including fringe benefits of $400)	3,000
Rent	2,000*
Utilities	600*
Advertising	350

	Inventories	
	June 1	*June 30*
Lumber	$ 1,200	$ 800
Glue, paint, etc.	250	300
Office supplies	75	90
Finished goods	12,000	8,000

* Sixty percent of these costs are assigned to manufacturing and 40 percent to selling and administration.

Production employee fringe benefits are classified as factory overhead. There is no beginning or ending inventory of work-in-process.

Requirements

a) Prepare a statement of cost of goods manufactured and an income statement. Actual overhead costs are assigned to products.

b) Determine each of the following:

Direct product costs.
Prime product costs.
Indirect product costs.
Conversion costs.

2–22 Statements: Cost of Goods Manufactured, Income

Presented at the top of page 57 is information from the records of the Charles River Production Company for the month of July, 19x3.

Purchases:	
Raw materials	$ 70,000
Manufacturing supplies	3,500
Office supplies	1,200
Sales	425,700
Administrative salaries	12,000
Direct labor	105,000
Production employee's fringe benefits	4,000*
Sales commissions	50,000
Production supervisors' salaries	7,200
Depreciation on plant	14,000
Depreciation on office	20,000
Plant maintenance	10,000
Plant utilities	35,000
Office utilities	8,000
Office maintenance	2,000
Production equipment rent	6,000
Office equipment rent	1,300

	Inventories	
	July 1	July 31
Raw materials	$17,000	$15,000
Manufacturing supplies	1,500	3,000
Office supplies	600	1,000
Work-in-process	51,000	40,000
Finished goods	35,000	27,100

* Classified as factory overhead.

Requirements

a) Prepare a statement of cost of goods manufactured and an income statement
Actual overhead costs are assigned to products.

b) Determine each of the following:

Direct product costs.
Prime product costs.
Indirect product costs.
Conversion costs.

2–23 Account Interrelationships: Missing Production Data

Supply the missing data in each independent case in the table at the top of page 58.

	Case 1	Case 2	Case 3	Case 4
Raw materials, beginning	$ 5,000	$ 3,000	$?	$ 3,000
Purchases	10,000	?	20,000	7,000
Raw materials, ending	8,000	5,000	6,000	2,000
Direct materials	?	20,000	30,000	?
Direct labor	12,000	?	40,000	?
Factory overhead	20,000	20,000	?	30,000
Current manufacturing costs	?	65,000	?	90,000
Work-in-process, beginning	15,000	?	10,000	5,000
Work-in-process, ending	16,000	35,000	20,000	?
Cost of goods manufactured	?	105,000	90,000	80,000
Finished goods, beginning	25,000	?	20,000	10,000
Finished goods, ending	10,000	10,000	50,000	?
Cost of goods sold	?	98,000	?	70,000

2–24 Account Interrelationships: Missing Data

Supply the missing data in each independent case.

	Case 1	Case 2	Case 3	Case 4
Sales	$50,000	$?	$?	$?
Raw materials, beginning	10,000	13,000	?	5,300
Purchases	?	13,000	2,500	31,400
Raw materials, ending	8,000	?	500	6,200
Direct materials	?	20,000	2,000	?
Direct labor	20,000	25,000	6,000	?
Factory overhead	10,000	8,000	?	29,200
Current manufacturing costs	55,000	?	12,000	?
Work-in-process, beginning	?	8,000	8,000	5,300
Work-in-process, ending	5,000	7,000	?	4,000
Cost of goods manufactured	55,000	?	19,000	82,000
Finished goods, beginning	?	6,000	1,500	8,000
Finished goods, ending	25,000	?	500	10,000
Cost of goods sold	?	55,000	?	?
Gross profit	10,000	9,000	?	10,500
Other expenses	8,000	?	5,000	3,500
Net income (loss)	?	(4,000)	1,000	?

2–25 Statement of Cost of Goods Manufactured and Sold from Percent Relationships

Information about the Ratio Company for the year ending December 31, 19x1 is given below.

- Sales $200,000
- Direct materials   32,000
- Factory overhead is 150 percent of direct labor.
- The beginning inventory of finished goods is 20 percent of the cost of goods sold.
- The ending inventory of finished goods is twice the beginning inventory.
- The gross profit is 20 percent of sales.

■ There is no beginning or ending work-in-process.

Required: Prepare a statement of cost of goods manufactured and sold for 19x1. *Hint:* Set up the statement format and start the solution from known information.

2–26 Income Statement and Statement of Cost of Goods Manufactured from Percent Relationships

Information about the Lots-O-Luck Company for the year ending December 31, 19x1 is given below.

■ Sales $350,000

■ Net income   5,000

■ Ending inventories:

Raw materials	18,000
Work-in-process	8,000
Finished goods	67,000

■ Inventory changes:
 Ending raw materials are twice beginning raw materials.
 Ending work-in-process is one-third larger than beginning work-in-process.
 Finished goods inventory increased by $15,000 during the year.

■ Selling and administrative expenses are five times net income.

■ Prime costs are 60 percent of manufacturing costs.

■ Conversion costs are 80 percent of manufacturing costs.

Required: Prepare an income statement and a statement of cost of goods manufactured for 19x1. *Hint:* Set up the statement formats and start the solution from known information.

2–27 Statement of Cost of Goods Manufactured with Predetermined Overhead and Labor Cost Classification

Presented is information pertaining to Little Bear Productions for the month of December, 19x4.

Purchases of raw materials	$ 41,000
Sales	310,000
Supervisors' salaries (production), including fringe benefits	20,000
Depreciation on office	17,500
Depreciation on plant	35,000
Plant utilities	51,000
Plant insurance	6,000
Purchases of office supplies	350
Plant property taxes	40,000

	Inventories	
	December 1	December 31
Raw materials	$ 3,000	$ 5,000
Office supplies	250	150
Work-in-process	25,000	15,000
Finished goods	12,000	18,000

Additional information:

- Factory overhead is applied to products at the rate of 200 percent of direct labor dollars.

- Employee base wages are $10 per hour.

- Employee fringe benefits amount to 50 percent of the base wage rate. They are classified as factory overhead.

- During December, production employees worked 9000 hours, including 8500 spent working on products.

Requirements

a) Prepare a statement of cost of goods manufactured.

b) Determine underapplied or overapplied overhead for December.

2–28 Statements: Cost of Goods Manufactured, Income with Predetermined Overhead and Labor Cost Classification

Presented is information pertaining to Big Bear, Incorporated for the month of April, 19x9.

Sales		$200,000
Purchases:		
Raw materials		35,000
Manufacturing supplies		800
Office supplies		500
Salaries (including fringe benefits)		
Administrative		6,000
Production supervisors		3,600
Sales		15,000
Depreciation:		
Plant and machinery		8,000
Office and office equipment		4,000
Utilities:		
Plant		5,250
Office		890

	Inventories	
	April 1	*April 30*
Raw materials	$5,000	$3,500
Manufacturing supplies	1,000	1,100
Office supplies	900	800
Work-in-process	2,000	2,300
Finished goods	8,000	9,000

Additional information:

- Factory overhead is applied to products at 80 percent of direct labor dollars.

- Employee base wages are $12 per hour.

- Employee fringe benefits amount to 40 percent of the base wage rate. They are classified as factory overhead.
- During April, production employees worked 5600 hours, including 4800 regular hours and 200 overtime hours spent working on products.
- Employees are paid a 50 percent overtime premium.

Requirements

a) Prepare a statement of cost of goods manufactured and an income statement.

b) Determine underapplied or overapplied overhead for April.

c) Recompute direct labor and actual factory overhead assuming employee fringe benefits for direct labor hours are classified as direct labor.

3

Cost Behavior Analysis

Activities undertaken to achieve an organization's short-range and long-range objectives result in the incurrence of various costs. Because economic resources are limited, managers must carefully control both costs and the activities that cause them. To plan and control costs, managers must know how costs respond to changes in activity. Some costs increase in direct proportion to changes in activity, whereas others do not change at all. Still others, which do not change throughout a range of activity, will then increase suddenly to a different amount. Managers need to know which costs will change, the circumstances that cause them to change, and the amount they will change.

The purpose of this chapter is to introduce **cost behavior analysis,** which is the study of how costs respond to changes in the volume of activity. We will study the major cost behavior patterns used in accounting models, mention several representative costs that display each pattern, and survey methods used to estimate cost behavior.

PLOTTING COST BEHAVIOR

The relationship between the volume and the total cost of an activity is often illustrated with a graph, such as the one in Exhibit 3–1(a). Volume, the independent variable that causes the incurrence of costs, is measured on the horizontal axis. Total cost, the dependent variable that responds to changes in volume, is measured on the vertical axis. Combinations of observed activity and cost are represented by dots. Total cost and total volume increase up and to the right from the origin, where the horizontal and vertical axes intersect. Each unit of activity, in Exhibit 3–1(a), results in the incurrence of an additional $1 in total costs.

By compressing the measurement scale, it is possible to move the individual dots so close together that the relationship between volume and total cost appears to be a solid line. In Exhibit 3–1(b) the unit cost is still $1, but the range of activity is now 0 to 500 units rather than 0 to 5 units. For ease of presentation, lines are often used to represent cost behavior even when the scale of activity is such that dots might be better. In cost behavior analysis, the horizontal axis is, by convention, labeled "volume" rather than "total volume of activity," "total activity," or "total volume." Because there are a variety of cost concepts, care should be taken to label the vertical axis "total cost," "average cost," "unit cost," or whatever other term is appropriate.

The slope of a line measures the change in the dependent variable for each unit of change in the independent variable. In cost behavior analysis, the slope indicates the responsiveness of costs to changes in volume.

EXHIBIT 3–1   Plotting Cost Behavior

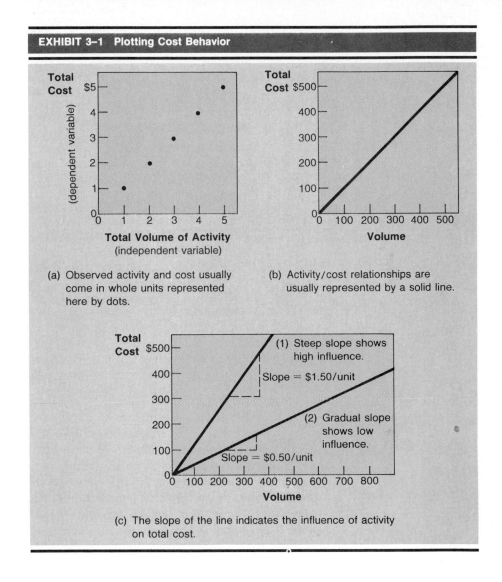

(a) Observed activity and cost usually come in whole units represented here by dots.

(b) Activity/cost relationships are usually represented by a solid line.

(c) The slope of the line indicates the influence of activity on total cost.

The slope of the total cost line is the incremental cost of one unit. In Exhibit 3–1(c) the slope of line (1) illustrates a situation where volume has a relatively large influence on total cost, whereas the slope of line (2) illustrates a situation where volume has a relatively small influence on total cost.

The slope of a straight line is computed as the change in the total cost between two selected volumes divided by the difference between the two volumes. The slopes of the two lines in Exhibit 3–1(c) are

$$\text{Slope of line (1)} = \frac{\$450 - \$300}{300 - 200} = \$1.50 \text{ per unit,}$$

and

$$\text{Slope of line (2)} = \frac{\$150 - \$100}{300 - 200} = \$0.50 \text{ per unit.}$$

The 300 and 200 unit volumes were randomly selected. Any pair of volumes on either line would give identical results.

IMPORTANT COST BEHAVIOR PATTERNS

Four cost behavior patterns — for variable, fixed, mixed (or semivariable), and step costs — are widely used in accounting models. Although the behavior of each is illustrated with a straight line drawn between zero units and an arbitrarily chosen high volume of activity, management is only interested in cost behavior within the range of *probable* activity. Illustrated cost behavior patterns are seldom valid over the entire range of *possible* activity. This limitation will be examined further immediately after the introduction of important total cost behavior patterns.

Variable Costs

A **variable cost** is the uniform incremental cost of each additional unit. Total variable costs change in direct proportion to changes in volume, equaling zero dollars when activity is zero and increasing at a constant amount per unit of activity. Typical variable costs include sales commissions, direct materials, direct labor, cost of goods sold in merchandising, postage in magazine publishing, gasoline in trucking, and asphalt in road maintenance. A behavior pattern for total variable costs is illustrated in Exhibit 3–2(a) by an upward sloping straight line that starts at the origin. The slope of this line represents the variable cost per unit. The equation for total variable costs is

$$\begin{array}{c}\text{Total variable} \\ \text{costs}\end{array} = \begin{array}{c}\text{Variable cost} \\ \text{per unit}\end{array} \times \begin{array}{c}\text{Unit} \\ \text{volume.}\end{array}$$

A 50 percent increase in volume results in a 50 percent increase in total variable costs. If hamburger patties cost Big Burger Restaurant $0.50 each, and Big Burger serves 10,000 hamburgers during February, the cost of hamburger patties consumed is $5000 (10,000 × $0.50). If volume increases 50 percent in March, the cost of hamburger patties consumed increases proportionally, to $7500 (15,000 × $0.50).

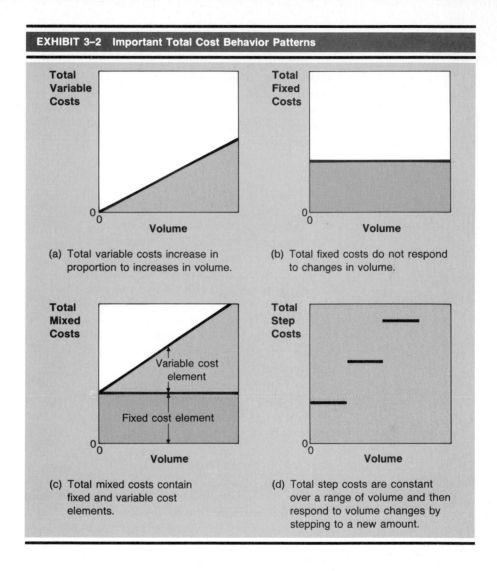

EXHIBIT 3–2   Important Total Cost Behavior Patterns

Total Variable Costs — Volume

(a) Total variable costs increase in proportion to increases in volume.

Total Fixed Costs — Volume

(b) Total fixed costs do not respond to changes in volume.

Total Mixed Costs — Volume

Variable cost element

Fixed cost element

(c) Total mixed costs contain fixed and variable cost elements.

Total Step Costs — Volume

(d) Total step costs are constant over a range of volume and then respond to volume changes by stepping to a new amount.

Fixed Costs

A **fixed cost** is a cost that does not respond to changes in the volume of activity within a given period. Total fixed costs are a constant amount per period regardless of the level of activity. Typical fixed costs include depreciation, supervisors' salaries, property taxes, rent, advertising, research and development, and charitable contributions. Total fixed costs are illustrated in Exhibit 3–2(b) by a straight line drawn parallel to the horizontal axis. Because fixed costs do not respond to changes in activity, the slope of the line is zero.

Organizations can control the relative portions of their variable and fixed costs by making long-run decisions about their methods of operation. For example, the frame of an automobile can be welded by skilled laborers or by robots. If the welding is performed by skilled labor, the direct labor cost per unit will be relatively high. If the welding is performed by a robot, fixed costs, such as depreciation, property taxes, and maintenance, will be relatively high. The trade-off between the fixed and variable costs of welding is summarized as follows:

	Relative Welding Costs	
	Skilled Labor	*Robot*
Variable	High	Low
Fixed	Low	High

Since the start of the industrial revolution more than 200 years ago, there has been a systematic shift toward more fixed and fewer variable costs. Though this shift has been generally beneficial, it has also reduced the flexibility of organizations, especially their ability to respond to decreases in activity. The decision to have welding operations performed automatically by a machine can provide an opportunity for great cost savings at high levels of output. However, this course of action is risky because the fixed costs of machine ownership are incurred regardless of the level of output. At low levels of output total costs might be lower if skilled labor were used.

Committed Fixed Costs Maintain Current Capacity. Fixed costs are classified as "committed" or "discretionary," depending on their immediate impact on the organization if they are changed. **Committed fixed costs** are required to maintain the current service or production capacity. Ordinarily, these costs can be reduced only by reducing the organization's capacity. Because they are related to capacity, committed fixed costs are frequently called **capacity costs.** Typical committed fixed costs include depreciation, supervisors' salaries, property taxes, and rent.

Committed fixed costs result from long-range decisions made by top management about the size and nature of the organization. For example, years ago the management of the Delaware and Hudson Railroad made a number of decisions about the railroad, including what communities the railroad would serve. Track was laid on the basis of these decisions, and the Delaware and Hudson now pays property taxes each year on the railroad's miles of track. These property taxes can be reduced by disposing of track. However, reducing the track will also reduce the railroad's capacity to serve.

Capacity is usually thought of in terms of a maximum *volume* of activity, such as the number of automobiles that can be produced in a month, the number of beds in a hospital, the number of seats in a church, and the monthly passenger seat miles in an airplane. There is also a *quality* dimension to current capacity. For example, a restaurant can retain its seating capacity while reducing its committed fixed costs by selling nonessential depreciable assets and reducing expenditures on entertainment, maintenance, heating, cooling, and so forth. The physical capacity remains, but the quality is lower; the restaurant is not what it was before the cost reductions.

Discretionary Fixed Costs Do Not Affect Current Capacity. **Discretionary fixed costs,** sometimes called **managed fixed costs,** are set at a fixed amount each year at the discretion of management. It is possible to change these costs and not change production or service capacity in the near-term. Typical discretionary fixed costs include advertising, charitable contributions, employee training programs, and research and development.

Expenditures on discretionary fixed costs are frequently regarded as investments in the future. Research and development, for example, is undertaken to produce new or improved products that can be profitably produced and sold in future periods. During periods of financial well-being, organizations may make large expenditures on discretionary cost items. Conversely, during periods of financial stress, organizations will likely reduce discretionary expenditures before reducing capacity costs. Managers should, of course, exercise care before making drastic changes in the level of funding of discretionary cost items. Fluctuations in funding reduce the effectiveness of long-range programs. A high quality research staff may be difficult to reassemble if key personnel are laid off; even the contemplation of such layoffs may reduce the staff's effectiveness. In all periods discretionary costs are subject to debate and are likely to be changed in the give and take of the budgeting process. The alternative designation, managed fixed costs, is intended to reflect the importance of management's judgment in setting their amount.

Mixed Costs

Mixed costs, sometimes called **semivariable costs,** contain a fixed and a variable cost element. Total mixed costs are positive (like fixed costs) when volume is zero, and they increase in a linear fashion (like total variable costs) as volume increases. Typical mixed costs include power, maintenance, and automobile rental charges. Some power is required to light buildings and to provide the heat necessary to keep water pipes from freezing in the winter, and additional power is required to operate machinery. Some maintenance is required to prevent the deterioration of buildings and equipment, and additional maintenance is required as the use of these assets increases. Finally, automobiles are frequently rented on the basis of a fixed charge per day plus an additional charge per mile driven. Total mixed costs are illustrated in Exhibit 3–2(c) by an upward sloping straight line that starts above the origin. The equation for total mixed costs is

$$\begin{array}{l} \text{Total mixed} \\ \text{costs} \end{array} = \begin{array}{l} \text{Fixed} \\ \text{costs} \end{array} + \left(\begin{array}{l} \text{Variable cost} \\ \text{per unit} \end{array} \times \begin{array}{l} \text{Unit} \\ \text{volume} \end{array} \right).$$

Because of the presence of fixed costs, total mixed costs do not increase in proportion to volume. Assume Big Burger Restaurant pays a franchise fee of $1000 per month plus 2 percent of sales. The franchise fee for a month when sales revenue totals $50,000 is $2000 [$1000 + ($50,000 × 0.02)]. If sales revenue increases by 50 percent, only the variable cost element of the franchise fee will increase, whereas the fixed element will remain $1000.

Step Costs

Step costs are constant within a range of activity but different between ranges of activity. Total step costs increase in a steplike fashion as volume increases. The steps are caused by input indivisibilities. Typical step costs include the salaries of quality inspectors and production supervisors. In some states the maximum legal first grade student to teacher ratio is 25 to 1. These laws cause first grade instructional costs to follow a step pattern. The first step is fixed over the range of 1 to 25 students. The 26th student requires the addition of a second full-time teacher. The third step starts with the 51st student, and so forth.

Step costs are illustrated in Exhibit 3–2(d) by a series of lines drawn parallel to the horizontal axis. Moving to the right, each line steps up to a level higher than the preceding line. The discontinuity that occurs at each increment makes step costs difficult to analyze, to represent by an equation, or to graphically illustrate in a chart depicting the total effect of several different costs. To overcome these problems, step costs are frequently approximated by mixed or fixed costs. The selection of a proxy depends on the range of activity included in each step and the cost difference between steps.

Step costs are approximated by mixed costs when there are many steps and the cost difference between steps is small. The illustration in Exhibit 3–3(a) shows that the mixed cost approximation passes through the midpoint of each step and intersects the vertical axis at one half the height of the first step. The mixed cost approximation is subject to a maximum error of one half the cost difference between steps. The mixed cost approximation may be used if this error is acceptable.

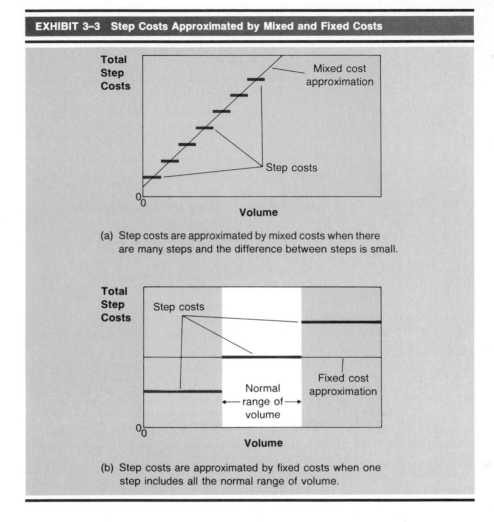

EXHIBIT 3–3   Step Costs Approximated by Mixed and Fixed Costs

(a) Step costs are approximated by mixed costs when there are many steps and the difference between steps is small.

(b) Step costs are approximated by fixed costs when one step includes all the normal range of volume.

Step costs are approximated by fixed costs when one step includes all the organization's probable range of volume. The illustration in Exhibit 3–3(b) shows that the fixed cost approximation is drawn through the step in the expected range of volume and extended parallel to the horizontal axis. The fixed cost approximation is only valid in the activity range of a single step. Large errors can occur if this approximation is used to predict step costs outside this range. If the difference between steps is large, and one step does not include the expected range of activity, step costs must be analyzed as step costs. In most textbook examples step costs are approximated by mixed costs.

Total Costs for the Organization

An organization's total costs consist of the sum of its variable, fixed, mixed, and step costs. With mixed costs approximating step costs, a behavior pattern for total costs is developed by combining variable, fixed, and mixed costs, as in Exhibit 3–4.

The equation for total costs is

$$\frac{\text{Total}}{\text{costs}} = \frac{\text{Fixed}}{\text{costs}} + \left(\frac{\text{Variable costs}}{\text{per unit}} \times \frac{\text{Unit}}{\text{volume}}\right).$$

In the equation for total costs, fixed costs and the fixed element of mixed costs are both included in the "fixed costs." Likewise, variable costs and the variable cost element of mixed costs are both included in the "variable costs." The equation for total costs corresponds to the general equation for a straight line:

$$Y = a + bX,$$

where Y = the value of the dependent variable,
  a = a constant term,
  b = the slope of the line, and
  X = the value of the independent variable.

To save space we will occasionally use the general equation.

EXHIBIT 3–4 Total Cost Behavior

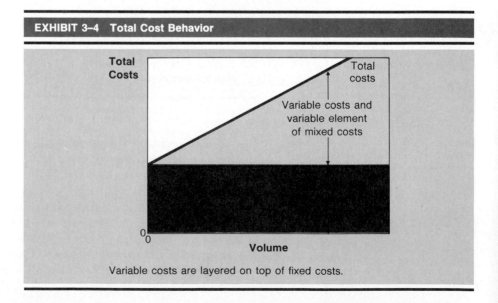

Variable costs are layered on top of fixed costs.

ECONOMIC COST PATTERNS AND THE RELEVANT RANGE

The use of straight lines in accounting models of cost behavior assumes a linear relationship between cost and volume, with each unit of additional volume being accompanied by a uniform increment in total costs. Accountants identify this uniform increment as the variable cost of one unit. The relationship between volume and the variable cost per unit is illustrated in Exhibit 3–5(a). Note that the vertical axis is labeled unit cost rather than total cost. Because the variable cost of each unit is identical, the slope of the unit cost line in Exhibit 3–5(a) is zero.

EXHIBIT 3–5   Incremental Costs in Accounting and Economic Cost Behavior Models

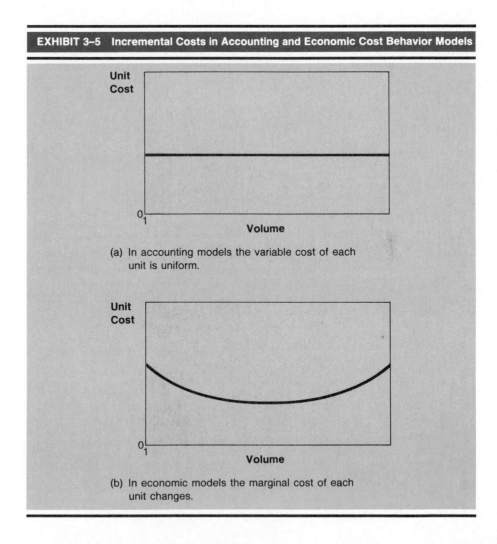

(a) In accounting models the variable cost of each unit is uniform.

(b) In economic models the marginal cost of each unit changes.

Economic models show a curvilinear relationship between cost and volume, with each unit of additional volume being accompanied by a varying increment in total cost. Economists identify the varying increment in total cost as the **marginal cost** of one unit. The relationship between volume and marginal cost is illustrated in Exhibit 3–5(b). At low volumes marginal costs are relatively high. They decline and level off as production becomes more efficient and then start to rise because of the existence of capacity constraints and increases in input costs.

The economists' short-run total cost pattern is illustrated in Exhibit 3–6(a). The vertical axis intercept represents capacity costs. Note the influ-

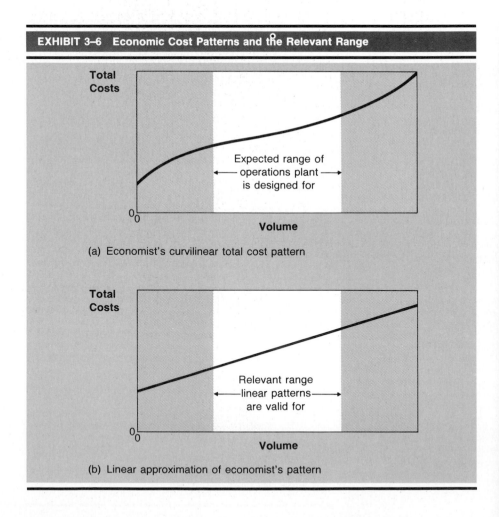

EXHIBIT 3–6 Economic Cost Patterns and the Relevant Range

Total Costs

Expected range of
operations plant
is designed for

Volume

(a) Economist's curvilinear total cost pattern

Total Costs

Relevant range
linear patterns
are valid for

Volume

(b) Linear approximation of economist's pattern

ence of marginal costs. The initial slope of the total cost line is quite steep in the range where marginal costs are high. The slope becomes less steep for a while as marginal costs decline and then increases again as marginal costs increase.

The economists' cost behavior patterns certainly sound plausible. The initially high marginal costs might represent a production situation where there is much excess capacity and idle time. Employees complete their assignments at a leisurely pace; indeed, they may try to make work. Marginal costs logically decline and then level off in the optimal range of production for which the plant was designed to operate. Again, we expect marginal costs to rise as capacity limits are reached. Near capacity, older equipment is brought out of retirement, new employees with little or no experience are hired, and experienced employees are paid overtime premiums to work additional hours.

If the economists' total cost pattern is valid, how can we reasonably approximate it with a straight line? The answer to this question is in the notion of a relevant range. A linear pattern may be a poor approximation of the economists' curvilinear pattern over the entire range of possible activity, but a linear pattern is often sufficiently accurate within the range of probable operations. The range of operations within which a linear cost function is a good approximation of the economists' curvilinear cost function is called the **relevant range.** Linear estimates of cost behavior are only valid within the relevant range. Managers and accountants must exercise extreme care when making statements about cost behavior outside the relevant range, which is illustrated in Exhibit 3–6(b).

AVERAGE COSTS

According to the absorption cost basis of external reporting, all manufacturing costs are product costs that are assigned to the units produced each period. For a single product company, the absorption cost of each unit is an average cost, computed as the cost of goods manufactured divided by the number of units produced. In the absence of beginning or ending inventories of work-in-process, the cost of goods manufactured is the same as the current manufacturing costs, and the average cost per unit is computed as the current manufacturing costs divided by the number of units produced. The following example illustrates the computation of average costs and the effect of volume on this amount.

The Springfield Bean Company manufactures bean bag chairs. The unit variable and monthly fixed production costs are as follows:

	Variable Costs	Fixed Costs
Direct materials	$2.75	
Direct labor	1.50	
Factory overhead	0.75	$3,000
Total	$5.00	$3,000

In the absence of beginning or ending inventories of work-in-process, the equations for the total manufacturing costs per month and the average cost per unit produced during a given month are

$$\text{Total manufacturing costs} = \$3000 + \$5X,$$

$$\text{Average cost per unit} = (\$3000 + \$5X)/X$$
$$= \$3000/X + \$5,$$

where X represents the unit volume.

The total and average production costs at several unit volumes are computed here and illustrated in Exhibit 3–7.

Volume	Total Fixed Costs	Total Variable Costs (Volume × $5)	Total Manufacturing Costs	Average Cost per Unit
100	$3,000	$ 500	$3,500	$35.00
200	3,000	1,000	4,000	20.00
300	3,000	1,500	4,500	15.00
400	3,000	2,000	5,000	12.50
500	3,000	2,500	5,500	11.00

The average cost declines as volume increases because fixed costs are spread over a larger number of units.

If the Springfield Bean Company regularly produced 300 bags per month, the average cost per unit would be $15. Although this cost would be used to value inventory and compute the cost of goods sold in external financial statements, it should not be used for internal planning and control. A manager may be tempted to conclude that the unit cost reported in external financial statements represents the incremental cost of producing one unit. If this cost is $15, the manager might budget production costs for 250 units as $3750 ($15 × 250) and conclude that production was ineffi-cient if the actual costs of producing 250 units were $4250. A proper analysis of cost behavior reveals that $4250 is, in fact, the expected production costs of 250 units:

$$\text{Total costs} = \$3000 + (\$5 \times 250) = \$4250.$$

EXHIBIT 3–7   Total and Average Costs

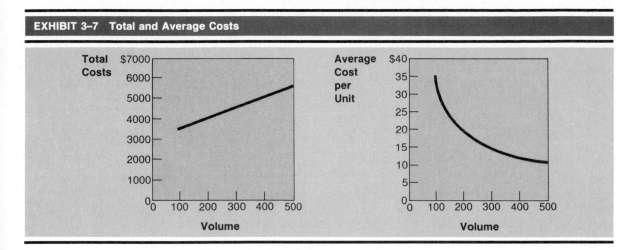

Here we see the significance of different costs for different purposes. Though average costs are widely used for external reporting, total costs should be used for internal planning and control. *Bad decisions can occur if cost information developed for one purpose is incorrectly used for another purpose.*

DETERMINING COST BEHAVIOR

Cost behavior is often determined through an analysis of historical cost data. To properly estimate the relationship between activity and cost, it is necessary (1) to be familiar with basic cost behavior patterns, (2) to understand the characteristics of the accounting data base, and (3) to be knowledgeable of cost estimating techniques. The first part of this chapter introduced important cost behavior patterns. A significant feature of the accounting data base, discussed in Chapter 2, is its orientation to information needed for external reporting. Managers must be very cautious in using these data for internal purposes. As illustrated in the preceding section, average costs presented in financial statements are of limited use in planning and control. To obtain appropriate data, it may be necessary to analyze individual cost elements rather than final cost figures.

Estimating Mixed Costs

Costs known to display a variable or a fixed cost pattern are readily estimated by studying the costs of a representative period. Unit variable costs are estimated by dividing total variable costs by unit volume, and fixed costs are estimated by totaling the known fixed costs of the period. It is the mixed costs that cause most cost estimation problems.

Assume the Springfield Bean Company incurred the following production costs in April, 19x3 when 4000 bean bag chairs were produced:

Direct materials		$11,000
Direct labor		6,000
Factory overhead:		
Supervisors' salaries	$1,800	
Depreciation	800	
Utilities and maintenance	3,400	6,000
Total		$23,000

Direct materials and direct labor are known to display variable cost patterns. Assuming April, 19x3 is a representative month, the variable costs of direct materials and direct labor are $2.75 and $1.50, respectively:

$$\frac{\text{Variable costs}}{\text{per unit}} = \frac{\text{Total variable costs}}{\text{Unit volume}},$$

$$\frac{\text{Variable cost}}{\text{of direct materials}} = \frac{\$11,000}{4000}$$

$$= \$2.75,$$

$$\frac{\text{Variable cost}}{\text{of direct labor}} = \frac{\$6,000}{4000}$$

$$= \$1.50.$$

Assuming supervisors' salaries and depreciation are fixed costs, total fixed costs amount to $2600:

Supervisors' salaries	$1,800
Depreciation	800
Total	$2,600

Utilities and maintenance are neither wholly variable nor wholly fixed; they are mixed costs that contain fixed and variable cost elements. According to a basic rule of algebra, two equations are needed to determine two unknowns. Following this rule at least two observations are needed to determine the variable and the fixed cost elements of a mixed cost.

High–Low Cost Estimation. The most straightforward approach to determining the variable and fixed elements of mixed costs is to use the **high-**

low method of cost estimation. This method utilizes data from two time periods, a representative high volume period and a representative low volume period, to estimate fixed and variable costs. Assuming identical fixed costs in both periods, the difference in total costs between these two periods is due entirely to the difference in total variable costs, and the variable costs per unit are found by dividing the difference in total costs by the difference in activity. The general formula to find variable costs using the high-low method is

$$\frac{\text{Variable costs}}{\text{per unit}} = \frac{\text{Difference in total costs}}{\text{Difference in activity}}.$$

Once the variable costs per unit are determined, the fixed costs, which are identical in both periods, are computed by estimating the total variable costs of either the high or the low volume period and subtracting them from the corresponding total costs:

$$\text{Fixed costs} = \text{Total costs} - \text{Variable costs}.$$

Assume April and May, 19x2 are representative high and low volume periods. The mixed costs and production volumes in these months are shown below.

	Utilities and Maintenance	Unit Production
April	$3,400	4,000
May	2,650	3,000

Equations for total mixed costs are

$$\text{April:} \quad \$3400 = a + b(4000),$$

$$\text{May:} \quad \$2650 = a + b(3000),$$

where a = fixed costs per month, and
b = variable costs per unit (the slope of the mixed cost line).

$$b = \frac{\$3400 - \$2650}{4000 - 3000}$$

$$= \frac{\$750}{1000}$$

$$= \$0.75$$

The variable cost element is $0.75 per unit.

The fixed element of Springfield's monthly utilities and maintenance costs is found by substituting the $0.75 for b in *either* the April or May total cost equation:

$$\text{April:} \quad \$3400 = a + \$0.75(4000)$$
$$a = \$3400 - \$0.75(4000)$$
$$= \$3400 - \$3000$$
$$= \$400,$$

or

$$\text{May:} \quad \$2650 = a + \$0.75(3000)$$
$$a = \$2650 - \$0.75(3000)$$
$$= \$2650 - \$2250$$
$$= \$400.$$

The fixed cost is $400 per month. The use of the high-low method to estimate the variable and fixed elements of this mixed cost is illustrated in Exhibit 3–8.

Springfield Bean Company's cost estimating equation for total monthly production costs is determined by adding together the total cost equations for variable and fixed costs.

	Fixed Costs		Variable Costs
Direct materials			$2.75X
Direct labor			1.50X
Factory overhead:			
Supervisors' salaries	$1,800		
Depreciation	800		
Utilities and maintenance	400		0.75X
Total costs =	$3,000	+	$5.00X

This cost estimating equation can be used to predict total production costs in a subsequent period. If July, 19x2 production is budgeted at 3800 units, the budgeted production costs are $22,000:

$$\$3000 + \$5.00(3800) = \$22,000.$$

If detailed cost information is not available, the high-low method can be applied to total cost data. Similar results are obtained because the total costs consist of fixed and variable cost elements.

In using the high-low method, *it is very important to select high and low volumes representative of normal operating conditions.* As illustrated in Exhibit 3–9, the periods of highest and lowest activity may not be representative of normal operating conditions. Even within the usual range of activity, the results of a particular period might not be representative if there was a strike, a materials shortage, a severe storm, or some other abnormal event. Because management is interested in predicting cost behav-

EXHIBIT 3–8 High-Low Cost Estimation

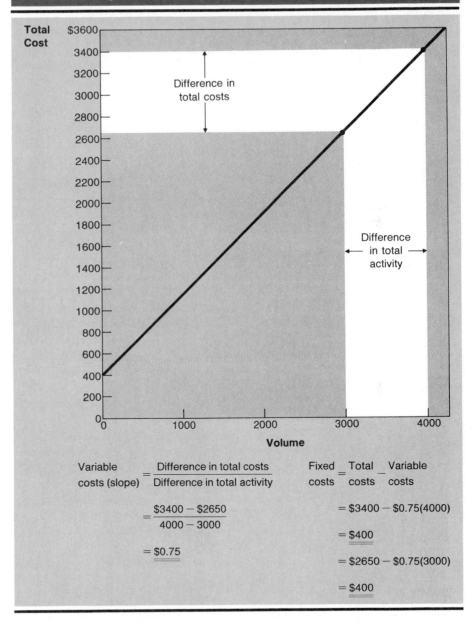

$$\frac{\text{Variable}}{\text{costs (slope)}} = \frac{\text{Difference in total costs}}{\text{Difference in total activity}} \qquad \frac{\text{Fixed}}{\text{costs}} = \frac{\text{Total}}{\text{costs}} - \frac{\text{Variable}}{\text{costs}}$$

$$= \frac{\$3400 - \$2650}{4000 - 3000} \qquad\qquad = \$3400 - \$0.75(4000)$$

$$= \$400$$

$$= \$0.75 \qquad\qquad = \$2650 - \$0.75(3000)$$

$$= \$400$$

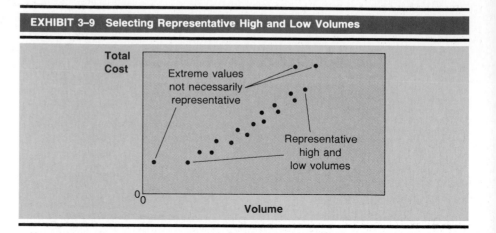

EXHIBIT 3–9   Selecting Representative High and Low Volumes

ior under normal operating conditions, cost estimating equations should be developed from data reflecting normal operating conditions. Professional judgment is required to select the appropriate data.

Scatter Diagrams. A **scatter diagram** is a graph of past volume and cost data, with individual observations represented by dots. Plotting historical volume and cost data on a scatter diagram is a useful approach to cost estimation, especially when used in conjunction with other cost estimating techniques such as the high-low method. The scatter diagram in Exhibit 3–9 would help identify representative high and low volumes. A scatter diagram is also useful in determining if costs can be reasonably approximated by a straight line.

Scatter diagrams are sometimes used alone as a basis of cost estimation. This requires the use of professional judgment to draw a representative straight line through the plot of historical data. Typically, the analyst tries to ensure that an equal number of observations are on either side of the line. Once a line is drawn, cost estimates at any representative volume are made by studying the line. Alternatively, an equation for the line may be developed by applying the high-low method to any two points on the line.

Exhibit 3–10(b) illustrates the use of the scatter diagram method to estimate the Springfield Bean Company's total production costs. The specific values of each observation are presented in Exhibit 3–10(a). Studying this line, the estimated production costs at 3000 units are approximately $18,000.

Least-Squares Method. The **least-squares method** of developing a cost estimating equation is conceptually similar to the scatter diagram method. However, the least-squares method uses a mathematical criterion, rather

EXHIBIT 3–10 Use of Scatter Diagram in Cost Estimation

Observation	Unit Volume	Total Production Costs
1	4000	$23,000
2	3000	18,000
3	2400	16,000
4	4400	24,000
5	2000	11,000
6	3600	23,000
7	2200	15,000

(a) Data

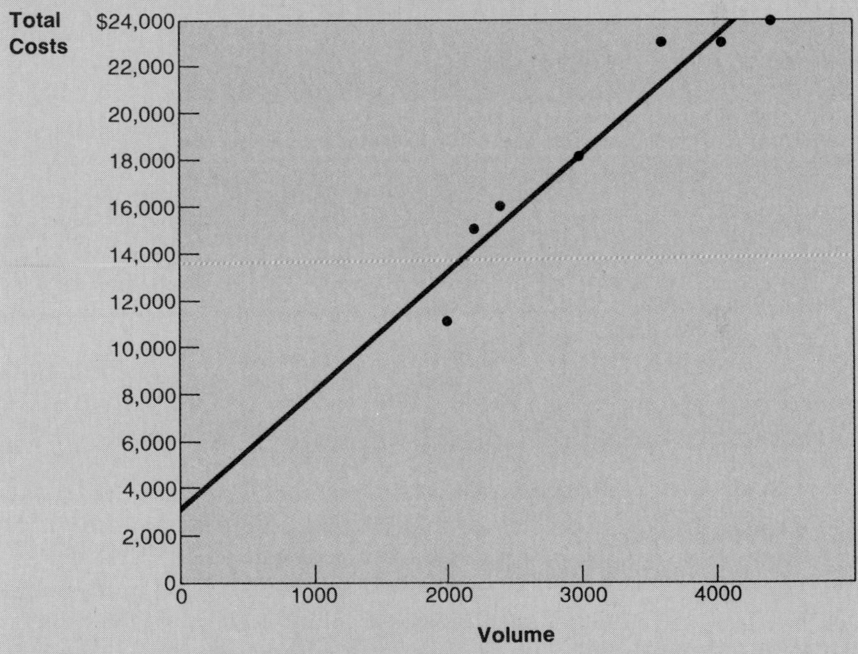

(b) Plot with cost estimating line

than professional judgment, to develop a cost estimating equation. The mathematical criterion is to fit a straight line to the observed data in a manner that minimizes the sum of the squared vertical differences between the observations and the line. The least-squares criterion is illustrated in Exhibit 3–11.

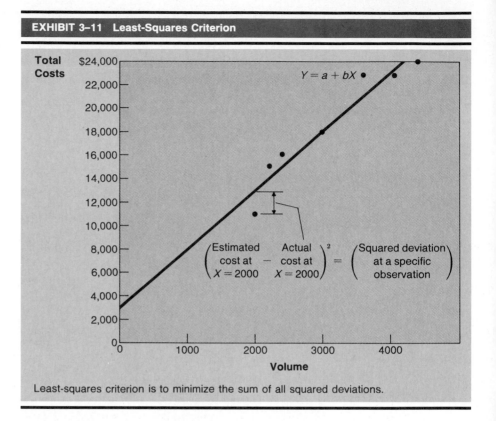

EXHIBIT 3–11   Least-Squares Criterion

Least-squares criterion is to minimize the sum of all squared deviations.

The observations plotted in Exhibit 3–11 are the same as in Exhibit 3–10. The line drawn through the data is based on an equation developed using the least-squares method. The deviations are measured as the differences between the estimated cost and the actual cost at each observation.

Many managers and management accountants believe the least-squares method is superior to the high-low and the scatter diagram methods of cost estimation. The least-squares method can use all available data, rather than just two observations, as does the high-low method. Its use of a mathematical criterion provides an objective approach to cost estimation, rather than the subjective approach involved in visually fitting a line through a scatter diagram. Most significant, the least-squares method can provide information on how good the cost estimating equation fits the historical cost data and information needed to construct probability intervals for cost estimates.

The computations required to estimate fixed and variable costs using the least-squares method are illustrated in Appendix A of this chapter.

Until recent years these computations were regarded as too complex for practical application. Today there is little need to perform them manually. Computers of all sizes and many hand calculators have programs available to perform least-squares calculations. Users need only provide paired observations of volume and cost.

With computational ease has come widespread application and an increased danger of inappropriate use. The analyst should not merely feed raw data into a computer and accept the output as truth. He or she must always be prepared to exercise professional judgment and evaluate the reasonableness of the least-squares approach, the solution, and the data. If the analyst's objective is to predict future costs expected under normal operating conditions, observations reflecting abnormal operating conditions should be deleted. The analyst should also verify that the cost behavior pattern is linear. Scatter diagrams assist in both of these judgmental activities.

Selecting the Independent Variable

The objective of cost behavior analysis is to determine how cost (the dependent variable) responds to changes in volume (the independent variable). The most appropriate measure of volume depends on the cost being studied. The measure of volume should have a logical relationship to the cost being studied, and it should be easy to measure. The sales volume of a department store in Miami, Florida is logically related to the number of persons who enter the store; the store's sales are not logically related to the number of fish in a New England pond. Although the factory overhead of a furniture manufacturer may be logically related to the amount of sawdust swept from the factory floor, difficulties in accurately measuring sawdust make this a bad basis for estimating overhead.

Care must also be taken to ensure that the independent and dependent variables are properly matched within each observation. In merchandising organizations, goods are purchased before they are sold. Though the cost of goods sold is matched with sales within each observation, the cost of purchases is matched with sales only when goods are purchased and sold in the same period. In manufacturing organizations, raw materials are purchased before they are used in production, and finished goods are produced before they are sold. Though the cost of goods sold is matched with sales within each observation, the current manufacturing costs are matched with sales only when goods are produced and sold in the same period. If production and sales differ, production volume rather than sales volume should be used as the independent variable in an analysis of manufacturing costs. In an analogous manner, if the purchases and use of raw materials differ, the volume of purchases rather than the volume of production should be used as the independent variable in an analysis of purchasing costs.

In selecting an independent variable for cost behavior analysis, it is important to determine the activity that causes the incurrence of the cost being analyzed. Professional judgment is very important in selecting an activity measure for a particular cost. Statistical measures, such as the correlation coefficient, are often used to assist in this effort. However, an activity measure should not be selected solely on the basis of a high past correlation with cost. A high correlation between two variables does not prove that one causes the other. Changes in both variables may be caused by a third variable, or the correlation between the two variables may be a chance event that will not recur. Factory overhead and sawdust may be correlated in a furniture plant, but unless sawdust is a major product of the plant it should not be treated as an independent variable. Both factory overhead and sawdust are caused by a third variable, the production of furniture. The correlation coefficient is discussed further in Appendix B of this chapter.

THE IMPACT OF CHANGING PRICES AND TECHNOLOGY

Cost estimation is the determination of previous or current relationships between cost and activity. Historical data from the accounting data base are used in cost estimation. **Cost prediction** is the forecasting of future relationships between cost and activity and is a frequent purpose of cost estimation. As a starting point in the prediction of future costs, management studies previous cost behavior by analyzing historical cost data.

Cost estimation and cost prediction are made difficult by changes in technology and prices. If an automobile manufacturer changes from skilled labor to computer controlled assembly procedures, the past data are of little or no value in predicting future costs. Only data accumulated subsequent to the initiation of the new assembly technique are useful in predicting the cost of robot assembly.

If prices have remained stable in the past but then uniformly increase by 20 percent, cost estimating equations developed for previous periods will underpredict future costs. In this example all that is required is a 20 percent increase in the prediction.

Unfortunately, adjustments for price changes are seldom this simple. The prices of various cost elements are likely to change at different rates and at different times. Furthermore, there are apt to be several different price levels included in the past data used to develop cost estimating equations. During periods of changing prices only data reflecting a single price level should be used in cost estimation and cost prediction. The analyst should always be suspicious of old data. If data from different price levels are used, an attempt should be made to restate the data to a single price level. Procedures used to do this are discussed in Chapter 17.

One response to the cost prediction problems resulting from changing prices is to use something other than cost as the dependent variable. It is, for example, possible to substitute direct labor hours for direct labor dollars and kilowatt hours for the cost of electricity. In terms of kilowatt hours the monthly use of electricity might be stated as

$$\text{Total kilowatt hours} = 20{,}000 + 50X,$$

where $X = $ unit volume.

If X is budgeted at 5000 units, the total use of electricity is predicted to be 270,000 [20,000 + (50 $\times$ 5000)] kilowatt hours. If the current cost of electricity is 12 cents per kilowatt hour, this translates into an electric bill of $32,400 ($0.12 $\times$ 270,000).

A disadvantage of this approach is that it must be implemented on a very disaggregated basis. Data for labor costs and electric costs can be added together and analyzed in total. Because labor hours and kilowatt hours cannot be added, they must be analyzed separately before totaling the final cost predictions for each cost element.

SUMMARY

Activities undertaken to achieve an organization's objectives result in the incurrence of costs. Because economic resources are limited, the costs that result from activity also limit activity. Consequently, managers must plan and control both costs and activities. To plan and control costs, managers must know how costs respond to changes in activity.

Managers must be familiar with variable, fixed, mixed, and step costs. A variable cost is the uniform incremental cost of each additional unit. Total variable costs change in direct proportion to changes in volume. A fixed cost does not respond to changes in the volume of activity within a given period. Total fixed costs are a constant amount regardless of the level of activity. Mixed costs contain a fixed and a variable cost element, they are positive when volume is zero, and they increase in a linear fashion as volume increases. Step costs are constant within a range of activity but different between ranges of activity. Total step costs increase in a step-like fashion as volume increases.

The cost behavior of a particular activity is often determined through an analysis of historical cost data. Three techniques used to develop an equation for total cost behavior are the high-low method, the scatter diagram method, and the least-squares method. The high-low method utilizes data from a representative high volume period and a representative low volume period. The scatter diagram method requires the use of professional judgment to draw a representative straight line through a plot of historical data. The least-squares method fits a straight line to the observed data in a manner that minimizes the sum of the squared deviations between individual observations and the line.

Regardless of the cost estimating technique used, the development of a cost estimating equation should be guided by professional judgment. The analyst must be familiar with the characteristics of the accounting data base, the data must display a linear trend within the relevant range, and observations reflecting abnormal operating conditions should be deleted from the analysis. Particular care should be taken to ensure that the data base reflects constant technology and a single price level. Even when proper precautions are taken, cost predictions are only valid within the relevant range and for the current technology and price level.

APPENDIX A
LEAST-SQUARES COST ESTIMATION

The equation for a straight line is

$$Y = a + bX,$$

where Y = the value of the dependent variable,
$\quad a$ = a constant term,
$\quad b$ = the slope of the line, and
$\quad X$ = the value of the independent variable.

The objective of least-squares cost estimation is to fit this equation to observations of X and Y in a manner that minimizes the sum of the squared deviations between the actual and estimated values of Y. Mathematicians have proved that the appropriate values of a and b can be found by the simultaneous solution of the following equations:

$$\sum XY = a \sum X + b \sum X^2, \qquad (3\text{–}1)$$

$$\sum Y = an + b \sum X, \qquad (3\text{–}2)$$

where Σ is a capital sigma, meaning "the sum of" (i.e., ΣXY means multiply X and the corresponding value of Y, and then sum the products) and
$\quad n$ = the number of observations.

The above equations, called the **normal equations,** are used to compute the constant term and the slope that best meets the least-squares criterion.

The computations required to apply the normal equations to the data in Exhibit 3–10(a) are shown below.

Observation	Unit Volume X	Total Costs Y	XY	X²
1	4,000	$ 23,000	92,000,000	16,000,000
2	3,000	18,000	54,000,000	9,000,000
3	2,400	16,000	38,400,000	5,760,000
4	4,400	24,000	105,600,000	19,360,000
5	2,000	11,000	22,000,000	4,000,000
6	3,600	23,000	82,800,000	12,960,000
7	2,200	15,000	33,000,000	4,840,000
	21,600	130,000	427,800,000	71,920,000

Substituting these values into the normal equations we obtain

$$427{,}800{,}000 = a21{,}600 + b71{,}920{,}000, \qquad (3\text{--}3)$$

$$130{,}000 = a7 + b21{,}600. \qquad (3\text{--}4)$$

We can solve for b by eliminating a from an equation for the difference between Eqs. (3–3) and (3–4). To do this, we must have the same coefficient for a in each equation. This can be accomplished in a number of ways. We will multiply Eq. (3–3) by 7 and Eq. (3–4) by 21,600. Doing this we obtain

$$2{,}994{,}600{,}000 = 151{,}200a + 503{,}440{,}000b \qquad (3\text{--}5)$$

$$2{,}808{,}000{,}000 = 151{,}200a + 466{,}560{,}000b \qquad (3\text{--}6)$$

$$186{,}600{,}000 = \qquad\qquad 36{,}880{,}000b \qquad (3\text{--}7)$$

Equation (3–7) is the difference between Eqs. (3–5) and (3–6). Solving Eq. (3–7) for b, we obtain

$$b = \frac{186{,}600{,}000}{36{,}880{,}000} = 5.06 \quad \text{(rounded)}.$$

We can solve for a by substituting the value of b in any equation containing a. Doing this in Eq. (3–4), we obtain

$$7a = 130{,}000 - (5.06)\,(21{,}600)$$

$$7a = 20{,}704$$

$$a = 20{,}704/7 = 2958 \quad \text{(rounded)}.$$

The resulting cost estimating equation is

$$\text{Total costs} = \$2958 + \$5.06X.$$

Computations involving large numbers are often simplified by expressing the numbers in thousands. In thousands, the unit volume and total cost of observation 1 are 4 and $23, respectively. The value of XY then becomes 92, and the value of X^2 becomes 16. Restating all seven observations into thousands and solving for a and b, we obtain $2.958 and $5.06. The slope of the line (value of b) is not affected when all data are expressed in thousands. However, the vertical axis intercept (value of b) is $2.958 thousand, that is, $2958, not $2.958.

In addition to the constant term and the slope, the correlation coefficient, the coefficient of determination, and the standard error of the estimate are often computed when the least-squares method is used. The **correlation coefficient,** a standardized measure of the degree to which two variables move together, is discussed in Appendix B of this chapter. The **coefficient of determination** is a measure of the percent of variation in the dependent variable that is explained by the cost estimating equation; it indicates how good the equation fits the historical data. The **standard error of the estimate** is a measure of the variability of actual costs around the cost estimating equation; it is used to construct probability intervals for cost estimates. Readers interested in studying this further should consult a basic statistics book.

APPENDIX B
THE CORRELATION COEFFICIENT

The **correlation coefficient** is a standardized measure of the degree to which two variables move together and can take on values between -1 and $+1$. Negative correlation implies that the two variables move in opposite directions; as one increases the other decreases. Positive correlation implies that the two variables move in the same direction; as one increases the other also increases. A correlation coefficient of zero implies that the movement of the two variables is unrelated.

When two variables that are logically related have a high correlation, knowledge of a change in one variable is useful in predicting a change in the other. Management accountants use the correlation coefficient to assist in selecting the best basis for overhead application and for cost estimation. In the selection process the management accountant is usually looking for the basis of activity measurement that has the highest correlation with total costs.

Assume we are trying to determine the best basis for applying overhead to products. We selected four possible bases and calculated their past correlation with total overhead.

Basis	Correlation with Total Overhead
Direct labor hours	0.752
Direct labor dollars	0.885
Machine hours	0.630
Number of employee coffee breaks	−0.100

We would select direct labor dollars as the basis of overhead application; it has the highest correlation with total overhead. Note that the number of employee coffee breaks had a small negative correlation with total overhead. This indicates a slight tendency for total overhead to decrease as the number of employee coffee breaks increases. This may be due to such factors as reduced power consumption by machines while employees are away on breaks.

The basis selected to apply overhead must also be logical and easy to implement. Direct labor dollars has a logical relationship to overhead and, in most organizations, it is easy to relate direct labor dollars to individual products. Even if the number of employee coffee breaks had the highest positive correlation with total overhead, we would not use it as a basis for overhead application. A large positive relationship between these variables does not seem logical. And it would be difficult to relate employee coffee breaks to individual products.

Mathematicians have developed the following equation to compute the correlation coefficient:

$$r = \frac{\Sigma(X - \bar{X})(Y - \bar{Y})}{\sqrt{\Sigma(X - \bar{X})^2 \; \Sigma(Y - \bar{Y})^2}},$$

where

r = the correlation coefficient

$\bar{X}$ = the average value of the independent variable, computed as ΣX divided by n

$\bar{Y}$ = the average value of the dependent variable, computed as ΣY divided by n

$(X - \bar{X})(Y - \bar{Y})$ = the sum of each difference between individual values of X and $\bar{X}$ multiplied by the corresponding difference between individual values of Y and $\bar{Y}$

$(X - \bar{X})^2$ = the sum of the squared differences between X and $\bar{X}$ and

$(Y - \bar{Y})^2$ = the sum of the squared differences between Y and $\bar{Y}$.

The average unit volume, $\bar{X}$, and the average total production cost, $\bar{Y}$, for the data in Exhibit 3–10(a) (as shown on page 83) are 3086 and $18,571,

EXHIBIT 3–12   Computation of the Correlation Coefficient

Observation	X	$(X - \bar{X})$	$(X - \bar{X})^2$	Y	$(Y - \bar{Y})$	$(Y - \bar{Y})^2$	$(X - \bar{X})(Y - \bar{Y})$
1	4,000	914	835,396	$23,000	4,429	19,616,041	4,048,106
2	3,000	− 86	7,396	18,000	− 571	326,041	49,106
3	2,400	− 686	470,596	16,000	− 2,571	6,610,041	1,763,706
4	4,400	1314	1,726,596	24,000	5,429	29,474,041	7,133,706
5	2,000	− 1086	1,179,396	11,000	− 7,571	57,320,041	8,222,106
6	3,600	514	264,196	23,000	4,429	19,616,041	2,276,506
7	2,200	− 886	784,996	15,000	− 3,571	12,752,041	3,163,906
			5,268,572			145,714,287	26,657,142

$$r = \frac{26,657,142}{\sqrt{(5,268,572)(145,714,287)}} = 0.962$$

respectively.

$\bar{X} = (4000 + 3000 + 2400 + 4400 + 2000 + 3600 + 2200)/7$
$= 3086$ (rounded)
$\bar{Y} = (\$23,000 + \$18,000 + \$16,000 + \$24,000 + \$11,000 + \$23,000 + \$15,000)/7$
$= \$18,571$ (rounded)

The computation of the correlation coefficient between unit volume and total production costs is presented in Exhibit 3–12. The correlation coefficient of 0.962 indicates a high positive relationship between these two variables. An increase in unit volume has a high statistical correlation with an increase in total production costs. It appears that unit volume is a good basis for estimating total production costs.

KEY TERMS

Cost behavior analysis

Variable cost

Fixed cost

Committed fixed cost

Capacity cost

Discretionary fixed cost

Managed fixed cost

Mixed cost

Semivariable cost

Step cost

Marginal cost

Relevant range

High-low method of cost estimation

Scatter diagram

Least-squares method of cost estimation

Cost estimation

Cost prediction

APPENDIX KEY TERMS

Normal equations

Correlation coefficient

Coefficient of determination

Standard error of the estimate

**REVIEW
QUESTIONS**

3–1 In cost behavior analysis, what is the relationship between the cost and the volume of an activity?

3–2 How do you compute the slope of a straight line?

3–3 Briefly describe four widely used total cost behavior patterns.

3–4 What long-run trade-offs are there between fixed and variable costs?

3–5 Under what circumstances are step costs approximated by mixed costs? By fixed costs?

3–6 In what range of activity is a straight line often a reasonable approximation of the economist's short-run total cost pattern?

3–7 Why do average unit costs decline as volume increases?

3–8 Average inventory costs are widely used for what purpose? Give an example of a purpose they should not be used for.

3–9 What minimum number of observations of past data are necessary to estimate the fixed and variable elements of mixed costs?

3–10 Why should we use data reflecting normal operating conditions as a basis for developing cost estimating equations?

3–11 Name two reasons why scatter diagrams are used in conjunction with the high-low and least-squares methods of cost estimation.

3–12 What is the least-squares criterion?

3–13 Why might current unit sales not be a good activity measure for the cost of current purchases in a manufacturing organization?

3–14 Distinguish between cost estimation and cost prediction on the basis of their time orientation.

3–15 Name two dynamic factors which limit the usefulness of historical cost data in cost prediction.

EXERCISES

3–1 Classifying Cost Behavior

Classify each of the following costs as variable, fixed, mixed, or step.

a) Depreciation on office equipment.

b) Pulpwood in a paper mill.

c) Salaries of two supervisors.

d) Real estate taxes.

e) Direct labor.

f) Salaries of quality inspectors.

g) Electric power in a factory.

h) Raw materials used in production.

i) Automobiles rented on the basis of a fixed charge per day plus an additional charge per mile driven.

j) Sales commissions.

3–2 Classifying Cost Behavior

For each situation, select the most appropriate cost behavior pattern. Lines represent the cost behavior pattern. The vertical axis represents total costs. The horizontal axis represents total volume. Dots represent actual costs. Each pattern may be used more than once.

Pattern

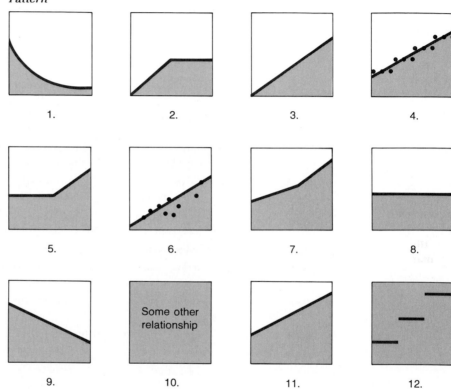

1.   2.   3.   4.

5.   6.   7.   8.

9.   10. Some other relationship   11.   12.

Situation

a) Total variable costs.

b) Variable costs per unit.

c) Total mixed costs.

d) Total fixed costs.

e) Average fixed costs per unit.

f) Total current manufacturing costs.

g) High-low cost estimation influenced by unusual observations.

h) Employees are paid $10 per hour for the first forty hours worked each week and $15 per each additional hour.

i) Employees are paid $10 per hour and guaranteed a minimum weekly wage of $200.

j) A consultant is paid $50 per hour with a guaranteed maximum fee of $1000.

k) Salaries of social workers where each social worker can handle a maximum of 20 cases.

l) A water bill where a flat fee of $800 is charged for the first 100,000 gallons and additional water costs $0.005 per gallon.

m) Variable costs properly used to estimate step costs.

n) Total direct materials costs.

o) Rent on exhibit space at a convention.

3–3 High-Low Cost Estimation

Tony's Taxi Company has the following information available about fleet miles and operating costs.

Year	Miles	Operating Costs
19x3	556,000	$125,060
19x4	684,000	142,340

Required: Use the high-low method to develop a cost estimating equation for annual operating costs.

3–4 High-Low Cost Estimation

An examination of monthly maintenance costs and direct labor hours reveals the following:

	Highest	Lowest
Maintenance	$51,000	$33,600
Direct labor hours	13,000	7,200

Required: Use the high-low method to develop a cost estimating equation for annual operating costs.

3–5 High-Low Cost Estimation

Jackson, Inc., is preparing a budget for 19x1 and requires a breakdown of the cost of steam used in its factory into the fixed and variable elements. The following data on the cost of steam used and direct labor hours worked are available for the last six months of 19x0:

Month	Cost of Steam	Direct Labor Hours
July	$ 15,850	3,000
August	13,400	2,050
September	16,370	2,900
October	19,800	3,650
November	17,600	2,670
December	18,500	2,650
Total	$101,520	16,920

Required: Use the high-low method to develop an equation for the monthly cost of steam.

(CPA Adapted)

3–6 High-Low Cost Estimation and Predetermined Overhead Rates

Presented is information on 19x7 and 19x8 factory overhead and direct labor hours:

	19x7	19x8
Factory overhead	$211,500	$258,600
Direct labor hours	55,500	71,200

Management predicts that 60,000 direct labor hours will be used in 19x9.

Required: Determine the 19x9 predetermined overhead rate per direct labor hour.

3–7 High-Low Cost Estimation and Predetermined Overhead Rates

Tastee-Treat Company prepares, packages, and distributes six frozen vegetables. The different vegetables are prepared in large batches. Manufacturing overhead is assigned to batches by a predetermined rate on the basis of direct labor hours. The manufacturing overhead costs incurred by the company during two recent years are presented below.

	Year 1	Year 2
Direct labor hours worked	2,760,000	2,160,000
Manufacturing overhead costs incurred (adjusted for changes in current prices and wage rates)		
Indirect labor	$11,040,000	$ 8,640,000
Employee benefits	4,140,000	3,240,000
Supplies	2,760,000	2,160,000
Power	2,208,000	1,728,000
Heat and light	552,000	552,000
Supervision	2,865,000	2,625,000
Depreciation	7,930,000	7,930,000
Property taxes and insurance	3,005,000	3,005,000
Total overhead costs	$34,500,000	$29,880,000

Required: Tastee-Treat Company expects to operate at a 2,300,000 direct labor hour level of activity in 19x4. Using the data from two recent years, calculate the rate Tastee-Treat should employ to assign manufacturing overhead to its products during 19x4.

(CMA Adapted)

3–8 Scatter Diagrams and High-Low Cost Estimation

Presented are monthly production and cost data.

Month	Volume	Total Cost
1	3,000	$40,000
2	1,500	28,000
3	4,000	65,000
4	2,800	39,000
5	2,300	32,000
6	1,000	20,000
7	2,000	30,000

Requirements

a) Using information from the high and low volume months, develop a cost estimating equation for monthly production costs.

b) Plot the data on a scatter diagram. Using information from *representative* high and low volume months, develop a cost estimating equation for monthly production costs.

c) What factors might cause the difference in the equations developed in requirements (a) and (b)?

3–9 Scatter Diagrams and High-Low Cost Estimation

From April 1 through October 31 the Central County Highway Department hires temporary employees to mow and clean the right-of-way along county roads. A county road commissioner has asked you to assist her in determining the variable labor cost of mowing and cleaning a mile of road. The following information is available regarding 19x5 operations.

Month	Miles Mowed and Cleaned	Labor Cost
April	350	$7,500
May	300	7,000
June	400	8,500
July	250	5,000
August	375	8,000
September	200	4,500
October	100	4,300

Requirements

a) Using information from the high and low volume months, develop a cost estimating equation for monthly labor costs.

b) Plot the information on a scatter diagram. Using information from *representa-*

tive high and low volume months, develop a cost estimating equation for monthly labor costs.

c) What factors might cause the difference in the equations developed in requirements (a) and (b)?

d) Adjust the equation developed in requirement (b) to incorporate the effect of a 7 percent increase in wages.

3–10 Computing Average Unit Costs

The total monthly operating costs of Laredo Chili To Go are

$$\$6000 + \$0.40X,$$

where $X =$ servings of chili.

Requirements

a) Determine the average cost per serving at each of the following monthly volumes: 10, 100, 200, 400, 600.

b) Determine the monthly volume at which the average cost per serving is $0.50.

3–11 Computing Average Unit Costs: Review of Relevant Costs

The local chapter of a professional organization is organizing a one-day continuing education program. Program costs are as follows:

Advertising	$1000 per program
Instructor's fee	600 per program
Room rental and set-up	200 per program
Instructional materials	20 per participant
Lunch and coffee breaks	15 per participant

Requirements

a) Develop an equation for total program costs.

b) Determine the average cost per participant at each of the following volumes: 10, 20, 30, 50.

c) Determine the volume at which the average cost per participant is $50.

d) The program is scheduled for October 1, 19x4. The budgeted advertising expenditures are made on September 1, and a $100 nonrefundable deposit for the room rental and set-up is made on September 15. All other costs, except the instructor's fee, are payable at the start of the program. The instructor's fee is payable at the end of the program.

One week before the scheduled date of the program, the chapter's director of continuing education becomes concerned about a lack of preregistered participants and considers whether or not to cancel the program. Identify the sunk and relevant costs for this decision, and develop a cost estimating equation that contains only relevant costs.

3–12 Developing an Equation from Average Costs

The average unit cost at a volume of 4000 units is $22.125, and the average unit cost at a volume of 8500 units is $21.000.

Required: Develop an estimating equation for total cost.

3–13 Developing an Equation from Average Costs

The Dog House is a pet hotel located on the outskirts of town. In March, when dog (occupancy) days were at an annual low of 500, the average cost per dog day was $18.50. In July, when dog days were at a capacity level of 3100, the average cost per dog day was $5.50.

Requirements

a) Develop an equation for *monthly* operating costs.

b) Determine the average cost per dog day at an *annual* volume of 24,000 dog days.

3–14 Mixed Cost Approximation of Step Costs

The Civic Center has asked you to develop a cost estimating equation for ticket takers. Ticket takers are on duty for a one-hour period starting 45 minutes before a performance is scheduled to begin. Ticket takers are paid $8 per hour, and each ticket taker can collect a maximum of 1000 tickets per hour.

Requirements

a) The labor cost of ticket takers is a step function with each step being 1000 tickets collected. Develop a mixed cost approximation of the cost of taking tickets.

b) Use the equation developed in requirement (a) to estimate the labor cost of collecting 10,000 and 10,001 tickets. What is the dollar amount of the error with this approximation?

3–15 Automatic Versus Manual Processing

The Fast Photo Company operates a 60-minute film development and print service. The current service, which relies extensively upon manual operations, has monthly operating costs of $5000 plus $2 per roll of film developed and printed. Management is evaluating the desirability of acquiring a machine that will automatically develop film and make prints. If the machine is acquired, the monthly fixed costs of the service will increase to $23,000, and the variable costs of developing and printing a roll of film will decline to $1.40.

Requirements

a) Determine the total costs of developing and printing 20,000 and 50,000 rolls per month:

With the current process.
With the automatic process.

b) Determine the monthly volume at which the total operating costs of both processes are identical.

3–16 Cost Behavior Analysis with Changing Prices

The Wildcat Auto Insurance Company has asked you to develop an equation that will be useful in predicting the labor cost of processing insurance claims. The following information regarding the operation of their claims office is available.

Year	Claims Processed	Labor Hours	Labor Dollars
19x2	3,300	3,700	$18,500
19x3	4,200	4,300	21,500
19x4	3,200	3,500	21,000
19x5	5,000	5,300	31,800
19x6	4,000	4,400	44,000
19x7	3,600	4,000	40,000

Wage rates have increased substantially over the six year period from 19x2 through 19x7. However, no additional increases are expected until 19x9.

Required: Develop an equation to predict the 19x8 labor cost of processing claims. Use the high-low method.

PROBLEMS

3–17 Cost Behavior Analysis in a Restaurant: High-Low Method

The Pizza House Restaurant has the following information available regarding costs at various levels of monthly sales.

Monthly sales in units	5,000	8,000	10,000
Cost of food sold	$ 5,250	$ 8,400	$10,500
Wages and fringe benefits of restaurant employees	4,250	4,400	4,500
Fees paid delivery help	1,250	2,000	2,500
Rent on building	1,200	1,200	1,200
Depreciation on equipment	300	300	300
Utilities	500	560	600
Supplies (soap, floor wax, etc.)	150	180	200
Administrative costs	1,300	1,300	1,300
Total	$14,200	$18,340	$21,100

Requirements

a) Identify each cost as being variable, fixed, or mixed.

b) Develop a schedule identifying the amount of each cost that is fixed or variable. Total the amounts under each category to develop an equation for total monthly costs.

c) Predict total costs for a monthly sales volume of 9500 units.

3–18 Cost Behavior Analysis in a Store: High-Low Method

The Eleventh Avenue Convenience Store has the following information available regarding costs and revenues for two recent months.

	April	May
Sales revenue	$60,000	$100,000
Cost of goods sold	−36,000	− 60,000
Gross profit	$24,000	$ 40,000
Less other expenses:		
Advertising	$ 600	$ 600
Utilities	4,200	5,600
Salaries and commissions	3,200	4,000
Supplies (bags, cleaning supplies, etc.)	320	400
Depreciation	2,300	2,300
Administrative costs	1,900	1,900
Total	−12,520	− 14,800
Net income	$11,480	$ 25,200

Requirements

a) Identify each cost as being fixed, variable, or mixed.

b) Develop a schedule identifying the amount of each cost that is fixed or variable. Express fixed costs as an amount per month and variable costs as a portion of sales revenue. Total the amounts under each category to develop an equation for total monthly costs.

c) Predict total costs for a monthly sales volume of $70,000.

3–19 Average Costs and Internal Decisions

The production supervisor of Confusion Reigns bursts into your office declaring that accounting information is of little or no use to him:

"Back in early August I asked the accounting department for production cost information. They told me that the July production costs were $13 per unit. Well, I knew that July was a typical month in which we had good cost control, so I used the $13 amount in my production cost budgets for August and September.

In August I was scheduled to produce 12,000 units, so I budgeted my costs at $156,000 (12,000 × $13). I figured that something was wrong when actual costs turned out to be $150,000. However, when the vice president congratulated me for saving $6000, I decided to keep my mouth shut. But last month was a disaster! In September I produced 5000 units at a budgeted cost of $65,000 (5000 × $13), and the V.P. is now demanding an explanation of the $15,000 difference between the budgeted costs and the actual costs of $80,000. I am totally confused because I believe I did an equally good job of controlling costs in all three months. You've got to help me!"

The first thing you did was obtain the following statements for the months in question.

Confusion Reigns
Statements of Cost of Goods Manufactured
For the Months of July, August, and September, 19x2

	July	August	September
Current manufacturing costs:			
Raw materials	$ 30,000	$ 36,000	$15,000
Direct labor	50,000	60,000	25,000
Factory overhead	50,000	54,000	40,000
Total	$130,000	$150,000	$80,000
Work-in-process, beginning	—	—	—
Total costs-in-process	$130,000	$150,000	$80,000
Work-in-process, ending	— —	— —	— —
Cost of goods manufactured	$130,000	$150,000	$80,000
Units manufactured	10,000	12,000	5,000

Required: Prepare a report explaining what happened. Based on your analysis, did the production supervisor do an equally good job of controlling costs in all three months?

3–20 Selecting an Independent Variable: Scatter Diagrams

Valley Production Company produces backpacks that are sold to sporting goods stores throughout the Rocky Mountains. Presented is information on production costs and inventory changes for five recent months.

	January	February	March	April	May
Finished goods inventory in units:					
Beginning	30,000	40,000	50,000	30,000	60,000
Manufactured	60,000	90,000	80,000	90,000	100,000
Available	90,000	130,000	130,000	120,000	160,000
Sold	− 50,000	− 80,000	−100,000	− 60,000	−120,000
Ending	40,000	50,000	30,000	60,000	40,000
Manufacturing costs	$300,000	$500,000	$450,000	$450,000	$550,000

Requirements

a) With the aid of scatter diagrams, determine whether units sold or units manufactured is a better predictor of manufacturing costs.

b) Prepare an explanation for your answer to requirement (a).

c) Which independent variable, units sold or units manufactured, should be a better predictor of selling costs? Why?

3–21 Selecting a Basis of Overhead Allocation: Scatter Diagrams

The Roth Company manufactures two products, A and B. In the past, factory overhead costs have been allocated equally to all products on the basis of the number of units produced. However, Mr. Roth is concerned that this method does not provide a proper cost basis for product pricing. Mr. Roth has noted that most of the company's factory overhead costs are related to the use of machinery, and that each unit of product A requires twice as many machine hours as a unit of product B. Consequently, he believes the allocation should be made on the basis of machine hours.

   You have been asked to study this matter and determine the more accurate basis of allocating factory overhead costs. The following information is available.

Month	Units Produced A	B	Total	Machine Hours	Factory Overhead
1	50	100	150	300	$30,000
2	200	100	300	500	40,000
3	100	50	150	250	25,000
4	150	50	200	350	30,000
5	50	350	400	450	32,000
6	100	300	400	500	35,000

Requirements

a) With the aid of scatter diagrams, determine whether units produced or machine hours is the better basis of overhead application.

b) Which product is assigned too few overhead costs, and which product is assigned too many overhead costs, when the allocation is made on the basis of units produced? Explain your answer. If prices are based on cost, what may happen to the prices Roth charges for its products compared to the prices of competitors' products?

3–22 Least-Squares Cost Estimation (Appendix A)

The Quartz Watch Repair Center is trying to determine the cost of repairing a quartz watch. The following information is available regarding the number of units repaired and labor hours.

Week	Watches Repaired	Labor Hours
1	150	45
2	50	20
3	75	25
4	200	60
5	175	40
6	250	50

Requirements

a) Determine the average and the incremental time to repair a quartz watch. Use the least-squares method to compute the incremental time. Round your answer to three decimal places.

b) Predict the total labor hours required for a week when 200 quartz watches are repaired. If the labor cost is $12 per hour, what is the predicted total labor cost for this week?

3–23 Least-Squares Cost Estimation (Appendix A)

The following information is available about shipping costs.

Month	Pounds Shipped	Total Shipping Cost
January	5,000	$12,000
February	7,000	16,000
March	6,000	15,000
April	9,000	17,000

Required: Use the least-squares method to develop an equation for total monthly shipping costs. Round answers to three decimal places. *Hint:* Perform calculations in thousands, and then adjust the constant term in your answer.

3–24 Predicting Selling Expenses (Appendix B)

The Grackly Company is trying to determine the best independent variable to use in predicting selling expenses. In the past this prediction has been made on the basis of expected unit sales. However, the increasing diversity of the company's products has led the sales manager to suggest that expected sales revenue might be a better predictor. You have gathered the following information:

Month	Units Sold	Sales Revenue	Selling Expense
1	5,000	$25,000	$2,200
2	7,000	35,000	2,400
3	6,000	20,000	1,800
4	9,000	40,000	3,200
5	8,000	30,000	2,400

Requirements

a) Use the correlation coefficient to determine the best predictor of selling expenses.

b) Use the least-squares method to develop an equation for predicting monthly selling expenses. Select the basis of prediction that has the highest correlation with actual selling expenses. If you select sales revenue as the independent variable, variable costs should be expressed as a portion of sales revenue.

3–25 Selecting a Basis of Overhead Application (Appendix B)

Presented is information on manufacturing activity and total overhead costs for five recent months.

Month	Direct Labor Hours	Machine Hours	Total Factory Overhead
April	20,000	6,000	$ 90,000
May	40,000	10,000	150,000
June	30,000	8,000	140,000
July	60,000	10,000	260,000
August	50,000	6,000	160,000

Requirements

a) Use the correlation coefficient to determine the best basis of overhead application.

b) Use the least-squares method to develop an equation to predict monthly overhead. Select the basis of prediction that has the highest correlation with actual overhead.

c) Modify the equation developed above to predict annual overhead, and then compute the predetermined overhead rate for a year when management predicts the use of 480,000 direct labor hours and 120,000 machine hours.

Cost–
Volume–
Profit
Analysis

Cost-volume-profit analysis is a technique used to examine the relationships between volume, total costs, total revenues, and profit. Cost-volume-profit analysis is particularly useful in the early stages of planning because it provides a framework for discussing planning issues and for organizing relevant data.

Cost-volume-profit analysis is widely used in for-profit and not-for-profit organizations, and it is equally applicable to service, merchandising, and manufacturing. In for-profit organizations cost-volume-profit analysis is used to answer such questions as: How many photocopies must the College Avenue Copy Service produce to earn a profit of $20,000? At what sales volume will Burger King's total costs and total revenues be equal? What profit will General Electric earn at an annual sales volume of 3 billion dollars? What will happen to the profits of Duff's Smorgasbord if there is a 20 percent increase in the cost of food and a 10 percent increase in the selling price of meals?

In not-for-profit organizations cost-volume-profit analysis is used to plan service levels, plan fund raising activities, and determine funding requirements: How many meals can the Downtown Salvation Army serve with an annual budget of $200,000? How many tickets must be sold for the benefit concert to raise $10,000? Given current tuition rates and projected enrollments, how much money must City University obtain from other sources?

The purpose of this chapter is to introduce cost-volume-profit analysis. We begin by developing a profit formula and presenting a new type of income statement based on that formula. Next we examine cost-volume-profit relationships and illustrate their use in planning. We conclude by summarizing the assumptions that are an inherent part of cost-volume-profit analysis.

A BASIC ASSUMPTION

In Chapter 2 *cost* was defined as a monetary measure of the economic sacrifice made to obtain some product or service. The cost of a product or service that has a future service or revenue generating potential is recorded as an asset, whereas the cost of a product or service that has been consumed or no longer has a revenue generating potential is recorded as an expense. An important distinction was made between product costs and period costs. *Product costs* — which include the cost of raw materials and other factors necessary to transform raw materials into finished goods — are recorded as assets until the finished goods are sold; at that time they become the expense cost of goods sold. *Period costs* — which are expired nonproduct costs, such as selling or administrative expenses — are recorded as expenses in the period they are incurred.

To simplify the discussion of cost-volume-profit relationships, inventories are assumed to be constant or at zero. All merchandise is sold and all supplies are consumed in the period they are purchased. In manufacturing organizations raw materials are converted into finished goods in the period they are purchased, and finished goods are sold in the period they are produced. *With this assumption product costs and period costs are both expenses of the period in which they are incurred.* By limiting the discussion to these two types of costs, the words "cost" and "expense" have equivalent meaning and may be used interchangeably. *In cost-volume-profit analysis the word "cost(s)" refers to product costs and periods costs that are expenses of the period in which they are incurred.* Additional assumptions of cost-volume-profit analysis are discussed at the end of this chapter.

THE PROFIT FORMULA

An organization's profit is equal to the difference between its total revenues and its total costs:

$$\text{Profit} = \text{Total revenues} - \text{Total costs.}$$

Total revenues are a function of the unit sales volume and the unit selling price:

$$\frac{\text{Total}}{\text{revenues}} = \frac{\text{Selling}}{\text{price}} \times \frac{\text{Unit}}{\text{volume.}}$$

The computation of profit can be expanded to include the detailed elements of revenues and costs:

$$\text{Profit} = \left(\frac{\text{Selling}}{\text{price}} \times \frac{\text{Unit}}{\text{volume}}\right) - \left[\frac{\text{Fixed}}{\text{costs}} + \left(\frac{\text{Variable costs}}{\text{per unit}} \times \frac{\text{Unit}}{\text{volume}}\right)\right].$$

Given information on the selling price, the fixed costs per period, and the variable costs per unit, this formula is used to determine profit at any specified volume. Consider the following example.

The Benchmark Card Company manufactures high-quality seasonal greeting cards that are sold at $8 per box of 100 cards. Variable and fixed costs are shown below.

Variable Costs per Box			Fixed Costs per Month	
Manufacturing:			Factory overhead	$ 5,000
Direct materials	$1.00		Selling and	
Direct labor	0.50		administrative	10,000
Factory overhead	0.50	$2.00	Total	$15,000
Selling and admin-				
istrative		1.00		
Total		$3.00		

If Benchmark produces and sells 4000 boxes of cards in October, 19x7, their profit would be $5000.

$$\text{Profit} = (\$8 \times 4000) - [\$15,000 + (\$3 \times 4000)]$$
$$= \$5000.$$

ALTERNATIVE INCOME STATEMENTS

Assuming Benchmark does not maintain beginning or ending inventories, and that monthly production equals monthly sales, the cost of goods manufactured is the cost of goods sold, and a detailed list of current manufacturing costs can be disclosed in the income statement as the cost of goods sold. There are two alternative formats for disclosing manufacturing and other costs in an income statement. Each is discussed and illustrated below.

Functional Income Statements Classify Expenses by Function

Benchmark Card Company's income statement is presented in Exhibit 4–1 in the form most frequently used for external reporting. This statement is called a **functional income statement** because costs are classified according to function, such as manufacturing or selling and administrative. Variable and fixed costs are included within each functional category. The cost of goods sold includes variable and fixed manufacturing costs; likewise, the selling and administrative expenses include variable and fixed costs. For the purpose of exposition, detailed computations of cost of goods sold and selling and administrative expenses are shown in Exhibit 4–1. In reality, it is unlikely that each functional cost would be further classified by cost behavior.

One immediate problem with a functional income statement is the difficulty of relating it to the profit formula where costs are classified according to behavior rather than function. The cost and profit consequences of changes in sales volume are not readily apparent in a functional income statement, especially when cost information is presented at an aggregated

---

EXHIBIT 4–1   Functional and Contribution Income Statements

Benchmark Card Company
Functional Income Statement
For the month of October, 19x7

Sales ($8 × 4000)		$32,000
Cost of goods sold:		
Direct materials ($1 × 4000)	$4,000	
Direct labor ($0.50 × 4000)	2,000	
Variable factory overhead ($0.50 × 4000)	2,000	
Fixed factory overhead	5,000	−13,000
Gross profit		$19,000
Selling and administrative expenses:		
Variable ($1 × 4000)	$ 4,000	
Fixed	10,000	−14,000
Net income		$ 5,000

Benchmark Card Company
Contribution Income Statement
For the month of October, 19x7

Sales ($8 × 4000)			$32,000
Less variable costs:			
Variable cost of goods sold:			
Direct materials ($1 × 4000)	$4,000		
Direct labor ($0.50 × 4000)	2,000		
Factory overhead ($0.50 × 4000)	2,000	$ 8,000	
Variable selling and administrative			
($1 × 4000)		4,000	−12,000
Contribution margin			$20,000
Less fixed costs:			
Fixed factory overhead		$ 5,000	
Fixed selling and administrative		10,000	−15,000
Net income			$ 5,000

---

level. *For planning and control purposes costs should be classified by behavior.* This classification assists in determining how costs and, hence, profits respond to changes in volume.

Contribution Income Statements Classify Expenses by Cost Behavior

The contribution income statement, which is also presented in Exhibit 4–1, is used for internal planning and control. In a **contribution income statement** costs are classified according to behavior. The variable manufacturing costs and the variable selling and administrative expenses are grouped together and subtracted from revenues. The difference between revenues and variable costs, called the **contribution margin,** is the amount of money contributed to cover fixed costs and to provide a profit. The fixed manufacturing costs and the fixed selling and administrative expenses are also grouped together and subtracted from the contribution margin to obtain net income.

When production and sales are equal (no beginning or ending inventories), the same net income will be obtained with either type of income statement. However, the gross profit (or gross margin) in a functional income statement will seldom be the same as the contribution margin in a contribution income statement. This is because the computation of gross profit includes a deduction for fixed manufacturing costs while excluding a deduction for variable selling and administrative expenses. The mixing of fixed and variable costs in the computation of a *manufacturing* firm's gross profit makes it difficult to determine how gross profit responds to changes in sales volume. Note, however, that a *merchandising* firm's cost of goods sold includes only the variable cost of goods purchased and sold; hence, the gross profit of a merchandising firm represents a contribution or margin that is available to cover selling and administrative costs and to provide for a profit. It should increase in direct proportion to changes in sales volume.

Unit Contribution Margin. For planning purposes it is useful to express sales, variable costs, and contribution margin by unit, percentage, or both. Condensing Benchmark's October, 19x7 contribution income statement, we obtain the following:

	Total	Per Unit	Percent of Sales
Sales (4000 units)	$32,000	$8	100.0
Variable costs	−12,000	−3	−37.5
Contribution margin	$20,000	$5	62.5
Fixed costs	−15,000		
Net income	$ 5,000		

The **unit contribution margin** is the difference between the unit selling price and the unit variable costs, including the variable cost of goods sold and the variable selling and administrative costs. The unit contribution margin is also described as the amount that each unit sold contributes to cover fixed costs and to provide for a profit. This notion is widely used to determine the profit impact of changes in sales volume. Management may want to know what will happen to Benchmark's profit if sales increase by 500 units. With a unit contribution margin of $5, the profit impact of a 500 unit increase in sales volume is quickly computed as $5 multiplied by 500:

$$\$5 \times 500 = \$2500 \quad \text{increase in profit.}$$

If the current profit is $5000 at a monthly volume of 4000 units, the new profit will be $7500 at a monthly volume 500 units higher.

Current profit	$5,000
Increase ($5 × 500)	2,500
New profit	$7,500

We could use the profit formula to compute the new profit and then subtract the current profit from this amount to determine the increase; however, this approach is more time consuming. Alternatively, we could start with the current contribution income statement and show the impact of the sales increase on revenues and variable costs:

	Current 4000 Units	Increase 500 Units	New 4500 Units
Sales ($8 per unit)	$32,000	$4,000	$36,000
Variable costs ($3 per unit)	−12,000	−1,500	−13,500
Contribution margin	$20,000	$2,500	$22,500
Fixed costs	−15,000	—	−15,000
Net income	$ 5,000	$2,500	$ 7,500

Not only is this a useful way of presenting information to management, it also illustrates one of the advantages of contribution income statements for internal planning. The effect of a volume change is much easier to illustrate with a contribution income statement than with a functional income statement.

Contribution Margin Ratio. The **contribution margin ratio,** which is the ratio of contribution margin to sales revenue, indicates the portion of each sales dollar that is available to cover fixed costs and provide for a profit. It is computed as the contribution margin divided by sales, which may be done in total ($20,000 ÷ $32,000 = 0.625) or per unit ($5 ÷ $8 = 0.625). It may also be computed as 1.00 minus the **variable cost ratio,**

that is, the ratio of variable costs to sales revenue. The variable cost ratio indicates the portion of each sales dollar that is used to cover variable costs and is computed as the variable costs divided by sales revenue. Again, this may be done in total ($12,000 ÷ $32,000 = 0.375) or per unit ($3 ÷ $8 = 0.375). Of each sales dollar received by the Benchmark Card Company, 37.5 percent goes to cover variable costs, and 62.5 percent goes to cover fixed costs and provide for a profit.

Using the contribution margin ratio, the profit impact of a change in sales revenue is easily determined as the change in sales revenue multiplied by the contribution margin ratio. Benchmark has a contribution margin ratio of 0.625. If Benchmark's monthly sales increase by $4000, their monthly profit will increase by $2500:

$$\$4000 \times 0.625 = \$2500 \quad \text{increase in profit.}$$

The unit contribution margin and the contribution margin ratio are equally useful in determining the effect on profit of volume changes in single product firms. However, *the contribution margin ratio is easier to work with in firms that sell several products in a constant sales mix.* Sales dollars provide a common denominator that can be meaningfully added across products. A furniture company may sell several different styles of desks, tables, and bookcases. Given the different selling prices, costs, and contributions of each product, the sum of the sales revenues is more meaningful than the sum of the unit sales.

COST-VOLUME-PROFIT RELATIONSHIPS

A **cost-volume-profit graph** illustrates the relationships between volume, total revenues, total costs, and profit. Its usefulness comes from its depicting revenue and cost relationships over a wide range of activity, rather than just at selected volumes. This visual representation of an organization's revenues and costs allows management to determine the value of these important variables at any graphed volume without making computations. A comparison of graphs illustrating the costs, revenues, and profits of alternative products or production procedures assists management in selecting the most desirable product or method of operation.

The Benchmark Card Company's cost-volume-profit graph is presented in Exhibit 4–2. Total revenues and total costs are measured on the vertical axis, and volume of activity is measured in units on the horizontal axis. Separate lines are drawn for total costs and total revenues. When total costs exceed total revenues, losses occur, and when total revenues exceed total costs, profits occur. The amount of profit or loss at a given volume is depicted by the vertical distance between the total revenue and the

EXHIBIT 4–2   Typical Cost-Volume-Profit Graph

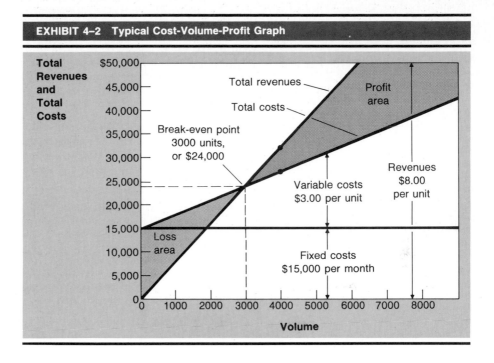

total cost lines. The **break-even point** occurs at the unit or dollar sales volume where total revenues equal total costs. Graphically, this happens when the total revenue and total cost lines intersect.

Before developing a cost-volume-profit graph it is necessary to obtain information on the behavior of costs and revenues. The three lines graphed in Exhibit 4–2 are developed as follows:

1. A line representing monthly fixed costs of $15,000 is drawn parallel to the horizontal axis. The distance between the horizontal axis and this line depicts Benchmark's monthly fixed costs.

2. Variable costs are layered on top of fixed costs to obtain total costs. To draw this line it is necessary to determine total costs at some randomly selected volume. At 4000 units Benchmark's total costs are $27,000 [$15,000 + ($3 × 4000)]. This point is plotted on the graph, and a straight line is drawn through it and the point where the fixed cost line inter-sects the vertical axis. The distance between the total cost line and the fixed cost line represents Benchmark's variable costs at each level of production.

3. A straight line depicting total revenues is drawn through the origin and a point representing total revenues at some other randomly selected

volume. At 4000 units Benchmark's total revenues are $32,000 ($8 ×
4000). The distance between the total revenue line and the horizontal
axis represents Benchmark's total revenues at each level of sales.

A widely used variation of the cost-volume-profit graph is presented
in Exhibit 4–3. Here a line is drawn first for variable costs with fixed costs
layered on top of variable costs to obtain total costs. By layering fixed
costs on top of variable costs, this graph emphasizes the contribution margin available to cover fixed costs and to provide for a profit. The contribution
margin is represented by the vertical distance between the total revenue
and the total variable cost lines. Up to the break-even point the entire
contribution margin goes to cover fixed costs, at the break-even point the
contribution margin equals the fixed costs, and beyond the break-even
point the contribution margin is large enough to cover fixed costs and
provide for a profit.

The lines in Exhibit 4–3 are developed in a manner similar to those
in Exhibit 4–2. Straight lines are drawn through plotted values at a randomly
selected volume and at the appropriate vertical axis intercepts. A useful
feature of this second graph is its relationship to the contribution income
statement. Compare the contribution income statement in Exhibit 4–1 with

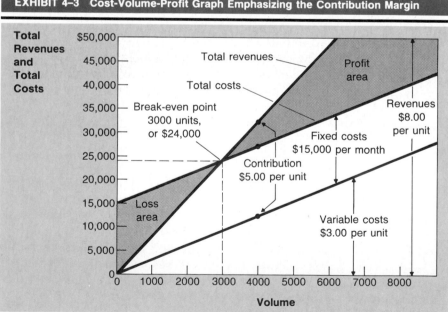

EXHIBIT 4–3 Cost-Volume-Profit Graph Emphasizing the Contribution Margin

the graph in Exhibit 4–3. The income statement is merely a formal presentation of the relationships graphed at 4000 units. With the graph it is easy to determine income statement amounts at other volumes.

Determining the Break-even Point

Three approaches are widely used to determine the break-even point: (1) the graphic approach, (2) the formula approach, and (3) the contribution approach. Each is used to determine the break-even point in units or sales dollars.

Graphic Approach The graphic approach involves the graphing of cost-volume-profit relationships. The break-even point in units or sales dollars is then determined by studying the graph. In Exhibits 4–2 and 4–3 the break-even point is 3000 units, or 24,000 sales dollars.

Formula Approach The formula approach to determining the break-even point involves the use of the profit formula with profits set equal to zero.

$$\text{Profit} = \left(\begin{matrix}\text{Selling}\\\text{price}\end{matrix} \times \begin{matrix}\text{Unit}\\\text{volume}\end{matrix}\right) - \left[\begin{matrix}\text{Fixed}\\\text{costs}\end{matrix} + \left(\begin{matrix}\text{Variable costs}\\\text{per unit}\end{matrix} \times \begin{matrix}\text{Unit}\\\text{volume}\end{matrix}\right)\right] = 0$$

With zero profits, total revenues equal total costs.

$$\underbrace{\begin{matrix}\text{Selling}\\\text{price}\end{matrix} \times \begin{matrix}\text{Unit}\\\text{volume}\end{matrix}}_{\textbf{Total Revenues}} = \underbrace{\begin{matrix}\text{Fixed}\\\text{costs}\end{matrix} + \left(\begin{matrix}\text{Variable costs}\\\text{per unit}\end{matrix} \times \begin{matrix}\text{Unit}\\\text{volume}\end{matrix}\right)}_{\textbf{Total Costs}}$$

The break-even unit volume is now computed by placing prices and costs in this equation and solving. Let X equal the break-even *unit* volume. Then, with a selling price of $8 per box, variable costs of $3 per box, and fixed costs of $15,000 per month:

$$\$8X = \$15,000 + \$3X.$$

Solving for X:

$$\$8X - \$3X = \$15,000$$
$$\$5X = \$15,000$$
$$X = \$15,000/\$5$$
$$= 3000 \text{ units.}$$

The break-even point in sales dollars is found by multiplying the unit selling price by the break-even unit volume:

$$\$8 \times 3000 = \$24,000.$$

Alternatively, using the variable cost ratio, the following equality also holds at the break-even dollar sales volume:

$$\text{Total revenue} = \text{Fixed costs} + \left(\text{Variable cost ratio} \times \text{Total revenue}\right).$$

The break-even dollar sales volume can be found by placing fixed costs and the variable cost ratio in this equation and solving. Let X equal the break-even *dollar* sales volume. Then, with fixed costs of $15,000 per month and variable costs equal to 37.5 percent of sales revenue,

$$X = \$15,000 + 0.375X.$$

Solving for X:

$$X - 0.375X = \$15,000$$
$$0.625X = \$15,000$$
$$X = \$15,000/0.625$$
$$= \$24,000.$$

Contribution Approach   Focusing on the final computation in the formula approach provides a third approach to determining the break-even unit or dollar sales volume. With fixed costs of $15,000 and a unit contribution margin of $5, the unit break-even point was computed as

$$\frac{\$15,000}{\$5} = 3000 \text{ units.}$$

The unit break-even volume indicates the number of units of contribution needed to cover the fixed costs. With fixed costs of $15,000 and a $5 unit contribution margin, 3000 units of contribution are required to break even. In general,

$$\text{Break-even point in units} = \frac{\text{Fixed costs}}{\text{Unit contribution margin}}.$$

In sales dollars, the break-even point was found as follows:

$$\frac{\$15,000}{0.625} = \$24,000,$$

where 0.625 is the contribution margin ratio.

To contribute $15,000 to cover fixed costs, a total revenue of $24,000 is required. This is verified as follows:

$$\$24,000 \times 0.625 = \$15,000.$$

In general,

$$\text{Break-even point in sales dollars} = \frac{\text{Fixed costs}}{\text{Contribution margin ratio}}.$$

Profit Planning

Cost-volume-profit relationships are used to determine profit or loss at any specified level of activity. The Benchmark Card Company, for example, anticipates a profit of $5000 at a sales volume of 4000 units, or 32,000 sales dollars. Using the graphs in Exhibits 4–2 and 4–3 (shown on pages 115 and 116), observe that a volume of 1000 units, or 8000 sales dollars, should result in a loss of $10,000.

Margin of Safety. The **margin of safety** is the excess of actual or budgeted sales over break-even sales. Expressed in units or sales dollars, the margin of safety indicates the amount that sales could decline before losses occur. The Benchmark Card Company's margin of safety for October, 19x7, is 1000 units, or $8000.

	Units	Sales Dollars
Anticipated sales	4,000	$32,000
Break-even sales	−3,000	−24,000
Margin of safety	1,000	$ 8,000

Activity Planning. Establishing profit objectives is an important part of planning in for-profit organizations. Profit objectives are determined in many ways. They can be computed as a percentage of last year's profits, as a percentage of total assets at the start of the current year, or as a percentage of average owner's equity over some past period. They might be based on a profit trend, or they might be expressed as a percent of sales. The economic outlook for the firm's products and anticipated changes in products, costs, and technology are also considered in establishing profit objectives.

Before incorporating profit plans into a detailed budget, it is useful to obtain some preliminary information on the feasibility of profit plans. Cost-volume-profit analysis is used for this purpose. By manipulating cost-volume-profit relationships, management can determine the sales volume required to obtain a desired profit. Management would then evaluate the feasibility of this sales volume. If the profit plans are feasible, a complete budget might be developed for this activity level. The required sales volume may be infeasible because of market conditions or because the required volume exceeds production capacity, in which case management might lower its profit objective or consider other ways of achieving it. Alternatively, the required sales volume might be less than management believes the firm is capable of producing and selling, in which case management would raise its profit objective.

Assume Benchmark's management desires to know the sales volume required to achieve a monthly profit of $12,000. Using the formula approach, the required unit sales volume is determined by setting profits equal to $12,000 and solving for X, the *unit* sales volume:

$$\text{Profit} = \text{Revenues} - \text{Costs}$$
$$\$12,000 = \$8X - (\$15,000 + \$3X)$$
$$\$8X - \$3X = \$15,000 + \$12,000$$
$$X = (\$15,000 + \$12,000)/\$5$$
$$= 5400 \text{ units.}$$

The required dollar sales volume is found by multiplying 5400 units times the unit selling price:

$$\$8 \times 5400 = \$43,200.$$

Alternatively, the dollar sales volume required to achieve a monthly profit of $12,000 can be found using the profit formula with the variable cost ratio:

$$\$12,000 = X - (\$15,000 + 0.375X)$$
$$X - 0.375X = \$15,000 + \$12,000$$
$$X = (\$15,000 + \$12,000)/0.625$$
$$= \$43,200,$$

where X equals the dollar sales volume.

Once again, the final computation in the formula approach provides a contribution approach to determining the required unit or dollar sales volume. The alternative computations using the contribution approach are shown below.

	Volume required to achieve a desired profit	
	$X = $ **units**	$X = $ **sales dollars**
In general:		
$X =$	$\dfrac{\text{Fixed costs} + \text{Desired profit}}{\text{Unit contribution margin}}$	$\dfrac{\text{Fixed costs} + \text{Desired profit}}{\text{Contribution margin ratio}}$
For Benchmark:		
$X =$	$\dfrac{\$15,000 + \$12,000}{\$5}$	$\dfrac{\$15,000 + \$12,000}{0.625}$
$=$	5400 units	$43,200

In units the contribution approach indicated the number of units of production and sales needed to cover the fixed costs and provide the desired profit. In sales dollars the contribution approach indicated the total sales revenue required to have a contribution equal to the fixed costs and the desired profit.

The Impact of Income Taxes. Income taxes are imposed on individuals and for-profit organizations by units of government. The amount of an individual's or an organization's income tax is determined by laws that specify the calculation of taxable income (the income subject to tax) and the calculation of the amount of tax on taxable income. Income taxes are computed as a percentage of taxable income with increases in taxable income usually subject to progressively higher tax rates. The laws governing the computation of taxable income differ in many ways from the accounting principles and standards that guide the computation of accounting income. Consequently, taxable income and accounting income are seldom the same.

In the *early stages* of profit planning, income taxes are sometimes incorporated into an organization's cost-volume-profit model by assuming that taxable income and accounting income are equal and that the tax rate is constant. Although these assumptions are seldom true, they are useful because they assist management in developing an early prediction of the sales volume required to earn a desired after-tax profit. Once management has developed a general plan, this early prediction should be refined with the advice of tax experts.

Assuming income taxes are imposed at a constant rate per dollar of before-tax profit, income taxes are computed as the tax rate times before-tax profit, and an organization's after-tax profit is equal to its before-tax profit minus income taxes:

$$\frac{\text{After-tax}}{\text{profit}} = \frac{\text{Before-tax}}{\text{profit}} - \left(\frac{\text{Tax}}{\text{rate}} \times \frac{\text{Before-tax}}{\text{profit}}\right).$$

After-tax profit can also be expressed as 1 minus the tax rate times before-tax profit:

$$\frac{\text{After-tax}}{\text{profit}} = \left(1 - \frac{\text{Tax}}{\text{rate}}\right) \times \frac{\text{Before-tax}}{\text{profit}}.$$

The relationship of before-tax profit to after-tax profit can be found by rearranging terms:

$$\frac{\text{Before-tax}}{\text{profit}} = \frac{\text{After-tax profit}}{(1 - \text{Tax rate})}.$$

With all costs and revenues in the profit formula expressed on a before-tax basis, the most straightforward way of determining the sales volume required to earn a desired after-tax profit is to

1. Determine the equivalent before-tax profit,
2. Substitute the desired before-tax profit into the profit formula,
3. Solve for the required sales volume using the formula or the contribution approach.

Assume that the Benchmark Card Company is subject to a 40 percent tax rate, and that management desires to earn a November, 19x3, after-tax profit of $12,000. The desired before-tax profit is readily determined to be $20,000:

$$\text{Desired before-tax profit} = \frac{\$12,000}{1 - 0.40}$$
$$= \$20,000.$$

Using the contribution approach, a sales volume of 7000 units or $56,000 is required to earn a before-tax profit of $20,000, as is shown below.

	Volume required to achieve a desired before-tax profit	
	X = **units**	*X* = **sales dollars**
In general: $X =$	$\dfrac{\text{Fixed costs} + \text{Desired before-tax profit}}{\text{Unit contribution margin}}$	$\dfrac{\text{Fixed costs} + \text{Desired before-tax profit}}{\text{Contribution margin ratio}}$
For Benchmark: $X =$	$\dfrac{\$15,000 + \$20,000}{\$5}$	$\dfrac{\$15,000 + \$20,000}{0.625}$
$=$	7000 units	$56,000

It is apparent that *income taxes increase the sales volume required to earn a desired profit.* A 40 percent tax rate increased the sales volume required for Benchmark to earn a profit of $12,000 from 5400 to 7000 units, or from $43,200 to $56,000. These amounts are verified in Exhibit 4–4.

Sensitivity Analysis

Sensitivity analysis is the study of the responsiveness of a model's dependent variable(s) to changes in one or more of the model's independent variables. It is often applied to an organization's cost-volume-profit model to determine how profits or some other variable will respond to some proposed change. Managers are particularly interested in performing sensitivity analysis on those variables that are most likely to change. Knowing what will happen to profits if cost or revenue or volume changes assists

---

EXHIBIT 4–4 Contribution Income Statement with Income Taxes

Benchmark Card Company
Contribution Income Statement
Planned for the month of November, 19x7

Sales ($8 × 7000)		$56,000
Less variable costs:		
Variable cost of goods sold ($2.00 × 7000)	$14,000	
Variable selling and administrative ($1.00 × 7000)	7,000	−21,000
Contribution margin		$35,000
Less fixed costs:		
Fixed factory overhead	$ 5,000	
Fixed selling and administrative	10,000	−15,000
Income before taxes		$20,000
Income taxes (0.40 × $20,000)		−8,000
Net income		$12,000

---

management in developing contingency plans that can be implemented as soon as an event occurs.

The management of the Benchmark Card Company might, for example, anticipate a decline in sales if the U.S. Post Office announces a December 15 increase in the cost of first class postage. To determine the possible profit impact of this change and to evaluate alternative responses, management would use sensitivity analysis. Possible responses might include doing nothing, instituting an offsetting reduction in selling prices, increasing advertising to encourage potential customers to mail early, lobbying to delay the postage increase, or introducing a new holiday postcard that can be mailed at a lower rate. By analyzing each alternative in advance, management will know what action to initiate if an increase in first class postage is announced.

To offset this increase in postage, management is considering a reduction in selling price from $8 to $7 per box of cards. Management needs to know the number of boxes Benchmark will have to sell at the new, lower price to earn a monthly before-tax profit of $20,000.

The $1 reduction in selling price would reduce the unit contribution margin from $5 to $4 ($7 − $3). With fixed costs of $15,000 the sales volume required to earn a before-tax profit of $20,000 is now 8750:

$$X = \frac{\$15,000 + \$20,000}{\$4}$$

$$= 8750 \text{ units.}$$

This is an increase of 1750 units:

Required sales volume at $7 selling price	8750
Required sales volume at $8 selling price	−7000
Increase in required sales volume	1750

PROFIT-VOLUME GRAPHS

In cost-volume-profit graphs, profits are represented by the difference between total revenues and total costs. When management is primarily interested in the profit impact of changes in sales volume, and less interested in the related revenues and costs, a profit-volume graph is sometimes used instead of a cost-volume-profit graph. A **profit-volume graph** illustrates the relationship between volume and profits; it does not illustrate revenues and costs. A manager primarily interested in profit-volume relationships will prefer a profit-volume graph because it provides a clear illustration of profits. Profits are read directly from a profit-volume graph rather than being computed as the difference between total revenues and total costs.

The Benchmark Card Company's monthly profit-volume graph is presented in Exhibit 4–5. Profit or loss is measured on the vertical axis, and

EXHIBIT 4–5   Typical Profit-Volume Graph

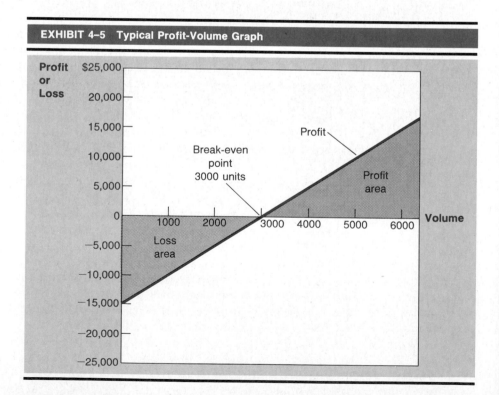

volume is measured in units on the horizontal axis, which intersects the vertical axis at zero profit. A single line, representing total profit, is drawn intersecting the vertical axis at a zero volume loss equal to the fixed costs. The profit line crosses the horizontal axis at the break-even unit sales volume. The profit or loss at any volume is depicted by the vertical distance between the profit line and the horizontal axis.

The profit line is drawn by determining and plotting profit or loss at two different volumes and then drawing a straight line through the plotted values. Perhaps the easiest values to select are the loss at a volume of zero (this amount is the fixed costs) and the volume at which the profit line crosses the horizontal axis (this is the break-even unit sales volume). It is also possible, using the profit formula, to determine profit or loss at any other volumes. Note that the slope of the profit line is equal to the unit contribution margin, the amount by which profits increase, or losses decrease, as one additional unit is sold.

NOT-FOR-PROFIT APPLICATIONS

Cost-volume-profit relationships and related break-even concepts are widely used in not-for-profit organizations. To make these concepts more acceptable in such organizations, they might be renamed "cost-volume-contribution" or "cost-volume-subsidy" relationships. Although managers of not-for-profit organizations are not specifically interested in earning a profit for the organization as a whole, they often desire that some activities provide a positive contribution that can be used to subsidize other activities. Consider the following example.

Martha Montgomery is a candidate for the U.S. House of Representatives. To obtain money to finance her campaign, a fund-raising dinner with a required donation of $100 per plate is scheduled in a rented hall. The costs of renting and decorating the hall are $3000. The variable cost of each meal served is $30. The total contribution to Martha Montgomery's campaign can be graphed as a function of the number of persons who attend the dinner. Substituting desired contribution for desired profits, campaign organizers can determine the number of tickets they must sell to net $25,000 from the dinner:

$$\frac{\$3000 + \$25,000}{\$100 - \$30} = 400 \text{ tickets.}$$

The concept of the break-even point is also widely used in not-for-profit organizations. The Student Association of City University will be interested in the break-even point for association-sponsored activities, such as concerts, festivals, and plays. They would also use cost-volume-profit relationships to determine the amount of any required subsidy if ticket sales fall short of the break-even point, or the amount of any contribution if ticket sales exceed the break-even point.

Many not-for-profit organizations provide goods or services for less than cost: The U.S. government subsidizes school lunches, civic orchestras stage children's concerts for a nominal fee, and the tuition charged by most colleges is inadequate to cover operating costs. Here cost-volume-profit relationships (or variations of the profit formula) are used to determine the required subsidy, or the activity level that can be supported with a given subsidy.

LIMITING ASSUMPTIONS

The models and graphs presented in this chapter are subject to a number of limiting assumptions. Although these assumptions do not negate the usefulness of these models in the early stages of planning, they do suggest the need for further analysis before plans are completed. This additional analysis will normally be reflected in an organization's budget for a coming period. Among the more important assumptions are the following:

1. *All costs are classified as fixed or variable.* Step costs must be approximated by fixed or mixed costs, and mixed costs must be broken down into their fixed and variable cost elements.

2. *The total cost function is linear.* This assumption may be valid only within a relevant range. Over the entire range of possible volumes, changes in productivity and efficiency are likely to result in a curvilinear cost function.

3. *The total revenue function is linear.* Unit selling prices are assumed to be constant over the entire range of possible volumes. This implies a purely competitive market for final products. In some economic models (monopolistic and oligopolistic), where the demand for a product responds to price changes, the revenue function is curvilinear. In these situations the linear approximation is accurate only within a limited range of activity.

4. *The sales mix is constant.* The **sales mix** refers to the relative portion of unit or dollar sales that is derived from each product or service. If multiple products have different unit costs or revenues, changes in the sales mix will cause changes in the slopes of total revenue or cost lines, or both. Changes in the sales mix are examined in the appendix to this chapter.

5. *Inventories are constant.* This assumption means that all current expenditures for acquiring or producing inventories are reported as expenses on the current income statement. In the absence of this assumption,

current manufacturing or inventory acquisition costs can be greater or less than the expenses reported on the income statement. This assumption, which was discussed at the beginning of this chapter, is examined further in Chapter 10.

SUMMARY

Cost-volume-profit analysis is used to examine the relationships between volume, total costs, total revenues, and profit. Because cost-volume-profit analysis provides a framework for discussing planning issues and organizing relevant data, it is widely used in the early stages of planning.

We illustrated the usefulness of this technique in determining the break-even point, the margin of safety, and the volume required to earn a desired profit with and without income taxes. In all these applications we used either the unit contribution margin or the contribution margin ratio. The unit contribution margin is the difference between the unit selling price and the unit variable costs. The contribution margin ratio is the ratio of contribution margin to sales dollars. In making short-run decisions managers should think in terms of these concepts. We will use them frequently in subsequent chapters.

APPENDIX
SALES MIX ANALYSIS

Sales mix refers to the relative portion of unit or dollar sales that are derived from each product or service. When the sales mix is constant, managers of multiple product organizations can use the average unit contribution margin, or the average contribution margin ratio, to determine the break-even point or the sales volume required to earn a desired profit. Often, however, management is interested in the effect of a change in the sales mix rather than a change in the sales volume at a constant mix. In this situation it is necessary to determine either the average unit contribution margin or the unit contribution margin ratio for each alternative mix.

Assume the Benchmark Card Company now sells posters as well as boxes of cards. Selling price and variable cost information is as follows:

	Posters per Unit	*Cards per Box*
Unit selling price	$5.00	$8.00
Unit variable costs:		
Manufacturing	$1.50	$2.00
Selling	1.00	1.00
Total	−2.50	−3.00
Unit contribution margin	$2.50	$5.00

The current sales mix in units is 50 percent posters and 50 percent cards. This mix produces an average unit selling price of $6.50 and an average unit contribution margin of $3.75:

Product	Unit Selling Price		Sales Mix (units)		Weight
Posters	$5.00	×	0.50	=	$2.50
Cards	8.00	×	0.50	=	4.00
Average unit selling price					$6.50

Product	Unit Contribution Margin		Sales Mix (units)		Weight
Posters	$2.50	×	0.50	=	$1.25
Cards	5.00	×	0.50	=	2.50
Average unit contribution margin					$3.75

With fixed costs of $15,000 per month, Benchmark's monthly break-even sales volume is 4,000 units ($15,000/$3.75). This 4,000 units consists of 2,000 posters and 2,000 boxes of cards:

Product	Total Sales (units)		Sales Mix (units)		Product Sales (units)
Posters	4000	×	0.50	=	2000
Cards	4000	×	0.50	=	2000

Benchmark's profit-volume graph is presented in Exhibit 4–6. The current mix is represented by the red line.

Benchmark's current break-even dollar sales volume can be computed by multiplying the break-even unit sales volume by the average unit selling price:

$$\text{Break-even dollar sales volume} = 4000 \times \$6.50 = \$26,000.$$

Alternatively, the break-even dollar sales volume is computed as the fixed costs divided by the average contribution margin ratio:

$$\text{Average contribution margin ratio} = \frac{\text{Average unit contribution margin}}{\text{Average unit selling price}} = \frac{\$3.75}{\$6.50} = 0.5769,$$

$$\text{Break-even dollar sales volume} = \frac{\$15,000}{0.5769} = \$26,000 \quad \text{(rounded)}.$$

Benchmark's management wants to know what the break-even unit and dollar sales volume will be if the sales mix in units becomes 20 percent

EXHIBIT 4–6   Sales Mix Analysis: Weighted Average Approach

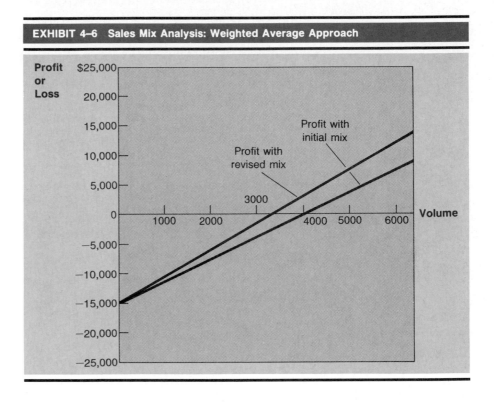

posters and 80 percent cards. There are no changes in costs or selling prices. The revised average unit selling price is $7.40, and the revised average unit contribution margin is $4.50:

Product	Unit Selling Price		Sales Mix (units)		Weight
Posters	$5.00	×	0.20	=	$1.00
Cards	8.00	×	0.80	=	6.40
Average unit selling price					$7.40

Product	Unit Contribution Margin		Sales Mix (units)		Weight
Posters	$2.50	×	0.20	=	$0.50
Cards	5.00	×	0.80	=	4.00
Average unit contribution margin					$4.50

The revised break-even sales volume is 3333 units ($15,000/$4.50) and consists of 667 posters (3333 × 0.20) and 2666 boxes of cards. Benchmark's revised mix is represented by the black line in Exhibit 4–6. The effect of shifting the mix from posters to cards is to reduce the break-even unit sales volume. This occurs because cards have a higher unit contribution margin. The revised average contribution margin ratio of 0.6081 ($4.50/$7.40) results in a break-even dollar sales volume of $24,667 ($15,000/0.6081).[1]

KEY TERMS

Cost-volume-profit analysis

Functional income statement

Contribution income statement

Contribution margin

Unit contribution margin

Contribution margin ratio

Variable cost ratio

Cost-volume-profit graph

Break-even point

Margin of safety

Sensitivity analysis

Profit-volume graph

Sales mix

REVIEW QUESTIONS

4–1   At what stage of planning is cost-volume-profit analysis particularly useful? Why?

4–2   Present the profit equation in detail.

4–3   Why is a contribution income statement superior to a functional income statement for planning and control purposes?

4–4   What is the unit contribution margin? What does it tell us?

4–5   Distinguish between the contribution margin ratio and the variable cost ratio.

4–6   Using the contribution approach, how is the unit break-even point computed? In words, what does it tell us?

4–7   Using the contribution approach, how is the break-even dollar sales volume computed?

4–8   Using the contribution approach, how do we determine the unit sales volume required to earn a desired profit?

4–9   Using the contribution approach, how do we determine the dollar sales volume required to earn a desired profit?

---

[1]In attempting to verify computations in this section you will find small discrepancies caused by rounding.

4–10 What assumptions are made when income taxes are incorporated into cost-volume-profit models?

4–11 Given a desired after-tax profit and a tax rate, how do we determine the desired before-tax profit?

4–12 Why is sensitivity analysis often applied to an organization's cost-volume-profit model?

4–13 Why do some managers prefer profit-volume graphs to cost-volume-profit graphs?

4–14 Name three uses of cost-volume-profit models in not-for-profit organizations.

4–15 Name five assumptions that limit the usefulness of cost-volume-profit models.

EXERCISES

4–1 Functional and Contribution Income Statements

The Ohio Company produces a product that is sold for $20 per unit. Variable and fixed costs are shown below.

Variable Costs per Unit			Fixed Costs per Month	
Manufacturing:			Factory overhead	$20,000
Direct materials	$3		Selling and	
Direct labor	2		administrative	10,000
Factory overhead	2	$ 7	Total	$30,000
Selling and				
administrative		3		
Total		$10		

The company produced and sold 5000 units during July of 19x1. There were no beginning or ending inventories.

Requirements

a) Prepare functional and contribution income statements for July.

b) Which of these income statements is more useful to management? Why?

c) Compute the unit contribution margin, and use it to determine the profit impact of a 600 unit decrease in sales.

d) Compute the contribution margin ratio, and use it to determine the profit impact of a $12,000 decrease in sales revenue.

4–2 Functional and Contribution Income Statements

The Ontario Company produces a product that is sold for $50 per unit. Variable and fixed costs are shown below.

Variable Costs per Unit			Fixed Costs per Month	
Manufacturing:			Factory overhead	$30,000
Direct materials	$ 8		Selling and	
Direct labor	12		administrative	15,000
Factory overhead	10	$30	Total	$45,000
Selling and				
administrative		5		
Total		$35		

The company produced and sold 10,000 units during May of 19x3. There were no beginning or ending inventories.

Requirements

a) Prepare functional and contribution income statements for May.

b) Explain why gross profit in the functional income statement differs from contribution margin in the contribution income statement.

c) Compute the unit contribution margin, and use it to determine the profit impact of a 200 unit increase in sales.

d) Compute the contribution margin ratio, and use it to determine the profit impact of a $10,000 increase in sales revenue.

4–3 Contribution Margin Concepts

At a price of $10 the estimated monthly sales of a product is 10,000 units. Variable costs include manufacturing, $6, and distribution, $1. Fixed costs are $12,000 per month.

Requirements

Determine each of the following:

a) Unit contribution margin.

b) Monthly break-even unit sales volume.

c) Monthly profit. (Ignore taxes.)

d) Monthly margin of safety in units.

4–4 Contribution Margin Concepts

At a monthly volume of $20,000 a company incurs variable costs of $4000 and fixed costs of $12,000.

Requirements

Determine each of the following:

a) Variable cost ratio.

b) Contribution margin ratio.

    c) Monthly break-even dollar sales volume.

    d) Monthly margin of safety in dollars.

4–5 Contribution Margin Concepts

In 19x5 the Duke Art Shop had the following experience:

	Fixed	Variable	
Sales			$800,000
Costs:			
Goods sold		$300,000	
Labor	$160,000	60,000	
Supplies	2,000	5,000	
Utilities	12,000	3,000	
Rent	24,000	—	
Advertising	6,000	2,000	
Miscellaneous	6,000	10,000	
Total costs	$210,000	$380,000	−633,000
Net income			$167,000

Requirements

a) Determine the annual break-even dollar sales volume.

b) Determine the current margin of safety in dollars.

c) What is the annual break-even dollar sales volume if management makes a decision that increases fixed costs by $52,500?

4–6 Cost-Volume-Profit Graphs with Sensitivity Analysis

Presented is a typical cost-volume-profit graph.

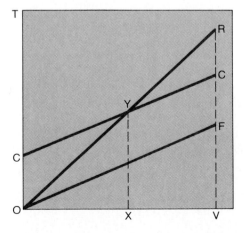

Requirements

a) Identify each of the following:

1. Line OF.

2. Line OR.

3. Line CC.

4. The difference between lines OF and OV.

5. The difference between lines CC and OF.

6. The difference between lines CC and OV.

7. The difference between lines OR and OF.

8. Point X.

9. Area CYO.

10. Area RCY.

b) Indicate the effect of each of the following independent events on lines CC, OR, and the break-even point:

1. A decrease in fixed costs.

2. An increase in the unit selling price.

3. An increase in unit variable costs.

4. An increase in fixed costs and a decrease in the unit selling price.

5. A decrease in fixed costs and a decrease in the unit variable costs.

4–7 Preparing Cost-Volume-Profit Graphs

Little Nero's Pizza Shop has the following monthly revenue and cost functions.

$$\text{Total revenues} = \$6.00X,$$

$$\text{Total costs} = \$9000 + \$1.50X.$$

Requirements

a) Prepare a graph, similar to that in Exhibit 4–2, illustrating Little Nero's cost-volume-profit relationships. The vertical axis should vary between $0 and $18,000, with increments of $3000. The horizontal axis should vary between 0 units and 3000 units, with increments of 500 units.

b) Prepare a graph, similar to that in Exhibit 4–3, illustrating Little Nero's cost-volume-profit relationships. Use the same scale for the graph as in requirement (a).

c) What does the graph prepared for requirement (b) emphasize?

4–8 Profit Planning with Taxes

In 19x5 the Huss Processing Company had the following income statement:

Sales		$950,000
Variable costs:		
Variable cost of goods sold	$420,000	
Variable selling and administrative expenses	150,000	−570,000
Contribution margin		$380,000
Fixed costs:		
Fixed factory overhead	$110,000	
Fixed selling and administrative expenses	70,000	−180,000
Net income before taxes		$200,000
Income taxes @ 0.36		−72,000
Net income		$128,000

Requirements

a) Determine the 19x5 break-even point in sales dollars.

b) Determine the 19x5 margin of safety in sales dollars.

c) What is the break-even point in sales dollars if management makes a decision that increases fixed costs by $50,000?

d) What dollar sales volume is required to provide an after-tax net income of $200,000? Assume fixed costs are $180,000.

e) Prepare an abbreviated contribution income statement to verify that the solution to requirement (d) will provide the desired after-tax income.

4–9 Profit Planning with Taxes

The Brown Manufacturing Company produces a product that is sold for $35 per unit. Variable and fixed costs are shown below.

Variable Costs per Unit		*Fixed Costs per Year*	
Manufacturing	$18	Manufacturing	$ 80,000
Selling and administrative	7	Selling and administrative	30,000
Total	$25	Total	$110,000

Last year Brown manufactured and sold 20,000 units to obtain a net income after taxes of $49,500.

Requirements

a) Determine the tax rate Brown paid last year.

b) What unit sales volume is required to provide an after-tax net income of $88,000?

c) If Brown reduces the unit variable cost by $2.50 and increases fixed manufacturing costs by $20,000, what unit sales volume is required to provide an after-tax income of $88,000?

d) What assumptions are made about taxable income and tax rates in requirements (a) through (c)?

4–10 Profit Planning with Taxes

Pawnee Company operated at normal capacity during the current year producing 50,000 units of its single product. Sales totaled 40,000 units at an average price of $20 per unit. Variable manufacturing costs were $8 per unit, and variable marketing costs were $4 per unit sold. Fixed costs were incurred uniformly throughout the year and amounted to $188,000 for manufacturing and $64,000 for marketing. There was no year-end work-in-process inventory.

Requirements

a) Determine Pawnee's break-even point in sales dollars for the current year.

b) Pawnee is subject to an income tax rate of 30 percent. Determine the number of units required to be sold in the current year to earn an after-tax income of $126,000.

c) Pawnee's variable manufacturing costs are expected to increase 10 percent in the coming year. Determine Pawnee's break-even point in sales dollars for the coming year.

d) Assuming Pawnee's variable manufacturing costs do increase by 10 percent in the coming year, determine the selling price that will yield the current contribution margin ratio in the coming year.

(CMA Adapted)

4–11 Profit-Volume Graph: Identification and Analysis

Presented is a typical profit-volume graph.

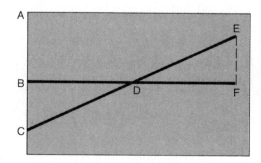

Requirements

a) Identify each of the following:

    1. Area BDC.

    2. Area DEF.

    3. Point D.

    4. Line AC.

    5. Line BC.

    6. Line EF.

b) Indicate the effect of each of the following on line CE and the break-even point.

    1. An increase in the unit selling price.

    2. An increase in the variable costs per unit.

    3. A decrease in fixed costs.

    4. An increase in fixed costs and a decrease in the unit selling price.

    5. A decrease in fixed costs and an increase in the variable costs per unit.

4–12 Preparing Cost-Volume-Profit and Profit-Volume Graphs

Fast Gas operates several self-service gas stations in the Maritime Provinces of Canada. Fast Gas has a selling price of $2.00 per imperial gallon. Variable operating costs are $1.80 per gallon, and fixed operating costs are $80,000 per month.

Requirements

a) Determine the monthly break-even point in gallons.

b) Prepare a cost-volume-profit graph for Fast Gas. Use a format that emphasizes the contribution margin. The vertical axis should vary between 0 dollars and $1,200,000, with increments of $200,000. The horizontal axis should vary between 0 gallons and 600,000 gallons, with increments of 100,000 gallons. Label the graph in thousands.

c) Prepare a profit-volume graph for Fast Gas. The vertical axis should vary between $(100,000) and $60,000, with increments of $20,000. The horizontal axis should vary between 0 gallons and 600,000 gallons, with increments of 100,000 gallons. Label the graph in thousands.

d) Evaluate the profit-volume graph. In what ways is it superior and in what ways is it inferior to the traditional cost-volume-profit graph?

4–13 Not-for-Profit Applications

Determine the solution to each of the following independent cases.

1. Lakeside College has annual fixed operating costs of $5,000,000 and variable operating costs of $1000 per student. Tuition is $4000 per student for the academic year. The projected enrollment for the coming year is 1500 students. Expected revenues from endowments and federal and state grants are $250,000. Determine the amount Lakeside must obtain from other sources.

2. The Lakeside College Student Association is planning a fall concert. Expected costs of renting a hall, hiring a band, and so forth are $30,000. Assuming 5000 persons attend the concert, determine the break-even price per ticket. How much will the association lose if this price is charged and only 4250 tickets are sold?

3. City Hospital has a contract with the city to provide indigent health care on an out-patient basis for $25 per visit. The patient will pay $5 of this amount, and the city will pay the balance of $20. Determine the amount the city will have to pay if the hospital has 10,000 patient visits.

4. A civic organization is engaged in a fund raising program. On Civic Sunday they will sell newspapers at $1.25 each. The organization will pay $0.75 for each newspaper. Costs of the necessary permits, signs, and so forth, are $500. Determine the amount they will raise if 5000 newspapers are sold.

5. Christmas for the Needy is a civic organization that provides Christmas presents to disadvantaged children. The annual costs of this activity are $5000 plus $10 per present. Determine the number of presents the organization can provide with $20,000.

4–14 High-Low Cost Estimation and Profit Planning

Presented are comparative 19x8 and 19x9 income statements for Montana Products, Inc.

Montana Products, Inc. Comparative Income Statements For the years ending December 31, 19x8 and 19x9		
	19x8	*19x9*
Unit sales	5,000	8,000
Sales revenue	$ 65,000	$104,000
Expenses	− 75,000	− 90,000
Net income (loss)	$(10,000)	$ 14,000

Requirements

a) Determine the break-even point in units.

b) Determine the unit sales volume required to earn a profit of $10,000.

4–15 High-Low Cost Estimation and Profit Planning

Presented are comparative 19y3 and 19y4 income statements for Nevada Products, Inc.

Nevada Products, Inc. Comparative Income Statements For the years ending 19y3 and 19y4		
	19y3	*19y4*
Sales revenue	$500,000	$300,000
Expenses	−440,000	−360,000
Net income (loss)	$ 60,000	$(60,000)

Requirements

a) Determine the break-even point in sales dollars.

b) Determine the dollar sales volume required to earn a profit of $180,000.

PROBLEMS

4–16 Cost-Volume-Profit Relationships: Missing Data

Supply the missing data in each independent case.

	Case 1	Case 2	Case 3	Case 4
Unit sales	1,000	800	?	?
Sales revenue	$20,000	?	?	$60,000
Variable cost per unit	$ 10	$ 1	$ 12	?
Contribution margin	?	$800	?	?
Fixed costs	$ 8,000	?	$80,000	?
Net income	?	$400	?	?
Unit contribution margin	?	?	?	$ 15
Break-even point (units)	?	?	4,000	2,000
Margin of safety (units)	?	?	300	1,000

4–17 Cost-Volume-Profit Relationships: Missing Data

Supply the missing data in each independent case.

	Case 1	Case 2	Case 3	Case 4
Sales revenue	$100,000	$80,000	?	?
Contribution margin	$ 60,000	?	$20,000	?
Fixed costs	$ 30,000	?	?	?
Net income	?	$15,000	$10,000	?
Variable cost ratio	?	0.25	?	0.20
Contribution margin ratio	?	?	0.40	?
Break-even point (dollars)	?	?	?	$25,000
Margin of safety (dollars)	?	?	?	$15,000

4–18 Cost Analysis

In 1979 Winnebago Industries Inc. reported a loss of $4.2 million on sales of $214.6 million. In an effort to save the company, John K. Hanson reduced the firm's employees to 1400 from 4000 and sold two assembly plants. This reduced Winnebago's break-even point to 100 million sales dollars. In 1981 Winnebago reported a profit of $10.1 million on sales of $146.6 million.

Required: Determine Winnebago's margin of safety, contribution margin ratio, variable cost ratio, and fixed costs during 1981. Round calculations to four decimal places.

4–19 Potpourri of Profit Planning without Taxes

1. Lindsay Company reported the following results from sales of 5000 units of product A for the month of June 19x1.

Sales	$200,000
Variable costs	120,000
Fixed costs	60,000
Operating income	20,000

Assume that Lindsay increases the selling price of product A by 10 percent on July 1, 19x1. How many units of product A would have to be sold in July 19x1 in order to generate an operating income of $20,000?

2. Singer, Inc., sells product R for $5 per unit. The fixed costs are $210,000, and the variable costs are 60 percent of the selling price. Determine the dollar sales volume required for Singer to realize a profit of 10 percent of sales.

3. Birney Company is planning its advertising campaign for 19x1 and has prepared the following budget data based on a zero advertising expenditure.

Normal plant capacity	200,000 units
Sales	150,000 units
Selling price	$25.00 per unit
Variable manufacturing costs	$15.00 per unit
Fixed costs:	
Manufacturing	$800,000
Selling and administrative	$700,000

An advertising agency claims that an aggressive advertising campaign would enable Birney to increase its unit sales by 20 percent. What is the maximum amount that Birney can pay for advertising and obtain an operating profit of $200,000?

4. Pitt Company is considering a proposal to replace existing machinery used for the manufacture of product A. The new machines are expected to cause increased annual fixed costs of $120,000; however, variable costs should decrease by 20 percent because of a reduction in direct labor hours and more efficient usage of direct materials. Before this change was under consideration, Pitt had budgeted product A sales and costs for 19x1 as follows:

Sales	$2,000,000
Variable costs	70 percent of sales
Fixed costs	$400,000

Assuming that Pitt implemented the above proposal by January 1, 19x1, what would be the increase in budgeted operating profit for product A for 19x1?

(CPA Adapted)

4–20 Cost-Volume-Profit Analysis of Alternative Products

Siberian Ski Company recently expanded its manufacturing capacity to allow production of up to 15,000 pairs of cross-country skis of the mountaineering model or the touring model. The sales department assures management that it can sell between 9000 and 13,000 of either product this year. Because the models are very similar, Siberian Ski will produce only one of the two models.

The following information was compiled by the accounting department.

	Model	
	Mountaineering	*Touring*
Selling price per unit	$88.00	$80.00
Variable costs per unit	$52.80	$52.80

Fixed costs will total $369,600 if the mountaineering model is produced but only $316,800 if the touring model is produced. Siberian Ski Company is subject to a 40 percent income tax rate.

Requirements

a) Determine the contribution margin ratio of the touring model.

b) If Siberian Ski Company desires an after-tax net income of $24,000, how many pairs of touring model skis will the company have to sell? Round answer to nearest unit.

c) Determine the *unit* sales volume at which Siberian Ski Company would make the same before-tax profit or loss regardless of the ski model it decides to produce. Also determine the resulting before-tax profit or loss.

d) Determine the *dollar* sales volume at which Siberian Ski Company would make the same before-tax profit or loss regardless of the ski model it decides to produce. Also determine the resulting before-tax profit or loss. *Hint:* Work with contribution margin ratios.

e) What action should Siberian Ski Company take if the annual sales of either model were guaranteed to be at least 12,000 pairs? Why?

f) Determine how much the unit variable costs of the touring model would have to change before both models have the same break-even point in units. Round calculations to the nearest cent.

g) Determine the new unit break-even point of the touring skis if their variable costs per unit decrease by 10 percent and their fixed costs increase by 10 percent. Round answer to nearest unit.

(CMA Adapted)

4–21 Break-even Point for Multiple Products (Appendix)

Presented is information regarding the Triangle Company's three products.

	A	B	C
Unit selling price	$5.00	$7.00	$6.00
Unit variable costs	−4.00	−5.00	−3.00
Unit contribution margin	$1.00	$2.00	$3.00

Triangle sells two units of A for each unit of B and three units of B for each unit of C. Fixed costs are $90,000 per month.

Required: Determine the unit sales of product A at the monthly break-even point.

4–22 Cost-Volume-Profit Relationships: Multiple Products (Appendix)

Doug's Tax Service prepares tax returns for low to middle income taxpayers. Doug's service operates January 2 through April 15 at a counter in a local department store. All jobs are classified into one of three categories: standard, multiform, and complex. Presented is information on each category.

	Standard	Multiform	Complex
Billing rate	$50	$125	$250
Average variable cost	−30	− 75	−150
Average contribution margin	$20	$ 50	$100
Returns prepared last year	1750	500	250

All employees are paid on a per-return basis. The fixed costs of rent, utilities, and so forth, were $30,000 last year.

Requirements

a) Determine Doug's break-even dollar sales volume.

b) Determine Doug's margin of safety in sales dollars and units. Round calculations to the nearest whole number.

c) Determine the number of multiform returns prepared at the break-even volume. Round calculations to the nearest whole number.

4–23 Sales Mix Analysis (Appendix)

Tennessee Instruments manufactures and sells two types of hand calculators: student and professional. Information about selling prices and costs follows:

	Student	Professional
Unit selling price	$20.00	$50.00
Unit variable costs:		
Manufacturing	$ 7.00	$15.00
Selling	3.00	5.00
Total	−10.00	−20.00
Unit contribution margin	$10.00	$30.00
Fixed costs are $60,000 per month.		

Monthly calculator sales total 5000 units. The current sales mix is 50 percent student calculators and 50 percent professional calculators. Management believes that a $10 reduction in the price of professional calculators will change the mix to 40 percent student calculators and 60 percent professional calculators while increasing the monthly calculator sales to 6000 units.

Requirements

a) Determine the current unit break-even point and monthly profit.

b) Determine the revised unit break-even point and monthly profit with the reduced price for professional calculators.

c) Prepare a profit-volume graph that contains profit lines for the current mix and prices as well as for the revised mix and prices.

d) Based on your analysis, what action do you recommend?

4–24 Sales Mix Analysis (Appendix)

The Fast Food Shop sells Super Burgers for $2.50 each. During a typical month Fast Food sells 20,000 Super Burgers, with variable costs of $1.00 per unit and fixed costs of $21,000 per month.

Management desires to introduce a new Super Chicken Sandwich. Super Chickens will sell for $2.75, with variable costs of $2. The introduction of Super Chickens will require Fast Food to hire additional help and purchase new equipment. These actions will increase monthly fixed costs by $9000.

In the short run, management believes that 10,000 Super Chickens will be sold each month. However, some of these sales will come from regular customers who will switch from Super Burgers to Super Chickens. Consequently, monthly sales of Super Burgers will decline to 15,000 units.

In the long run, management believes Super Chicken sales will increase to 15,000 units per month, and Super Burger sales will increase to 30,000 units per month.

Requirements

a) Determine each of the following:

1. Current unit break-even point and monthly profit.

2. Short-run unit break-even point and monthly profit subsequent to the introduction of Super Chickens. Indicate how many units of each product are included in the break-even volume.

3. Long-run unit break-even point and monthly profit subsequent to the introduction of Super Chickens. Indicate how many units of each product are included in the break-even volume.

b) Prepare a profit-volume graph that contains profit-lines for the current, short-run, and long-run mixes.

5

Relevant Costs for Management Decisions

In Chapter 4 cost-volume-profit analysis was presented as a useful framework for discussing planning issues and organizing relevant data. Cost-volume-profit analysis is especially useful in the early stages of planning. By providing a view of the "big picture" it helps managers avoid getting lost in the details of individual decisions. Yet, despite the immense value of cost-volume-profit analysis, a sharper focus is often needed to make specific decisions. This need is particularly evident in multiple-product or multiple-service organizations. Here managers are frequently faced with the problem of too much rather than too little information.

When evaluating alternative actions, management should not place all information within the framework of their organization's overall cost-volume-profit model or profit formula. Instead, they should focus their attention on those costs and revenues that differ under alternative actions.

The purpose of this chapter is to examine concepts used to identify and analyze cost information for specific management decisions. While examining these concepts a number of decision situations are discussed: whether to accept or reject a special order, whether to make or buy a part or service, how best to use limited capacity, whether to sell a product or process it further, and what price to charge for a product or service.

The decision situations presented here are not exhaustive; they are only intended to illustrate relevant cost concepts. Once these concepts are understood, they can be applied to a variety of management decisions. Because income taxes would unnecessarily complicate the discussion of relevant cost concepts, they are omitted from the examples presented in this chapter.

Although the emphasis in this chapter is on identifying and analyzing cost information, it is important to keep in mind that decisions should not be based solely on the criterion of short-run cost minimization or profit maximization. A proper analysis of cost information *assists* management in making decisions; however, management must also consider legal, ethical, social, and other nonquantitative factors. These factors may lead management to select a course of action other than that suggested by cost information alone.

RELEVANT COSTS AND DIFFERENTIAL ANALYSIS

Cost concepts for management action were introduced in Chapter 2. *Relevant costs* were defined as future costs that differ among competing alternatives, and *sunk costs* were defined as costs that result from past decisions management no longer has control over. Management must avoid being influenced by sunk costs that cannot be changed or by future costs that are not affected by the decision at hand. *The key to effective cost analysis is to (1) identify the relevant costs (and revenues), and (2) organize them in a manner that clearly indicates how they differ under each alternative.* Consider the following equipment replacement decision.

The Ace Stamping Company uses a Model I stamping machine to produce 10,000 widgets per year. Widgets sell for $15 each. Ace's variable and fixed costs are as follows:

Variable:	
Direct materials	$3 per unit
Direct labor	4 per unit
Factory overhead	1 per unit
Selling and administrative	1 per unit
Fixed:	
Factory overhead other than depreciation	$19,000 per year
Depreciation of Model I stamping machine	15,000 per year
Selling and administrative	12,000 per year

The Model I stamping machine is two years old and has a remaining useful life of four years. It cost $90,000 and has an estimated salvage value of zero dollars at the end of its useful life. Its current book value (original cost less accumulated depreciation) is $60,000, but its current disposal value is only $35,000.

Management is evaluating the desirability of replacing the Model I stamping machine with a new Model II stamping machine. The new machine costs $80,000, has a useful life of four years, and a predicted salvage value of zero dollars at the end of its useful life. Though the new machine has the same productive capacity as the old machine, its operating costs would be lower because it would require only one operator rather than the two needed by the old machine. Furthermore, it has fewer moving parts, so it would require less maintenance and use less power. The new labor and overhead costs are predicted to be as follows:

Direct labor	$2.00 per unit
Variable factory overhead	0.80 per unit
Fixed factory overhead other than depreciation	$16,000 per year

All other costs would be the same as for the old machine.

Identifying Relevant Costs

The decision at hand is either to keep the old Model I stamping machine or to replace it with a new Model II stamping machine. To assist management in making this decision, the accountant should prepare an analysis of those costs and revenues that differ under each alternative. Although the clearest presentation is one that contains only those costs and revenues that differ, the first objective of this chapter is to study the distinction between relevant and irrelevant items. To help accomplish this objective, a complete analysis of all costs and revenues under each alternative is presented in Exhibit 5–1. After evaluating the relevance of each item in

---

EXHIBIT 5–1   Complete Analysis of All Costs and Revenues

	Complete Analysis of Four Year Totals		
	(1) Keep Old Model I Machine	(2) Replace with New Model II Machine	(1) - (2) Difference (Effect of Replacement on Income)
Sales (10,000 units × $15 × 4 years)	$600,000	$600,000	
Costs:			
Direct materials (10,000 × $3 × 4)	$120,000	$120,000	
Direct labor:			
Old (10,000 × $4 × 4)	160,000		
New (10,000 × $2 × 4)		80,000	$80,000
Variable overhead:			
Old (10,000 × $1 × 4)	40,000		
New (10,000 × $0.80 × 4)		32,000	8,000
Variable selling and administrative (10,000 × $1 × 4)	40,000	40,000	
Fixed overhead except depreciation:			
Old ($19,000 × 4)	76,000		
New ($16,000 × 4)		64,000	12,000
Depreciation or write-off of old machine	60,000	60,000*	
Disposal value of old machine		(35,000)*	35,000
Cost of new machine		80,000	(80,000)
Fixed selling and administrative ($12,000 × 4)	48,000	48,000	
Total costs	−544,000	−489,000	
Net income	$56,000	$111,000	$55,000
Advantage of replacement		$55,000	

---

* A single loss on disposal of $25,000 ($60,000 − $35,000) would be shown on an income statement prepared for external users.

Exhibit 5–1, a more focused differential analysis of relevant costs will be prepared.

The first thing to notice about Exhibit 5–1 is that many costs and revenues are the same under each alternative. These items are not relevant to the replacement decision. The only relevant items are those that have an entry in the difference column.

Future Revenues May Be Relevant. Revenues, which are inflows of resources from operations, are relevant if they differ under decision alternatives. Revenues in this example are not relevant because they are identical under each alternative. They would be relevant if the new machine had greater capacity that would be utilized, or if management intended to change the unit selling price should they acquire the new machine.

The keep or replace decision facing Ace's management might be called a **cost reduction proposal** because it is based on the assumption that the organization is committed to an activity and that management desires to minimize the cost of the activity. Here the alternatives are (1) continue operating with the old machine or (2) replace with a new machine.

Although this approach is appropriate for many activities, managers of for-profit organizations should always remember that they have another alternative; namely, discontinue operations. To simplify the analysis, managers normally do not consider the alternative to discontinue when operations appear to be profitable. However, if there is any doubt about an operation's profitability, this alternative should be considered. Failure to do so may result in throwing good money after bad. Because revenues will change if an operation is discontinued, revenues are relevant whenever this alternative is considered.

Outlay Costs May Be Relevant. **Outlay costs** are future costs that require future expenditures of cash or other resources. Outlay costs that differ under the decision alternatives at hand are relevant; those that do not differ are irrelevant. It is a mistake to assume that variable costs are always relevant and fixed costs always irrelevant. The relevant and the irrelevant outlay costs for Ace Stamping Company's equipment replacement decision are as follows:

Relevant Outlay Costs	*Irrelevant Outlay Costs*
Direct labor	Direct materials
Variable factory overhead	Variable selling and administrative
Fixed factory overhead except depreciation	Fixed selling and administrative
Cost of new machine	

Variable and fixed costs are included in both categories.

Because variable costs respond to changes in the volume of activity, they are relevant when decision alternatives have different activity levels. *Variable costs may not be relevant when decision alternatives have the same activity level.* In this case, variable costs will differ only if there is a difference in the variable cost per unit of activity.

The Model II stamping machine requires fewer operators, less maintenance, and less power. Hence, direct labor and variable overhead are relevant to the replacement decision. Because there is no change in the production and sales volume, nor any other change in selling or administrative procedures, the variable selling and administrative costs are not relevant.

Fixed costs may be relevant. A decision to increase activity may necessitate an increase in capacity and an accompanying increase in fixed costs. Conversely, a decision to reduce activity may provide an opportunity to reduce fixed costs. Alternative production or service procedures may have different fixed costs at the same activity level. This is the situation faced by the Ace Stamping Company. The Model II machine's fixed factory overhead is lower than the Model I's.

Because the fixed administrative costs are the same with both machines, they are irrelevant to the replacement decision. Indeed, fixed administrative costs, such as those incurred to pay the president's salary, have little or nothing to do with the operation of the stamping machine. These costs are not associated with the decision at hand.[1] The acquisition cost of the new machine is obviously relevant. This cost will be incurred only if the replacement alternative is selected.

Sunk Costs Are Never Relevant. *Though the relevance of outlay costs is determined by the decision at hand, sunk costs are never relevant.* Sunk costs result from past expenditures that cannot be changed. The cost of the Model I machine is a historical cost, not a future cost. This historical cost, and the related depreciation, result from the past decision to acquire the old machine. Even though all the outlay costs discussed above would be relevant to a decision to continue or discontinue operations, the sunk cost of the Model I machine is not relevant even to this decision.

If management elects to keep the old machine, its book value will be depreciated over its remaining useful life of four years, whereas if management elects to replace the old machine, its book value will be written off when it is replaced. Even if management elects to discontinue operations, the book value of the old machine must be disposed of.

Although the book value of the old machine has no economic signifi-

---

[1] In textbook examples and problems, and in professional examinations, it is assumed, in the absence of specific information, that fixed costs do not differ between decision alternatives. This is a simplifying assumption. In practice the manager or the management accountant would have to ask many questions to determine whether or not fixed outlay costs are relevant to a decision situation.

cance, the accounting treatment of past costs can make it difficult for managers to regard them as irrelevant. If management replaces the old machine, a loss from disposal of $25,000 will be recorded in the year of replacement:

Book value	$60,000
Disposal value	−35,000
Loss on disposal	$25,000

Managers are often reluctant to have such a loss recorded out of fear that it will lead superiors to question the wisdom of past decisions. The loss acts as an attention-getting flag. A manager might prefer using the old machine, with lower total profits over the four-year period, to replacing it and being forced to record a loss on disposal.

From an economic viewpoint, a mistake made in acquiring the old machine cannot be corrected by continuing to use the old machine. When a preferred alternative is available, continued commitment to the original decision compounds the first mistake with a second. Though there is no easy solution to this behavioral problem, managers and management accountants should be aware of its potential impact.

Disposal and Salvage Values. Revenues are inflows of resources from operations. The Ace Stamping Company's revenues, which are from the sale of widgets, were discussed above. The sale of fixed assets is also a source of resources. Because the sale of fixed assets is a nonoperating item, cash inflows obtained from these sales are discussed separately.

The disposal value of the Model I machine is a relevant cash inflow. It is obtained only if the replacement alternative is selected. Any salvage value available at the end of the useful life of either machine would also be relevant. A loss on disposal may have a favorable tax impact if the loss can be offset against taxable gains or taxable income. In this case, though the book value of the old asset remains irrelevant, the expected tax reduction would be relevant.

Differential Analysis of Relevant Costs

Differential cost analysis is an approach to the analysis of relevant costs that focuses on the costs that differ under alternative actions. A differential analysis of relevant costs for the Ace Stamping Company's equipment replacement decision is presented in Exhibit 5–2. Replacement provides a net advantage of $55,000 over the life of both machines.[2]

---

[2] Our current objectives are (1) to distinguish between relevant and irrelevant costs and (2) to demonstrate the advantages of analyzing only relevant costs. An analysis of long-lived projects should also consider the time value of money. The time value of money is discussed in Chapter 14 and in the appendix to this book.

EXHIBIT 5–2   Differential Analysis of Relevant Costs

	(1) *Keep Old Model I Machine*	*(2)* *Replace with New Model II Machine*	*(1) - (2)* *Difference (Effect of Replacement on Income)*
		Differential Analysis of Four-Year Totals	
Costs:			
Direct labor:			
Old (10,000 × $4 × 4)	$160,000		
New (10,000 × $2 × 4)		$ 80,000	$80,000
Variable overhead:			
Old (10,000 × $1 × 4)	40,000		
New (10,000 × $0.80 × 4)		32,000	8,000
Fixed overhead except depreciation:			
Old ($19,000 × 4)	76,000		
New ($16,000 × 4)		64,000	12,000
Disposal value of old machine		(35,000)	35,000
Cost of new machine		80,000	(80,000)
Total	$276,000	$221,000	$55,000
Advantage of replacement		$55,000	

A differential analysis of relevant costs and revenues (such as the one in Exhibit 5–2) is superior to a complete analysis of all costs and revenues (such as the one in Exhibit 5–1) for a number of reasons:

- Focusing only on those items that differ provides a clearer picture of the impact of the decision at hand. Management is less apt to be confused by a differential analysis than by an analysis that intermingles relevant and irrelevant items.

- Because a differential analysis contains fewer items, it is easier and quicker to prepare.

- In complex situations, such as those encountered by multiple-product or multiple-plant firms, it is difficult, if not impossible, to develop complete firmwide statements to analyze all decision alternatives.

Predicting Relevant Costs

Information on relevant costs is almost always given in textbook examples and problems. Here the task is to (1) distinguish between relevant and irrelevant costs and (2) properly classify the relevant costs. In practice the analyst would also have the difficult job of obtaining the relevant cost information, which is a very time consuming process that requires questioning, observing, and analyzing. Obviously, an understanding of relevant cost concepts is a prerequisite to obtaining relevant cost information. Simply stated, the analyst must know what to look for. The knowledge of this helps guide the search for the few pieces of relevant information contained in a sea of data.

Predicting relevant costs may involve an examination of past cost trends. If one of the alternatives under consideration is to continue operations as in the past, the techniques discussed in Chapter 3 can be used to estimate past costs and to develop predictions of future costs. The predicted operating costs of the Model I stamping machine would be developed in this manner.

It is more difficult to predict costs when technology changes. The substitution of the Model II for the Model I stamping machine is an example of a technological change. Because the Model II is new, the Ace Stamping Company's historical information is of little or no value in predicting its future operating costs. Cost predictions for the Model II machine must be deduced from information obtained from the manufacturer, other users, trade associations and publications, and engineers employed by Ace. Management should carefully evaluate the credibility of this information.

A **cost prediction error** is the difference between a predicted future cost and the actual amount of the cost when, or if, it is incurred. Because cost predictions may be inaccurate, management should determine how sensitive a decision is to prediction errors. This would include, for example, determining how much a prediction could change before affecting the decision.

The Ace Stamping Company's new machine has a net advantage of $55,000 over its four-year life; hence, cost predictions could increase by $55,000 before affecting the decision.[3] Given the magnitude of the operating costs, a $55,000 prediction error seems unlikely. If the net advantage of the new machine were smaller, say $10,000, management might want to consider the likelihood of a $10,000 prediction error.

APPLICATIONS OF DIFFERENTIAL ANALYSIS

Differential analysis is used to provide information for a variety of planning and decision situations. Illustrated in this section are some of the more frequently encountered applications of differential analysis, including multiple changes in profit plans, whether to accept or reject a special order,

---

[3] See footnote 2.

whether to make or buy a product or service, how best to use limited resources, and whether to sell a product or process it further.

Multiple Changes in Profit Plans

Mind Trek, Ltd. manufactures an electronic game that is sold to distributors for $22 per unit. Manufacturing and other costs are as follows:

Variable Costs per Unit			*Fixed Costs per Month*	
Manufacturing:			Factory overhead	$30,000
Direct materials	$5.00		Selling and administrative	15,000
Direct labor	3.00		Total	$45,000
Factory overhead	2.00	$10.00		
Selling and administrative		2.00		
Total		$12.00		

The unit contribution margin is $10 ($22 selling price − $12 variable costs). Mind Trek's April, 19x6 Contribution Income Statement is presented in Exhibit 5–3. The April, 19x6 operations are typical. Monthly production and sales average 5000 units, and monthly profits average $5000.

Management wants to know the effect on monthly profits of the following three alternative actions.

EXHIBIT 5–3   Contribution Income Statement

Mind Trek, Ltd.
Contribution Income Statement
For the month of April, 19x6

Sales ($22 x 5000)			$110,000
Less variable costs:			
Variable cost of goods sold:			
Direct materials ($5 x 5000)	$25,000		
Direct labor ($3 x 5000)	15,000		
Factory overhead ($2 x 5000)	10,000	$50,000	
Variable selling and administrative			
($2 x 5000)		10,000	−60,000
Contribution margin			$ 50,000
Less fixed costs:			
Fixed factory overhead		$30,000	
Fixed selling and administrative		15,000	−45,000
Net income			$ 5,000

1. Increasing the monthly advertising budget by $4000, which should result in a 1000 unit increase in monthly sales.

2. Increasing the unit selling price by $3, which should result in a 2000 unit decrease in monthly sales.

3. Decreasing the unit selling price by $2, which should result in a 2000 unit increase in monthly sales. However, because of capacity constraints, the last 1000 units would be produced during overtime, when the direct labor costs increase by $1 per unit.

It is possible to develop contribution income statements for each alternative and then determine the profit impact of the proposed change by comparing the new net income with the current net income. A more direct approach is to use differential analysis and focus only on those items that differ under each alternative.

Alternative 1:

Profit increase from increased sales (1000 × $10)	$ 10,000
Profit decrease from increased advertising	(4,000)
Increase in monthly profit	$ 6,000

Alternative 2:

Profit decrease from reduced sales if there were no changes in prices or costs (2000 × $10)	$(20,000)
Profit increase from increased selling price [(5000 − 2000) × $3]	9,000
Decrease in monthly profit	$(11,000)

Alternative 3:

Profit increase from increased sales if there were no changes in prices or costs (2000 × $10)	$ 20,000
Profit decrease from reduced selling price of all units [(5000 + 2000) × $2]	(14,000)
Profit decrease from increased direct labor costs of the last 1000 units (1000 × $1)	(1,000)
Increase in monthly profit	$ 5,000

Alternative 2 is undesirable because it would result in a decrease in monthly profit. Because Alternative 1 results in a larger increase in monthly profit, it is preferred to Alternative 3.

Special Orders

Assume a Brazilian distributor has proposed to place a special, one-time order for 1000 units next month, at a reduced price of $12 per unit. The distributor will pay all packing and transportation costs, and there will be no incremental selling or administrative expenses associated with the order. Mind Trek has sufficient production capacity to produce the additional units without reducing sales to other customers. Management desires to know the profit impact of accepting the order. The following analysis focuses on those costs and revenues that will differ if the order is accepted.

Increase in revenues (1000 × $12)		$12,000
Increase in costs:		
Direct materials (1000 × $5)	$ 5,000	
Direct labor (1000 × $3)	3,000	
Variable factory overhead (1000 × $2)	2,000	−10,000
Increase in profits		$ 2,000

Accepting the order will result in a profit increase of $2000.

If management were unaware of management accounting concepts, they might be tempted to compare the special order price to the average unit cost of goods sold used for financial accounting purposes. If management made their decision by comparing the special order price to the unit cost of goods sold found in Mind Trek's April, 19x6 financial statements, they might reject the order. With all manufacturing costs assigned to the units produced, the April cost of goods sold averaged $16 per unit:

Cost of goods sold:		
Direct materials ($5 × 5000)		$25,000
Direct labor ($3 × 5000)		15,000
Factory overhead:		
Variable ($2 × 5000)	10,000	
Fixed	30,000	40,000
Total		$80,000
Unit production and sales		÷ 5,000
Average unit cost of goods sold		$ 16

Comparing the special order price of $12 per unit to the average unit cost of goods sold of $16, management might conclude the order would result in a loss of $4 per unit.

It is apparent that the $16 figure is composed of variable manufacturing costs of $10 per unit and fixed manufacturing costs of $30,000 spread over 5000 units. But remember that management may not have detailed cost information. To obtain appropriate information for decision-making purposes, management must ask their accounting staff for the specific information needed. Different configurations of cost information are provided for different purposes. In the absence of special instructions the accounting staff will probably supply the most readily available data, namely, that used for financial reporting.

Importance of Time Span. The special order is a one-time order for 1000 units that will use current excess capacity. Because no special setups or equipment are required to produce the order, it is appropriate to consider only variable costs in computing the order's profitability.

But what if the Brazilian distributor wanted Mind Trek to sign a multi-year contract to provide 1000 units per month at $12 each? Under these circumstances management would be well advised to reject the order because there is a high probability that cost increases would make the order unprofitable in later years. At the very least, management should insist that a cost escalation clause be added to the purchase agreement, specifying that the selling price be increased to cover any cost increases and detailing how cost is computed.

Of more concern is the variable nature of all long-run costs. *In the long run all costs, including costs classified as fixed in a given period, are variable.* To remain in business in the long run, Mind Trek must replace equipment, pay property taxes, pay administrative salaries, and so forth. Consequently, management should consider all costs (fixed and variable, manufacturing and nonmanufacturing) in evaluating a long-term contract.

Full costs include all (fixed and variable) product and period costs. The average full cost per unit is sometimes used to approximate long-run variable costs. If accepting a long-term contract increases the monthly production and sales volume to 11,000 units, the average full cost per unit will be $16.09:

Direct materials	$ 5.00
Direct labor	3.00
Variable factory overhead	2.00
Fixed factory overhead ($30,000 ÷ 11,000)	2.73
Variable selling and administrative costs	2.00
Fixed selling and administrative costs ($15,000 ÷ 11,000)	1.36
Average full cost per unit	$16.09

If the Brazilian distributor agrees to pay separately all variable selling and administrative expenses associated with the contract, the estimated long-run variable costs are $14.09 per unit ($16.09 − $2.00). Many managers would say this is the minimum acceptable unit selling price for the order, especially if the order extends over a long period of time.

Opportunity Costs May Also Be Relevant. Recall from Chapter 2 that an *opportunity cost* is the net cash inflow that could be obtained if the resources committed to one action were used in the most desirable other alternative. Because Mind Trek has excess productive capacity, no opportunity cost is associated with accepting the Brazilian distributor's one-time order. There is no alternative use of the productive capacity in the short run, so there is no opportunity cost.

But what if Mind Trek were operating with no excess capacity? In this case accepting the special order would require either reducing regular sales or using overtime. To simplify the illustration, assume overtime production is not possible. Because Mind Trek is operating at capacity, there is an alternative use of the productive capacity and, hence, an opportunity cost associated with its use to fill the special order. Each unit sold to the Brazilian distributor could generate a $10 contribution from regular customers. Accepting the special order would cause Mind Trek to incur an opportunity cost of $10,000, the net benefit of the most desirable other action, selling to regular customers:

Lost sales to regular customers	1,000 units
Regular unit contribution margin	×$10
Opportunity cost of accepting special order	$10,000

Because this opportunity cost exceeds the $2000 contribution derived from the special order, management should reject the special order. Accepting the order will reduce profits by $8000 ($2000 − $10,000).

Nonquantitative Considerations. Although an analysis of cost and revenue information may indicate that a special order would be profitable in the near term, management might still reject the order because of nonquantitative, short-run or long-run considerations. Because of a concern for the order's impact on regular customers, management might reject an order even if they had excess capacity. If the order involves a special low price, regular customers might demand a similar price reduction and threaten to take their business elsewhere. Alternatively, management might accept the special order even though they were operating at capacity if they believed there were long-term benefits associated with penetrating a new market. Legal factors must also be considered if the special order is from a buyer who competes with regular customers. These legal factors are discussed later in this chapter.

Make or Buy Decisions

Now suppose a foreign manufacturer has offered a one-year contract to supply Mind Trek with an electronic component at a cost of $2.20 per unit. If Mind Trek accepts the offer, they will be able to reduce materials costs by 10 percent and direct labor and variable factory overhead costs

EXHIBIT 5–4   Differential Analysis for Make or Buy Decision

	(1) Cost to Make	(2) Cost to Buy	(1) - (2) Difference (Effect of Buying on Income)
Cost to buy ($2.20 × 60,000*)		$132,000	$(132,000)
Cost to make:			
Direct materials			
($5 × 0.10 × 60,000*)	$ 30,000		30,000
Direct labor			
($3 × 0.20 × 60,000*)	36,000		36,000
Variable factory overhead			
($2 × 0.20 × 60,000*)	24,000		24,000
Fixed factory overhead	20,000		20,000
Total	$110,000	$132,000	$ (22,000)
Advantage of making		$22,000	

* 5000 units per month × 12 months = 60,000 units.

by 20 percent. Fixed factory overhead can be reduced by $20,000 per year. A differential analysis of Mind Trek's make or buy decision is presented in Exhibit 5–4. Making the component has a net advantage of $22,000.

But what if the space currently used to manufacture the electronic component can be rented to a third party for $40,000 per year? In this case the productive capacity has an alternative use, and the net cash flow from this alternative use is an opportunity cost of making the component. In analyzing the make or buy decision, this opportunity cost should be treated as a cost of making. Buying now has a net advantage of $18,000:

	Cost to Make	Cost to Buy	Difference (Effect of Buying on Income)
Cost to buy		$132,000	$(132,000)
Cost to make:			
Outlay*	$110,000		110,000
Opportunity	40,000		40,000
Total	$150,000	$132,000	$ 18,000
Advantage of buying		$18,000	

* See Exhibit 5–4.

Even if buying appears financially advantageous in the short run, management should not decide to buy before considering a variety of nonquantitative factors. Is the outside supplier attempting to use some temporarily idle capacity? If so, what will happen at the end of the contract period? Will the supplier extend the contract at all, or at a higher price? What impact would a decision to buy have on the morale of Mind Trek's employees? Will Mind Trek have to rehire laid-off employees after the contract expires? Will the outside supplier meet delivery schedules? Does the supplied part meet Mind Trek's quality standards, and will it continue to meet them? Organizations often manufacture products or provide services they can obtain elsewhere in order to control quality and have an assured source of supply with on-time delivery.

How Best to Use Limited Resources

No doubt you have experienced time as a limiting resource. With two exams the day after tomorrow and a paper due next week, your problem was how to allocate limited study time. The solution depended on your objectives, your current status (grades, knowledge, skill levels, and so forth), and the available time. Given this information, you devised a work plan to most nearly meet your objectives.

Managers must also decide how best to use limited resources to accomplish organizational goals. A supermarket may lose sales because limited shelf space prevents stocking all available brands of cereal. A manufacturer may lose sales because limited machine or labor hours prevents filling all orders. Managers of for-profit organizations will likely find the problems of capacity constraints less troublesome than the problems of excess capacity; nonetheless, these problems are real.

The long-run solution to these problems may be to expand capacity. However, this is usually not feasible in the short run. Economic models suggest that another solution is to reduce demand by increasing the price. Again, this may not be desirable. The supermarket, for example, may want to maintain competitive prices, and the manufacturer might want to maintain a long-run price or to avoid accusations of "price-gouging."

The allocation of limited resources should be made only after a careful consideration of many nonquantitative factors. The following rule provides a useful starting point in making short-run decisions of how best to use limited resources: *To achieve short-run profit maximization, a for-profit organization should allocate limited resources in a manner that maximizes the contribution per unit of constraining factor.* The application of this rule is illustrated in the following example.

The Delta Manufacturing Company produces three products: A, B, and C. A limitation of 100 machine hours per week prevents Delta from meeting the sales demand for these products. Product information is as follows:

	A	B	C
Unit selling price	$100	$ 80	$ 50
Unit variable costs	− 90	− 50	− 25
Unit contribution margin	$ 10	$ 30	$ 25
Machine hours per unit	2	2	1

Product A has the highest selling price, product B has the highest unit contribution margin, and product C is shown below to have the highest contribution per machine hour.

	A	B	C
Unit contribution margin	$ 10	$ 30	$ 25
Machine hours per unit	÷ 2	÷ 2	÷ 1
Contribution per machine hour	$ 5	$ 15	$ 25

Following the rule of maximizing the contribution per unit of constraining factor, Delta should use its limited machine hours to produce product C. As shown in the following analysis, any other plan would result in lower profits.

	A	B	C
	Highest Selling Price	Highest Contribution per Unit	Highest Contribution per Unit of Constraining Factor
Machine hours available	100	100	100
Machine hours per unit	÷ 2	÷ 2	÷ 1
Weekly production	50	50	100
Unit contribution margin	×$10	×$30	×$25
Total contribution	$500	$1500	$2500

Despite this analysis, management may decide to produce some units of A, or B, or both to satisfy the requests of some "good" customers, or to offer a full product line. However, such decisions sacrifice short-run profits. Each machine hour used to produce A or B has an opportunity cost of $25, the net cash flow from using that hour to produce a unit of C, the most desirable other alternative. Producing all A, for example, results in an opportunity cost of $2500 (100 × $25). The net disadvantage of producing all A is $2000:

Contribution from A	$ 500
Opportunity cost of not producing C	− 2500
Net disadvantage of producing A	$(2000)

The opportunity cost of producing all C is $1500. This is the net cash flow from the most desirable other alternative, producing B. However, when compared to producing B, producing C has a net advantage of $1000:

Contribution from C	$ 2500
Opportunity cost of not producing B	− 1500
Net advantage of producing C	$ 1000

When an organization has alternative uses for several (rather than one) limiting resources, the optimal use of those resources cannot be determined using the rule for short-run profit maximization. In these situations linear programming (discussed in Chapter 13) is used to determine the optimal mix of products or services.

Sell or Process Further

Single Product Decisions. When a product is saleable at various stages of completion, management must determine the product's most advantageous selling point. As each stage is completed, management must determine whether to sell it then or to process it further. Assume the Boston Rocking Company manufactures rocking chairs from precut and shaped wood. The chairs are saleable once they are assembled; however, Boston Rocking sands and paints all chairs before they are sold. Management wishes to know if this is the optimal selling point.

A complete listing of unit costs and revenues for the alternative selling points is as follows:

	Per Chair		
	Sell After Assembly	Sell After Painting	Difference (Effect of Painting on Income)
Selling price	$40	$75	$35
Assembly costs	(25)	(25)	
Sanding and painting costs		(12)	(12)
Contribution margin	$15	$38	$23
Advantage of painting		$23	

The chairs should be sold after they are painted. The sanding and painting operation has an additional contribution of $23 per unit.

Note that the assembly costs are the same under both alternatives. This illustrates that *all costs incurred prior to the decision point are irrelevant.* Given the existence of an assembled chair, the decision alternatives are to sell it now or process it further. A differential analysis for the decision to sell or process further should include only revenues and the incremental costs of further processing:

Increase in revenues:		
Sell after painting	$75	
Sell after assembly	−40	$35
Additional costs of sanding		
and painting		−12
Advantage of sanding and painting		$23

The identical solution is obtained if the selling price without further processing is treated as an opportunity cost:

Revenues after painting		$75
Additional costs of sanding		
and painting	$12	
Opportunity cost of not selling		
after assembly	40	−52
Advantage of sanding and painting		$23

By processing the chairs further, Boston Rocking has forgone the opportunity to receive $40 from its sale. Since the chair is already made, this $40 is the net cash inflow from the most desirable alternative; hence, it is the opportunity cost of painting.

Joint Product Decisions.   Two or more products simultaneously produced from a common set of inputs by a single process are called **joint products.** Joint products are often found in basic industries that process natural raw materials, such as dairy products, chemicals, meat products, petroleum, and wood products. In the petroleum industry, crude oil is refined into fuel oil, gasoline, kerosene, lubricating oil, and other products.

The point in the process where the joint products emerge as separately identifiable products is called the **split-off point,** and product costs incurred prior to the split-off point are called **joint costs.** For external reporting purposes a number of techniques are used to allocate joint costs among joint products. (Some of these techniques are considered in the appendix to Chapter 12.) We are not interested in these techniques here, except to note that none of them provides information that is useful in determining what to do with a joint product once it is produced. Because joint costs are incurred prior to the decision point, they are sunk costs. Consequently, *joint costs are irrelevant to a decision to sell a joint product or process it further.*

THE PRICING DECISION

Product pricing is one of the most important and complex decisions facing management. The saleability of individual products or services is directly affected by pricing decisions, as is the profitability and even the survival of the organization. Although we cannot give a thorough treatment of the topic here, we can introduce some basic concepts and indicate the important role of costs in pricing decisions.

Economic Approaches to Product Pricing

In economic models, the firm has a profit maximizing goal and known cost and revenue functions. The firm continues to produce as long as the marginal revenue derived from the sale of each additional unit exceeds the marginal cost of producing that unit. **Marginal revenue** is the varying increment in total revenue derived from the sale of an additional unit. **Marginal cost** is the varying increment in total cost required to produce and sell an additional unit. Profits are maximized by producing until marginal revenue equals marginal cost.

Economic models provide a useful framework for thinking about pricing decisions, but they are seldom used for day-to-day pricing decisions. Their primary weaknesses stem from the assumptions of profit maximization and known cost and revenue functions. Most for-profit organizations attempt to achieve a target profit rather than a maximum profit. One reason for this is an inability to determine the single set of actions out of all possible actions that will lead to profit maximization. Furthermore, managers are more apt to strive to satisfy a number of goals (such as profits for owners, job security for themselves and their employees, and being a "good" corporate citizen) than to strive for the maximization of a single profit goal. In any case, to maximize profits a company's management would have to know the cost and revenue functions of every product their firm sells. Unfortunately, for most products this information either cannot be developed or cannot be developed at a reasonable cost.

Cost Based Approaches to Product Pricing

Though cost is not the only consideration in product pricing, it is important. There are several reasons for this.

- *Cost data are readily available*. When hundreds of different prices must be set in a short time, cost may be the only feasible basis for product pricing.
- *Cost based prices are defensible*. Managers threatened by legal action or public scrutiny may feel secure using cost based pricing. They can argue that prices are set in a manner that provides a "fair" profit.
- *Revenues must exceed costs if the firm is to remain in business*. In the long run the unit selling price must exceed the full cost of each unit, including the product cost of the unit and a portion of all other costs.

In a typical pricing decision management uses cost information to arrive at an initial selling price. Other available information about the market, competitors, and so forth is then evaluated in arriving at a final selling price.

Price Setting in Single Product Companies. Determining the initial cost based price in a single product company is straightforward if everything is known but the selling price. In this case all known information can be substituted into the profit formula, which is then solved for the variable price.

Assume that Bright Rug Cleaning Company has annual fixed costs of $200,000 and variable costs of $10 per rug cleaned. Management desires to achieve a target profit of $30,000. The estimated annual volume is 10,000 units. As a matter of policy, management charges the same price regardless of the type, size, or shape of the rug. Using the profit formula, the unit price required to achieve the target profit is determined to be $33:

	Total Costs		
Total Revenue	**Fixed**	**Variable**	**Profit**

$$(\text{Price} \times 10{,}000) - [\$200{,}000 + (\$10 \times 10{,}000)] = \$30{,}000.$$

Solving for the price:

$$(\text{Price} \times 10{,}000) - \$300{,}000 = \$30{,}000$$
$$\text{Price} = \$330{,}000/10{,}000$$
$$= \$33.$$

To achieve its target profit, Bright would charge $33 to clean a rug.

Price Setting in Multiple Product Companies. In multiple product companies, desired profits are determined for the company as a whole, and standard procedures are established for determining the initial selling price of each product. These procedures typically specify the initial selling price as cost, plus a markup stated as a percentage of cost, which is determined by the cost base used in the computations. The larger the cost base for a given product the smaller the markup. Two possible cost bases that we will consider are variable costs and manufacturing costs.

When the markup is based on variable costs, it must be large enough to cover all fixed costs and the target profit:

$$\textbf{Variable cost markup} = \frac{\text{Predicted fixed costs} + \text{Target profit}}{\text{Predicted variable costs}}.$$

Once the variable cost markup is determined it is then used to determine the initial selling price of each product:

$$\textbf{Initial selling price} = \frac{\text{Variable costs}}{\text{per unit}} + \left(\frac{\text{Variable costs}}{\text{per unit}} \times \frac{\text{Variable}}{\text{cost markup}}\right).$$

Assume the predicted 19x9 variable and fixed costs for Magnum Enterprises are as follows:

Variable Costs		*Fixed Costs*	
Manufacturing	$600,000	Manufacturing	$400,000
Selling and		Selling and	
administrative	200,000	administrative	200,000
Total	$800,000	Total	$600,000

To achieve a target profit of $200,000, Magnum Enterprises needs a 100 percent markup on variable costs:

$$\frac{\text{Variable}}{\text{cost markup}} = \frac{\$600,000 + \$200,000}{\$800,000} = 1.00.$$

Assume the following information is available about product A:

		Unit
Direct material		$ 4
Direct labor		4
Factory overhead:		
Variable	$2	
Fixed	5	7
Total manufacturing costs		$15
Variable selling and administrative costs		$ 2

Variable costs for Product A are $12 per unit:

	Unit
Direct material	$ 4
Direct labor	4
Variable factory overhead	2
Variable selling and administrative	2
Total variable costs	$12

Using the variable cost markup, we find that the initial selling price of A is $24:

$$\text{Initial selling price} = \$12 + (\$12 \times 1.00)$$
$$= \$24.$$

To make appropriate pricing decisions, management must be aware of the variable costs of a product or service and the markup required to cover fixed costs and to provide for a target profit. One way of doing this is to break the markup on variable costs into two parts: one part to cover fixed costs and another part to provide for a profit. For Magnum Enterprises this might be done as follows:

	Product A
Variable costs	$12
Markup to cover fixed costs [($600,000/$800,000 = 0.75) × $12]	9
Markup to achieve target profit [($200,000/$800,000 = 0.25) × $12]	3
Initial price	$24

With this information management can readily see that any price in excess of $12 increases short-run profits or reduces short-term losses. However, all products must have an average markup of 75 percent on variable costs if the firm is to be profitable in the long run. Using this guideline, we realize that the suggested markup for product A is at least $9. To achieve target profits, all products must have an additional average markup of 25 percent on variable costs. We see that the suggested additional markup for product A is $3 using this guideline. Management would modify this initial price to reflect current market conditions and other factors.

When the markup percent is based on manufacturing costs, it must be large enough both to cover selling and administrative costs and to provide for the desired profit:

$$\textbf{Manufacturing cost markup} = \frac{\text{Predicted selling and administrative costs} + \text{Desired profit}}{\text{Predicted manufacturing costs}}.$$

To compute the manufacturing cost markup, it is necessary to determine the desired profit and to predict all costs for the pricing period. The initial prices of individual products are then computed as their unit manufacturing costs plus the markup.

$$\text{Initial selling price} = \text{Manufacturing costs per unit} + \left(\text{Manufacturing costs per unit} \times \text{Manufacturing cost markup} \right)$$

Magnum Enterprises has the following cost predictions for 19x9:

	Manufacturing Costs		Selling and Administrative Costs
Variable	$ 600,000	Variable	$200,000
Fixed	400,000	Fixed	200,000
Total	$1,000,000	Total	$400,000

To achieve a target profit of $200,000, Magnum Enterprises needs a 60 percent markup on manufacturing costs:

$$\text{Manufacturing cost markup} = \frac{\$400,000 + \$200,000}{\$1,000,000}$$
$$= 0.60.$$

Using the manufacturing cost markup, with total manufacturing costs of $15, we find that the initial selling price of product A is $24:

$$\text{Initial selling price} = \$15 + (\$15 \times 0.60)$$
$$= \$24.$$

Because of the availability of manufacturing cost data, this approach to product pricing is widely used. Nevertheless, we do not recommend it. The manufacturing cost markup indiscriminately mixes fixed and variable costs in the base and in the markup. If the variable selling and administrative expenses can be identified with individual products, they should be included in the base rather than in the markup. Conversely, the nonvarying nature of fixed manufacturing costs and the difficulty of accurately associating them with individual products suggest that they should be included in the markup rather than in the base.

Legal Forces Increase the Role of Costs

Cost has always been an important determinant of price in regulated industries such as utilities, communications, and transportation. In recent years a number of legal forces have greatly increased the role of costs in many other industries. Large government defense contracts, for example, are often awarded on the basis of cost, which is determined in a manner specified by government regulations, plus an allowance for profit. Medicare and medicaid reimbursements to hospitals are based on cost as well, which again is determined in a specified manner.

The **Robinson–Patman Act** prohibits charging purchasers different prices when these purchasers compete with one another in the sale of their products or services. There are three exceptions to the act:

1. The discriminatory lower price is in response to changing conditions in the market for, or the marketability of, the commodities involved (such as the sale of discontinued products);

2. The discriminatory lower price is made to meet an equally low price of a competitor; and

3. The discriminatory lower price makes only due allowance for specific cost differences, such as those resulting from long production runs and bulk shipments.

Management must always take care to ensure that accepting a special order does not violate the provisions of the Robinson–Patman Act.

SUMMARY

A number of decision situations were presented in this chapter, including whether to accept or reject a special order, whether to make or buy a product or service, how best to use limited resources, and whether to sell a product or process it further. When evaluating alternative actions such as these, managers should focus their attention on the decision at hand. They should evaluate only those costs and revenues that differ under each alternative.

Relevant costs include all future costs that differ among competing alternatives, namely, outlay costs that differ under each alternative, and sometimes an opportunity cost. An outlay cost is a future cost that requires a future expenditure. An opportunity cost is the net cash flow from the most desirable other alternative. When resources are limited, the initiation of one action requires management to forgo competing alternative actions.

Exhibit 5–5 Summary Classification of Relevant and Irrelevant Costs

Relevant Costs		Irrelevant Costs	
Future costs that differ among competing alternatives		Costs that do not differ among competing alternatives	
Opportunity Cost	**Outlay Costs**		**Sunk Cost**
Net cash flow from the best alternative	Future costs requiring future expenditures that differ	Future costs requiring future expenditures that do not differ	A historical cost resulting from a past decision

The net cash flow from the most desirable other alternative is the opportunity cost of the action selected.

Irrelevant costs, which include sunk costs and certain outlay costs, do not differ among competing alternatives. Sunk costs are historical costs resulting from past decisions. There is absolutely nothing management can do to change the total amount of these costs. All outlay costs are relevant to some decisions, such as the decision to continue or discontinue operations, but not all outlay costs are relevant to all decisions. Outlay costs that do not differ under decision alternatives are not relevant to that decision. A summary classification of relevant and irrelevant costs is presented in Exhibit 5–5.

Although this chapter has focused on short-run decisions, decisions should not be based solely on short-run cost minimization or profit maximization. This is especially true in price setting and determining whether to accept or reject a special order. Any price in excess of variable cost will increase current profits. In the long run, all costs are variable. Accordingly, average prices must exceed the full cost of products or services if the firm is to remain in business in the long run.

KEY TERMS

Cost reduction proposal

Outlay costs

Differential cost analysis

Cost prediction error

Full cost

Joint products

Split-off point

Joint costs

Marginal revenue

Marginal cost

Variable cost markup

Manufacturing cost markup

Robinson–Patman Act

REVIEW QUESTIONS

5-1 Distinguish between relevant and irrelevant revenues.

5-2 In evaluating a cost reduction proposal, what three alternatives are available to the management of a for-profit organization?

5-3 When are outlay costs relevant? When are outlay costs irrelevant?

5-4 Are variable costs always relevant? Why or why not?

5-5 Are fixed costs always irrelevant? Why or why not?

5-6 Are sunk costs ever relevant? Why or why not?

5-7 Why is a differential analysis of relevant items preferred to a detailed listing of all costs and revenues associated with each alternative?

5-8 In evaluating a special order management might erroneously compare the special price to the average unit cost of goods sold. Mention two ways that management can avoid this error.

5-9 What costs should be considered in evaluating a special order that will extend over several years?

5-10 When are opportunity costs relevant to the evaluation of a special order?

5-11 How should limited resources be utilized to achieve short-run profit maximization?

5-12 In the decision to sell or process further, of what relevance are costs incurred prior to the decision point? Explain your answer.

5-13 How is the optimal production and sales volume determined in economic models?

5-14 Why are cost data widely used as a starting point in pricing decisions?

5-15 In cost based pricing, what is the most useful way of presenting the variable cost markup to management?

EXERCISES

5-1 Relevant Cost Terms: Matching

A company that produces three products, M, N, and O, is evaluating a proposal that will result in doubling the production of N and discontinuing the production of O. The facilities that are currently used to produce O will be devoted to the production of N. Furthermore, additional machinery will be acquired to produce N. The production of M will not be affected. All products have a positive contribution margin.

Presented are a number of phrases or statements related to the proposal. For each phrase or statement, select the most appropriate cost term. Each term is used only once.

1. Increased revenues from the sale of N
2. Increased variable costs of N
3. Property taxes on the new machinery
4. Revenues from the sale of M

a. Opportunity cost
b. Sunk cost
c. Irrelevant variable outlay cost

5. Cost of the equipment used to produce O
6. Contribution margin of O
7. Variable costs of M
8. The salary of the company president

d. Irrelevant fixed outlay cost
e. Relevant variable outlay cost
f. Relevant fixed outlay cost
g. Relevant revenues
h. Irrelevant revenues

5–2 Identifying Relevant Costs and Revenues

The Ames Company manufactures two components (A and B) and assembles them into a final product. Ames is evaluating two alternative proposals.

Proposal 1 calls for buying component B. This action would free up facilities to manufacture more units of component A and assemble more units of final product. Management believes the additional production can be sold at the current market price.

Proposal 2 calls for replacing the equipment currently used to manufacture component B. The new equipment would operate with fewer workers and less power. The salvage value of the old equipment is equal to its removal costs.

Presented are a number of cost and revenue terms related to the operations of the Ames Company. Under the columns for proposals 1 and 2 indicate whether each item is relevant or irrelevant to that proposal.

	Proposal 1	**Proposal 2**
1. Sales revenue		
2. Variable costs of assembling final product		
3. Direct materials — component A		
4. Direct materials — component B		
5. Direct labor — component A		
6. Direct labor — component B		
7. Variable overhead — component A		
8. Variable overhead — component B		
9. Cost of final assembly equipment		
10. Cost of A manufacturing equipment		
11. Cost of old B manufacturing equipment		
12. Cost of new B manufacturing equipment		
13. Variable selling and administrative costs		
14. Fixed selling and administrative costs		

5–3 Classifying Relevant and Irrelevant Items

Taylor, Taylor, and Tower, Attorneys at Law, have been asked to represent a local client in proceedings to be held in Washington, D.C. Classify each of the following items on the basis of their relationship to this engagement. Items may have multiple classifications.

	Relevant Costs		Irrelevant Costs	
	Opportunity	Outlay	Outlay	Sunk

1. The case will require 3 attorneys to stay 4 nights in a Washington hotel. The predicted hotel bill is $1200.

2. Taylor, Taylor, and Tower's professional staff is paid $800 per day for out-of-town assignments.

3. Last year, depreciation on Taylor, Taylor, and Tower's office was $12,000.

4. Round-trip transportation to Washington is expected to cost $250 per person for the engagement.

5. The firm has recently accepted an engagement that will require them to spend 2 weeks in Atlanta. The predicted out-of-pocket costs of this engagement are $8500.

6. The firm has a maintenance contract on its word processing equipment that will cost $2200 next year.

7. If the firm accepts the engagement in Washington, it will have to decline a conflicting engagement in Hilton Head that would have provided a net cash inflow of $7200.

8. The firm's variable overhead is $8 per client hour.

9. The firm pays for Mr. Tower's cigars, which cost $25 per box.

10. Last year the firm paid $3500 to increase the insulation in its building.

5–4 Classifying Relevant and Irrelevant Items

Baltimore Computer Services maintains records and prepares reports for area businesses. Fantastic Clipper Hair Shoppes has asked Baltimore to maintain their payroll records for an annual fee of $800. Classify each of the following items on the basis of its relationship to the decision to accept or reject Fantastic Clipper's order. Items may have multiple classifications.

	Relevant Costs		Irrelevant Costs	
	Opportunity	**Outlay**	**Outlay**	**Sunk**

1. Baltimore Computer's President earned $60,000 last year.

2. Baltimore Computer intends to spend $10,000 on advertising next year.

3. Baltimore Computer owns 5 printers that cost $6000 each.

4. The Fantastic Clipper job would require 2 labor hours per month for data entry at $15 per hour.

5. The sales manager is paid a 2 percent commission on gross revenues.

6. Baltimore Computer's utility bills were $15,000 last year.

7. The Fantastic Clipper job would use supplies costing $75 per year.

8. Sam's Head House, a major competitor of Fantastic Clipper, currently uses Baltimore Computer Services. Sam indicated he will take his business elsewhere if Baltimore accepts Fantastic's order. Sam's business provides an annual net cash inflow of $150.

9. Depreciation on Baltimore's computer will be $5200 next year.

10. Variable overhead is $8.50 per labor hour.

5–5 Special Order

The Vegetable Garden is a new health food restaurant situated on a busy highway in Pomona, California. The Vegetable Garden specializes in a chef's salad dinner selling for $5. Daily fixed costs are $1500, and variable costs are $2.50 per meal.

An average of 750 meals are served each day even though the capacity is 800 meals per day.

Requirements

a) Determine the current average cost per meal.

b) A bus load of 40 girl scouts, on their way home from the San Bernadino National Forest, stops by and the scoutmaster offers to bring them in if the scouts can all be served a meal for a total of $150. The owner refuses, saying he would lose $0.75 per meal if he accepted this offer. Comment.

c) A local businessman on a tomato juice break overhears the conversation with the scoutmaster and offers the owner a one-year contract to feed 300 of his employees at the special price of $3.75 per meal. Should the restaurant owner accept? Why or why not?

5–6 Special Order: High-Low Cost Estimation

The Knox Belt Company produces seat belts that are sold to North American automobile manufacturers. Although the company has a capacity of 300,000 belts per year, it is currently producing at an annual rate of 180,000 belts.

Knox Belt has received an order from a German manufacturer to purchase 60,000 belts at $10 each. Budgeted costs for 180,000 and 240,000 units are as follows:

Units	180,000	240,000
Manufacturing costs:		
Direct materials	$ 450,000	$ 600,000
Direct labor	315,000	420,000
Factory overhead	1,215,000	1,260,000
Total	$1,980,000	$2,280,000
Selling and administrative	765,000	780,000
Total	$2,745,000	$3,060,000
Costs per unit:		
Manufacturing	$11.00	$ 9.50
Selling and administrative	4.25	3.25
Total	$15.25	$12.75

Sales to North American manufacturers are priced at $20 per unit, but the sales manager believes Knox Belt should aggressively seek the German business even if it results in a loss of $2.75 per unit. She believes obtaining this order would open up several new markets for the company's product. The general manager is concerned about the ethical and legal problems associated with accepting the order. He also commented that Knox Belt cannot tighten its belt enough to absorb the $165,000 loss ($2.75 × 60,000) they would incur if the order is accepted.

Requirements

a) Determine the financial implications of accepting the order.

b) How would your analysis differ if Knox Belt were operating at capacity? Determine the net advantage or disadvantage of accepting the order under these circumstances.

c) Comment on the legal implications of accepting the order.

5–7 Make or Buy

Pure Air Limited manufactures a line of room air fresheners. Management is currently evaluating the possible production of an air freshener for the passenger compartment of automobiles. Based on an annual volume of 10,000 units, the predicted cost of an auto air freshener is as shown below.

Direct materials	$ 8.00 per unit
Direct labor	1.50 per unit
Factory overhead	7.00 per unit
Total	$16.50 per unit

These cost predictions include an allocation of $50,000 in fixed factory overhead.

One of the component parts of the auto air freshener is a battery operated electric motor. Pure Air does not currently manufacture battery operated electric motors. However, the above cost predictions are based on the assumption that Pure Air will purchase and assemble such a motor.

The Mini Motor Company has offered to supply an assembled battery operated motor at a cost of $4.50 per unit, with a minimum annual order of 5000 units. If Pure Air accepts this offer, it will be able to reduce the variable labor and variable overhead costs of the auto air freshener by 50 percent. The electric motor's components will cost $2.00 if Pure Air assembles the motors themselves.

Requirements

a) Determine whether Pure Air should make or buy the electric motor.

b) If Pure Air could rent the space the motors would be assembled in for $8000 per year, should they make or buy this component?

c) What additional factors should Pure Air consider in deciding whether they should make or buy the electric motors?

5–8 Make or Buy

John Madison, III, MD, is a general practitioner whose offices are located in the South Falls Professional Building. In the past Dr. Madison has operated his practice with a nurse, a receptionist/secretary, and a part-time bookkeeper. Dr. Madison, like many small town physicians, has billed his patients and their insurance companies from his own office. The part-time bookkeeper, who works 10 hours per week, is employed exclusively for this purpose.

The North Falls Physician's Service Center has offered to take over all of Dr. Madison's billings and collections for an annual fee of $6000. If Dr. Madison accepts this offer, he will no longer need the bookkeeper. The bookkeeper's wages and fringe benefits amount to $6 per hour, and the bookkeeper works 50 weeks per year. With all the billings and collections done elsewhere, Dr. Madison will have 2 additional hours available per week to see patients. Dr. Madison sees an average of 3 patients per hour at an average fee of $30 per visit. His practice is expanding, and new patients often have to wait several weeks for an appointment. Dr. Madison has resisted expanding his office hours or working more than 50 weeks per year. Finally, if Dr. Madison subscribes to the computer service, he will no longer need to rent a records storage locker in the basement of the Professional Building. The locker rents for $100 per month.

Required: Determine whether or not Dr. Madison should subscribe to the service.

5–9 Limited Resources

The Cape Town Manufacturing Company, Ltd. produces three products: X, Y, and Z. A limitation of 200 labor hours per week prevents Cape Town Manufacturing from meeting the sales demand for these products. Product information is as follows:

	X	Y	Z
Unit selling price	$160	$100	$200
Unit variable costs	−100	−50	−180
Unit contribution margin	$ 60	$ 50	$ 20
Labor hours per unit	4	2	4

Requirements

a) Determine the weekly contribution from each product when the labor hours are allocated on the basis of the following:

  1. Unit selling price.
  2. Unit contribution margin.
  3. Contribution per labor hour.

b) What generalization can be made regarding the allocation of limited resources to achieve short-run profit maximization?

c) Determine the opportunity cost Cape Town Manufacturing will incur if management requires the weekly production of 10 units of X.

5–10 Limited Resources

John Drive, a regional sales representative for the Byte Computer Supply Company, has been working more than 80 hours per week calling on a total of 140 regular customers each month. Because of considerations of family and health, he has decided to spend no more than 40 hours per week, or 160 per month, with customers. Unfortunately, this cutback will require John to turn away some of his regular customers, or at least serve them less frequently than once a month. John has developed the following information to assist him in determining how to best allocate his time.

	Customer Classification		
	Large Business	Small Business	Individual
Number of customers	10	50	80
Average monthly sales per customer	$2000	$1000	$500
Commission percentage	5%	7%	10%
Hours per customer per monthly visit	4.0	2.0	2.5

Required: Develop a monthly plan indicating the number of customers he should call on in each classification to maximize his monthly sales commissions. Determine the monthly commissions he will earn if he implements this plan.

5–11 Sell or Process Further

The Great Lakes Boat Company manufactures sailboat hulls at a cost of $4200 per unit. The hulls are sold to boatyards for $5000. Great Lakes Boat Company is evaluating the desirability of adding masts, sails, and rigging to the hulls prior to sale. These additional parts would cost $1500. However, the completed sailboats could then be sold for $5500 each.

Required: Determine whether the Great Lakes Boat Company should sell sailboat hulls or process them further into complete sailboats.

5–12 Sell or Process Further

The Cooktown Chemical Company processes raw material D into joint products E and F. Each 100 liters of D yields 60 liters of E and 40 liters of F. Raw material D costs $5 per liter, and it costs $100 to convert 100 liters of D into E and F. Product F can be sold immediately for $5 per liter or processed further into product G at an additional cost of $4 per liter. Product G can then be sold for $12 per liter.

Required: Determine whether product F should be sold or processed further into product G.

5–13 Single Product Price Setting

Presented is the 19y2 contribution income statement of Ampex Products.

Ampex Products
Contribution Income Statement
For the year ending December 31,19y2

Sales (12,000 units)		$1,440,000
Less variable costs:		
Variable cost of goods sold	$480,000	
Variable selling and administrative	132,000	−612,000
Contribution margin		$ 828,000
Less fixed costs:		
Fixed factory overhead	$520,000	
Fixed selling and administrative	210,000	−730,000
Net income		$ 98,000

During the coming year it is expected that variable manufacturing costs will increase by $6 per unit and fixed manufacturing costs will increase by $70,000.

Requirements

a) If sales remain at 12,000 units, what price should Ampex charge to produce the same profit as last year? Round your answer to the nearest cent.

b) Management believes that sales can be increased to 15,000 units if the selling price is lowered to $110. Is this action desirable?

c) After taking into consideration the expected increases in costs, what sales volume is needed to earn a profit of $98,000 with a unit selling price of $110? Round your answer to the nearest whole unit.

5–14 Single Product Price Setting

Mary Snow is planning to open a soft ice cream franchise. The franchise will operate in a resort community during June, July, and August. Fixed operating costs for the three-month period are projected to be $4450. Variable costs per serving include the cost of the ice cream and cone, $0.25, and a franchise fee payable to Snowdrift Cooler, $0.05. A market analysis prepared by Snowdrift Cooler indicates that summer sales in the resort community should total 21,000 units.

Required: Determine the price Mary Snow should charge for each Snowdrift Cooler to achieve a profit of $5000 for the three-month period.

PROBLEMS

5–15 Multiple Changes in Profit Plans

Presented is the Mountainside Company's April, 19x6 contribution income statement.

Mountainside Company
Contribution Income Statement
For the month of April, 19x6

Sales ($40 × 10,000)			$400,000
Less variable costs:			
Variable cost of goods sold:			
Direct materials ($5 × 10,000)	$ 50,000		
Direct labor ($14 × 10,000)	140,000		
Variable factory overhead			
($6 × 10,000)	60,000	$250,000	
Variable selling and administrative			
($5 × 10,000)		50,000	−300,000
Contribution margin ($10 × 10,000)			$100,000
Less fixed costs:			
Fixed factory overhead		$ 50,000	
Fixed selling and administrative		60,000	−110,000
Net income (loss)			$ (10,000)

In an attempt to improve the company's profit performance, management is considering a number of alternative actions. They have asked your help in evaluating the consequences of each.

Requirements: Determine the effect of each of the following on monthly profit. Each situation is to be evaluated independent of all others.

a) Purchasing automated assembly equipment. This action should reduce direct labor costs by $6 per unit. It will also increase variable overhead costs by $2 per unit and fixed factory overhead by $20,000 per month.

b) Reducing the unit selling price by $5 per unit. This should increase the monthly sales by 5000 units. At this higher volume additional equipment and salaried personnel would be required. This will increase fixed factory overhead by $3000 per month and fixed selling and administrative costs by $2500 per month.

c) Buying rather than manufacturing a component of Mountainside's final product. This will increase direct materials costs by $15 per unit. However, direct labor will decline $4 per unit, variable factory overhead will decline $1 per unit, and fixed factory overhead will decline $10,000 per month.

d) Increasing the unit selling price by $3 per unit. This action should result in a 1000 unit decrease in monthly sales.

e) Combining requirements (a) and (d).

5–16 Multiple Changes in Profit Plans: Multiple Products

Information on Flamingo Bay's three products follow.

	A	B	C
Unit sales per month	800	1400	900
Selling price per unit	$5.00	$7.50	$4.00
Variable costs per unit	−5.20	−6.00	−2.00
Unit contribution margin	$(0.20)	$1.50	$2.00

Requirements: Determine the effect of each of the following on monthly profits. Each situation is to be evaluated independent of all others.

a) Product A is discontinued.

b) Product A is discontinued, and the subsequent loss of customers causes sales of B to decline by 100 units.

c) The selling price of A is increased to $5.50 with a sales decrease of 200 units.

d) The price of B is increased to $8.00 with a sales decrease of 200 units. However, some of these customers shift to product A, and sales of product A increase by 100 units.

e) Product A is discontinued, and the plant in which A was produced is used to produce D, a new product. Product D has a unit contribution margin of $0.30. Monthly sales of product D are predicted to be 700 units.

f) The selling price of product C is increased to $5, and the selling price of product B is decreased to $7. Sales of C decline by 200 units, and sales of B increase by 300 units.

5–17 Multiple Product Price Setting   The Sussex Company's predicted 19x0 variable and fixed costs are as follows:

Variable Costs		Fixed Costs	
Manufacturing	$400,000	Manufacturing	$200,000
Selling and administrative	100,000	Selling and administrative	50,000
Total	$500,000	Total	$250,000

Sussex produces a wide variety of small tools. Information about one of these products, the type A clamp, is as follows:

	Unit
Direct materials	$ 5
Direct labor	7
Factory overhead:	
Variable	6
Fixed	6
Total manufacturing costs	$24
Variable selling and administrative costs	$ 3

Management has set a $150,000 profit goal for 19x1.

Requirements

a) Determine the percentage markup on variable costs required to earn the desired profit.

b) Use variable cost markup to determine a suggested selling price for the type A clamp.

c) For the type A clamp, break the markup on variable costs into separate parts for fixed costs and profit. Explain the significance of each part.

d) Determine the percentage markup on manufacturing costs required to earn the desired profit.

e) Use the manufacturing cost markup to determine a suggested selling price for the type A clamp.

f) Evaluate the variable and the manufacturing cost approaches to determining the percentage markup.

5–18 Multiple Product Price Setting

The Chesapeake Tackle Company produces a wide variety of commercial fishing equipment. In the past the prices of individual products have been set by product managers on the basis of professional judgment. John Marlin, the new Controller, believes this practice has led to the significant underpricing of some products (and lost profits) and the significant overpricing of other products (and lost sales volume). You have been asked to assist Mr. Marlin in developing a corporate approach to pricing. The output of your work should be a cost-based formula that can be used to develop initial selling prices for each product. Though product managers will be allowed to adjust these prices to meet competition and take advantage of market opportunities, they will be required to explain such deviations in writing.

You have obtained the following 19x4 cost information from the accounting records.

Manufacturing Costs		Selling and Administrative Costs	
Variable	$350,000	Variable	$ 50,000
Fixed	150,000	Fixed	200,000
Total	$500,000	Total	$250,000

In 19x4 Chesapeake reported earnings of $80,000. However, the Controller believes that proper pricing should produce earnings of at least $120,000 on the same sales mix and unit volume. Accordingly, you are to use the above cost information and a target profit of $120,000 in developing a pricing formula.

Selling and administrative expenses are not currently associated with individual products. However, you have obtained the following unit production cost information for the Tigershark Reel.

Variable manufacturing costs	$120 per unit
Fixed factory overhead	60 per unit
Total	$180 per unit

Requirements

a) Determine the standard markup percent for each of the following cost bases. Round answers to three decimal places.

1. Full cost, including fixed and variable manufacturing costs, and fixed and variable selling and administrative costs.

2. Manufacturing costs plus variable selling and administrative costs.

3. Manufacturing costs.

4. Variable costs.

5. Variable manufacturing costs.

b) Explain why the markup percentages became progressively larger between parts 1 and 5 of requirement (a).

c) Determine the initial price of a Tigershark Reel using the manufacturing cost markup and the variable manufacturing cost markup.

d) Do you believe the Controller's approach to product pricing is reasonable? Why or why not?

5–19 Relevant Costs and Differential Analysis

The Third National Bank of Outback paid $50,000 for a check sorting machine in January of 19x1. The machine had an estimated life of 10 years and annual operating costs of $40,000, excluding depreciation. Although management is pleased with the machine, recent technological advances have made it obsolete. Consequently, as of January, 19x5 the machine has a book value of $30,000, a remaining operating life of 6 years, and a salvage value of $0.

The manager of operations is evaluating a proposal to acquire a new Perfect Reader II—Optical Scanning and Sorting Machine. The new machine would cost $60,000 and reduce annual operating costs to $25,000, excluding depreciation. Because of expected technological improvements, the manager believes the new machine will have an economic life of only 6 years and no salvage value at the end of that life.

Prior to signing the papers authorizing the acquisition of the new machine, the president of The Third National Bank prepared the following analysis:

Six-year savings [($40,000 – $25,000) × 6]	$ 90,000
Cost of new machine	(60,000)
Loss on disposal of old machine	(30,000)
Advantage (disadvantage) of replacement	$ —

After looking at these numbers he rejected the proposal and commented that he was ". . . tired of looking at marginal projects. This bank is in business to make a profit, not to break even. If you want to break even, go work for the government."

Requirements

a) Evaluate the president's analysis.

b) Prepare a differential analysis of six-year totals for the old and the new machine.

5–20 Cost Plus Pricing and a Special Order

Thousand Islands Propulsion Company produces a variety of electric trolling motors. Management follows a pricing policy of manufacturing cost plus 60 percent. In response to a request from Northern Sporting Goods, the following price has been developed for an order of 300 Minnow Motors (this is the smallest motor Thousand Island produces):

Manufacturing costs:	
Direct materials	$10,000
Direct labor	12,000
Factory overhead	18,000
Total	$40,000
Markup (60 percent)	24,000
Selling price	$64,000

Mr. Bass, the president of Northern Sporting Goods, rejected this price as too high and offered to purchase the 300 Minnow Motors at a price of $44,000.

Additional information:

- Thousand Islands has sufficient excess capacity to produce the motors.
- Factory overhead is applied on the basis of direct-labor dollars.
- Budgeted factory overhead is $400,000 for the current year. Of this amount, $100,000 is fixed.
- Selling and administrative expenses are budgeted as follows:

Fixed	$90,000 per year
Variable	$20 per unit manufactured and sold

Requirements

a) The president of Thousand Islands Propulsion wants to know if he should allow Mr. Bass to have the Minnows for $44,000. Determine the effect on profits of accepting Mr. Bass' offer.

b) Briefly explain why you omitted certain costs from your analysis in requirement (a).

c) Assume Thousand Islands is operating at capacity and that they could sell the 300 Minnows at their regular markup.

  1. Determine the opportunity cost of accepting Mr. Bass' offer.

  2. Determine the effect on profits of accepting Mr. Bass' offer.

5–21 Special Order

Every Halloween the Glacier Ice Cream Shop offers a Trick-or-Treat package of 20 coupons for $3. The coupons are redeemable, by children of 12 or under, for a single-scoop cone of Glacier ice cream, with a limit of one coupon per child per visit. Coupon sales average 500 books per year. The printing costs are $60.

A single-scoop cone of Glacier Ice Cream normally sells for $0.60. The variable costs of a single scoop cone are $0.40.

Requirements

a) Determine the loss if all coupons are redeemed without any other effect on sales.

b) Not all coupons will be redeemed. Assuming regular sales are not affected, determine the coupon redemption rate at which Glacier will break even on the offer.

c) Assuming regular sales are not affected and that each time a coupon is redeemed one additional single-scoop cone is sold at the regular price, determine the coupon redemption rate at which Glacier will break even on the offer.

d) Determine the profit or loss incurred on the offer if

  ▪ The coupon redemption rate is 60 percent.

  ▪ One fourth of the redeemed coupons have no effect on sales.

  ▪ One fourth of the redeemed coupons result in additional sales of 2 single-scoop cones.

  ▪ One fourth of the redeemed coupons result in additional sales of 3 single-scoop cones.

  ▪ One fourth of the redeemed coupons come out of regular sales of single-scoop cones.

5–22 Relevant Costs for Various Decisions

The income statement for Davann Co. presented below represents the operating results for the fiscal year just ended. Davann had sales of 1,800 tons of product during the current year. The manufacturing capacity of Davann's facilities is 3,000 tons of product.

Davann Co.
Income Statement
For the year ended December 31, 19y0

Sales	$900,000
Variable costs:	
Manufacturing	$315,000
Selling	180,000
Total variable costs	−495,000
Contribution margin	$405,000
Fixed costs:	
Manufacturing	$ 90,000
Selling	112,500
Administrative	45,000
Total fixed costs	−247,500
Net income before taxes	$157,500
Income taxes (40%)	− 63,000
Net income	$ 94,500

Requirements

a) Determine the 19y0 break-even volume in tons of product.

b) Determine the expected 19y1 after-tax net income, assuming a sales volume of 2100 tons and no changes in selling prices or cost behavior.

c) Assume demand from regular customers equals 1800 tons in 19y1 and there are no changes in regular selling prices or cost behavior. Davann has a potential foreign customer that has offered to buy 1500 tons at $450 per ton. What net income after taxes would Davann make in 19y1 if it took this order and rejected some business from regular customers so as not to exceed capacity?

d) Assume Davann will have additional capacity in 19y1 and there are no changes in sales to regular customers, selling prices, or cost behavior. Davann plans to market its product at the regular price in a new territory. This will require an additional promotion program costing $61,500 annually. Additionally, an extra $25 per ton sales commission, over and above the current sales commission, would be required in the new territory. How many tons would have to be sold in the new territory to maintain Davann's current after-tax income of $94,500?

e) Davann is considering replacing a highly labor intensive process with an automatic machine. This would result in an increase of $58,500 in annual fixed manufacturing costs. The variable manufacturing costs would decrease by $25 per ton. Determine the new break-even volume in tons.

f) Davann estimates the per ton selling price will decline by 10 percent next year. If variable costs increase $40 per ton and fixed costs remain unchanged, what sales volume *in dollars* would be required to earn an after-tax net income of $94,500?

(CMA Adapted)

5–23 Potpourri of Relevant Costs

1. Plainfield Company manufactures Part G for use in its production cycle. The costs per unit for 10,000 units of Part G are as follows:

Direct materials	$ 3
Direct labor	15
Variable overhead	6
Fixed overhead	8
	$32

Verona Company has offered to sell Plainfield 10,000 units of Part G for $30 per unit. If Plainfield accepts Verona's offer, the released facilities could be used to save $45,000 in relevant costs in the manufacture of Part H. In addition $5 per unit of the fixed overhead applied to Part G would be totally eliminated. What alternative is more desirable and by what amount is it more desirable?

Alternative	Amount
a) Manufacture	$10,000
b) Manufacture	$15,000
c) Buy	$35,000
d) Buy	$65,000

2. Boyer Company manufactures basketballs. The forecasted income statement for the year before any special orders is as follows:

	Amount	Per Unit
Sales	$4,000,000	$10.00
Manufacturing cost of goods sold	−3,200,000	−8.00
Gross profit	$ 800,000	$ 2.00
Selling expenses	− 300,000	−0.75
Operating income	$ 500,000	$ 1.25

Fixed costs included in the above forecasted income statement are $1,200,000 in manufacturing cost of goods sold and $100,000 in selling expenses. A special order offering to buy 50,000 basketballs for $7.50 each was made to Boyer. There will be no additional selling expenses if the special order is accepted. Assuming Boyer has sufficient capacity to manufacture 50,000 more basketballs, by what amount would operating income be increased or decreased as a result of accepting the special order?

a) $25,000 decrease

b) $62,500 decrease

c) $100,000 increase

d) $125,000 increase

3. Gandy Company has 5000 obsolete desk lamps that are carried in inventory at a manufacturing cost of $50,000. If the lamps are reworked for $20,000, they could be sold for $35,000. Alternatively, the lamps could be sold for $8,000 to a jobber located in a distant city. In a decision model analyzing these alternatives, the sunk would be?

a) $8,000

b) $15,000

c) $20,000

d) $50,000

4. Kingston Company needs 10,000 units of a certain part to be used in its production cycle. The following information is available.

Cost to Kingston Company to make the part:	
Direct materials	$ 6
Direct labor	24
Variable overhead	12
Fixed overhead applied	15
	$57
Cost to buy the part from Utica Company	$53

If Kingston buys the part from Utica instead of making it, Kingston could not use the released facilities in another manufacturing activity. Sixty percent of the fixed overhead applied will continue regardless of what decision is made.

In deciding whether to make or buy the part, which of the following is the total relevant cost to make the part?

a) $342,000

b) $480,000

c) $530,000

d) $570,000

5. Yardley Corporation uses a joint process to produce products A, B, and C. Each product may be sold at its split-off point or processed further. Additional processing costs are entirely variable and are traceable to the respective products produced. Joint production costs for 19x5 were $50,000. Relevant data follow.

Product	Units Produced	Sales Value at Split-Off	Sales Values	Additional Costs
		Sales Values and Additional Costs If Processed Further		
A	20,000	$ 45,000	$60,000	$20,000
B	15,000	75,000	98,000	20,000
C	15,000	30,000	62,000	18,000
		$150,000		

To maximize profits, which products should Yardley subject to further processing?

a) A only

b) C only

c) B and C only

d) None, because of joint costs

6. Brike Company, which manufactures robes, has enough idle capacity available to accept a special order of 10,000 robes at $8 a robe. A predicted income statement for the year without this special order is as follows:

	Per Unit	Total
Sales	$12.50	$1,250,000
Manufacturing costs (variable)	$ 6.25	$ 625,000
Manufacturing costs (fixed)	1.75	175,000
Manufacturing costs (total)	−8.00	−800,000
Gross profit	$ 4.50	$ 450,000
Selling expenses (variable)	$ 1.80	$ 180,000
Selling expenses (fixed)	1.45	145,000
Selling expenses (total)	−3.25	−325,000
Operating income	$ 1.25	$ 125,000

Assuming no additional selling expenses, what would be the effect on operating income if the special order were accepted?

a) $8,000 increase

b) $17,500 increase

c) $32,500 decrease

d) $40,000 increase

5–24 Analysis of Relevant Costs for Decision Alternatives   Auer Company had received an order for a piece of special machinery from Jay Company. Just as Auer Company completed the machine, Jay Company declared bankruptcy, defaulted on the order, and forfeited the 10 percent deposit paid on the selling price of $72,500.

Auer's manufacturing manager identified the costs already incurred in the production of the special machinery for Jay as follows:

Direct materials used		$16,600
Direct labor incurred		21,400
Overhead applied:		
Manufacturing:		
Variable	$10,700	
Fixed	5,350	16,050
Fixed selling and administrative		5,405
Total cost		$59,455

Another company, Kaytell Corp., would be interested in buying the special machinery if it were reworked to Kaytell's specifications. Auer offered to sell the reworked special machinery to Kaytell as a special order for a net price of $68,400. Kaytell has agreed to pay the net price when it takes delivery in two months. The additional identifiable costs to rework the machinery to the specifications of Kaytell are as follows:

Direct materials	$ 6,200
Direct labor	4,200
Total	$10,400

A second alternative available to Auer is to convert the special machinery to the standard model. The standard model lists for $62,500. The additional identifiable costs to convert the special machinery to the standard model are:

Direct materials	$ 2,850
Direct labor	3,300
Total	$ 6,150

A third alternative for the Auer Company is to sell, as a special order, the machine as is (e.g., without modification) for a net price of $52,000. However, the potential buyer of the unmodified machine does not want it for 60 days. The buyer offers a $7000 down payment with final payment upon delivery.

The following additional information is available regarding Auer's operations:

- The sales commission rate on sales of standard models is 2 percent, whereas the sales commission rate on special orders is 3 percent. All sales commissions are calculated on net sales price (i.e., list price less cash discount, if any).

- Normal credit terms for sales of standard models are 2/10, net/30, that is, customers who pay within 10 days receive a 2 percent cash discount; otherwise, the full sales price is due within 30 days. Ordinarily, customers take the discounts. Credit terms for special orders are negotiated with the customer.

- The application rates for manufacturing overhead and the fixed selling and administrative costs are as follows:

Manufacturing:	
Variable	50 percent of direct labor cost
Fixed	25 percent of direct labor costs
Selling and administrative:	
Fixed	10 percent of the total of direct material, direct labor and manufacturing overhead costs

- Normal time required for rework is 1 month.

- A surcharge of 5 percent of the sales price is placed on all customer requests for minor modifications of standard models.

- Auer normally sells a sufficient number of standard models for the company to operate at a volume in excess of the break-even point.

Auer does not consider the time value of money in analyses of special orders and projects whenever the time period is less than one year, because the effect is not significant.

Requirements

a) Determine the dollar contribution each of the three alternatives will make to the Auer Company's before-tax profits.

b) If Kaytell makes Auer a counteroffer, what is the lowest price Auer should accept for the reworked machinery from Kaytell? Explain your answer.

c) Discuss the influence fixed factory overhead cost should have on the sales prices quoted by Auer Company for special orders when

    1. A firm is operating at or below the break-even point.

    2. A firm's special orders constitute efficient utilization of unused capacity above the break-even volume.

(CMA Adapted)

5–25 Differential Analysis with Joint Costs

Helene's, a high fashion women's dress manufacturer, is planning to market a new cocktail dress for the coming season. Helene's supplies retailers in the east and mid-Atlantic states.

Four yards of material are required to lay out the dress pattern. Some material remains after cutting that can be sold as remnants.

The leftover material could also be used to manufacture a matching cape and handbag. However, if the leftover material is to be used for the cape and handbag, more care will be required in the cutting, which will increase the cutting costs.

The company expected to sell 1250 dresses if no matching capes or handbags were available. Helene's market research reveals that dress sales will be 20 percent higher if a matching cape and handbag are available. The market research indicates that the cape or handbag will only sell well as optional accessories with the dress. The various combinations of dresses, capes, and handbags that are expected to be manufactured by Helene's and sold by retailers are as follows:

	Percent of Total
Complete sets of dress, cape, and handbag	70
Dress and cape	6
Dress and handbag	15
Dress only	9
Total	100

The material used in the dress costs $12.50 a yard or $50.00 for each dress. The cost of cutting the dress if the cape and handbag are not manufactured is estimated at $20.00 a dress, and the resulting remnants can be sold for $5.00 for each dress cut out. If the cape and handbag are to be manufactured, the cutting costs will be increased by $9.00 per dress. There will be no saleable remnants if the capes and handbags are manufactured in the quantities estimated.

The selling prices and the costs to complete the three items once they are cut are presented below.

	Selling Price Per Unit	Unit Cost to Complete (Excludes Cost of Material and Cutting Operation)
Dress	$200.00	$80.00
Cape	27.50	19.50
Handbag	9.50	6.50

Requirements

a) Calculate Helene's incremental profit or loss from manufacturing the capes and handbags in conjunction with the dresses.

b) Identify any nonquantitative factors that could influence Helene's management in its decision to manufacture the matching capes and handbags.

(CMA Adapted)

II

Planning and Control

Operating
Budgets

Planning and controlling involves anticipating future activities before they happen and undertaking measures to ensure they occur in a way that has the best impact on the organization. More than simply forecasting what will take place and reporting what actually did take place, planning and controlling is an ongoing process of guiding, monitoring, and governing an organization. In this and the next five chapters a structure for planning and controlling is developed, along with alternative procedures for reporting activities within this structure. One purpose of this chapter is to develop a basic framework for financial planning.

The process of projecting the operations of the organization and their financial impact into the future is called operations budgeting. An **operating budget** is a formal financial document that reports expected revenues and expenses, as well as all other expected operating and financing transactions for a future period of time (usually one year). Another purpose of this chapter is to discuss the basic concepts and benefits of operating budgets. This is presented by considering some alternative approaches to budget preparation. Next, an example of a complete operations budget is developed, starting with the forecasting of sales and concluding with the preparation of pro forma financial statements. Also included is an examination of the behavioral implications of budgeting and a discussion of some of the difficulties and problems that are often encountered in operations budgeting.

JUSTIFICATIONS OF BUDGETING

Preparing budgets is an important function in all organizations. It requires making estimates about future needs and developments that may be difficult to predict and even more difficult to control. Many future events almost defy accurate prediction (e.g., a company trying to anticipate the cost of complying with union demands or federal regulations). In spite of the difficulty and the inherent uncertainty involved in budgeting, there are several important benefits that are expected to accrue to the users of operations budgeting. These are discussed below.

Future Planning

Budgeting is planning for a future period, and as applied to the accounting aspects of an organization, requires management to examine what is anticipated in its financial environment. This look into the future invariably compels management to establish goals and objectives for the future and, maybe more important, it helps management to identify major problems that may develop later if corrective action is not taken. Budgeting moves the organization from an informal reaction method of management to a formal controlled method of management. Less time is spent on solving unanticipated problems, and more time is spent on positive measures and preventive actions.

Improved Communication

Operating budgets are prepared for the entire organization, and budget preparation requires the participation of all levels of management. The process of compiling, reviewing, and revising budget data opens up seldom-used lines of communication within organizations (vertically), between subordinates and superiors, and (horizontally) between managers of various departments, whose operations are related and interdependent.

Functional Coordination

Once completed, the operating budget becomes the plan of action for the entire organization and must therefore reflect the coordinated efforts of all components of the organization. The production and sales managers cannot make their plans independent of each other. The personnel department must know the needs of all other departments before it can budget its needs for new employees and training costs. The final version of the operating budget emerges after an extensive, and often lengthy, process of communication and coordination. It represents a synthesis of the experience and knowledge of management at every level of the organization.

Performance Evaluation

Effective planning and control require a basis for evaluating performance. The traditional bases for measuring performance are historical, industry, and budgeted data. The first two measures have some disadvantages. If *historical data* regarding the firm's performance are used for measuring current performance, past inefficiencies may be allowed to continue as long as the organization operates at the same level. Also, changes in the organization's operating environment will not be reflected in the basis on which performance is evaluated—for example, a machine losing its value because of technological advances.

Using *industry data* to measure performance has the disadvantage of comparing one organization to other companies that may be substantially different from it, thus leading to erroneous conclusions. Comparisons of one organization with others in an industry may be interesting, and they may provide a general perspective of how well one firm is doing compared to similar ones, but it is usually a poor basis for evaluating management's performance for a particular operating period.

Budgeted data prepared for the period under review is a more realistic way of evaluating performance because the benchmarks are current. They are compared to actual results and produce meaningful variances that can be useful evaluation measures. The use of budgeted data will minimize the carry-over of past inefficiencies and will reflect environmental changes.

An organization's budgeted data are relevant only for a specific operating period, thereby reflecting all the unique conditions affecting managment's performance.

Regardless of the types of data used, they must be communicated properly to those being evaluated through a feedback process. Such a process compares actual performance to some type of standard, budget, or benchmark. Receiving feedback on actual operations serves as a basis for evaluating performance and taking corrective action.

Motivation Aspects and Human Behavior

All organizations are made up of individuals who carry out a wide variety of activities in pursuit of the common goal of the organization. To accomplish this objective, it is important for management to recognize what effects its chosen tools and techniques have on the behavior of the people in the organization.

Properly used, the operating budget can be an effective mechanism for motivating workers to higher levels of performance and productivity. Improperly developed and administered, it can foster feelings of animosity toward both management and the budget process. When workers participate in the preparation of budgets and feel that the budgets represent fair standards for evaluating their performance, they receive personal satisfaction from accomplishing the goals set forth in the budgets.

Budgeting often engenders strong reactions in people. It is possible for some managers to use budgets in such a way that employees perceive the budgets as a means of squeezing the last unit of productivity out of them, or merely as a means of identifying the poor performers. Because people inherently dislike restrictions on their behavior, we often see only the negative aspects of budgeting. Budgeting can and should be used as a positive motivator, as a means of bringing out the best in people without threatening their security and self-esteem.

Another important motivational aspect of operating budgets is related to management's recognition that the budget is not infallible. Mistakes in prediction and judgment are sometimes made, and unforeseen circumstances often develop, necessitating modification of the budget. Unless top management is willing to recognize these needs for change in the budget, support for the budget at lower levels can quickly erode. If the organization is to receive maximum benefit from the budget process, support for the budget at the top management level, as well as at lower levels, must be maintained. Achieving this goal may be the most difficult challenge facing an organization undertaking budgeting for the first time.

Lower level managers will not respect the budget and the related performance reports if they perceive a lack of commitment by top management. Violations of the budget by top management can quickly destroy the effectiveness of the budget throughout the organization.

Managers who follow the suggestions below may be successful in using budgets as a positive tool for accomplishing organizational goals through people.

1. Emphasize the importance of budgeting as a planning device.

2. Encourage wide participation in budget preparation at all levels of management.

3. Demonstrate through appropriate communications that the budget has the complete support of top management.

4. Recognize that the budget is not immutable, that it may require modification if conditions change.

5. Use budget performance reports not just to identify the poor performer; use them also to recognize good performance.

6. Conduct programs in budget education to provide new managers with information about the purposes of budgets and to dispel erroneous misconceptions that may exist.

FORMAL PLANNING CONCEPTS

Before an organization can develop operating budgets, management must decide which approaches to budgeting will be used for various activities. Widely used approaches to budgeting include (1) the input/output approach, (2) the incremental approach, and (3) the minimum level approach. Notice in Exhibit 6–1 the relationships between budget approaches and typical cost characteristics.

Input/Output Approach

The **input/output approach** budgets physical inputs and costs as a function of planned activity. This approach is often used for manufacturing and distribution activities where there are clearly defined relationships between effort and accomplishment. For example, if each unit produced requires two pounds of raw materials that cost $5 each, and the planned production volume is 25 units, then the budgeted inputs and costs for raw materials are 50 (25 × 2) pounds and $250 (50 × $5). Notice that the budgeted inputs

---

EXHIBIT 6–1 Planning Concepts

Approach to Budgeting	Typical Cost Characteristic
Input/output	Variable and mixed costs
Incremental	Discretionary fixed costs
Minimum level	Committed fixed costs

are a function of the planned outputs. Using the input/output approach, we start with the planned outputs and work backward to budget the inputs. In evaluating the proposed budget, management would focus its attention on the physical and cost relationships between the inputs and the outputs. Any time that variable costs exist the input/output approach is most appropriate. This approach is seldom used for activities that do not have clearly defined input/output relationships, such as advertising, research and development, and executive training.

Incremental Approach

The **incremental approach** budgets costs for a coming period as a dollar or percentage change from the amount budgeted for (or spent during) the previous period. This approach is often used where the relationships between inputs and outputs are weak or nonexistent, particularly where fixed costs dominate. It is difficult to establish a clear relationship between sales volume and advertising expenditures. Consequently, the budgeted amount of advertising for some coming period is often based on the budgeted or actual advertising expenditures in a previous period. If budgeted advertising expenditures for 19x1 were $200,000, the budgeted expenditures for 19x2 would be some increment based on $200,000. In evaluating the proposed 19x2 budget, management would accept the $200,000 base and focus its attention on a justification for the increment.

This approach to budgeting has been more widely used in government than in business organizations (see the appendix to this chapter). In seeking an annual budget appropriation, a department operating under the incremental approach would be required to justify only proposed expenditures in excess of its previous budget appropriation.

The primary advantage of the incremental approach is that it simplifies the budget process by having it consider only the increments in the various budget items, which in most cases would be smaller and easier to handle than the total budgeted amount. On the other hand, a major disadvantage is that existing waste and inefficiencies may be pyramided year after year without ever being discovered.

Minimum Level Approach

Using the **minimum level approach,** an organization establishes a base amount for all budget items and requires explanation or justification for any budgeted amount above the minimum. Under this method an absolute minimum amount of expenditures is presumed necessary to support ongoing activity in the organization. This method is very useful where many committed costs continue from period to period. Proponents of this approach maintain that requiring extensive justifications of budget items up to the minimum amount is an ineffective use of managerial time. Like the incremental approach, the minimum level approach is often used for activities that do not have clearly defined input/output relationships. The corporate director of product development would need some minimum provision in the budget to support a minimum level of activity for ongoing projects. Additional increments might also be included first to support the current level of product development and second to undertake desirable new projects.

All three approaches are often used in the same organization. A manufacturing firm might, for example, use the input/output approach to budget manufacturing and distribution expenditures; the incremental approach to budget administrative salaries, advertising, and contributions; and the minimum level approach to budget research and development, employee training, and computer operations.

BUDGET PREPARATION

There are probably no two organizations that prepare budgets in exactly the same way, but there are two approaches to budgeting that seem to characterize budget preparation in most organizations: the *imposed budget* and the *participation budget*. These are sometimes referred to as, respectively, the *top-down* approach and the *bottom-up* approach.

Under the **imposed budget,** or **top-down,** approach to budget preparation, top management decides on the goals and objectives for the whole organization and communicates these to lower management levels. As we discussed earlier, this *nonparticipative approach* to budgeting can have serious motivational consequences. Although the imposed budget approach was used quite frequently in the past, today most companies encourage greater participation in budget preparation.

The **participation budget** utilizes the benefits of improved communication, coordination, and motivation. The participation budget requires managers at all levels, and in some cases even nonmanagers, to become involved in budget preparation. This approach is sometimes referred to as the **bottom-up** approach. Budget proposals are made first at the lowest level of management and then are integrated into the proposals for the next level, and so on, until the proposals reach the top level of management where the budget is completed.

Also important to the preparation are the types of forecasts used. Though the sales forecast is primary to most organizations, the other types of forecasts vary in importance. Other forecasts or predictions often used are estimates of uncollectibles, production output as a ratio of resources input, production days available, employee turnover and subsequent training of new employees, and cash balance needs per month. Because of the diverse sources of these estimates, the preparation process requires coordination of most of the functions in an organization. Unfortunately, with the forecasts come new and additional demands by those providing input: Marketing wants to change the product unit, production wants to operate only four days a week, and the treasurer wants a smaller daily cash balance, just to list a few.

Obviously, all requests cannot be included in the budget. Someone must be responsible for deciding which requests are most important to the organization. Most organizations have a **budget committee** that is responsible for supervising budget preparation and that serves as a review board for evaluating requests for discretionary cost items and new projects. The final responsibility for decisions rests with the budget committee, which is usually composed of top-level managers. In addition, larger companies frequently will have a *budget office,* responsible to the controller, that performs a staff function of assisting the budget committee. The budget office is responsible for the preparation, distribution, and processing of forms used in gathering budget data and handles most of the work of actually formulating the budget schedules and reports. The budget office staff may also assist the budget committee by preparing various analyses and special reports as the need arises.

Large organizations frequently have a full-time budgeting staff that works year-round on the budget. This does not mean that it takes twelve months to prepare the budget, or that once the annual budget is completed the budgeting staff has nothing else to do until the next year. Preparing a budget may take most of the year in some companies; also, the final budget is really never final — it may have to be revised several times during the course of the budget period. Furthermore, the multiyear, long-range plans of many companies are updated constantly to reflect changing conditions. Revisions and updating are part of the responsibility of the budget office.

BUDGETING PERIODS

Up to this point the normal budget period has been assumed to be one year. Although the annual budget period is certainly the most common, many organizations budget for shorter periods (such as a month or a quarter of a year) and for longer periods (such as two years, five years, or more). In addition to fixed length budget periods, two other types of budget periods are commonly used, *cycle budgeting* and *continuous budgeting.*

For some businesses, a fixed time period is not particularly relevant to the planning of operations. A company engaged in large construction projects might find it more advantageous to prepare a budget for the entire project life, which may be more than a year in some cases and less than a year in others. In these cases the firm may use **cycle budgeting,** which is appropriate when the entire life of the cycle or project represents a more useful planning horizon than an artificial period of one year. Such cycles could be reduced to shorter planning periods by breaking the overall project into several components, such as construction phases.

Another type of budgeting that is gaining in popularity is *continuous,* or *perpetual,* budgeting. Under **continuous budgeting,** the budget is based on a moving time frame that extends over a fixed period. For example, an organization on a continuous four-quarter budget system adds a quarter into the future at the end of each quarter of operations, thereby always maintaining a four-quarter budget. Under this system plans for a full year into the future are always available; whereas under a fixed annual budget operating plans for a full year ahead are available only at the beginning of the budget year. Because management is constantly involved in this type of budgeting, the budget process becomes an active and integral part of the management process. Management is forced to be future-oriented throughout the year, rather than just once each year. Continuous budgeting helps to elevate the level of visibility and recognition of the planning function.

TYPES OF BUDGETS

The types of budgets that must be prepared depend on the nature of the business and the types of its activities. The operating budget is actually a model of the operating cycles of a business. Most organizations have two basic cycles, expenditure and revenue, as shown in Exhibit 6–2. The complete business cycle evolves from cash to purchases, to sales, to cash, although many organizations, such as General Motors, have far more complex cycles. Exhibit 6–2 illustrates the cycle for a merchandising company.

In most organizations the budgeting process begins with the development of the sales budget and concludes with the development of pro forma financial statements. The illustration in Exhibit 6–3 highlights the budget assembly process in a manufacturing firm. Here, the critical aspects of sales and manufacturing converge upward toward cash and inward toward the pro forma statements.

To illustrate the procedures involved in budget assembly, an operating budget will be developed for the All American Automobile Company (AAA) for the year 19x5. The assembly sequence will follow the overview in Exhibit 6–3. AAA is a manufacturer of two primary products, A-Cars and B-Cars, both of which are marketed throughout the Western Hemisphere.

The activities of a business can be summarized under three broad categories: operating activities, financing activities, and investing activities. For our purposes, and to simplify our discussion, assume that All American Automobile Company engaged in no investing activities during the budget

---

EXHIBIT 6–2 Operating Cycles

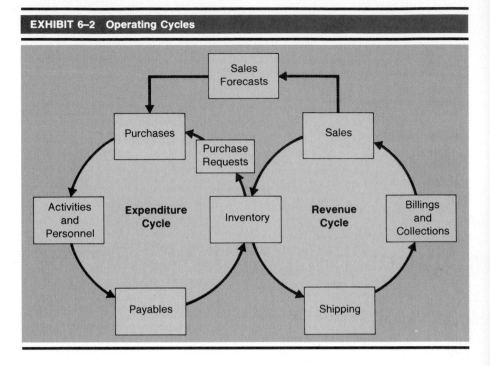

---

period and that the only financing activity is short-term borrowing. Activities performed in conducting the daily affairs of an organization are called **operating activities.** These, of course, are the major concern of management in preparing operating budgets. The operating activities of the All American Automobile Company include:

1. Sales of goods or services.
2. Purchase of materials, labor, and overhead for the manufacture of saleable goods.
3. Purchase and use of goods and services classified as selling expenses.
4. Purchase and use of goods and services classified as general and administrative expenses.

In addition to preparing the budget for each operating activity, a cash budget is prepared that summarizes the projected cash receipts and disbursement for the budget period. The importance of cash planning makes the cash budget a vital part of the total budget process. Management must, for example, be aware of the need to borrow and have some idea when borrowed funds can be repaid.

EXHIBIT 6–3   Overview of Budget Assembly in a Manufacturing Firm

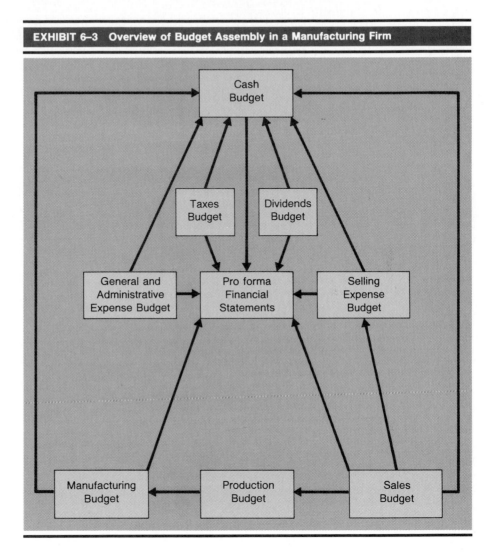

The budgets for AAA provide information for each of the four quarters in 19x5 and totals for the year. The balance sheet at the end of 19x4, presented in Exhibit 6–4, contains information to use as a starting point in preparing the various budgets. We will adopt the input/output approach to budget variable production and selling costs. The budgets for other costs were developed using either the incremental or the minimum level approach. Budgets to be prepared include sales, production, manufacturing, selling expense, general and administrative, and cash.

EXHIBIT 6–4   Initial Balance Sheet

All American Automobile Company
Balance Sheet
December 31, 19x4
(*In thousands*)

Assets

Current assets:			
Cash		$ 15,000	
Accounts receivable (net)		22,000	
Inventory, raw materials		23,600	
Inventory, finished goods (1800 units)		9,800	$ 70,400
Property, plant and equipment:			
Land		$ 60,000	
Buildings and equipment	$ 260,000		
Less accumulated depreciation	−124,800	135,200	195,200
Total assets			$265,600

Liabilities and stockholders' equity

Current liabilities:			
Accounts payable			$ 17,200
Stockholders' equity:			
Capital stock		$150,000	
Retained earnings		98,400	248,400
Total liabilities and stockholders' equity			$265,600

Sales Budget

The **sales budget** contains a forecast of unit sales volume and sales dollars, and it may also contain a forecast of sales collections. The sales budget is a critical element in the overall operating budget process because so many of the other elements, such as inventory purchases, manufacturing requirements, and labor needs, are based on projected sales. Management uses the best available information to forecast future market conditions accurately. These forecasts, when considered along with product development plans, promotion and advertising plans, and expected pricing policies, should lead to the most dependable sales predictions. The sales budget for 19x5 is presented in Exhibit 6–5.

Once the sales predictions are made, information on credit terms, collections policy, and past collection experience are utilized to develop a sales collections budget. Collections on sales normally include receipts from the current period's sales and the collections from sales of prior periods. An allowance for bad debts, which reduces each period's collections, is also predicted. Other items often included are sales discounts, allowances for volume discounts, and seasonal changes of sales prices and collections. For AAA 75 percent of the cash is collected in the quarter of sales and 24 percent in the quarter after the sales take place. Bad debts are budgeted at 1 percent of sales.

Production Budget   The **production budget** is based on sales predictions with adjustments for beginning inventory and desired ending inventory. It establishes the production quotas for each period necessary to cover sales and provide desired ending inventory levels. Assume AAA's experience indicates ending inventories should amount to 20 percent of the next quarter's expected sales. First we determine the total needs for sales and desired ending inventories and then subtract the expected beginning inventories from this

---

EXHIBIT 6–5   Sales Budget

All American Automobile Company
Sales Budget
For the year ended December 31, 19x5

	First Quarter	Second Quarter	Third Quarter	Fourth Quarter	Year Total
Sales (units)					
A-Cars	5,000	6,000	8,500	5,500	25,000
B-Cars	4,000	6,000	7,400	6,000	23,400
Total	9,000	12,000	15,900	11,500	48,400
Sales (dollars*)					
(In thousands)					
A-Cars	$30,000	$ 36,000	$ 51,000	$ 33,000	$150,000
B-Cars	64,000	96,000	118,400	96,000	374,400
Total	$94,000	$132,000	$169,400	$129,000†	$524,400
Collections on sales					
For current quarter					
(75% of sales)	$70,500	$ 99,000	$127,050	$ 96,750†	$393,300
For previous quarter					
(24% of sales)	22,000‡	22,560	31,680	40,656	116,896
Total	$92,500	$121,560	$158,730	$137,406	$510,196
Budgeted bad debts					
(1% of current					
quarter sales)	$ 940	$ 1,320	$ 1,694	$ 1,290†	$ 5,244

* Average selling price per unit is expected to be $6000 for A-Cars and $16,000 for B-Cars.

† Accounts receivable at December 31, 19x5, is $30,960 ($129,000 − $96,750 − $1,290).

‡ Uncollected balance at December 31, 19x4, is expected to be collected in the first quarter of 19x5.

EXHIBIT 6–6   Production Budget

All American Automobile Company
Production Budget
For the year ended December 31, 19x5
(In units)

	First Quarter	Second Quarter	Third Quarter	Fourth Quarter	Year Total
A-Cars					
Budgeted sales (from Exhibit 6–5)	5,000	6,000	8,500	5,500	25,000
Plus required ending inventory*	1,200	1,700	1,100	1,000	1,000
Total inventory requirements	6,200	7,700	9,600	6,500	26,000
Less beginning inventory	−1,000	−1,200	−1,700	−1,100	− 1,000
Budgeted production A-Cars	5,200	6,500	7,900	5,400	25,000
B-Cars					
Budgeted sales (from Exhibit 6–5)	4,000	6,000	7,400	6,000	23,400
Plus required ending inventory*	1,200	1,480	1,200	800	800
Total inventory requirements	5,200	7,480	8,600	6,800	24,200
Less beginning inventory	− 800	−1,200	−1,480	−1,200	− 800
Budgeted production B-Cars	4,400	6,280	7,120	5,600	23,400

* Budgeted at 20 percent of the next quarter's expected sales.

amount. The difference is what the company needs to produce. The production budget for 19x5 is presented in Exhibit 6–6.

Notice in Exhibit 6–6 that the inventories at the beginning of the first quarter and at the end of the last quarter are the same. This is because management expects 19x6 first quarter sales to be the same as 19x5 first quarter sales.

Manufacturing Budget

The **manufacturing budget,** based on an analysis of the production budget, is used to plan the materials, labor, and factory overhead requirements of the budgeted volume of production. These requirements are then converted into actual disbursement dollars and presented as an additional section of the manufacturing budget. Some companies also develop a separate section for budget manufacturing costs (a budgeted statement of cost of goods manufactured). Because of our focus on activities rather than product costs, this section is omitted.

Production costs for each type of car produced by AAA have been estimated by management to be as follows:

	A-Cars	B-Cars
Direct materials	$2,000	$3,000
Direct labor (50 hrs at $20)	1,000	1,000
Variable overhead ($10 per hour)	500	500
Total variable cost per unit	$3,500	$4,500

Common fixed manufacturing costs are as follows:

Fixed overhead requiring cash expenditures	$25 million per quarter
Fixed overhead not requiring cash expenditures (depreciation)	$ 5 million per quarter

Direct labor and overhead, except for depreciation, are acquired and paid for in the quarter they are used. Direct materials are purchased in the quarter preceding their use. Information on budgeted labor hours and budgeted dollar purchases is presented in the upper portion of Exhibit 6–7. Payments for purchases of direct materials are made 50 percent in the quarter they are purchased and 50 percent in the following quarter. The budgeted manufacturing disbursements are presented in the lower portion of Exhibit 6–7. Depreciation is not included as a budgeted manufacturing disbursement because cash flow is not associated with depreciation but is incurred in connection with the acquisition of assets.

Selling Expense Budget

The **selling expense budget** indicates the costs and disbursements the organization plans to incur in connection with sales and distribution. Budgeted selling expenses include variable selling expenses and fixed selling expenses other than depreciation of $50,000 per quarter. Notice in the Selling Expense Budget, Exhibit 6–8, that the budgeted variable selling expenses are based on budgeted sales as a percentage of budgeted sales dollars. The budgeted fixed selling expenses are given amounts obtained from the manager of the sales department. Budgeted selling costs for AAA are paid in the quarter they are incurred.

General and Administrative Expense Budget

The **general and administrative expense budget** presents the expected costs and disbursements for the overall administration of the organization, such as the accounting department, the computer center, and the president's office. Depreciation of $150,000 per quarter is omitted since no cash disbursement is required. Notice in Exhibit 6–9 that there are no variable general and administrative costs. This is because most expenditures categorized as general and administrative are related to top management opera-

EXHIBIT 6–7   Manufacturing Budget

All American Automobile Company
Manufacturing Budget
For the year ended December 31, 19x5

	First Quarter	Second Quarter	Third Quarter	Fourth Quarter	Year Total
Budgeted production (*units*)					
A-Cars (From Exhibit 6–6)	5,200	6,500	7,900	5,400	25,000
B-Cars (From Exhibit 6–6)	4,400	6,280	7,120	5,600	23,400
Total	9,600	12,780	15,020	11,000	48,400
Budgeted labor hours					
(50 hours per unit)	480,000	639,000	751,000	550,000	2,420,000
*Materials purchases**					
(*In thousands*)					
For A-Cars ($2000 per unit)	$13,000	$15,800	$10,800	$10,400	$50,000
For B-Cars ($3000 per unit)	18,840	21,360	16,800	13,200	70,200
Total	$31,840	$37,160	$27,600	$23,600	$120,200
Manufacturing disbursements					
(*In thousands*)					
Payments on materials purchases:					
For current quarter (50%)	$15,920	$18,580	$13,800	$11,800	$ 60,100
For last quarter (50%)	17,200†	15,920	18,580	13,800	65,500
Total	$33,120	$34,500	$32,380	$25,600	$125,600
Direct labor:					
$20 per hour	9,600	12,780	15,020	11,000	48,400
Variable overhead					
$10 per hour	4,800	6,390	7,510	5,500	24,200
Fixed overhead:	25,000	25,000	25,000	25,000	100,000
Total budgeted manufacturing					
expenditures	$72,520	$78,670	$79,910	$67,100	$298,200

* *Example:* Purchases in the first quarter are based on the production needs of the second quarter, 6500 × $2000 = $13,000,000.
† Unpaid balance at December 31, 19x4 reflects prior year payment terms.

tions that do not vary with current sales or production. For AAA all general and administrative costs except depreciation are assumed to be paid in the quarter they are incurred.

Cash Budget

The **cash budget** summarizes all cash receipts and disbursements expected to occur during the budget period. Almost all activities affect cash sooner or later. AAA's cash budget, presented in Exhibit 6–10, is affected by credit policies, sales discounts taken by customers, collection experiences, pay-

EXHIBIT 6–8 Selling Expense Budget

All American Automobile Company
Selling Expense Budget
For the year ended December 31, 19x5
(*In thousands*)

	First Quarter	Second Quarter	Third Quarter	Fourth Quarter	Year Total
Budgeted sales (*from Exhibit 6–5*)	$94,000	$132,000	$169,400	$129,000	$524,400
Selling costs and disbursements					
Variable costs:					
Delivery (1% of sales)	$ 940	$ 1,320	$ 1,694	$ 1,290	$ 5,244
Commissions (2% of sales)	1,880	2,640	3,388	2,580	10,488
Miscellaneous (1% of sales)	940	1,320	1,694	1,290	5,244
Total	$ 3,760	$ 5,280	$ 6,776	$ 5,160	$ 20,976
Fixed costs:					
Promotion and advertising	$ 2,250	$ 2,250	$ 2,250	$ 2,250	$ 9,000
Office expenses	125	125	125	125	500
Miscellaneous	100	100	100	100	400
Total	2,475	2,475	2,475	2,475	9,900
Total selling costs and disbursements	$ 6,235	$ 7,755	$ 9,251	$ 7,635	$ 30,876

EXHIBIT 6–9 General and Administrative Expense Budget

All American Automobile Company
General and Administrative Expense Budget
For the year ended December 31, 19x5
(*In thousands*)

	First Quarter	Second Quarter	Third Quarter	Fourth Quarter	Year Total
General and administrative costs and disbursements (all fixed)					
Compensation	$2,500	$2,500	$2,500	$2,500	$10,000
Research and development	2,000	2,000	2,000	2,000	8,000
Insurance	200	200	200	200	800
Property taxes	300	300	300	300	1,200
Miscellaneous	100	100	100	100	400
Total budgeted general and administrative costs and disbursements	$5,100	$5,100	$5,100	$5,100	$20,400

ment policies, purchase and volume discounts taken, and a myriad of other factors. In Exhibit 6–10 the information for taxes is furnished by AAA's tax department, and the information for dividends by the Board of Directors. The cash budget shows the cash operating deficiencies and surpluses expected to occur at the end of each quarter. This information is used to predict cash borrowing, loan payment, and cash investment needs.

The cash maintenance policy for All American Automobile Company requires a minimum balance of $15 million to be maintained at the end

---

EXHIBIT 6–10 Cash Budgets

All American Automobile Company
Cash Budget
For the year ended December 31, 19x5
(*In thousands*)

	First Quarter	Second Quarter	Third Quarter	Fourth Quarter	Year Total
Cash balance, beginning	$ 15,000	$ 15,365	$ 15,252	$ 15,462	$ 15,000
Plus cash collections on sales					
(from Exhibit 6–5)	92,500	121,560	158,730	137,406	510,196
Total available from operations	$107,500	$136,925	$173,982	$152,868	$525,196
Less budgeted disbursements:					
Manufacturing					
(from Exhibit 6–7)	$ 72,520	$ 78,670	$ 79,910	$ 67,100	$298,200
Selling (from Exhibit 6–8)	6,235	7,755	9,251	7,635	30,876
General and administrative					
(from Exhibit 6–9)	5,100	5,100	5,100	5,100	20,400
Other:					
Income taxes	14,280	15,148	16,739	9,319	55,486
Dividends	10,000	25,000	25,000	25,000	85,000
Total	−108,135	−131,673	−136,000	−114,154	−489,962
Excess (deficiency) cash					
Available over disbursements	$ (635)	$ 5,252	$ 37,982	$ 38,714	$ 35,234
Short-term financing:*					
New loans	$ 16,000	$ 10,000	—	—	$ 26,000
Repayments	—	—	$(20,000)	$ (6,000)	(26,000)
Interest	—	—	(2,520)†	(540)	(3,060)
Net cash flow from financing	16,000	10,000	(22,520)	(6,540)	(3,060)
Cash balance, ending	$ 15,365	$ 15,252	$ 15,462	$ 32,174	$ 32,174

* Short-term loans are obtained to maintain cash at a minimum balance of $15 million at all times. Accordingly, new loans required are budgeted for the beginning of the quarter and repayments are budgeted for the end of the quarter. Loan repayments are made on a first-in first-out basis and interest is paid only at the time of repayment.

† Sample interest computation for first repayment of $20,000,000 is ($16,000,000 × 9 months × 1.5 percent = $2,160,000) + ($4,000,000 × 6 months × 1.5 percent = $360,000) = $2,520,000.

of each quarter. AAA has a line of credit with a major bank, with any interest on borrowed funds computed at the rate of 18 percent per year, or 1.5 percent per month. All necessary borrowing is assumed to occur at the start of each quarter in increments of one million dollars. The cash budget presented in Exhibit 6–10 indicates that AAA will need to borrow $16 million at the beginning of the first quarter and $10 million at the beginning of the second. At the end of the third quarter, AAA will be able to repay $20 million of the loan, and the balance of $6 million will be repaid at the end of the fourth quarter.

PRO FORMA STATEMENTS

The preparation of operating budgets culminates in the preparation of *pro forma financial statements*. **Pro forma financial statements** are hypothetical statements that reflect the "as if" effects of the budgeted activities on the actual financial position of the organization. That is, the statements

---

EXHIBIT 6–11 Pro Forma Income Statement

All American Automobile Company
Pro Forma Income Statement
For the year ended December 31, 19x5
(*In thousands*)

Sales (Exhibit 6–5)			$524,400
Less variable costs			
Costs of goods sold:			
Direct materials (Exhibit 6–7)	$120,200		
Direct labor (Exhibit 6–7)	48,400		
Variable overhead (Exhibit 6–7)	24,200	$192,800	
Selling (Exhibit 6–8)		20,976	
Bad debts expense (Exhibit 6–5)		5,244	−219,020
Contribution margin			$305,380
Less fixed expenses			
Manufacturing (Exhibit 6–7)		$100,000	
Depreciation (manufacturing)		20,000	
Selling (Exhibit 6–8)		9,900	
Depreciation (selling)		200	
General and administrative (Exhibit 6–9)		20,400	
Depreciation (general and administrative)		600	−151,100
Net income from operations			$154,280
Less interest expense (Exhibit 6–10)			− 3,060
Net income before income taxes			$151,220
Less provision for estimated income taxes			− 55,486
Net income			$ 95,734

EXHIBIT 6–12   Pro Forma Balance Sheet

All American Automobile Company
Pro Forma Balance Sheet
December 31, 19x5
(*In thousands*)

Assets

Current assets:

Cash (Exhibit 6–10)	$ 32,174	
Accounts receivable (net) (Exhibit 6–5)	30,960	
Inventory, raw materials (Exhibit 6–7)	23,600	
Inventory, finished goods (1800 units)	9,800	$ 96,534

Property, plant and equipment:

Land		$ 60,000	
Buildings and equipment	$260,000		
Less accumulated depreciation	−145,600	114,400	174,400
Total assets			$270,934

Liabilities and stockholders' equity

Current liabilities:

Accounts payable (Exhibit 6–7)		$ 11,800
Stockholders' equity:		
Capital stock	$150,000	
Retained earnings	109,134	259,134
Total liabilities and stockholders' equity		$270,934

Sources of data:

1. Cash balance was obtained from the cash budget.
2. Accounts receivable represents 24 percent of the fourth quarter 19x5 sales that are expected to be collected in 19x6.
3. Raw materials inventory represents the purchases of direct materials in the fourth quarter of 19x5 that will be used in manufacturing in 19x6.
4. Finished goods inventory represents an inventory level of 20 percent of the first quarter's sales of 19x6. The inventory value at 12/31/x5 is the same as at 12/31/x4 because last-in first-out inventory valuation is used.
5. Land and buildings and equipment are the same as at the end of 19x4.
6. Accumulated depreciation is equal to the balance at the end of 19x4 increased by the 19x5 depreciation expense from the pro forma income statement.
7. The balance in accounts payable is 50 percent of the fourth quarter 19x5 purchases of direct materials.
8. Capital stock is the same as at the end of 19x4.
9. Retained earnings is equal to the balance at the end of 19x4 plus 19x5 pro forma net income, less budgeted dividends of $85 million reported in the cash budget.

reflect what the results of operations will be if all the predictions in the budget are completely correct. Such predictions have been simplified greatly by computer programs designed especially for financial planning. These models permit the user to determine immediately the impact of any assumed changes.

Exhibit 6–11 presents the pro forma income statement for the year ended December 31, 19x5 using the contribution format. If all the predictions made in the operating budget are correct, All American will produce a net income for the year of $95.7 million. Note that just about every item on the pro forma income statement comes from one of the budget schedules. The only exceptions are depreciation expense and taxes. Depreciation expense is predicted by the company's chief accountant; it is based on historical asset costs. The $55 million for estimated income taxes is provided by the company's tax department. This figure is determined on the basis of taxable income following rules established by the Internal Revenue Service. It is unlikely that taxable income will be the same as net income before income taxes.

The pro forma balance sheet, presented in Exhibit 6–12, shows the financial position of AAA at the end of 19x5, assuming all the budget predictions are correct. Sources of the pro forma balance sheet data are included as part of the exhibit.

POTENTIAL PROBLEMS OF BUDGETING

Like many other tools available to managers, budgeting offers the potential for vast benefits; however, it is not without potential pitfalls and problems. This section briefly mentions some of the more important problems that may be encountered in budgeting.

Preparation Time

A budget can be a massive task for a large company, requiring hundreds, and perhaps thousands, of hours of valuable management time. It requires careful coordination and planning to keep budget preparation from becoming too onerous for managers or from interfering with their other responsibilities. The budget preparation calendar should be carefully planned, and easy-to-use forms should be provided to minimize the time required by each manager.

Accuracy

Budgets are not infallible because the prediction ability of management is very limited in some cases. The more limited management's ability to make the accurate forecasts and predictions that are necessary for the budget, the more limited the usefulness of a single budget becomes. This is particularly true for newer businesses. Rapidly changing economic conditions also make budgeting difficult. Even then, however, managers who study the budgetary impact of possible changes can learn what factors to monitor most closely and to develop contingency plans that can be implemented if needed. Many statistical and mathematical techniques, such as those discussed in the appendix to Chapter 3, are available to improve the reliability of the budget data.

Budgetary Slack

Budgetary slack, sometimes referred to as "padding the budget," occurs when managers intentionally request more funds in the budget for their departments than they need to support the anticipated level of operations. If a department consistently produces large favorable variances — or even small favorable variances with little apparent effort — this may be a symptom of slack built into the budget. That managers feel a need to pad their budgets may indicate poor relations between upper and lower management, or poor administration of the budget.

Economy and Industry Relations

Although each organization is a unique entity whose peculiar characteristics are reflected in its operations budget, most organizations are also affected by general economic or industry conditions. Any inability to obtain accurate and reliable information about these conditions can pose serious problems for managers trying to make predictions about their own companies. For example, many organizations that depend on banks and other financial institutions for funds have found it very difficult to predict not only the cost of capital funds but also their availability.

SUMMARY

Operating budgets are an integral part of the overall planning and control system. They represent management's expectations about the events and activities scheduled to occur during a specified future period. Budgets provide the basis for evaluating actual performance and modifying subsequent plans. Budgeting offers many potential benefits for organizations, including forcing managers to look at the future of the company, improving communication, improving coordination between various departments and functions in the organization, and motivating managers to achieve organizational objectives.

The input/output approach is based on clearly defined relationships between effort and accomplishment. The incremental approach requires budget review of proposals in excess of the budgeted (or actual) expenditures for the previous period. The minimum level approach requires review of any budgeted amounts in excess of some minimum amount. The budgeting process is usually implemented on an annual schedule, although companies in certain industries find the cyclical approach more feasible. Continuous budgeting consists of adding a new time unit to the end of the budget period upon completing a unit of time.

Most manufacturing organizations prepare budgets for sales, production and manufacturing, selling expenses, general and administrative expenses, and cash. Budget preparation culminates with the presentation of pro forma financial statements reflecting the "as if" effects on the company, assuming the budget is actually carried out.

Feedback is an essential part of budgeting. Without interpretation of actual performance much of the benefit, including that of motivating people, would be lost. To receive maximum benefits from budgeting requires participation by all management levels, commitments by top management, and both positive and negative feedback.

Pitfalls of operations budgeting include placing excessive time demands on managers, expecting accurate and reliable predictions of all general economic and industry conditions, failure of top management to support the budget, poorly established organizational lines of authority and responsibility, and possible budgetary slack.

APPENDIX
NOT-FOR-PROFIT BUDGETING

In not-for-profit organizations, budgeting plays a vital role in planning and monitoring the effective and efficient use of scarce resources. In most not-for-profit organizations, the key element is budgeted revenue. It is often the primary determinant of all the expenditures in the rest of the budget. The budget is essentially a legal document for governmental units and a limiting document for nongovernmental units. Not-for-profit organizational agencies or units cannot exceed budgeted amounts until the proper authorities have approved budget amendments.

For most not-for-profit organizations the budget is the primary control element. It is through the budget process that the projected revenues and expenditures for each of the accounts are established. Two types of budgets, revenue budgets and appropriation budgets, are used by many organizations. **Revenue budgets** establish the amount expected to be collected from each revenue source during the upcoming period. **Appropriation budgets** provide the authorization for expenditures during the specified period.[1] Very seldom do the agencies or units have equal revenues and expenditures.

---

[1] An appropriation is an authorization to make expenditures and incur obligations with limitations on amount, purpose, and time period.

For example, many units of a municipality generate revenue, but others receive no revenue. The city-supported college receives revenue through student fees and contributions, whereas the city prison system receives no revenues. To make up for the deficits, the city will usually impose either income taxes, sales taxes, or property taxes, which are allocated to the different agencies that do not raise enough revenue to be self-supporting.

Once the budget is approved, it is considered the authority for expenditures of funds to carry out the goals and objectives of each organizational unit. The budgetary control accounts are then created for the coming period (see Exhibit 6–13). The parent group (a state, a religious organization, a private college) establishes the general control accounts that break the budget process into its major elements. For the Ohio Valley Children's Foundation these accounts are Contributions, Service Fees, Interest Income, Children's Home, Summer Camp, and Emergency Care.

The revenue accounts are an accounting of revenues from all sources and are used to maintain control of all revenues, much as the master budget does for a corporation. The estimated revenues are a function of the various revenue generating activities of an organizational unit. The appropriations accounts are an accounting of budgeted appropriations. The detailed appropriations accounts specify the funds allocated to the different areas of the organization.

Organizations use two types of budgeting to control the different operational units. A **lump-sum budget** is where only general areas are allocated revenues and expenditures. Appropriations for such a budget appear in Exhibit 6–13. In this budget the Children's Home was allocated $1,500,000 for the period. The other type of budget is a **line-item budget,** which assigns revenues and expenditures to specific categories and items of responsibility. This method would allocate the $1,500,000 to the Children's

---

EXHIBIT 6–13   Control Budget

Ohio Valley Children's Foundation
Budget for 19x6

Estimated revenues:		
Contributions	$1,000,000	
Service fees	600,000	
Interest income	400,000	$2,000,000
Appropriations:		
Children's Home	$1,500,000	
Summer Camp	200,000	
Emergency Care	275,000	−1,975,000
Balance to general fund		$ 25,000

EXHIBIT 6–14 Line-Item Budget

Children's Home
Ohio Valley Children's Foundation
Budget for 19x6

Estimated revenues:		
Contributions		$ 700,000
Appropriations:		
Building maintenance	$200,000	
Staff salaries and benefits	300,000	
Food and clothing	600,000	
Utilities	100,000	
Equipment	150,000	
Schooling	150,000	−1,500,000
Excess appropriations over revenues		$(800,000)
Balance from general fund		800,000
Fund balance		$

Home by major categories. A line-item budget for the Children's Home might appear as in Exhibit 6–14. Using this budget, the management of the Children's Home would be required to adhere to the appropriation limits set for each category. Most organizations resist shifting funds from one line item to another without approval of the governing body. This type of budgeting places tight control over the expenditures, but it does not attempt to measure the efficiency or effectiveness of the expenditures.

Revenue and Appropriation Budgets

Because revenues in most not-for-profit organizations come from many sources, each major source of revenue should be itemized, as in Exhibit 6–15 for the City of Dothan. For comparison purposes Exhibit 6–15 also shows the actual revenues of the prior period.

The itemization of the revenue budget allows the city to evaluate each revenue source separately. Some revenue sources are more susceptible to prediction errors than others. For example, it is much easier to predict the revenue received from property taxes than it is to predict the fees collected from exhibitors in the city park. Although not an easy task, this uncertainty must be allowed for in the budget.

Appropriation budgets show how each organizational unit is authorized to spend its resources or allocations during the budget period. The format of a given budget depends on the type of organizational unit and budget being used. The overall appropriation budget for the City of Dothan and a line-item budget for the fire department are shown in Exhibit 6–16. In this case there are only five line items.

EXHIBIT 6–15   Revenue Budgets

City of Dothan
Budgeted Revenue
Fiscal year 19x6–x7

	Actual 19x5–x6	Budget 19x6–x7
Taxes:		
Property	$2,000,000	$2,300,000
Sales	600,000	750,000
Total taxes	$2,600,000	$3,050,000
Fees and licenses:		
Business	$ 20,000	$ 25,000
Water sales	310,000	315,000
Police	32,000	40,000
Total fees and licenses	362,000	380,000
Other revenues:		
Federal and state grants	$ 150,000	$ 150,000
Investment income	25,000	30,000
Sales of equipment	10,000	25,000
Total other revenues	185,000	205,000
Total revenues budgeted	$3,147,000	$3,635,000

Appropriation budgets are the primary basis for the evaluation and control of not-for-profit organizations. Nonprofit organizations generally emphasize accountability of funds rather than efficiency of operation; therefore, each operating period is measured by the funds expended (cash payments) rather than by the matching of revenues and expenses. To ensure that budgets are adhered to, the manager of each operating unit is responsible for accepting the budget as the operating plan for the next period. Performance reports that compare actual results with the budgets are prepared to see whether the plans were carried out. The City of Dothan fire department performance report for fiscal year 19x5–x6 is also illustrated in Exhibit 6–16.

For most not-for-profit organizations, the performance report is the key means of evaluating a unit. Each item should be evaluated separately and favorable variances should receive as detailed an analysis as unfavorable variances. For example, a department could have a favorable variance for salaries simply because not enough people were employed to carry out its services. In such a situation management would be able to evaluate whether or not the services were weakened because of the lack of personnel or if, in fact, the category was overbudgeted at the beginning of the period.

EXHIBIT 6–16   Budget Relationships

City of Dothan
Appropriation Budget
Fiscal year 19x6–x7

	Actual 19x5–x6	Budget 19x6–x7
Schools	$1,300,000	$1,350,000
Police	800,000	900,000
Fire	200,000	220,000
Water	47,000	50,000
Street maintenance	500,000	600,000
Administration and courts	200,000	275,000
Parks and recreation	100,000	240,000
Totals	$3,147,000	$3,635,000

City of Dothan
Fire Protection Budget
Fiscal year 19x6–x7

	Actual 19x5–x6	Budget 19x6–x7
Salaries	$160,000	$175,000
Maintenance (equipment)	20,000	10,000
Supplies	11,000	22,000
Operating expenses	5,000	8,000
Gas and oil	4,000	5,000
Total	$200,000	$220,000

City of Dothan
Fire Protection
Performance Report
Fiscal year 19x5–x6

	Actual	Budget	Variances*
Salaries	$160,000	$162,000	$ 2,000 F
Maintenance (equipment)	20,000	9,000	11,000 U
Supplies	11,000	18,000	7,000 F
Operating expenses	5,000	5,500	500 F
Gas and oil	4,000	4,000	—
Total	$200,000	$198,500	$ 1,500 U

*F = Favorable
 U = Unfavorable

Approaches to Budget Preparation

The budgets of governmental units are authorized by law. The collection of revenues and the appropriation of expenses must conform with constitutional law and must be specifically authorized through an approved budgetary process. Once the budgets of governmental units are approved, they have binding legal authority. Rather than just being a guide to action, the budget of a governmental unit is a mandate to act. Frequently used approaches to preparing budgets in governments and other not-for-profit organizations include incremental budgeting, programming budgeting, and zero base budgeting.

Incremental budgeting, a simplistic and often used approach to budgeting in not-for-profit organizations, which was discussed earlier in the chapter, is often used where the relationships between inputs and outputs are weak or nonexistent. The input/output approach, also discussed earlier, is often difficult to use in not-for-profit organizations, thereby resulting in the popularity of incremental budgeting. As an example, the cost of police protection is not necessarily a function of the measurable output of the agency (arrests) but of the inputs (size of city, previous crime rate, and level of trained personnel).

In seeking an annual appropriation, an agency is required to justify only proposed expenditures in excess of its previous budget. Because input/output relationships are difficult to determine, this method considers only the increments from an established base. The biggest advantages of incremental budgeting are simplicity and ease of preparation. However, a major disadvantage is that current inefficiencies may continue undetected for years.

Planning, programming, and budgeting systems (PPBS) emphasize outputs of an organization in programmed areas rather than inputs. A program is a specific activity or set of activities established to achieve a desired objective, such as fire protection. PPBS is based on three control ideas: (1) It is a formal planning system, (2) it uses a program budget, and (3) it emphasizes cost-benefit analysis. PPBS requires a careful specification and analysis of program objectives for each area or agency as a first step. Next, the process analyzes, insofar as possible, the output of a program in terms of its objectives. The third step is to measure the total costs of the program for several periods into the future. Next, the concept analyzes alternatives and seeks those that have the greatest benefits as related to the stated objectives. The last step is the systematic implementation of the selected alternatives.

PPBS emphasizes control through responsibility accounting. The key to successful PPBS is forcing agencies to back away from their current operations and to evaluate their overall objectives. Through such evaluations each agency head accepts the responsibility of current and planned activities and must account for the results. Unfortunately, PPBS has not been well received in recent years because of its difficulty in implementation. All managers involved in the process must be familiar with it, and its implementation is very time consuming.

Zero base budgeting begins with the premise that every dollar of a budgeted expenditure must be justified, including current expenditures that are to be continued. Incremental budgeting starts with the current level of expenditures and requires justification only for any proposed increases. Unlike incremental budgeting, which usually allows account increase differentiation but often requires spending cuts across the board, zero base budgeting permits each program to receive any allocations that can be justified and supported.

Zero base budgeting, as a planning tool, forces management to identify the activities that each agency or department engages in, to evaluate these activities, and to rank them in order of priority. The availability of funds will determine how many of the activities will be implemented.

The zero base budgeting approach often assumes that decision makers have the capacity to eliminate programs. However, the political forces in any jurisdiction are such that few programs, if any, can be eliminated in any given year. For this reason zero base budgeting may be better applied to selected programs than to entire organizations. Proposals for zero base budgeting for the federal government would have program review only once every four or five years, with all programs of a given agency or department reviewed in the same year.[2]

The basic steps in zero base budgeting are (1) development of decision packages consisting of departmental or agency activities, (2) evaluation of each decision package, (3) ranking of decision packages, (4) compilation of acceptable decision packages into the budget, and (5) monitoring, control, and follow-up.

A **decision package** identifies each activity or department or agency. Decision packages may relate to goods, services, geographic areas, capital projects, or any other activity that relates to the organization's goals and objectives. Each decision package must be complete and able to stand alone, and it must include all direct costs and the cost of support activities. The budget of a city library could be defined as a decision package.

Decision packages should include an evaluation of what the organization is getting for each proposed expenditure and an identification of the cost and benefit relationships. The effects of different spending levels on costs and benefits should also be determined. Because cost and benefit relationships are not always linear, significant increases in total benefits may be accomplished by small increases in total costs. By comparing the incremental effect of additional expenditures on different programs, deci-

---

[2] Joel Havemann, "Congress Tries to Break Ground Zero in Evaluating Federal Programs," *National Journal,* Volume 8, 1976, p. 708.

sion makers are better able to determine the optimal funding level. For the city library the cost of adding video packages would have to be evaluated against the increased service to the public and the public's acceptance of the new service.

Starting at the lowest decision level in the organization, decision packages are ranked and reranked until some upper level of management establishes a final order of priority. For example, the library director ranked the new video packages as the top priority for the coming year, the city budget review committee ranked it in the top 20 percent of the new requests, and the city council placed it in the middle of all new budgetary needs. Starting with the highest ranked package, the organization approves decision packages as long as uncommitted funds exist. The rankings are made on a variety of economic, social, bureaucratic, and political criteria. The funds available will determine the number of decision packages accepted; generally, they are accepted in descending order. Therefore, any reduction in funds should result in dropping only the marginal decision packages.

Budgeting Problems

Like for-profit organizations, not-for-profit organizations have used budgeting for many years. The emphasis on formalized budgeting programs in government began long before that of most businesses. Although the benefit of experience has been a positive influence, there have also been some negative effects. Because many not-for-profit organizations have used budgeting for compliance rather than for coordinating and planning, many negative attitudes toward budgeting have developed.

For governments a budget is an authorization to spend that is founded in law. If an unusual occurrence causes activities to increase, the funding may be inadequate, but if the activities fall below planned levels, there will likely be an abundance of funds. For a given period the not-for-profit budget usually does not change. Another detrimental effect of the static (nonflexible) budget of not-for-profit organizations is that when a program does not spend all its budgeted funds, it may receive a smaller appropriation the following year. The fear of this sends many managers into a spending frenzy at the end of the fiscal year, which usually results in wasted resources.

The inability of managers to obtain additional resources as their activities increase also has a negative effect. Because their agencies are funded for a definite period, usually one year, additional resources are usually unavailable. Managers often build slack into their budget, preparing their requests for all possible situations. These budget manipulations destroy confidence in the process and create situations where managers falsify inputs to ensure proper operations of their departments.

From these negative experiences two improvements can be suggested. First, organizations can strive to maintain flexible budgets where resources are related directly to activities. Second, organizations should commit their objectives to writing. Planning and control can be facilitated by the establishment of specific objectives, with funds appropriated on the basis of these objectives.

In not-for-profit organizations the revenue budget strongly influences the quantity and quality of services and programs. However, it should be remembered that revenue is not a goal in itself; it merely provides the means of operating the various programs and services that are desired. The appropriations budget is the organization's plan for using the resources that it has available. Revenue and appropriations budgets should be prepared in sufficient detail to provide control over the activities of not-for-profit organizations.

The budget plays a critical role in not-for-profit organizations because it represents approval for expenditures at each operating level. It is also a critical tool for management accounting. Traditional budgeting has focused on input and accountability, but recent advances in management accounting in not-for-profit organizations include the program budget and zero base budgeting. Management is provided with a structure that establishes priorities and allows allocation of resources based on priorities. Zero base budgeting has application in most areas of the not-for-profit sector. If possible, unit evaluations should also consider both efficiency and effective measures.

KEY TERMS

Operating budget

Incremental approach

Participation budget

Bottom-up approach

Cycle budgeting

Operating activities

Production budget

Selling expense budget

Pro forma financial statements

Input/output approach

Minimum level approach

Imposed budget

Top-down approach

Budget committee

Continuous budgeting

Sales budget

Manufacturing budget

General and administrative expense budget

Cash budget

Budgetary slack

APPENDIX KEY TERMS

Revenue budget

Appropriations budget

Lump-sum budget

Line-item budget

PPBS

Zero base budgeting

Decision package

**REVIEW
QUESTIONS**

6–1   What is the relationship between budgeting and planning and control?

6–2   Does budgeting require formal planning? Identify and briefly describe three budget planning concepts.

6–3   Identify the types of organizations or situations the incremental approach to budgeting is best suited for.

6–4   Identify the advantages and disadvantages of the incremental approach to budgeting.

6–5   Discuss the three bases used for performance evaluation.

6–6   Why should motivational considerations be a part of budget planning and utilization?

6–7   Contrast the top-down and bottom-up approaches to budget preparation.

6–8   What is the role of the budget committee? Who should be on the budget committee?

6–9   Why are annual budgets not always desirable? What are some alternative budget periods?

6–10   Explain how continuous budgeting works.

6–11   Which budget brings together all other budgets? How is this accomplished?

6–12   What are pro forma statements?

6–13   Why is prediction ability important to budgeting?

6–14   Is budgetary slack a desirable feature? Can it be prevented?

EXERCISES

**6–1 Production
Budget**

Western Jeans Company is now in the process of preparing a production budget for the first quarter. The company's sales forecast for the next four months is as follows:

Month	Unit Sales	Month	Unit Sales
January	50,000	March	58,000
February	60,000	April	70,000

End-of-month inventory levels must equal 15 percent of the following month's sales. The inventory at the end of December was 10,000 units.

Required: How many units must be produced during each month of the first quarter? Include a summary for the entire quarter.

6–2 Cash Budget

Jackson Hardware Company is planning a cash budget for the next three months. Estimated sales revenue is as follows:

Month	Sales Revenue	Month	Sales Revenue
January	$200,000	March	$125,000
February	150,000	April	140,000

All sales are on credit. Forty percent of the sales are collected during the month of sale, and 60 percent are collected during the next month.

Cost of goods sold is 70 percent of sales. Payments for merchandise sold are made in the month following the month of sale. Operating expenses to be paid amount to $41,000 each month and are paid during the month incurred.

Required: Prepare monthly cash budgets for February, March, and April.

6–3 Sales Budget

Florida Sand Company sells three products. The seasonal sales pattern for 19x6 is as follows:

	Products		
Quarter	Gravel	Limestone	Sand
1	10%	25%	20%
2	20	25	30
3	30	25	40
4	40	25	10
	100%	100%	100%

The annual sales budget shows forecasts of: Gravel, 150,000 tons; Limestone, 120,000 tons; and Sand, 180,000 tons. Next year's selling prices per ton will be: Gravel, $10; Limestone, $5; and Sand, $9.

Required: Prepare a sales budget by quarters for the company for the coming year.

6–4 Budgeted Items

Ohio Products Company has a sales budget for next year of $16,000,000. Cost of goods sold is expected to be 65 percent of sales. The beginning inventory of merchandise is $750,000. Ending inventory is budgeted at $900,000. All goods are purchased on account and paid for in the next month. Beginning accounts payable are $750,000. Ending accounts payable should be equal to one month's average purchases.

Requirements

Compute the following budgeted amounts for the year:

a) Cost of goods sold.

b) Purchases.

c) Ending accounts payable. (Round answer to the nearest dollar.)

d) Cash needed to pay accounts payable.

6–5 Cash Receipts Budget

The sales budget for Roses and Flowers, Inc. is forecasted as follows:

Month	Sales Revenue	Month	Sales Revenue
May	$55,000	July	$90,000
June	75,000	August	80,000

In order to prepare a cash budget, the company must determine the budgeted cash collections from sales. Historically, the following trend has been established regarding cash collection of sales:

60 percent in month of sale,
20 percent in month following sale,
15 percent in second month following sale,
 5 percent uncollectible.

The company gives a 2 percent cash discount for payments made by customers during the month of sale. The accounts receivable balance on April 30 is $24,000, of which $7000 represents uncollected March sales, and $17,000 represents uncollected April sales.

Required: Prepare a schedule showing the budgeted cash collections from sales for May, June, and July. Include a three-month summary of estimated cash collections.

6–6 Job Product Cash Budget

Little Red Wagon Company has a contract to manufacture 200 wagons at a unit price of $1000 each. The customer agrees to pay 50 percent of the contract upon delivery in November and the balance in December.

Production will take place in October. Materials for the contract are estimated to cost $65,000 and will be delivered and paid for in the month preceding the month of production. Other costs are estimated at $80,000 and will be incurred during the month of production. These costs include depreciation of plant and equipment of $20,000. The other costs will be paid during the month of production.

Required: For each month (September through December), determine the cash receipts and disbursements relating to the contract.

6–7 Cash Budget

Boston Tea Company began July with a cash balance of $142,000. A cash receipts and payment budget for each six-month period is prepared in advance. Sales have been estimated as follows:

Month	Sales Revenue	Month	Sales Revenue
May	$120,000	September	$ 80,000
June	140,000	October	100,000
July	80,000	November	100,000
August	60,000	December	120,000

All sales are on credit with 75 percent collected during the month of sale, 20 percent collected during the next month, and 5 percent collected during the second month following the month of sale.

Cost of goods sold averages 70 percent of sales revenue. Ending inventory is one half of the next month's predicted cost of sales. The other half of the merchandise is acquired during the month of sale. All purchases are paid for in the month after purchase.

Operating costs are estimated at $18,000 each month and are paid for during the month incurred.

Required: Prepare monthly cash budgets for six months from July to December.

6–8 Purchases Budget in Dollars

Cotton Shirt Company, a merchandising firm, has the following sales budget for the first four months of next year.

Month	Sales Revenue	Month	Sales Revenue
January	$100,000	March	$105,000
February	110,000	April	120,000

Cost of sales averages $6 for each shirt. The average sales price is $10. One half of estimated sales for the next month are maintained in inventory merchandise if possible. The finished goods inventory on January 1 was $30,000.

Required: Compute budgeted purchases for January, February, and March.

6–9 Cash Receipts Budget

Chicago Metal Company is currently estimating cash receipts for the next six months. The accounts receivable balance is to be estimated at the end of each month also. Cash sales are estimated at 10 percent of sales for the month. The balance of sales should be collected as follows:

50 percent during the month of sale,
40 percent during the following month,
10 percent during the second month following month of sale.

The accounts receivable balance at April 1 was $110,000. Budgeted and actual sales are as follows:

Month	Sales Revenue	Month	Sales Revenue
January	$200,000	April	$150,000
February	190,000	May	180,000
March	170,000	June	200,000

Required: Prepare a cash collections budget for each month of the second quarter. Determine the estimated balance of accounts receivable at the end of each month.

6–10 Pro Forma Income Statement

Big Burger Drive-in is planning a budget for the next fiscal year. Sales revenue has been estimated at $1,000,000. The cost of goods sold has been estimated at 70 percent of sales revenue. Depreciation on the office building and fixtures is budgeted at $50,000. Salaries and wages should amount to 15 percent of sales revenue. Advertising has been budgeted at $75,000, and utilities should amount to $20,000. Income tax is estimated at 40 percent of operating income.

Required: Prepare a pro forma income statement for the next fiscal year.

6–11 Cash Disbursements Budget

Oregon Timber Company is in the process of preparing its budget for next year. Cost of goods sold has been estimated at 70 percent of sales, and payments on lumber purchases are to be made during the month preceding the month of sale. Wages are estimated at 15 percent of sales and are paid during the month of sale. Other operating costs amounting to 10 percent of sales are to be paid in the month following the month of sale. Additionally, a monthly lease payment of $10,000 is paid to BMI for computer services. Sales revenue is forecast as follows:

Month	Sales Revenue	Month	Sales Revenue
February	$100,000	May	210,000
March	160,000	June	180,000
April	180,000	July	230,000

Required: Prepare cash disbursements budgets for April, May, and June.

6–12 Purchases Budget

Budgeted sales of The Record Shop for the first six months of 19x3 are as follows:

Month	Unit Sales	Month	Unit Sales
January	120,000	April	210,000
February	160,000	May	180,000
March	200,000	June	240,000

Beginning inventory for 19x3 is 40,000 units. The budgeted inventory at the end of a month is 40 percent of units to be sold the following month. Purchase price per unit is $3.

Required: Prepare a purchases budget in units and dollars for each month, January through May.

6–13 Profit Planning   The goals of the Evergreen Tree Company for the coming winter quarter are as follows:

Increase in sales	15%
Increase in net income	25%
Income-to-sales ratio	10%
Income-to-owners' equity ratio	15%

Results for the current quarter and budgeted figures for winter quarter are as follows:

	Current Quarter	Winter Quarter Budget
Sales	$50,000	$54,000
Cost of sales	27,000	30,000
Net income	3,500	5,050
Owners' equity	22,000	24,000

Required: Analyze the individual budget figures in terms of the corresponding goal.

6–14 Purchases Budget in Units and Dollars   Unit sales estimates for Snow King Plow Company for next year are as follows:

Month	Units Sales	Month	Units Sales
January	45,000	March	90,000
February	60,000	April	93,000

There were 10,000 units of finished goods in inventory at the beginning of January. Plans are to have an inventory of finished product equal to one third of the sales for the next month.

Four hundred pounds of materials are required for each unit produced. Each pound of material costs $10. Inventory levels for materials are to be equal to one fourth of the needs for the next month. Materials inventory on January 1 was 5.5 million pounds.

Requirements

a) Prepare production budgets for January, February, and March.

b) Prepare a purchases budget in pounds and dollars for January and February.

6–15 Labor Budget

Teddy Bear Toy Company is preparing a labor cost budget. Each employee is paid a regular rate of $10 per hour and receives an overtime rate equal to 1.5 times the regular rate. The company has estimated that vacation pay is equal to $1 for each regular hour of work and that other fringe benefits, such as medical plans, pensions, and sick leave are equal to $2 per regular hour worked. The labor hour budget for the third quarter is as follows:

	Regular	Overtime	Total
July	8800	700	9500
August	8200	600	8800
September	8400	500	8900

Required: Compute the total labor cost per month including fringe benefits.

6–16 Manufacturing Budget

Lexington Marble Company's product budget for the first two months of next year is as follows:

	January	February	Total
Units to be manufactured	90,000	80,000	170,000

Direct materials purchases will be $480,000. Direct materials of $275,000 will be used for production during January, and $250,000 will be used during February. Labor is paid at the rate of $10 per hour, and two hours are needed for the production of each unit. Variable factory overhead is $3 per direct labor hour. The fixed factory overhead is applied at a rate of $5 per unit of product on the basis of a standard production of 90,000 units per month.

Required: Prepare manufacturing cost budgets for January and February.

6–17 General Budget (Appendix)

The City of Taylorsville has budgeted the following general fund revenues and appropriations for the 19x3 fiscal year.

Revenue forecasts:	
Property taxes	$400,000
Sales taxes	100,000
Income taxes	220,000
State revenue sharing	70,000
Appropriations:	
Police protection	$300,000
Fire protection	180,000
Public works	90,000
Administration	125,000
Health and welfare	100,000

Requirements

a) Set up a revenue and appropriation budget for 19x3.

b) Is this a lump-sum or line-item budget? Explain.

6–18 General Budget (Appendix)

The Clayton Research Foundation has established the following revenue and appropriation budgets for 19x1.

Revenues:	
Donations	$700,000
Interest and dividends	250,000
Federal grants	620,000
Appropriations:	
Administration	$110,000
Research and development	980,000
Lab equipment	470,000

Requirements

a) Set up a revenue and appropriation budget for 19x1.

b) What happens if projected revenues do not equal appropriations?

6–19 General Budget (Appendix)

From the list of general accounts below, prepare a budget for the City of Plitchard for June 30, 19x0.

Revenues (utilities)	$189,000	Revenues (taxes)	$430,000
Maintenance	421,000	Salaries	400,000
Autos, police	14,000	Notes payable	100,000
Equipment	15,000	Library expenses	2,000

6–20 General Budget (Appendix)

The following accounts are from the general fund of the St. Louis General Hospital for October, 19x4.

Cash	$100,000	Investments	$500,000
Taxes receivable	80,000	Accounts payable	86,000
Food preparation	44,000	Maintenance	41,000
Nursing services	781,000	Cafeteria revenue	15,000
Security costs	6,000	Patient charges	837,000
Supplies	41,000	Notes payable	400,000

Required: Prepare a revenue and appropriation budget for October, 19x4.

**6–21 Cash Budget
(Appendix)**

Tulsa Water Service had the following sales of water for selected months of 19x8.

Month	Sales Revenue	Month	Sales Revenue
February	$120,000	May	$150,000
March	130,000	June	170,000
April	140,000	July	190,000

All sales are on credit. Historically, 60 percent is collected in the month of sale, 30 percent during the first month following sale, and 10 percent in the second month following sale.

Cost of water averages 70 percent of sales revenue. Ending inventory is estimated at 5 percent of the next month's sales. All purchases are paid during the month following purchase.

Operating costs of $20,000 are paid each month.

Required: Prepare a cash budget for the months of April, May, and June.

PROBLEMS

**6–22 Inventory and
Purchases
Budgets**

The Midwest Belt Company sells men's and boys' belts that are cut to order. Each foot or fraction thereof sells for $2.00. Small belts average two feet, and large belts average three feet in length. The leather is purchased from a local tannery for 90 cents per foot. The buckles are purchased at $2.00 for the small size and $2.50 for the large size. No changes are expected in any of the purchasing and selling prices.

Sales should increase 20 percent this year over last year. Last year the company sold 300 small belts and 140 large belts during January and February. The inventories are as follows:

December 31 Actual		February 28 Target	
Leather (feet)	900	Leather (feet)	800
Small buckles	200	Small buckles	200
Large buckles	300	Large buckles	250

Purchases are made to provide sufficient stock for each two-month period.

Requirements

a) Compute total belts, buckles, and leather needed for January and February.

b) Compute the budgeted materials costs of small belts for January and February.

c) Compute budgeted materials costs of large belts for January and February.

6–23 Cash Budget

The Mobile Supply Company sells one product that is purchased for $20 and sold for $30. Budgeted sales in total dollars for next year are $720,000. The sales information needed for preparing the July budget is as follows:

Month	Sales Revenue	Month	Sales Revenue
May	$30,000	July	$48,000
June	40,000	August	60,000

Account balances at July 1 include:

Cash	$15,000
Merchandise inventory	16,000
Accounts receivable (sales)	30,000
Accounts payable (purchases)	20,000

The company pays for one half of its purchases in the month of purchase, and the remainder in the following month. End-of-month inventory must be 50 percent of the budgeted sales in units for the next month.

A 2 percent cash discount on sales is allowed if payment is made during the month of sale. Experience indicates that 50 percent of the billings will be collected during the month of sale, 40 percent in the following month, 8 percent in the next following month, and 2 percent will be uncollectible.

Total budgeted selling and administrative expenses (excluding bad debts) for the fiscal year are estimated at $186,000, of which half is fixed expense (inclusive of a $20,000 annual depreciation charge). Fixed expenses are incurred evenly during the year. The other selling and administrative expenses vary with sales. Expenses are paid during the month incurred.

Requirements

a) Prepare a schedule of estimated cash collections of accounts receivable for July.

b) Prepare a schedule of estimated cash payments for merchandise and payables for July. (Round calculations to the nearest dollar.)

c) Prepare a schedule of selling and administrative expenses, including estimated cash payments, for July.

d) Prepare a cash budget in summary form using the above information.

6–24 Materials Budget

Topper Toys makes plastic riding tractors that require 3 pounds of material. The company wants raw materials on hand at the beginning of each month equal to one half of the month's production needs. This requirement was met on April 1, the start of the second quarter. There are no work-in-process inventories. A sales budget in units for the next four months is given below.

Month	Unit Sales	Month	Unit Sales
April	15,000	June	24,000
May	18,000	July	26,000

Finished goods inventory at the end of each month must be equal to 40 percent of the next month's sales. On March 31 the finished goods inventory totaled 7500 units.

Requirements

a) Prepare a production budget for April, May, and June.

b) Prepare a purchases budget for April and May.

6–25 Purchases Budget

Crown Candy Company manufactures various products to sell to retail stores. A sales budget for pecan turtles for the next several months is shown below.

Month	Budgeted Units in Boxes
June	20,000
July	24,000
August	30,000
September	36,000
October	40,000

There is no inventory of turtles on hand at June 1. During the summer the company desires an ending inventory of 10 percent of the following month's sales. The raw materials must be purchased one month before they are needed in production. The June 1 raw materials inventory meets these requirements.

Pecan turtles require direct materials as follows:

	Pounds of Materials per Box of Product
Caramel	3
Pecans	2
Chocolate	5

Required: Prepare a purchases budget in pounds of each ingredient for June and July.

6–26 Pro Forma Income Statement

Pendleton Company, a merchandising company, is developing its master budget for 19x2. The income statement for 19x1 is as follows:

Pendleton Company Income Statement For the year ending December 31, 19x1	
Gross sales	$750,000
Less estimated uncollectible accounts	− 7,500
Net sales	$742,500
Cost of goods sold	−430,000
Gross profit	$312,500
Operating expenses (including $25,000 depreciation)	−200,500
Net income	$112,000

The following are management's goals and forecasts for 19x2.

1. Selling prices will increase by 8 percent, and sales volume will increase by 5 percent.
2. The cost of merchandise will increase by 4 percent.
3. All operating expenses are fixed and are paid in the month incurred. Price increases for operating expenses will be 10 percent.
4. The estimated uncollectibles are 1 percent of budgeted sales.

Required: Prepare a budgeted income statement for 19x2.

6–27 Pro Forma Statements

Madison Butter Sales Company is preparing a budget for January and February of next year. The balance sheet as of December 31, 19x1 is given below.

Madison Butter Sales Company Balance Sheet December 31, 19x1			
Assets		*Equities*	
Cash	$100,000	Accounts payable	$125,000
Accounts receivable	60,000	Operating expenses payable	30,000
Inventory	30,000	Miscellaneous payable	20,000
Equipment leasehold	60,000	Capital stock	25,000
		Retained earnings	50,000
Total assets	$250,000	Total equities	$250,000

Monthly sales data for the current year and the budgeted data for next year are as follows:

November 19x1	$180,000	February 19x2	$250,000
December 19x1	200,000	March 19x2	260,000
January 19x2	240,000	April 19x2	280,000

Forty percent of the sales revenue is collected during the month of sale, with the balance collected during the following month.

Cost of goods sold is 60 percent of sales. Merchandise inventory equal to 20 percent of next month's sales is to be maintained at the end of each month. All butter purchased for resale is paid for in the month following the month of purchase.

Operating expenses for each month are estimated at 10 percent of sales revenue. All operating expenses are paid during the following month.

Income taxes are estimated at 40 percent of income before taxes. Income taxes are paid fifteen days after the end of the quarter. There were no taxes payable on December 31. The miscellaneous payables at December 31, 19x1 are to be paid during January of 19x2.

Requirements

a) Prepare a budgeted income statement for the quarter ending March 31, 19x2. Do not prepare monthly statements.

b) Prepare a pro forma balance sheet as of March 31, 19x2.

6–28 Cash Budget

Cash budgeting of Kentucky Fried Fish is done on a quarterly basis. The company is planning its cash needs for the third quarter of 19x1 and the following information is available to assist in preparing a cash budget.

Budgeted income statements for July through October 19x1 are as follows:

	July	August	September	October
Sales	$18,000	$24,000	$28,000	$36,000
Cost of goods sold	−10,000	−14,000	−16,000	−20,000
Gross profit	$ 8,000	$10,000	$12,000	$16,000
Less other expenses:				
Selling	$ 2,300	$ 3,000	$ 3,400	$ 4,200
Administrative	2,600	3,000	3,200	3,600
Total	− 4,900	− 6,000	− 6,600	− 7,800
Net income	$ 3,100	$ 4,000	$ 5,400	$ 8,200

Additional information:

1. Other expenses, which are paid monthly, include $1000 a month of depreciation.

2. Sales are 20 percent for cash and 80 percent on credit.

3. Credit sales are collected 20 percent in the month of sale, 70 percent one month after sale, and 10 percent two months after sale.

4. March sales were $15,000, and June sales were $16,000. Merchandise is paid for 50 percent in the month of purchase. The remaining 50 percent is paid in the following month. Accounts payable for merchandise at June 30 totaled $6000.

5. The company maintains its ending inventory levels at 25 percent of the cost of goods to be sold in the following month. The inventory at June 30 is $2500.

6. An equipment note of $5000 per month is being paid through August.

7. The company must maintain a cash balance of at least $5000 at the end of each month. The cash balance on June 30 is $5100.

8. The company can borrow from its bank as needed. Borrowings must be in multiples of $100. All borrowings take place at the beginning of a month, and all repayments are made at the end of a month. At the time the principal is repaid, interest is also paid on the portion of the principal repaid. The interest rate is 12 percent per annum.

Requirements

a) Prepare a monthly schedule of budgeted operating cash receipts for July, August, and September.

b) Prepare a monthly schedule of budgeted cash payments for purchases for July, August, and September.

c) Prepare a monthly cash budget for July, August, and September. Show borrowings from the company's bank and repayments to the bank as needed to maintain the minimum cash balance.

6–29 Budgets

The Peyton Department Store prepares budgets quarterly. The following information is available for use in planning the second quarter budgets for 19x1.

Peyton Department Stores
Balance Sheet
March 31, 19x1

Assets		Equities	
Cash	$ 3,000	Accounts payable	$26,000
Accounts receivable	25,000	Dividends payable	17,000
Inventory	30,000	Rent payable	2,000
Prepaid insurance	2,000	Stockholders' equity	40,000
Fixtures	25,000		
Total assets	$85,000	Total equities	$85,000

Actual and forecasted monthly sales for the coming months in 19x1 are as follows:

Month	Sales Revenue	Month	Sales Revenue
January	$60,000	May	$60,000
February	50,000	June	70,000
March	40,000	July	90,000
April	50,000	August	80,000

Monthly operating expenses are as follows:

Wages and salaries	$25,000
Depreciation	100
Utilities	1,000
Rent	2,000

Cash dividends of $17,000 are paid during the first month of each quarter and declared during the third month of each quarter for the next quarter. Operating expenses are paid as incurred, except insurance, rent, and depreciation. Rent is paid during the following month. The prepaid insurance is for five more months. Cost of goods sold is equal to one half of sales.

Inventories equal 120 percent of the next month's sales. Purchases during any given month are paid in full during the following month. All sales are on account, with 50 percent collected during the month of sale, 40 percent during the next month, and 10 percent during the month thereafter.

Money can be borrowed and repaid in multiples of $1000 at an interest rate of 12 percent per annum. The company desires a minimum cash balance of $3000 at the first of each month. At the time the principal is repaid, interest is paid on the portion of principal that is repaid. All borrowing is at the start of the month, and all repayment is at the end of the month. Money is never repaid at the end of the month it is borrowed.

Requirements

a) Prepare a purchases budget for each month of the quarter ending June 30, 19x1.

b) Prepare a cash receipts schedule for each month of the quarter ending June 30, 19x1. Do not include borrowings.

c) Prepare a cash disbursements schedule for each month of the second quarter ending June 30, 19x1. Do not include repayments of borrowings.

d) Prepare a cash budget for each month of the quarter ending June 30, 19x1.

e) Prepare an income statement for each month of the quarter ending June 30, 19x1.

f) Prepare a pro forma balance sheet as of June 30, 19x1.

6–30 Production Budget

The sales of Richmond Paint Company are expected to be 200,000 gallons of paint during the second quarter of 19x1. The sales budget calls for a selling price of $15 per gallon. Finished goods inventory at the end of the second quarter is planned to be 16,000 gallons. There is no beginning inventory.

Only two minutes of direct labor time are required to produce each gallon. The direct labor rate is $10 per hour. Two different raw materials ingredients go into each gallon. Liquid L costs $1 per quart, and three quarts are used per gallon. Powder P costs $3 per pound, and two pounds are used per gallon. The following inventory levels are planned for the second quarter.

	Beginning	Ending
Material L	80,000 quarts	60,000 quarts
Material P	45,000 pounds	60,000 pounds

Other variable costs include manufacturing overhead of 25 cents per gallon, and selling and administrative expenses of 20 cents per gallon. Fixed manufacturing overhead is $100,000, and fixed selling and administrative expenses are $50,000.

Requirements

a) Prepare a production budget for Richmond Paint for the second quarter.

b) Prepare a raw materials purchases budget for both Liquid L and Powder P for the second quarter. Show both units and dollars.

6–31 Production Budget with Inventory Reorder Points and Lead Times[3]

The Press Company manufactures and sells industrial components. The Whitmore Plant is responsible for producing two components referred to as AD-5 and FX-3. Plastic, brass, and aluminum are used in the production of these two products.

Press Company has adopted a thirteen-period reporting cycle in all its plants for budgeting purposes. Each period is four weeks long and has 20 working days. The projected inventory levels for AD-5 and FX-3 at the end of the current (seventh) period and the projected sales for these two products for the next three four-week periods are presented below:

---

[3] This problem assumes the student has a basic familiarity with inventory models.

Projected Inventory Level (*in units*)		Projected Sales (*in units*)		
End of Seventh Period		Eighth Period	Ninth Period	Tenth Period
AD-5	3000	7500	8750	9500
FX-3	2800	7000	4500	4000

Past experience has shown that adequate inventory levels for AD-5 and FX-3 can be maintained if 40 percent of the next period's projected sales are on hand at the end of a reporting period. Based on this experience and the projected sales, the Whitmore Plant has budgeted production of 8000 units of AD-5 and 6000 units of FX-3 in the eighth period. Production is assumed to be uniform for both products within each four-week period.

The raw materials specifications for AD-5 and FX-3 are as follows:

	AD-5	FX-3
Plastic	2.0 lb.	1.0 lb.
Brass	0.5 lb.	—
Aluminum	—	1.5 lb.

Data relating to the purchase of raw materials are presented below.

	Purchase Price (*per lb.*)	Standard Purchase Lot (*in lb.*)	Reorder Point (*in lb.*)	Projected Inventory Status at the End of the Seventh Period (*in lb.*)		Lead Time in Working Days
				on Hand	on Order	
Plastic	$0.40	15,000	12,000	16,000	15,000	10
Brass	0.95	5,000	7,500	9,000	—	30
Aluminum	0.55	10,000	10,000	14,000	10,000	20

The sales of AD-5 and FX-3 do not vary significantly from month to month. Consequently, the safety stock incorporated into the reorder point for each of the raw materials is adequate to compensate for variations in the sales of the finished products.

Raw materials orders are placed the day the quantity on hand falls below the reorder point. Whitmore Plant's suppliers are very dependable so that the given lead times are reliable. The outstanding orders for plastic and aluminum are due to arrive on the tenth and fourth working days of the eighth period, respectively. Payments for all raw materials orders are remitted in the month of delivery.

Requirements

The Whitmore Plant is required to submit a report to corporate headquarters of Press Company summarizing the projected raw material activities before each period commences. The data for the eighth-period report are being assembled. Determine the following items for plastic, brass, and aluminum for inclusion in the eighth-period report:

a) Projected quantities (in pounds) of each raw material to be issued to production.

b) Projected quantities (in pounds) of each raw material ordered and the date (in terms of working days) the order is to be placed.

c) The projected inventory balance (in pounds) of each raw material at the end of the period.

d) The payments for purchases of each raw material.

(CMA Adapted)

6–32 Reporting (Appendix)

Washington County makes the following public report on July 31 of each year for its educational program.

Washington County Annual Report Education Program July 31, 19x4		
	Budget	*Actual*
Revenues (all sources)	$4,500,000	$4,400,000
Expenditures:		
Salaries	2,250,000	2,270,000
Maintenance	600,000	700,000
Other	1,650,000	1,580,000

Notes to report:

1. Revenues were lower than expected.

2. Teachers did not get a pay raise.

3. Twelve new buses were purchased.

Requirements

a) As a commissioner of Washington County, what additional information would you want in the body of the financial report?

b) What management accounting information could be furnished?

c) How could the notes section be improved?

6–33 Financial Statement (Appendix)

The City of Naples conducts all its activities through a general fund account. At the beginning of the 19x1 fiscal year the town's assets consisted of cash, $12,000; city hall, $132,000; city park, $19,500; and equipment, $68,000.

At the beginning of the year the town council approved the following line-item budget.

Budgeted revenues:	Taxes, $75,000; other revenues, $28,600
Appropriations:	Salaries, $56,000; supplies, $2000; equipment, $3000; contractual services, $14,000; miscellaneous, $2000

Actual transactions for the year were as follows:

Revenues:	Taxes, $80,000; other revenues, $25,000
Expenditures:	Salaries, $55,500; supplies, $1400; equipment, $3000; contractual services, $14,000; miscellaneous, $1500

Requirements

a) Prepare a budget statement of revenues and expenditures for the fiscal year ending October 31, 19x1 for the general fund of Naples.

b) Prepare a performance report for the year ended October 31, 19x1.

c) One citizen group complained that the cut in expenditures hurt the town park; another group complained that not enough was spent on streets. In preparing the next budget, what could you do to be more responsive to citizen groups?

6–34 Budget by Function (Appendix)

The city of Flowershine prepares functional budgets based on the estimated needs of its managers. These are limited by the general budget, which is approved by the city council.

For 19x5 the council approved the following line-item general budget.

Salaries and wages	$ 800,000
Supplies	100,000
Repairs and parts	212,000
Capital expenditures (buildings)	400,000
Equipment purchases	170,000
General and miscellaneous	62,000
Total	$1,744,000

This budget is then allocated to the service functions based on a program evaluation of services. For 19x5 the needs are as follows:

	Utilities	Fire Protection	Police Protection	Welfare	Administration
Salaries and wages	10%	20%	30%	15%	25%
Supplies	40	15	20	10	15
Repairs and parts	20	30	40	5	5
Capital expenditures	50	5	10	5	30
Equipment purchases	30	35	20	5	10
General and miscellaneous	15	20	20	25	20

Required: Prepare a budget for each fund.

6-35 Budget Preparation (Appendix)

The Board of Education of the Victoria School District is developing a budget for the school year ending June 30, 19x1. The budgeted expenditures follow.

Victoria School District
Budgeted Expenditures
For the year ending June 30, 19x1

Current operating expenditures:			
Instruction:			
General	$1,401,600		
Vocational training	112,000	$1,513,600	
Pupil service:			
Bus transportation	$ 36,300		
School lunches	51,700	88,000	
Attendance and health service		14,000	
Administration		46,000	
Operation and maintenance of plant		208,000	
Pensions, insurance, etc.		154,000	
Total current operating expenditures			$2,023,600
Other expenditures:			
Capital outlays from revenues		$ 75,000	
Debt service (annual installment and interest on long-term debt)		150,000	
Total other expenditures			225,000
Total budgeted expenditures			$2,248,600

The following data are available.

1. The estimated average daily school enrollment of the school district is 5000 pupils, including 200 pupils enrolled in a vocational training program.

2. Estimated revenues include equalizing grants-in-aid from the state of $150 per pupil. The grants were established by state law under a plan intended to encourage raising the level of education.

3. The federal government matches 60 percent of state grants-in-aid for pupils enrolled in a vocational training program. In addition, the federal government contributes toward the cost of bus transportation and school lunches a maximum of $12 per pupil based on total enrollment within the school district but not to exceed $6\frac{2}{3}$ percent of the state per-pupil equalization grants-in-aid.

4. Interest on temporary investment of school tax receipts and rents of school facilities are expected to be $75,000 and are earmarked for special equipment acquisitions listed as "Capital outlays from revenues" in the budgeted expenditures. Cost of the special equipment acquisitions will be limited to the amount derived from these miscellaneous receipts.

5. The remaining funds needed to finance the budgeted expenditures of the school district are to be raised from local taxation. An allowance of 9 percent of the local tax levy is necessary for possible tax abatements and losses. The assessed valuation of the property located within the school district is $80,000,000.

Requirements

a) Prepare a schedule computing the estimated total funds to be obtained from local taxation for the ensuing school year ending June 30, 19x1 for the Victoria School District.

b) Prepare a schedule computing the estimated current operating cost per regular pupil and per vocational pupil to be met by local tax funds. Assume that costs other than instructional costs are assignable on a per capita basis to regular and vocational students.

c) Without prejudice to your solution to requirement (a), assume that the estimated total tax levy for the ensuing school year ending June 30, 19x1 is $1,092,000. Prepare a schedule computing the estimated tax rate per $100 of assessed valuation of the property within the Victoria School District.

(CPA Adapted)

7

Responsibility Accounting and Flexible Budgets

Feedback in the form of performance reports is essential if the benefits of budgeting are to be fully realized. Managers need to know how actual results compare with the current budget in order to control current operations and improve budgets for future periods. Consider a relatively simple situation where the unit cost of raw materials exceeds the cost allowed in the budget. A performance report addressed to the appropriate manager indicates the existence of the disparity, and the manager initiates an investigation to determine its cause. The manager may find that a new employee in the Purchasing Department is buying from unauthorized vendors or in small lots. In this case the manager will take action to bring performance into line with plans, perhaps by having the new employee work closely with a more experienced colleague. Alternatively, the investigation may reveal unanticipated price increases. In this case the budget should be revised to reflect the price increases, and the new prices should also be used in future budgets.

The importance of feedback to budgeting is illustrated in Exhibit 7–1. Here budgeting and performance evaluation are presented as a continuous cycle. Assume the cycle starts with the current budget. As the year passes, actual operating data are accumulated and compared with the current budget in the form of performance reports. The appropriate managers receive these reports and then obtain additional information to explain significant deviations from the budget. Based on this information, management attempts to improve current operations and plans for the future, which are summarized in the new budget. The new budget becomes the current budget and the cycle continues.

The purpose of this chapter is to examine the nature of performance reports and the concepts that underlie their development and use. We will study the relationship between performance reports and organization

EXHIBIT 7–1 The Budgeting–Performance Evaluation Cycle

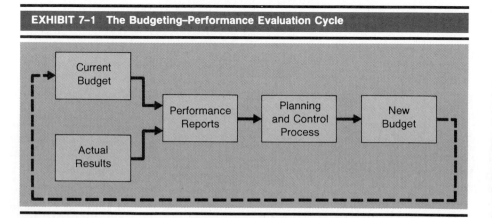

structure, as well as determine the types of performance reports that are best suited to various activities. Much of the material presented here is examined in greater detail in later chapters.

RESPONSIBILITY ACCOUNTING

By serving as a scorecard and an attention director, performance reports, which contain comparisons of actual results and plans, help managers determine and control the organization's activities. In accordance with the concept of management by exception, the absence of significant differences indicates that activities are proceeding as planned, whereas the presence of significant differences indicates a need either to take corrective action or to revise plans.

Performance reports should be prepared in accordance with the concept of **responsibility accounting,** which is the structuring of performance reports addressed to individual or group members of an organization in a manner that emphasizes the factors controllable by them. In responsibility accounting the focus is on specific units within the organization that are responsible for the accomplishment of specific activities or objectives. Performance reports are customized to emphasize the activities of each specific organizational unit. For example, a performance report addressed to the head of a production department contains manufacturing costs controllable by the department head; it does not contain costs (such as advertising, sales commissions, or the president's salary) that the department head cannot control. Including noncontrollable costs distracts the manager's attention from controllable costs and thereby dilutes the manager's efforts to deal with controllable items. Lower level managers may also become frustrated with the entire performance reporting system if they believe upper level managers expect them to control costs they cannot influence.

Performance Reports and Corporate Structure

Before implementing a responsibility-accounting system all areas of authority and responsibility within an organization must be clearly defined. Organization charts and other documents should be examined to determine an organization's authority and responsibility structure. However, when an attempt is made to implement a responsibility-accounting system, management may find many instances of overlapping duties, of authority not commensurate with responsibility, and of expenditures for which no one appears responsible. These circumstances make the development of a responsibility-accounting system difficult, but their resolution is a benefit of successful installation.

Though performance reports can be developed for areas of responsibility as narrow as a single worker, the basic responsibility unit in most organizations is the department. In manufacturing plants, separate responsibility centers are set up for individual production and service departments. When a large department performs a number of diverse and significant activities, responsibility accounting may be further refined so that a single department contains several responsibility centers with performance reports prepared for each.

An abbreviated organization chart for a manufacturing firm is presented in Exhibit 7–2. The short-run objective of the firm is to earn a profit by the production and sale of finished goods. The president and the executive

EXHIBIT 7–2   Partial Organization Chart of a Manufacturing Firm

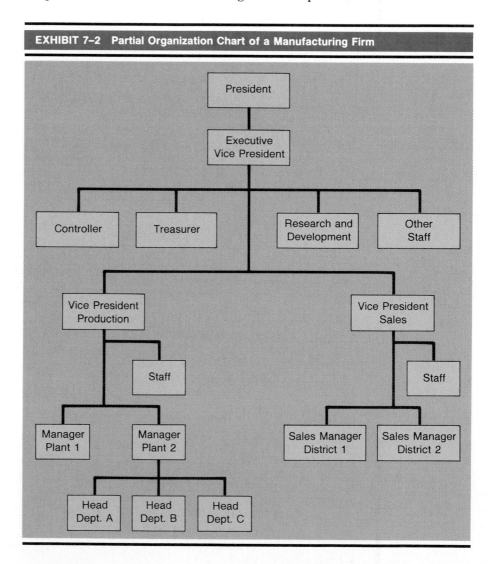

vice president are responsible for overall operations and profitability. The authority to set selling prices and to incur costs in connection with the sale of goods is delegated to the vice president of sales, who in turn delegates a portion of this authority to each of two district sales managers. The authority to incur costs in connection with the manufacture of goods is delegated to the vice president of production, who in turn delegates a portion of this authority to each of two plant managers. Finally, each plant manager delegates the authority to incur costs, in connection with specific manufacturing activities, to department heads.

Commensurate with their authority, the responsibility of individual department heads is quite narrow. And, commensurate with greater authority, responsibility is broader at higher levels in the organization. A series of performance reports, illustrating expanding authority for manufacturing costs, is presented in Exhibit 7–3. A plant manager is responsible for more costs than is a department head, and the vice president of production is responsible for more costs than is a single plant manager. Notice how the performance reports tie together. The totals for the head of Department C are included as one line in the plant manager's report, and the totals for the manager of Plant 2 are included as one line in the report for the vice president of production. This aggregation takes place because the managers closest to actual activities need detailed information to control day-to-day activities, whereas upper level managers spend less time controlling activities and more time planning them.

Nonmonetary Performance Measures

An organization's basic performance reports are almost always stated in terms of dollars, which provide a common, additive unit of measure for all activities. Once the dollar impact of each activity is determined, the dollar measures can be summarized and reported up the corporate ladder. Furthermore, both the immediate supervisor of an activity and other managers far removed from the activity can understand the impact of dollars on cash flow and income. Dollars should not, however, be used to the exclusion of nondollar performance measures. A favorable variance that resulted from an unethical or illegal action should not be rewarded. Short-sighted managers may also take actions that appear favorable in the short run but are detrimental to the organization in the long run. Excessive pressures for employee productivity may result in strikes and employee turnover, and bargain purchases of raw materials may result in excess waste. These examples illustrate the need for upper level management to inquire about the causes of favorable as well as unfavorable variances. What is more, there should be some legitimate way for concerned employees to communicate with upper management without violating the chain-of-command. For example, an employee in a waste treatment department should be able to legitimately express a concern to upper management

EXHIBIT 7-3   Responsibility Accounting Reports for Manufacturing

	Actual Cost	Allowed Cost	Variance*
Vice president: Production			
Plant 1	$ 55,000	$ 54,800	$ 200 U
Plant 2	69,600	68,400	1,200 U
Vice president's office (itemized)	10,900	12,000	1,100 F
Total	$135,500	$135,200	$ 300 U

	Actual Cost	Allowed Cost	Variance*
Manager: Plant 2			
Department A	$ 25,400	$ 24,700	$ 700 U
Department B	17,500	18,000	500 F
Department C	20,500	19,900	600 U
Plant manager's office (itemized)	6,200	5,800	400 U
Total	$ 69,600	$ 68,400	$1,200 U

	Actual Cost	Allowed Cost	Variance*
Head: Department C			
Direct materials	$ 6,000	$ 5,000	$1,000 U
Direct labor	6,500	7,000	500 F
Factory overhead (itemized)	8,000	7,900	100 U
Total	$ 20,500	$ 19,900	$ 600 U

* F = Favorable, if actual costs are less than allowed costs.
  U = Unfavorable, if actual costs are greater than allowed costs.

about a supervisor's illegal cost cutting measures. A corporate ombudsman might be useful in this regard.

The persons responsible for the accomplishment of specific activities, especially first line supervisors, should be routinely provided with dollar and nondollar performance measures. The nondollar measures should be stated in terms of the activities or resources for which first line supervisors are responsible. The head of a production department, for example, should receive information on materials use, labor hours, machine hours, units produced, defective units, scrap, and so forth. A district sales manager would like information on market share, number of orders, number of salespersons' visits, and customer complaints.

**Frequency of
Performance
Reports**

Performance reports must be provided with sufficient frequency for managers to take timely corrective action. Although performance reports for an entire year may assist in developing plans and evaluating managers' performance, they are of no use in adjusting operations during the year. On the other hand, daily or hourly performance reports may be of great value to some managers but a distraction to others. The solution to this dilemma is to recognize that different levels of management, and different personnel at each level, have differing needs for performance information. The head of a production department may require daily, hourly, or even continuous information about operations under his or her control, whereas a plant manager may need only weekly reports from each department head. Similarly, the vice president of production may require only monthly performance reports from each plant. The further a manager is from actual operations, the less the manager's need for frequent feedback. Higher level managers spend more time planning operations and motivating personnel to execute these plans, and lower level managers spend more time executing plans. Hence, lower level managers have greater need for frequent and fast feedback.

**Types of
Responsibility
Centers**

Under responsibility accounting, performance reports are prepared for departments, segments of departments, or groupings of departments that operate under the control and authority of a responsible manager. Each organizational unit for which performance reports are prepared is identified as a **responsibility center.** Depending on the nature of their assigned activities, responsibility centers may be classified as investment centers, profit centers, revenue centers, or cost centers.

An **investment center** is responsible for the relationship between its profits and the total assets invested in the center. In general, the management of an investment center is expected to earn a target profit per dollar invested. Investment center managers are evaluated on the basis of how well they use the total resources entrusted to their care to earn a profit.

An investment center is the broadest and most inclusive type of responsibility center. The entire organization depicted in Exhibit 7–2 would be regarded as an investment center, with the president and the executive vice president being the investment center's management. These officials have more authority and responsibility than other managers and are primarily responsible for planning, organizing, and controlling firm activities. Their decisions regarding the size of the company determine the total assets for which they are responsible. Because of their authority regarding the size of corporate assets, they are held responsible for the relationship between profits and assets.

A **profit center** is responsible for the difference between revenues and costs. A profit center may refer to an entire organization but is more frequently a segment of an organization, such as a product line, marketing territory, or store. In the context of performance evaluation the word "profit" may not refer to the bottom line of an income statement; instead, it is likely to refer to the profit center's contribution to common corporate costs and profit. Profit is computed as the center's revenues less all costs identified with operating the center.

A large retail organization might evaluate each of its stores as a profit center, with the store manager being the administrative officer. The store manager, who has responsibility for the overall operation of the store, accepts the store's physical structure and the organization's investment in the store as a given. Though the store manager may request that additional investments be made for a variety of purposes, the manager seldom has the authority to make investment or financing decisions. Having limited authority regarding the size of the store's total assets, the store manager is not held responsible for the relationship between profits and assets. For making special analyses, management may, of course, evaluate the store as an investment center.

A **revenue center** is responsible for the generation of sales revenues. In Exhibit 7–2 there are three revenue centers: District 1, District 2, and the Vice President of Sales. A performance report is prepared for each district and the Vice President of Sales. Even though the basic performance report of a revenue center emphasizes sales, revenue centers are likely to be assigned responsibility for the controllable costs they incur in generating revenues. If revenues and costs are evaluated separately, the center has dual responsibility as a revenue center and as a cost center. If controllable costs are deducted from revenues to obtain some bottom-line contribution, the center is, in fact, being treated as a quasi-profit center.

A **cost center** is only responsible for the incurrence of costs; it does not have a revenue responsibility. A cost center may be as small as a segment of a department or large enough to include a major aspect of the organization, such as all manufacturing activities. The performance reports in Exhibit 7–3 illustrate an increasing responsibility for manufacturing costs. The head of a production department is responsible only for costs incurred in his or her department, but the vice president of manufacturing is responsible for all manufacturing costs. Cost centers are established for nonmanufacturing as well as for manufacturing activities. In Exhibit 7–2 each of the staff departments, such as the Controller's Department, is evaluated as a cost center. Cost centers are also established in merchandising, service, and not-for-profit organizations. Typical examples of these cost centers include the following:

Organization	Cost Center
Retail store	Advertising department
	Maintenance department
TV station	Audio/video engineering
	Buildings and grounds
College	History department
	Power plant
City government	Public safety (police and fire)
	Welfare

In the remainder of this chapter we introduce concepts that are important to the development of performance reports for cost and revenue centers. We conclude by illustrating how the performance reports of cost centers and revenue centers can be combined to reconcile the difference between an organization's budgeted and actual income. We will take a closer look at cost center performance reports in Chapter 8, investment centers are considered in Chapter 9, and performance reports for important segments of a business (profit centers) are examined in Chapter 10.

PERFORMANCE REPORTS FOR COST CENTERS

Performance reports for cost centers should always include a comparison of actual and allowed costs, with the difference identified as a variance. The variance is favorable if actual costs are less than allowed costs and unfavorable if actual costs are greater than allowed costs. These comparisons are made in total and for each type of controllable cost assigned to the cost center. The allowed costs used in performance reports are based on a flexible budget for the actual level of activity.

Development of Flexible Budgets

A budget that is based on a prior prediction of expected sales and production is called a **static budget.** The operating budget explained in Chapter 6 is a static budget. Budgets may also be drawn up for a series of possible production and sales volumes or adjusted to a particular level of production after the fact. These budgets, based on cost-volume-profit or cost-volume relationships, are called **flexible budgets;** they are used to determine what costs should have been for an attained volume of activity. Before a flexible budget can be developed, management must understand how costs respond to changes in activity.

Assume the Meridian Clock Company contains three departments, Production, Sales, and Administration. In this chapter we will develop performance reports for each of them, starting with the Production Department. The flexible budget cost estimating equation for total monthly production costs is as follows:

	Fixed Costs	**Variable Costs**
Direct materials		$10X$
Direct labor		$6X$
Factory overhead	$50,000	$4X$
Total cost $\quad=$	$50,000 $\quad+$	$20X$

where X equals the number of units produced.

If management planned to produce 10,000 units in July of 19x7, the budgeted manufacturing costs for July would amount to $250,000:

Meridian Clock Company	
Manufacturing Budget	
For the month of July, 19x7	
Manufacturing costs:	
Direct materials (10,000 × $10)	$100,000
Direct labor (10,000 × $6)	60,000
Variable overhead (10,000 × $4)	40,000
Fixed overhead	50,000
Total	$250,000

If actual July production happened to equal 10,000 units, the performance report for the Production Department should be based on a comparison of actual and budgeted manufacturing costs. But if production was at some volume other than that specified in the manufacturing budget, such as 11,000 units, it would be inappropriate to compare actual and budgeted manufacturing costs. Fixed costs should be the same at all levels of production; variable costs will fluctuate. In this case, for the purpose of performance evaluation, a flexible budget is tailored, after the fact, to the actual level of activity. Examples of performance reports for July manufacturing costs, based on static and flexible budgets, are presented in Exhibit 7–4. When the Production Department is evaluated using the static budget, the actual costs of producing 11,000 units are compared to the budgeted costs of producing 10,000 units. The result is a series of large, unfavorable variances, totaling $23,000. When the Production Department is evaluated by comparing actual costs to the costs allowed in a flexible budget drawn

EXHIBIT 7–4   Flexible Budgets and Performance Evaluation

Meridian Clock Company
Production Department Performance Report
For the month of July, 19x7

	Based on Static Budget			Based on Flexible Budget		
	Actual	*Original Budget*	*Variance**	*Actual*	*Flexible Budget*	*Variance**
Volume	11,000	10,000		11,000	11,000	
Manufacturing costs:						
Direct materials	$108,000	$100,000	$ 8,000 U	$108,000	$110,000	$2,000 F
Direct labor	70,000	60,000	10,000 U	70,000	66,000	4,000 U
Variable overhead	44,000	40,000	4,000 U	44,000	44,000	—
Fixed overhead	51,000	50,000	1,000 U	51,000	50,000	1,000 U
Total	$273,000	$250,000	$23,000 U	$273,000	$270,000	$3,000 U

*F = Favorable
U = Unfavorable

up for the actual production volume, the results are mixed. Direct materials have a $2000 favorable variance. Direct labor has a $4000 unfavorable variance. There is no variable overhead variance. And fixed overhead has a $1000 unfavorable variance. The net unfavorable variances amount to $3000.

Flexible Budgets Emphasize Efficiency

The initial production and manufacturing budgets are based on sales forecasts and management's inventory policy. If actual sales differ from budgeted sales, the actual production volume may differ from the budgeted production volume. If sales increase, the production volume should be increased to support this level of sales. If sales decrease, the production volume should be decreased to avoid carrying excess inventories. Since manufacturing costs are a function of production volume, it is inappropriate to compare actual manufacturing costs to the original budget if actual production differs from budgeted production. If this were done, a production supervisor might gladly respond to reductions in production orders (with the resulting favorable manufacturing cost variances) but be very reluctant to increase production in response to unanticipated orders. An increase in sales, as illustrated in Exhibit 7–4, would result in a performance report containing many large unfavorable variances, even if the production supervisor had done a good job of controlling costs.

To make production personnel more willing to respond to changes in the desired production volume, they should be evaluated on the basis of flexible budgets drawn up for the actual level of production. Use of flexible budgets is an acknowledgment that production personnel control costs, not volume. Management wishes to evaluate them on the basis of their **efficiency,** which means operating with the lowest use of resources possible under the circumstances. Flexible budgets using standard costs are widely used to measure the efficiency of production activities.

Standard Costs

A **standard cost,** a budget for one unit of product, indicates what it should cost to produce one unit of product under efficient operating conditions. Standard costs can be developed from an engineering analysis or from an analysis of historical data adjusted for expected changes in the product, production technology, or costs. When standards are developed using historical data, management must be careful to ensure that past inefficiencies are excluded from current standards. The standard variable product costs for the Meridian Clock Company are $20 per unit, including direct materials, direct labor, and factory overhead costs of $10, $6, and $4, respectively. These standard costs were used in developing the flexible budget in Exhibit 7–4.

Standard costs are used for budgeting, performance evaluation, and product costing. In Chapter 6 standard costs for materials, labor, and overhead were used in developing the operating budget for the All American Automobile Company. In this chapter and in Chapter 8 standard costs are used for performance evaluation. In Appendix B of Chapter 11, standard costs are used for product costing. When standard costs are used to value product inventories in external financial statements, the unit standard cost must also include an element for fixed overhead.[1] For purposes of internal planning and control, it is better to classify costs by their behavior. Accordingly, since fixed costs are constant in the short run without regard to the level of operations, they are treated as a lump sum in this chapter. In the Meridian Clock Company's flexible budget for manufacturing costs (see Exhibit 7–4), the budgeted fixed overhead does not vary with production volume.

To obtain the full benefit of standard costs, the standards must be based on realistic expectations. Some organizations intentionally set "tight" standards to motivate employees toward higher levels of production. The management of the Meridian Clock Company might set their standard for direct labor at $4 per unit, rather than at the expected $6 per unit, hoping that employees will strive toward the lower cost. The use of tight standards often causes planning and behavioral problems. Management expects them to result in unfavorable variances. Accordingly, tight standards should not

---

[1] External reporting requires that inventories be stated on an absorption cost basis in which all manufacturing costs, including fixed costs, are product costs.

be used to budget input requirements and cash flows — management expects to incur more labor costs than the standards allow. The use of tight standards can have undesirable behavioral effects if lower level managers and employees find that a second set of standards are used in the "real" budget or if they are constantly subject to unfavorable performance reports. They may come to distrust the entire budgeting and performance evaluation system, or they may quit trying to achieve any of the organization's standards.

Tight standards are more likely to occur in an imposed budget and less likely to occur in a participation budget where employees are actively involved in budget preparation. In a participation budget the problems may be to avoid loose standards that are easily attained and to avoid overstating the costs required to produce a product. Loose standards may fail to properly motivate employees; what is more, they may lead the company into an uncompetitive market position with costs and prices that are higher than competitors'.

Standard and Discretionary Cost Centers

A distinction is often made between standard and discretionary cost centers. A **standard cost center** is a cost center that has clearly defined relationships between effort and accomplishment. A **discretionary cost center** is a cost center that does not have clearly defined relationships between effort and accomplishment.

Standard cost centers are evaluated with the aid of flexible budgets drawn up for the actual level of activity. A production department is the most obvious example of a standard cost center. However, the growth of services and service industries, and the resultant need to control service costs, has led to an expanding use of standard cost centers. Standard cost centers can be established for any segment of a business for which it is possible to develop standard costs per unit of activity. Possible applications include the costs of packaging, transportation, commissions, utilities, room cleaning, residential fire inspection, laundry, automobile repair, and processing loan applications.

Recall that discretionary costs are set at a fixed amount at the discretion of management. Changing these costs does not affect production or service capacity in the near term. Because of the absence of a relationship between effort and accomplishment, the performance of a discretionary cost center cannot be evaluated with the aid of a flexible budget. Indeed, it is difficult to evaluate the performance of a discretionary cost center by any means. The best monetary evaluation is based on a comparison of the actual and budgeted costs for a given period, with the results identified as over-budget or under-budget.

If a research and development budget for 19x9 contained authorized expenditures of $1.5 million, but the actual 19x9 expenditures amounted to $1.2 million, the $300,000 difference is not necessarily favorable. Research and development was $300,000 under-budget. Whether or not this is good or bad depends on what was accomplished during the year. If the money was saved by canceling a program critical to the future of the organization, the net result is hardly favorable. Again, all the variance does is inform management that actual results were not in line with plans. Management must investigate further to determine the significance of the variance.

Though it is difficult to evaluate the under-budget performance of a discretionary cost center, an over-budget performance has an undesirable implication regardless of the results achieved. If, after the budget is approved, the manager of a discretionary cost center realizes the center's budget is inadequate, the manager should immediately request additional funds, or notify his or her supervisor of the need to reduce activity. Going over-budget implies that the manager is unable to operate with the budgeted resources. Obviously, a manager should not be allowed unlimited use of the organization's resources. To control such use, the organization's treasurer is often prohibited from providing financial resources in excess of an authorized limit (like the limit on a bank credit card). If this limit is exceeded, the matter should immediately be brought to the attention of the next level of management.

In for-profit organizations, an increase in demand for a product or service is usually accompanied by an increase in resources that more than covers the increase in variable costs. This is often not the case in not-for-profit organizations. Here the funds provided for an activity may be fixed regardless of the level of the activity. A city in upstate New York might budget $1,000,000 per year for snow removal with the money collected from property taxes. If this budget is based on an average of five snowfalls per year at an average removal cost of $200,000 per snowfall, the city department responsible for snow removal may have to operate with this amount even if there are seven snowfalls. The problem is that the department, a natural standard cost center, receives resources as if it were a discretionary cost center. Consequently, the department may not have enough resources to do its job in periods of high activity, and it may have excess resources (which it might be tempted to waste) in periods of low activity. The unique problems of planning and control in not-for-profit organizations are considered further in the appendix to Chapter 6.

As management's ability to define the relationships between effort and accomplishment becomes more refined, there is a tendency for managers to replace discretionary cost centers with standard cost centers. A computer center that was initially established as a discretionary cost center may be changed to a standard cost center, once management determines the relationships between the computer's operating costs and some measure of its activity. A management that desires to better plan and control costs will encourage the evolution from discretionary to standard cost centers wherever practicable.

PERFORMANCE REPORTS FOR REVENUE CENTERS

The performance reports for revenue centers include a comparison of actual and budgeted revenues, with the difference identified as a variance. Revenue centers are sometimes assigned responsibility for controllable costs they incur in generating revenues. In this case they have a dual responsibility as a revenue center and as a cost center. Controllable costs may be deducted from revenues to obtain some bottom-line contribution. If the center is then evaluated on the basis of this contribution, it is being treated as a profit center.

Revenue Center Reports Emphasize Effectiveness

Effectiveness is getting the job done. If the organization is to meet its budgeted profit goal for a period, with its budgeted fixed and variable costs, the organization's revenue centers must meet their original revenue budgets. Consequently, the original budget (a static budget), rather than a flexible budget, is used to evaluate revenue centers.

Assume the Meridian Clock Company's sales budget for July, 19x7 called for the sale of 10,000 units at $40 each. If Meridian actually sold 11,000 units at $39 each, the total revenue variance would be $29,000:

Actual revenues (11,000 × $39)	$429,000
Budgeted revenues (10,000 × $40)	−400,000
Revenue variance	$ 29,000 F

Because actual revenues exceeded budgeted revenues, the revenue variance is favorable. Note that two distinct events occurred to create the $29,000 favorable variance: The selling price declined from $40 to $39, and the sales volume increased from 10,000 to 11,000 units. These two causes of the total revenue variance are identified as the sales price variance and the sales volume variance.

The **sales price variance** indicates the impact on revenues of a change in selling price, given the actual sales volume. It is computed as the change in selling price times the actual sales volume:

$$\begin{matrix} \text{Sales} \\ \text{price} \\ \text{variance} \end{matrix} = \left(\begin{matrix} \text{Actual} \\ \text{selling} \\ \text{price} \end{matrix} - \begin{matrix} \text{Budgeted} \\ \text{selling} \\ \text{price} \end{matrix} \right) \begin{matrix} \text{Actual} \\ \times \text{sales} \\ \text{volume.} \end{matrix}$$

The **sales volume variance** indicates the impact on revenues of the change in sales volume, assuming there was no change in selling price. It is computed as the difference between the actual and the budgeted sales volume times the budgeted selling price:

$$\begin{matrix} \text{Sales} \\ \text{volume} \\ \text{variance} \end{matrix} = \left(\begin{matrix} \text{Actual} \\ \text{sales} \\ \text{volume} \end{matrix} - \begin{matrix} \text{Budgeted} \\ \text{sales} \\ \text{volume} \end{matrix} \right) \begin{matrix} \text{Budgeted} \\ \times \text{selling} \\ \text{price.} \end{matrix}$$

The July sales price and volume variances for the Meridian Clock Company are $11,000 U and $40,000 F, respectively:

Sales price variance   = ($39 − $40) × 11,000   = $11,000 U
Sales volume variance   = (11,000 − 10,000) × $40 =   40,000 F
Total revenue variance $29,000 F

The interpretation of variances is subjective. In this case we might say that if the increase in sales volume had not been accompanied by a decline in selling price, revenues would have increased $40,000. The $1 per unit decline in selling price cost the company $11,000 in revenues. Alternatively, we might note that a $1 reduction in the unit selling price was more than offset by an increase in sales volume.

In any case, variances are merely signals that actual results are not proceeding according to plan. They help managers identify potential problems and opportunities. An investigation into their cause(s) may even indicate that a manager who received a favorable variance was doing a poor job, whereas a manager who received an unfavorable variance was doing an outstanding job. Consider Meridian's favorable sales volume variance. This occurred because actual sales exceeded budgeted sales by 1000 units or 10 percent, which on the surface indicates good performance. But what if the total market for the company's products exceeded the company's forecast by 20 percent? In this case Meridian's sales volume fell below its expected percentage share of the market, and the favorable variance may have occurred, despite a poor marketing effort, because of strong customer demand that competitors could not fill.

Revenue Center Reports Sometimes Include Costs

Controllable costs should also be considered when evaluating the overall performance of revenue centers. A failure to consider costs might encourage uneconomic selling practices, such as excessive advertising and entertaining, and spending too much time on small accounts. The controllable costs of revenue centers include variable and fixed selling costs. These costs are sometimes further classified into order getting and order filling costs. **Order getting costs** are costs incurred to obtain a customer's order, for example, advertising, salespersons' salaries and commissions, travel, telephone, and entertainment. **Order filling costs** are costs incurred to place finished goods in the hands of purchasers, for example, storing, packaging, and transportation. Many of these costs are fixed (committed and discretionary); others are variable.

The performance of a revenue center in controlling costs can be evaluated with the aid of a flexible budget drawn up for the actual level of activity. Assume the Meridian Clock Company's July 19x7 budget for the Sales Department calls for fixed costs of $10,000 and variable costs of $5 per unit sold. If the actual fixed and variable selling expenses for July are $9500 and $65,000, respectively, the total cost variances assigned to the Sales Department are $9500 unfavorable:

Meridian Clock Company
Sales Department Performance Report for Costs
For the month of July, 19x7

	Actual	Flexible Budget	Variance*
Volume	11,000	11,000	
Selling expenses:			
Variable	$65,000	$55,000	$10,000 U
Fixed	9,500	10,000	500 F
Total	$74,500	$65,000	$ 9,500 U

*F = Favorable
U = Unfavorable

In evaluating the performance of the Sales Department as both a cost center and a revenue center, management would consider these cost variances as well as the revenue variances.

Revenue Centers Are Sometimes Evaluated As Profit Centers

Even though we have computed revenue and cost variances for Meridian's Sales Department, we are still left with an incomplete picture of the performance of this revenue center. Is the Sales Department's performance best represented by the $29,000 favorable revenue variance, by the $9500 unfavorable cost variance, or by the net favorable variance of $19,500 ($29,000 F + $9500 U)? Actually, it is inappropriate to attempt to obtain an overall measure of the Sales Department's performance by combining these separate revenue and cost variances. The combination of revenue and cost variances is only appropriate for a profit center and, so far, we have left out one important cost that must be assigned to the Sales Department before it can be treated as a profit center. That cost is the standard variable cost of goods sold.

As a profit center, the Sales Department acquires units from the Production Department and sells them outside the firm. Its total responsibilities include revenues, the standard variable cost of goods sold, and actual selling expenses. Notice that the Sales Department is assigned the standard, rather than the actual, variable cost of goods sold. Because the Sales Department does not control production activities, it should not be assigned actual production costs. Doing so would result in the Production Department's variances being passed on to the Sales Department. Fixed manufacturing costs are not assigned to the Sales Department because short-run variations in sales volume do not normally affect the total amount of these costs.

To evaluate the Sales Department as a profit center, the computation of the sales volume variance must be adjusted for the corresponding variations in allowed costs. In its current form the sales volume variance does not consider that costs as well as revenues respond to changes in sales volume. Consequently, to evaluate the performance of a profit center, this variance must be stated net of its impact on the flexible budgets for manufacturing and selling costs. The standard variable costs that respond to changes in sales volume are as follows:

Direct materials	$10
Direct labor	6
Factory overhead	4
Selling	5
Total	$25

When standard variable costs are considered, the net impact of the sales volume variance is $15,000 favorable:

Sales volume variance [(11,000 − 10,000) × $40]	$40,000 F
Less increase in standard variable costs	
[(11,000 − 10,000) × $25]	−25,000
Net sales volume variance	$15,000 F

In general, the **net sales volume variance** indicates the impact of a change in sales volume on the contribution margin, given the budgeted selling price and the standard variable costs. It is computed as the difference between the actual and the budgeted sales volume times the budgeted unit contribution margin. The budgeted unit contribution margin is the budgeted selling price minus the standard variable costs per unit:

$$\begin{array}{c} \text{Net sales} \\ \text{volume} \\ \text{variance} \end{array} = \left(\begin{array}{cc} \text{Actual} & \text{Budgeted} \\ \text{sales} & - \text{sales} \\ \text{volume} & \text{volume} \end{array} \right) \times \begin{array}{c} \text{Budgeted} \\ \text{unit contribution} \\ \text{margin.} \end{array}$$

The Meridian Clock Company's budgeted unit contribution margin is $15:

Budgeted unit selling price	$40
Standard unit variable costs	−25
Budgeted unit contribution margin	$15

Using the formula presented above, the net sales volume variance is computed as follows:

$$\text{Net sales volume variance} = [(11,000 - 10,000) \times \$15]$$
$$= \$15,000 \text{ F.}$$

In summary, as a profit center the Sales Department has responsibility for the sales price variance, the net sales volume variance, and any cost variances associated with its operations. The Meridian Clock Company's sales price variance was previously computed to be $11,000 U, the $1 reduction in selling price times the actual sales volume of 11,000 units. The net sales volume variance was determined to be $15,000 F, the 1000 unit increase in sales volume times the budgeted unit contribution margin of $15. The cost variances assigned to the Sales Department net to $9500 U, the difference between $74,500 in actual selling costs and $65,000 in selling costs allowed for the actual sales volume. As a profit center, the Sales Department's net variances are $5500 unfavorable:

Sales price variance	$11,000 U
Net sales volume variance	15,000 F
Selling expense variances	9,500 U
Net Sales Department variances	$ 5,500 U

In an attempt to improve their overall performance, managers often commit themselves to unfavorable variances in some areas, believing these variances will be more than offset by other favorable variances. In the case above, it appears that the favorable net sales volume variance was not sufficient to offset the price reductions and the higher selling expenses.

Also notice that the more complete evaluation of the Sales Department as a profit center (with a $5500 unfavorable variance) gives a very different impression than the evaluation of the Sales Department as a revenue center (with a $29,000 favorable variance) or as a dual revenue and cost center (with additional $9500 unfavorable cost variances).

RECONCILING BUDGETED AND ACTUAL INCOME

It is possible to reconcile the difference between budgeted and actual net income for an entire organization. This can be done either by (1) assigning all costs and revenues to responsibility centers and summarizing the performance of each responsibility center or (2) developing a detailed reconciliation of actual and budgeted costs and revenues for the organization as a whole. Assume the Meridian Clock Company's budgeted and actual income statements, in a contribution format, for July, 19x7 are as presented in Exhibit 7–5.

Following the first reconciliation approach, assume that the Meridian Clock Company contains three responsibility centers: a Production Department, a Sales Department, and an Administration Department. Further assume that the Production and the Administration Departments are cost centers and that the Sales Department is a profit center. The Production Department's variances, as itemized in Exhibit 7–4, net to $3000 U. The Sales Department's variances, as summarized above, net to $5500 U. The only variance for the Administration Department is the $200 difference between actual and budgeted fixed administrative costs ($3800 actual — $4000 budget). Because the Administration Department is a discretionary cost center, this variance is best identified as under-budget. For consistency in the performance reports, however, it is labeled favorable. Assigning all previously computed variances to these three responsibility centers, the reconciliation of budgeted and actual income is as follows:

Budgeted net income		$86,000
Sales Department variances		
(a profit center)	$5,500 U	
Production Department variances		
(a standard cost center)	3,000 U	
Administration Department variances		
(a discretionary cost center)	200 F	− 8,300 U
Actual net income		$77,700

EXHIBIT 7–5   Budgeted and Actual Income Statements

Meridian Clock Company
Budgeted Income Statement
For the month of July, 19x7

Sales ($40 × 10,000)			$400,000
Less variable costs:			
Variable cost of goods sold:			
Direct materials ($10 × 10,000)	$100,000		
Direct labor ($6 × 10,000)	60,000		
Factory overhead ($4 × 10,000)	40,000	$200,000	
Selling ($5 × 10,000)		50,000	−250,000
Contribution margin			$150,000
Less fixed costs:			
Factory overhead		$ 50,000	
Selling		10,000	
Administrative		4,000	− 64,000
Net income			$ 86,000

Meridian Clock Company
Actual Income Statement
For the month of July, 19x7

Sales ($39 × 11,000)			$429,000
Less variable costs:			
Variable cost of goods sold:			
Direct materials	$108,000		
Direct labor	70,000		
Factory overhead	44,000	$222,000	
Selling		65,000	−287,000
Contribution margin			$142,000
Less fixed costs:			
Factory overhead		$ 51,000	
Selling		9,500	
Administrative		3,800	− 64,300
Net income			$ 77,700

Following the second approach, a detailed reconciliation of budgeted and actual costs and revenues for the organization as a whole is presented in Exhibit 7–6. Column (1) presents Meridian's actual income statement. The budgeted income statement is presented in column (7). Variance computations are presented in columns (2), (4), and (6). The cost variances in column (2) reconcile actual costs with costs allowed in a flexible budget

EXHIBIT 7-6 Reconciliation of Budgeted and Actual Income

	(1) Actual Volume, Actual Prices, Actual Costs	(2) Cost Variances	(3) Actual Volume, Actual Prices, Standard Costs	(4) Sales Price Variance	(5) Actual Volume, Budgeted Prices, Standard Costs	(6) Net Sales Volume Variance	(7) Original (Static) Budget
Volume (units)	11,000		11,000		11,000	1,000	10,000
Sales	$429,000		$429,000	$11,000 U	$440,000	$40,000	$400,000
Less variable costs:							
Direct materials	$108,000	$(2,000) F	$110,000		$110,000	$10,000	$100,000
Direct labor	70,000	4,000 U	66,000		66,000	6,000	60,000
Factory overhead	44,000	—	44,000		44,000	4,000	40,000
Selling	65,000	10,000 U	55,000		55,000	5,000	50,000
Total	−287,000		−275,000		−275,000	−25,000	−250,000
Contribution margin	$142,000		$154,000		$165,000	$15,000 F	$150,000
Less fixed costs:							
Factory overhead	$ 51,000	1,000 U	$ 50,000		$ 50,000		$ 50,000
Selling	9,500	(500) F	10,000		10,000		10,000
Administrative	3,800	(200) F	4,000		4,000		4,000
Total	− 64,300		− 64,000		− 64,000		− 64,000
Net income	$ 77,700	$12,300 U	$ 90,000	$11,000 U	$101,000	$15,000 F	$ 86,000

drawn up for the actual level of activity. Included in column (2) are the manufacturing cost variances (materials, labor, variable overhead, and fixed overhead, all totaling $3000 U), the selling expense variances (variable and fixed, both totaling $9500 U), and the administrative cost variance (all fixed, totaling $200 F). The sales price variance is presented in column (4). A detailed computation of the net sales volume variance is presented in column (6). The sales volume variance is shown at the top of the column followed by adjustments for the impact of the change in volume on allowed standard costs.

SUMMARY

Responsibility accounting is the structuring of performance reports addressed to individual members of an organization in a manner that emphasizes the factors controllable by them. Each administrative unit for which performance reports are prepared is identified as a responsibility center. Depending on the nature of their assigned activities, responsibility centers are classified as investment centers, profit centers, revenue centers, or cost centers. An investment center is responsible for the relationship between its profits and the total assets invested in the center. A profit center is responsible for the difference between revenues and costs. Although a revenue center is responsible for the generation of sales revenue, it is often assigned responsibility for the controllable costs incurred in generating revenues. If this is done, the revenue center has a dual responsibility as a revenue and cost center. If controllable costs are deducted from revenues, the center is, in fact, being treated as a profit center. A cost center is only responsible for the incurrence of costs and is often further classified as either standard or discretionary.

A standard cost center is a cost center that has clearly defined relationships between effort and accomplishment. The performance of a standard cost center is evaluated by comparing actual costs with the costs allowed in a flexible budget drawn up for the actual level of activity. A discretionary cost center is a cost center that does not have clearly defined relationships between activity and accomplishment. Discretionary cost centers are evaluated, for accounting purposes, by comparing the actual and budgeted costs for a given period. The difference is identified as over-budget or under-budget.

It is possible to reconcile the difference between budgeted and actual income for an entire organization. This can be done by (1) assigning all costs and revenues to responsibility centers and then summarizing the performance of each responsibility center or (2) developing a detailed reconciliation of all costs and revenues for the organization as a whole.

KEY TERMS

Responsibility
  accounting

Responsibility center

Investment center

Profit center

Revenue center

Cost center

Static budget

Flexible budget

Efficiency

Standard cost

Standard cost center

Discretionary cost
  center

Effectiveness

Sales price variance

Sales volume variance

Order getting costs

Order filling costs

Net sales volume
  variance

**REVIEW
QUESTIONS**

7–1 Briefly describe the budgeting and performance evaluation cycle.

7–2 What is responsibility accounting? Why should noncontrollable costs be excluded from performance reports prepared in accordance with responsibility accounting?

7–3 Why are an organization's basic performance reports stated in terms of dollars?

7–4 Why does a production supervisor need more frequent performance measurements than the vice president of production?

7–5 Distinguish between investment and profit centers.

7–6 Why is a flexible budget rather than a static budget used to evaluate production departments?

7–7 Identify three alternative uses of standard costs.

7–8 What problems can result from the use of tight standards?

7–9 Distinguish between standard and discretionary cost centers.

7–10 Why are revenue center performance reports based on the original (static) budget?

7–11 How are the sales price and the sales volume variances computed?

7–12 Why are revenue centers often assigned responsibility for controllable costs?

7–13 Why is a sales department, when it is evaluated as a profit center, assigned responsibility for the standard variable cost of goods sold rather than the actual cost of goods sold?

7–14 How is the net sales volume variance computed?

7–15 Briefly describe two alternative approaches to reconciling the differences between budgeted and actual income.

EXERCISES

7–1 Developing a Flexible Budget

Complete the following flexible budget for each level of activity.

		Annual Production (units)		
	Standard Cost	10,000	15,000	20,000
Direct materials	$ 5.00/unit			
Direct labor	10.00/unit			
Variable overhead:				
Indirect materials	0.75/unit			
Equipment maintenance	0.10/unit			
Utilities	0.50/unit			
Overtime	0.05/unit			
Fringe benefits	4.00/unit			
Fixed overhead:				
Depreciation	$220,000/year			
Supervision	40,000/year			
Insurance	25,000/year			
Property taxes	28,000/year			
Building maintenance	35,000/year			
Total				

7–2 Flexible Budgets and Performance Evaluation

Presented is the January, 19x1 performance report for the production department of the Johnson Company.

Johnson Company
Production Department Performance Report
For the month of January, 19x1

	Actual	Budget	Variance
Volume	32,000	28,000	
Manufacturing costs:			
Direct materials	$ 89,600	$ 84,000	$ 5,600 U
Direct labor	165,000	140,000	25,000 U
Variable overhead	64,000	56,000	8,000 U
Fixed overhead	27,500	28,000	500 F
Total	$346,100	$308,000	$38,100 U

Requirements

a) Evaluate the performance report.

b) Prepare a more appropriate performance report.

7–3 Flexible Budgets and Performance Reports

Presented is the March, 19x3 performance report for the Finishing Department of the E-Z Person Chair Company.

E-Z Person Chair Company
Finishing Department Performance Report
For the month of March, 19x3

	Actual	Budget	Variance
Volume	15,000	20,000	
Manufacturing costs:			
Direct materials	$ 35,000	$ 40,000	$ 5,000 F
Direct labor	150,000	200,000	50,000 F
Variable overhead	73,000	100,000	27,000 F
Fixed overhead	13,000	12,000	1,000 U
Total	$271,000	$352,000	$81,000 F

Requirements

a) Evaluate the performance report.

b) Prepare a more appropriate performance report.

7–4 Sales Revenue Variances

The following information is available regarding a product sold by the Wilson Company.

	Actual	Budget
Unit selling price	$ 88	$ 80
Unit sales	× 5,000	× 6,000
Revenue	$440,000	$480,000

Required: Compute the sales price and the sales volume variances. Use these variances to reconcile the difference between budgeted and actual revenues.

7–5 Sales Revenue Variances

The following information is available regarding a product sold by the Smith Company.

	Actual	Budget
Unit selling price	$ 25	$ 30
Unit sales	× 11,000	× 8,000
Revenue	$275,000	$240,000

Required: Compute the sales price and the sales volume variances. Use these variances to reconcile the difference between budgeted and actual revenues.

7–6 Sales Revenue Variances

The gross profit of Reade Company for each of the years ended December 31, 19x1 and 19x0 was as follows:

	19x1	19x0
Sales	$792,000	$800,000
Cost of goods sold	−464,000	−480,000
Gross profit	$328,000	$320,000

Selling prices were 10 percent lower during 19x1.

Required: Compute the sales price and the sales volume variances. Use these variances to reconcile the difference between 19x0 and 19x1 revenues. Treat 19x0 as the base or standard.

(CPA Adapted)

7–7 Sales Variances

Presented is information pertaining to an item sold by the Crooked Creek General Store.

	Actual	Budget
Unit sales	150	120
Unit selling price	$ 26	$ 25
Unit standard variable costs	− 20	− 20
Unit contribution margin	$ 6	$ 5
Revenues	$3900	$3000
Standard variable costs	−3000	−2400
Contribution margin at standard costs	$ 900	$ 600

Requirements

a) Compute the sales price and the sales volume variances.

b) Use the variances computed in requirement (a) to reconcile the budgeted and the actual revenues.

c) Compute the net sales volume variance.

d) Use the sales price and the net sales volume variances to reconcile the difference between the budgeted and the actual contribution margin at standard costs.

7–8 Sales Variances

Presented is information pertaining to a product of the Boise Mountain Supply Company.

	Actual	Budget
Unit sales	600	800
Unit selling price	$ 10	$ 8
Unit standard variable costs	− 5	− 5
Unit contribution margin	$ 5	$ 3
Revenues	$6000	$6400
Standard variable costs	−3000	−4000
Contribution margin at standard costs	$3000	$2400

Requirements

a) Compute the sales price and the sales volume variances.

b) Use the variances computed in requirement (a) to reconcile the budgeted and the actual revenues.

c) Compute the net sales volume variance.

d) Use the sales price and the net sales volume variances to reconcile the difference between the budgeted and the actual contribution margin at standard costs.

7–9 Reconciling Budgeted and Actual Gross Profit

The Johnson Company is a merchandising firm that buys and sells a single product. Presented is information from Johnson's 19y4 and 19y3 income statements.

	19y4	19y3
Unit sales	220,000	250,000
Sales revenue	$990,000	$750,000
Cost of goods sold	−506,000	−500,000
Gross profit	$484,000	$250,000

Requirements

a) Reconcile the variation in sales revenue using appropriate sales variances. Treat 19y3 as the base or standard.

b) Reconcile the variation in gross profit using appropriate sales and cost variances. Treat 19y3 as the base or standard.

7–10 Reconciling Budgeted and Actual Gross Profit

Garfield Company is a merchandising firm that buys and sells a single product. Presented is information from Garfield's 19x8 and 19x7 income statements.

	19x8	19x7
Unit sales	150,000	180,000
Sales revenue	$750,000	$720,000
Cost of goods sold	−525,000	−576,000
Gross profit	$225,000	$144,000

Requirements

a) Reconcile the variation in sales revenue using appropriate sales variances. Treat 19x7 as the base or standard.

b) Reconcile the variation in gross profit using appropriate sales and cost variances. Treat 19x7 as the base or standard.

(CPA Adapted)

7–11 Profit Center Performance Reports

The Record Rack is a store that specializes in the sale of recordings of classical music. There has been a recent upsurge in the popularity of J. S. Bach's works. Because of this, the Record Rack has established a separate room, Bach's Concert Room, dealing only in recordings of Bach's music. The albums are purchased from a wholesaler for $4.25 each. Though the standard retail price is $7.75 per album, the manager of Bach's Concert Room may undertake price reductions and other sales promotions in an attempt to increase sales volume. With the exception of the cost of albums, the operating costs of Bach's Concert Room are fixed.

Presented are the budgeted and the actual August, 19x3 contribution statements of Bach's Concert Room.

Record Rack: Bach's Concert Room
Budgeted and Actual Contribution Statements
For the month of August, 19x3

	Actual	Budget
Unit sales	4,200	4,000
Unit selling price	$ 7.25	$ 7.75
Sales revenue	$30,450	$31,000
Cost of goods sold	−17,850	−17,000
Gross profit	$12,600	$14,000
Operating costs	− 5,000	− 6,000
Contribution to corporate costs and profits	$ 7,600	$ 8,000

Required: Compute variances to assist in evaluating the performance of Bach's Concert Room as a profit center. Use these variances to reconcile the budgeted and actual contribution to corporate costs and profits.

7-12 Profit Center Performance Reports

Dip-In Donuts produces donuts in a central Chicago bakery and ships them to Dip-In Donut Shops throughout the Chicago area. Each shop is evaluated as a profit center. The shops purchase the Dip-In Donuts from the bakery at $1.50 per dozen. The standard retail price is $3.00 per dozen; however, individual shop managers may issue coupons and undertake other promotions in order to increase sales volume. With the exception of the cost of donuts, each shop's operating costs are fixed.

Presented are the budgeted and the actual May, 19x6 contribution statements of the Wicker Park Shop.

Dip-In Donuts: Wicker Park Shop
Budgeted and Actual Contribution Statements
For the month of May, 19x6

	Actual	*Budget*
Unit sales (dozen)	15,500	14,000
Unit selling price (dozen)	$ 2.80	$ 3.00
Sales revenue	$43,400	$42,000
Cost of food sold	−23,250	−21,000
Gross profit	$20,150	$21,000
Operating costs	−19,500	−17,000
Contribution to corporate costs and profits	$ 650	$ 4,000

Required: Compute variances to assist in evaluating the performance of the Wicker Park Shop as a profit center. Use these variances to reconcile the budgeted and actual contribution to corporate costs and profits.

PROBLEMS

7-13 Evaluating Cost Center Performance Reports with Behavioral Implications

Denny Daniels is production manager of the Alumalloy Division of WRT Inc. Alumalloy has limited contact with outside customers and has no sales staff. Most of its customers are other divisions of WRT. All sales and purchases with outside customers are handled by other corporate divisions. Therefore, Alumalloy is treated as a cost center for reporting and evaluation purposes rather than as a revenue or profit center.

Daniels perceives accounting as an historical number generating process that provides little useful information for conducting his job. Consequently, the entire accounting process is regarded as a negative motivational device that does not reflect how hard or how effectively he works as a production manager. Daniels tried to discuss these perceptions and concerns with John Scott, the Controller for the Alumalloy Division. Daniels told Scott, "I think the cost report is misleading.

I know I've had better production over a number of operating periods, but the cost report still says I have excessive costs. Look, I'm not an accountant, I'm a production manager. I know how to get a good quality product out. Over a number of years, I've even cut the raw materials used to do it. But the cost report doesn't show any of this. Basically, it's always negative, no matter what I do. There's no way you can win with accounting or the people at corporate headquarters who use those reports."

Scott gave Daniels little consolation. The accounting system and the cost reports generated by headquarters, Scott stated, are just part of the corporate game and almost impossible for an individual to change. "Although these accounting reports are pretty much the basis for evaluating the efficiency of your division and the means corporate management uses to determine whether you have done the job they want, you shouldn't worry too much. You haven't been fired yet! Besides, these cost reports have been used by WRT for the last twenty-five years."

Daniels perceived from talking to the production manager of the Zinc Division that most of what Scott said was probably true. However, some minor cost reporting changes for Zinc had been agreed to by corporate headquarters. He also knew from the trade grapevine that the turnover of production managers was considered high at WRT, even though relatively few were fired. Most seemed to end up quitting, usually in disgust, because of beliefs that they were not being evaluated fairly. Typical comments of production managers who have left WRT are:

- "Corporate headquarters doesn't really listen to us. All they consider are those misleading cost reports. They don't want them changed, and they don't want any supplemental information."

- "The accountants may be quick with numbers, but they don't know anything about production. As it was, I either had to ignore the cost reports entirely or pretend they are important even though they didn't tell how good a job I had done. No matter what they say about not firing people, negative reports mean negative evaluations. I'm better off working for another company."

A recent copy of the cost report prepared by corporate headquarters for the Alumalloy Division is shown below. Daniels does not like this report because he believes it fails to reflect the division's operations properly, thereby resulting in an unfair evaluation of performance.

Alumalloy Division
Cost Report
For the month of April, 19x0

	Original Budget	Actual Cost	Excess Cost
Aluminum	$ 400,000	$ 437,000	$37,000
Labor	560,000	540,000	
Overhead	100,000	134,000	34,000
Total	$1,060,000	$1,111,000	

Requirements

a) Comment on Denny Daniels' perception of John Scott, the controller; corporate headquarters; the cost report; and himself as a production manager. Discuss how his perceptions affect his behavior and probable performance as a production manager and employee of WRT.

b) Identify and explain three changes that could be made in the cost information presented to the production managers that would make the information more meaningful and less threatening to them.

(CMA Adapted)

7–14 Reconciling Budgeted and Actual Income

JK Enterprises sold 550,000 units during the first quarter ended March 31, 19y1. These sales represented a 10 percent increase over the number of units budgeted for the quarter. In spite of the sales increase, profits were below budget, as is shown in the condensed income statement presented below.

JK Enterprises Income Statement For the first quarter ended March 31, 19y1	Budget	Actual
Sales	$2,500,000	$2,530,000
Variable expenses:		
Cost of goods sold	$1,475,000	$1,540,000
Selling	400,000	440,000
Total variable expenses	−1,875,000	−1,980,000
Contribution margin	$ 625,000	$ 550,000
Fixed expenses:		
Selling	$ 125,000	$ 150,000
Administration	275,000	300,000
Total fixed expenses	− 400,000	− 450,000
Income before taxes	$ 225,000	$ 100,000
Income taxes (40 percent)	− 90,000	− 40,000
Net income	$ 135,000	$ 60,000

The accounting department always prepares a brief analysis that explains the difference between budgeted net income and actual net income. This analysis, which has not yet been completed for the first quarter, is submitted to top management with the income statement.

Required: Prepare an explanation of the $125,000 unfavorable variance between the first quarter budgeted and actual before-tax income for JK Enterprises by calculating a single amount for each of the following:

1. Sales price variance.

2. Variable cost variance.

3. Net sales volume variance.

4. Fixed cost variance.

(CMA Adapted)

7–15 Reconciling Budgeted and Actual Income

Presented are the budgeted and actual contribution income statements of Queen's Encyclopedia, Limited, for the month of October, 19x8.

Queen's Encyclopedia, Limited
Budgeted Contribution Income Statement
For the month of October, 19x8

Sales ($300 × 900)			$270,000
Less variable costs:			
Variable cost of goods sold:			
Direct materials ($50 × 900)	$45,000		
Direct labor ($20 × 900)	18,000		
Factory overhead ($30 × 900)	27,000	$ 90,000	
Selling ($70 × 900)		63,000	−153,000
Contribution margin			$117,000
Less fixed costs:			
Factory overhead		$ 40,000	
Selling		50,000	
Administration		10,500	−100,500
Net income			$ 16,500

Queen's Encyclopedia, Limited
Actual Contribution Income Statement
For the month of October, 19x8

Sales ($320 × 1000)			$320,000
Less variable costs:			
Variable cost of goods sold:			
Direct materials	$50,000		
Direct labor	22,000		
Factory overhead	35,000	$107,000	
Selling		100,000	−207,000
Contribution			$113,000
Less fixed costs:			
Factory overhead		$ 38,000	
Selling		65,000	
Administration		12,000	−115,000
Net income (loss)			$ (2,000)

Queen's Encyclopedia contains three responsibility centers: a production department, a sales department, and an administration department. The production and administration departments are cost centers, and the sales department is a profit center.

Requirements

a) Prepare a performance report for the production department that compares actual and allowed costs.

b) Prepare a performance report for selling expenses that compares actual and allowed costs.

c) Determine the sales price and the net sales volume variances.

d) Prepare a report that summarizes the performance of the sales department.

e) Determine the amount the administration department was over or under budget.

f) Prepare a report reconciling budgeted and actual net income. Your report should focus on the performance of each responsibility center.

7–16 Reconciling Budgeted and Actual Income

The budgeted and the actual income statements of Queen's Encyclopedia, Limited, for the month of October, 19x8 are presented in Problem 7–15.

Required: Prepare a detailed reconciliation of actual and budgeted costs, revenues, and income for the organization as a whole.

7–17 Reconciling Budgeted and Actual Income

Presented are the budgeted and the actual income statements of the Jones Valve Company, for the year ended December 31, 19x2.

Jones Valve Company
Budgeted and Actual Income Statements
For the year ending December 31, 19x2

	Budget	Actual
Unit sales	20,000	18,000
Unit selling price	$ 18	$ 21
Sales	$360,000	$378,000
Less variable costs:		
Direct materials ($2 per unit standard)	$ 40,000	$ 45,000
Direct labor ($3 per unit standard)	60,000	54,000
Factory overhead ($3 per unit standard)	60,000	50,400
Selling ($1 per unit standard)	20,000	20,000
Total	−180,000	−169,400
Contribution margin	$180,000	$208,600
Less fixed costs:		
Factory overhead	$ 55,000	$ 56,000
Selling	60,000	54,000
Administration	40,000	47,500
Total	−155,000	−157,500
Net income	$ 25,000	$ 51,100

The Jones Valve Company contains three responsibility centers: a production department, a sales department, and an administration department. The production and administration departments are cost centers, and the sales department is a profit center.

Requirements

a) Prepare a performance report for the production department that compares actual and allowed costs.

b) Prepare a performance report for selling expenses that compares actual and allowed costs.

c) Determine the sales price and the net sales volume variances.

d) Prepare a report that summarizes the performance of the sales department.

e) Determine the amount the administration department was over or under budget.

f) Prepare a report reconciling budgeted and actual net income. Your report should focus on the performance of each responsibility center.

7–18 Reconciling Budgeted and Actual Income

The budgeted and the actual income statements of the Jones Valve Company, for the year ended December 31, 19x2 are presented in Problem 7–17.

Required: Prepare a detailed reconciliation of actual and budgeted costs, revenues, and income for the organization as a whole.

7–19 Evaluating a Sales Compensation Plan

Betterbuilt Corporation manufactures a full line of windows and doors, including casement windows, bow windows, and patio doors. The bow windows and patio doors have a significantly higher gross profit per unit than casement windows, as is shown in the schedule below.

	Unit Price and Cost Data		
	Casement Windows	Bow Windows	Patio Doors
Sales price	$130	$250	$260
Manufacturing costs:			
Direct materials	$ 25	$ 40	$ 50
Direct labor	20	35	30
Variable overhead*	16	28	24
Fixed overhead†	24	42	36
Total manufacturing costs	− 85	−145	−140
Gross profit	$ 45	$105	$120

* Variable manufacturing overhead is applied at the rate of 80 percent of direct labor cost.

† Fixed manufacturing overhead is applied at the rate of 120 percent of direct labor cost.

The company sells almost entirely to general contractors of residential housing. Most of these contractors complete and sell fifteen to fifty houses per year. Each contractor builds tract houses that are similar, with some variations in exteriors and rooflines.

When contractors contact Betterbuilt, they are likely to seek bids for all the windows in the houses they plan to build in the next year. At this point, the Betterbuilt salespeople have an opportunity to influence the window configuration of these houses by suggesting patio doors or bow windows as variations for one or more casement windows for each of the several exteriors and rooflines built by the contractor.

The bow windows and patio doors are approximately twice as wide as the casement windows. A bow window or a patio door usually is substituted for two casement windows. Casement windows are usually ordered in pairs and placed side-by-side in those houses that could be modified to accept bow windows and patio doors.

Joseph Hite, President of Betterbuilt Corporation, is perplexed with the company's profit performance. In a conversation with his sales manager he declared, "Our total dollars sales volume is growing, but our net income has not increased as it should. Our unit sales of casement windows have increased proportionately more than the sale of bow windows or patio doors. Why aren't our salespeople pushing our more profitable products?" The sales manager responded with a sense of frustration, "I don't know what else can be done. The salespeople have been told which type of windows we want sold because of the greater profit margin. Furthermore, they have the best compensation plan in the industry, with $500 monthly draw against their commissions of 10 percent on sales dollars."

Requirements

a) Explain why Betterbuilt's present compensation program for its salespeople does not support the President's objectives to sell the more profitable units.

b) Identify and explain alternative compensation program(s) that may be more appropriate for motivating Betterbuilt Corporation's salespeople to sell the more profitable units.

(CMA Adapted)

7–20 Evaluating Alternative Sales Compensation Plans

Pre-Fab Corporation, a relatively large company in the manufactured housing industry, is known for its aggressive sales promotion campaigns. Pre-Fab's innovative advertising and sales strategies have resulted in generally satisfactory performance in the last few years.

One of Pre-Fab's objectives is to increase sales revenue by at least 10 percent annually. This objective has been attained. Return on investment is considered good and had increased annually until last year when net income decreased for the first time in nine years. The latest economic recession could be the cause of the change, but other factors, such as sales growth, discount this reason.

A significant portion of Pre-Fab's administrative expenses are fixed, but the majority of the manufacturing expenses are variable in nature. The increases in selling prices have been consistent with the 12 percent increase in manufacturing expenses. Pre-Fab has consistently been able to maintain a companywide contribution margin of approximately 30 percent. However, the contribution margin on individual product lines varies from 15 to 45 percent.

Sales commission expenses increased 30 percent over the past year. The prefabricated housing industry has always been sales oriented and Pre-Fab's management has believed in generously rewarding the efforts of its sales personnel. The sales force compensation plan consists of three segments:

- A guaranteed annual salary, which is increased annually at about a 6 percent rate. The salary is below industry average.

- A sales commission of 9 percent of total sales dollars. This is higher than the industry average.

- A year-end bonus of 5 percent of total sales dollars to each salesperson when their total sales dollars exceed the prior year by at least 12 percent.

The current compensation plan has resulted in an average annual income of $42,500 per sales employee, compared with an industry annual average of $30,000. However, the compensation plan has been effective in generating increased sales. Further, the sales department employees are satisfied with the plan. Management, however, is concerned about the financial implications of the current plan. They believe the plan has caused higher selling expenses and a lower net income relative to the sales revenue increase.

At the last staff meeting the controller suggested that the sales compensation plan be modified so that sales employees could earn an annual average income of $37,500. The controller believed that such a plan still would be attractive to its sales personnel and, at the same time, allow the company to earn a more satisfactory profit.

The vice president for sales voiced strong objection to altering the current compensation plan because employee morale and incentive would drop significantly if there were any change. Nevertheless, most of the staff believed that the area of sales compensation merited a review. The president stated that all phases of a company operation can benefit from a periodic review, no matter how successful they have been in the past.

Several compensation plans known to be used by other companies in the manufactured housing industry are:

- Straight commission as a percentage of sales.
- Straight salary.
- Salary plus compensation based upon sales to new customers.
- Salary plus compensation based upon contribution margin.
- Salary plus compensation based upon unit sales volume.

Requirements

a) Discuss the advantages and disadvantages of Pre-Fab Corporation's current sales compensation plan with respect to (1) the financial aspects of the company and (2) the behavioral aspects of the sales personnel.

b) For each of the alternative compensation plans known to be used by other companies in the manufactured housing industry, discuss whether the plan would be an improvement over the current plan in terms of (1) the financial performance of the company and (2) the behavioral implications for the sales personnel.

(CMA Adapted)

7–21 Evaluating a Sales Compensation Plan

Prior to 19y3 the Carbon Chemical Company paid its sales representatives a straight salary plus selling expenses. In an attempt to better motivate them, the company changed their basis of compensation from salary to commissions based on gross sales. The commission rate was computed as 19y2 sales salaries divided by 19y2 gross sales revenues.

Early in 19y4 Martha Childs, the company president, was reviewing Carbon Chemical's 19y3 performance, as compared to its 19y2 performance. She is concerned that the commissions are not motivating the sales representatives to work in the company's best interest, and she wants your advice.

Presented is comparative 19y2 and 19y3 information.

	19y2	19y3
Gross sales	$648,000	$934,000
Less sales returns and allowances	− 8,000	− 34,000
Net sales	$640,000	$900,000
Variable costs:		
Cost of goods sold	$388,800	$560,400
Commissions	—	74,720
Total	−388,800	−635,120
Contribution margin	$251,200	$264,880
Fixed costs:		
Sales salaries	$ 51,840	$ —
Other selling	20,000	55,000
Administration	80,000	90,000
Total	−151,840	−145,000
Net income	$ 99,360	$119,880

Required: Evaluate the sales compensation plan, and suggest some alternative plans that might better motivate the sales representatives to work in the company's interest.

7–22 Evaluating a Companywide Performance Report

Mr. Micawber, the production supervisor, bursts into your office carrying the Crupp Company's 19y2 performance report:

"There is villainy here, sir! And I shall get to the bottom of it. I will not stop searching until I have found the answer! Why is Mr. Heep so down on my department? I thought we did a good job last year. But Heep claims I and my production people cost the company $31,500! I plead with you, sir, explain this performance report to me.''

Trying to calm Mr. Micawber, you take the report from him and ask to be left alone for 15 minutes. The report is presented below.

Crupp Company, Limited
Performance Report
For the year 19y2

	Actual	Budget	Variance
Unit sales	7,500	5,000	
Sales	$262,500	$225,000	$37,500 F
Less manufacturing costs:			
Direct materials	$ 55,500	$ 47,500	$ 8,000 U
Direct labor	48,000	32,500	15,500 U
Factory overhead	40,000	32,000*	8,000 U
Total	−143,500	−112,000	−31,500 U
Gross profit	$119,000	$113,000	$ 6,000 F
Less selling and administrative expenses:			
Selling (all fixed)	$ 60,000	$ 40,000	$20,000 U
Administrative (all fixed)	55,000	50,000	5,000 U
Total	−115,000	− 90,000	−25,000 U
Net income	$ 4,000	$ 23,000	$19,000 U
Performance summary:			
Budgeted net income			$23,000
Sales department variances:			
Sales revenue	$ 37,500 F		
Selling expenses	20,000 U	$ 17,500 F	
Administration department variances		5,000 U	
Production department variances		31,500 U	19,000 U
Actual net income			$ 4,000

* Includes fixed factory overhead of $22,000.

Requirements

a) Evaluate the performance report. Is Mr. Heep correct? Or, is there ''villainy here''?

b) Assume that the sales department is a profit center and that the production and administration departments are cost centers. Determine the responsibility of each for cost, revenue, and income variances, and prepare a report reconciling budgeted and actual net income. Your report should focus on the performance of each responsibility center.

8

Performance Evaluation of Standard Cost Centers

In Chapter 7 two types of cost centers were introduced, standard cost centers and discretionary cost centers. This chapter discusses standard cost centers in greater depth. You recall that standard cost centers are cost centers that have clearly defined relationships between effort (inputs) and accomplishment (outputs) that can be expressed in terms of standard costs per unit produced. These unit standard costs help to make up the budget formula that is used to prepare each period's flexible budget for the firm's actual production output. Manager performance, then, is evaluated by comparing actual costs incurred with flexible budget costs. Because of their role in determining flexible budget costs, standard costs are the basis for evaluating managers in standard cost centers.

The standard cost of making one finished unit of product is determined separately for direct materials, direct labor, and variable factory overhead.[1] In addition, each of these cost components is broken down into price and quantity factors. For example, the standard direct materials cost of manufacturing neckties might be stated at $5 per necktie, consisting of $\frac{1}{3}$ yard of fabric at a rate of $15 per yard. Because of the amount of detail that goes into establishing cost standards, variances between actual costs and flexible budget costs can be rigorously analyzed. This analysis involves separating flexible budget variances into component variances that indicate the specific causes for the flexible budget variances. When reported to the cost center manager, detailed cost variance information can be used to evaluate performance and facilitate substantive cost control decisions.

The purpose of this chapter is to discuss how standard costs are established for direct materials, direct labor, and variable factory overhead, and to show how they are used in evaluating standard cost centers. To use and interpret standard cost variances properly, it is essential for managers to understand both the standard-setting process and the framework for computing and analyzing standard cost variances. In this chapter we focus on these aspects of standard cost planning and control systems.

BASIC VARIANCE ANALYSIS CONCEPTS

In a standard cost system **variance analysis** is the process of analyzing the difference between *actual costs* and *standard costs allowed by the flexible budget* for manufacturing a product or providing a service. In other words, standard cost variance analysis is the process of analyzing

---

[1] Standard unit costs ordinarily are not determined for fixed factory overhead costs for performance evaluation purposes because these costs are incurred based on the production capacity provided, not the production capacity used. Accordingly, they are not controlled on a per unit of production basis.

flexible budget variances. To illustrate, assume that Wonderful Widgets, Inc. has determined that the standard cost of making widgets is $10 per unit. If the company manufactures 250 widgets in July at an actual cost of $2805, the total flexible budget variance is $305:

Actual costs incurred	$2,805
Less standard costs allowed (250 outputs at $10 each)	−2,500
Total flexible budget variance	$ 305 U

Since actual costs exceeded the standard costs allowed, the variance is unfavorable. To analyze the $305 total flexible budget variance, we must understand the two numbers that produced the variance — the actual costs incurred and the standard costs allowed by the flexible budget.

Actual costs incurred and standard costs allowed differ because one is based on *actual inputs,* and the other is based on *actual outputs.* The $2805 of actual costs incurred is an historical cost measure of the materials, labor, and overhead actually put into production to manufacture the widgets. Assume that the actual cost incurred of $2805 consisted of 255 units of inputs, purchased for $11 per unit. To simplify the initial analysis, also assume that each unit of input contained some materials, labor, and overhead. "Actual costs," therefore, is an input concept.

Standard costs allowed represents the predetermined, or standard, amount that should have been incurred, and thus was allowed by the flexible budget, to produce the output of 250 widgets; it is the total input cost allowed for the actual outputs achieved. "Standard costs allowed," therefore, is primarily an output concept. To produce 250 widgets, management was allowed $2500, or $10 of input costs per unit produced. The relationships between production inputs, outputs, and costs are illustrated in Exhibit 8–1. The standard cost of units produced is always measured in terms of the standard input cost allowed for the actual outputs produced. *The total flexible budget variance is the difference between the actual costs of actual inputs (materials, labor, and overhead) and the standard cost of inputs allowed by the flexible budget for the actual outputs produced.* A flexible budget variance will result any time the quantity of actual inputs is different from the standard inputs allowed, or the actual input price is different from the standard input price.

By adding another cost value to our analysis — *the standard cost of actual inputs* — the total flexible budget variance can be broken down into two component variances, the *price variance* and the *quantity variance.* For Wonderful Widgets, Inc. the standard cost of actual inputs was $2550 (255 actual input units × $10 standard cost per unit of input). According

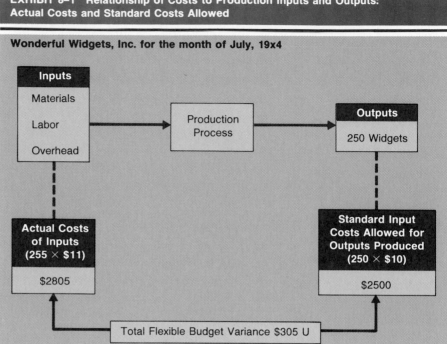

EXHIBIT 8–1 Relationship of Costs to Production Inputs and Outputs: Actual Costs and Standard Costs Allowed

Wonderful Widgets, Inc. for the month of July, 19x4

to the standards, each finished widget should use one input unit costing $10. Since 250 widgets were produced, the standard cost allowed in the flexible budget was $2500 (250 units of output × 1 input unit for each output × $10 standard cost per unit of input).

Exhibit 8–2 shows how input and output costs relate to produce the total flexible budget variance, and the price and quantity variances. Notice that the price variance results from comparing the actual inputs with the standard cost of actual inputs, and the quantity variance results from comparing the standard cost of actual inputs with the standard cost of allowed inputs. The allowed inputs are based on the actual output of 250 widgets.

Graphical presentations are often helpful in understanding standard cost variances. Exhibit 8–3 presents, through a series of graphs, the (a) actual cost of actual inputs, (b) standard cost of allowed inputs, (c) total flexible budget variance, and (d) price and quantity variances.

Exhibits 8–2 and 8–3 are helpful in gaining a conceptual understanding of variance analysis; however, for purposes of computing price and quantity variances, a more direct approach, which is presented in the box at the top of page 295, is used throughout this chapter.

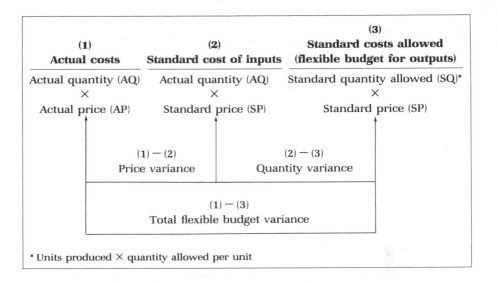

	(1) **Actual costs**	(2) **Standard cost of inputs**	(3) **Standard costs allowed (flexible budget for outputs)**
	Actual quantity (AQ) × Actual price (AP)	Actual quantity (AQ) × Standard price (SP)	Standard quantity allowed (SQ)* × Standard price (SP)

(1) — (2)
Price variance

(2) — (3)
Quantity variance

(1) — (3)
Total flexible budget variance

* Units produced × quantity allowed per unit

EXHIBIT 8–2 Relationship of Production Inputs and Outputs to Actual Costs, Standard Cost of Inputs, and Standard Costs Allowed

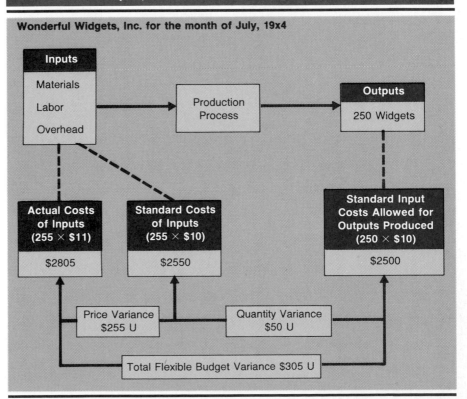

Wonderful Widgets, Inc. for the month of July, 19x4

Inputs

Materials

Labor

Overhead

Production
Process

Outputs

250 Widgets

**Actual Costs
of Inputs
(255 × $11)**

$2805

**Standard Costs
of Inputs
(255 × $10)**

$2550

**Standard Input
Costs Allowed for
Outputs Produced
(250 × $10)**

$2500

Price Variance
$255 U

Quantity Variance
$50 U

Total Flexible Budget Variance $305 U

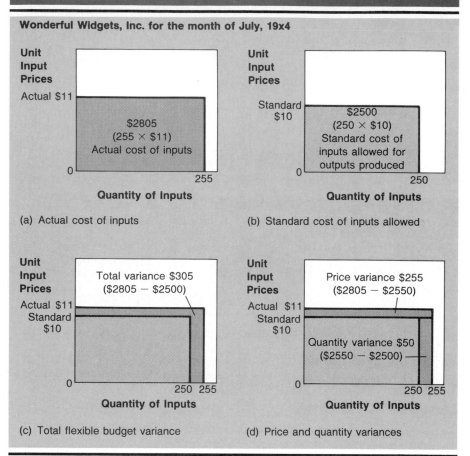

EXHIBIT 8–3   Graphic Illustrations of Actual Costs, Standard Costs, and Basic Variances

Wonderful Widgets, Inc. for the month of July, 19x4

(a) Actual cost of inputs

(b) Standard cost of inputs allowed

(c) Total flexible budget variance

(d) Price and quantity variances

To summarize the above computations, the *price variance* equals the actual costs incurred minus the standard cost of actual inputs:

$$\text{Price variance} = (AQ \times AP) - (AQ \times SP).$$

Alternatively, by factoring the above equation the price variance can be computed:

$$\text{Price variance} = AQ(AP - SP).$$

The *quantity variance* equals the standard cost of actual inputs minus the standard cost of inputs allowed by the flexible budget for the outputs produced:

$$\text{Quantity variance} = (AQ \times SP) - (SQ \times SP).$$

Alternatively, the quantity variance can be computed:

$$\text{Quantity variance} = SP(AQ - SQ).$$

The general variance computation model is illustrated below for Wonderful Widgets, Inc.

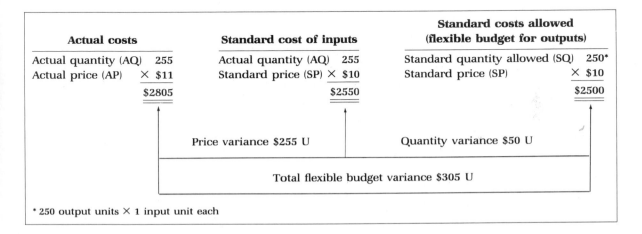

Actual costs		Standard cost of inputs		Standard costs allowed (flexible budget for outputs)	
Actual quantity (AQ)	255	Actual quantity (AQ)	255	Standard quantity allowed (SQ)	250*
Actual price (AP)	× $11	Standard price (SP)	× $10	Standard price (SP)	× $10
	$2805		$2550		$2500

Price variance $255 U   Quantity variance $50 U

Total flexible budget variance $305 U

* 250 output units × 1 input unit each

The total unfavorable flexible budget variance of $305 consists of a $255 unfavorable price variance and a $50 unfavorable quantity variance. The price variance was *unfavorable* because the price paid for inputs ($11) was greater than the standard price of inputs ($10). The quantity variance was *unfavorable* because the actual quantity of inputs used (255) was greater than the inputs allowed (250) by the flexible budget for the level of outputs achieved. The standards allowed only 1 unit of input per unit of output; therefore production of 250 widgets should have required only 250 units of input, not the 255 units actually used.

In the Wonderful Widgets example we assumed that each input unit contained some amount of materials, labor, and overhead. In an actual manufacturing situation these three production components are acquired, used, and controlled separately—which is the reason that, in the following sections of this chapter, these cost components are discussed separately. For each of these cost components, price and quantity variances are computed; however, these variances are ordinarily referred to by different names for direct labor and variable factory overhead. The commonly used names of the price and quantity variances for materials, labor, and variable overhead are as follows:

Cost Component	Price Variance Name	Quantity Variance Name
Direct materials	Materials price variance	Materials quantity variance
Direct labor	Labor rate variance	Labor efficiency variance
Variable overhead	Variable overhead spending variance	Variable overhead efficiency variance

To facilitate our discussion of materials, labor, and variable overhead variance analysis, we will use the March, 19x6 standard and actual cost information for Execupens, Inc. presented in Exhibit 8–4. Execupens manufactures gold casings for high priced writing pens. Except for minor design differences, the casings are identical. Completed casings are sold to other manufacturers, who add their own writing element and a spring. Each casing has a standard cost of $68.

Notice in Exhibit 8–4 that the $68 standard cost per unit includes only direct materials, direct labor, and variable overhead. These costs vary in total with the volume of production. As production increases, the direct materials, direct labor, and variable overhead costs allowed also increase.

EXHIBIT 8–4   Cost and Production Data

Execupens, Inc.
Cost and Production Data
For the month of March, 19x6

	Standard Quantity		Standard Price		Standard Cost (Flexible Budget Formula)
Standard cost per unit manufactured:					
Direct materials	6 hours	×	$ 8	=	$48
Direct labor	1 hour	×	$14	=	14
Variable overhead	1 hour	×	$ 6	=	6
Total standard cost per unit					$68
Budgeted fixed overhead per month					$198,000
Number of units manufactured during March, 19x6					20,000
Actual production costs:					
Direct materials	124,000 grams at $7.96				$ 987,040
Direct labor	19,200 hours at $14.84				284,928
Variable overhead					126,000
Fixed overhead					200,000
Total actual costs					$1,597,968

Fixed overhead is *excluded* because, within the relevant range of normal activity, it does not vary with the volume of production. For the purpose of internal planning and control, fixed costs are budgeted and evaluated as a *lump sum*. Our focus in the body of this chapter is on internal planning and control. For external reporting fixed overhead costs are normally assigned to products on a per unit basis. Also, to facilitate product costing, many organizations develop a standard fixed overhead cost per unit. Standard cost variances that arise under these circumstances are discussed in the appendix to this chapter.

The performance report showing the flexible budget variances for Execupens, Inc. is presented in Exhibit 8–5. In the following sections we will analyze the flexible budget cost variances for each of the variable cost components and compute the appropriate price and quantity variances. Control of the fixed factory overhead flexible budget variance will also be discussed.

EXHIBIT 8–5   Performance Report

Execupens, Inc.
Production Department Performance Report
For the month of March, 19x6

	Flexible Budget Formula	Actual Costs	Flexible Budget Costs	Flexible Budget Variances
Volume		20,000	20,000	
Manufacturing costs:				
Direct materials	$48/unit	$987,040	$960,000	$27,040 U
Direct labor	$14/unit	284,928	280,000	4,928 U
Variable overhead	$6/unit	126,000	120,000	6,000 U
Fixed overhead	$198,000/month	200,000	198,000	2,000 U
Totals		$1,597,968	$1,558,000	$39,968 U

MATERIALS STANDARDS AND VARIANCES

There are two basic elements contained in the standards for direct materials — the *standard price* and the *standard quantity*. Materials standards indicate (1) how much should be paid for each unit of direct materials used and (2) the quantity of direct materials that should be used to produce one unit of output. The standard price per unit of direct materials should include all reasonable costs necessary to acquire the materials. These costs include the invoice price of materials, less planned discounts, plus freight, insurance, special handling, and any other costs related to the acquisition of the materials.

The standard quantity represents the number of units of raw materials *allowed* for the production of one unit of finished product. The standard quantity of raw materials allowed to produce a unit of finished product should include the amount dictated by the physical characteristics of the process and the product, plus a reasonable allowance for normal spoilage, waste, and other inefficiencies. The quantity standard may be determined by engineering analysis, professional judgment, or by averaging the actual amount used for several periods. An average of actual past materials usage is generally considered not to be a good standard because it includes excessive wastes and inefficiencies in the standard quantity. Execupens, Inc. has a direct materials quantity standard of 6 grams per finished unit produced. In fact, each unit may physically contain only 5 grams of raw materials, with the additional gram representing the amount allowed by the standards for normal spoilage, waste, and other inefficiencies.

Materials Variances Illustrated

Using the general variance analysis model introduced earlier, we can compute the materials price and quantity variances. The **materials price variance** is the difference between the actual cost of the actual materials inputs and the standard cost of the actual materials inputs. The **materials quantity variance** is the difference between the standard cost of actual materials inputs and the standard cost of materials inputs allowed for the actual outputs.

Actual costs		Standard cost of inputs		Standard costs allowed (flexible budget for outputs)	
Actual quantity (AQ)	124,000	Actual quantity (AQ)	124,000	Standard quantity allowed (SQ)	120,000*
Actual price (AP)	× $7.96	Standard price (SP)	× $8.00	Standard price (SP)	× $8.00
	$987,040		$992,000		$960,000

Materials price variance $4,960 F

Materials quantity variance $32,000 U

Total flexible budget materials variance $27,040 U

* 20,000 units × 6 grams per unit

Execupens, Inc. had a favorable materials price variance of $4960 because the actual cost of materials used ($987,040) was less than the standard cost of materials used ($992,000). Stated another way, for the materials actually used, the total price paid was $4960 less than the price allowed by the standards. The price variance can also be viewed as the actual quantity used times the difference between the actual price and the standard price. Execupens, Inc. paid 4 cents below the standard price for 124,000 grams of gold purchased, for a total savings of $4960:

$$\text{Materials price variance} = AQ(AP - SP)$$
$$= 124,000 \ (\$7.96 - \$8.00)$$
$$= 124,000 \times \$0.04$$
$$= \$4,960 \ F.$$

The unfavorable quantity variance of $32,000 occurred because the standard cost of materials used ($992,000) was greater than the standard cost of the quantity allowed ($960,000). A total of 120,000 grams of raw materials is allowed to produce 20,000 units of finished outputs. This is computed as 20,000 finished units times 6 grams of raw materials per unit. The materials quantity variance may also be computed as the standard cost per gram times the difference between the number of grams actually used and the number of grams allowed. Four thousand grams of gold more than the standard amount allowed were used at a standard cost of $8 per gram, resulting in an additional cost of $32,000:

$$\text{Materials quantity variance} = SP(AQ - SQ)$$
$$= \$8.00 \ (124,000 - 120,000)$$
$$= \$8.00 \times 4000$$
$$= \$32,000 \ U.$$

In the Execupens example, the computation of the price variance was based on the *materials actually used* during the period. However, since materials prices are ordinarily controlled at the point of purchase, rather than at the point of usage, many managers prefer to compute the materials price variance on the basis of *materials purchased* instead of materials used. If 125,000 grams of materials were purchased at $7.96 but only 124,000 were used, the materials variances would be computed as follows in the box insert at the top of page 302.

Actual costs		Standard cost of inputs		Standard costs allowed (flexible budget for outputs)	
Actual quantity purchased (AQ)	125,000	Actual quantity purchased (AQ)	125,000		
Actual price (AP)	× $7.96	Standard price (SP)	× $8.00		
	$995,000	Standard cost of materials purchased	$1,000,000		
		Materials purchased price variance $5000 F			
		Actual quantity used (AQ)	124,000	Standard quantity allowed (SQ)	120,000*
		Standard price (SP)	× $8.00	Standard price (SP)	× $8.00
		Standard cost of materials used	$ 992,000		$960,000
				Materials quantity variance $32,000 U	
				Total flexible budget materials variance $32,000 U	

* 20,000 units × 6 grams per unit

Notice that now there are two actual quantities for materials. First, the actual quantity *purchased* is used to compute the materials price variance. The **materials purchased price variance** is the actual cost of materials purchased minus the standard cost of materials purchased. Second, the actual quantity *used* is utilized in computing the materials quantity variance. When the materials price variance is computed at the point of purchasing, all units of materials are charged to production at the standard price. Therefore, the materials price variance is not charged to production, and the total flexible budget variance consists entirely of the quantity variance.

Measuring the price variance at the point of materials purchases is desirable in situations where raw materials purchases vary substantially from the amount used during a given period. The purchasing manager, who controls materials purchases, needs to receive price variance information as soon as possible after the actual purchase of materials. If the price variance is measured when materials are used (which may be weeks or months after materials are purchased), the price variance information may be received too late to be useful in controlling materials prices. Also, timely reporting of price variance information is necessary for making pricing decisions, as it is for making other decisions based on current replacement costs.

Interpreting Materials Variances

Accountants often overemphasize the computation of variances and forget that the main objectives of variance analysis are reporting and interpreting the variances. It is necessary to understand how variances are computed, but it is even more important to know what to do with the variances after they are computed.

A *favorable materials price variance* indicates that the manager responsible for materials purchases paid less per unit than the price allowed by the standards. This may result from receiving discounts for purchasing in larger than normal quantities, effective bargaining by the manager, purchasing substandard quality materials, purchasing from a distress seller, or other factors. Ordinarily when a favorable price variance is reported, the manager's performance will be interpreted as favorable. However, if the favorable price variance resulted from the purchase of materials of lower than standard quality, or purchasing in larger than desirable quantities, the manager's performance would be questionable.

An *unfavorable materials price variance* means that the purchasing manager paid more per unit than the price allowed by the standards. This may be caused by failure to buy in sufficient quantities to get normal discounts, failure to place materials orders on a timely basis thereby requiring a more expensive shipping alternative, uncontrollable price changes in the market for raw materials, failure to bargain for the best available prices, or other factors. It should be emphasized that the type of evaluation the purchasing manager receives depends on the reasons for the variance. An unfavorable variance does not always mean that the manager performed unfavorably, and a favorable variance does not always indicate favorable performance.

A *favorable materials quantity variance* means that the actual quantity of raw materials used was less than the quantity allowed for the units produced. This may result from factors such as less materials waste than allowed by the standards, better than expected machine efficiency, raw materials of higher quality than required by the standards, and more efficient use of raw materials by the employees.

An *unfavorable materials quantity variance* occurs when the quantity of raw materials used exceeds the quantity allowed for the units produced. This may result from incurring more waste than provided for in the standards, poorly maintained machinery requiring larger amounts of raw materials, raw materials of lower quality than required by the standards, or poorly trained employees who were unable to utilize the materials at the level of efficiency required by the standards.

One possible cause for any standard cost variance (materials, labor, or overhead) is that the standard quantity or price used in computing the variance was too high or too low. A necessary consideration in evaluating any variance is that an inappropriate standard value may have been used in its computation. When investigating the possible causes for a given variance, one should always consider that the standards may be inappropriate. If the standards are determined to be incorrect, they should be revised to reflect current efficient operating conditions. Higher level managers should always be eager to revise the standards to reflect changes in the environment not controllable by their subordinate managers. This attitude will encourage responsibility center managers to have greater respect for both the reported variances and the entire performance evaluation system.

LABOR STANDARDS AND VARIANCES

Direct labor standards, like direct materials standards, consist of two components, *quantity* and *price*. The direct labor quantity standard is usually referred to as the labor efficiency, or usage, standard; the price standard is referred to as the labor rate standard. To evaluate management performance in controlling labor costs by using a standard cost system, it is necessary to determine the *standard labor time allowed* to produce a unit and the *standard labor rate* for each hour of labor allowed.

The standard labor time per unit can be determined by an engineering approach or an empirical observation approach. When using an engineering approach, industrial engineers ascertain the amount of labor required to produce a unit of finished product by applying time and motion methods or other available techniques. Normal operating conditions are assumed in arriving at the labor efficiency standard; therefore, allowances must be made for normal machine downtime, employee personal breaks, and so forth. Under the empirical approach, the long-run average time required in the past to produce a unit under normal operating conditions is used as a basis for the standard. By using normal operating conditions, inefficiencies such as machine downtime and employee breaks are automatically factored into the standard. The tightness of the standard can be adjusted by increasing or decreasing the observed average.

Setting labor rate standards may be quite simple or extremely complex, depending on the particular circumstances. If only one class of employees is used to make each product, and all employees earn the same wages, determination of the standard cost is relatively easy: simply adopt the normal wage rate as the standard labor rate. If several different classes of employees are utilized in making each unit of product, it is necessary to establish separate efficiency and rate standards for each class. For example, the standard direct labor cost per unit for making heavy machine components may be stated as follows:

Millwright labor (3 hr at $15 per hr)	$ 45
Machinist labor (5 hr at $12 per hr)	60
Standard labor cost per unit produced	$105

If wage rates vary for a given class of employees because of seniority or other differences, an average wage rate is ordinarily used for the labor rate standard. In these cases any variance caused by using an average rate should be negligible, unless there are large variations in wage rates within a particular employee class. To simplify our examples, we assume there is only one class of employees with all employees earning the same wage rate. As stated in Chapter 2, labor related fringe benefit costs are usually considered to be factory overhead and, therefore, are not included in the actual or standard labor rate.

Labor Variances Illustrated

Using the general variance model, we can compute the labor rate and efficiency variances. The **labor rate variance** is the difference between the actual cost of the actual labor hours and the standard cost of the actual labor hours. The **labor efficiency variance** is the difference between the standard cost of the actual labor hours and the standard cost of the labor hours allowed for the actual outputs.

Actual costs		Standard cost of inputs		Standard costs allowed (flexible budget for outputs)	
Actual hours (AH)	19,200	Actual hours (AH)	19,200	Standard hours allowed (SH)	20,000*
Actual rate (AR)	× $14.84	Standard rate (SR)	× $14.00	Standard rate (SR)	× $14.00
	$284,928		$268,800		$280,000
		Labor rate variance $16,128 U		Labor efficiency variance $11,200 F	
		Total flexible budget labor variance $4,928 U			

* 20,000 units × 1 hour per unit

Execupens' direct labor standards and labor usage data for March, 19x6 are presented in Exhibit 8–4. Notice that the standards provide for 1 hour of direct labor time per unit at a cost of $14 per hour. During the month of March, 19x6, 19,200 hours were used at a cost of $14.84 per hour. Using these data, the labor rate (price) variance and labor efficiency (quantity) variance can be computed as shown in the box insert at the bottom of page 305.

Notice in the computation of the labor rate variance that the quantity of labor inputs is held constant at the actual quantity of 19,200 direct labor hours, whereas the labor rate is varied between actual and standard. The labor rate variance can also be computed as the actual hours used times the difference between the actual labor rate and the standard labor rate:

$$
\begin{aligned}
\text{Labor rate variance} &= \text{AH(AR} - \text{SR)} \\
&= 19,200(\$14.84 - \$14.00) \\
&= 19,200 \times \$0.84 \\
&= \$16,128 \text{ U.}
\end{aligned}
$$

This computation of the labor rate variance shows that the company paid 84 cents above the standard rate for each of the 19,200 hours worked.

In computing the labor efficiency variance, the labor rate is held constant at the standard of $14, whereas total labor hours is varied between the actual and standard hours allowed for the work done. Since 20,000 units of product were finished during the period, and 1 hour of labor was allowed for each unit, the total standard hours allowed was 20,000. The labor efficiency variance can also be computed as the standard rate times the difference between the actual direct labor hours and the standard allowed hours for the output achieved:

$$
\begin{aligned}
\text{Labor efficiency variance} &= \text{SR(AH} - \text{SH)} \\
&= \$14(19,200 - 20,000) \\
&= \$14 \times 800 \\
&= \$11,200 \text{ F.}
\end{aligned}
$$

This computation of the labor efficiency variance indicates that the company used 800 fewer direct labor hours than the budget permitted, and that each of these hours saved $14, or a total of $11,200.

Interpreting Labor Variances

The possible explanations for labor rate variances are rather limited. An *unfavorable labor rate variance* may be caused by the use of higher skilled (and thus higher paid) laborers than provided for by the standards. Also, a new labor union contract increasing wages may have been implemented after the standards were set. In this case the standards should have been revised to account for the wage rate change. In a nonunion situation, where wages are not controlled by negotiated contract, there is the possibility that a manager may arbitrarily increase employee wages above the standard rate. This would also give rise to an unfavorable labor rate variance.

A *favorable labor rate variance* would occur if lower skilled (and thus lower paid) workers were used or if actual wage rates were reduced below standard labor rates. As an example of falling wage rates, in the early 1980s economic problems in the automobile industry forced some union negotiators to relinquish previously awarded employee benefits. Such adjustments, however, should be reflected in the standards before the variances are reported.

Unfavorable labor efficiency variances occur whenever workers require more than the number of hours allowed by the standards to produce a given amount of product. This may be caused by a management decision to use poorly trained workers, or because of the use of poorly maintained machinery or low quality materials that cause downtime or other production problems. Low employee morale, and generally bad working conditions, may also adversely affect the efficiency of workers, resulting in an unfavorable labor efficiency variance.

A *favorable labor efficiency variance* will occur when fewer labor hours are used than are allowed by the standards. This above normal efficiency may be caused by the company's use of higher skilled (and higher paid) workers, better machinery, or raw materials of higher quality than provided for in the standards. High employee morale, improved job satisfaction, or generally improved working conditions, may also account for the above normal efficiency of the workers.

It is important to understand the potential interactive effect of the use of raw materials, direct labor, and machinery on the overall efficiency of the production process. These three factors must be combined efficiently to produce a unit of finished product of optimal quality. The quality of one factor usually affects the efficiency in using the other two components. For example, low quality materials will ordinarily reduce the efficiency of the workers and the machinery. Likewise, poorly maintained machinery reduces the efficiency of the workers and causes excessive waste of raw materials. And use of poorly trained workers often results in lower than normal output from the use of materials and machinery. Because of these interactive relationships, the interpretation of one variance is often interrelated with the interpretation of other variances. Seldom are there clear-cut and isolated explanations for each variance reported. Because of complexities of this sort, *using* variances is far more challenging than *computing* them.

VARIABLE OVERHEAD STANDARDS
AND VARIANCES

Factory overhead costs are usually separated into fixed and variable elements for control purposes. Such a division is necessary because the variance between actual costs and expected costs is caused by different factors for fixed and variable costs. In this section we discuss the standards and variances related to variable overhead costs. Fixed overhead costs will be discussed in the next section.

In Chapter 2 factory overhead was defined as manufacturing costs other than direct materials and direct labor. Variable factory overhead includes all variable manufacturing costs other than direct materials and direct labor. Examples of variable factory overhead are indirect materials and supplies, indirect labor, overtime costs, employee fringe benefits, utilities, and so forth.

Unlike direct materials and direct labor costs that represent specific cost components, factory overhead represents a *group* of different costs. Consequently, setting standards is often more difficult for overhead costs than for materials or labor costs. Because of the difficulty of tracing overhead costs to the finished product, the engineering approach to setting overhead standards is seldom used. For mixed factory overhead costs (those that have variable and fixed components), an estimation technique, such as the high-low, least-squares, or scatter-graph method, is often used to separate the fixed and variable overhead components. These techniques were discussed in Chapter 3. If management believes the observations used in estimating variable costs reflect normal operating conditions, the estimate will probably be adopted as the standard variable cost.

Because it includes many heterogeneous costs, variable factory overhead poses a unique problem in standard costing related to measuring standard quantity and standard price. Direct materials have a natural physical measure of quantity such as tons, barrels, pounds, and meters. Similarly, all direct labor is measurable in hours. However, no natural quantity is common to all variable overhead items. Variable overhead is a cost group that may include, at the same time, costs measurable in hours, pounds, grams, kilowatts, and gallons.

To deal with the problem of multiple quantity measures in variable factory overhead, most companies use an artificial, or substitute, measure of quantity for all items in the group. Typical substitute measures are *direct labor hours* and *machine hours*. The variable overhead standard then is stated in terms of this *common activity base,* and the amount of variable overhead budgeted is based on this artificial activity measure. To illustrate, assume that Execupens' standard variable overhead rate of $6 per direct labor hour consists of the following:

Variable Overhead Cost Item	Quantity Consumed per Direct Labor Hour	Standard Cost per Direct Labor Hour
Indirect materials:		
Silicon coating	2 fluid ounces	$0.25
Machine lubricants	3 centimeters	0.20
Cleaning supplies	3 grams	0.15
Indirect labor:		
Inspection	5 minutes	0.40
Fringe benefits	1 direct labor hour	3.50
Electricity	1 kilowatt hour	0.05
Machine depreciation	1 hour of machine time	1.45
Total variable factory overhead cost per direct labor hour		$6.00

Execupens, Inc. chose to measure variable factory overhead in terms of direct labor hours because a large portion of these costs is related to direct labor activity. Thus *direct labor hours worked* is better than *units of product finished* as a measure of how much variable overhead cost should be incurred because these costs tend to vary in relation to direct labor hours worked whether or not the workers are producing the standard 1 finished unit per direct labor hour. Also, if common facilities are used to produce two or more products that use unequal amounts of overhead, the same hourly overhead rate can be used to budget and charge different amounts of overhead for production of the products. For example, if one product required $\frac{1}{2}$ standard hour of direct labor and another required 1 hour, at a rate of $6 per direct labor hour, $3 of variable overhead would be allowed for making the first product, and $6 would be allowed for the second. The use of activity bases for allocating common costs, such as variable overhead, is discussed in greater depth in Chapter 12.

Variable Overhead Variances Illustrated

The general model for computing standard cost variances for materials and labor can also be used in computing variable overhead variances. However, the actual costs of inputs, such as indirect materials, indirect labor, and utilities, are ordinarily obtained directly from the accounting records rather than being computed as quantity times price.

The **variable overhead spending variance** is the difference between the actual variable overhead cost incurred and the standard variable overhead cost for the actual activity base inputs (direct labor hours). The **variable overhead efficiency variance** is the difference between the standard variable overhead cost for the actual activity base inputs and the standard variable overhead cost of the activity base inputs allowed for the actual outputs.

For Execupens, Inc. the total actual cost of variable overhead is given at $126,000. This represents the actual cost of indirect materials, indirect labor, utilities, and machine depreciation recorded during the period. Since actual variable overhead is expected to vary with the actual level of labor hours, the standard cost of inputs is 19,200 actual direct labor hours times the standard variable overhead rate of $6, or $115,200. The variable overhead allowed for the actual outputs is based on the 20,000 direct labor hours allowed (20,000 units × 1 hour) for the units produced during the period. Consequently, the standard cost allowed is 20,000 labor hours times the variable overhead rate of $6, or $120,000. Using these data, the variable overhead spending (price) variance and the variable overhead efficiency (quantity) variance can be computed:

Actual costs			**Standard cost of inputs**		**Standard costs allowed (flexible budget for outputs)**	
Actual hours (AH)		n/a*	Actual hours (AH)	19,200	Standard hours allowed (SH)	20,000†
Actual rate (AR)	×	n/a	Standard rate (SR)	× $6.00	Standard rate (SR)	× $6.00
		$126,000		$115,200		$120,000

Variable overhead spending variance $10,800 U

Variable overhead efficiency variance $4,800 F

Total flexible budget variable overhead variance $6,000 U

* Not applicable
† 20,000 units × 1 hour per unit

Notice that the spaces for actual hours and actual rate are left blank in the actual costs section. Since variable overhead is assumed to be incurred as direct labor hours are incurred, we could say that the actual quantity of inputs of variable overhead was 19,200 direct labor hours. Using 19,200 as the quantity of overhead inputs, we can now determine the actual average variable overhead per labor hour by dividing the actual variable overhead cost of $126,000 by 19,200 hours to get $6.56 per hour. Because variable overhead costs are not actually purchased in units of direct labor hours, it is probably less confusing to omit this computation. A more compelling reason for not making the computation is that it provides no benefit to management in controlling variable overhead costs.

An alternative to the above computation of the variable overhead efficiency variance is as follows:

$$\text{Variable overhead efficiency variance} = SR(AH - SH)$$
$$= \$6.00(19{,}200 - 20{,}000)$$
$$= \$6.00 \times 800$$
$$= \$4800 \text{ F.}$$

This approach emphasizes that the 800 labor hours saved should have produced a variable overhead savings of $4800, at the standard rate of $6 per direct labor hour.

Interpreting Variable Overhead Variances

The variable overhead spending variance measures the difference between actual variable overhead incurred and the amount of overhead cost expected for the actual activity inputs used. Operating at 19,200 actual hours, with a standard rate of $6 per hour, management expected $115,200 (19,200 $\times$ $6) to be spent on variable overhead. Since $126,000 was actually incurred, management overspent, and a $10,800 unfavorable spending variance resulted.

Why did Execupens spend $10,800 too much? Was it caused by increasing prices for indirect materials, by higher than expected wage rates for indirect labor, or by higher than expected kilowatt rates for electricity? Or was it caused by workers' use of excessive quantities of indirect materials, indirect labor, and electricity for the actual direct labor hours worked? The answer is that the unfavorable spending variance could have resulted *both* from increasing prices for variable overhead goods and services used *and* from excessive consumption of these goods and services. Thus the term *spending* variance is used instead of the term *price* variance.

For variable overhead the *unfavorable spending variance* encompasses all factors that cause actual expenditures to exceed the amount expected for the actual labor hours, including purchasing excessive quantities of variable overhead items, as well as paying too much for the variable overhead items purchased. Conversely, a *favorable spending variance* results when the actual expenditures are less than expected for the actual labor hours attained. This is caused by purchasing fewer overhead items than expected, or by paying less than the expected amount for overhead items, or by both of these.

The key to understanding the variable overhead spending variance is recognizing that the amount of variable overhead cost that can be incurred without exceeding the variable overhead spending budget is based on the actual level of the activity base chosen for budgeting variable overhead cost. For Execupens actual direct labor hours determine the spending budget for variable overhead. Any deviation from this spending budget — due to mismanagement of variable overhead price or quantity variables — causes a spending variance to occur.

The variable overhead efficiency variance measures the difference between the standard variable overhead cost for the actual labor hours used and the standard variable overhead cost for the allowed labor hours. In computing the variable overhead efficiency variance, the variable overhead rate per hour remains constant, whereas the labor hours vary between actual and allowed. Consequently, this variance measures the additional amount of variable overhead that should have been incurred or saved because of the efficient or inefficient use of labor. It provides no information about the degree of efficiency in utilizing variable overhead items such as indirect materials and indirect labor. This information is reflected in the spending variance. Since overhead is being measured and budgeted on the basis of labor hours, it is logical to expect overhead costs to be affected by the degree of labor efficiency. This effect is measured by the variable overhead efficiency variance. Because of the connection of this variance to labor efficiency, it will always move in the *same direction* as the labor efficiency variance; when the labor efficiency variance is favorable, the variable overhead efficiency variance will be favorable, and vice versa.

In this discussion of variable overhead variances the activity base selected for budgeting variable overhead cost was direct labor hours. Observations similar to those made above for direct labor hours could also be made for other activity bases such as machine hours.

FIXED OVERHEAD STANDARDS AND VARIANCES

Because of the nature of fixed costs, the quantity of goods and services purchased by fixed expenditures does not change in proportion to changes in the level of production. For example, in the short run the production level does not affect the amount of depreciation on buildings, the number of fixed salaried employees, or the amount of real property subject to property taxes. Whether 20,000 or 30,000 units are produced, the same amount of fixed overhead is expected to be incurred so long as the production level is within the relevant range of activity provided by the current fixed overhead items. Therefore a quantity or efficiency variance is ordinarily not computed for fixed overhead costs.

Even though the components of fixed overhead are not affected by the production activity level in the short run, the actual amount spent for fixed overhead items can differ from the amount budgeted by management. For example, higher than budgeted supervisors' salaries can be paid, extreme temperatures can cause heating costs to exceed budget, and price increases can cause the amounts paid for fixed property maintenance costs to be higher than expected. Fixed overhead costs in excess of the amount budgeted are reflected in the fixed overhead budget variance. The **fixed overhead budget variance** is the difference between budgeted and actual fixed overhead.

$$\frac{\text{Fixed overhead}}{\text{budget variance}} = \text{Actual fixed overhead} - \text{Budgeted fixed overhead.}$$

Using the fixed overhead data in Exhibit 8–4 for Execupens, Inc., the fixed overhead budget variance is computed as $2000, or $198,000 of actual fixed overhead costs minus $200,000 of budgeted fixed overhead costs. The fixed overhead budget variance is always the *same* as the total fixed overhead flexible budget variance. Because budgeted fixed overhead is the same for all outputs within the relevant range, the budget variance accounts for the total flexible budget variance between actual and allowed fixed overhead.

REPORTING STANDARD COST VARIANCES

Two critical factors in the operation of a responsibility accounting system are (1) the reporting of variances to the appropriate managers and (2) management's responding with explanations and control decisions. The method and format used to report variances to managers should be tailored to the specific needs of each situation. Exhibit 8–6 illustrates for Execupens, Inc. one approach that is available for reporting performance results and standard cost variances for a standard cost center. This report is an expanded version of the flexible budget performance report presented in Exhibit 8–5. In the standard cost performance report, purchasing costs are separated from production costs. Notice, however, that the total unfavorable flexible budget variance of $39,968 in Exhibit 8–5 is equal to the total purchasing and production variance in Exhibit 8–6. These amounts would not be the same if materials purchased differed from materials used.

Managers receiving performance reports are usually required to respond to their immediate superiors within a designated period of time with explanations for variances that are significant in amount. Ordinarily, it is not economically feasible to investigate all variances. Each company must determine what constitutes a significant variance warranting managerial attention. All significant variances, both *unfavorable* and *favorable,* should be investigated. As stated before, a favorable variance does not necessarily indicate favorable managerial performance.

EXHIBIT 8–6   Standard Cost Performance Report

Execupens, Inc.
Standard Cost Performance Report
For the month of March, 19x6

	Actual Costs	Standard Costs Allowed (Flexible Budget)	Flexible Budget Variance	Variance Analysis	
Purchasing costs					
Direct materials purchased	$ 987,040	$ 992,000	$ 4,960 F	$ 4,960 F	Materials purchased price variance
Production costs					
Direct materials used	$ 992,000*	$ 960,000	$32,000 U	$32,000 U	Materials quantity variance
Direct labor	284,928	280,000	4,928 U	16,128 U	Labor rate variance
				11,200 F	Labor efficiency variance
Variable factory overhead	126,000	120,000	6,000 U	10,800 U	Variable overhead spending variance
				4,800 F	Variable overhead efficiency variance
Fixed factory overhead	200,000	198,000	2,000 U	2,000 U	Fixed overhead budget variance
Totals	$1,602,928	$1,558,000	$44,928 U	44,928 U	
Total purchasing and production variance				$39,968 U	

* Represents standard cost of raw materials requisitioned since the production manager has no control over the price paid for materials.

APPLICATIONS AND BENEFITS
OF VARIANCE ANALYSIS

Standard costs are used primarily for performance evaluation, budgeting, and product costing. Throughout this chapter we have emphasized the performance evaluation aspect of standard costing. Closely related to the objective of performance evaluation is the objective of cost control, which is an important part of management responsibility that must be routinely evaluated. Although cost control is not a manager's only important responsibility, in a cost center it is a high priority with upper management. Standard costs provide a logical basis for evaluating a manager's performance. Standard cost reports are an important part of a responsibility reporting system for standard cost centers, and, as such, help to identify good and bad performers.

Standard cost reports can assist in formulating performance evaluations of managers by providing a beginning point, but serious consequences can result if standard cost reports are used exclusively to evaluate managers. Managers may learn quickly how to manipulate the system in order to generate favorable variances. For example, purchasing managers may buy substandard raw materials, and production managers may sacrifice quality for quantity, or sacrifice employee satisfaction for higher productivity. Though these ploys may produce favorable variances in the short run, often they have negative effects on the organization in the long run. To avoid these types of manipulations, standard cost performance reports should be used as only *a part of an overall performance evaluation system* that considers all areas of manager performance.

Another use of standard costs is to provide information useful in performing operations budgeting procedures, which we discussed in Chapter 6. If cost standards exist and are current, they can be used to budget manufacturing costs after sales and inventory requirements are budgeted. Having standard costs readily available significantly reduces the time and effort required to establish the budgeted costs for the planned production.

Standard costing is also useful in product costing. In a standard product costing system, manufactured inventory is always costed at standard allowed cost. Consequently, the cost of the finished inventory can be readily determined as the number of units in inventory times the standard cost per unit. This eliminates the product costing delays usually associated with using actual costs for product costing. Chapter 11 is devoted to the topic of product costing, and Appendix B to that chapter explains standard product costing systems.

SUMMARY

Cost centers that have a predictable relationship between production inputs and outputs often use a standard cost system for controlling costs and evaluating manager performance. Standard cost control systems require that cost standards be developed for each type of product produced (or service provided) and that they include unit budgeted costs for materials, labor, and overhead. Periodically, actual costs are compared with standard costs, and cost variances are reported to managers for possible corrective action.

Variance analysis involves breaking down flexible budget variances to show specific variances caused by price and quantity departures from the standards. Price and quantity variances are reported for materials, labor, and overhead. For variable overhead, price and quantity variances are combined in the variable overhead spending variance, and the variable overhead efficiency variance measures the impact of quantity variations in the variable overhead activity base.

For standard costing, most companies measure the quantity of variable overhead consumed in terms of a substitute activity base, such as direct labor hours, rather than in terms of the quantity of overhead goods and services consumed. Therefore the variable overhead quantity, or efficiency variance, measures the impact on overhead cost of the efficiency with which the activity base is used. The variable overhead price, or spending variance, measures the combined impact of price and quantity deviations from standard for variable overhead goods and services used.

For internal planning and control, fixed overhead is budgeted and reported in a lump sum and, therefore, is not affected by the level of activity achieved during the period. The fixed overhead budget variance is the difference between actual fixed overhead and budgeted fixed overhead. An additional fixed overhead variance is often computed when fixed overhead is applied to products on a unit basis for external reporting purposes. This variance is discussed in the following appendix.

APPENDIX
A CLOSER LOOK AT FIXED
OVERHEAD VARIANCES

The absorption cost method of external reporting treats all manufacturing costs as product costs. In Chapter 2 we indicated that most firms use a predetermined rate to assign factory overhead to products. This predetermined factory overhead rate is established at the start of the year by dividing the predicted overhead costs for the year by the predicted activity for the year. Many firms prefer to use separate overhead rates for fixed and variable overhead. When this is done, often variable overhead is assigned using the standard variable overhead rate, and fixed overhead assigned using a separate *standard fixed overhead rate*.

The development of the variable overhead rate and its subsequent use in computing standard cost variances was considered in the body of this chapter. In this appendix we consider the development of the standard fixed overhead rate and its subsequent use in computing standard cost variances.

The motivation for using a standard fixed overhead rate is the same as the motivation for using a predetermined overhead rate, namely, more rapid product costing and smoothing the bookkeeping work load. Furthermore, the use of a standard fixed overhead rate results in identical fixed costs being assigned to identical products regardless of when they are produced during the year.

When a standard fixed overhead rate is used, *total fixed overhead* costs assigned to production behave as *variable* costs. As production increases, the total fixed overhead assigned to production increases. Because total fixed overhead does not vary, differences arise between actual and assigned fixed overhead, and managers often inquire about the cause of the differences.

The standard fixed overhead rate is computed as the *budgeted fixed costs* divided by some *budgeted standard level of activity*. Since budgeted fixed overhead is the same for all levels of output (within the relevant production range), the standard fixed overhead rate will vary depending on the budgeted level of activity. In our example of Execupens, Inc. (see Exhibit 8–4), budgeted monthly fixed overhead is $198,000. To simplify the illustration, assume that Execupens develops their standard fixed overhead rate monthly, instead of annually, and that Execupens bases the rate on a standard activity level of 22,000 labor hours per month. The standard fixed overhead rate per direct labor hour is $9:

$$\text{Standard fixed overhead rate} = \frac{\text{Budgeted total fixed overhead}}{\text{Standard activity level}}$$

$$= \frac{\$198,000}{22,000 \text{ hours}}$$

$$= \$9.$$

The total fixed overhead assigned to production is computed as the standard rate of $9 multiplied by the standard hours allowed for the units produced. Therefore the assigned fixed overhead equals the budgeted monthly fixed overhead only if the allowed activity is 22,000 hours. This is illustrated in Exhibit 8–7(a). If the company operates below 22,000 allowed hours, the fixed overhead assigned to production is less than the $198,000 budgeted; if it operates above 22,000 allowed hours, the fixed overhead assigned to production is more than the amount budgeted.

Even though total fixed overhead is not affected by producing below or above the standard activity level, the fixed overhead assigned to production increases at the rate of $9 per allowed labor hour. The difference between total budgeted fixed overhead and total standard fixed overhead assigned to production is called the **volume variance.** This variance is sometimes referred to as the **denominator variance,** a term that emphasizes the accounting origin of the variance. The volume variance indicates neither good nor bad performance by the production personnel. Instead, it merely indicates a difference between the activity allowed for the actual

EXHIBIT 8–7   Graphic Analysis of Fixed Overhead Costs and Variances

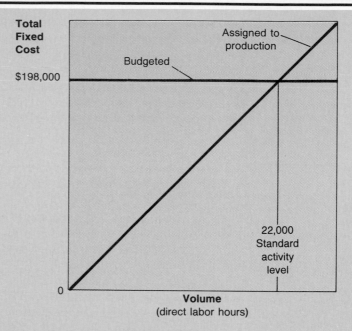

(a) Budgeted and assigned fixed overhead

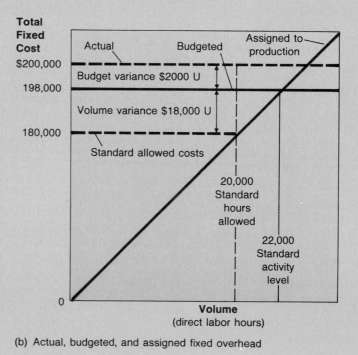

(b) Actual, budgeted, and assigned fixed overhead

output and the activity level used as the denominator in computing the standard fixed overhead rate.

To explain the difference between actual fixed overhead and standard fixed overhead assigned to production, two fixed overhead variances are computed, the budget variance and the volume variance. These variances are illustrated in graphic form in Exhibit 8–7(b). They are computed below for Execupens, Inc., assuming the following data:

Budgeted fixed overhead	$198,000
Actual fixed overhead	$200,000
Denominator activity level	22,000 standard allowed hours (or 22,000 units)
Actual activity level	20,000 standard allowed hours (or 20,000 units)

Actual costs			**Budgeted costs**			**Standard costs assigned**	
Actual hours (AH)		n/a*	Budgeted hours (BH)		n/a	Standard hours allowed (SH)	20,000†
Actual rate (AR)	×	n/a	Standard rate (SR)	×	n/a	Standard rate (SR)	× $9.00
		$200,000			$198,000		$180,000

Fixed overhead budget variance $2,000 U‡

Fixed overhead volume variance $18,000 U

Total fixed overhead variance $20,000 U

* Not applicable

† 20,000 units × 1 hour per unit

‡ Also the flexible budget fixed overhead variance.

Because actual and budgeted fixed overhead do not vary for activity within the relevant range, their amounts are stated in total rather than computed as a function of some volume of activity. The amount of fixed overhead assigned to production does vary with activity and is computed as the standard hours allowed for the actual outputs times the standard fixed overhead rate per hour. The fixed overhead budget variance represents the difference between actual fixed overhead and budgeted fixed overhead. The budget variance is caused by a combination of price and quantity factors related to the use of fixed overhead goods and services (e.g., heating costs, indirect labor, etc.). The $2000 unfavorable budget variance for Execupens was caused either by using excessive quantities of fixed overhead goods and services, or by paying higher prices than expected for those items, or both.

The volume variance represents the difference between budgeted and assigned fixed overhead and is caused by a difference between the allowed activity and the denominator activity used in computing the fixed overhead rate. The $18,000 unfavorable volume variance for Execupens means that the company operated at an output activity level below the denominator activity level. As stated above, this variance ordinarily cannot be used to control costs. If the denominator activity level is based on production capacity, this variance can be used only to alert management that facilities are underutilized, or utilized above management's expectations.

KEY TERMS

Variance analysis

Standard cost variance

Quantity variance

Price variance

Materials price variance

Materials quantity variance

Materials purchased price variance

Labor rate variance

Labor efficiency variance

Variable overhead spending variance

Variable overhead efficiency variance

Fixed overhead budget variance

REVIEW QUESTIONS

8–1   What is a standard cost variance, and what is the objective of variance analysis?

8–2   How do production inputs affect the cost of production outputs?

8–3   The total standard cost variance can usually be broken down into two basic types of variances. Name and define these two types of variances.

8–4   Give the general model presented in the chapter for computing the basic standard cost variances. Show both the abbreviations and the complete component terms.

8–5   Identify two ways that materials standards can be determined. Which method is more precise?

8–6   Should the materials quantity variance be determined on the basis of materials purchased or materials used? Explain.

8–7   List possible causes for (1) a materials price variance and (2) a materials quantity variance.

8–8   Show two ways of computing the labor rate variance.

8–9 Explain how an unfavorable labor efficiency variance may be related to a favorable materials price variance.

8–10 What is the appropriate treatment in the standard cost system of a change in wage rates in the contract with the labor union?

8–11 How is the variable overhead spending variance computed, and what factors may cause it to occur?

8–12 If prices of indirect materials exceed the prices used in budgeting variable overhead, which variance is likely to be affected? Explain.

8–13 If the basic monthly rate for telephone service (not including long distance calls) increases beyond the amount budgeted, which variance will be affected?

8–14 Explain why only one variance is computed for fixed overhead for companies that use the contribution approach to internal reporting.

EXERCISES

8–1 Input/Output Analysis

Delio Company manufactures a product called "micropack." The standard input allowed for each unit of output is 5 units. Each unit of input has a standard cost of $8.00. During a recent period 9000 units of input, acquired at a cost of $7.75 per unit, were used to manufacture 1500 actual units of output.

Requirements

a) Determine the price variance.

b) Determine the quantity variance.

8–2 Graphical Representations

Prepare a graph depicting the variances computed in Exercise 8–1.

8–3 Materials Variances

Mcgrath Company uses standard costs to control materials costs. The standards call for 2 pounds of materials for each finished unit produced. The standard cost per pound of materials is $1.50. During the month of May, 4500 finished units were manufactured and 8800 pounds of materials were used. The price paid for the materials was $1.52 per pound. There were no beginning or ending materials inventories.

Requirements

a) Determine the total materials cost allowed for the manufacture of 4500 finished units.

b) Determine the total materials cost actually incurred for the manufacture of 4500 finished units, and compute the total materials variance.

c) How much of the difference between the answers to requirements (a) and (b) was related to the price paid for the purchase of materials?

d) How much of the difference between the answers to requirements (a) and (b) was related to the quantity of materials used?

8–4 Materials Price Variance Based on Purchases and on Usage

The Charleston Company manufactures decorative weather vanes that have a standard cost of $1.50 per pound for direct materials used in the manufacturing process. During September 11,000 pounds of materials were purchased for $1.55 per pound, and 10,000 pounds were actually used in making weather vanes. There were no beginning inventories.

Requirements

a) Determine the materials price variance assuming that materials costs are the responsibility of the purchaser of materials.

b) Determine the materials price variance assuming that materials costs are the responsibility of the user of materials.

8–5 Direct Labor Variances

Dolex Company manufactures specialty electronic circuitry through a unique photoelectronic process. One of the primary products, Model ZX40, has a standard labor time of $\frac{3}{4}$ hour, and a standard labor rate of $13.50 per hour. During February the following activities pertaining to direct labor for ZX40 were recorded.

Direct labor hours used	3,220
Direct labor cost	$44,000
Units of ZX40 manufactured	4,600

Requirements

a) Determine the total labor cost variance.

b) Determine the labor rate variance.

c) Determine the labor efficiency variance.

8–6 Variable Overhead Variances

Murduct Company bases standard variable overhead costs on direct labor hours. Standard variable overhead costs have been set at $15 per unit of output, based on $5 per direct labor hour for three hours allowed to produce one finished unit. Last month 4300 direct labor hours were used and 1400 units of output were manufactured. The following actual variable overhead costs were incurred.

Indirect materials	$ 3,500
Indirect labor	8,200
Utilities	5,800
Miscellaneous	3,500
Total variable overhead	$21,000

Requirements

a) Determine the variable overhead spending variance.

b) Determine the variable overhead efficiency variance.

c) How is the variable overhead efficiency variance related to labor efficiency?

d) If the company were to use smaller quantities of indirect materials than allowed by the standards, in which variance would the resulting cost savings be reflected? Explain.

8–7 Fixed Overhead Budget Variance

The Tallahassee Company uses standard costs for cost control and internal reporting. Fixed costs are budgeted at $7500 per month at a normal operating level of 10,000 units of production output. During October actual fixed costs were $7900, and actual production output was 10,500 units.

Requirements

a) Determine the fixed overhead budget variance.

b) Was the fixed overhead budget variance affected because the company operated above the normal activity level of 10,000 units?

8–8 Fixed Overhead Volume Variance (Appendix)

Assume that the Tallahassee Company in Exercise 8–7 applied fixed overhead to inventory on a per unit basis.

Requirements

a) Determine the fixed overhead volume variance.

b) Explain the reason for the volume variance. How is reporting of the volume variance useful to management?

8–9 Causes for Variances

During January the May Company reported the following variances in the production of flagpoles, its only product.

1. Materials price variance (based on purchases)
2. Materials quantity variance
3. Labor rate variance
4. Labor efficiency variance
5. Variable overhead spending variance
6. Variable overhead efficiency variance
7. Fixed overhead budget variance

Requirements

a) Identify the variances that are caused by price factors only.

b) Identify the variances that are caused by quantity usage factors only.

c) Identify the variances that are caused by both price and quantity factors.

PROBLEMS
8–10 Standard Costs and the Flexible Budget

The following performance report was prepared for a cost center in the Hoosier Company for March, 19x2. The production volume was 1800 units.

	Actual Costs	Flexible Budget Costs	Flexible Budget Variances
Direct materials	$8,200	$ 9,000	$800 F
Direct labor	5,550	5,400	150 U
Variable overhead:			
Supplies	680	630	50 U
Inspection	700	810	110 F
Indirect labor	900	990	90 F
Utilities	1,335	1,170	165 U
Fixed overhead:			
Depreciation	400	400	—
Supervision	950	900	50 U
Other	485	550	65 F
Totals	$19,200	$19,850	$650 F

Requirements

a) Determine the flexible budget formula for this cost center.

b) Determine the variable standard cost per unit.

8–11 Computation of Variable Cost Variances

Information pertaining to the standard costs and actual activity for the Tyler Company for September is presented below.

Standard cost per unit	
Direct materials	4 units of material A at $2 per unit
	1 unit of material B at $3 per unit
Direct labor	3 hours at $8 per hour
Variable overhead	$1.50 per direct labor hour
Activity for September	
Materials purchased:	
Material A	4500 units for $9225
Material B	1100 units for $3410
Materials used:	
Material A	4150 units
Material B	995 units

There were no beginning raw materials inventories.

Direct labor used	2950 hours at $8.20 per hour
Variable overhead costs incurred	$3800
Production output	1000 units

Requirements

a) Determine the materials price and quantity variances assuming materials prices are the responsibility of the purchasing manager.

b) Determine the labor rate and efficiency variances.

c) Determine the variable overhead spending and efficiency variances.

8–12 Materials and Labor Variances; Alternative Computations; Interpretation of Variances

The Galaxy Company manufactures bookcases that have the following unit standard costs for direct materials and direct labor.

Direct materials — lumber	
(36 feet at $0.70 per foot)	$25.20
Direct labor	
($\frac{1}{2}$ hour at $7.50 per hour)	3.75
Total standard direct cost	
per bookcase	$28.95

The following activities were recorded for the month of March.

- 1400 bookcases were manufactured.
- 51,200 feet of lumber costing $34,272 was purchased and used.
- $5775 was paid for 770 hours of direct labor.

There were no beginning or ending work-in-process inventories.

Requirements

a) Compute the direct materials variances using two different computational techniques. (Round computations to four decimal places and round answers to the nearest dollar.)

b) Compute the direct labor variances using two different computational techniques.

c) Give one possible reason that each of the above variances occurred.

8–13 Variance Computations: Performance Report

The Outdoor Company is a new firm that manufactures camping tents from a lightweight synthetic fabric. Each tent has a standard materials cost of $20, consisting of 4 yards of fabric at $5 per yard. The standard call for 2 hours of direct labor at $12 per hour and variable overhead at the rate of $2.50 per direct labor hour. Fixed costs are budgeted at $10,000 per month.

The following data were recorded for October 19x5, the first month of operations.

Fabric purchased	10,000 yards for $49,000
Fabric used in production of 1,700 tents	7,000 yards
Direct labor used	3,600 hours costing $45,000
Variable overhead costs incurred	$8,900
Fixed overhead costs incurred	$12,500

Requirements

a) Compute all standard variable cost variances for the month (materials, labor, and overhead).

b) Determine the fixed overhead budget variance.

c) Determine the standard variable cost of the 1700 tents produced, broken down into direct materials, direct labor, and variable overhead.

d) Prepare a performance report using the format illustrated in Exhibit 8–6.

8–14 Determining Unit Costs: Variance Analysis and Interpretation

The Harmon Company, a manufacturer of dog food, produces its product in 1000 bag batches. The standard cost of each batch consists of 8000 pounds of direct materials at $0.30 per pound, 48 direct labor hours at $8.50 per hour, and variable cost (based on machine hours) at the rate of $10 per hour for 16 machine hours per batch.

The following variable costs were incurred for the last 1000 bag batch produced.

Direct materials	8200 pounds costing $2378 were purchased and used
Direct labor	45 hours costing $405
Variable overhead	$200
Machine hours used	18

Requirements

a) Determine the actual and standard variable costs per bag of dog food produced, broken down into direct materials, direct labor, and variable overhead.

b) For the last 1000 bag batch, determine the standard cost variances for direct materials, direct labor, and variable overhead.

c) Explain the probable causes for each of the variances determined in requirement (b).

8–15 Computation of Variances and Other Missing Data

The following data for the Jones Company pertain to the production of 300 units of product X during the month of December. Selected data items are omitted.

Direct materials (All materials purchased were used in current production.)
Standard cost per unit: ___(a)___ pounds at $3.20 per pound
Total actual cost: 1830 pounds costing ___(b)___
Standard cost allowed for units produced: $5760

Materials price variance: $183 F

Materials quantity variance: ___(c)___

Direct labor

Standard cost: 2 hours at $7.00

Actual cost per hour: $7.25

Total actual cost: ___(d)___

Labor rate variance: ___(e)___

Labor efficiency variance: $140 U

Variable overhead

Standard costs: ___(f)___ hours at $4 per direct labor hour

Actual cost: $2250

Variable overhead spending variance: ___(g)___

Variable overhead efficiency variance: ___(h)___

Total units produced were 300.

Required: Fill in the missing amounts in the blanks lettered (a) through (h).

8–16 Computation of Missing Variances and Other Data

The following data pertaining to the production of the Dalko Company's primary product are for a recent month, with selected items omitted. Two thousand units of product were produced during the month, and the total flexible budget cost allowed was $100,000.

Direct materials

Standard cost per unit: 4 gallons at $7.90 per gallon

Total actual cost of materials used: ___(a)___ gallons at $8.00 per gallon

Total standard cost allowed: ___(b)___

Total flexible budget variance: ___(c)___

Materials price variance: ___(d)___

Materials quantity variance: $553 U

Direct labor

Standard cost per unit: $\frac{1}{2}$ hour at $12 per hour

Total actual cost of labor: ___(e)___ hours at ___(f)___ per hour

Total standard cost allowed: ___(g)___

Total flexible budget variance: $485 F

Labor rate variance: $235 U

Labor efficiency variance: ___(h)___

Variable overhead

Standard cost per unit: ___(i)___ labor hours at $4 per hour

Actual cost: $4200

Total standard cost allowed: ___(j)___

Total flexible budget variance: ___(k)___

Variable overhead spending variance: ___(l)___

Variable overhead efficiency variance: ___(m)___

Fixed overhead

Actual cost: ___(n)___

Budgeted cost: ___(o)___

Budget variance: $1000 U

Required: Fill in the missing amounts in the blanks lettered (a) through (o).

8–17 Overhead Variances

The Grogan Coach Company controls variable overhead costs based on direct labor hours, and controls fixed costs on the basis of total budgeted costs. Each unit of output has 10 standard direct labor hours. The standard variable overhead cost per unit of output, broken down by cost components, is presented below.

Indirect materials	$125
Indirect labor	90
Plant and facilities cost	65
Miscellaneous variable overhead	50
Standard variable overhead cost per unit of output	$330

Budgeted fixed costs per month are as follows:

Indirect labor	$8,000
Plant and facilities cost	3,000
Depreciation	2,500
Miscellaneous fixed costs	1,200
Total budgeted fixed costs	$14,700

During July 2100 actual direct labor hours were worked, and the production output was 200 units. Actual costs incurred were as follows:

	Variable	Fixed
Indirect materials	$23,500	—
Indirect labor	19,000	$ 8,800
Plant and facilities	12,200	3,750
Depreciation	—	2,500
Miscellaneous	10,400	1,100
Total actual overhead costs	$65,100	$16,150

Required: Prepare a performance report that shows variable and fixed overhead variances broken down by cost items. Use the following column headings for your report.

				Variance Analysis	
		Standard Costs	Total	Spending	
Cost Item	Actual Costs	(Flexible Budget)	Variance	or Budget	Efficiency
	$	$	$	$	$

8–18 Causes of Standard Cost Variances

Below are ten unrelated situations that would ordinarily be expected to affect one or more standard cost variances.

1. A salaried production foreman is given a raise, and no adjustment is made in the labor cost standards.

2. The materials purchasing manager gets a special reduced price on raw materials by purchasing a train carload. A warehouse had to be rented to accommodate the unusually large amount of raw materials. The rental fee was charged to rent expense, a fixed overhead item.

3. An unusually hot month of August caused the company to use 25,000 kilowatts more electricity than provided for in the variable overhead standards.

4. The local electric utility raised the charge per kilowatt hour. No adjustment was made in the variable overhead standards.

5. The plant manager traded in his leased company car for a new Cadillac in July, increasing the monthly lease payment by $150.

6. A machine malfunction on the assembly line caused by using cheap and inferior raw materials resulted in decreased output by the machine operator and higher than normal machine repair costs. Repairs are treated as variable overhead costs.

7. The production maintenance supervisor decreased routine maintenance checks, resulting in lower production output. Maintenance costs are treated as fixed costs.

8. An announcement that vacation benefits had been increased resulted in improved employee morale. Consequently, raw materials pilferage and waste declined, and production efficiency increased.

9. The plant manager reclassified her secretary to administrative assistant and gave him an increase in salary.

10. A union contract agreement was signed calling for an immediate 5 percent increase in production worker wages. No changes were made in the standards.

Required: For each of the above situations indicate by letter which of the following standard cost variances would be affected. More than one variance will be affected in some cases.

a) Material price variance

b) Material quantity variance

c) Labor rate variance

d) Labor efficiency variance

e) Variable overhead spending variance

f) Variable overhead efficiency variance

g) Fixed overhead budget variance

8–19 Measuring the Effects of Decisions on Standard Cost Variances

Below are five unrelated situations that affect one or more standard cost variances for materials, labor, and overhead.

1. Lois Jones, a production worker, announced her intentions to resign in order to accept another job paying $1.20 per hour more. To keep from losing her, the production manager agreed to raise her salary from $7.00 to $8.50 per hour. Lois works an average of 175 hours per month.

2. At the beginning of the month a supplier of a component used in our product notified us that, because of a minor design improvement, the price will be increased by 15 percent above the current standard price of $100 per unit. As a result of the improved design, we expect the number of defective components to decrease by 80 units per month. On the average 1200 units of the component are purchased each month. Defective units are identified prior to use and are not returnable.

3. In an effort to meet a deadline on a rush order in Department A, the plant manager reassigned several higher skilled workers from Department B, for a total of 300 labor hours. The average salary of the Department B workers was $1.85 more than the standard $7.00 per hour rate of the Department A workers. Since they were not accustomed to the work, the average Department B worker was able to produce only 36 units per hour instead of the standard 48 units per hour. (Consider only the effect on Department A labor variances.)

4. Rob Celiba is an inspector who earns a flat salary of $700 per month plus a piece rate of 20 cents per bundle inspected. His company accounts for inspection costs as factory overhead. Because of a payroll department error in June, Rob was paid $500 plus a piece rate of 30 cents per bundle. He received gross wages totaling $1100.

5. The materials purchasing manager purchased 5000 units of component K2X from a new source at a price $12 below the standard unit price of $200. These components turned out to be of extremely poor quality with defects occurring at three times the standard rate of 5 percent. The higher rate of defects reduced the output of workers (who earn $8 per hour) from 20 units per hour to 15 units per hour on the units containing the discount components. Each finished unit contains one K2X component. To appease the workers, who were irate at having to work with the inferior components, the production manager agreed to pay the workers an additional 25 cents for each of the components (good and bad) in the discount batch. Variable factory overhead is applied at the rate of $4 per direct labor hour. The defective units also caused a 20 hour increase in total machine hours. The actual cost of electricity to run the machines is $2 per hour.

Required: For each of the above situations determine which standard cost variance(s) will be affected, and compute the amount of the effect for one month on each variance. Indicate whether the effect is favorable or unfavorable. Assume the standards are not changed in response to these situations. (Round calculations to two decimal places.)

8–20 Developing Cost Standards for Materials and Labor

After several years of operating without a formal system of cost control, the Carlsen Company, a tools manufacturer, has decided to implement a standard cost system. The system will be established first for the department that makes lug wrenches for automobile mechanics. The standard production batch size is 100 wrenches. The actual materials and labor required for eight batches selected randomly from last year's production are as follows:

Batch	Materials used (in pounds)	Labor Used (in hours)
1	504	10
2	508	9
3	506	9
4	521	5
5	516	8
6	518	7
7	520	6
8	515	8
Average	513.5	7.75

Management has obtained the following recommendations concerning what the materials and labor quantity standards should be.

- The manufacturer of the equipment used in making the wrenches advertises in the toolmakers' trade journal that the machine Carlsen uses can produce 100 wrenches with 500 pounds of raw materials and 5 labor hours. Carlsen's engineers believe the standards should be based on these data.

- The accounting department believes a more realistic standard would be 504 pounds and 5 hours.

- The production supervisor believes the standard should be 513.5 pounds and 7.75 hours.

- The production workers argue for standards of 515 pounds and 8 hours.

Requirements

a) State the arguments for and against each of the recommendations and the probable effects of each recommendation on the quantity variances for materials and labor.

b) Which recommendation provides the best combination of cost control and motivation to the production workers? Explain.

8–21 Variance Analysis for Services Costs

Atlantic Manufacturers Bank uses standard costs in its commercial loan department. The standard cost to process a loan has been determined as follows:

Direct materials (20 pages of forms at 10 cents per page)	$ 2
Direct labor (2 hr at $8)	16
Variable overhead cost (2 hr at $1 per labor hr)	2
Total variable standard cost per loan application	$20

Fixed costs in the commercial loan department are budgeted at $1500 per month. Last month 160 loan applications were processed, and the following costs were incurred.

Direct materials	3500 pages of forms totalling $350
Direct labor	345 hr at $8.20 per hr
Variable overhead	$400
Fixed overhead	$1350

Requirements

a) Determine all standard variable cost variances discussed in this chapter for direct materials, direct labor, and variable overhead.

b) Determine the fixed overhead budget variance.

8–22 Compiling and Reporting Standard Cost Variances

The Carberg Corporation manufactures and sells a single product. The cost system used by the company is a standard cost system. The variable standard cost per unit of product is shown below:

Material (1 lb of plastic at $2)	$ 2.00
Direct labor (1.6 hr at $4)	6.40
Variable overhead cost	3.00
	$11.40

The overhead cost per unit was calculated from the following annual overhead cost budget for a 60,000 unit volume.

Variable overhead cost:		
Indirect labor (30,000 hr at $4)	$120,000	
Supplies—oil (60,000 gal at $0.50)	30,000	
Utilities	30,000	$180,000
Fixed overhead costs:		
Supervision	$ 27,000	
Depreciation	45,000	
Other fixed costs	15,000	87,000
Total budgeted overhead costs for 60,000 units		$267,000

The charges to the manufacturing department for November, when 5000 units were produced, are given below.

Materials (5300 lb at $2)	$10,600
Direct labor (8200 hr at $4.10)	33,620
Indirect labor (2400 hr at $4.10)	9,840
Supplies — oil (6000 gal at $0.55)	3,300
Utilities	3,200
Supervision	2,475
Depreciation	3,750
Other fixed costs	1,250
Total	$68,035

The purchasing department normally buys about the same quantity as is used in production during a month. In November 5200 pounds were purchased at a price of $2.10 per pound.

Requirements

a) Calculate the following variances from standard costs for the data given below.

1. Materials purchased price variance

2. Materials quantity variance

3. Direct labor rate variance

4. Direct labor efficiency variance

5. Total flexible budget variance for each overhead item.

b) The company has divided its responsibilities so that the purchasing department is responsible for the price at which materials and supplies are purchased, and the manufacturing department is responsible for the quantities of materials used. Does this division of responsibilities solve the conflict between price and quantity variances? Explain.

c) Prepare a report that details the flexible overhead budget variances. The report, which will be given to the manufacturing department manager, should display only that part of each variance that is the obvious responsibility of the manager. It should highlight the information in ways that would be useful to that manager in evaluating departmental performance and when considering corrective action. *Hint:* This part requires considerable thought, rather than technical analysis.

d) Assume that the department manager performs the timekeeping function for this manufacturing department. From time to time an analysis of overhead and direct labor variances has shown that the department manager has deliberately misclassified labor hours (e.g., listed direct labor hours as indirect labor hours, and vice versa) so that only one of the two labor variances is unfavorable. It is not feasible economically to hire a separate timekeeper. What should the company do, if anything, to resolve this problem?

(CMA Adapted)

8–23 Data Computations from Variance Information

On May 1, 19x5, Bovar Company began the manufacture of a new mechanical device known as "Dandy." The company installed a standard cost system in accounting for manufacturing costs. The standard costs for a unit of "Dandy" are as follows:

Raw materials (6 lb at $1 per lb)	$ 6
Direct labor (1 hr at $4 per hr)	4
Overhead (75% of direct labor costs)	3
	$13

The following data were obtained from Bovar's records for the month of May.

Actual production of "Dandy"	4,000 units
Unsold units of "Dandy"	2,500 units
Sales	$50,000
Purchases	$27,300
Materials purchased price variance	$ 1,300 U
Materials quantity variance	$ 1,000 U
Direct labor rate variance	$ 760 U
Direct labor efficiency variance	$ 800 F
Total overhead flexible budget variance	$ 500 U

Required: Compute each of the following items for Bovar for the month of May.

1. Total standard quantity of raw materials allowed (in pounds)

2. Total actual quantity of raw materials used (in pounds)

3. Total standard labor hours allowed

4. Total actual hours worked

5. Actual direct labor rate per hour

6. Actual total overhead costs

(CPA Adapted)

8–24 Variance Analysis: Factory Overhead Based on Labor Cost

Armando Corporation manufactures a product with the following standard costs.

Direct materials (20 yd at $1.35 per yd)	$	27
Direct labor (4 hr at $9 per hr)		36
Variable factory overhead (4 per direct labor hr) costs		20
Total variable standard cost per unit of output	$	83
Total budgeted fixed factory overhead per month	$ 6,000	

The following information pertains to the month of July, 19x1.

Direct materials purchased (18,000 yd at $1.38)	$24,840
Direct materials used (9500 yd)	
Direct labor (2100 hr at $9.15)	19,215
Total factory overhead ($6800 fixed)	16,650
Total actual costs	$60,705

500 units of product were actually produced in July, 19x1.

Requirements

a) Determine the variable overhead rate per direct labor hour.

b) Compute the following variances:

Materials purchased price variance
Materials quantity variance
Labor rate variance
Labor efficiency variance
Variable overhead spending variance
Variable overhead efficiency variance
Fixed overhead budget variance

c) Prepare a performance report showing actual costs, flexible budget costs, total flexible budget variances, and standard cost variances for the month of July.

(CPA Adapted)

8–25 Fixed Overhead Budget and Volume Variances (Appendix)

The Starling Company assigns fixed overhead costs to inventory for external reporting purposes by using a predetermined standard overhead rate based on direct labor hours. The standard rate is based on a normal (or denominator) activity level of 10,000 standard allowed direct labor hours per year. There are 5 standard allowed hours for each unit of output. Budgeted fixed overhead costs are $200,000 per year. During 19x8 the Starling Company produced 1900 units of output, and actual fixed costs were $195,000.

Requirements

a) Determine the standard fixed overhead rate used to assign fixed costs to inventory.

b) Determine the amount of fixed overhead assigned to inventory in 19x8.

c) Determine the fixed overhead budget variance.

d) Determine the fixed overhead volume variance.

e) What information does the fixed overhead volume variance computed above convey to management?

8–26 Variance Computations with Fixed Cost Assigned on a Unit Basis (Appendix)

The Terry Company manufactures a commercial solvent that is used for industrial maintenance. This solvent is sold by the drum and generally has a stable selling price. Because of a decrease in demand for this product, Terry produced and sold 60,000 drums in December, 19x6, which is 50 percent of normal capacity. The following information is available regarding Terry's operations for the month of December 19x6.

Standard costs per drum of product manufactured were as follows:

Materials:
10 gallons of raw materials at $2 per gallon	$20
1 empty drum	1
Total materials cost	$21
Direct labor: 1 hour	$ 7
Variable factory overhead: per labor hour	$ 4
Fixed factory overhead: per labor hour	$ 6
(Fixed overhead is assigned to production based on a normal production volume of 120,000 allowed direct labor hours.)	

Costs incurred during December 19x6 were as follows:

Raw materials:
  600,000 gallons were purchased at a cost of
    $1,150,000.
  700,000 gallons were used.
Empty drums:
  85,000 drums were purchased at a cost of $85,000.
  60,000 drums were used, and 60,000 drums of product were produced.
Direct labor: 65,000 hours for a total of $470,000.
Factory overhead:

Variable factory overhead	$ 76,500
Supervision and indirect labor (contains $320,000 variable and $140,000 fixed)	460,000
Depreciation (fixed)	330,000
Total factory overhead	$866,500

Required: Compute the following variances.

1. Materials purchased price variance
2. Materials quantity variance
3. Labor rate variance
4. Labor efficiency variance
5. Variable overhead spending variance
6. Variable overhead efficiency variance
7. Fixed overhead budget variance
8. Fixed overhead volume variance

(CPA Adapted)

8–27 Sales, Flexible Budget, and Standard Cost Variances: Reconciliation of Actual and Budgeted Net Income

The Boise Company's Copperhill plant produces copper rods for industrial use. Oscar Santos, who was recently appointed general manager, just received the following income statement for his plant for May, 19x6, his first month as manager.

	Actual	Budgeted	Variance
Units	11,000	12,000	1000 U
Sales	$132,000	$120,000	$12,000 F
Less variable costs:			
Direct materials	$ 22,275	$ 23,400	$ 1,125 F
Direct labor	20,805	21,000	195 F
Factory overhead	15,860	16,500	640 F
Total variable costs	− 58,940	− 60,900	1,960 F
Contribution margin	$ 73,060	$ 59,100	$13,960 F
Less fixed manufacturing costs	− 26,500	− 25,000	− 1,500 U
Plant net income	$ 46,560	$ 34,100	$12,460 F

There were no beginning or ending inventories. The variable standard costs per unit are as follows:

Direct materials $1\frac{1}{2}$ kilograms at $1.30 per kilogram
Direct labor $\frac{1}{2}$ hour at $3.50 per hour
Variable overhead $\frac{1}{2}$ direct labor hour at $2.75 per hour

The following actual data were collected.

Direct materials used: 16,500 kilograms
Direct labor hours used: 5700 hours

Requirements

a) Determine the amount of the net income variance traceable to the decision to raise the selling price. *Hint:* Compute the sales price variance.

b) Determine the amount of the net income variance traceable to selling 1000 units below the budget. *Hint:* Compute the net sales volume variance.

c) Determine the amount of the net income variance traceable to manufacturing cost control factors. *Hint:* Compute the flexible budget variance for total manufacturing costs, including variable and fixed.

d) What does the sum of the answers to requirements (a) through (c) represent?

e) Determine the total flexible budget variance for direct materials and the appropriate standard cost variances.

f) Repeat requirement (e) for direct labor.

g) Repeat requirement (e) for variable factory overhead.

h) Repeat requirement (e) for fixed factory overhead.

i) Santos is feeling very good about exceeding the original budgeted net income in spite of selling 1000 fewer units of product than budgeted. From a cost control standpoint, does he have any reason to be pleased about his performance? Explain.

9

Control of Decentralized Operations

Businesses that operate in several different industries, or widely dispersed geographic areas, are often organized into many quasi-independent parts. Although a centralized organizational structure is appropriate for many organizations, it has several limitations and is often replaced by a decentralized structure in diverse and complex organizations.

The purpose of this chapter is to present techniques used to measure and evaluate the performance of segments of decentralized organizations. We examine the various ways in which such operations can be evaluated, how they interact with each other, and the problems large organizations encounter when they have decentralized operations.

The decentralized units normally become quasi-independent, often having their own controller function, computer system, and administrative and marketing staffs. When this occurs, the corporate office faces several problems in keeping the units properly functioning for the benefit of the entire organization. Several of these problem areas are discussed in the last section of the chapter.

MANAGEMENT PHILOSOPHIES OF DECENTRALIZED OPERATIONS

To establish a proper framework for *decentralization,* it is necessary to examine some of the issues surrounding *centralization.* **Centralization** exists when the major functions of an organization (such as manufacturing, sales, accounting, computer operations, marketing, research and development, and management control) are controlled by top management. Reasons for centralization include the following:

- Economies of scale — Centralized resources can be more fully utilized than the same resources divided into smaller groupings.

- Sophistication of applications — By combining the firm's resources, greater efficiency may be achieved and more complex tasks performed.

- Improved control — More direct lines of authority provide better control of resources. Improved control permits the organization to rapidly shift resources to achieve changing corporate goals. Centralization also permits a greater perspective by top managers because they are in contact with a larger proportion of activities than if decentralized.

However, centralization does have its limitations, the most significant of which are given below:

- Span of control — After the size of a given function increases to a certain level, it becomes difficult to control from the top of an organization.

- Complexity — Combining activities into large centralized functions may create organizations of such complexity that they become unmanageable.

- Diseconomies of scale — When functions become too large, problems of control and efficiency begin to occur. Almost every organizational function has a point of diminishing returns where adding another employee, work task, or manager does little toward reaching the overall organizational objectives.

Decentralization is the delegation of decision-making authority to successively lower management levels in an organization. The lower in the organization the authority is delegated, the greater the decentralization. This approach offers several advantages that tend to counter the problems of centralization. The most compelling arguments for decentralization are based on the need for management to be more responsive to the various operating units and segments of the organization. The advantages of decentralization include the following:

- First-hand decision making — Personnel closely associated with problems and situations are allowed to make decisions. Experience in decision making at low management levels results in trained managers when higher level positions become available.

- Faster decisions — Decisions are made locally without having to feed information up the chain of command and then wait for a response.

- Specialization — Corporate management can concentrate on strategic planning and policy, and divisional management can concentrate on operating decisions.

- Motivation — Managers who actively participate in decision making are more committed to the success of their programs and are more willing to accept responsibility for the consequences of their actions.

Before accepting decentralization as the answer to organizational problems, its disadvantages must be considered. The primary problems associated with this type of organizational structure are given below:

- Competent personnel — Division management may not be able to carry out and control its operations in accordance with company policy because of a lack of competent personnel.

- Consistency — It is difficult to keep all operating units on the same measurement system in a large organization. This includes reporting periods, methods of reporting, and consistency of data collection.

- Suboptimization — It is difficult to keep each unit operating for the benefit of the entire organization rather than for its own selfish benefit.

As organizations expand in size and complexity, centralized control becomes more difficult. Planning, controlling, coordinating, budgeting, and a variety of other functions may overwhelm top management in a large centralized organization. The solution to this problem is the decentralization of the organization into smaller operating units. With proper planning and staffing of each unit or division, the organization can often overcome the disadvantages of decentralization and improve overall organizational performance.

In most large decentralized organizations, the primary operating units are called divisions. Each division is largely autonomous, with the division manager usually being responsible for sales, production, and administration of the unit. Division managers usually have control over all activities, although capital budgeting and long-range planning activities are often

EXHIBIT 9–1   Decentralized Organizational Chart

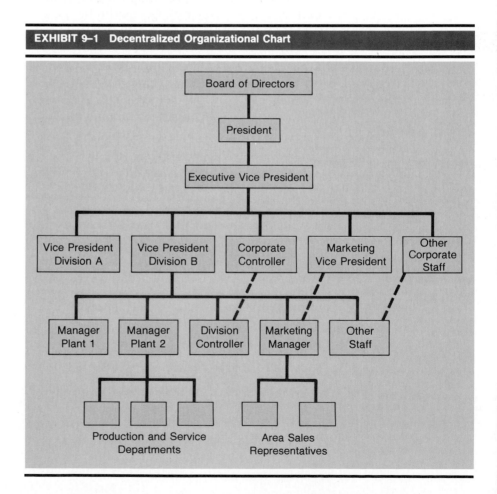

limited. These two activities are often centralized within corporate headquarters, with the various division managers given control over the investments once they are made. As generally organized, divisions are the most common example of investment centers.

A decentralized organizational structure is illustrated in Exhibit 9–1. The theory behind this structure is to delegate most responsibilities to each division and let each division operate as a quasi-independent business. You might want to contrast this with the centralized organizational chart in Exhibit 7–2.

The division management group usually includes managers from the computer center, personnel, marketing, controller's office, production, and other necessary functions. One potential problem of such a structure is the conflict of two superiors. The dashed lines in Exhibit 9–1 represent each staff's responsibility to corporate headquarters, whereas the solid lines connect each staff to the division vice president who has day-to-day authority. For example, the controller has a dual responsibility: (1) to the divisional vice president who exercises line authority and (2) to the corporate controller who exercises functional authority. The divisional controller performs at the division level most of the controllership tasks outlined in Chapter 1. In performing assignments the divisional controller must follow certain firmwide accounting procedures specified by the corporate controller. Sometimes the divisional controller is regarded as an extension of the corporate controller or as a "front-office employee." In this case the divisional controller has a direct-line relationship with the corporate controller and a staff-line relationship with the division manager.

EVALUATION METHODS

Recall from Chapter 7 that responsibility accounting is the structuring of performance reports addressed to individual members of an organization in a manner that emphasizes the factors controllable by them. Responsibility accounting reports may be prepared for cost centers, revenue centers, profit centers, or investment centers. Cost centers are evaluated by comparing actual with allowed costs, and revenue centers are evaluated by comparing actual with budgeted revenues. Because divisions operate as quasi-independent businesses with significant authority over their activities and the size of their investments, they are evaluated as investment centers. When the investment center concept is implemented, the use of net income as a performance measure is not sufficient because different centers may have substantially different asset bases. In these situations net income does not properly reflect the efficient utilization of the assets employed. Today, most organizations use the *return on investment* ratio as the primary basis for evaluating investment centers. This concept is more relevant than traditional net income because investment center performance reports need to emphasize the relationship between each investment center's income and the size of its asset base. A closely related concept, *residual income,* is also frequently used.

Return on Investment (ROI)

Return on investment is a measure of the earnings per dollar of investment.[1] The return on investment of an investment center is computed by dividing the income of the center by its asset base (usually total assets):

$$\text{ROI} = \frac{\text{Investment center income}}{\text{Investment center asset base}}.$$

It can also be computed as investment turnover times the return-on-sales ratio (also called margin, income percentage of revenue, and income-sales ratio):

$$\text{ROI} = \text{Investment turnover} \times \text{Return-on-sales ratio,}$$

where,
$$\text{Investment turnover} = \frac{\text{Sales}}{\text{Investment center asset base}}, \text{ and}$$

$$\text{Return-on-sales ratio} = \frac{\text{Investment center income}}{\text{Sales}}.$$

When investment turnover is multiplied by income as a percentage of sales, the product is the same as investment center income divided by investment center asset base:

$$\text{ROI} = \frac{\text{Sales}}{\text{Investment center asset base}} \times \frac{\text{Investment center income}}{\text{Sales}}$$

$$= \frac{\text{Investment center income}}{\text{Investment center asset base}}.$$

Once ROI is computed, it is compared to some previously identified performance criteria, such as the investment center's previous ROI, overall company ROI, the ROI of similar divisions, or the ROI of nonaffiliated companies that operate in similar markets, produce similar products, or provide similar services. The breakdown of ROI into investment turnover and return-on-sales ratio is useful in determining the source of variance in overall performance.

---

[1] Other similar concepts that are often used to supplement or replace ROI, but are not discussed here, include return on assets, return on net assets, and return on production assets.

To illustrate the computation and use of ROI, the following information is available concerning the 19x3 operations of the Maine Division of North American Steel:

Sales	$1,200,000
Income	144,000
Investment base	800,000

From these facts ROI can be computed as

$$\text{ROI} = \frac{\text{Investment center income}}{\text{Investment center asset base}}$$

$$= \frac{\$144,000}{\$800,000}$$

$$= 0.18, \text{ or } 18 \text{ percent,}$$

or as

$$\text{ROI} = \frac{\text{Sales}}{\text{Investment center asset base}} \times \frac{\text{Investment center income}}{\text{Sales}}$$

$$= \frac{\$1,200,000}{\$800,000} \times \frac{\$144,000}{\$1,200,000}$$

$$= 1.5 \times 0.12$$

$$= 0.18, \text{ or } 18 \text{ percent.}$$

During 19x3, Maine Division earned a return on its investment base of 18 percent, consisting of an investment turnover of 1.5 times and a return-on-sales ratio of 0.12. Using such an analysis, the company has three measurement criteria with which to evaluate the performance of Maine Division: (1) ROI, (2) investment turnover, and (3) return-on-sales ratio.

For 19x3, North American chose to evaluate its divisions based on company ROI and its interrelated components of investment turnover and income-sales ratio. The information for each division is shown in Exhibit 9–2. For each division the 19x3 performance measures are presented along with the company's criteria. Because each division is different in size, the company evaluation standard is not a simple average of the divisions but is based on desired levels of company sales, assets, and income.

Based on ROI, the Tijuana Division had the best performance, Alberta excelled in investment turnover, and Utah had the highest return-on-sales ratio. From Exhibit 9–2 it is obvious that Tijuana had the best year because it was the only division that exceeded each of the company's criteria. For

---

EXHIBIT 9–2   Division Evaluation Data

North American Steel
Performance Measures
For the year ended June 30, 19x3

	Performance Measures		
	ROI	Investment Turnover	Return-on-Sales Ratio
Operating unit:			
Maine division	0.18	1.5	0.12
Alberta division	0.24	3.0	0.08
Utah division	0.22	1.1	0.20
Tijuana division	0.27	1.5	0.18
Average	0.21	1.4	0.15
Company criteria:			
Projected minimum	0.18	1.2	0.15

19x3 each division equaled or exceeded the minimum ROI established by the company, even though the component criteria of ROI were not always achieved. For example, Maine Division achieved the minimum ROI even though its return-on-sales ratio was below 0.15. It accomplished this by having an investment turnover that exceeded the minimum by 0.3 (1.5 less 1.2).

To properly evaluate each division the company should study the underlying components of ROI. For the Maine Division, management would want to know why the minimum investment turnover was achieved when the return-on-sales ratio minimum was not achieved. By achieving the investment turnover minimum, the Maine Division may have produced inefficiently in reaching its minimum sales level. As a result of inefficient production, the return-on-sales ratio declined to a point below the minimum desired level. It is difficult to evaluate a large operating division based on one financial figure. Management should select several key indicators of performance when conducting periodic reviews of its operating segments.

A similar analysis of ROI and its components can be made when planning for future periods. In developing plans for 19x4, management wants to know the possible effect of changes in the major elements of ROI for Maine Division. Sensitivity analysis can be used to predict the impact of changes in sales, the investment center asset base, or investment center income.

Assuming the investment base is unchanged, a projected ROI can be determined for Maine Division for a sales goal of $1,600,000 and an income goal of $160,000:

$$\text{ROI} = \frac{\text{Sales}}{\text{Investment center asset base}} \times \frac{\text{Investment center income}}{\text{Sales}}$$

$$= \frac{\$1,600,000}{\$800,000} \times \frac{\$160,000}{\$1,600,000}$$

$$= 2.0 \times 0.10$$

$$= 0.20, \text{ or 20 percent.}$$

Notice that ROI increased from 18 to 20 percent, even though the return-on-sales ratio decreased from 12 to 10 percent. The change in turnover from 1.5 to 2.0 more than offset the reduced return-on-sales ratio.

Starting from Maine's 19x3 performance, now assume that projected operating efficiencies reduce expenses by $12,000, and that sales remain constant, thereby increasing income to $156,000. The ROI increases from 18 percent to 19.5 percent:

$$\text{ROI} = \frac{\text{Sales}}{\text{Investment center asset base}} \times \frac{\text{Investment center income}}{\text{Sales}}$$

$$= \frac{\$1,200,000}{\$800,000} \times \frac{\$156,000}{\$1,200,000}$$

$$= 1.5 \times 0.13$$

$$= 0.195, \text{ or 19.5 percent.}$$

Sensitivity analysis may involve changing only one factor in the ROI model or a combination of factors. When more than one factor is changed, the user must be careful to properly analyze exactly how much change is caused by each factor.

Management may desire a minimum ROI. In this case the major elements of the ROI model can be manipulated to determine the best way to meet this minimum. If, for example, ROI is set at 24 percent, it may be obtained by changing only the investment base (from $800,000 to $600,000):

$$\text{ROI} = \frac{\text{Sales}}{\text{Investment center asset base}} \times \frac{\text{Investment center income}}{\text{Sales}}$$

$$= \frac{\$1,200,000}{\$600,000} \times \frac{\$144,000}{\$1,200,000}$$

$$= 2.0 \times 0.12$$

$$= 0.24, \text{ or 24 percent.}$$

Or it may be obtained by changing a combination of the investment base (from \$800,000 to \$900,000) and income (from \$144,000 to \$216,000):

$$\text{ROI} = \frac{\text{Sales}}{\text{Investment center asset base}} \times \frac{\text{Investment center income}}{\text{Sales}}$$

$$= \frac{\$1,200,000}{\$900,000} \times \frac{\$216,000}{\$1,200,000}$$

$$= 1.333 \times 0.18$$

$$= 0.24, \text{ or } 24 \text{ percent.}$$

It may also be obtained by changing any combination of the three factors, together or separately.

Statistics such as ROI, investment turnover, and return-on-sales ratio mean little by themselves. They take on meaning only when compared with an objective, a trend, another division, a competitor, or an industry average. Many businesses establish minimum ROIs for each of their divisions, which are expected to attain or exceed this minimum return. The salaries, bonuses, and promotions of division managers may be tied directly to the ROI of their divisions. Without other evaluation techniques, managers often strive for ROI maximization, sometimes to the long-run detriment of the entire organization.

Investment Base. Despite the relevance and conceptual simplicity of ROI, a division's ROI cannot be computed until management determines how divisional investment and income are to be measured. Because the primary purpose for computing ROI is to evaluate the effectiveness of a division's operating management in utilizing the assets entrusted to them, most organizations define investment as the average total assets of a division during the evaluation period.

The first difficulty in defining the investment base relates to current assets. Corporate cash and receivables are sometimes held by corporate headquarters, which permits more efficiency in billings and collections. This enables the corporation to hold a smaller total amount of cash than would be required if each division had its own bank account. Although it is relatively easy to assign receivables to divisions (on the basis of their origin) for ROI computations, the assignment of cash presents some problems. Because of operating economies, the total cash requirements of the entire organization are less than the cash requirements of all divisions acting as independent units. However, assigning cash on the basis of the division's independent cash needs is likely to raise objections. The best approach seems to be to allocate cash based on the amount of incremental cash needed to support each division as compared to the company as a whole; nevertheless, cash allocations are most frequently based on relative sales or cash expenditures.

The next problem relates to general corporate assets. It is not advisable to allocate the cost of physical assets utilized by corporate headquarters to the operating divisions (see Chapter 10 for a complete discussion of this topic). Though the divisions might need additional administrative facilities if they were truly independent, they have no control over the headquarter's facilities. Additionally, the joint nature and use of these facilities make any allocation arbitrary.

One of the problems with the comparisons of ROI among divisions is the difference in the historical cost of each division's assets. It is somewhat difficult to compare a division whose asset base is measured in 1985 dollars with one that has most of its asset base measured in 1974 dollars. To overcome this problem, many companies require all divisions to use some common dollar base.

Investment Center Income. Divisional income is equal to divisional revenues less divisional operating expenses. Except for service expenses that can be clearly identified with the activities of individual divisions (such as the variable costs of processing accounts receivable), the expenses of operating corporate headquarters should not be allocated to the division for ROI purposes. Some companies advocate not allocating even if the absence of corporate headquarters would cause the divisions to incur additional expenses. In many decentralized operations, corporate general and administrative expenses are often allocated to divisions for internal reporting purposes, but they are excluded when computing divisional ROI.

Some companies allocate all expenses in determining ROI because these expenses represent the value of services rendered by the home office. Other companies believe that allocated expenses should not be included because division management has no control over the incurrence or allocation of the expenses. Also, the allocations are often for items of questionable value to the division, such as the corporation's legal costs.

Generally, such allocations are not included in the computation of divisional ROI. Only when the expenses can be directly associated with the division should they be included in the ROI computation. An example of this is the interest expense on debt associated with the financing of divisional operations. The amount of expenses allocated should be approximately the same as it would be if the division had incurred the services on its own. If allocated corporate costs are substantially greater than a division's independently incurred costs would be, then costs are allocated in excess of benefits received, which is a very undesirable situation.

Asset Measurement. Once divisional investment and income have been operationally defined and ROI computations have been made, the significance of the resulting ratios may still be questioned. Return on investment may be overstated in terms of constant dollars because inflation and arbitrary depreciation procedures cause an undervaluation of the inventory and fixed assets included in the investment center asset base. Asset measurement is particularly troublesome if inventories are valued at last-in, first-out (LIFO) cost and fixed assets were acquired many years ago. A division manager may hesitate to replace an old inefficient asset with a new efficient one because the replacement may lower income and ROI through an increased investment base and increased depreciation.

To improve the comparability between divisions' old and new assets, some firms value assets at original cost rather than at net book value (cost less accumulated depreciation) in ROI computations. This procedure does not reflect inflation, however. An old asset that cost $120,000 ten years ago is still being compared with an asset that costs $200,000 today. A better solution might be to value old assets at their replacement cost, although depreciation values can become a problem. This raises issues about the cost and value of information and about whether or not the old asset would be replaced in kind at today's prices.

Residual Income

Residual income is an often-mentioned alternative to measuring investment center performance. **Residual income** is the excess of investment center income over the minimum return set by the corporation. The minimum return is computed as a percentage of the investment center's asset base. If residual income is the primary basis of evaluation, the management of each investment center is encouraged to maximize residual income rather than ROI.

To illustrate the computation, assume a company requires each division to earn 12 percent on its investment base. A division of the company has an annual net operating income of $200,000 and an investment base of $1,500,000. The residual income for these assumptions would be $20,000, computed as follows:

Division income	$200,000
Minimum return ($1,500,000 × 0.12)	−180,000
Residual income	$ 20,000

Many executives view residual income as a better measure of performance than ROI. They believe that residual income encourages managers to make profitable investments that would otherwise be rejected by managers who are being measured by ROI. To illustrate, assume that two divisions of Color Company have an opportunity to make an investment of $100,000 that will generate a return of 20 percent. The manager of Green Division is evaluated using ROI, and the manager of Orange Division is evaluated using residual income. The current ROI of each division is 24 percent, and each division has a current income of $120,000 and a minimum rate of 18 percent on invested capital. If each division has a current investment base of $500,000, the investment can be analyzed as follows:

	Current	+	Proposed	=	Total
Green division:					
Investment center income	$120,000		$ 20,000		$140,000
Asset base	$500,000		$100,000		$600,000
ROI	0.24 or 24 percent		0.20 or 20 percent		0.233 or 23.3 percent
Orange division:					
Asset base	$500,000		$100,000		$600,000
Investment center income	$120,000		$ 20,000		$140,000
Minimum return (0.18 × base)	−90,000		−18,000		−108,000
Residual income	$ 30,000		$ 2,000		$ 32,000

Since the performance of the Green Division is being measured according to the best rate of return that can be generated, the manager will not want to make the new investment because it reduces the current ROI of 24 percent to 23.3 percent. This is true, even though the company's minimum return is 18 percent. The manager will probably reject the opportunity even though it may have benefited the company as a whole. Nor does the manager want to have to explain a decline in the division's ROI.

The Orange Division manager will probably be happy to accept the new project because it increases residual income by $2000. Any investment that provides a return greater than the required minimum of 18 percent will be acceptable to the Orange Division manager. Given a profit maximization goal for the organization the residual income method is preferred because it maximizes the investment opportunities of the organization by accepting all projects with returns above the 18 percent cutoff.

The primary disadvantage of the residual income method is that it measures performance in dollars. It cannot be used to compare the performance of divisions of different sizes; for example the residual income of a multimillion dollar sales division would be expected to be larger than that of a half-million dollar sales division. Where such situations exist and management desires something other than ROI, the **residual income ratio** is sometimes used. This is simply the residual income divided by the investment base:

$$\text{Residual income ratio (RIR)} = \frac{\text{Residual income}}{\text{Investment base}},$$

or

$$\text{RIR} = \text{ROI} - \text{Minimum rate of return.}$$

This assists in analyzing divisions with diverse investment base amounts because it provides a percentage of the amount earned over and above the minimum required return. For example, Division 291 has an investment base of $100,000, and Division 436 has a base of $400,000. The minimum return is 15 percent. During 19x8, Division 291 earns $20,000, and Division 436 earns $70,000. A comparative analysis is as follows:

	Division 291	Division 436
Income	$20,000	$70,000
Minimum return:		
$100,000 × 0.15	−15,000	
$400,000 × 0.15		−60,000
Residual income	$ 5,000	$10,000
RIR	$\frac{5,000}{\$100,000} = 0.05$	$\frac{\$10,000}{400,000} = 0.025$

Even though Division 436 has twice as much residual income as Division 291, its RIR is half that of Division 291.

If an organization desires to maximize dollars of profit, residual income should be used. However, if it desires financial information to assist in performance evaluation (especially between division managers), ROI should be used because it has, regardless of division size, a common base of comparison — the ratio of income to investment.

TRANSFER PRICING

Transfer pricing is used when products or services are exchanged between units of an organization. A **transfer price** is the internal value assigned a product or service that one division provides to another. All cost allocations are a form of transfer pricing, although the term is generally restricted to transfer prices in excess of cost. Assigning maintenance costs to production departments is an example of cost allocation, not an example of transfer pricing. In a transfer-pricing situation the exchange is typically between profit or investment centers rather than between cost centers.

The objective of transfer pricing is to transmit financial data between departments or divisions of a company as they use each other's goods and services. Transfer-pricing systems are normally used in decentralized operations to determine whether organizational objectives are being achieved in each division. For division managers to be accountable for all transactions, both external and internal, transfer prices must be determined for the internal transfers of goods and services.

Management Considerations

The desire of the selling and buying divisions of the same company to maximize their individual performance measures often creates a transfer pricing problem. Acting as independent units, the divisions may take actions that are not in the best interest of the organization as a whole. The two examples that follow illustrate the need for the organization to maintain a profit-maximizing objective while attempting to allow divisional autonomy and responsibility.

Assume that Division 6 of Rex Manufacturing is operating at 80 percent capacity and that it manufactures two products, Alpha and Beta. Alpha is sold outside the organization for $50, and Beta is sold to Division 13 at a transfer price of $60. The costs associated with these two products are given below:

	Product	
	Alpha	Beta
Direct materials	$15	$14
Direct labor	5	10
Variable manufacturing overhead	5	16
Fixed manufacturing overhead	6	15
Variable selling	4	—
Total	$35	$55

A proposal has just been received from another company to supply Division 13 with a substitute product similar to Beta at a price of $52. From the company's viewpoint, this is merely a make-or-buy decision. The relevant costs are the differential outlay costs of the alternative actions. If the fixed manufacturing costs of Division 6 cannot be reduced, the relevant costs are as follows:

Buy		$52
Make:		
Direct materials	$14	
Direct labor	10	
Variable manufacturing	16	−40
Difference favors making		$12

From the viewpoint of Division 13, this is a cost minimization decision — that is, buy from the source that charges the lowest price. If Division 6 does not lower its price, the costs of Division 13 are minimized, and profits are maximized by purchasing outside.

From the viewpoint of Division 6, this is a decision to accept (lower price) or reject a special sales order at $52. Although a sale at $52 provides a $12 contribution toward fixed costs and profits, Division 6 might elect not to lower its price. If central management forced Division 6 to lower the price of Beta, divisional autonomy would be reduced.

To examine a slightly different transfer-pricing conflict, assume that Division 6 can sell all the Beta in the above situation that it can produce (it is operating at capacity), and that there is a one-to-one trade-off between the production of Alpha and Beta. They both use equal amounts of the limited capacity of Division 6.

The corporation still regards this as a make-or-buy decision, but the costs of producing Beta have changed. Beta now includes an avoidable cost and an opportunity cost. The avoidable cost is the variable cost of $40 ($14 + $10 + $16) computed above. The opportunity cost is the net benefit forgone if the limited capacity of Division 6 is used to produce Beta:

Selling price of Alpha		$50
Avoidable costs of Alpha:		
Direct materials	$15	
Direct labor	5	
Variable manufacturing overhead	5	
Variable selling	4	−29
Opportunity cost of making Beta		$21

Accordingly, the relevant costs in the make-or-buy decision are as shown at the top of page 355.

Make		
Avoidable cost of Beta	$40	
Opportunity cost of Beta	21	$61
Buy		$51

Product Beta should be purchased from the outside supplier. If there were no outside suppliers, the relevant cost of manufacturing Beta would still be $61 — which is another way of saying that Beta should not be produced and processed further in Division 13 unless the resultant revenues cover all outlay costs (including the $40 in Division 6) and provide a contribution of at least $21 ($61 — $40). From the viewpoint of the corporation, the relevant costs in a make-or-buy decision are the external price, the outlay costs of manufacture, and the opportunity cost to manufacture. The opportunity cost is zero if there is excess capacity.

Determining Transfer Prices

As illustrated above, the transfer price of goods or services may be subject to much controversy. Although a price must be agreed upon for each item or service transferred between divisions, the selection of the pricing method is dependent upon many factors. The conditions surrounding the transfer will determine which of the alternative methods discussed below is selected.

In considering each method, observe that each transfer results in a revenue entry on the books of the supplier and a cost entry on the books of the receiver. Transfers may be considered as sales by the supplier and as inventory purchases by the receiver. Although no method is likely to be ideal, one must be selected if the profit or investment center concept is used.

Market Price. When there is an existing market with established prices for an intermediate product and the actions of the company will not affect prices, market prices are ideal transfer prices. If divisions are free to buy and sell outside the firm, the use of market prices preserves divisional autonomy and leads divisions to act in a manner that maximizes corporate goal congruence. Unfortunately, not all product transfers have equivalent external markets. Furthermore, the divisions should carefully evaluate whether the market price is competitive or controlled by one or two large companies.

When there are substantial selling expenses associated with outside sales, many firms specify the transfer price as market price less selling expenses. The internal sale may not require the incurrence of costs to get and fill the order.

To illustrate, assume that product Alpha of Division 6 can be sold competitively at $50 per unit or transferred to Division 24 for additional processing. Under most situations, Division 6 will never sell Alpha for less than $50, and Division 24 will likewise never pay more than $50 for it. However, if any variable expenses related to marketing and shipping can be eliminated by divisional transfers, these costs are generally subtracted from the competitive market price. In our illustration, where variable selling expenses are $4 for Alpha, the transfer price could be reduced to $46 ($50 − $4). A price between $45 and $50 would probably be better than either extreme price.

Variable Costs. If there is excess capacity in the supplying division, establishing a transfer price equal to variable costs leads the purchasing division to act in a manner that is optimal from the corporation's viewpoint. The buying division has the corporation's variable costs as its own variable cost as it enters the external market. Unfortunately, establishing the transfer price at variable cost causes the supplying division to report zero profits or a loss equal to any fixed costs. If excess capacity does not exist, establishing a transfer price at variable cost may not lead to optimal action because the supplying division may have to forgo sales that include a markup for fixed costs and profits. In the above example, Division 6 would not want to transfer Beta to Division 13 if it received only a $40 transfer price based on the following variable costs:

Direct materials	$14
Direct labor	10
Variable manufacturing overhead	16
Total variable costs	$40

Division 6 would much rather sell outside the company if it can receive a price of $60, which covers variable costs and provides for a profit contribution margin of $20:

Selling price of Beta	$60
Variable costs	−40
Contribution margin	$20

Variable Costs Plus Opportunity Costs. From the viewpoint of the corporation this is the optimal transfer price. Because all relevant costs are included in the transfer price, the purchasing division is led to act in an optimal manner regardless of whether or not excess capacity exists.

With excess capacity in the supplying division, the transfer price is the variable cost per unit. Without excess capacity the transfer price is the sum of the variable and opportunity costs. Following this rule in the above example, if Division 6 had excess capacity, the transfer price of Beta would be set at Beta's variable costs of $40 per unit. At this transfer price, Division 13 would buy Beta internally rather than externally at $52 per unit. If Division 6 can sell all that it can produce and is operating at capacity, the transfer price per unit would be set at $61, the sum of Beta's variable and opportunity costs ($40 + $21) computed previously. At this transfer price, Division 13 would buy Betas externally for $52. In both situations, Division 13 has acted in accordance with the profit-maximizing viewpoint of the organization as a whole.

However, there are two problems with this method. First, when the supplying division has excess capacity, establishing the transfer price at variable cost causes the supplying division to report zero profits or a loss equal to any fixed costs. Second, it is difficult to determine opportunity costs when the supplying division produces several products. If the problems with the previously mentioned transfer pricing methods are too great, three other often used methods are available; they are absorption cost plus mark-up, negotiated prices, and dual prices.

Absorption Costs Plus Mark-up. According to absorption costing all variable and fixed manufacturing costs are product costs. Pricing internal transfers at *absorption cost* eliminates the supplying division's reported loss on each product that may occur using a variable cost transfer price. *Absorption cost plus mark-up* provides the supplying division with a contribution toward unallocated costs. Even though such transfer prices may not maximize company profits, they are widely used. Their popularity stems from several factors including ease of implementation, justifiability, and perceived fairness. Once everyone agrees on "absorption cost plus mark-up" pricing rules, internal disputes are minimized.

In "cost plus" transfer pricing, "cost" should be defined as standard cost rather than actual cost. This prevents the supplying division from passing on the cost of inefficient operations to other divisions, and it allows the buying division to know its cost in advance of purchase.

Negotiated Prices. Negotiated transfer prices are used when the supplying and buying divisions independently agree on a price. Like market-based transfer prices, negotiated transfer prices are believed to preserve divisional autonomy. Negotiated transfer prices may lead to some suboptimal decisions, but this is regarded as a small price to pay for other benefits of decentralization. When negotiated transfer prices are used, some corporations establish arbitration procedures to help settle disputes between divisions. However, the existence of an arbitrator with any real or perceived authority reduces divisional autonomy.

Dual Prices. Dual prices exist when a company allows a difference in the supplier's transfer price and the receiver's transfer price for the same product. This method allegedly minimizes internal squabbles of division managers and problems of conflicting divisional goals. The supplier's price normally approximates market price, which allows the selling division to show a "normal" profit on items that it transfers internally. The receiver's price is usually variable cost or absorption cost. Dual prices eliminate the receiver's need for covering internally transferred profits when the final external price is established. The receiver is also allowed to make a profit from the final product that was transferred in.

Applying Transfer Pricing

Once the transfer prices have been determined, they can be used to reflect interdivision sales. Although most divisional income statements are very complex, the following illustration concentrates only on the elements related to the transfer of goods and services. Leigh Ann's Fashions, a dress manufacturer, has two divisions, Sewing and Sales. The Sewing Division sells to the Sales Division and to other distributors. During the first quarter of 19x7 the Sewing Division incurred the following unit costs:

Direct materials	$ 8
Direct labor	5
Other variable manufacturing costs	3
Variable selling costs	1
Total	$17

Total production for the quarter was 30,000 dresses, of which 20,000 were sold to the Sales Division for $18 each. External sales were $25 for each dress. There were no beginning or ending inventories. Fixed manufacturing costs totaled $60,000.

After the Sales Division receives the dresses, they affix private labels where necessary and then package and ship to retail customers. The variable unit costs are $4, and the Sales Division incurs $40,000 in fixed costs each quarter. The Division sold all dresses received during the first quarter for $30 each.

Exhibit 9–3 provides a simple illustration of how transfer pricing affects each division's income statement and the company as a whole. The 20,000 units transferred from Sewing to Sales shows up as $360,000 of internal sales for Sewing and as $360,000 of transferred-in cost to Sales. Notice that both amounts are ignored for the overall company income statement. The

EXHIBIT 9–3 Divisional and Company Income Statements

Leigh Ann's Fashions
Divisional and Company Income Statements
First Quarter, 19x7

	Sewing Division	Sales Division	Company
Sales:			
External*	$250,000	$600,000	$850,000
Internal†	360,000	—	—
Total	$610,000	$600,000	$850,000
Variable costs:			
Incurred‡	$510,000	$ 80,000	$590,000
Transferred-in§	—	360,000	—
Total	−510,000	−440,000	−590,000
Contribution margin	$100,000	$160,000	$260,000
Fixed costs	− 60,000	− 40,000	−100,000
Net income	$ 40,000	$120,000	$160,000

* 10,000 × $25 = $250,000, and 20,000 × $30 = $600,000.

† 20,000 × $18 = $360,000.

‡ 30,000 × $17 = $510,000, and 20,000 × $4 = $80,000.

§ Transferred-in costs is the same as internal sales.

reason for this elimination at the company level is the desire to provide external users of financial statements information related to economic activities with outside parties and not internal transfers.

Although evaluating divisional income statements with transfer prices is very beneficial, it is often necessary to determine their impact on the company to fully assess the results of decisions involving transfer pricing. Divisional and overall statement analysis may be necessary when one division is at or near capacity, is substantially below capacity, has offers of either buying or selling externally items normally transferred internally, or is considering eliminating products currently transferred to other divisions. Depending on how these types of decisions are resolved, divisional managers often suboptimize corporate performance.

SUBOPTIMIZATION

A transfer-pricing problem exists when divisions, acting in their own best interest, set transfer prices or make decisions based on transfer prices that are not in the best interest of the organization as a whole. The seriousness of the transfer-pricing problem depends on the extent to which the affairs of divisions are intertwined. When intermediate products have established markets and divisions are free to buy and sell outside the firm, the use of market prices avoids the transfer-pricing problem.

A potential transfer-pricing problem exists when divisions exchange goods or services for which there is not an established market. If the actual or potential amount of such transfers is relatively small, the use of cost-plus or negotiated prices seems most appropriate. The benefits of decentralization are believed to more than offset any loss of profit on individual products.

Though suboptimization may be tolerated on some products to obtain the benefits of decentralization, the problem sometimes becomes so severe that cost and revenue centers should be used in place of investment or profit centers. Consider a single-product firm that attempts to operate its manufacturing and marketing activities as separate profit or investment centers. The affairs of these two divisions cannot be disentangled, and any attempt to do so will reduce the profits of the entire business.

The ideal solutions for the supplying division and for the buying division generally conflict. From the organization's perspective, the desired transfers may not occur because the division managers, pursuing their own best interests, could decide against a transfer. These conflicts sometimes are overcome by having a higher ranking manager impose a transfer price and insist that a transfer be made. But the managers of divisions in an organization that has a policy of decentralization often regard these orders as undermining their autonomy. So the imposition of a price may solve the goal congruence and incentive problem but exacerbate the autonomy problem. Transfer pricing thus becomes a problem with no ideal solutions.

It has been pointed out that there is seldom a single transfer price that will meet all the criteria for inducing top management's desired decisions. The best transfer price depends on the circumstances at hand. Furthermore, the optimal price for either division may differ from that employed for external needs, including tax requirements.

SUMMARY

When an organization expands in size, management must decide whether to adopt a centralized or decentralized structure. As individual units within an organization become large enough to be separately evaluated as quasi-independent businesses, management generally decides to decentralize its operations into investment centers. During such a change, sound practices of responsibility accounting must be developed.

The selection of the evaluation method to be used for each responsibility center is generally determined by what the center can realistically be responsible for in its operations. Centers that receive no revenues can hardly be labeled profit centers, but centers that have unique product lines sold externally can be considered profit or investment centers.

In order to properly evaluate each responsibility center, management must select some type of measurement system. The two most popular methods of evaluating investment center performance are return on investment (ROI) and residual income. In most situations it is recommended that both methods be used if feasible.

Organizations that have internal transfers between profit or investment centers are faced with using transfer pricing and its related problems of goal congruence. Although there are no easy solutions to transfer-pricing problems, several workable alternatives were discussed in this chapter.

KEY TERMS

Centralization	**Residual income**
Decentralization	**Residual income ratio**
Return on investment	**Transfer price**

REVIEW QUESTIONS

9–1 What are the primary advantages of having a centralized organizational structure?

9–2 What are the primary advantages of having a decentralized organizational structure?

9–3 What criteria should management use when changing from one organizational structure to the other?

9–4 How can the problems of decentralization be minimized?

9–5 For what purpose do organizations use return on investment? Why is this measure preferred to net income?

9–6 How does residual income assist in the evaluation process?

9–7 List the elements in the ROI equation, and tell how they are related.

9–8 How is an investment center's asset base determined?

9–9 How is overhead allocated to divisions using ROI? Why?

9–10 What information does residual income provide that ROI does not?

9–11 Should rates of return for each division using residual income be the same? Why? How are they determined?

9–12 In what types of organizations and for what purpose are transfer prices used?

9–13 What problems arise when transfer pricing is used?

9–14 From the viewpoint of the corporation, what is the best method of transfer pricing? What problems may limit the use of this method?

9–15   When do transfer prices lead to suboptimization? How can suboptimization be minimized? Can it bé eliminated? Why or why not?

EXERCISES

9–1 ROI and Residual Income: Basic Computations

The Firebird Division of Central Motors had an operating income of $90,000 and net assets of $400,000. Central Motors has a target rate of return of 16 percent.

Requirements

a) Compute the return on investment.

b) Compute the residual income.

9–2 ROI and Residual Income: Impact of a New Investment

From Exercise 9–1 above, Firebird has an opportunity to increase operating income by $20,000 with an investment in assets of $85,000.

Requirements

a) Compute the Firebird Division's return on investment if the project is undertaken. (Round your answer to three decimal places.)

b) Compute the Firebird Division's residual income if the project is undertaken.

9–3 ROI and Residual Income with Different Bases

Forward Trinket Company is considering evaluating its divisions on both an historical and replacement cost basis. The following information is available for 19x1.

Division	Assets		Income	
	Book Value	Replacement Value	Book Value	Replacement Value
Trinket	$ 600,000	$ 900,000	$120,000	$110,000
Gadget	700,000	700,000	120,000	120,000
Widget	1,000,000	1,400,000	200,000	180,000

The company has a minimum desired rate of 15 percent.

Requirements

a) Compute return on investment using book value and replacement value amounts for each division. (Round your answer to two decimal places.)

b) Compute residual income using book value and replacement value amounts for each division.

c) Does book value or replacement value provide the better basis for performance evaluation? Which division do you consider the most successful?

9–4 ROI: Basic Computations

Keystone Company uses return on investment as one of the evaluation tools for division managers.

Selected operating data for three divisions of the company are given below.

	East Division	West Division	Central Division
Sales	$600,000	$750,000	$900,000
Operating assets	300,000	250,000	350,000
Net operating income	51,000	56,000	59,000

Requirements

a) Compute the return on investment for each division. (Round answers to three decimal places.)

b) Which divisional manager is doing the best job based on ROI? Why?

9–5 ROI: Fill in the Blanks

Provide the missing data in the following situations:

	Division K	Division L	Division M
Sales	$?	$5,000,000	$?
Net operating income	$100,000	$ 200,000	$144,000
Operating assets	$?	$?	$800,000
Return on investment	16%	10%	?
Return-on-sales ratio	0.04	?	0.12
Investment turnover	?	?	1.5

9–6 ROI and Residual Income: Basic Computations

The three divisions of the Atta Moore Company had the following results for 19x6:

	Division A	Division B	Division C
Sales	$60,000	$80,000	$100,000
Operating income	9,000	9,500	10,000
Investment base	60,000	61,000	62,000

The company has a minimum desired rate of return on investment of 15 percent.

Requirements

a) Compute each division's return on investment. (Round answers to three decimal places.)

b) Compute each division's residual income.

9–7 Transfer Pricing and Division Gross Profit

Greenwood Paper Company has two divisions. The Pulp Division prepares the wood for processing. The Paper Division processes the pulp into paper. No inventories exist in either division at the beginning of 19x3. During the year, the Pulp Division prepared 40,000 cords of wood at a cost of $240,000. All the pulp was transferred to the Paper Division where additional operating costs of $5 per cord were incurred. The 400,000 pounds of finished paper were sold for $1,000,000.

Requirements

a) Determine the gross profit for each division and for the company as a whole if the transfer price from Pulp to Paper is, at cost, $6 per cord.

b) Determine the gross profit for each division and for the company as a whole if the transfer price is $5 per cord.

c) Determine the gross profit for each division and for the company as a whole if the transfer price is $7 per cord.

9–8 Internal or External Acquisition: No Opportunity Costs

The Truck Division of the CP Corporation has offered to purchase 180,000 wheels from the Wheel Division for $52 per wheel. At a normal volume of 500,000 wheels per year, production costs per wheel for the Wheel Division are as follows:

Direct materials	$20
Direct labor	10
Variable overhead	6
Fixed overhead	20
Total	$56

The Wheel Division has been selling 500,000 wheels per year to outside buyers at $70 each. Capacity is 700,000 wheels per year. The Truck Division has been buying wheels from outside suppliers at $67 per wheel.

Requirements

a) Should the Wheel Division manager accept the offer? Show computations.

b) From the standpoint of the company, will the internal sale be beneficial?

9–9 Appropriate Transfer Prices: Opportunity Costs

The Plains Peanut Butter Company recently acquired a peanut processing company that has a normal annual capacity of 4,000,000 pounds and that sold 2,800,000 pounds last year at a price of $2 per pound. The purpose of the acquisition is to furnish peanuts for the peanut butter plant. The peanut butter plant needs 1,600,000 pounds of peanuts per year. It has been purchasing peanuts from suppliers at the market price.

Production costs of the peanut processing company per pound are as follows:

Direct materials	$0.50
Direct labor	0.25
Variable overhead	0.12
Fixed overhead at normal capacity	0.20
Total	$1.07

Management is trying to decide what transfer price to use for sales from the newly acquired Peanut Division to the Peanut Butter Division. The manager of the Peanut

Division argues that $2, the market price, is appropriate. The manager of the Peanut Butter Division argues that the cost price of $1.07 should be used — or perhaps even less, since fixed overhead costs should be recomputed.

Any output of the Peanut Division, up to 2,800,000 pounds, not sold to the Peanut Butter Division could be sold to regular customers at $2 per pound.

Requirements

a) Compute the annual gross profit for the Peanut Division using a transfer price of $2.00.

b) Compute the annual gross profit for the Peanut Division using a transfer price of $1.07.

c) What transfer price(s) will lead the manager of the Peanut Butter Division to act in a manner that will maximize company profits?

9–10 Negotiating a Transfer Price with Excess Capacity

The Weaving Division of Carolina Textiles, Inc., produces cloth that is sold to the Company's Dyeing Division and to outside customers. Operating data for the Weaving Division for 19x3 are as follows:

	To the Dyeing Division	To Outside Customers
Sales:		
300,000 yards at $5	$1,500,000	
200,000 yards at $6		$1,200,000
Variable expenses at $2	− 600,000	− 400,000
Contribution margin	$ 900,000	$ 800,000
Fixed expenses*	− 750,000	− 500,000
Net income	$ 150,000	$ 300,000

* Allocated on the basis of unit sales

The Dyeing Division has just received an offer from an outside supplier to supply cloth at $4.30 per yard. The manager of the Weaving Division is not willing to meet the $4.30 price. She argues that it costs her $4.50 per yard to produce and sell to the Dyeing Division, so she would show no profit on the Dyeing Division sales. Sales to outside customers are at a maximum, 200,000 yards.

Requirements

a) Verify the Weaving Division's $4.50 unit cost figure.

b) Should the Weaving Division meet the outside price of $4.30 for Dyeing Division sales? Explain.

c) Could the $4.30 be met and still show a profit for the Weaving Division sales to the Dyeing Division? Show computations.

9–11 ROI and Residual Income: Impact of a New Investment

The Oak Division of the Hardwood Company reported an operating income of $2,100,000 for 19x3 with an investment of $9,000,000. The division manager desires to know the effect on the division's performance of an incremental investment of $5,000,000, which will increase annual operating income by $820,000 per year.

Required: Determine the impact of the new investment on ROI and residual income. Assume that an 18 percent return on investment is considered acceptable. (Round calculations to three decimal places.)

9–12 Dual Transfer Pricing

The Alpha Company has two divisions, Beta and Gamma. Gamma Division produces a product at a variable cost of $8 per unit and sells 150,000 units to outside customers at $10 per unit and 40,000 units to Beta Division at variable cost plus 40 percent. Under the dual transfer price system, Beta Division pays only the variable cost per unit. The fixed costs of Gamma Division are $250,000 per year.

Beta Division sells its finished product to outside customers at $23 per unit. Beta has variable costs of $6 per unit in addition to the costs from Gamma Division. The annual fixed costs of Beta Division are $170,000. There are no beginning or ending inventories.

Required: Prepare the income statements for the two divisions and the company as a whole. Why is the income for the company less than the sum of the profit figures shown on the income statements for the two divisions? Explain.

9–13 Transfer Pricing and Divisional Gross Profit

Jefferson Company has two divisions. Division Jeff manufactures chocks and Division Sam finishes them. The unfinished chocks can be sold for $2.50 each or finished and sold for $3.625 each. After Jeff manufactures the chocks, some are sold to outsiders and some are transferred to Division Sam, which finishes them. The following information pertains to 19x7:

Manufacturing cost of Division Jeff to produce 2,000,000 units	$3,000,000
Sales revenue from 800,000 units sold by Jeff to outside market	2,000,000
Market value of 1,200,000 units when transferred to Sam	3,000,000
Sales revenue from 800,000 units processed by Sam and sold	2,900,000
Total additional processing cost of Sam	750,000

Required: Prepare income statements for the company and for each division. Use market value as the transfer price.

9–14 Transfer Prices at Full Cost with Excess Capacity: Divisional Viewpoint

The Dairy Company has a Cheese Division that produces cheese that sells for $12 per unit in the open market. The cost of the product is $8 (variable manufacturing of $5 plus fixed manufacturing of $3). Total fixed manufacturing costs are $210,000 at the normal annual production volume of 70,000 units.

The Overseas Division has offered to buy 15,000 units at the full cost of $8. The producing division has excess capacity, and the 15,000 units can be produced without interfering with the current outside sales of 70,000 units. The total fixed cost of the Cheese Division will not change.

Required: Explain whether the Cheese Division should accept or reject the offer. Show calculations.

9–15 Transfer Pricing with Excess Capacity: Divisional and Corporate Viewpoints

The Boyett Art Company has a Print Division that is currently producing 100,000 prints per year but has a capacity of 150,000 prints. The variable costs of each print are $30, and the annual fixed costs are $900,000. The prints sell for $40 in the open market.

The Retail Division of the company wants to buy 50,000 prints at $28 each. The Print Division manager refuses the order because the price is below variable cost. The Retail Division manager argues that the order should be accepted because it will lower the fixed cost per print from $9 to $6.

Requirements

a) Should the order from Retail Division be accepted? Why or why not?

b) From the viewpoints of the Print Division and the company, should the order be accepted if the manager of the Retail Division intends to sell each print in the outside market for $42 after incurring additional costs of $10 per print?

c) What action should the company take assuming it believes in divisional autonomy?

PROBLEMS

9–16 Transfer Pricing

The International Building Company owns its own clay mine, which supplies clay for the Brick Division. The clay is charged to the Brick Division at market price. Income statements for 19x5 were as follows:

International Building Company
Divisional Income Statements
For the year ended December 31, 19x5

	Clay Mine	Brick Division
Sales	$ 800,000	$2,000,000
Production costs:		
Materials	$ —	$ 800,000
Labor	380,000	500,000
Overhead	160,000	300,000
Total	− 540,000	−1,600,000
Gross profit	$ 260,000	$ 400,000
Selling and administrative costs	− 120,000	− 300,000
Income of division	$ 140,000	$ 100,000

In 19x5 and 19x6 the clay mine sold 20,000 tons of clay. In 19x6 the market prices of clay increased 50 percent and conversion costs increased 10 percent, whereas the Brick Division increased its price by 10 percent. Income statements for 19x6 were as shown at the top of page 368.

International Building Company
Divisional Income Statements
For the year ended December 31, 19x6

	Clay Mine	Brick Division
Sales	$1,200,000	$2,200,000
Production costs:		
Materials	$ —	$1,200,000
Labor	418,000	550,000
Overhead	176,000	330,000
Total	− 594,000	−2,080,000
Gross profit	$ 606,000	$ 120,000
Selling and administrative costs	− 120,000	− 330,000
Income (loss) of division	$ 486,000	$ (210,000)

Corporate management is concerned about the Brick Division's 19x6 loss.

Requirements

a) Prepare income statements for the company in 19x5 and 19x6.

b) Evaluate the company's performance in 19x6.

c) What should be the transfer price for clay? Discuss.

9–17 ROI and Residual Income: Impact of a New Investment

Office Equipment, Inc., is a decentralized organization with four autonomous divisions. The divisions are evaluated on the basis of the change in their return on invested assets. Operating results in the Modern Division for 19x1 are given below:

Office Equipment, Inc.
Modern Division Income Statement
For the year ended December 31, 19x1

Sales	$2,500,000
Less variable expenses	−1,250,000
Contribution margin	$1,250,000
Less fixed expenses	− 900,000
Net operating income	$ 350,000

Operating assets for Modern Division currently average $1,800,000. The Modern Division can add a new product line for an investment of $300,000. Relevant data for the new product line are as follows:

Sales	$800,000
Variable expenses	0.60 of sales
Fixed expenses	$300,000

Requirements

a) Determine the effect on ROI of accepting the new product line. (Round calculations to three decimal places.)

b) If a return of 6 percent is the minimum that should be earned by any division, and residual income is used to evaluate managers, would this encourage the division to accept the new product line? Explain and show computations.

9–18 Transfer Pricing at Absorption Cost

Division 23 of Numbers Company produces large metal numbers that are sold to Division 86. This division uses numbers in constructing signs that are sold to highway departments of local governments.

Division 23 contains two operations, stamping and finishing. The unit variable cost of materials and labor used in the stamping operation is $100. The fixed stamping overhead is $800,000 per year. Current production of 20,000 units is at full capacity.

The variable cost of labor used in the finishing operation is $12 per number. The fixed overhead in this operation is $340,000 per year.

The company uses an absorption-cost transfer price. The price data for each operation presented to Division 86 by Division 23 are shown below:

Stamping:		
Variable cost per unit	$100	
Fixed overhead cost per unit ($800,000/20,000 units)	40	$140
Finishing:		
Labor cost per unit	$ 12	
Fixed overhead cost per unit ($340,000/20,000 units)	17	29
Total cost per unit		$169

An outside company has offered to lease Division 86 machinery that would perform the finishing part of the number manufacturing. The lease is $200,000 per year. With the new machinery, the labor cost per frame would remain at $12. If Division 23 transfers the units for $140, the following analysis can be made:

Current process:		
Finishing process costs (20,000 × $29)		$580,000
New process:		
Machine rental cost per year	$200,000	
Labor cost ($12 × 20,000 units)	240,000	−440,000
Savings		$140,000

The manager of Division 86 wants approval to acquire the new machinery.

Requirements

a) How would you advise the company concerning the proposed lease?

b) How could the transfer-pricing system be modified or the transfer-pricing problem eliminated?

9–19 Transfer Pricing with and without Capacity Constraints

The National Carpet Company has just acquired a new Backing Division. The Backing Division produces a rubber backing, which it sells for $2.00 per square yard. Sales are about 1,200,000 square yards a year. Since the Division has a capacity of 2,000,000 yards a year, top management is thinking that it might be wise for the company's Assembly Division to start purchasing from the newly acquired Backing Division.

The Assembly Division now purchases 600,000 square yards a year from an outside supplier at a price of $1.80 per square yard. That the current price is lower than the competitive $2.00 price is a result of the large quantity discounts. The Backing Division's cost per square yard is shown below:

Direct materials	$1.00
Direct labor	0.20
Variable overhead	0.25
Fixed overhead (1,200,000 level)	0.10
Total cost	$1.55

Requirements

a) If both divisions are to be treated as investment centers, and their performance evaluated by the ROI formula, what transfer price would you recommend? Why?

b) What will be the effect on the profits of the company using your transfer price?

c) Based on your transfer price, would you expect the ROI in the Backing Division to increase, decrease, or remain unchanged? Explain.

d) What would be the effect on the ROI of the Assembly Division using your transfer price? Explain.

e) Assume that the Backing Division is now selling 2,000,000 square yards a year to retail outlets. What transfer price would you recommend? Explain what will happen between Backing and Assembly.

f) If the Backing Division is at capacity and decides to sell to the Assembly Division for $1.80 per square yard, what will be the effect on the profits of the company?

9–20 Transfer Pricing with and without Capacity Constraints

The Northern Clock Company is a decentralized organization containing three divisions. The Windup Division has asked the Dial Division, which is operating at capacity, to supply it with a large quantity of dials. The Dial Division sells dials outside for $2.50 each. The Windup Division, which is operating at 50 percent of capacity, wants to pay $2.00 each for the dials.

The Dial Division has a variable cost of production of $1.80. The current costs of the clock being built by the Windup Division are shown below:

Materials (except dials)	$30.00
Dials	2.00
Other variable costs	18.00
Fixed overhead	10.00
Total cost per clock	$60.00

The manager of the Windup Division believes that the $2.00 price from the Dial Division is necessary if the division is to compete with its competitor, Clockex.

Requirements

a) As division controller of the Dial Division, would you recommend that your division supply Windup Division as requested? Why?

b) If the Dial Division has excess capacity, would it be desirable for the Dial Division to supply the Windup Division with the fittings at $2.00 each? Explain.

c) Assuming the Dial Division has excess capacity, as the corporate controller, what would you advise?

9–21 Transfer Pricing and Special Orders　Atlantic Telephone Company has several manufacturing divisions. The Pacific Division produces a component part that is used in the manufacture of electronic equipment. The cost per part for July is as follows:

Variable cost	$ 90
Fixed cost (at 2000 units per month capacity)	60
Total cost per part	$150

Some of Pacific Division's output is sold to outside manufacturers, and some is sold internally to the Electronics Division. The price per part is $175.

The Electronics Division's cost and revenue structure is shown below:

Selling price per unit		$1000
Less variable costs per unit:		
Cost of parts from the Pacific Division	$175	
Other variable costs	400	
Total variable costs		− 575
Contribution margin per unit		$ 425
Less fixed costs per unit (at 200 units		
per month)		− 100
Net income per unit		$ 325

The Electronics Division received an order for 10 units. The buyer wants to pay only $500 per unit.

Requirements

a) From the perspective of the Electronics Division, should the $500 price be accepted? Explain.

b) If both divisions have excess capacity, would the Electronics Division's action benefit the company as a whole? Explain.

c) If the Electronics Division has excess capacity, but the Pacific Division does not, and can sell all its parts to outside manufacturers, what would be the advantage or disadvantage to the Electronics Division of accepting the 10 unit order at the $500 price?

d) In order to make a decision that is in the best interest of Atlantic Telephone, what transfer pricing information is needed by the Electronics Division?

9–22 Transfer Pricing with an Outside Market

French Vision has four divisions, Frame, Glass, Plastic, and Assembly, that collectively produce protective industrial eyeglasses. The Frame, Glass, and Plastic Divisions supply parts to the Assembly Division, which produces the final product.

The monthly fixed outlay costs of all divisions, except the Plastic Division, are identical at $150,000 each. Plastic's monthly fixed outlay costs are $300,000. In addition, fixed costs that do not require the use of cash amount to $50,000 per month per division, except for Plastic, where these costs are $100,000. Average production is 50,000 eyeglasses per month.

The full costs of each component are shown below:

Division	Part	Variable Cost per Unit	+	Fixed Cost per Unit	=	Full Cost per Unit
Frame	Frame	$15		$4		$19
Glass	Glass	20		4		24
Plastic	Ear pieces	5		4		9
Plastic	Nose pieces	2		4		6

Full absorption-cost transfer prices are used. In the Assembly Division, the manager has authority to buy inside the company or to buy from an outside supplier. The outside prices vary somewhat throughout the year. For next month the outside prices are as follows:

Part	Outside Price
Frame	$20
Glass	26
Ear pieces	7
Nose pieces	6

The Assembly Division manager notices that the outside purchase price of ear pieces is $2 lower than the transfer price and places an order with an outside supplier. Consequently, the Plastic Division stops producing ear pieces, reallocates all its fixed cost to the remaining units of nose pieces, and adjusts the full cost transfer price.

Requirements

a) Reallocate the fixed cost in the Plastic Division, and determine the adjusted transfer prices for nose pieces. What action might the manager of the Assembly Division take? What are the likely consequences of this action?

b) What action might French Vision take in establishing transfer prices and organizing its operations to avoid similar problems in the future?

9–23 Evaluating ROI The Independent Consulting Company has several decentralized divisions. Each division manager is responsible for service revenue, cost of operations, acquisition and financing of divisional assets, and working capital management.

The vice president of general operations is considering changing from annual to multiyear evaluations of division managers. Currently, a review of the performance, attitudes, and skills of management is undertaken annually. As a trial run, two managers will be selected for the new evaluation procedure. The selection has been narrowed to the managers of Divisions 11 and 14.

Both managers became division managers in 19x1. Their divisions have the following operating results for the last three years:

	Division 11			Division 14		
(*in thousands*)	*19x1*	*19x2*	*19x3*	*19x1*	*19x2*	*19x3*
Estimated industry sales	$1,000,000	$1,200,000	$1,300,000	$500,000	$600,000	$650,000
Division sales	$ 100,000	$ 110,000	$ 121,000	$ 45,000	$ 60,000	$ 75,000
Variable costs	$ 30,000	$ 32,000	$ 34,500	$ 13,500	$ 17,500	$ 21,000
Fixed operating costs	40,000	40,500	42,000	17,000	20,000	23,000
Fixed administrative costs	27,500	32,500	32,500	14,000	20,000	25,000
Total costs	− 97,500	− 105,000	− 109,000	− 44,500	− 57,500	− 69,000
Net income	$ 2,500	$ 5,000	$ 12,000	$ 500	$ 2,500	$ 6,000
Net assets	$ 22,700	$ 23,500	$ 24,500	$ 12,300	$ 14,000	$ 17,000
Return on investment	?	?	?	?	?	?

Requirements

a) Determine ROI for each year for each manager.

b) Is ROI an appropriate measurement for manager evaluation? Why?

c) What additional measures might be used?

d) Per year, which manager performed the best?

e) Over three years, which manager performed the best?

(CMA Adapted)

9–24 Decentralization and Autonomy

Edwin Hall, Chairman of the Board and President of Arrow Works Products Company, founded the company in the mid-1960s. He is a talented and creative engineer. Arrow Works was started with one of his inventions, an intricate die-cast item that required a minimum of finish work. The item was manufactured for Arrow Works by a Gary, Indiana foundry. The product sold well in a wide market.

The company issued common stock in 1972 to finance the purchase of the Gary foundry. Additional shares were issued in 1975 when Arrow purchased a fabricating plant in Cleveland to meet the capacity requirement of a defense contract.

The company now consists of five divisions. Each division is headed by a manager who reports to Hall. The Chicago Division contains the product development and engineering department and the finishing (assembly) operation for the basic products. The Gary Plant and Cleveland Plant are the other two divisions engaged in manufacturing operations. All products manufactured are sold through two selling divisions. The Eastern Sales Division is located in Pittsburgh and covers the country from Chicago to the east coast. The Western Sales Division, which covers the rest of the country, is located in Denver. The Western Sales Division is the newest operation and was established just eight months ago.

Hall, who still owns 53 percent of the outstanding stock, actively participates in the management of the company. He travels frequently and regularly to all the company's plants and offices. He says, "Having a business with locations in five different cities spread over half the country requires all of my time." Despite his regular and frequent visits, he believes the company is decentralized with the managers having complete autonomy. "They make all the decisions and run their own shops. Of course they don't understand the total business as I do, so I have to straighten them out once in a while. My managers are all good men, but they can't be expected to handle everything alone. I try to help all I can."

The last two months have been a period of considerable stress for Mr. Hall. During this period, John Staple, manager of the fabricating plant, was advised by his physician to request a six-month sick leave to relieve the work pressures that had made him nervous and tense. This request had followed by three days a phone call in which Hall had directly and bluntly blamed Staple for the lagging production output and increased rework and scrap of the fabricating plant. Hall made no allowances for the pressures created by the operation of the plant at volumes in excess of normal and close to its maximum rated capacity for the previous nine months.

Hall thought Staple and he had had a long and good relationship before this event. Hall attributed his loss of temper in this case to his frustration with several other management problems that had arisen in the past two months. The sales manager of the Denver office had resigned shortly after a visit from Hall. The letter of resignation stated he was seeking a position with greater responsibility. The sales manager in Pittsburgh asked to be reassigned to a sales position in the field; he did not feel he could cope with the pressure of management.

Requirements

a) Explain the difference between centralized and decentralized management.

b) Is Arrow Works Products Company decentralized, as Edwin Hall believes? Explain your answer.

c) Could the events that have occurred over the past two months in Arrow Works Products Company have been expected? Explain your answer.

(CMA Adapted)

9–25 An Evaluation of Market Based Transfer Prices

A large, diversified corporation operates its divisions on a decentralized basis. Division A makes Product X, which can be sold either to Division B or to outside customers.

At current levels of production, the variable cost of making Product X is $1.40 per unit, the fixed cost is 30 cents, and the market price is $2.75 per unit.

Division B processes Product X into Product Y. The additional variable cost of producing Product Y is $1.00 per unit.

Top management is developing a corporate transfer pricing policy. The bases for setting transfer prices being reviewed are full absorption cost, total variable costs, and market price.

Requirements

a) In order to avoid waste and maximize efficiency up to the transfer point, which of the transfer price bases being reviewed should be used and why?

b) Which of the transfer price bases in the short run would tend to encourage the best utilization of the corporation's productive capacity? Why would this not be true in the long run?

c) Identify *two* possible advantages that Division B might expect if it purchased Product X from Division A at the current market price.

d) What possible disadvantage might accrue to Division A if it was committed to sell all its production of X to Division B at the current market price?

(CIA Adapted)

9–26 A Transfer Pricing Dispute

MBR Inc. consists of three divisions that formerly were three independent manufacturing companies. Bader Corporation and Roper Company merged in 19x5, and the merged corporation acquired Mitchell Company in 19x6. The name of the corporation was subsequently changed to MBR Inc., and each company became a separate division retaining the name of its former company.

The three divisions have operated as if they were still independent companies. Each division has its own sales force and production facilities. Each division management is responsible for sales, cost of operations, acquisition and financing of divisional assets, and working capital management. The corporate management of MBR evaluates the performance of the divisions and division managements on the basis of return on investment.

Mitchell Division has just been awarded a contract for a product that uses a component manufactured by the Roper Division as well as by outside suppliers. Mitchell used a cost figure of $3.80 for the component manufactured by Roper in preparing its bid for the new product. This cost figure was supplied by Roper in response to Mitchell's request for the average variable cost of the component and represents the standard variable manufacturing cost and variable selling and distribution expense.

Roper has an active sales force that is continually soliciting new prospects. Roper's regular selling price for the component Mitchell needs for the new product is $6.50. Sales of this component are expected to increase. However, the Roper management has indicated that it could supply Mitchell with the required quantities of the component at the regular selling price less variable selling and distribution expenses. Mitchell's management has responded by offering to pay standard variable manufacturing cost plus 20 percent.

The two divisions have been unable to agree on a transfer price. Corporate management has never established a transfer price policy because interdivisional transactions have never occurred. As a compromise, the corporate vice president of finance has suggested a price equal to the standard full manufacturing cost (i.e., no selling and distribution expenses) plus a 15 percent markup. This price has also been rejected by the two division managers because each considered it grossly unfair.

The unit cost structure for the Roper component and the three suggested prices are shown below:

Standard variable manufacturing cost	$3.20
Standard fixed manufacturing cost	1.20
Variable selling and distribution expenses	0.60
	$5.00
Regular selling price less variable selling and distribution expenses ($6.50 − $0.60)	$5.90
Standard full manufacturing cost plus 15% ($4.40 × 1.15)	$5.06
Variable manufacturing plus 20% ($3.20 × 1.20)	$3.84

Requirements

a) What should be the attitude of the Roper Division's management toward the three proposed prices?

b) Is the negotiation of a price between the Mitchell and Roper Divisions a satisfactory method of solving the transfer price problem? Explain your answer.

c) Should the corporate management of MBR Inc. become involved in this transfer price controversy? Explain your answer.

(CMA Adapted)

10

Inventory Valuation Approaches and Segment Reporting

A fundamental internal reporting decision that every manufacturing company makes is how to account for fixed factory overhead. The outcome of this decision affects inventory valuation and, thus, income measurement. Though the absorption costing procedures used for external reporting purposes treat fixed factory overhead as a product cost, an alternative concept, called variable costing, is often used for internal reporting. Variable costing procedures assign only variable manufacturing costs to products. All other costs, including fixed manufacturing overhead, are treated as period costs.[1]

One of the purposes of this chapter is to present an analysis of absorption and variable costing. Each method is defined and its effects on inventory valuation and income measurement are illustrated. The advantages and limitations of each procedure are also discussed.

Organizations with multiple products, multiple plants, or multiple markets for their products often find it desirable to report the profits of each segment of the organization separately. Segment reporting allows a company's internal profitability reports to be prepared by divisions, products, territories, or on some other basis. Basic issues in segment reporting include the definition of business segments and the assignment of costs and revenues to each segment.

Another purpose of this chapter is to illustrate the development of segment reports and to discuss their usefulness in internal decision making, especially the decision to continue or discontinue a segment. In our discussion, special attention is given to problems caused by costs that are common to several segments of a business.

ABSORPTION COSTING AND VARIABLE COSTING

Under **absorption costing,** also called **full costing,** all manufacturing costs are assigned to products. Direct materials, direct labor, variable factory overhead, and fixed factory overhead costs are assigned to inventory, whereas selling and administrative costs, both fixed and variable, are immediately expensed as period costs.

Under **variable costing,** also called **direct costing,** only variable manufacturing costs are assigned to products. Direct materials, direct labor, and variable factory overhead costs are assigned to inventory, whereas fixed factory overhead and both fixed and variable selling and administrative costs are immediately expensed as period costs. A summary of product

---

[1] Recall from Chapter 2 that *product costs* are costs assigned to products. They are expensed when the products are sold. *Period costs* are expired nonproduct costs. They are treated as an expense in the period they are incurred.

EXHIBIT 10–1   A Comparison of Absorption and Variable Costing

Absorption Costing	Variable Costing
Product costs	
Direct materials	Direct materials
Direct labor	Direct labor
Variable factory overhead	Variable factory overhead
Fixed factory overhead	
Period costs	
Variable selling and administrative	Fixed factory overhead
Fixed selling and administrative	Variable selling and administrative
	Fixed selling and administrative

and period costs under absorption costing and variable costing is presented in Exhibit 10–1.

The difference between absorption costing and variable costing is the inclusion or exclusion of fixed factory overhead as a product cost. Under absorption costing, fixed factory overhead is assigned to products and expensed as part of the cost of goods sold when inventories are sold. Under variable costing, fixed factory overhead is immediately expensed as a period cost.

Inventory Valuations

The differing treatments of fixed factory overhead under absorption and variable costing result in different inventory valuations. To illustrate these differences, consider the following predicted cost data for the Morehart Company at a monthly volume of 4000 units.

Direct materials	$7 per unit
Direct labor	$5 per unit
Variable factory overhead	$4 per unit
Total fixed factory overhead	$8000 per month

To determine the unit cost of inventory using absorption costing, it is necessary to compute the average fixed overhead cost per unit by dividing the predicted monthly fixed overhead of $8000 by the predicted monthly activity level of 4000 units ($2 per unit). This per unit fixed overhead figure is essentially a predetermined factory overhead rate. Even though fixed factory overhead is not a variable cost, under absorption costing it is applied to inventory on a per unit basis the same as variable costs.

At a monthly volume of 4000 units, Morehart's inventory costs per unit under variable and absorption costing are as shown below:

Costs Category	Cost per Unit	
	Variable Costing	Absorption Costing
Direct materials	$ 7	$ 7
Direct labor	5	5
Variable factory overhead	4	4
Fixed factory overhead ($8000/4000 units)	—	2
Total unit costs	$16	$18

The $2 difference in unit costs results from assigning fixed costs to the product by the absorption method, but not by the variable method.

Assume that Morehart had no beginning inventory in March of 19x4 but produced 4000 units and sold 3500 units. The March 31 ending inventories under absorption costing and variable costing are $9000 and $8000, respectively (see Exhibit 10–2).

The $1000 difference in ending inventory between the two costing methods is due entirely to the treatment of fixed manufacturing costs. Under the variable costing method, all fixed manufacturing costs are treated as period costs and expensed. The difference can be explained as follows:

Inventory difference = Ending inventory units × Fixed costs per unit
= 500 units × $2
= $1000.

Reconciliations of absorption costing and variable costing inventory valuations may be more complex where product costs vary from period to period, or if production volume differs from period to period. Variations in cost behavior or production volume require explicit considerations of

EXHIBIT 10–2   Absorption and Variable Costing Inventory Valuation

March 19x4	Absorption Costing			Variable Costing		
	Units	Costs	Dollars	Units	Costs	Dollars
Beginning inventory	—		$ —	—		$ —
Product costs	4,000	$18	72,000	4,000	$16	64,000
Goods available for sale	4,000		$72,000	4,000		$64,000
Cost of goods sold	−3,500	$18	−63,000	−3,500	$16	−56,000
Ending inventory	500	$18	$ 9,000	500	$16	$ 8,000

the treatment of over- or underabsorbed overhead and inventory cost flow assumptions, such as LIFO, FIFO, or weighted average.

Income Determination

The different treatments of fixed factory overhead under absorption costing and variable costing require different income statement formats and often result in different net income amounts. Under absorption costing, variable and fixed manufacturing costs are mixed together in the cost of goods sold. Under variable costing, the cost of goods sold includes only variable manufacturing costs.

Income statements presented in a functional format are used in connection with absorption costing. In functional income statements, costs are classified according to business *function,* such as manufacturing, selling, or administration. Both variable and fixed costs are included within each category. Manufacturing costs (cost of goods sold) are subtracted from sales to determine gross profit, and selling and administration costs are subtracted from gross profit to obtain net income.

Income statements presented in the contribution format are ordinarily used in connection with variable costing. In contribution income statements, costs are classified according to *behavior.* The difference between revenues and variable costs is identified as the contribution margin—the amount contributed to cover fixed costs and provide for a profit. Accordingly, contribution margin minus fixed costs equals net income.

To compare functional and contribution income statements for variable and absorption costing, assume the following additional information is available for the Morehart Company.

Selling price	$30 per unit
Variable selling and administrative expenses	$3 per unit
Fixed selling and administrative expenses	$10,000 per month

Sales Varying and Production Constant. Assume production remains constant at 4000 units per month during June, July, and August while sales are 4000 units, 2500 units, and 5500 units respectively. Previously, the unit cost at this production level was computed to be $18 under absorption costing and $16 under variable costing. Absorption costing and variable costing income statements for June, July, and August of 19x4 are presented in Exhibit 10–3. A summary of unit inventory changes is presented at the bottom of the exhibit.

The first set of statements is prepared in a functional format using absorption costing. The second set of statements is prepared in a contribution format using variable costing.

EXHIBIT 10–3   Absorption and Variable Costing Income (Production Constant)

Morehart Company
Absorption Costing Income Statements
For June, July, and August, 19x4

	Sales Equal Production	Production Exceeds Sales	Sales Exceed Production
	June	July	August
Unit sales	4,000	2,500	5,500
Sales (at $30 per unit)	$120,000	$75,000	$165,000
Cost of goods sold (at $18 per unit)	− 72,000	−45,000	− 99,000
Gross profit	$ 48,000	$30,000	$ 66,000
Selling and administrative expenses:			
Variable (at $3 per unit)	$ 12,000	$10,500	$ 16,500
Fixed	10,000	10,000	10,000
Total	− 22,000	−20,500	− 26,500
Net income	$ 26,000	$ 9,500	$ 39,500

Morehart Company
Variable Costing Income Statements
For June, July, and August, 19x4

	June	July	August
Unit sales	4,000	2,500	5,500
Sales (at $30 per unit)	$120,000	$75,000	$165,000
Variable expenses:			
Cost of goods sold (at $16 per unit)	$ 64,000	$40,000	$ 88,000
Selling and administrative (at $3 per unit)	12,000	10,500	16,500
Total	− 76,000	−50,500	−104,500
Contribution margin	$ 44,000	$24,500	$ 60,500
Fixed expenses:			
Factory overhead	$ 8,000	$ 8,000	$ 8,000
Selling and administrative	10,000	10,000	10,000
Total	− 18,000	−18,000	− 18,000
Net income	$ 26,000	$ 6,500	$ 42,500

Summary of Unit Inventory Changes

	June	July	August
Beginning inventory	—	—	1,500
Production	4,000	4,000	4,000
Total available	4,000	4,000	5,500
Sales	− 4,000	− 2,500	− 5,500
Ending inventory	—	1,500	—

In June production and sales were equal, resulting in no deferral of costs in inventory. All current costs were deducted under both methods, as either product or period costs, resulting in the same net income under both methods.

In July production exceeded sales (4000 produced; 2500 sold). Absorption costing results in deferring part of the current fixed overhead costs in the ending inventory of finished goods as product costs, whereas direct costing expenses all current fixed overhead costs as period costs. Consequently, absorption costing net income for July exceeded variable costing net income by $3000, the increase in inventory (1500 units) times the fixed overhead per unit ($2).

In August sales exceeded production (5500 produced; 4000 sold). All production and all beginning inventory were sold. Consequently, under absorption costing, all the current period's fixed factory overhead and fixed factory overhead previously deferred in Finished Goods Inventory are expensed through cost of goods sold. Under variable costing, the prior period's ending inventory sold during August included only variable cost. The only fixed costs deducted on the August variable costing income statement are those incurred in August. As a result, expenses are greater and net income is smaller under absorption costing than under variable costing. The difference in net income of $3000 is equal to the change in inventory (1500 units) times the fixed overhead per unit ($2).

Sales Constant and Production Varying. Assume that sales remain constant at 4000 units for the Morehart Company during October, November, and December of 19x4. Production units were 4000 for October, 5000 for November, and 3000 for December. Unlike the previous illustration where production was constant and fixed factory overhead costs were $2 per unit, this illustration (assuming an actual overhead rate is used) has the following fixed factory overhead costs per unit.

	October	November	December
Fixed factory overhead	$8,000	$8,000	$8,000
Units produced	÷4,000	÷5,000	÷3,000
Fixed costs per unit	$ 2.00	$ 1.60	$ 2.67

As a result of this situation, the unit cost of inventory and, subsequently, the cost of goods sold, will vary each period. Given the variable unit costs of $16 from the previous illustration, the total unit manufacturing costs for these months are as follows:

	October	November	December
Variable costs per unit	$16.00	$16.00	$16.00
Fixed costs per unit	2.00	1.60	2.67
Total manufacturing costs per unit	$18.00	$17.60	$18.67

If sales remain the same over several periods, it is expected that income should be the same, especially if cost behavior is constant. However, as Exhibit 10–4 shows, absorption income varies even though sales and cost behavior remained constant. Under the variable costing method income remains constant when both sales and cost behavior are the same for different periods.

EXHIBIT 10–4   Absorption and Variable Costing Income (Sales Constant)

Morehart Company
Absorption Costing Income Statements
For October, November, and December, 19x4

	Sales Equal Production	Production Exceeds Sales	Sales Exceed Production
	October	November	December
Unit sales	4,000	4,000	4,000
Sales (at $30 per unit)	$120,000	$120,000	$120,000
Cost of goods sold:			
Beginning inventory	$ —	$ —	$ 17,600
Variable manufacturing costs	64,000	80,000	48,000
Fixed factory overhead	8,000	8,000	8,000
Cost of goods available	$ 72,000	$ 88,000	$ 73,600
Less: Ending inventory	— —	− 17,600	— —
Cost of goods sold	− 72,000	− 70,400	− 73,600
Gross profit	$ 48,000	$ 49,600	$ 46,400
Selling and administrative expenses:			
Variable (at $3 per unit)	$ 12,000	$ 12,000	$ 12,000
Fixed	10,000	10,000	10,000
Total	− 22,000	− 22,000	− 22,000
Net income	$ 26,000	$ 27,600	$ 24,400

Under the absorption costing method, income changes with production even if sales and cost behavior are constant. When sales equal production, the income under both methods is the same (see June in Exhibit 10–3, and October in Exhibit 10–4). All other things being equal, absorption income increases when production goes up and declines when production goes down.

Reconciliation of Income Differences

An examination of the previous illustrations reveals several important differences between absorption costing and variable costing.

- When production equals sales, absorption costing net income equals variable costing net income.

Morehart Company
Variable Costing Income Statements
For October, November, and December, 19x4

	Sales Equal Production	Production Exceeds Sales	Sales Exceed Production
	October	November	December
Unit sales	4,000	4,000	4,000
Sales (at $30 per unit)	$120,000	$120,000	$120,000
Variable expenses:			
Cost of goods sold (at $16 per unit)	$ 64,000	$ 64,000	$ 64,000
Selling and administrative (at $3 per unit)	12,000	12,000	12,000
Total	− 76,000	− 76,000	− 76,000
Contribution margin	$ 44,000	$ 44,000	$ 44,000
Fixed expenses:			
Factory overhead	$ 8,000	$ 8,000	$ 8,000
Selling and administrative	10,000	10,000	10,000
Total	− 18,000	− 18,000	− 18,000
Net income	$ 26,000	$ 26,000	$ 26,000

Summary of Unit Inventory Changes

	October	November	December
Beginning inventory	—	—	1,000
Production	4,000	5,000	3,000
Total available	4,000	5,000	4,000
Sales	− 4,000	− 4,000	− 4,000
Ending inventory	—	1,000	—

- When production exceeds sales, absorption costing net income exceeds variable costing net income.
- When production is less than sales, absorption costing net income is less than variable costing net income.

For each period, the income differences between absorption and direct costing can be explained by analyzing the change in inventoried fixed factory overhead under absorption costing net income. In general,

$$\begin{matrix} \text{Variable} & & \text{Increase (or minus decrease)} & & \text{Absorption} \\ \text{costing} & + & \text{in inventoried fixed} & = & \text{costing} \\ \text{net income} & & \text{factory overhead} & & \text{net income} \end{matrix}$$

This equation may be reversed to reconcile from absorption costing net income to variable costing net income:

$$\begin{matrix} \text{Absorption} & & \text{Decrease (or minus increase)} & & \text{Variable} \\ \text{costing} & + & \text{in inventoried fixed} & = & \text{costing} \\ \text{net income} & & \text{factory overhead} & & \text{net income} \end{matrix}$$

Exhibit 10–5 presents a set of reconciliations for June, July, and August, which reconciles from variable income to absorption income, as well as a set for October, November and December, which reconciles in the reverse order.

EXHIBIT 10–5   Reconciliation of Absorption and Variable Costing Net Income

	June	July	August
Variable costing net income	$26,000	$ 6,500	$42,500
Change in inventoried fixed costs:			
Fixed overhead in ending inventory units	$ —	$ 3,000*	$ —
Less fixed overhead in beginning inventory	– —	– —	– 3,000‡
Increase (decrease) in inventoried fixed costs	—	3,000	(3,000)
Absorption costing net income	$26,000	$ 9,500	$39,500

	October	November	December
Absorption costing net income	$26,000	$27,600	$24,400
Change in inventoried fixed costs:			
Fixed overhead in beginning inventory units	$ —	$ —	$ 1,600‡
Less fixed overhead in ending inventory	– —	– 1,600†	– —
Increase (decrease) in inventoried fixed costs	—	(1,600)	1,600
Variable costing net income	$26,000	$26,000	$26,000

* 1500 units × $2.00 of fixed factory costs per unit
† 1000 units × $1.60 of fixed factory costs per unit
‡ Ending of July is beginning of August and ending of November is beginning of December.

Notice in the following totals for the three-month period (June to August) that total production equals total sales and total absorption costing net income equals total variable costing net income.

Month	Production	Sales	Absorption Costing Income	Variable Costing Income
June	4,000	4,000	$26,000	$26,000
July	4,000	2,500	9,500	6,500
August	4,000	5,500	39,500	42,500
Total	12,000	12,000	$75,000	$75,000

For any given time period, regardless of length, if total units produced equals total units sold, net income will be the same for absorption costing and variable costing, all other things being equal. Under absorption costing, all fixed factory overhead is released as a product cost through cost of goods sold when inventory is sold. Under variable costing, all fixed factory overhead is reported as a period cost and expensed in the period incurred. Consequently, over the life of a product the income differences within periods are offset since they are caused only by the timing of the release of fixed factory overhead to the income statement.

An Evaluation of Variable Costing

Few accounting topics have generated as much controversy as variable costing. The central theoretical issue in this controversy is whether or not the incurrence of fixed manufacturing costs adds value to products. Proponents of variable costing argue that the incurrence of these costs does not add value to a product. Fixed costs are incurred to provide the capacity to produce during a given period, and these costs expire with the passage of time regardless of whether the related capacity was used. Variable manufacturing costs, on the other hand, are incurred only if production takes place. Consequently, these costs are properly assignable to the units produced.

Proponents of variable costing also argue that inventories have value only to the extent that they avoid the necessity for incurring costs in the future. Having inventory available for sale does avoid the necessity of incurring some future variable costs, but the availability of finished goods inventory does not avoid the incurrence of future fixed manufacturing costs. They conclude that inventories should be valued at their variable manufacturing cost, and fixed manufacturing costs should be expensed as incurred.

When considering the accounting principle of matching, variable costing has an advantage over absorption costing because it matches revenues with the direct cost of producing the revenues. This results in net income varying only with sales and not with both sales and production, as is often found in absorption costing. In absorption costing, overproduction especially distorts net income during a period because the excess inventory is assigned fixed costs that would otherwise be assigned to the units produced and sold. Using absorption costing, a company can always increase net operating income by simply producing more than it sells.

Opponents of variable costing argue that fixed manufacturing costs are incurred for only one purpose, namely, to manufacture the product. Because they are incurred to manufacture the product, they should be assigned to the product. It is also argued that in the long run all costs are variable. Consequently, by omitting fixed costs, variable costing understates long-run variable costs and misleads decision makers into underestimating true production costs.

On a pragmatic level, the central arguments for variable costing center around the fact that the use of variable costing facilitates the development of contribution income statements and cost-volume-profit analysis when production and sales are not equal. If all costs are accumulated on an absorption costing basis, contribution income statements are difficult to develop, and cost-volume-profit analysis becomes very complicated unless production and sales are equal.

Variable costing is now widely used for internal reporting. However, it is not acceptable for external reporting in published financial statements or for income tax determination. Consequently, accountants should routinely use variable costing for internal reports and absorption costing for external reports. The simultaneous use of variable and absorption costing is a prime example of the use of different costs for different purposes.

SEGMENT REPORTING

Most top-level managers must have more than cost reports to aid them in evaluating large operating units. Income statements are often a vital part of the evaluation process. In this section of the chapter, emphasis is on cost classifications and the evaluation of individual segments.

Segment reports are income statements that show operating results for portions or segments of a business. When the reporting of operating activities is presented for product lines, it is often labeled **product reporting.** Segment reporting is used primarily for internal purposes, although generally accepted accounting principles also require disclosure of segment information for some public corporations.

Segment reporting is very common in organizations where there are distinct divisions of product lines, geographic territories, or organizational units. The segments or products of the organization for which reports are prepared depend on the information needs of management. The four most common types of segment reports are as follows:

1. Income statements for each plant or division.
2. Income statements for each product line.
3. Income statements for each sales territory.
4. Cost reports for cost centers (segments without sales or revenue).

Segment reports usually include the costs of both manufacturing and non-manufacturing activities. Divisional income statements and product reports include product costs and appropriate selling and administrative costs. A given report may often include operating data for several products or territories, which may require further segmentation.

The format and frequency of segment reports is limited only by the decision needs and willingness of management to pay for preparing the reports. Although there are many different types of segment reports, three functions basic to the preparation of every report are:

1. Identification of the reporting objective.
2. Assignment of direct costs to the reporting objective.
3. Allocation of indirect costs to the reporting objective.

Segment reporting requires careful control over data collection and storage because of the different reporting formats. To properly compute the income for each segment or product, all costs, fixed and variable, must be considered. To effectively report the activities of a business segment, management should use the contribution approach, which focuses on the contribution made by each segment to cover common costs and to provide for a profit. The contribution approach discussed in the first section of this chapter (and in Chapter 4) is used for detailed segment statements.

Reporting Objective   A company with a single product or a homogeneous activity has little difficulty defining the activities to be included in its operating report, but the reporting structure of a multisegment business is not so easily defined. For example, if management wants to know the profit contributed by a certain product in a particular sales region, cost determination may be complicated in that certain marketing efforts promote several products, whereas others overlap different sales territories. Each reporting objective must be identified and described as precisely as possible to ensure that only relevant revenues and costs are assigned to each reporting segment.

Contribution Margin   In preparing segment income statements, management must decide whether to use the functional (absorption) approach or the contribution (variable) approach. Segment reports are more useful if they emphasize the segment's contribution to profit. To compute the contribution margin by segments, sales and variable expenses must be assigned to each reporting segment. Since records are generally kept by segments, the accumulation of these data is relatively easy.

Segment reporting is an excellent example of how the contribution margin approach can be used for evaluation purposes. It can be used for determining the effect on profit of certain types of short-run changes when other types are held constant. Examples include changes in sales volume and product mix and temporary changes in capacity, special orders, and product promotions. As sales volume changes in a particular segment, the impact on net income can be determined by multiplying the segment contribution margin per unit by the change in units sold, or by multiplying the contribution margin ratio by the changes in sales dollars. Many decisions relating to the short run involve only variable costs and sales.

Segment Report Configurations

The nature and extent of segmentation of operating reports depends on the organizational structure of the company. A highly decentralized multilevel organization with different levels of operation may use a reporting structure similar to that presented in Exhibit 10–6 for the Offshore Refining Company for 19x4. The benefits accruing to management from such a series of segment reports are many. Segment reporting can aid in identifying trends, percentage relationships, and other income information that management uses to evaluate the performance of the various activities of the organization.

For the reports in Exhibit 10–6 the reporting objective was defined by territories. Sales and expense data are presented for the two reporting territories of Offshore Refining. The direct manufacturing costs (variable costs) are deducted from territory sales to determine the **manufacturing margin.** The variable expenses of nonmanufacturing activities are then deducted to obtain the contribution margin. All direct fixed expenses identifiable with each territory are subtracted from the contribution margin to arrive at the territory margin, which is the amount that each territory contributes toward covering common corporate expenses and generating corporate profits. Common corporate expenses include the general administrative expenses of operating the corporate offices and conducting corporate activities. These expenses are necessary in the operations of the company, but they are not identifiable with specific territories or divisions.

Multilevel Segment Report Configurations

The needs of large organizations are usually not met with just one segment report, whether segmented by territory, product, division, or other reporting objective. Exhibit 10–7 illustrates a set of multilevel reports for the Offshore Refining Company. Exhibit 10–7(a) segments the totals for the company in terms of divisions, Exhibit 10–7(b) further segments one of these divisions in terms of the product lines sold within the division, and Exhibit

EXHIBIT 10–6   Segment Report Configuration by Territory (*in thousands*)

Offshore Refining Company
Territory and Company Income Statements
For the year ended December 31, 19x4

	Segments		Company Totals
	Atlantic	Gulf	
Sales	$150,000	$150,000	$300,000
Less: Variable manufacturing expenses	−30,000	−40,000	− 70,000
Manufacturing margin	$120,000	$110,000	$230,000
Less: Variable selling expenses	$ 14,000	$ 11,000	$ 25,000
Variable administrative expenses	25,000	30,000	55,000
Total	−39,000	−41,000	− 80,000
Contribution margin	$ 81,000	$ 69,000	$150,000
Less direct fixed expenses:			
Manufacturing	$ 30,000	$ 32,000	$ 62,000
Selling	9,000	11,000	20,000
Administrative	18,000	12,000	30,000
Total	−57,000	−55,000	−112,000
Territory margin	$ 24,000	$ 14,000	$ 38,000
Less common expenses:			
Manufacturing			$ 9,000
Selling			4,000
Administrative			2,000
Total			− 15,000
Net income			$ 23,000

10–7(c) divides one of these product lines into the areas where it is sold. As each segment is further divided, the report shows more detailed aspects of the company.

The *first-level statements* for Offshore Refining show the company totals and a set of income statements segmented by its major reporting objective, operating divisions. Sales and cost data are presented for Offshore's two divisions in Exhibit 10–7(a). The column company totals includes the same total sales and expenses as the same column in Exhibit 10–6, except that the fixed costs are allocated differently below the contribution margin level. All direct fixed expenses identifiable with each division are subtracted from the contribution margin to arrive at the **divisional segment margin,** which is the amount each division contributes toward covering common corporate expenses and generating corporate profits.

Second-level statements may be presented for each first-level reporting objective. In our illustration, a product line contribution statement is pre-

(a) Segment margins by divisions of Offshore Refining Company (first level)

| | Segments | | Company |
	Division A	Division B	Totals
Sales	$100,000	$200,000	$300,000
Less: Variable manufacturing expenses	− 20,000	− 50,000	− 70,000
Manufacturing margin	$ 80,000	$150,000	$230,000
Less: Variable selling expenses	$ 10,000	$ 15,000	$ 25,000
Variable administrative expenses	25,000	30,000	55,000
Total	− 35,000	− 45,000	− 80,000
Contribution margin	$ 45,000	$105,000	$150,000
Less direct fixed expenses:			
Manufacturing	$ 15,000	$ 50,000	$ 65,000
Selling	5,000	17,000	22,000
Administrative	10,000	18,000	28,000
Total	− 30,000	− 85,000	−115,000
Divisional margin	$ 15,000	$ 20,000	$ 35,000
Less common expenses:			
Manufacturing			$ 6,000
Selling			2,000
Administrative			4,000
Total			− 12,000
Net income			$ 23,000

(b) Segment margins by products within Division A of Offshore Refining Company (second level)

| | Segments | | Division A |
	Oil Products	Gas Products	Totals
Sales	$ 40,000	$ 60,000	$100,000
Less: Variable manufacturing expenses	− 5,000	− 15,000	− 20,000
Manufacturing margin	$ 35,000	$ 45,000	$ 80,000
Less: Variable selling expenses	$ 5,000	$ 5,000	$ 10,000
Variable administrative expenses	12,000	13,000	25,000
Total	− 17,000	− 18,000	− 35,000
Contribution margin	$ 18,000	$ 27,000	$ 45,000
Less direct fixed expenses:			
Manufacturing	$ 4,000	$ 8,000	$ 12,000
Selling	1,000	3,000	4,000
Administrative	4,000	4,000	8,000
Total	− 9,000	− 15,000	− 24,000
Product margin	$ 9,000	$ 12,000	$ 21,000

EXHIBIT 10–7   (Continued)

	Segments		Division A
	Oil Products	Gas Products	Totals
Less common expenses:			
Manufacturing			$ 3,000
Selling			1,000
Administrative			2,000
Total			− 6,000
Divisional margin			$ 15,000

**(c) Segment margins by territories of
Oil Products within Division A of
Offshore Refining Company (third level)**

	Segments		Oil Products
	Atlantic	Gulf	Totals
Sales	$ 12,000	$ 28,000	$ 40,000
Less: Variable manufacturing expenses	− 1,500	− 3,500	− 5,000
Manufacturing margin	$ 10,500	$ 24,500	$ 35,000
Less: Variable selling expenses	$ 2,000	$ 3,000	$ 5,000
Variable administrative expenses	4,000	8,000	12,000
Totals	− 6,000	− 11,000	− 17,000
Contribution margin	$ 4,500	$ 13,500	$ 18,000
Less direct fixed expenses:			
Selling	$ 100	$ 400	$ 500
Administrative	1,000	2,000	3,000
Total	− 1,100	− 2,400	− 3,500
Territory margin	$ 3,400	$ 11,100	$ 14,500
Less common expenses:			
Manufacturing			$ 4,000
Selling			500
Administrative			1,000
Total			− 5,500
Product margin			$ 9,000

sented for each product of Division A. These reports, in Exhibit 10–7(b),
are useful to management in making decisions related to product pricing,
sales strategy, inventory levels, product breakeven, and production scheduling. The decision to continue or discontinue a product may also be based,
in part, on information provided by these statements.

In Exhibit 10–7(b), the computations of the manufacturing margin and
the contribution margin follow the same format as for the divisional contribution statement. However, the computation of the **product margin**
(product sales less direct segment costs) is somewhat different from the

computation of the divisional contribution. This difference occurs because some of the fixed expenses regarded as direct at the divisional segment level are not direct at the product level. These fixed expenses include such items as divisional office salaries and plant security which pertain to the general operation of the division rather than to the products. Therefore only part of the fixed expenses of the division is assigned to products, with the resulting balance of $6,000,000 reported as common costs. These divisional expenses are similar to the common fixed expenses of the company in the divisional contribution statement.

The next set of reports, *third-level statements,* is a breakdown of a second-level reporting objective. Exhibit 10–7(c) shows the amount of contribution margin of Oil Products in Division A generated by each sales region. The **territory margin** is the contribution margin less direct fixed expenses associated with a given market area. The margins for the same product often vary because of different environments. For example, the company office that serves the Atlantic area may experience significantly higher marketing and distribution costs than the office serving the Gulf area. Though the Atlantic area is more populated, it is farther from the refineries. Additionally, the company may have a better reputation in the Gulf area, thereby making sales easier.

Notice from Exhibit 10–7 that fewer fixed expenses are allocated to segments as the reporting process is broken down to more specific segments of the business. Because the allocation would be very subjective, none of the fixed manufacturing expense is assignable to the sales territories in Exhibit 10–7(c), and smaller amounts of the selling and administrative expenses are allocated at this level. Each level has certain costs that can be defined as direct or indirect, and at each subsequent level the total expenses are smaller because the indirect expenses are not carried forward from the previous level. This reduction is evident for the Atlantic and Gulf areas where the territorial margins totaled $14,500,000, while the total product margin was only $9,000,000.

Other Configurations

In addition to, or instead of, the segments shown in Exhibits 10–6 and 10–7, management may desire first-level statements for other reporting objectives. For example, Exhibit 10–8 illustrates how the company can be segmented into first-level reporting by products. The product segment report, when used as a first-level statement, includes the products of both Divisions A and B.

In Exhibits 10–6, 10–7(a), and 10–8, the same total costs and revenues are allocated and assigned through the contribution margin level. Because of differences in allocating fixed costs, the company's total fixed costs of $127,000,000 (direct plus common) are treated differently in each of the different first-level statements.

EXHIBIT 10–8   Alternative Reporting Examples (*in thousands*)

**Segment margins by products
of Offshore Refining Company
(first level)**

	Oil Products	Gas Products	Chemical Products	Saline Products	Company Totals
			Segments		
Sales	$40,000	$60,000	$120,000	$80,000	$300,000
Less: Variable manufacturing expenses	− 5,000	−15,000	− 35,000	−15,000	− 70,000
Manufacturing margin	$35,000	$45,000	$ 85,000	$65,000	$230,000
Less: Variable selling expenses	$ 5,000	$ 5,000	$ 14,000	$ 1,000	$ 25,000
Variable administrative expenses	12,000	13,000	22,000	8,000	55,000
Total	−17,000	−18,000	− 36,000	− 9,000	−80,000
Contribution margin	$18,000	$27,000	$ 49,000	$56,000	$150,000
Less direct fixed expenses:					
Manufacturing	$ 4,000	$ 8,000	$ 24,000	$28,000	$ 64,000
Selling	1,000	3,000	5,000	6,000	15,000
Administrative	4,000	4,000	4,000	4,000	16,000
Total	− 9,000	−15,000	− 33,000	−38,000	− 95,000
Product margin	$ 9,000	$12,000	$ 16,000	$18,000	$ 55,000
Less common expenses:					
Manufacturing					$ 7,000
Selling					9,000
Administrative					16,000
Total					− 32,000
Net Income					$ 23,000

In Exhibit 10–6, $112,000,000 of fixed costs is assigned to segments with $15,000,000 treated as common costs to both territories. For the division segment reports (Exhibit 10–7a), $115,000,000 of fixed costs is assigned and $12,000,000 is common. And for the product reports (Exhibit 10–8), $95,000,000 is assigned and $32,000,000 is common.

It is possible for the common costs to be different for each type of first-level segment report because cost traceability for each reporting objective is different. Because manufacturing expenses are assumed to occur at the divisional level, they should all be assigned to the division incurring them. Even though manufacturing expenses are incurred to produce the products, it is often difficult to assign every expense to a specific product. In Exhibit 10–6, only $62,000,000 is assigned to products, with $9,000,000 treated as common expenses; and in Exhibit 10–8, $64,000,000 is assigned to the territories, with $7,000,000 treated as common expenses.

Other segment configurations are used by organizations to meet different management needs. Although reports segmented by division, product line and territory are the most common, segment reports can also be based on plants, single products, industries (for conglomerates), and domestic and foreign operations. Because segment reporting allows a company to examine itself from various perspectives, management will select the types of segment reports that are most beneficial for decision making.

Segment Margin

The **segment margin** represents the amount that a segment contributes toward the common (indirect) costs of the organization and toward profits.[2] It is generally considered one of the best gauges of profitability for a given segment of a company.

At the operating management level, segment margins are helpful in making decisions related to production, such as those pertaining to capacity changes and long-range pricing policies. The contribution margin is most useful in those situations involving short-run operating decisions, such as pricing of special orders, and accepting or rejecting special projects.

Direct Versus Common Segment Costs

It is not always easy to distinguish between direct and common costs. **Direct segment costs** are often defined as costs that would not be incurred if the segment being evaluated were to be discontinued. They are specifically identifiable with a particular segment. For example, if the Gas Products segment in Exhibit 10–8 were discontinued, Gas Product advertising would probably be discontinued; therefore it should be classified as a direct cost of Gas Products. Other examples include equipment depreciation and segment management salaries. On the other hand, the divisional vice president would probably not be terminated even if Gas Products was discontinued. Therefore the vice president's salary is common to both product lines. **Common segment costs,** also called **indirect segment costs,** are those costs related to more than one segment and not directly traceable to a particular segment.

These costs are referred to as common costs because they are incurred at one level for the benefit of two or more segments at a lower level. Nonmanufacturing activities often produce numerous indirect costs. A large organization, for example, may provide a centralized computer operation to serve all its production and marketing activities. Other examples of com-

---

[2] Segment margin can also be used to assist in measuring the segment return on investment, a very popular evaluation tool in decentralized organizations. See Chapter 9 for a detailed discussion.

mon costs include salaries of corporate management, companywide sales promotion, and expenses of the corporate accounting department.

Notice from Exhibit 10–7(a) that when segments are defined as divisions, Division A has $30,000,000 in direct fixed costs. In Exhibit 10–7(b), only $24,000,000 of this amount remains direct when we narrow our definition of a segment from divisions to that of product lines in a division. The other $6,000,000 becomes a common cost of Division A product lines.

There are several possible reasons that the $6,000,000 of direct fixed costs is a common cost when the division is broken down into product line segments; for example, the amount could include the monthly salary of the division manager. The division manager's salary is a direct cost when considering the division as a whole, but it is common to the separate product lines within the divisions. Other items that might be treated the same way include plant depreciation, security costs, computer costs, or office equipment.

The $24,000,000 of fixed costs that remain direct ($9,000,000 for Oil and $15,000,000 for Gas) after the division is separated into product line segments consists of items that can be assigned to the products. These might include product research, equipment rental, and product advertising.

Common segment costs should not be allocated; they should simply be deducted from the segment margin in total to arrive at the net income for the company or the segment income for the next higher level segment. Nothing is added to the usefulness of segment reports by allocating common costs to the various segments; in fact, allocations of this sort will significantly reduce the usefulness of the information. These arbitrary allocations will draw attention away from direct segment costs toward those items that are not directly traceable to a given segment. Lastly, any attempt to allocate common fixed costs at any segment level will inevitably result in arbitrary and misleading data, thereby obscuring important relationships between revenues and earnings.

Segment Decisions

Decisions to continue or drop a segment are frequently based on segment reports. A problem (similar to that previously discussed in comparing direct and common segment costs) arises when determining whether a cost is relevant to a segment or product being considered for continuation or noncontinuation. When a company is able to identify relatively small segments, accountants generally find that the smaller the segments used for reporting, the more the costs tend to be common and, therefore, irrelevant to most short-term decisions.

The isolation of direct costs is complicated in that accounting reports often show allocations of common costs among various segments as expenses in the segment reports. To illustrate, if common facilities are used by a dairy processor in the manufacture of various milk products, the

EXHIBIT 10–9   Continuing or Discontinuing a Product

(a) Current period product income statements (partial)

| | Segments | | | Company |
	Cream	Ice Cream	Yogurt	Totals
Sales (liters)	500,000	300,000	200,000	
	× $0.22	× $0.30	× $0.40	
	$110,000	$ 90,000	$ 80,000	$280,000
Variable costs	− 40,000	− 30,000	− 65,000	−135,000
Contribution margin	$ 70,000	$ 60,000	$ 15,000	$145,000
Depreciation expense	− 50,000	− 30,000	− 20,000	−100,000
Segment and company income	$ 20,000	$ 30,000	$ (5,000)	$ 45,000

(b) Pro forma product income statements (partial)

| | Segments | | Company |
	Cream	Ice Cream	Totals
Sales	$110,000	$ 90,000	$200,000
Variable costs	− 40,000	− 30,000	− 70,000
Contribution margin	$ 70,000	$ 60,000	$130,000
Depreciation expense	− 62,500	− 37,500	−100,000
Segment and company income	$ 7,500	$ 22,500	$ 30,000

income statement for each product would probably include a portion of the depreciation on these facilities. In Exhibit 10–9(a), Yogurt appears unprofitable, and management might be tempted to discontinue it. If the depreciation is $100,000 per year and a total of 1,000,000 liters of all products are made, each liter of product could be charged with $0.10. Suppose that Yogurt, with current sales of 200,000 liters, is dropped. The $20,000 depreciation expense now allocated to Yogurt will not be avoided, but the remaining 800,000 liters of the other products must be charged with $0.125 per liter. As a result, the apparent profitability of the remaining products would be reduced, and company profits would decline, as shown in Exhibit 10–9(b). In fact, the profit decline is due to the decision to drop Yogurt. When a segment is dropped, there may be no short-run reduction in common costs. For this reason allocated common costs are generally irrelevant to a decision about whether a particular segment should be dropped. In making these decisions, managers must be wary of any sunk costs. Even if they are direct costs of a segment, they should be ignored in the decision analysis.

SUMMARY

Absorption costing and variable (sometimes called direct) costing are two alternative approaches to inventory valuation. The essential difference between absorption and variable costing is the inclusion, or exclusion, of fixed factory overhead as a product cost. Under absorption costing, fixed factory overhead is assigned to products and expensed as part of the cost of goods sold when inventories are sold. Under variable costing, fixed factory overhead is immediately expensed as a period cost.

Although absorption costing is generally accepted for external and income tax reporting, variable costing provides better information for use internally by management in evaluating the consequences of short-run decisions and in planning operations in the near term. Variable costing is superior primarily because it permits the development of contribution income statements. Contribution income statements classify costs by behavior and assist management in understanding cost-volume-profit relationships.

Segment reports are income statements that show operating results for portions or segments of a business. The format and frequency of segment reports is limited only by management's decision needs and willingness to incur the cost for these reports.

The distinction between direct segment costs and indirect, or common, segment costs is very important in segment reporting. Direct segment costs are costs specifically identifiable with a particular segment of a business. By subtracting a segment's direct costs from its revenues, segment margin is obtained. Indirect, or common, segment costs are costs that are not directly traceable to a particular segment but are necessary to support the activities of two or more segments. Indirect segment costs may be allocated to segments for a variety of reporting purposes, but unavoidable indirect segment costs should not be allocated in internal reports that are to be used for management decisions such as whether to continue or discontinue a segment.

KEY TERMS

Absorption costing	**Direct segment costs**
Full costing	**Indirect segment costs**
Variable costing	**Common segment costs**
Direct costing	**Manufacturing margin**
Product costs	**Divisional segment margin**
Period costs	**Product margin**
Segment reports	**Segment margin**
Product reporting	**Territory margin**

REVIEW QUESTIONS

10–1 Explain the difference between product costs and period costs.

10–2 Can period costs exist under the absorption method? If so, give some examples.

10–3 How can full costing be a synonym for absorption costing?

10–4 Explain the basic difference between variable and absorption costing.

10–5 Is inventory more consistently valued using variable or absorption costing? Why?

10–6 What is the relationship between variable costing and the contribution income method?

10–7 How do you reconcile the differences in net income between the variable costing and absorption costing methods of inventory valuation?

10–8 What is the relationship between segment reports and product reports?

10–9 How are contribution margins and segment margins similar? How are they different?

10–10 What is a reporting objective? How is it determined?

10–11 How do you distinguish between direct and indirect segment costs?

10–12 Can a company have more than one type of first-level statements in segment reporting?

10–13 Explain the relationships between any two levels of statements in segment reporting.

10–14 What types of information are needed before management should decide on dropping a product?

EXERCISES

10–1 Absorption and Variable Costing Inventory Valuations

Wall Street Paper Company had the following information available for 19x1.

Direct labor	$900,000
Variable manufacturing overhead	300,000
Direct materials	500,000
Variable selling and administrative expenses	400,000
Fixed selling and administrative expenses	400,000
Fixed manufacturing overhead	800,000

For the period sales were 75,000 units, and production totaled 100,000 units.

Requirements

a) Compute the ending finished goods inventory under both absorption costing and variable costing.

b) Would income be higher or lower under variable costing? Why or why not? Provide supporting computations.

10–2 Absorption and Variable Costing Income Statements

The Littlejohn Company sells its product at a unit price of $10.00. Unit manufacturing costs are direct materials, $2.00; direct labor, $3.00; and variable factory overhead, $1.50. Total fixed manufacturing costs are $30,000 per year. Selling and administrative expenses are $1.00 per unit variable and $10,000 per year fixed. Though 24,000 units were produced during 19x1, only 20,000 units were sold. There was no beginning inventory.

Requirements

a) Prepare an income statement using absorption costing.

b) Prepare an income statement using variable costing.

10–3 Absorption and Variable Costing Inventory Valuation

Rosebud Perfume Company projects the following costs for 19x1.

	Per Unit
Direct materials	$5
Direct labor	$6
Variable overhead	$1
Fixed overhead ($40,000 for 20,000 units)	$2

During May, 20,000 units were produced, but only 10,000 were sold. During June, 20,000 units were produced and sold. During July, 20,000 units were produced, and 24,000 units were sold. There was no inventory on May 1.

Required: Compute the amount of ending inventory and cost of goods sold under variable costing and absorption costing for each month.

10–4 Contribution Income Statement

The Columbia Company began operation on January 1, 19x1. The 19x1 income statement on an absorption costing basis is as follows:

Columbia Company
Absorption Costing Income Statement
For the year ended December 31, 19x1

Sales (15,000 units)		$300,000
Less cost of goods sold:		
Beginning inventory	$ —	
Cost of goods manufactured (20,000 units)	280,000	
Ending inventory (5000 units)	− 70,000	−210,000
Gross profit		$ 90,000
Selling and administrative expenses		− 35,000
Net income		$ 55,000

All the selling and administrative expenses are fixed. Manufacturing costs include the following:

Direct materials	$ 4
Direct labor	5
Variable manufacturing overhead	2
Fixed manufacturing overhead	3
Total	$14

Required: Prepare an income statement in a contribution format with inventory valued using the variable costing method.

10–5 Absorption and Variable Costing Inventory Valuations

During 19x1 the Edwards Manufacturing Company produced 20,000 units and sold 16,000 units. There were no beginning inventories. Related costs were as follows:

Direct labor	$700,000
Direct materials	800,000
Variable factory overhead	420,000
Variable selling and administrative expenses	350,000
Fixed selling and administrative expenses	500,000
Fixed factory overhead	600,000

Required: Compute the ending finished goods inventory using absorption costing and variable costing.

10–6 Absorption and Variable Costing Income Statements

Start-up Company began the year 19x1 with great optimism. During 19x1 it had no sales, but there were $60,000 in variable manufacturing costs and $20,000 in fixed manufacturing costs. In 19x2 it sold half of the finished goods inventory from 19x1 for $50,000, but it had no manufacturing costs. In 19x3 it sold the remainder of the inventory, did no manufacturing, and went out of business December 31. Selling and administrative expenses were all fixed at $5000 each year.

Required: Prepare income statements for each year under both absorption costing and variable costing.

10–7 Absorption and Variable Costing Comparisons: Production Equals Sales

Continental Candy Company manufactures and sells 15,000 cases of candy each quarter. The following data are available for the third quarter of 19x3.

Sales price per case	$ 20
Direct materials per case	10
Direct labor per case	3
Variable manufacturing overhead per case	2
Total fixed manufacturing overhead	30,000
Fixed selling and administrative expenses	10,000

Requirements

a) Compute the cost per case under both absorption costing and variable costing.

b) Compute net income under both absorption costing and variable costing.

c) Reconcile the income difference, if any. Explain.

10–8 Absorption and Variable Costing Income Statements

The Overhead Door Company had no beginning 19x1 inventory. The following data are available for 19x1 operations.

Actual production	8000 units
Sales: 7000 units at $15 each	$105,000
Variable manufacturing costs	40,000
Fixed manufacturing costs	24,000
Variable selling and administrative costs	28,000
Fixed selling and administrative costs	48,000

Requirements

a) Prepare income statements for 19x1, using absorption costing and variable costing.

b) Compute the cost assigned to December 31, 19x1 inventory for both methods.

10–9 Income Statements Segmented by Territory

The Dual Manufacturing Company has two product lines. The 19x1 income statements of each product line and the company are as follows:

Dual Manufacturing Company
Product Line and company Income Statements
For the year ended December 31, 19x1

	Product Lines		
	Pens	Pencils	Total
Sales	$20,000	$30,000	$50,000
Less variable expenses	− 8,000	−12,000	−20,000
Contribution margin	$12,000	$18,000	$30,000
Less direct fixed expenses	− 8,000	− 7,000	−15,000
Product margin	$ 4,000	$11,000	$15,000
Less common fixed expenses			− 6,000
Net income			$ 9,000

The pens and pencils are sold in two territories, Alaska and Alabama, as follows:

	Alaska	Alabama
Pen sales	$12,000	$ 8,000
Pencil sales	9,000	21,000
Total sales	$21,000	$29,000

The common fixed expenses above are traceable to each territory as follows:

Alaska fixed expenses	$2,000
Alabama fixed expenses	3,000
Home office administration fixed expenses	1,000
Total common fixed expenses	$6,000

The direct fixed expenses of pens, $8000, and of pencils, $7000, cannot be identified with either territory.

Requirements

a) Prepare income statements segmented by territory for 19x1, and include a column for the entire firm.

b) Why are direct expenses of one type of segment reports not necessarily direct expenses of another type of segment reports?

10–10 Income Statements Segmented by Products

Collins Consulting Firm provides three types of client services. The income statement for 19x2 is as follows:

Collins Consulting Firm
Income Statement
For the year ended December 31, 19x2

Sales		$800,000
Less variable expenses:		
Services	$535,000	
Selling and administrative	65,000	−600,000
Contribution margin		$200,000
Less fixed expenses		− 70,000
Net income		$130,000

The sales, contribution margin ratios, and direct fixed expenses for the three types of services are as follows:

	Service 14	Service 28	Service 33
Sales	$250,000	$250,000	$300,000
Contribution margin ratio	30%	40%	30%
Direct fixed expenses	$ 28,000	$ 17,000	$ 15,000

Required: Prepare income statements segmented by products, and include a column for the entire firm in the statement.

10–11 Profit Planning with Absorption Costing

The Profit Control Corporation wants to ensure that its profits do not decline in proportion to sales declines. To prevent profits from decreasing, Profit Control plans to increase production above normal capacity. For 19x1 and 19x2 the following budget information is available.

	19x1	19x2
Sales volume estimates	500,000 units	400,000 units
Normal production capacity	500,000 units	500,000 units
Planned production	500,000 units	700,000 units
Fixed manufacturing overhead	$1,000,000	$1,000,000
Fixed selling and administrative expenses	$ 100,000	$ 100,000
Total variable manufacturing costs	$10 per unit	$10 per unit
Sales	$20 per unit	$20 per unit

Requirements

a) Prepare pro forma income statements using absorption costing for 19x1 and 19x2. (Round computations to the nearest dollar.)

b) Prepare pro forma income statements using variable costing for 19x1 and 19x2.

c) Can the company actually control profits? Explain.

10–12 Absorption and Variable Costing Income Statements

The Uncontrolled Profit Corporation was disappointed to find that increased sales volume in 19x2 did not result in increased profits. Both variable unit and total fixed manufacturing costs for 19x1 and 19x2 remained constant at $10 and $1,000,000, respectively.

In 19x1 the company produced 100,000 units and sold 80,000 units at a price of $25 per unit. There was no inventory at the beginning of 19x1. In 19x2 the company made 70,000 units and sold 90,000 units at a price of $25 per unit. Selling and administrative expenses, all fixed, were $50,000 each year.

Requirements

a) Prepare income statements for 19x1 and 19x2 using the absorption costing method.

b) Prepare income statements for 19x1 and 19x2 using the variable costing method.

c) Explain why the profit was different each year using the two methods. Show computations.

PROBLEMS

10–13 Variable Costing Income Statement

For the first three quarters of 19x4, Mustang Motor Company has had wide fluctuations in production and sales. Sales volume and the variable cost of production have increased with no increase in the selling price. Variable manufacturing costs per unit were as follows:

	Quarter		
	First	Second	Third
Direct materials	$1,500	$2,000	$2,500
Direct labor	2,000	2,000	3,000
Variable factory overhead	500	1,000	2,000

The motors sell for $10,000 each. The fixed manufacturing costs are $250,000,000 each quarter. The variable selling and administrative expenses are $600 for each unit sold, and the fixed selling and administrative expenses are $80,000,000 a quarter. Beginning motor inventory at the start of the first quarter, 20,000 units, was recorded at $80,000,000. The company uses the FIFO inventory method. Production and sales data are as follows:

Quarter	Produced	Sold
First	150,000	140,000
Second	160,000	150,000
Third	160,000	170,000

Required: Prepare income statements for each quarter using variable costing.

10–14 Absorption and Variable Costing Income Statements with Income Taxes

The operating data for the Western Paddle Company are given below.

	19x1	19x2	19x3
Units manufactured	80,000	100,000	80,000
Units sold	70,000	90,000	100,000
Unit selling price	$10	$10	$10
Variable manufacturing costs per unit	$4	$4	$4
Fixed manufacturing cost	$200,000	$250,000	$300,000

There was no inventory on hand on January 1, 19x1. The company uses the FIFO method to maintain its inventories. Variable selling and administrative expenses are $1.20 per unit, and fixed selling and administrative expenses for each year are $60,000. Income tax is estimated at 40 percent of before-tax income.

Required: Prepare income statements for each year using both absorption costing and variable costing. *Hint:* Variable costing is not acceptable for tax purposes.

10–15 Variable Costing Income Statements with Income Taxes

The manager of a newly organized division of Johnson Manufacturing does not understand why income went down when sales went up.

Information for the first and second quarters of 19x1 is given below for Greenhouse Division.

Johnson Manufacturing Company
Absorption Costing Income Statements
For the first two quarters of 19x1

	First Quarter	Second Quarter
Units produced	20,000	15,000
Units sold	15,000	20,000
Sales	$300,000	$400,000
Cost of goods sold:		
Inventory, beginning of quarter	$ —	$ 75,000
Current production cost	300,000	275,000
Cost of merchandise available for sale	$300,000	$350,000
Less inventory, end of quarter	− 75,000	− —
Cost of goods sold	−225,000	−350,000
Gross profit	$ 75,000	$ 50,000
Selling and administrative expenses	− 25,000	− 25,000
Income before income taxes	$ 50,000	$ 25,000
Income tax (40%)	− 20,000	− 10,000
Net income	$ 30,000	$ 15,000

The company operated at normal capacity during the first quarter. Variable manufacturing cost per unit was $5, and the fixed cost was $200,000. Selling and administrative expenses are all fixed.

Requirements

a) Revise the statement for each of the two quarters on the variable costing basis. *Hint:* Variable costing is not acceptable for tax purposes.

b) Explain the profit differences. How would variable costing help the manager avoid confusion?

10–16 Absorption Costing and Variable Costing Income Statements: All Fixed Costs

The Fixed Rock Company has only fixed costs. It built its building over a pile of rocks and simply sells them when customers visit the plant.

All employees of the plant are paid a fixed annual wage. There are no material costs and no variable overhead because the rocks came with the land and they do not need processing. They are washed in a creek that flows through the property. Costs are estimated as follows for 19x5 and 19x6.

Labor	$200,000
Depreciation	50,000
Insurance	20,000
Administration	40,000

Production capacity is 2000 tons per year. Rocks sell for $200 per ton. Results for two years are as follows:

	19x5	19x6
Tons produced	1600	2000
Tons sold	1500	2100

Required: Prepare income statements for each year under both absorption costing and variable costing. Which method is better? Why?

10–17 Absorption and Variable Costing Comparisons

The March Manufacturing Company had two identical divisions, Left and Right. Their sales, production volume, and fixed manufacturing costs have been the same for both divisions for the last five years. These amounts for each division are as follows:

	19x1	19x2	19x3	19x4	19x5
Units produced	100,000	110,000	110,000	88,000	88,000
Units sold	90,000	90,000	100,000	100,000	100,000
Fixed manufacturing costs	$110,000	$110,000	$110,000	$110,000	$110,000

Left uses absorption costing, and Right uses variable costing. Both use FIFO inventory methods. Variable manufacturing costs are $5 per unit. Both have identical selling prices and selling and administrative expenses. There were no 1/1/x1 inventories.

Required: Which division reports the higher income in each year? Explain.

10–18 Absorption and Variable Costing Comparisons

Never Quit Shoe Company is concerned with changing to the variable costing method of inventory valuation for making internal decisions. The absorption statements of income for January and February are shown below.

Never Quit Shoe Company
Absorption Costing Income Statements
For January and February, 19x9

	January	February
Sales (8000 units)	$160,000	$160,000
Cost of goods sold	− 99,200	−108,800
Gross profit	$ 60,800	$ 51,200
Selling and administrative expense	− 30,000	− 30,000
Net income	$ 30,800	$ 21,200

Production data are as shown below.

	January	February
Production units	10,000	6,000
Variable costs per unit	$10	$10
Fixed overhead costs	$24,000	$24,000

Variable selling and administrative expenses are $1 per unit sold.

Requirements

a) Compute the absorption cost per unit manufactured in January and February.

b) Explain why the net income for January was higher than the net income for February when the same number of units was sold in each month.

c) Prepare income statements for both months using variable costing.

d) Reconcile the absorption costing and variable costing net income figures for each month. Start with variable costing net income.

10–19 Absorption and Variable Costing Comparisons

The Jam Company manufactures strawberry jam. Because of bad weather, the crop was small. The following data have been gathered for the summer quarter of 19x3.

Beginning inventory, cases	—
Cases produced	10,000
Cases sold	9,600
Sales price per case	$30
Direct materials per case	$6
Direct labor per case	$5
Variable manufacturing overhead per case	$3
Total fixed manufacturing overhead	$400,000
Variable selling and administrative cost per case	$1
Fixed selling and administrative cost	$48,000

Requirements

a) Prepare an income statement for the quarter using absorption costing.

b) Prepare an income statement for the quarter using variable costing.

c) What is the value of ending inventory under absorption costing?

d) What is the value of ending inventory under variable costing?

e) Explain the difference in ending inventory under absorption costing and variable costing.

10–20 Conversion from Absorption to Variable Costing Statements

The income statement for Wall-to-Wall Company has been prepared on an absorption costing basis.

Wall-to-Wall Company		
Absorption Costing Income Statement		
For the month ended December 31, 19x1		
Sales (5000 units)		$20,000
Cost of goods sold:		
Inventory, beginning	$ 5,000	
Cost of goods manufactured	10,000	
Cost of products available for sale	$15,000	
Less inventory ending	− 2,500	12,500
Gross profit		$ 7,500
Selling and administrative expenses		− 2,000
Net income		$ 5,500

Variable unit costs have remained unchanged during the year. In 19x1 the monthly fixed factory overhead was $2000. During December 4000 units were manufactured.

Requirements

a) Recast the income statement for December to place it on a variable costing basis.

b) Reconcile the two statements.

10–21 Segment Reporting

Friday Company has provided you with the following information about its operations.

1. There are two products, Wednesdays and Saturdays.

2. There are two sales territories, Southeast and Northwest.

3. Monthly traceable direct fixed costs are $14,000 in the Southeast territory and $12,000 in the Northwest territory.

4. During January of 19x3, Southeast sold $40,000 of Wednesdays and $20,000 of Saturdays, and Northwest sold $10,000 of Wednesdays and $30,000 of Saturdays.

5. Variable cost of sales and selling expenses total 40 percent for Wednesdays and 70 percent for Saturdays.

6. Of Northwest's direct fixed costs, $5000 is traceable to Wednesdays and $5000 to Saturdays.

7. Of Southeast's direct fixed costs, $4000 is traceable to Wednesdays and $2000 to Saturdays.

8. Total fixed costs of the Friday Company were $40,000 during January.

9. Total variable costs of the Friday Company were $55,000 during January.

Requirements

a) Prepare January, 19x3 segment income statements for both territories, and include a column for the entire firm.

b) Prepare income statements segmented by product within each territory, and include a column for the entire firm.

10–22 Multiple Segment Reports

Ottawa Snow Company has two divisions: Snow and Ice. Because of increasing costs, the president wants to review overall operations by means of segment reporting. For 19x7 total revenue was $40,000,000: $14,000,000 for Snow and $26,000,000 for Ice. For Ice, $20,000,000 was generated by retail customers and $6,000,000 by manufacturing customers.

Total variable costs were $8,000,000 for Snow and $14,000,000 for Ice. For Ice, $11,500,000 was for retail customers and $2,500,000 for manufacturing customers. Total direct fixed costs were $2,000,000 for Snow and $10,000,000 for Ice. For Ice, $7,000,000 was for retail customers and $3,000,000 was for manufacturing customers.

In addition to the above, there were common corporate fixed costs of $4,000,000 for selling and administrative facilities. Common corporate fixed costs of $1,000,000 were also incurred for administrative personnel and supplies. These costs are not allocated to divisions.

Requirements

a) Prepare segment income statements for the divisions, and include a column for the entire firm.

b) Prepare segment income statements for the separate parts of the Ice Division, and include a column for the entire division.

10–23 Multiple Segment Reports

Earth Products, Incorporated sells throughout the world in three sales territories: Europe, the East, and the West. For July of 19x3 all $50,000 of administrative expense are allocated, except $10,000, which is common to all units and cannot be traced to the sales territories. The percentage of product line sales made in each of the sales territories and the allocations of traceable fixed expenses are shown below.

	Sales Territory			
	Europe	East	West	Total
Cookware sales	40%	50%	10%	100%
China sales	40	40	20	100
Vases sales	20	20	60	100
Fixed administrative expense	$15,000	$15,000	$10,000	$ 40,000
Fixed selling expense	30,000	60,000	60,000	150,000

The manufacturing takes place in one large facility with three distinct manufacturing operations. Selected cost data are shown below.

| | Product Line | | | |
	Cookware	China	Vases	Total
Variable costs	$ 9	$ 9	$ 5	
Depreciation and supervision	15,000	15,000	12,000	$ 45,000*
Other factory overhead (common)				10,000
Fixed administrative expense				
(common)				50,000
Fixed selling expense (common)				150,000

* Includes common costs of $3000

The unit sales and selling price for each product are shown below.

	Unit Sales	Selling Price
Cookware	10,000	$10
China	20,000	15
Vases	15,000	20

Requirements

a) Prepare an income statement for July 19x3 segmented by product line, and include a column for the entire firm.

b) Prepare an income statement for July 19x3 segmented by sales territories and include a column for the entire firm.

10–24 Segment Reporting and Analysis

Neighborhood Bakery, Incorporated bakes three products: donuts, pies, and cakes. It sells them in the cities of Irmo and Jackson. For March 19x4 the following absorption costing income statement was prepared.

Neighborhood Bakery, Inc.
Territory and Company Income Statements
For the month of March, 19x1

	Irmo	Jackson	Total
Sales	$2,100	$500	$2,600
Cost of goods sold	−1,500	−300	−1,800
Gross profit	$ 600	$200	$ 800
Selling and administrative expenses	− 400	−100	− 500
Net income	$ 200	$100	$ 300

Sales and selected variable expense data are as follows:

	Products		
	Donuts	*Pies*	*Cakes*
Fixed baking expenses	$200	$140	$100
Variable baking expenses as a percentage of sales	50%	50%	60%
Variable selling expenses as a percentage of sales	4%	4%	5%
City of Irmo, sales	$800	$900	$400
City of Jackson, sales	$200	$100	$200

The fixed selling expenses were $260 for March, of which $210 was a direct expense of the Irmo market and $50 a direct expense of the Jackson market. Fixed administrative expenses were $130, which management has decided not to allocate when using the contribution approach.

Requirements

a) Prepare a segment income statement for each sales territory for March, and include a column for the entire firm.

b) Prepare segment income statements for each product, and include a column for the entire firm.

c) Should any products or territories be dropped?

10–25 Segment Reporting and Analysis

The Hardback Book Company has prepared income statements segmented by divisions, but management is still uncertain about actual performance. Financial information for 19x8 is given below.

	Segments		
	Textbook Division	*Professional Division*	*Total Company*
Sales	$180,000	$410,000	$590,000
Less variable expenses:			
Manufacturing	$ 32,000	$205,000	$237,000
Selling and administration	4,000	20,500	24,500
Total	−36,000	−225,500	−261,500
Contribution margin	$144,000	$184,500	$328,500
Less direct fixed expenses	−15,000	−220,000	−235,000
Net income	$129,000	$ (35,500)	$ 93,500

The Professional Division is of concern to management and needs additional analysis. Additional information regarding the 19x8 operations of the Professional Division is as follows:

	Accounting	Executive	Management
Sales	$140,000	$140,000	$130,000
Variable manufacturing expenses as a percentage of sales	60%	40%	50%
Other variable expenses as a percentage of sales	5%	5%	5%
Direct fixed expenses	$ 50,000	$ 75,000	$ 50,000

The professional accounting books are sold to auditors and controllers. The current information on these markets is as follows:

	Sales Market	
	Auditors	Controllers
Sales	$30,000	$110,000
Variable manufacturing expenses as a percentage of sales	60%	60%
Other variable expenses as a percentage of sales	16%	2%
Direct fixed expenses	$20,000	$ 25,000

Requirements

a) Prepare an income statement segmented by products of the Professional Division, and include a column for the division as a whole.

b) Prepare an income statement segmented by markets of the accounting books of the Professional Division.

c) Evaluate which accounting books the Professional Division should keep or discontinue.

10–26 Segment Reports

The Justa Corporation produces and sells three products. The three products, A, B, and C, are sold in a local market and in a regional market. After the end of the first quarter of 19x2, the following income statement was prepared.

Justa Corporation
Territory and Company Income Statements
For the first quarter of 19x2

	Local	Regional	Total
Sales	$1,000,000	$300,000	$1,300,000
Cost of goods sold	− 775,000	−235,000	−1,010,000
Gross profit	$ 225,000	$ 65,000	$ 290,000
Selling expenses	$ 60,000	$ 45,000	$ 105,000
Administrative expenses	40,000	12,000	52,000
Total	− 100,000	− 57,000	− 157,000
Net income	$ 125,000	$ 8,000	$ 133,000

Management has expressed special concern with the regional market because of the extremely poor return on sales. This market was entered a year ago because of excess capacity. It was originally believed that the return on sales would improve with time, but after a year no noticeable improvement can be seen from the results as reported in the above quarterly statement.

In attempting to decide whether to eliminate the regional market, the following information has been gathered.

		Products	
	A	B	C
Sales	$500,000	$400,000	$400,000
Variable manufacturing expenses as a percentage of sales	60%	70%	60%
Variable selling expenses as a percentage of sales	3%	2%	2%

	Sales by Markets	
Product	Local	Regional
A	$400,000	$100,000
B	300,000	100,000
C	300,000	100,000

All administrative expenses and fixed manufacturing expenses are common to the three products and the two markets and are fixed for the period. The remaining selling expenses are fixed for the period and separable by market. All fixed expenses are based on a prorated yearly amount.

Requirements

a) Prepare the quarterly income statement showing contribution margins by markets (territories), and include a column for the company as a whole.

b) Assuming there are no alternative uses for the Justa Corporation's present capacity, would you recommend dropping the regional market? Why or why not?

c) Prepare the quarterly income statement showing contribution margins by products and include a column for the company as a whole.

d) It is believed that a new product can be ready for sale next year if the Justa Corporation decides to go ahead with continued research. The new product can be produced by simply converting equipment now used in producing Product C. This conversion will increase fixed costs by $10,000 per quarter. What must be the minimum contribution margin per quarter for the new product to make the changeover financially feasible?

(CMA Adapted)

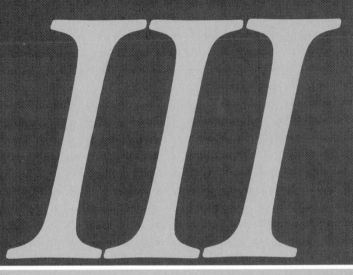

III

Product Costing and Cost Allocation

Product Costing

Product costing is the process of assigning costs to inventories as they are converted from raw materials into finished goods. Determining product costs is necessary for inventory valuations and expense measurement in general purpose financial statements, and it is useful for internal planning and control purposes, such as product pricing, operations budgeting, and profit planning.

The purpose of this chapter is to examine the two major product costing methods used in manufacturing organizations. These methods are *job-order costing* and *process costing*. We begin with a review of product cost systems introduced in Chapter 2.

MANUFACTURING INVENTORIES AND COSTS

Manufacturing organizations have three major inventory categories:

- *Raw materials* inventories contain the physically existing items that are to be converted into finished products.
- *Work-in-process* inventories contain the raw materials that are in the process of being converted into finished products.
- *Finished goods* inventories contain the manufactured products that are available for sale to customers.

The cost of manufacturing products from raw materials consists of three elements:

- *Direct materials* costs represent outlays for primary raw materials used in processing finished goods. Examples of primary raw materials are lumber used in making furniture, crude oil used in refining petrochemicals, and fabric used in making garments.
- *Direct labor* costs consist of the wages earned by production employees for the time they actually spend working on the product. Examples of direct labor are the wages paid to welders in an automobile assembly plant and to carpenters on a construction job.
- *Factory overhead* costs are all manufacturing costs other than direct materials and direct labor. They include indirect materials (materials other than primary raw materials), indirect labor (all labor costs other than direct labor, such as wages paid for supervision, maintenance, and factory security), and other manufacturing costs (such as depreciation on factory buildings and equipment, insurance on factory facilities, and lubricants and cleaning supplies used).

Raw materials, work-in-process, and finished goods are the physical inventory categories in a manufacturing company, and the cost of these inventories is measured by the product costing system. Direct materials, direct labor, and factory overhead represent the cost components of the various inventory categories. The Raw Materials[1] account in the ledger includes only direct materials cost. In the processing stage, direct labor and factory overhead are added to direct materials; therefore Work-in-Process and Finished Goods Inventory valuations include direct materials cost, direct labor cost, and factory overhead cost. As goods move through the typical manufacturing process, direct materials costs represent a progressively smaller proportion of total inventory cost, and direct labor and factory overhead costs represent a progressively larger proportion of total inventory cost.

MANUFACTURING COST FLOWS

Inventory costs in a manufacturing organization flow in a very logical pattern through the accounting system. Purchased raw materials are recorded initially in the Raw Materials account, and other incidental supplies are recorded as Manufacturing Supplies. As primary raw materials are requisitioned from materials stores to the factory, direct materials costs are assigned to Work-in-Process. Direct labor costs are added to Work-in-Process as labor hours are devoted to processing raw materials. All other manufacturing costs, as incurred, are collected temporarily in an account called Factory Overhead. These costs include indirect materials, indirect labor, and other manufacturing costs (such as depreciation, utilities, rents, and taxes). Periodically, these factory overhead costs are assigned to Work-in-Process. In effect, Factory Overhead is a clearing account that collects all manufacturing costs, other than direct materials and direct labor costs, until they are assigned to Work-in-Process.

When products are completed by the manufacturing department and transferred to the finished goods warehouse, the accumulated costs of processing these goods are transferred from Work-in-Process to Finished Goods Inventory. The final transfer of product costs, which occurs when the products are sold, is from Finished Goods Inventory to Cost of Goods Sold. The general pattern of cost flows for a manufacturing organization is illustrated in T-accounts in Exhibit 11–1.

---

[1] As stated in Chapter 2, account titles are capitalized to distinguish them from physical items with the same name. For example, raw materials refers to the physical goods, whereas Raw Materials refers to the account.

EXHIBIT 11–1   Manufacturing Cost Flows

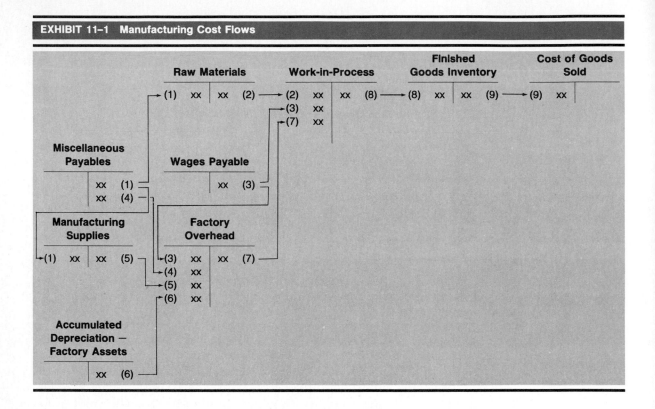

The numbered journal entries posted to the account in Exhibit 11–1 are presented on page 425 with the appropriate explanations. Before the above journal entries can be recorded, the supporting data must be collected and documented. These supporting data are provided by the **product costing system,** which consists of the records of manufacturing inventories and the records of manufacturing transactions.

JOB-ORDER COSTING AND PROCESS COSTING

Product costs always flow through the accounts in the manner illustrated in the previous section, whether a job-order cost system or process cost system is used. The basic distinction between these cost systems is related to two factors; the *production level* and the *time period* chosen for accumulating manufacturing costs, both of which depend on the nature of the product. Some products, such as a bridge or a space shuttle, are designed for the specific needs of the customer. Other products, such as furniture

Journal entries

(1)	Raw Materials	xx	
	Manufacturing Supplies	xx	
	Accounts Payable		xx
	To record purchase of raw materials and manufacturing supplies on account.		
(2)	Work-in-Process	xx	
	Raw Materials		xx
	To record requisition and transfer of raw materials to the factory from materials stores.		
(3)	Work-in-Process	xx	
	Factory Overhead	xx	
	Wages Payable		xx
	To assign direct labor cost incurred to Work-in-Process and indirect labor cost to Factory Overhead.		
(4)	Factory Overhead	xx	
	Miscellaneous Payables[2]		xx
	To record incurrence of various factory overhead costs, such as repairs and maintenance, and property taxes.		
(5)	Factory Overhead	xx	
	Manufacturing Supplies		xx
	To record supplies used in manufacturing.		
(6)	Factory Overhead	xx	
	Accumulated Depreciation — Factory Assets		xx
	To recognize depreciation on factory assets.		
(7)	Work-in-Process	xx	
	Factory Overhead		xx
	To assign factory overhead costs to Work-in-Process.		
(8)	Finished Goods Inventory	xx	
	Work-in-Process		xx
	To record transfer of finished goods from work-in-process inventory to finished goods inventory.		
(9)	Cost of Goods Sold	xx	
	Finished Goods Inventory		xx
	To record the cost of finished goods sold.		

and clothing, are usually produced in batches. Still other products, such as petrochemicals and newsprint paper, are produced in large quantities through a continuous process.

---

[2] The account Miscellaneous Payables is used for convenience in this example to record any liability other than wages and inventory purchases. Miscellaneous payables include utilities payable, taxes payable, and rent payable.

Production Level

Job-order costing is used when unique products are produced, or when products are produced in batches. In job-order costing, manufacturing costs are accumulated at the level of the job. Accordingly, the cost of a particular job can be determined from the cost records maintained for that job. If the job consists of a batch of units, the cost of each unit is determined by dividing the total cost of the job by the number of units in the batch. For example, if 20 bookcases are manufactured in a batch at a total cost of $2000, the cost per bookcase is $100.

Process costing is used when large quantities of a product are manufactured through a continuous process. In process costing systems, costs are accumulated at the level of the manufacturing department, and the cost of a single unit is equal to the total accumulated product costs for the department divided by the number of units produced. For example, if a process manufacturing department produces 4000 gallons of paint during the month at a total cost of $16,000, the cost per gallon is $4.

In Exhibit 11–1 the various components of manufacturing costs are accumulated in Work-in-Process. In a job-order costing system, the costs recorded in Work-in-Process must also be recorded on the appropriate job cost records for specific jobs. At any given time, the balance in Work-in-Process should equal the total costs on the job cost records for all jobs in process.

In a process costing system, the costs recorded in Work-in-Process must also be recorded on appropriate departmental cost records. Therefore, at any given time, the balance in Work-in-Process will be equal to the total costs on the departmental cost records for all departments. For all manufacturing organizations, Work-in-Process is, in effect, a *control account* that is backed up by subsidiary job cost records in a job-order cost system and subsidiary departmental cost records in a process cost system.

Time Dimension

Another important distinction between job-order and process costing is related to the time dimension in accounting for manufacturing costs. In a job-order cost system, all job costs are accumulated in Work-in-Process inventory until the job is completed. A job is not considered completed until all units comprised by the job are finished. For example, during July, 19x3, Brocks Brothers, Inc., a manufacturer of sport coats and suits for men and women, began work on a production job to make 1000 gray suits. Although some of the suits were finished at the end of July, the job was not considered completed until all suits were finished and transferred to finished goods. In a job-order cost system the job is a discrete production unit, and the cost of the completed job is determined when the job is finished, which will not necessarily coincide with the end of an accounting period.

In a process costing system, the manufacturing process consists of a continuous stream of homogeneous goods entering and leaving the production process. During each accounting period the goods worked on usually consist of three groups: (1) goods started in the previous period and completed in the current period, (2) goods both started and completed in the current period, and (3) goods started but not completed in the current period. In a process cost system, costs are accumulated for each accounting period (e.g., month or year) and assigned to the units produced during the period. Since some goods are only partially processed during the period, it is necessary to determine the total production for the period in terms of the equivalent number of completed units. For example, if 100 units were started and completed through 50 percent of the process during the period, the equivalent of 50 fully completed units would have been produced. The total number of equivalent units is divided into the total costs for the period to determine the average cost per unit.

To summarize, in a job-order costing system, costs are accumulated at the level of the job, and unit production costs are determined when each job is completed. In process costing, manufacturing costs are accumulated at the level of the department, and average unit production costs are determined for each accounting period.

BASIC COST SYSTEM RECORDS

In any product cost system — job-order or process — several basic records must be maintained to support the system. These records can be classified as (1) *inventory records* and (2) *transaction records*. Separate inventory records must be maintained for raw materials, work-in-process, and finished goods inventories. In addition, records must be prepared to document transactions that increase or decrease the inventory balances. Exhibit 11–2 shows a typical **raw materials inventory record** used to record increases and decreases and the available balance for each type of raw material, a **materials requisition form** used to record transfers of direct materials from raw materials to work-in-process, and a **direct labor ticket** used to record direct labor hours and costs. These three records are virtually identical for job-order and process costing systems, except that in a process cost system the materials requisition form and direct labor ticket would indicate the department number instead of the job number.

Exhibit 11–2 also includes a typical **finished goods inventory record.** This record is maintained for each product in a process cost system; however, in a job-order system individual finished goods inventory records are required only when goods are produced for open stock. If products are manufactured for specific customers (which is often the case in companies that use job-order systems), job cost records for completed but undelivered jobs provide the necessary detail and documentation for the balance in Finished Goods Inventory. The basic records illustrated in Exhibit 11–2

EXHIBIT 11–2 Basic Cost System Records

Raw Materials Inventory Record

Inventory Number . . . .   Description . . . .

	Purchased			Issued			Balance		
Date	Units	Unit Cost	Total Cost	Units	Unit Cost	Total Cost	Units	Unit Cost	Total Cost

Materials Requisition Form

Requisition No. . . . .   Job No. . . . . . .

Date . . . .

Inventory Number	Quantity	Unit Cost	Total Cost

Issued by . . . .

Received by . . . .

Direct Labor Ticket

Employee No. . . . . .   Job No. . . . . . .

Employee Name . . . .

Date . . . .

Time Work   Time Work
Started . . . .   Completed . . . .

Office Use		
Hours . . . . . Rate . . . . . Charge		

Finished Goods Inventory Record

Inventory No. . . . .   Description . . . .

	Received from Factory			Sold			Balance		
Date	Units	Unit Cost	Total Cost	Units	Unit Cost	Total Cost	Units	Unit Cost	Total Cost

serve the dual purpose of keeping track of physical quantities and providing cost information for accounting transactions.

JOB-ORDER COSTING PROCEDURES

Job Cost Sheet

In job-order costing it is necessary to assign manufacturing costs simultaneously to (1) Work-in-Process and (2) specific jobs. **Job cost sheets** are used to accumulate the costs for specific jobs in process. As manufacturing costs are assigned to Work-in-Process, they are also recorded on the appropriate job cost sheets. The job cost sheets, therefore, constitute the subsidiary records for Work-in-Process. Each job cost sheet has a place for recording the different elements of manufacturing costs — direct materials, direct labor, and factory overhead. A reproduction of a typical job cost sheet is presented in Exhibit 11–3.

EXHIBIT 11–3   Job Cost Sheet

Job Cost Sheet

Job No. . . . .　　Date Started. . . . .

Description . . . .　　Target Completion Date . . . .

Number of Units in Job . . . .　　Date Completed. . . . .

	Materials		Labor		Factory Overhead	
Date	Requisition Number	Amount	Hours	Amount	Rate per Hour	Amount
Totals						

Total Job Cost _____　　　　　　Cost per Unit _____

Job-Order Costing Illustrated

To illustrate how manufacturing costs flow through the accounts in a job-order cost accounting system, the manufacturing transactions recorded by Brocks Brothers, Inc. in August, 19x3 are presented below. Included are the transactions recorded in the general ledger and the procedures performed in the cost system records. Total inventories were $193,565 at the beginning of August and consisted of Raw Materials, $18,800; Work-in-Process, $97,315; and Finished Goods, $77,450. The components of these inventories are summarized below.

Raw Materials			
Description	Quantity	Unit Cost	Total Cost
Gray fabric	800 yards	$10	$ 8,000
Blue fabric	500 yards	14	7,000
Brown fabric	200 yards	19	3,800
			$18,800

Work-in-Process		Finished Goods Inventory	
Job	Total Cost	Job	Total Cost
325	$55,245	323	$52,250
326	42,070	324	25,200
	$97,315		$77,450

The manufacturing transactions recorded by Brocks Brothers, Inc. for the month of August are described below, along with the required *journal entries* and descriptions of the required product *cost system procedures*.

1. Purchased 1000 yards of blue fabric at $14 per yard and 300 yards of brown fabric at $19 per yard.

Journal entry

Raw Materials	19,700	
Accounts Payable		19,700
To record purchase of fabrics.		

Cost system procedures

Record purchases on raw materials inventory records:
   Blue fabric   1,000 yards @ $14 = $14,000
   Brown fabric   300 yards @ $19 = $ 5,700

2. Requisitioned the following raw materials to the factory: 200 yards of gray fabric to Job 326 and 900 yards of blue fabric to Job 327, a new job started in August.

Journal entry			

Work-in-Process	14,600	
Raw Materials		14,600
To record requisition of raw materials		
to factory.		

Cost system procedures

a) Prepare materials requisition forms.

b) Record raw materials issued on inventory records:
    Gray fabric   200 yards @ $10 = $ 2,000
    Blue fabric   900 yards @ $14 = $12,600

c) Record direct materials costs on individual job cost sheets:
    Job 326 $ 2,000
    Job 327 $12,600

3. Manufacturing payroll for the month of August is summarized below.

	Cost	Hours
Direct labor		
Job 325	$ 9,460	1,150
Job 326	16,845	2,100
Job 327	1,680	195
Total direct labor	$27,985	3,445
Indirect labor	7,200	
Total labor	$35,185	

Journal entry

Work-in-Process	27,985	
Factory Overhead	7,200	
Wages Payable		35,185
To record wages for the month and		
assign direct labor cost to Work-in-		
Process and indirect labor		
cost to Factory Overhead.		

Cost system procedures

a) Prepare labor tickets.

b) Record direct labor hours and costs on individual job cost sheets:

Job 325	1,150 hours	$ 9,460
Job 326	2,100 hours	$16,845
Job 327	195 hours	$ 1,680

4. Recorded the following factory overhead costs:

Factory supplies used		$ 950
Factory depreciation		1,500
Other factory expenses:		
Maintenance and repairs	$1,740	
Property taxes	500	
Utilities	2,400	4,640
Total		$7,090

Journal entry

Factory Overhead	7,090	
Prepaid Factory Supplies[3]		950
Accumulated Depreciation — Factory Assets		1,500
Miscellaneous Payables		4,640
To record actual factory overhead expenses incurred for the month of August.		

Cost system procedures

None is required since the manufacturing inventory accounts are not affected by this transaction.

5. Applied factory overhead cost to Work-in-Process for the month of August using a predetermined rate of $4 per direct labor hour.

---

[3] In this example Prepaid Factory Supplies is treated as only a general ledger account. In many cost systems this account would have detailed subsidiary accounts (the same as other inventory accounts) showing the transactions and balances for specific supply items.

Job Number	Direct Labor Hours	Applied Factory Overhead
325	1,150	$ 4,600
326	2,100	8,400
327	195	780
	3,445	$13,780

Journal entry

Work-in-Process	13,780	
Factory Overhead		13,780
To apply factory overhead to Work-in-Process at the rate of $4 per direct labor hour.		

Cost system procedures

Record factory overhead applied on job cost sheets:
Job 325	$4,600
Job 326	$8,400
Job 327	$ 780

6. Completed jobs 325 and 326.

Cost Summary	Job 325	Job 326
Total cost, beginning of month	$55,245	$42,070
Job costs assigned in August:		
Direct materials	—	2,000
Direct labor	9,460	16,845
Factory overhead	4,600	8,400
	$69,305	$69,315
Total cost of Jobs 325 and 326		$138,620

Journal entry

Finished Goods Inventory	138,620	
Work-in-Process		138,620
To record completion and transfer of Jobs 325 and 326 to finished goods inventory.		

Cost system procedures	Transfer job cost sheets for Jobs 325 and 326 from Work-in-Process subsidiary file to Finished Goods subsidiary file. Unit costs are computed as follows:

	Job 325	*Job 326*
(a) Total job cost	$69,305	$69,315
(b) Total units per job	1,500	1,000
Unit cost (a) ÷ (b)	$46.20	$69.32

7. Delivered the following jobs to customers:

	Total Cost
Job 323 (completed at beginning of month)	$ 52,250
Job 324 (completed at beginning of month)	25,200
Job 325 (completed in August, see transaction 6)	69,305
	$146,755

Journal entry	Cost of Goods Sold 146,755
	Finished Goods Inventory 146,755
	To record delivery of Jobs 323, 324, and 325 to customers.

Cost system procedures	Transfer job cost sheets for Jobs 323, 324, and 325 from Finished Goods subsidiary file to Completed and Delivered Jobs file.

Exhibit 11–4 shows the various manufacturing inventory accounts, Cost of Goods Sold, and the cost system records reflecting the above transactions. Notice how the cost system records provide supporting documentation for the general ledger account balances.

ACCOUNTING FOR FACTORY OVERHEAD

In the illustration of Brocks Brothers, Inc., we assigned factory overhead costs to Work-in-Process and to specific jobs at the predetermined rate of $4 per direct labor hour. By using a predetermined overhead rate the total cost of a particular job can be determined as soon as the job is completed

EXHIBIT 11–4   General Ledger Accounts and Supporting Job-Order Cost System Records for Brocks Brothers, Inc.

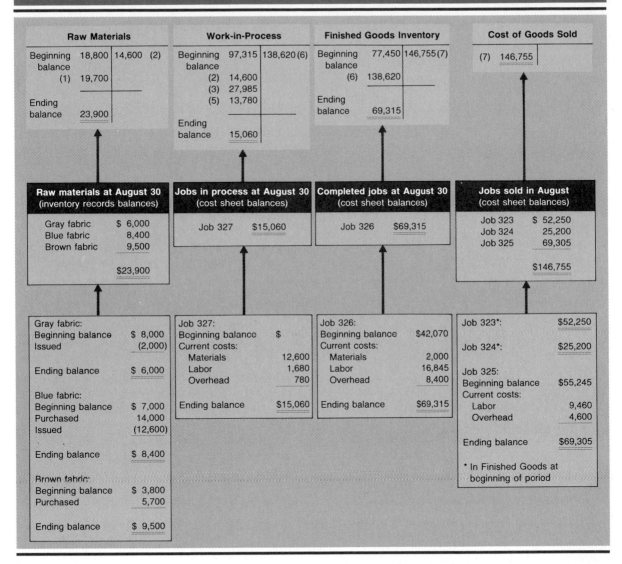

Raw Materials			
Beginning balance	18,800	14,600	(2)
(1)	19,700		
Ending balance	23,900		

Work-in-Process			
Beginning balance	97,315	138,620	(6)
(2)	14,600		
(3)	27,985		
(5)	13,780		
Ending balance	15,060		

Finished Goods Inventory			
Beginning balance	77,450	146,755	(7)
(6)	138,620		
Ending balance	69,315		

Cost of Goods Sold	
(7) 146,755	

Raw materials at August 30
(inventory records balances)

Gray fabric	$ 6,000
Blue fabric	8,400
Brown fabric	9,500
	$23,900

Jobs in process at August 30
(cost sheet balances)

Job 327	$15,060

Completed jobs at August 30
(cost sheet balances)

Job 326	$69,315

Jobs sold in August
(cost sheet balances)

Job 323	$ 52,250
Job 324	25,200
Job 325	69,305
	$146,755

Gray fabric:

Beginning balance	$ 8,000
Issued	(2,000)
Ending balance	$ 6,000

Blue fabric:

Beginning balance	$ 7,000
Purchased	14,000
Issued	(12,600)
Ending balance	$ 8,400

Brown fabric:

Beginning balance	$ 3,800
Purchased	5,700
Ending balance	$ 9,500

Job 327:

Beginning balance	$
Current costs:	
Materials	12,600
Labor	1,680
Overhead	780
Ending balance	$15,060

Job 326:

Beginning balance	$42,070
Current costs:	
Materials	2,000
Labor	16,845
Overhead	8,400
Ending balance	$69,315

Job 323*: $52,250

Job 324*: $25,200

Job 325:

Beginning balance	$55,245
Current costs:	
Labor	9,460
Overhead	4,600
Ending balance	$69,305

* In Finished Goods at beginning of period

and the number of labor hours is tabulated. If actual overhead costs were assigned to jobs, total costs could not be determined until the *end of the period* when total factory overhead costs are known.

The predetermined factory overhead rate is computed by dividing predicted overhead costs for the year by the predicted activity for the year.

Assuming Brocks Brothers, Inc. estimates total factory overhead costs for the year to be $100,000 and total production activity (measured in terms of direct labor hours) to be 25,000 direct labor hours, the predetermined factory overhead rate is $4 per direct labor hour:

$$\text{Predetermined factory overhead rate} = \frac{\text{Predicted total overhead for the year}}{\text{Predicted total direct labor hours for the year}}$$
$$= \frac{\$100,000}{25,000 \text{ hours}}$$
$$= \$4.$$

Two important questions must be addressed whenever predetermined factory overhead rates are used: (1) What is the appropriate basis for overhead allocation, and (2) what disposition should be made of any underapplied or overapplied balances in factory overhead at the end of the period?

Basis for Overhead Allocation

In addition to direct labor hours, other common bases for overhead allocation include machine hours, direct labor costs, and number of units produced. Examples of predetermined overhead rates using these bases are $2 per machine hour, 40 percent of direct labor cost, and $10 per unit completed.

A company, such as a clothing manufacturer, that has a labor intensive manufacturing process would probably select a labor-related activity base, such as direct labor hours or direct labor costs. Labor intensive companies usually find a close correlation between the amount of factory overhead costs incurred and the volume of labor-related activities. On the other hand, a company whose production is machine intensive, such as a chemical company, would probably use an activity base reflecting machine activity, such as machine hours. Companies that have more than one production department may use a different base for each department.

The primary goal in selecting an allocation base is to make sure that a logical association exists between the base and the significant factory overhead cost components. Also, the quantity of the base for each period, and for each job or department, should be fairly easy to measure. Direct labor hours is a widely used base because the annual prediction of direct labor hours is easily determined when the units of planned production and the number of plant employees are known. Moreover, the actual number of direct labor hours for each period, and for each job or department, is available in the product costing system.

Overapplied and Underapplied Overhead

Using the Brocks Brothers example (where predicted factory overhead costs for the year were $100,000, and direct labor hours were 25,000), assume that the company actually incurred $100,000 in factory overhead costs and that actual direct labor hours for the year were 25,000. Summary entries for actual and applied overhead costs are as follows:

Journal entry

Factory Overhead	100,000	
Various balance sheet accounts		100,000
To record actual factory overhead costs for the year.		
Work-in-Process	100,000	
Factory Overhead		100,000
To apply factory overhead to Work-in-Process for 25,000 direct labor hours at the rate of $4 per direct labor hour.		

Because the actual costs recorded are equal to the applied costs, there is no balance in Factory Overhead at the end of the year. However, if either the actual overhead costs or the actual level of the production activity base differed from its predicted value, there would be a balance in Factory Overhead, representing overapplied or underapplied overhead.

Now assume that the prediction of 25,000 direct labor hours was correct but that actual overhead costs were $105,000. In this case, Factory Overhead shows a $5000 debit balance representing underapplied factory overhead:

Factory Overhead

Actual costs 105,000	100,000 Applied costs
Underapplied 5,000	
factory overhead	

If actual costs were only $98,000, Factory Overhead would show a $2000 credit balance, representing overapplied factory overhead:

Factory Overhead

Actual costs 98,000	100,000 Applied costs
	2,000 Overapplied
	factory overhead

It is apparent from these examples that if the *predictions* of factory overhead costs are not accurate, there will be an underapplied or overapplied balance in Factory Overhead at the end of the year. A similar result occurs when the actual production activity level is different from the predicted activity level used in computing the predetermined rate. Any balances in Factory Overhead during the year representing overapplied or underapplied overhead are usually allowed to accumulate from month to month. Any balance in Factory Overhead at the end of the year is usually disposed of by one of the two methods discussed in the following section.

Disposition of Factory Overhead Balances

To illustrate the disposition of the Factory Overhead balance at the end of the accounting period, assume the following year-end account balances (all debits) for a manufacturing company:

Work-in-Process	$300,000
Finished Goods Inventory	200,000
Cost of Goods Sold	500,000
Factory Overhead (underapplied)	8,000

The first method for disposing of the $8,000 debit balance in Factory Overhead at the end of the period is merely to write the balance off to Cost of Goods Sold by the following journal entry:

Journal entry

Cost of Goods Sold	8,000	
Factory Overhead		8,000

The effect of this entry is to close out the Factory Overhead account and to charge the overapplied balance to Cost of Goods Sold, thus increasing total expenses on the income statement and reducing net income. If Factory Overhead has a credit balance, representing overapplied overhead, Factory Overhead would be debited, and Cost of Goods Sold would be credited. Crediting Cost of Goods Sold reduces total expenses and increases net income.

The second method of disposing of an end-of-period balance in Factory Overhead is to allocate it among Work-in-Process, Finished Goods Inventory, and Cost of Goods Sold. This allocation is frequently made on the basis of the relative total costs in each account at the end of the period. The following computations show how the $8000 would be allocated to these accounts.

	Account Balance	Relative Portion of Total		Underapplied Factory Overhead		Allocation
Work-in-Process	$ 300,000	0.30	×	$8,000	=	$2,400
Finished Goods	200,000	0.20	×	8,000	=	1,600
Cost of Goods Sold	500,000	0.50	×	8,000	=	4,000
Total	$1,000,000	1.00				$8,000

The entry to record the assignment of the Factory Overhead balance to Work-in-Process, Finished Goods Inventory, and Cost of Goods Sold is shown in the journal entry on the following page.

Journal entry	Work-in-Process	2,400	
	Finished Goods Inventory	1,600	
	Cost of Goods Sold	4,000	
	Factory Overhead		8,000

The rationale for writing the Factory Overhead balance off against Cost of Goods Sold is that it is convenient and simple. And, if the predicted amounts used in calculating the predetermined rate are relatively accurate, the underapplied or overapplied amount should be relatively small, thereby justifying the use of the most convenient method.

The allocation method, however, is more desirable if the Factory Overhead balance is relatively large. An overapplied or underapplied balance in factory overhead is always caused by the use of a predetermined overhead rate that differs from the actual overhead rate. If we waited until the end of the period to apply overhead, an accurate overhead rate based on actual costs could be used. Therefore it is logical to allocate the ending balance in Factory Overhead to the accounts affected by the predetermined rate, that is, to Work-in-Process, Finished Goods Inventory, and Cost of Goods Sold. After the allocation, the balance in each account should be approximately the same as it would be if the actual rate had been used. An expanded discussion of factory overhead and other common cost assignments is provided in Chapter 12.

PROCESS COSTING PROCEDURES

Because many elements of process costing systems are similar to those discussed previously for job-order systems, only the concepts and procedures unique to process costing are emphasized in this section. Recall that process costing systems differ from job-order systems in two respects — the production level at which costs are accumulated and the period of time for which costs are accumulated. In a *process costing system* costs are accumulated at the level of the *department,* and the cost accumulation time period is the *accounting period.*

We saw, in a job-order cost system, how job cost sheets collect the essential cost information for all goods in process. Cost collection is much simpler in a process cost system because each department's production is treated as if it were one job worked on during the period. In a company that has only one manufacturing department, process costing is particularly simple because the Work-in-Process account is, in fact, the departmental cost record. Where a company has more than one department, a separate Work-in-Process account is established for each department.

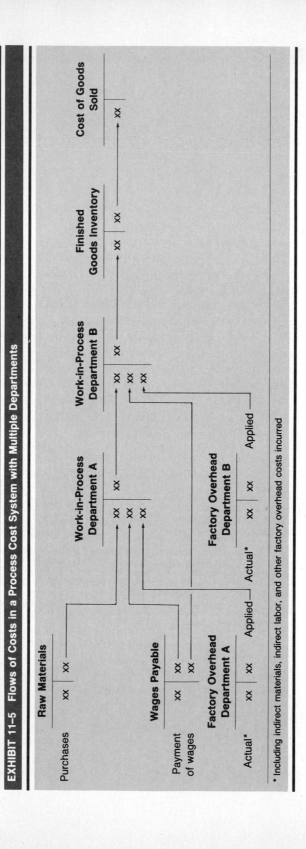

EXHIBIT 11–5 Flows of Costs in a Process Cost System with Multiple Departments

* Including indirect materials, indirect labor, and other factory overhead costs incurred

The general model of cost flows in a two-department process costing system is shown in Exhibit 11–5. It is assumed in this diagram that all materials are added in the first department and that all products are worked on in both departments, first in Department A and then in Department B. Many products, however, do not require multiple departments. For example, candy bars are usually made in one highly automated process that converts raw materials into finished products, wrapped and packaged for sale.

Single Department Company

To illustrate process costing in a company that has only one department, assume that Micro Systems Co. began business in 19x3 to manufacture memory chips for microcomputers. Sophisticated machinery has been purchased for manufacturing the chips in a one-step process. Each finished unit requires that one unit of raw materials be added at the beginning of the manufacturing process. The production and cost data for the first year of operations for Micro Systems are as follows:

Production Data	Units
Raw materials transferred to processing	20,000
Completed units transferred to finished goods	16,000
Units in process, end of period (75% converted)	4,000

Current Manufacturing Costs		Dollars
Raw materials transferred to processing		$ 80,000
Conversion costs:		
Direct labor for the period	$38,000	
Factory overhead applied (50% of direct labor cost)	19,000	57,000
Total costs for period		$137,000

The key to mastering process costing is understanding the **cost of production report,** which summarizes unit and cost data for each department. It consists of the following sections:

- Flow of whole or partial units.
- Equivalent units.
- Total costs to be accounted for and cost per equivalent unit.
- Accounting for total costs.

EXHIBIT 11–6   Process Costing without Beginning Inventories

Micro Systems Co.
Cost of Production Report
For the year ended December 31,19x3

Flow of Whole or Partial Units

Beginning	—
Units started	20,000
In process	20,000
Completed	−16,000
Ending	4,000

Equivalent Units in Process	*Materials*	*Conversion*
Units completed	16,000	16,000
Plus: equivalent units in ending inventory	4,000	3,000*
Equivalent units in process	20,000	19,000

Total Costs to Be Accounted for and Cost per Equivalent Unit in Process	*Materials*	*Conversion*	*Total*
Work-in-Process, beginning	$ —	$ —	$ —
Current costs	80,000	57,000†	137,000
Total costs in process	$80,000	57,000	$137,000
Equivalent units in process	÷20,000	÷19,000	
Cost per equivalent in unit process	$ 4	$ 3	$ 7

Accounting for Total Costs			
Transferred out (16,000 × $7)			$112,000
Work-in-Process, ending:			
Materials (4000 × $4)		$16,000	
Conversion (3000 × $3)		9,000	25,000
Total costs accounted for			$137,000

* 4000 units 75% converted
† Includes direct labor of $38,000 and applied factory overhead of $19,000

The cost of production report for Micro Systems Co. is shown in Exhibit 11–6, and its four sections are discussed below.

Flow of Whole or Partial Units. This section of the report provides a summary of all units on which some work was done in the department during the period. Units in process at the beginning of the period plus units started equals the total units in process in the department during the period. Units in process during the period either were completed or were still on hand at the end of the period.[4]

All units are treated the same in this section regardless of the amount of processing that took place on them during the period. The objective here is merely to account for all the units of product worked on during the period. Note in Exhibit 11–6 that 20,000 individual units were worked on to some extent during the period, 16,000 units were completed, and 4,000 units were still in process at the end of the period.

Equivalent Units. In this section of the cost of production report, the objective is to translate the number of units worked on during the period into equivalent completed units. **Equivalent completed units** represents the number of completed units that is equal to a given number of partially completed units. For example, 80 units 50 percent completed are the equivalent of 40 completed units in terms of processing costs. Micro Systems Co. adds all materials at the beginning of the process, and all conversion costs — direct labor and factory overhead — are added evenly throughout the manufacturing process. Therefore, separate computations must be made for equivalent units of *materials cost* and equivalent units of *conversion cost*. Although the department worked on 20,000 units during the period, the total number of equivalent units completed with respect to conversion costs was only 19,000 units, 16,000 finished units plus 3000 equivalent units (4000 units 75 percent converted). All 20,000 units (16,000 finished and 4000 in process) were completed with respect to materials cost.

Total Costs to Be Accounted for and Cost per Equivalent Unit. This section of the report summarizes the total costs assigned to the department during the period. The disposition of these costs is summarized in the next section of the report. Since there were no units in process at the beginning of the period, the only production costs that Micro Systems Co. had to account for during 19x3 were the current period's costs. Therefore, to compute the average cost per unit, the total cost charged to the department is divided by the equivalent units worked on during the period. Because the number of equivalent units in process differs for materials cost and conversion cost, separate computations of units cost are made for these cost components. The total cost per equivalent unit in process during the period is determined by adding together the unit costs of materials and conversion.

Accounting for Total Costs. This section shows the disposition of the total costs charged to the department during the period. The general rule

---

[4] In some processes units may be lost through spoilage or pilferage. These special situations are covered in advanced courses in cost accounting.

in assigning costs to units of production is that manufacturing costs follow the units worked on. Therefore the total costs to be accounted for are assigned to two groups of units: (1) the units completed during the period and (2) the units in process at the end of the period. The 16,000 units finished during the period are complete with respect to materials and conversion; hence, their total cost is $7 per unit — the unit materials cost of $4 plus the unit conversion cost of $3. The 4000 units in ending work-in-process are assigned a full equivalent unit of cost for materials, or $4 per unit. However, only the costs for 3000 equivalent units are assigned to ending Work-in-Process because the 4000 units in process have gone through only 75 percent of the conversion (or manufacturing) process. Processing will be completed on these units in a subsequent period. The total costs accounted for should equal the total costs in process. In this example both are $137,000.

Journal Entries. The cost of production report summarizes all the manufacturing costs assigned to Work-in-Process during the period and provides information for preparing the journal entry to record the cost of goods completed and transferred to finished goods inventory during the period. The journal entries and the supporting documents to record the assignment of costs to Work-in-Process are essentially the same as those discussed for job-order costing. The entries for Micro Systems Co. for 19x3 are as follows:

Journal entries

(1) Work-in-Process	80,000	
Raw Materials		80,000
To record materials requisitioned to factory.		
(2) Work-in-Process	38,000	
Wages Payable		38,000
To record wages for the period.		
(3) Work-in-Process	19,000	
Factory Overhead		19,000
To apply factory overhead at 50 percent of direct labor cost.		
(4) Finished Goods Inventory	112,000	
Work-in-Process		112,000
To record transfer of completed units to finished goods.		

After the above entries are posted, Work-in-Process appears as follows:

Work-in-Process

(1) Direct materials	80,000	112,000	(4) To Finished Goods Inventory
(2) Direct labor	38,000		
(3) Factory overhead	19,000		
Ending balance	25,000		

Notice in Exhibit 11–6 that the $112,000 assigned to 16,000 units transferred out is equal to the amount credited to Work-in-Process for costs transferred to Finished Goods Inventory. Also, the $25,000 balance in Work-in-Process is equal to the amount assigned to ending work-in-process on the cost of production report.

Process Costing with Beginning Inventories

In the previous example, Micro Systems Co. was in its first year of operations and had no beginning inventories. Continuing the example into 19x4, the second year of operations, we can illustrate process costing procedures for a company that has both *beginning* and *ending* inventories. The pertinent information for 19x4 is summarized below.

Production Data	*Units*
Units in process, beginning of period (75% converted)	4,000
Raw materials transferred to processing	30,000
Completed and transferred to finished goods	29,000
Units in process, end of period (40% converted)	5,000

Current Manufacturing Costs		*Dollars*
Raw materials transferred to processing		$123,400
Conversion costs:		
Direct labor for the period	$62,200	
Factory overhead applied		
(50% of direct labor)	31,100	93,300
Total costs for period		$216,700

Weighted Average Process Costing. Several different methods are used in process costing systems to account for partially completed units in beginning inventory. We will discuss two of these methods, the *weighted average* method and the *FIFO* (first-in first-out) method. Other methods are covered in advanced courses in cost accounting. In the **weighted average method,** the costs of partially completed units in beginning work-in-process are combined with current manufacturing costs, and the total is assigned on an average basis to all equivalent units in process during the period. In

EXHIBIT 11–7   Weighted Average Process Costing with Beginning Inventories

Micro Systems Co.
Cost of Production Report
For the year ended December 31, 19x4

Flow of Whole or Partial Units

Beginning	4,000
Units started	30,000
In process	34,000
Completed	−29,000
Ending	5,000

Equivalent Units in Process	*Materials*	*Conversion*	
Units completed	29,000	29,000	
Plus: Equivalent units in ending inventory	5,000	2,000*	
Equivalent units in process	34,000	31,000	

Total Costs to Be Accounted for and Cost per Equivalent Unit in Process	*Materials*	*Conversion*	*Total*
Work-in-Process, beginning	$ 16,000	$ 9,000	$ 25,000
Current costs	123,400	93,300†	216,700
Total costs in process	$139,400	$102,300	$241,700
Equivalent units in process	÷ 34,000	÷ 31,000	
Cost per equivalent unit in process	$ 4.10	$ 3.30	$ 7.40

Accounting for Total Costs			
Transferred out (29,000 × $7.40)			$214,600
Work-in-Process, ending:			
Materials (5000 × $4.10)		$ 20,500	
Conversion (2000 × $3.30)		6,600	27,100
Total costs accounted for			$241,700

* 5000 units 40% converted

† Includes direct labor of $62,200 and factory overhead applied of $31,100

this context, "in process" means being physically located in the production department at some time during the period. The weighted average method makes no distinction between beginning inventory units worked on during the period and units started during the current period.

Micro Systems' cost of production report for 19x4, prepared under the weighted average method, is shown in Exhibit 11–7. Note that the equivalent units of 34,000 for materials and 31,000 for conversion are called *equivalent units in process.* These amounts include the number of equivalent units in process during the period — partially completed units in beginning inventory plus units started during the period. Similarly, the cost computations of $139,400 and $102,300 are called *total costs in process* and include beginning Work-in-Process plus current manufacturing costs. Consequently, the unit cost figures represent the costs per equivalent unit "in process." The total unit cost of $7.40 is assigned to all units transferred out during the period, whether they were started in the previous period or in the current period.

FIFO Inventory Method. Under the **FIFO inventory method,** partially completed units held at the beginning of the period are not combined with currently produced units for costing purposes. Instead, the units in beginning inventory are costed as a separate group consisting of two components — the portion processed in the previous period is assigned the unit costs for that period, and the portion processed in the current period is assigned the current period's unit costs. For example, assume a company using the FIFO method had unit conversion costs of $5 in 19x3 and $6 in 19x4 and had one unit of inventory 60 percent converted at the end of 19x3. In 19x4 when the unit is completed, the conversion cost assigned to that unit would be $5.40:

Portion processed in 19x3:	$0.60 \times \$5.00 =$	$3.00
Portion processed in 19x4:	$0.40 \times \$6.00 =$	2.40
Total unit cost		$5.40

This method of computing costs for units partially processed in two different periods is the distinguishing characteristic of the FIFO method of process costing. A FIFO cost of production report for Micro Systems for 19x4 is shown in Exhibit 11–8. Notice in the computation of equivalent units that the FIFO method identifies the number of *equivalent units manufactured* during the current period by subtracting the partially completed equivalent units contained in beginning inventory from the equivalent units in process. In the weighted average method, the computation of equivalent units was based on total *equivalent units in process.*

In the FIFO method, the cost per equivalent unit manufactured consists of only *current manufacturing costs,* computed by dividing current costs (not total costs) by the equivalent units manufactured in the current period. This unit cost is then used to determine the cost of (1) currently completed units in beginning inventory, (2) units started and completed during the period, and (3) units started but not completed. Notice in the last section of Exhibit 11–8 that the FIFO method assumes the units completed first

EXHIBIT 11–8   FIFO Process Costing with Beginning Inventories

Micro Systems Co.
Cost of Production Report
For the year ended December 31, 19x4

Flow of Whole or Partial Units

Beginning	4,000
Units started	30,000
In process	34,000
Completed	−29,000
Ending	5,000

Equivalent Units Manufactured	*Materials*	*Conversion*
Units completed	29,000	29,000
Plus: Equivalent units in ending inventory	5,000	2,000*
Equivalent units in process	34,000	31,000
Less: Equivalent units in beginning inventory	− 4,000	− 3,000†
Equivalent units manufactured	30,000	28,000

Total Costs to Be Accounted for and Cost per Equivalent Unit Manufactured	*Materials*	*Conversion*	*Total*
Work-in-Process, beginning	$ omit ‡	$ omit ‡	$ 25,000
Current costs	123,400	93,300§	216,700
Total costs in process	$ omit ‡	$ omit ‡	$241,700 #
Equivalent units manufactured	÷ 30,000	÷ 28,000	
Cost per equivalent unit manufactured	$ 4.113	$ 3.332	$ 7.445

Accounting for Total Costs

Transferred out:			
Work-in-Process, beginning	$ 25,000		
Cost to complete (1000 × $3.332)	3,332	$ 28,332	
Started and completed this period			
(25,000 × $7.445)		186,125	$214,457
Work-in-Process, ending:			
Materials (5000 × $4.113)		$ 20,565	
Conversion (2000 × $3.332)		6,664	27,229
Total costs accounted for			$241,686 #

---

* 5000 units 40% converted

† 4000 units 75% converted

‡ Cost per equivalent unit manufactured is based on current costs only.

§ Includes direct labor of $62,200 and applied factory overhead of $31,100

\# Answer reflects $14 rounding error ($241,700 − $241,686).

are the units started in the previous period and completed in the current period. These units are assigned a cost based partially on the previous year's cost and partially on current unit costs. The next units completed are those that were both started and completed in the current period. These units are valued using only the current period's unit costs. The remaining units — those started but not completed — are assigned a full unit of current materials cost and a partial unit of current conversion cost based on their percentage of completion.

In the case of Micro Systems Co., the difference in the cost valuations between the weighted average method and the FIFO method was only $129 ($27,100 − $27,229) for ending work-in-process and $143 ($214,600 − $214,457) for goods completed and transferred to finished goods. These *differences* in inventory cost valuations between weighted average and FIFO costing tend to be *small* if the change in unit manufacturing costs (materials, labor, and overhead) from one period to the next is small or if the equivalent units in beginning work-in-process represent a small percentage of the total equivalent units worked on during the year.

Under the weighted average method, the cost of goods completed was larger and the cost of ending work-in-process was smaller than under the FIFO method. These relationships between FIFO and weighted average will prevail as long as prices are rising from period to period. In times of falling prices, FIFO will produce a higher valuation for completed units and a lower valuation for units in process.

Multiple Departments

In the previous section we assumed that the product was converted from raw materials into finished goods in a single department. It is common in many manufacturing organizations for products to be processed in more than one department before they are completed. For example, a company that manufactures appliances may have separate departments for sheet metal stamping, assembly, painting, and inspection. A textile mill has several departments, including spinning, weaving, and bleaching.

To illustrate process costing for a multiple-department manufacturing organization, assume that at the beginning of 19x5, because of quality control problems, Micro Systems Co. is forced to add another department to its manufacturing process to test and inspect its products before they are shipped to customers. It now has two departments, the Molding Department where the memory chips are molded from raw materials and the Testing Department where the chips are tested for defects. When units are completed in the Molding Department, they are transferred to the Testing Department for further processing. Separate departmental cost records are maintained for Molding and Testing, including separate Work-in-Process accounts. When goods are completed in the Molding Department, their accumulated costs are transferred to the Testing Department by the following entry:

Journal entry	Work-in-Process, Testing Department	xx	
	Work-in-Process, Molding Department		xx

Assume that all materials are added at the beginning of the Molding Department process and that only additional conversion costs — direct labor and factory overhead — are added in the Testing Department. When a unit of product is completed through both departments, its total cost consists of the following components:

- Direct materials, Molding Department.
- Conversion costs, Molding Department.
- Conversion costs, Testing Department.

To illustrate the costing procedures for 19x5 for Micro Systems Co., assume the following data:

	Units	
	Molding	Testing
Production Data	Department	Department
Units in process, beginning of period		
(40% converted in Molding)	5,000	—
Raw materials transferred to Molding	35,000	—
Units transferred to Testing	33,000	—
Units received from Molding	—	33,000
Transferred to finished goods	—	28,000
Units in process, end of period		
(50% converted in Molding and Testing)	7,000	5,000

	Dollars	
	Molding	Testing
Current Manufacturing Costs	Department	Department
Raw materials transferred to Molding	$155,500	—
Conversion costs:		
Direct labor cost for the period	$ 83,200	16,800
Factory overhead applied		
(50% of direct labor cost)	41,600	8,400
Total	$124,800	$25,200

Exhibit 11–9 presents the combined cost of production reports for the Molding and Testing Departments for 19x5 using the weighted average method. A few differences should be noted in comparing Exhibit 11–9 with

EXHIBIT 11–9   Weighted Average Process Costing with Beginning Inventories and Two Departments

Micro Systems Co.
Cost of Production Report
For the year ended December 31, 19x5

Flow of Whole or Partial Units

	Molding	Testing
Beginning	5,000	—
Units started	35,000	33,000
In process	40,000	33,000
Completed	−33,000	−28,000
Ending	7,000	5,000

Equivalent Units in Process	Molding Department		Testing Department	
	Materials	Conversion	Transferred-in	Conversion
Units completed	33,000	33,000	28,000	28,000
Plus: Equivalent units in ending inventory	7,000	3,500*	5,000	2,500‡
Equivalent units in process	40,000	36,500	33,000	30,500

Total Costs to Be Accounted for and Cost per Equivalent Unit in Process	Molding Department		Testing Department	
	Materials	Conversion	Transferred-in	Conversion
Work-in-Process, beginning	$ 20,500	$ 6,600	$ —	—
Current costs	155,500	124,800‡	264,000	25,200§
Total costs in process	$176,000	$131,400	$264,000	$ 25,200
Total department costs	$307,400		$289,200	
Equivalent units in process	÷ 40,000	÷ 36,500	÷ 33,000	÷ 30,500
Cost per equivalent unit in process	$ 4.40	$ 3.60	$ 8.00	$ 0.826
Total department unit cost	$8.00		$8.826	

Accounting for Total Costs

Molding department:
  Transferred out (33,000 × $8.00) $264,000
Work-in-Process, ending:
  Materials (7000 × $4.40) $ 30,800
  Conversion (3500 × $3.60)   12,600   43,400
Total molding department costs
  accounted for $307,400

Testing department:
  Transferred out (28,000 × $8.826) $247,128
  Work-in-Process, ending:
    Transferred-in cost (5000 × $8.00) $ 40,000
    Conversion (2500 × $0.826)   2,065   42,065
Total testing department
  costs accounted for $289,193 #

---

* 7000 units 50% converted

† 3000 units 50% converted

‡ Includes direct labor of $83,200 and applied factory overhead of $41,600

§ Includes direct labor of $16,800 and applied factory overhead of $8,400

Answer reflects $7 rounding error ($289,200 − $289,193).

the cost of production reports prepared for Micro Systems Co. in 19x3 and 19x4, when it was a single department company. First, there are two cost components (materials and conversion) added to units processed by the Molding Department. However, when units are transferred to the Testing Department, these costs are combined and called **transferred-in costs,** with no further separation into materials and conversion costs. Additional conversion costs are added to transferred-in costs in the Testing Department.

The total cost per unit transferred out of the Testing Department into finished goods in 19x5 is computed by adding the Testing Department conversion cost of $0.826 per unit and transferred-in costs of $8 per unit for a total unit cost of $8.826. Another way to get the total unit cost of $8.826 is to add the Molding Department materials cost of $4.40 and conversion cost of $3.60 to the conversion cost of $0.826 added in the Testing Department. Exhibit 11–9 presents the cost of production reports for Molding and Testing in a combined format to make it easier to see the transfer of costs from Molding to Testing. Most companies, however, ordinarily prepare separate reports for each department.

SUMMARY

Product costing is the process of assigning costs to inventories as they flow through the manufacturing process. The costs assigned to manufactured products establish the values reported in the external financial statements for Work-in-Process and Finished Goods Inventories, and Cost of Goods Sold expense. Product cost information is also useful in many areas of internal management, such as product pricing, profit planning, and cost control.

Job-order costing and process costing are the two primary product costing methods used by manufacturing organizations. Job-order costing involves accumulating costs by specific jobs, or batches of product, and is used primarily by companies that have a noncontinuous manufacturing process or that manufacture on a custom-order basis. Process costing involves accumulating costs by the departments that manufacture a product in a continuous process. When units worked on are not completely processed in one period, process costing uses the concept of equivalent units in computing unit costs for the period. Both job-order costing systems and process costing systems ordinarily assign factory overhead to the product on the basis of a predetermined overhead rate.

Two methods are available in process costing for accounting for beginning Work-in-Process. The weighted average method combines beginning inventory costs with current costs and computes an average cost per equivalent unit in process. The FIFO method separates the inventory worked on during the current period into two batches for costing purposes. The first batch consists of beginning inventory. Upon completion in the current period, its total cost equals the beginning Work-in-Process balance plus the current costs required to complete the beginning inventory. The second batch consists of units started in the current period to which only current period costs are assigned. Therefore, units started and completed in the current period and units started in the current period but not completed contain only current period costs. The weighted average method is simpler to use than the FIFO method; moreover, in many cases the valuations for inventory and cost of goods sold will not differ significantly between the two methods.

For manufacturing processes involving two or more departments, costs transferred out of one department are carried forward to the next department as transferred-in costs. These costs are accounted for as a separate component by the receiving department in addition to materials and conversion costs added in the receiving department.

APPENDIX A
NORMAL FACTORY OVERHEAD ACCOUNTING

Many companies use an accounting method for factory overhead, called **normal factory overhead accounting,** that does not close the balance in factory overhead at the end of the accounting period. As indicated earlier, total factory overhead cost tends to be rather stable from year to year because many of the components of factory overhead are not related to the level of production activity. Accordingly, predetermined overhead rates based on predicted activity for each year will vary if production activity is expected to change from year to year. For example, assume that a company predicts its factory overhead costs to be fixed at $100,000 per year. When predicted activity is 25,000 direct labor hours, the factory overhead rate is $4; when predicted activity is 20,000 direct labor hours, the factory overhead rate is $5. This difference will affect gross profit for the product and may affect managers' evaluations of firm profitability.

Assume that it takes 1 direct labor hour to make 1 finished unit, and that direct materials and direct labor costs total $10 per unit. If the product sells for $18 per unit, the gross profit per unit decreases from $4 to $3 when direct labor hours (the factory overhead activity base) are decreased from 25,000 to 20,000:

	Overhead based on direct labor hours	
Direct labor hours	25,000	20,000
Selling price per unit	$18	$18
Direct materials and direct labor per unit	$10	$10
Factory overhead per unit (1 hr per unit)	4	5
Total cost per unit	−14	−15
Gross profit per unit	$ 4	$ 3

To illustrate further the impact of annual estimated factory overhead rates on reported profits, assume that the above company produced 25,000 units in 19x3 operating at a production level of 25,000 direct labor hours and produced 20,000 units in 19x4 operating at a production level of 20,000 units. Also, assume that actual sales for each of the two years was 22,500 units. The gross profit for each of the two years is presented below.

	19x3	19x4
Sales (22,500 units at $18)	$405,000	$405,000
Cost of goods sold:		
(22,500 units at $14)	−315,000	—
(2500 units at $14 left over from 19x3 plus 20,000 units at $15)	—	−335,000
Gross profit	$ 90,000	$ 70,000

In this example gross profit varied by $20,000 in successive years that had the same amount of sales. The difference was caused entirely by the variation in the production level for the two years. In 19x4 the total fixed cost was spread over 5000 fewer units, causing the cost per unit produced to be $1 higher than the units produced in 19x3. As discussed in Chapter 10, most managers feel that profits should not vary with the production activity level, but rather with changes in sales. Uniform unit costs from year to year will be achieved only if the production level is uniform and the factory overhead rate is based on annual predicted production activity. For the above company, the expected cost of producing a unit would be $15 each year only if it maintained its production level at 20,000 units each year.

In most manufacturing situations the operating level cannot be held constant. It is likely to vary from year to year because of fluctuating demand for the product, or other factors such as difficulty in obtaining raw materials, or the work force going on strike during the year. It would be infeasible, and in many cases impossible, to maintain production at a constant level just to keep product cost at a uniform level.

The effect of uniform production levels on unit production costs can be achieved by using a factory overhead rate based on a long-run normal production activity level. If the company above normally operated at a level of 25,000 direct labor hours, under normal overhead accounting $4 per unit would be used in costing the product, even in years when the production level is different from 25,000 direct labor hours. Using a normal factory overhead rate, the gross profit statements for 19x3 and 19x4 would appear as follows:

	19x3	19x4
Sales (22,500 units at $18)	$405,000	$405,000
Cost of goods sold (22,500 units at $14)	−315,000	−315,000
Gross profit	$ 90,000	$ 90,000

From the standpoint of profit measurement, the use of a normal overhead rate clearly overcomes the problem of fluctuating profits caused by fixed costs and fluctuating production levels. But how do normal overhead rates affect the entries in the cost system? In the example above the normal rate was based on estimated factory overhead costs of $100,000 and normal production activity of 25,000 direct labor hours. In 19x3, when production activity was actually 25,000 direct labor hours and actual factory overhead costs were $100,000, the Factory Overhead account appeared as follows:

Factory Overhead

Actual costs 100,000	100,000 Applied costs

In 19x4, with a production level of 20,000 direct labor hours and using the normal factory overhead rate of $4 per direct labor hour, applied factory overhead was $80,000, which produced a balance in Factory Overhead of $20,000, as shown below.

Factory Overhead

Actual costs 100,000	80,000 Applied costs
Underapplied 20,000 factory overhead	

Unlike the treatment discussed in this chapter for disposing of the underapplied or overapplied factory overhead balance, when normal overhead rates are used, any balance left in Factory Overhead at the end of the period is not closed out. Because fluctuations in production activity are expected to occur from time to time, it is anticipated that over a period of years the underapplied and overapplied factory overhead amounts will offset each other. Therefore, these amounts are usually not closed out to Cost of Goods Sold or to the inventory accounts, but instead are reported on the balance sheet as Deferred Charges (if underapplied) or as Deferred Credits (if overapplied). If the underapplied or overapplied Factory Overhead balance is a material amount, generally accepted accounting principles do not permit it to be carried forward on the balance sheet for financial accounting purposes. In this case the balance should be either closed to Cost of Goods Sold or allocated to Cost of Goods Sold and the inventory accounts.

APPENDIX B
PRODUCT COSTING USING STANDARD COSTS

In Chapter 8 we discussed the concept of standard costs and developed a model for computing standard cost variances. The main focus of that discussion of standard costs and variance analysis was cost control and management performance evaluation. Standard costs are often integrated into the product costing system in which they are used for inventory valuation. When this is done, the manufacturing accounts are charged with standard costs instead of actual costs, and the differences between standard costs and actual costs are recorded as standard cost variances. These variances are then disposed of in a manner similar to the disposition of underapplied and overapplied factory overhead, which was discussed in this chapter.

To illustrate standard product costing, assume that Execupens, Inc. (discussed in Chapter 8) uses standard costs in costing its only product, gold casings for writing pens. For product costing purposes, standard costs usually include both variable costs and fixed costs. Therefore the standard product cost of one casing is $77, consisting of $68 of variable costs and $9 of assigned fixed costs:

Materials (6 gm at $8)	$48
Direct labor (1 hr at $14)	14
Variable overhead (1 hr at $6)	6
Total variable cost	$68
Fixed overhead (1 hr at $9)	9
Standard cost per unit	$77

The fixed overhead rate of $9 is computed by dividing budgeted annual fixed overhead of $198,000 by 22,000 standard direct labor hours allowed for a normal level of 22,000 units of output. Execupens' transactions for March, 19x6, summarized from Chapter 8, were as follows:

- There were no beginning or ending units in process.
- 124,000 grams of materials were purchased at $7.96 per gram for a total of $987,040.
- All 124,000 grams of materials were issued to processing.
- The direct labor payroll was $284,928 for 19,200 hours, an average of $14.84 per hour.
- Actual overhead costs were $126,000 variable and $200,000 fixed.
- 20,000 units were produced during the year.
- 16,000 units were sold.

Standard Cost Variances

The standard cost variances for Execupens, Inc. are summarized below. These variances were computed and discussed in Chapter 8.

Materials purchased price variance	$ 4,960 F
Materials quantity variance	32,000 U
Labor rate variance	16,128 U
Labor efficiency variance	11,200 F
Variable overhead spending variance	10,800 U
Variable overhead efficiency variance	4,800 F
Fixed overhead budget variance	2,000 U
Fixed overhead volume variance	18,000 U

Journal Entries

The cost of materials purchases are usually recorded at standard cost with any price variance recognized at the time of purchase. The entry to record Execupens' materials acquisitions at the time of purchase is as follows:

Journal entry

Raw Materials	992,000	
Materials Purchased Price Variance		4,960
Accounts Payable		987,040
To record at standard cost, $8, the purchase		
of 124,000 grams of gold.		

As units are transferred out of processing to finished goods inventory, the following entry is made.

	Journal entry		
	Finished Goods Inventory	1,540,000	
	Work-in-Process		1,540,000
	To record completion of 20,000 units at the standard cost of $77.		

As units are sold, the following entry is made to record the cost of goods sold.

Journal entry

Cost of Goods Sold	1,232,000	
Finished Goods Inventory		1,232,000
To record the Cost of Goods Sold and decrease in Finished Goods Inventory at the standard cost of $77 for 16,000 units sold.		

At the end of the period when actual costs are determined, the following entries are made to assign costs to Work-in-Process, to recognize actual costs, and to record standard cost variances. Work-in-Process is debited for the standard cost per unit for the 20,000 units produced in the following entries for materials, labor, variable overhead, and fixed overhead.

Journal entries

Work-in-Process (20,000 × $48)	960,000	
Materials Quantity Variance	32,000	
Raw Materials		992,000
To record raw materials cost assigned to Work-in-Process at standard cost.		
Work-in-Process (20,000 × $14)	280,000	
Labor Rate Variance	16,128	
Labor Efficiency Variance		11,200
Wages Payable		284,928
To record direct labor assigned to Work-in-Process at standard cost.		
Work-in-Process (20,000 × $6)	120,000	
Variable Overhead Spending Variance	10,800	
Variable Overhead Efficiency Variance		4,800
Factory Overhead		126,000
To record variable factory overhead assigned to Work-in-Process at standard cost.		
Work-in-Process (20,000 × $9)	180,000	
Fixed Overhead Budget Variance	2,000	
Fixed Overhead Volume Variance	18,000	
Factory Overhead		200,000
To record fixed factory overhead assigned to Work-in-Process at standard cost.		

Notice in the journal entries that *unfavorable variances* are recorded as *debits* and *favorable variances* are recorded as *credits*. Unfavorable variances are viewed as current manufacturing costs incurred but not charged to processing, whereas favorable variances are viewed as excess charges of manufacturing costs to processing. At the end of the period after standard manufacturing costs and the cost variances have been recorded, it is necessary to dispose of the balances in the variance accounts. Probably the most common procedure for disposing of standard cost variances is to close them out with the net variance debited or credited to Cost of Goods Sold. Another method sometimes used is to allocate them pro rata among Work-in-Process, Finished Goods, and Cost of Goods Sold. This is the same procedure that was discussed earlier for allocating overapplied and underapplied factory overhead.

KEY TERMS

Product costing system

Raw materials
   inventory record

Materials requisition form

Direct labor ticket

Finished goods
   inventory record

Job cost sheet

Cost of production report

Equivalent completed units

Weighted average
   inventory method

FIFO inventory method

Transferred-in costs

REVIEW QUESTIONS

11–1 How are the cost measurements that are generated by the product costing system used in financial accounting? In management accounting?

11–2 Name three types of inventories and three components of product cost in a manufacturing organization.

11–3 Trace the flow of manufacturing costs through the inventory accounts into Cost of Goods Sold.

11–4 Describe the difference between job-order and process costing in terms of the production level and time period for which costs are accumulated.

11–5 What is the function of job-cost sheets, and what is their relationship to work-in-process inventory?

11–6 Name the job-order cost system records that provide supporting detail for the following general ledger accounts: Raw Materials, Work-in-Process, Finished Goods Inventory, and Cost of Goods Sold.

11–7 Which record in a process cost system provides cost data used to record the transfer of completed goods from work-in-process to finished goods?

11–8 Present the general equation for computing a predetermined factory overhead rate.

11–9 What are the primary benefits of using a predetermined factory overhead rate?

11–10 Briefly explain two methods for disposing of underapplied or overapplied factory overhead.

11–11 For each of the following examples of factory overhead rates, name the production activity base and describe the probable characteristics of the company's manufacturing process: $3 per direct labor hour, 25 percent of direct labor cost, and $0.80 per machine hour.

11–12 Explain the difference between equivalent units in process and equivalent units manufactured.

11–13 Contrast weighted average and FIFO process costing in terms of the treatment of beginning work-in-process inventory.

11–14 Present the general equation for computing cost per equivalent unit for the weighted average method and the FIFO method.

11–15 Under what circumstances will a department show "transferred-in cost" in its cost of production report?

EXERCISES

11–1 Job-Order Cost System and Predetermined Factory Overhead

The following information was taken from the job cost sheet for Job 101 for A-1 Sign Company.

Date started: December 27, 19x3
Date completed: January 13, 19x4

Date	Direct Materials	Direct Labor	Factory Overhead	Job Total
12–27–x3	$1,400			
12–30–x3		$ 370		
12–31–x3			$ 296	
1–04–x4	250	480		
1–11–x4		250		
1–13–x4		150	704	
Totals	$1,650	$1,250	$1,000	$3,900

Requirements

a) Prepare the journal entries to record the costs incurred for Job 101 in 19x4 for direct materials, direct labor, and factory overhead.

b) Prepare the journal entry to record the completion of Job 101.

c) Assume that A-1 Sign Company applies factory overhead costs at the end of each month and as jobs are completed on the basis of direct labor cost. What is its predetermined factory overhead rate?

11–2 Factory Overhead Account Entries

The December 31, 19x4 Factory Overhead account for Athens Manufacturing Company is as follows:

Factory Overhead

265,000	250,000
Balance 15,000	

Requirements

a) What were the actual factory overhead costs?

b) How much factory overhead cost was applied to Work-in-Process?

c) What does the $15,000 balance represent?

d) Describe two alternatives that are available for disposing of the $15,000 balance.

e) Which of the alternatives in requirement (d) will result in the largest net income for the year? Explain.

11–3 Cost of Production Report: No Beginning Inventories

Rider Paving Products Company manufactures asphalt paving materials for highway construction through a single-step process in which all materials are added at the beginning of the process. During October 19x4, Rider accumulated the following data in its process costing system.

Production data:	
Work-in-process, October 1	0 tons
Raw materials transferred to processing	25,000 tons
Work-in-process, October 31 (75% converted)	5,000 tons
Cost data:	
Raw materials transferred to processing	$300,000
Conversion costs:	
Direct labor cost incurred	14,375
Factory overhead applied	?

Factory overhead is applied at the rate of $1 per equivalent unit (ton) processed.

Required: Prepare a cost of production report for October, 19x4. (Round calculations to four decimal places.)

11–4 Equivalent Units Computations

During February 19x5, Apex Co. had 15,000 units of product in its Mixing Department, of which 3000 were still in process (25 percent converted) at the end of the period.

Requirements

a) Determine the equivalent units in process for conversion costs assuming that there was no beginning inventory.

b) Determine the equivalent units in process for conversion costs assuming that 2800 of the 15,000 units were in beginning work-in-process, 30 percent converted, and that Apex uses weighted average costing.

c) Determine the equivalent units manufactured for conversion costs assuming that 2800 of the 15,000 units were in beginning work-in-process, 30 percent converted, and that Apex uses FIFO costing.

11–5 Job-Order Costing and Process Costing Applications

For each of the following situations indicate whether job-order or process costing is more appropriate and why.

a) A building contractor for residential dwellings.

b) A manufacturer of nylon yarn that sells to textile companies that make fabric.

c) A clothing manufacturer that makes suits in several different fabrics, colors, styles, and sizes.

d) A hosiery mill that manufactures one product that fits all sizes.

e) A vehicle battery manufacturer that has just received an order for 500,000 identical batteries to be delivered as manufactured over the next twelve months.

11–6 Costing Work-in-Process and Finished Goods Using Weighted Average Costing

Wadkins Manufacturing Company makes one product that is produced on a continuous basis in one department. All materials are added at the beginning of production. The total cost per equivalent unit in process in March 19x4 was $4.60, consisting of $3 for materials and $1.60 for conversion. During the month, 10,000 units of product were transferred to finished goods inventory, and on March 31, 2000 units were in process, 10 percent converted. Wadkins uses weighted average costing.

Requirements

a) Determine the cost of goods transferred to finished goods inventory.

b) Determine the cost of the ending work-in-process inventory.

c) What was the total cost of the beginning work-in-process, plus the current manufacturing costs?

11–7 Normal Factory Overhead (Appendix)

Chippendale Furniture Company predicted factory overhead to be $5 million for 19x6. Predicted production activity measured in direct labor hours was 400,000 hours. This level of activity is below the normal five-year average activity level of 500,000 hours. Planned production reductions for the year were made because of expected lower sales caused by a national economic recession. The recession is expected to end in a few months.

Requirements

a) If Chippendale uses a predetermined factory overhead rate based on predicted actual activity, what is the application rate?

b) If the predetermined factory overhead rate is based on long-term normal activity, what is the application rate?

c) If a normal factory overhead rate is used and the actual activity is 400,000 direct labor hours (as predicted), and if actual factory overhead costs are $5 million (as predicted), what is the balance in Factory Overhead at the end of the year?

d) What are the alternative methods of disposing of the balance determined in requirement (c)?

PROBLEMS

11–8 Manufacturing Cost Flows: Journal Entries

Springfield Manufacturing Co. completed the following transactions with respect to its manufacturing operations during November, 19x5.

- Raw materials costing $60,000 and manufacturing supplies costing $12,000 were purchased on account.

- A total of $30,000 of raw materials were requisitioned to the factory for manufacturing operations conducted during November.

- Manufacturing payroll for the month consisted of 2250 hours of direct labor and 400 hours of indirect labor, both at $10 per hour.

- Manufacturing supplies costing $3000 were used.

- Depreciation on the factory building and equipment was $15,000.

- Miscellaneous factory overhead expenses totaled $3600 for November.

- Factory overhead cost was applied to Work-in-Process at the rate of $11 per direct labor hour.

- Units of product with a total manufacturing cost of $45,000 were completed and transferred to the finished goods warehouse.

- Finished goods costing $36,000 were sold during November.

Requirements

a) Prepare journal entries for each of the transactions that occurred during November, 19x5.

b) Prepare T-accounts for the ledger accounts used in recording the transactions in requirement (a), and post all entries to the appropriate accounts.

11–9 Job-Order Costing: Journal Entries

Tri-star Publishing Company prints sales fliers and catalogs for retail and mail-order companies. Production costs are accounted for using a job-order cost system. At the beginning of June, 19x5, two jobs were in process, Job 425 with assigned costs of $13,750 and Job 426 with assigned costs of $1800. The following information summarizes manufacturing activities for June.

- Raw materials costing $80,000 were purchased on account.

- Manufacturing supplies costing $9000 were purchased on account.

- Raw materials and manufacturing supplies requisitioned during June were as follows:

Raw materials:	
Job 426	$ 2,400
Job 427	18,000
Job 428	14,400
Total direct materials	$34,800
Factory supplies	6,500
Total	$41,300

■ Salaries and wages were recorded as follows:

Direct labor (4800 hr at $10 per hr):	
Job 425	$ 5,000
Job 426	15,000
Job 427	20,000
Job 428	8,000
Total direct labor cost	$48,000
Indirect labor cost	7,000
Total payroll	$55,000

■ Depreciation of $5000 was recorded on the plant and equipment.

■ Miscellaneous factory overhead costs of $8750 were incurred on account.

■ Factory overhead was applied to production at the rate of $5 per direct labor hour.

■ Jobs 425, 426, and 427 were completed.

Requirements

a) Prepare journal entries to record the manufacturing activities for June, 19x5.

b) Compute the balance in Work-in-Process at June 30. Show the job cost breakdown by individual jobs to support the balance in Work-in-Process and Finished Goods Inventory.

11–10 Job-Order Costing and Predetermined Factory Overhead: Journal Entries

United Fabricators accounts for production using a job-order cost system. Actual costs for direct materials and direct labor are assigned to the jobs; however, factory overhead costs are assigned using a predetermined rate based on machine hours. Annual factory overhead for 19x4 was predicted at the beginning of the year to be $40,000. Predicted machine hours for the year were 5000. The following information is provided for the jobs worked on during November, 19x4.

	Job 1007	Job 1008	Job 1009
Work-in-Process, November 1	$10,500	$8,000	$4,200
November production activity:			
Materials requisitioned (units)	1,200	1,400	
Materials cost per unit	$4	$5	$3
Direct labor hours	250	1,800	400
Direct labor cost per hour	$8	$8	$8
Machine hours	1,250	2,000	1,500

Actual November factory overhead costs were $43,000.

Requirements

a) Prepare journal entries to record direct materials and direct labor assigned to production during November.

b) Compute the predetermined factory overhead rate.

c) Prepare the journal entry to apply factory overhead costs to Work-in-Process.

d) Assuming Jobs 1007 and 1008 were completed during November, what was the total cost for each job?

e) Assuming there was no November 1 balance in Factory Overhead, what was the balance at November 30? Does the balance represent overapplied or under-applied factory overhead?

11–11 Predetermined Factory Overhead: Determination of Rate and Disposition of Balance

The Dunwoody Company has decided to use a predetermined rate to assign factory overhead costs to production. Based on several years' experience the following predictions have been made for the current year, 19x4.

Predicted total factory overhead costs	$270,000
Predicted direct labor hours	30,000 hours
Predicted direct labor costs	$300,000
Predicted machine hours	45,000 hours

Requirements

a) Compute the predetermined factory overhead rate under three different bases: (1) direct labor hours, (2) direct labor costs, and (3) machine hours.

b) Assume that actual factory overhead costs were $298,000 and that Dunwoody elected to apply factory overhead to Work-in-Process based on direct labor hours. If actual direct labor was 32,000 hours for 19x4, was factory overhead overapplied or underapplied? By how much?

c) The Dunwoody Company follows the policy of writing off any under- or overapplied factory overhead balance to Cost of Goods Sold at the end of the year. Make the entry necessary at the end of 19x4 to dispose of the factory overhead balance determined in requirement (b).

11–12 Job-Order Costing with Predetermined Factory Overhead Rate

Avondale Foundries uses a job-order costing system and a predetermined factory overhead rate based on machine hours. For 19x4 predicted total factory overhead cost is $120,000 and predicted total machine usage is 20,000 hours. During the year the following activities were completed. There were no beginning inventories. Each ton of raw materials makes one ton of finished product.

- Purchased 2000 tons of raw materials at $150 per ton.
- Purchased manufacturing supplies for $38,000.
- Issued to work-in-process 1500 tons of raw materials and $32,000 in manufacturing supplies.
- Used 18,000 labor hours at $12 per hour and 22,000 machine hours. Ten percent of the total labor was indirect.
- Recorded the following manufacturing costs:

Depreciation	$32,500
Utilities	15,000
Maintenance and repairs	8,500
Miscellaneous	7,800
Total	$63,800

- Completed jobs with a total cost of $510,000 during 19x4.
- Jobs costing $480,000 were sold during 19x4.

Requirements

a) Prepare the journal entries to record the manufacturing activities for Avondale Foundries for 19x4.

b) Prepare a T-account for Factory Overhead showing the actual and applied factory overhead. Indicate whether the balance represents under- or overapplied factory overhead.

c) Prepare the journal entries to dispose of the under- or overapplied factory overhead under two separate assumptions:

1. It is written off to Cost of Goods Sold.
2. It is allocated to Work-in-Process, Finished Goods Inventory, and Cost of Goods Sold. (Round calculations to three decimal places.)

11–13 Disposition of Factory Overhead Balance

The Mouser Company had the following selected account balances (all debit balances) at the end of 19x4.

Work-in-Process	$ 55,000
Finished Goods Inventory	75,000
Cost of Goods Sold	370,000
Factory Overhead	32,000

Requirements

a) Was factory overhead cost underapplied or overapplied in 19x4? Explain.

b) Prepare the journal entry to dispose of the Factory Overhead balance assuming it is written off to Cost of Goods Sold.

c) Prepare the journal entry to dispose of the Factory Overhead balance assuming it is allocated among Work-in-Process, Finished Goods Inventory, and Cost of Goods Sold.

d) Which method of disposing of under- or overapplied factory overhead cost is more accurate? Explain.

11–14 Selecting a Basis for Factory Overhead Application

Delicious Peach Company operates a peach processing and packing plant consisting of two departments, Grading and Packaging. The grading process is carried out primarily by an automated system that separates the fruit based on size and firmness. Packing the fruit is done primarily by hand. Delicious has decided to apply factory overhead costs to Work-in-Process using a predetermined rate. The following information has been collected for both departments at the beginning of 19x5.

	Grading	Packaging
Predicted factory overhead costs	$40,000	$ 25,000
Predicted direct labor hours	2,000	25,000
Predicted direct labor costs	$12,000	$120,000
Predicted machine hours	20,000	5,000

Requirements

a) Compute a predetermined factory overhead rate for each department for each of the following bases:

1. Direct labor hours
2. Direct labor costs
3. Machine hours

b) Which method (or methods) is probably best suited for each department? Explain.

11–15 Process Costing: No Beginning Inventories

Selected production and cost data for April, 19x4, the first month of operations for Clark Manufacturing Company, are presented below.

Raw materials transferred to processing	8,500 units
Completed and transferred to finished goods	6,000 units
Direct materials cost debited to Work-in-Process	$29,750
Direct labor cost debited to Work-in-Process	$54,000

Each unit of production requires one unit of raw materials, which is added at the beginning of the process. Factory overhead is applied to Work-in-Process based on 40 percent of direct labor cost. Units in ending Work-in-Process were 30 percent converted.

Requirements

a) Determine the number of equivalent units in process for April for (1) materials and (2) conversion.

b) Determine the total cost per equivalent unit in process.

c) Determine the total cost of (1) units completed and transferred to finished goods and (2) units in process at the end of the month.

11–16 Process Costing: Computation of Manufacturing Costs

The Universal Company determined the cost per equivalent unit in process for materials to be $6 for August, 19x5. There were no inventories at the beginning of August. There were 25,000 units finished during the period and ending work-in-process contained 5000 units 80 percent converted. The combined cost of units finished and units in ending work-in-process was $299,625. Factory overhead is applied at the rate of 25 percent of direct labor cost. All materials are added at the beginning of the process.

Requirements

a) Determine the equivalent units in processing for materials and conversion costs.

b) Determine the total current cost incurred for (1) direct materials, (2) direct labor, and (3) factory overhead.

c) Determine the cost per equivalent unit in process for materials and conversion costs.

11–17 Weighted Average Process Costing with Beginning Inventories: Production Report and Journal Entries

Chamblee Processing Company manufactures a product on a continuous basis in two departments, Processing and Finishing. All materials are added at the beginning of work on the product in the Processing Department. During December, 19x5, the following events occurred in the Processing Department.

- Units started .... 16,000 units
- Units completed and transferred to Finishing .... 15,000 units
- Costs assigned to Processing:

Raw materials (one unit of raw materials for each unit of product)	$142,000
Manufacturing supplies used	18,000
Direct labor costs incurred	67,000
Supervisors' salaries	12,000
Other production labor costs	14,000
Depreciation on equipment	16,000
Other production costs	18,000

Additional information:

- Chamblee uses weighted average costing and applies factory overhead to Work-in-Process at the rate of 100 percent of direct labor cost.

- Ending inventory in the Processing Department consists of 3000 units that are one-third converted.

- Beginning inventory contained 2000 units one-half converted, with a cost of $27,300 ($17,300 for materials and $10,000 for conversion).

Requirements

a) Prepare a cost of production report for the Processing Department for December.

b) Prepare all journal entries to record costs incurred by the Processing Department in December and to record the transfer of units to the Finishing Department. Overapplied or underapplied factory overhead is written off to Cost of Goods Sold at the end of each month.

11–18 Cost of Production Report: FIFO and Beginning Inventories

Agrikill Chemical Co. manufactures a patented chemical product called WPK that is used by farmers to kill weeds and pests. WPK is produced through a continuous process, entirely in one department, with all materials added at the beginning of processing. Production and cost data for the company for February, 19x8 are as follows:

Production data:	
In process, beginning of month (50% converted)	15,000 units
Started during February	95,000 units
Completed and transferred to finished goods	100,000 units
In process, end of month (40% converted)	10,000 units
Manufacturing costs:	
Work-in-process, beginning	$ 55,000
Raw materials transferred to processing	275,000
Conversion costs:	
Direct labor cost for February	80,000
Factory overhead (applied at the rate of $1 per equivalent unit processed)	?

Required: Prepare a cost of production report for February, 19x8. (Round calculations to three decimal places.)

11–19 Process Costing: Work-in-Process Analysis: FIFO Costing

Karkare Products, Inc. manufactures automobile polish through a process involving two departments (Mixing and Bottling). All materials are added at the beginning of the Mixing Department process. Factory overhead is applied at the rate of 125 percent of direct labor costs. The Work-in-Process account for the Mixing Department for May, 19x5 is presented below.

Work-in-Process:
Mixing

May 1 balance (100,000 units, 40% converted)	120,000	(c) ?	Finished and transferred to Bottling Department (a) (? units)
May costs assigned:			
Raw materials (400,000 units)	460,000		
Direct labor	(b) ?		
Factory overhead	125,000		
May 31 balance (60,000 units, 45% converted)	(d) ?		

Required: Determine the values for the missing items lettered (a) through (d) in the Mixing Department Work-in-Process account. Assume the company uses FIFO costing. Show all computations, and round calculations to three decimal places. *Hint:* You may want to prepare a cost of production report.

11–20 Work-in-Process Analysis: Weighted Average Costing

Determine the values of the missing items (a) through (d) in Problem 11–19 for Karkare Products, Inc. assuming the company uses weighted average costing. Also assume the raw materials portion of the beginning inventory had a cost of $1 per unit in process. (Round calculations to three decimal places.)

11–21 Process Costing: Two-Department Cost of Production Report

Atlantic Paper Company manufactures paper used in printing newspapers. The process involves two departments, Processing and Bleaching. Raw materials are added at the beginning of the Processing Department. Goods are transferred from the Processing Department to the Bleaching Department and from Bleaching to finished goods inventory. Production and cost data for Atlantic Paper Company are presented below for the month of January, 19x5.

	Processing	Bleaching
Production data (units):		
In process, January 1 ($33\frac{1}{3}$% converted in Processing, 25% converted in Bleaching)	150,000	80,000
Raw materials transferred to Processing	450,000	
Transferred to Bleaching from Processing	500,000	500,000
Transferred to Finished Goods		520,000
Cost data:		
Raw materials transferred to Processing	$3,600,000	
Conversion costs:		
Direct labor cost	2,000,000	$3,000,000
Factory overhead applied (210% of direct labor cost for Processing and 120% of direct labor cost for Bleaching)	4,200,000	3,600,000

Additional information:

- Assume that 1 unit of raw materials is required to produce 1 unit of product.
- Ending work-in-process inventory was 50 percent converted in the Processing Department and 20 percent converted in the Bleaching Department.
- The company uses weighted average costing.
- Beginning work-in-process consisted of the following:

	Processing	Bleaching
Raw materials	$1,125,000	
Transferred-in costs		$1,520,000
Conversion costs	575,000	242,400
Total	$1,700,000	$1,762,400

Requirements

a) Prepare a combined cost of production report for the Processing and Bleaching Departments using the format illustrated in Exhibit 11–9. (Round calculations to three decimal places.)

b) Prepare the journal entries to record (1) transfer of units from the Processing Department to the Bleaching Department and (2) the transfer of units from the Bleaching Department to finished goods inventory.

11–22 Manufacturing Cost Flows: Standard Cost System: Journal Entries (Appendix)

Konrad Company uses a standard cost system in accounting for the production of its only product, a gadget called "de-slicer" that attaches to golf clubs to help golfers hit the ball straighter. The standard cost of producing one de-slicer has been determined to be $7.65. During a recent month the following activities occurred:

- Raw materials with a standard cost of $72,000 were purchased for $75,000.
- There were 20,000 units completed during the month.
- There were 18,500 units sold during the month.

At the end of the month, actual manufacturing activities were summarized as follows:

- Actual raw materials issued to processing had a standard cost of $70,000. There was an unfavorable materials quantity variance of $2000.
- The standard cost of direct labor for the units produced during the period was $50,000, whereas actual direct labor cost was $47,500. The difference was caused by an unfavorable labor rate variance of $800 and a favorable labor efficiency variance of $3300.
- Actual factory overhead was $38,000 and the standard factory overhead allowed for the units produced was $35,000.

Factory overhead standard cost variances were as follows:

Variable overhead spending variance	$1,200 U
Variable overhead efficiency variance	1,100 F
Fixed overhead spending variance	1,400 F
Fixed overhead volume variance	4,300 U

Required: Prepare journal entries to record (1) the purchase of raw materials; (2) the completion of finished goods; (3) the sale of finished goods; and (4) actual and standard costs for direct materials used, direct labor, and factory overhead.

11–23 Job-Order Costing: Preparation of Statement of Cost of Goods Manufactured

The Helper Corporation manufactures one product and accounts for costs by a job-order cost system. You have obtained the following information for the year ended December 31, 19x3 from the corporation's books and records.

- Total manufacturing costs added during 19x3 were $1,000,000, based on actual direct materials, actual direct labor, and applied factory overhead based on actual direct labor dollars.

- Cost of goods manufactured was $970,000, also based on actual direct material, actual direct labor, and applied factory overhead.

- Factory overhead was applied to Work-in-Process at 75 percent of direct labor dollars. Applied factory overhead for the year was 27 percent of the total manufacturing cost.

- Beginning Work-in-Process at January 1 was 80 percent of ending Work-in-Process at December 31.

Requirements

a) Prepare a formal statement of cost of goods manufactured for the year ended December 31, 19x3 for Helper Corporation. Use actual direct materials used, actual direct labor, and applied factory overhead. Show supporting computations.

b) Job 37, manufactured entirely in 19x3, had $2500 of direct labor cost and $5700 of direct materials cost. What was the total cost of manufacturing Job 37?

(CPA Adapted)

11–24 Multiple-Choice Questions: Job-order and Process Costing

1. Worrell Corporation has a job-order cost system. The following debits (credits) appeared in the general ledger account Work-in-Process for the month of March, 19x2.

March 1, balance	$ 12,000
March 31, direct materials	40,000
March 31, direct labor	30,000
March 31, factory overhead	27,000
March 31, to Finished Goods	(100,000)

Worrell applies overhead to production at a predetermined rate of 90 percent based on direct labor cost. Job No. 232, the only job still in process at the end of March 19x2, has been charged with factory overhead of $2250. What was the amount of direct materials charged to Job No. 232?

a) $2250

b) $2500

c) $4250

d) $9000

2. Information for the month of January 19x2, concerning Department A, the first stage of Ogden Corporation's production cycle, is as follows:

	Materials	Conversion
Work-in-Process, beginning	$ 8,000	$ 6,000
Current costs	40,000	32,000
Total costs	$ 48,000	$38,000
Equivalent units in process using weighted average method	100,000	95,000
Average unit costs	$ 0.48	$ 0.40
Goods completed	90,000 units	
Work-in-process, ending	10,000 units	

Materials are added at the beginning of the process. The ending work-in-process inventory was 50 percent complete in conversion costs. How would the total costs accounted for be distributed using the weighted average method?

	Units Completed	Ending Work-in-Process
a)	$79,200	$6,800
b)	$79,200	$8,800
c)	$86,000	—
d)	$88,000	$6,800

3. Richardson Company computed the flow of physical units completed for Department M for the month of March, 19x2 as follows:

Units completed:	
From work-in-process on March 1, 19x2	15,000
From March production	45,000
Total	60,000

Materials are added at the beginning of the process. The 12,000 units of work-in-process at March 31, 19x2 were 80 percent complete in conversion costs. The work-in-process at March 1, 19x2 was 60 percent complete in conversion costs. Using the FIFO method, what were the equivalent units for March conversion costs?

a) 55,200

b) 57,000

c) 60,600

d) 63,600

4. Tooker Company adds materials at the beginning of the process in Department A. Information concerning the materials used in April, 19x2 production is as follows:

Work-in-process at April 1	10,000 units
Started during April	50,000 units
Completed and transferred to next	
department during April	36,000 units
Work-in process at April 30	24,000 units

Using the weighted average method, what are the equivalent units for the materials unit cost calculation for the month of April?

a) 52,000

b) 55,000

c) 57,000

d) 60,000

5. Roy Company manufactures product X in a two-stage production cycle in Departments A and B. Materials are added at the beginning of the process in Department B. Roy uses the weighted average method. Conversion costs for Department B were 50 percent complete in the 6000 units in the beginning work-in-process and 75 percent complete in the 8000 units in the ending work-in-process. During February, 19x0, 12,000 units were completed and transferred out of Department B. An analysis of the Work-in-Process costs and production activity in Department B for February, 19x0 is as follows:

	Transferred-in	Materials	Conversion
Work-in-Process, February 1	$12,000	$2,500	$1,000
February costs incurred	29,000	5,500	5,000

What was the total cost per equivalent unit of product X transferred out for February 19x0 (rounded to the nearest penny)?

a) $2.75

b) $2.78

c) $2.82

d) $2.85

(CPA Adapted)

11–25 Process Costing: Two-Department Cost of Production Report

The Dexter Production Company manufactures a single product. Its operations are a continuing process carried on in two departments — Machining and Finishing. In the production process, materials are added to the product in each department without increasing the number of units produced. For the month of June, 19x5, the company records indicated the following production statistics for each department.

	Machining	Finishing
Units in process, June 1	—	—
Units transferred from previous department	—	60,000
Units started in production	80,000	—
Units completed and transferred out	60,000	50,000
Units in process, June 30	20,000	10,000
Percent of completion of units in process at June 30:		
Materials	100	100
Conversion	50	70
Cost records showed the following charges for the month of June:		
Materials	$240,000	$ 88,500
Labor	140,000	141,500
Overhead	65,000	25,700

Required: Prepare a combined cost of production report for the Machining and Finishing Departments for June, 19x5. (Round calculations to three decimal places.)

(CPA Adapted)

11–26 Process Costing with Beginning Inventories: FIFO Method

Zeus Company has two production departments — Fabricating and Finishing. In the Fabricating Department, Polyplast is prepared from Miracle Mix and Bypro. In the Finishing Department, each unit of Polyplast is converted into six Tetraplexes and three Uniplexes. The Fabricating and Finishing Departments use process cost systems. Actual production costs are assigned monthly to Work-in-Process. Raw materials and work-in-process inventories are costed on a FIFO basis. The following data were taken from the Fabricating Department's records for December, 19x1.

Quantities (units of Polyplast):	
In process, December 1	3,000
Started in process during the month	25,000
Total units to be accounted for	28,000
Transferred to Finishing Department	19,000
In process, December 31	9,000
Total units accounted for	28,000
Cost of work-in-process, December 1:	
Materials	$ 13,000
Labor	17,500
Overhead	21,500
Total	$ 52,000
Direct labor costs for December	$154,000
Factory overhead for December	$198,000

Polyplast work-in-process at the beginning and end of the month was partially completed as follows:

	Materials	Conversion
December 1	66⅔%	50%
December 31	100%	75%

The following data were taken from raw materials inventory records for December.

	Miracle Mix		Bypro	
	Quantity	Amount	Quantity	Amount
Balance, December 1	62,000	$62,000	265,000	$18,550
Purchases:				
December 12	39,500	$49,375		
December 20	28,500	$34,200		

The Fabricating Department used 83,200 units of Miracle Mix and 50,000 units of Bypro during the month.

Requirements

a) Compute the equivalent number of units of Polyplast manufactured during December, with separate calculations for materials and conversion.

b) Compute the following items to be included in the Fabricating Department's cost of production report for December, 19x1, with separate calculations for materials and conversion. Prepare supporting schedules.

1. Total costs to be accounted for.
2. Unit costs for equivalent units manufactured. (Round calculations to three decimal places.)
3. Transfers to Finishing Department during December and Work-in-Process at December 31. Reconcile your answer to requirement (b1).

(CPA Adapted)

12

The Assignment of Common Costs

In Chapter 2, *cost objectives* were defined as the objects or activities to which costs are assigned. All cost measurements involve assigning costs to cost objectives. Management may be concerned with determining the cost of constructing a building, or with manufacturing 500 units of inventory, or with that of operating the personnel department. These are all examples of cost assignment.

Cost assignment is complicated by two main problems: (1) the existence of multiple cost objectives and (2) the inability to relate costs directly with the specific cost objectives for which they were incurred. To illustrate the first problem, assume that a company with a centralized corporate computer system assigns the costs of computer services to all operating units as well as to the product (for computer monitored machinery). The manufacturing division consists of three levels of operations: product lines, plants, and departments within plants. When one of the plant departments uses the computer, the costs incurred must be assigned to all the cost objectives for the various responsibility center managers. In addition, the costs must be recognized in the product costing system for measuring the cost of manufacturing the inventory. Computer operations costs must also be assigned to the computer center cost objective to provide a basis for evaluating the computer center manager's performance.

The second problem is also illustrated by the above example. When computer services are used by a production department, it is impossible to measure directly the exact costs assignable to the department. As computer services are provided, many costs are incurred. For instance things such as including equipment lease and depreciation costs, electricity, operators' labor costs, building costs, intangible software development costs, insurance, taxes, and so forth. These costs cannot feasibly be traced directly to each user of computer services. Many of them, however, can be traced directly to the computer center. Consequently, all these costs are assigned to the computer center cost objective and are subsequently reassigned to the various users in a manner similar to how factory overhead is allocated to production.

By assigning the costs initially to the computer center cost objective, computer operations costs are included in the performance report of the computer center manager. By reassigning the costs to the users, the managers of the operating departments are held responsible for the amount of computer services they consume. And by including the assigned computer costs in the production department factory overhead rates, these costs are applied to the product.

The purpose of this chapter is to discuss the nature and basic concepts of common cost allocation, as well as its uses and limitations. The allocation of manufacturing service department costs is also discussed, including various allocation techniques. Finally, there is a brief discussion of the assignment of corporate home office costs and of common costs in not-for-profit organizations.

THE NATURE OF COMMON COSTS

Costs are incurred at many different levels within an organization. Manufacturing costs, for example, may be incurred at the following levels: plant administration (plant manager's costs), plant services (maintenance, personnel, and cafeteria costs), production departments (direct department costs), and jobs (direct product costs). All costs are directly assignable to a cost objective at some level. When initially incurred, costs are charged, or assigned, to the cost objectives to which direct assignment can be made. For this reason, when raw materials are issued, their costs are assigned to specific departments and jobs, whereas the costs of cleaning supplies (which cannot be traced to specific jobs) are assigned to departments as overhead. Departmental overhead is then allocated, or reassigned, to the products using an overhead application rate. This is an example of common cost allocation.

Common costs then are costs incurred at a given level for the benefit of two or more cost objectives. For the factory mentioned above with four levels of cost objectives, three separate common cost allocations are required for *product costing purposes*. First, Plant Administration costs are allocated to the service and production departments that are supervised by the manager. Second, service department costs (including Plant Administration cost allocations) are allocated to the producing departments that receive the services. Third, all production department overhead costs (including allocated service department costs) are applied to the product.

To summarize, at the point of incurrence all costs are directly assignable to some cost objective, even though the initial assignment may be to a general cost objective (such as factory overhead) that exists only for the purpose of facilitating reassignment to other cost objectives. When costs are incurred for the specific benefit of a given cost objective, the costs are said to be direct costs. Costs assigned to a cost objective by allocation from another cost objective are indirect costs. Hence, a **direct department cost** is a cost assigned to a department upon its incurrence, and an **indirect department cost** is a cost reassigned to a department from another cost objective. In the example above, the plant manager's salary is a direct department cost to the Plant Administration Department, and the reassigned Plant Administration Department costs are indirect department costs to the service departments. All service department costs are indirect department costs when reassigned to the production departments.

USES AND LIMITATIONS OF COMMON COST ASSIGNMENTS

For product costing purposes all manufacturing costs must be assigned to the product under the full absorption costing method. Full cost assignment to the product can be achieved only through the indirect assignment of all manufacturing costs not directly traceable to the product. However, just because costs are reassigned to a department for product costing purposes does not mean that these cost allocations can be used effectively for other purposes, such as cost control and performance evaluation.

For control purposes, costs should be reported at the level at which they are *controllable* — that is, at the *level of incurrence*. For example, even though the costs of operating the plant manager's office are appropriately allocated to the production departments for product costing purposes, they should not be included in the production department performance and cost control reports. Serious management morale problems may result if managers are held responsible for costs over which they have no control.

Indirect cost allocations may be made simply to inform managers of the cost of services they are receiving so that managers will not feel the services are free. Such assignments designed to provide information to managers are often useful; however, they should not be used for performance evaluation purposes unless managers have some control over the amount of services received or over the costs incurred in providing the services. Managers will resist any cost allocations for services over which they have no control. Even if cost allocations can be justified for performance evaluation purposes, they should be based on the *standard cost* of services provided, not on the basis of *actual costs* incurred. Allocating standard costs prevents actual cost inefficiencies from being passed on to the users of the services.

In other cases, the costs of services are intentionally not allocated to user departments to encourage managers to take full advantage of service departments. For example, if top management is trying to encourage managers to increase computer applications in their departments, computer center costs may intentionally not be allocated to users, or they may be allocated at arbitrarily very low rates.

Indirect department costs should be used carefully when considering the overall profitability of a particular department or segment of a company. As discussed in Chapters 5 and 10, assigned costs that are unavoidable (and thus continue to be incurred whether or not the department is continued) should be disregarded in measuring the department's contribution to total company profits. To illustrate, assume that a department store's Toy Department reported a loss of $3000 for the year, after deducting a cost allocation of $5000 for the store manager's salary. The store manager's salary will be incurred whether or not the Toy Department continues; therefore, this cost should be ignored in a decision regarding continuation of the department. The department is contributing $2000 (before the $5000 unavoidable expense allocation) to the overall profitability of the store; therefore, overall profit will decline by that amount if the department is discontinued (assuming there is no alternative use for the space).

The key to using allocated common costs effectively is recognizing their uses and limitations. Allocated costs are fundamentally different from direct controllable costs and thus should be treated differently by users of cost information.

ALLOCATION OF COMMON COSTS

A major difference between direct cost assignments and indirect cost allocations is related to measurement precision. Initial cost assignment is a *direct measurement* of costs incurred for a specific cost objective, whereas subsequent indirect allocations are, at best, *estimates* of the costs incurred for the services provided to each cost objective.

To illustrate indirect cost allocation, assume that Company X has a factory with two departments, A and B. Labor cost can be traced to a specific department for all employees except the factory manager, who earns $30,000 per year. If Company X wants to assign all costs to the departments, the factory manager's salary must be reassigned to departments A and B using an allocation base. One possibility is to make the allocation according to the number of employees in each department, which is a reasonable basis if most of the factory manager's time is spent dealing with employee-related problems. If there are 20 employees in Department A and 30 employees in Department B, 40 percent (20 ÷ 50) of the factory manager's salary, or $12,000, would be allocated to Department A and 60 percent (30 ÷ 50), or $18,000, would be allocated to Department B.

Since common cost allocations are just estimates of the actual costs incurred for each cost objective, the amount assigned to a given cost objective is only as reliable as the allocation system used. Frequently, allocated costs are combined with direct costs (such as in product costing); therefore, any error in the allocation of common costs affects not only the allocated cost component but also the total cost for the cost objective.

For a better understanding of common cost allocation, it is necessary to examine further the basic components of common cost allocation systems. These basic components are as follows:

- Cost objectives
- Cost pools
- Allocation bases

In the example of Company X, the two plant departments are the *cost objectives,* the factory manager's salary is the *cost pool,* and the number of employees in the departments is the *allocation base.*

COST OBJECTIVES

Before cost pools and allocation bases can be determined, it is necessary to know the objectives to which costs are to be allocated. In establishing cost objectives, management should consider potential allocation problems

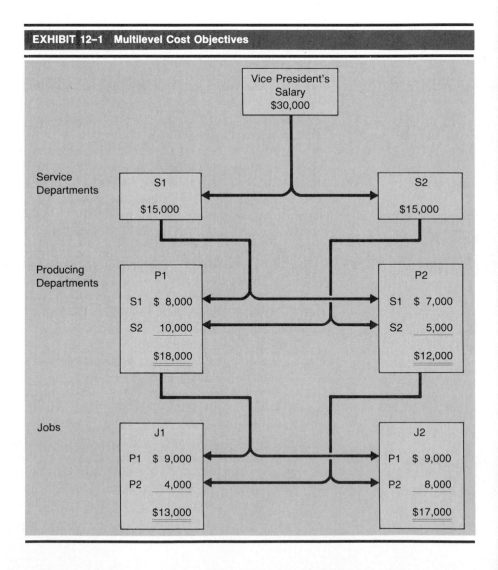

EXHIBIT 12–1   Multilevel Cost Objectives

that may be encountered. Managers often feel that accountants have an unlimited ability to measure costs — that they can measure the cost of every activity, product, service, and operating component of the business. Although it is true that anything that has a cost is subject to cost measurement, consideration should always be given to the efforts and benefits of providing the cost measurement, as well as to the reliability of the cost information.

To illustrate how costs flow through the various cost objectives, assume that a company vice president who earns $30,000 per year supervises the managers of two service departments, which, in turn, provide services for two producing departments. During the year the company worked on two separate production jobs.

Exhibit 12–1 shows how the vice president's salary might be allocated through three levels of cost objectives — service departments, producing departments, and jobs. The $30,000 is allocated first to the service department cost objectives, then to the producing department cost objectives, and finally to the job cost objectives. It should be noted that Exhibit 12–1, for illustrative purposes, follows one cost item through all three levels of cost objectives. In the normal course of events other costs would be combined with the vice president's salary in the service department cost pools. Similarly, other costs would be combined with the allocations shown in the producing department cost pools and the job cost pools.

COST POOLS

A **cost pool** is a group of common costs, such as factory overhead, that is allocated to other cost objectives. As a practical matter it is not feasible in many situations to allocate each item of cost (such as the factory manager's salary) separately. Instead, several similar costs are combined into a cost pool, and the entire pool is allocated as a single item. Common costs are often pooled along departmental lines, such as payroll department costs, computer center costs, or maintenance department costs. Pooling all common labor-related costs or building-related costs, or the costs for any other natural function, is also frequently done. Sometimes these functional cost pools are referred to as departments even though they may not exist as such on the organization chart. For example, all building-related costs (depreciation, insurance, repairs, etc.) are often pooled together to form building department costs, which are then allocated to the departments that use the building.

The key consideration in establishing cost pools is that the items pooled together should be relatively homogeneous and have a logical *cause-and-effect* relation to the allocation base. For instance, a building cost pool would include all costs related to the maintenance and operation of the building and might be allocated on the basis of square footage occupied. The costs in this pool, such as insurance, property taxes, and depreciation have a logical cause-and-effect relation to the amount of square footage provided. As the square footage increases, these costs are naturally expected to increase.

Within functional cost pools it may be useful to provide separate pools for fixed costs and variable costs. For example, instead of forming one cost pool for the maintenance department, fixed maintenance department costs might be accumulated in one pool, and variable maintenance department costs might be accumulated in another. Using separate pools gives greater flexibility in selecting allocation bases — fixed costs may be allocated on one basis and variable costs on another.

To illustrate common cost allocation for fixed and variable costs, assume that Alco Manufacturing Company has one factory with three producing departments: Stamping, Assembly, and Inspection. There is also a Maintenance Department that provides services to the producing departments. Costs incurred by the Maintenance Department are allocated to the producing departments each period in separate pools for fixed costs and variable costs. Fixed costs consist of maintenance staff salaries, depreciation, insurance, and utilities on the maintenance shop facilities. Variable costs consist of supplies and parts used in performing maintenance services for the producing departments. Maintenance Department costs for 19x3 were as follows:

Fixed costs	$60,000
Variable costs	37,500
Total Maintenance Department costs	$97,500

Five hundred standard hours of services were performed for the three producing departments as follows:

Stamping Department	250
Assembly Department	200
Inspection Department	50
Total standard service hours	500

In setting up the Maintenance Department, Alco's management decided on a maintenance service *capacity* of 800 standard service hours per year. This capacity was based on a maximum need of 400 hours for the Stamping Department, and 200 hours each for the Assembly and Inspection Departments. It was also determined that *fixed costs* should be allocated to the producing departments on the basis of *capacity provided* for each depart-

---

EXHIBIT 12–2   Allocation of Fixed and Variable Costs Allocation

---

Fixed Cost Allocation

| Department | Capacity Provided | | Total Fixed Cost | | Fixed Cost Allocation |
	Service Hours	Percent			
Stamping	400	50	× $60,000	=	$30,000
Assembly	200	25	× 60,000	=	15,000
Inspection	200	25	× 60,000	=	15,000
Total	800	100			$60,000

Variable Cost Allocation

Department	Actual Service Hours		Variable Cost per Hour*		Variable Cost Allocation	Percent of Allocation
Stamping	250	×	$75	=	$18,750	50
Assembly	200	×	75	=	15,000	40
Inspection	50	×	75	=	3,750	10
Total	500				$37,500	100

Total Maintenance Department Cost Allocation

Department	Fixed Cost	Variable Cost	Total Allocation
Stamping	$30,000	$18,750	$48,750
Assembly	15,000	15,000	30,000
Inspection	15,000	3,750	18,750
Total	$60,000	$37,500	$97,500

* Variable cost per service hour:

Total variable cost		Number of hours used		Variable cost per hour used,
$37,500	÷	500	=	$75.

---

ment, and that *variable costs* should be allocated on the basis of *actual usage* of Maintenance Department services. Exhibit 12–2 shows the allocation computations for fixed and variable Maintenance Department costs. The fixed cost allocation percentages reflect the cost of the capacity provided for each department, whereas the variable cost allocation percentages reflect the variable costs actually incurred for each department during the period.

ALLOCATION BASES

The allocation base is the connecting link between cost objectives and cost pools. The **allocation base** is the factor, or characteristic, common to the cost objectives that determines how much of the cost pool is assigned to each cost objective. The allocation base selected varies depending on the nature of the common costs and the nature of the cost objectives. For example, labor-related costs may be allocated according to some measure (or estimate) of the labor time devoted to the various cost objectives, and depreciation and other building-related costs are often allocated on the basis of square footage occupied. Other examples of common costs and frequently used allocation bases include the following:

Cost Category	Allocation Base
Employee health services	Number of employees or calls
Personnel	Number of employees or new hires
Plant and grounds	Square footage occupied
Maintenance repairs	Number of repair orders
Purchasing	Number of orders placed
Warehouse	Square footage used or value of materials stored.

The most important consideration in selecting an allocation base is making sure there is a logical association between the base selected and the costs incurred. For instance, it is logical to allocate personnel department costs according to the number of employees because the function of the personnel department is to provide employee-related services to the various departments. Thus personnel costs are incurred as these services are provided. It follows that departments with a large number of employees should ordinarily receive a larger allocation of personnel department costs than departments with few employees.

Another consideration in selecting an allocation base is whether to reflect the service capacity provided or only the actual services used. Refer to Exhibit 12–2, where we use different bases for allocating fixed and variable costs. Fixed costs are allocated based on the capacity provided, and variable costs are allocated according to the actual services used. Basing fixed costs on capacity provided eliminates the possibility that the amount of the cost allocation to one department is affected by the level of services utilized by other departments. In Exhibit 12–2, the Assembly Department used 200 service hours during the year, equaling the capacity provided for it. The 200 hours represent 25 percent (200 hours ÷ 800 hours) of the total capacity of the service department, but they represent 40 percent (200 hours ÷ 500 total actual hours) of the total actual services rendered. If fixed costs were allocated based on actual services used rather than on capacity provided, $24,000 (40 percent of the fixed costs), instead of $15,000, would be allocated to the Assembly Department. This additional charge of $9000 results from other producing departments failing to use the capacity provided for them. When fixed service department costs are allocated according to capacity provided, managers of producing departments are charged for the capacity provided whether they use it or not, and their use of services has no effect on the amount of costs allocated to other departments. A benefit of this allocation system is that it reduces the temptation for managers to avoid or delay services in order to minimize fixed cost allocations to their departments.

SERVICE DEPARTMENT COST ALLOCATION

A **service department** is generally a department that provides support functions for one or more production departments. Examples of service departments are maintenance, personnel, payroll, cost accounting, internal audit, data processing, food services, and health services. These departments, which are considered essential elements in the overall manufacturing process, do not work directly on the "product," but they do provide auxiliary support to the producing departments. In addition to providing support for the various producing departments, some service departments also provide services to *other service departments.* For example, the payroll and personnel departments may provide services for all departments, both production and service; data processing may provide services only for other service departments; and cost accounting may provide services for the producing departments as well as limited services for food and health services. Services provided by one service department to other service departments are called **interdepartmental services.**

Three methods are discussed in this section for allocating service department costs: the *direct method,* the *step method,* and the *linear algebra method.* To illustrate each method we will allocate common service department costs for the Kona Kola Company for 19x3. Kona Kola has two producing departments, Mixing and Bottling, and three service departments. The service departments and their respective service functions and cost allocation bases are as follows:

Department	Service Functions	Allocations Base
Administrative Services	Accounting, audit, payroll, and inventory control	Total department capital investment
Human Resources	Personnel, training, and health services	Number of employees
Plant and Facilities	Maintenance, security, depreciation, and insurance	Square footage occupied

Kona Kola readily determined the appropriate allocation bases for the Human Resources Department and the Plant and Facilities Department; however, for Administrative Services the choice was much less clear. Because of the diversity of services provided by this department, no logical allocation base emerged as the obvious choice. After conducting correlation studies it was determined that the most equitable base for allocating Administrative Services costs was total capital investment in each department. Although this base does not correlate closely with each of the cost components incurred in the department, the company felt it represented a good compromise that should be acceptable to management at all levels and for all cost assignment purposes.

Difficulty in choosing an allocation base for service department costs is not uncommon. This example simply illustrates that when there is no obvious allocation base an effort should be made to find a substitute that is both *realistic and fair* in distributing costs to the various producing departments. *If an appropriate allocation base cannot be found, the decision to allocate the costs should be reconsidered.*

The data used to illustrate the service department cost allocations for Kona Kola Company for 19x3 are summarized below.

	Direct Department Costs	Number of Employees	Square Footage Occupied	Department Capital Investment
Service departments:				
Administrative Services	$ 27,000	15	4,000	$ 75,000
Human Resources	20,000	10	2,000	45,000
Plant and Facilities	10,000	5	3,000	50,000
Producing departments:				
Mixing	40,000*	24	11,000	180,000
Bottling	90,000*	56	33,000	270,000
Total	$187,000	110	53,000	$620,000

* Direct department overhead

Direct Allocation Method

The **direct method** allocates all service department costs directly to the producing departments without any recognition of interdepartmental services. Exhibit 12–3 shows the flow of costs using the direct allocation method. Note that all arrows depicting the cost flows extend only from service departments to producing departments; there are no cost allocations between the service departments.

Exhibit 12–4 shows the service department cost allocations for the direct method. To explain the basic approach of the direct method, notice the cost allocations of the Human Resources department based on the number

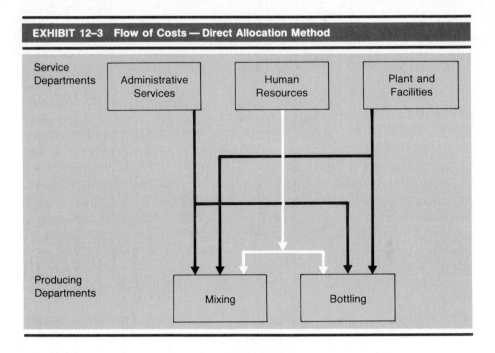

EXHIBIT 12–3   Flow of Costs — Direct Allocation Method

Service Departments: Administrative Services | Human Resources | Plant and Facilities

Producing Departments: Mixing | Bottling

of employees. Only the number of employees in the producing departments is considered in computing the allocation percentages — 24 in the Mixing Department and 56 in the Bottling Department, for a total of 80 employees. Thirty percent (24 ÷ 80) of the producing department employees work in the Mixing Department; therefore, 30 percent of the Human Resources Department costs are allocated to the Mixing Department. Applying the same reasoning, 70 percent of the Human Resources Department costs are allocated to the Bottling Department. Similar logic is followed in computing the cost allocations for the Plant and Facilities Department and the Administrative Services Department.

The cost allocation summary at the bottom of Exhibit 12–4 shows that all service department costs have been allocated, increasing the producing department balances by the amounts of the respective allocations. Also note that total direct costs are not affected by the allocations — the total of $187,000 was merely redistributed so that all costs are assigned to the producing departments.

The total department costs of the producing departments after allocation of service department costs are $59,300 for the Mixing Department and $127,700 for the Bottling Department. These amounts represent the total actual factory overhead costs for the producing departments for the period. If Kona Kola applies actual factory overhead costs to production,

EXHIBIT 12-4   Service Department Cost Allocations — Direct Allocation Method

		Total	Mixing	Bottling
Administrative Services Department:				
Allocation base (capital investment)		$450,000	$180,000	$270,000
Percent of total base		100%	40%	60%
Cost allocation		$ 27,000	$ 10,800	$ 16,200
Human Resources Department:				
Allocation base (number of employees)		80	24	56
Percent of total base		100%	30%	70%
Cost allocation		$ 20,000	$ 6,000	$ 14,000
Plant and Facilities Department:				
Allocation base (square footage occupied)		44,000	11,000	33,000
Percent of total base		100%	25%	75%
Cost allocation		$ 10,000	$ 2,500	$ 7,500

Cost Allocation Summary:

	Administrative Services	Human Resources	Plant and Facilities	Mixing	Bottling	Total
Department costs before allocations	$27,000	$20,000	$10,000	$40,000	$ 90,000	$187,000
Cost allocations:						
Administrative Services	(27,000)			10,800	16,200	—
Human Resources		(20,000)		6,000	14,000	—
Plant and Facilities			(10,000)	2,500	7,500	—
Department costs after allocations	$ —	$ —	$ —	$59,300	$127,700	$187,000

these amounts will be applied to the Mixing Department and Bottling Department Work-in-Process accounts at the end of the period. If the company uses a predetermined overhead rate, the difference between the overhead applied and total actual overhead costs (after service department cost allocations) is the underapplied or overapplied Factory Overhead balance.

Step Allocation Method

Unlike the direct method, which gives no recognition to interdepartmental services, the **step method** of allocating service department costs gives at least partial recognition to interdepartmental services among service departments. Under the step method, first management determines the service department that provides the most interdepartmental services. Costs for that department are then allocated to the other service departments and the producing departments. The service department whose costs are allocated first receives no allocations from other service departments even though it may receive services from them. Costs for the service department allocated second (including costs received from the first department) are allocated to the remaining service departments (excluding the first department) and to the producing departments. Costs for the last service department to be allocated (including all costs received from other service departments) are allocated only to the producing departments.

Exhibit 12–5 shows the flow of costs for Kona Kola Company under the step allocation method. Notice that Human Resources costs are allocated to the remaining two service departments and to the producing departments. Administrative Services costs are allocated to Plant and Facilities and to the producing departments. Plant and Facilities costs are allocated only to the producing departments.

Although there is no generally accepted rule for determining the order for allocating service department costs under the step method, as explained above costs for the department that provides the most services to other service departments are usually allocated first. Allocations of other service department costs follow in order based on their relative levels of *interdepartmental services*.

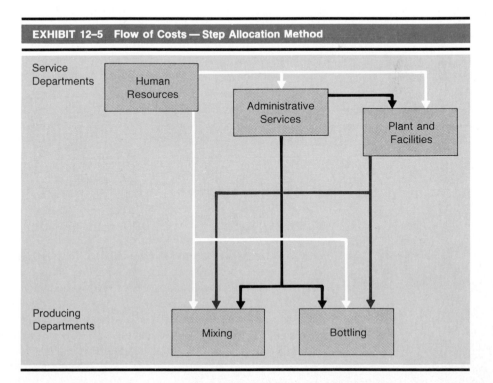

EXHIBIT 12–5   Flow of Costs — Step Allocation Method

EXHIBIT 12–6   Allocation Sequence for Step Allocation Method

	Administrative Services	Human Resources	Plant and Facilities
Allocation base	Capital investment	Number of employees	Square footage
(a) Total base for other service and producing departments	$545,000	100	50,000
(b) Total base for other service departments	$ 95,000	20	6,000
Portion of total services provided to other service departments			
((b) ÷ (a))	17.4%	20%	12%
Allocation sequence	Second	First	Third

Exhibit 12–6 shows the computations for determining the sequence of cost allocations for Kona Kola's service departments. The measure of services provided by the service departments is stated in terms of the *allocation base*. For example, the services provided by the Administrative Services Department are measured in terms of total investment. The total investment in all departments other than Administrative Services is $545,000, and the total investment in other service departments is $95,000. Therefore, in terms of its allocation base, Administrative Services provided 17.4 percent ($95,000 ÷ $545,000) of its total services to other service departments. The total investment in all departments of $545,000 excludes the investment in Administrative Services, since only services to other departments are considered. The amounts of interdepartmental services are 20.0 percent for Human Resources and 12.0 percent for Plant and Facilities; therefore, the sequence of allocation of service department costs under the step method is Human Resources first, followed by Administrative Services and then Plant and Facilities.

Allocation of service department costs using the step method is shown in Exhibit 12–7. The mathematical procedures are essentially the same as in the direct method. Notice, however, that under the step method the allocation base includes the appropriate base measure for the producing and service departments to which costs are allocated. For example, the Human Resources cost allocation base includes the number of employees in the producing departments and the other service departments. For Administrative Services, the base includes capital investment for the producing departments and for the Plant and Facilities Department. For Plant and Facilities, the base includes only the square footage for the producing departments since its costs are allocated to only these departments.

EXHIBIT 12–7 Service Department Cost Allocations — Step Allocation Method

	Total	Administrative Services	Plant and Facilities	Mixing	Bottling
Human Resources Department:					
Allocation base (number of employees)	100	15	5	24	56
Percent of total base	100%	15%	5%	24%	56%
Cost allocation	$ 20,000	$3,000	$ 1,000	$ 4,800	$ 11,200
Administrative Services Department:					
Allocation base (capital investment)	$500,000		$50,000	$180,000	$270,000
Percent of total base	100%		10%	36%	54%
Cost allocation	$ 30,000		$ 3,000	$ 10,800	$ 16,200
Plant and Facilities Department:					
Allocation base (square footage occupied)	44,000			11,000	33,000
Percent of total base	100%			25%	75%
Cost allocation	$ 14,000			$ 3,500	$ 10,500

Cost Allocation Summary:

	Human Resources	Administrative Services	Plant and Facilities	Mixing	Bottling	Total
Department costs before allocation	$20,000	$27,000	$10,000	$40,000	$ 90,000	$187,000
Cost allocations:						
Human Resources	(20,000)	3,000	1,000	4,800	11,200	—
Administrative Services		(30,000)	3,000	10,800	16,200	—
Plant and Facilities			(14,000)	3,500	10,500	—
Department costs after allocation	$ —	$ —	$ —	$59,100	$127,900	$187,000

Notice in Exhibit 12–7 that under the step method the total cost allocated from each service department includes the department's direct costs plus any costs received in previous allocations from other service departments. Since Human Resources costs are allocated first, they include only direct department costs. However, Administrative Services costs include $27,000 of direct department costs plus $3000 of costs allocated from Human Resources. Plant and Facilities costs include $10,000 of direct department costs plus allocations of $1000 from Human Resources and $3000 from

Administrative Services. These interdepartmental cost allocations are summarized at the bottom of Exhibit 12–7.

Linear Algebra Method

The *direct method* provides an easy way of allocating the costs of service departments to producing departments. Its primary weakness is that it does not recognize *any* interdepartmental services among service departments. This weakness is not crucial so long as all service departments are providing approximately the same level of services to all producing departments. When the quantity of services provided to the producing departments is significantly disproportionate, the service department cost allocations may be distorted using the direct method.

The *step method* recognizes interdepartmental services *only partially* because a service department cannot receive an allocation from other departments once its costs have been allocated. Although the step method overcomes much of the distortion inherent in direct allocations, significant distortions may remain under some circumstances. The only sure way of eliminating all distortions of this type is to recognize all interdepartmental services simultaneously.

The **linear algebra** method allocates all service department costs simultaneously to service departments and to producing departments. To use this method, a linear algebraic equation is developed for each service and production department. Each equation represents total departmental costs, that is, direct department costs plus a percentage of allocated service department costs. To illustrate the equations, assume a company has two service departments (S1 and S2) and two producing departments (P1 and P2). The percentage distribution of services is shown below for each department.

Services Provided from	Services Provided to				Total
	S1	S2	P1	P2	
S1	—	5%	40%	55%	100%
S2	10%	—	30%	60%	100%

Total direct department costs for the service and producing departments are as follows:

S1	$ 20,000
S2	$ 35,000
P1	$150,000
P2	$ 90,000

The algebraic equations expressing the total costs (direct and allocated) for each department are as follows:

$$S1 = 20{,}000 + 0.10\ S2$$
$$S2 = 35{,}000 + 0.05\ S1$$
$$P1 = 150{,}000 + 0.40\ S1 + 0.30\ S2$$
$$P2 = 90{,}000 + 0.55\ S1 + 0.60\ S2$$

Using the substitution method, these equations are solved as shown below.
Substituting S2 into S1:

$$S1 = 20{,}000 + 0.10(35{,}000 + 0.05\ S1)$$
$$S1 = 20{,}000 + 3500 + 0.005\ S1$$
$$0.995\ S1 = 23{,}500$$
$$S1 = 23{,}618.$$

Substituting the solution of S1 into S2:

$$S2 = 35{,}000 + 0.05(23{,}618)$$
$$= 35{,}000 + 1{,}181$$
$$= 36{,}181.$$

Substituting the solutions of S1 and S2 into P1:

$$P1 = 150{,}000 + 0.40(23{,}618) + 0.30(36{,}181)$$
$$= 150{,}000 + 9{,}447 + 10{,}854$$
$$= 170{,}301.$$

Substituting the solutions of S1 and S2 into P2:

$$P2 = 90{,}000 + 0.55(23{,}618) + 0.60(36{,}181)$$
$$= 90{,}000 + 12{,}990 + 21{,}709$$
$$= 124{,}699.$$

How do we interpret these solutions? First, notice that the solutions to P1 and P2 consist of three components. P1 consists of $150,000 plus $9447 plus $10,854, and P2 consists of $90,000 plus $12,990 plus $21,709. For each of these producing department variables, the first component represents the *direct costs* of the department. The second component represents the allocation of S1 costs to the producing department after interdepartmental cost allocation, and the third component represents the allocation of S2 costs to the producing departments after interdepartmental cost allocation. These components are summarized as follows:

	Direct Department Costs	Allocated Costs		Total Producing Department Costs
		S1 Component	S2 Component	
P1	$150,000	$ 9,447	$10,854	$170,301
P2	$ 90,000	12,990	21,709	$124,699
Total allocations		$22,437	$32,563	
Less: Direct service department costs		−20,000	−35,000	
Net interdepartmental cost allocation		$ 2,437	$ (2,437)	

The net interdepartmental cost allocation consists of an allocation of $3618 from S2 to S1, and a $1181 allocation from S1 to S2.

	S1	S2
Value after interdepartmental allocation	$23,618	$36,181
Direct department costs	−20,000	−35,000
Cost allocation received	$ 3,618	$ 1,181
Net interdepartmental cost allocation		$2,437

A summary of all cost allocations among service departments and producing departments is shown below, and a diagram of these allocations is provided in Exhibit 12–8.

	S1	S2	P1	P2	Total
Department costs before allocation	$20,000	$35,000	$150,000	$ 90,000	$295,000
S1 allocation	(23,618)	1,181	9,447	12,990	—
S2 allocation	3,618	(36,181)	10,854	21,709	—
Department costs after allocation	$ —	$ —	$170,301	$124,699	$295,000

The substitution method of simultaneously solving linear equations is inefficient except in the simplest of situations (such as our example). Where there are more than two service departments providing interdepart-

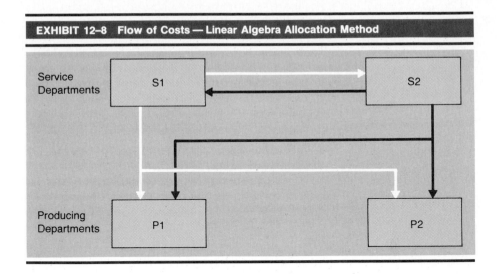

EXHIBIT 12–8   Flow of Costs — Linear Algebra Allocation Method

mental services, it is necessary to use matrix algebra for solving equations simultaneously. Using matrix algebra would also be very laborious were it not for the aid of computers. If you have access to a computer and software for solving matrix algebra problems, we recommend that you use them to solve the equations in our example. (A detailed discussion of matrix algebra is beyond the scope of this text.)

THE ALLOCATION OF NONMANUFACTURING COSTS

Many of the allocation concepts discussed in this chapter are often applied to nonmanufacturing costs in manufacturing organizations and to operating costs in service organizations, both for-profit and not-for-profit. Some of these applications are discussed below.

Home Office Expenses

Many top-level managers feel that all costs, including home office expenses, should be assigned for internal reporting purposes to the operating divisions of companies. **Home office expenses** consist of central corporate expenses, including the salaries of the president and other executive officers, public relations expenses (such as corporate advertising and corporate contributions), expenses of the legal and tax department, and corporate planning and development costs. The functions provided by these costs are vitally important to the operation of the organization, but some of these functions (such as the president's activities) are often not considered to directly benefit the operating divisions and profit centers. Because there is no direct association between profit producing functions and central home office functions, it is often difficult, if not impossible, to find a widely supported basis for allocating these costs to the divisions.

One of the most frequently used bases for allocating home office expenses is total revenues of the divisions. Using this basis, a division producing 30 percent of the company's total revenues is allocated 30 percent of all home office expenses, whereas another producing only 5 percent of total revenues is allocated just 5 percent. This allocation basis is often denounced by managers as a "soak the rich" approach that does not reflect an appropriate matching of effort and accomplishment. Managers of successful divisions argue that a disproportionate share of home office efforts is often devoted to struggling divisions and product lines, and to new or potential endeavors of the company, and not to the most successful divisions and product lines, which nevertheless carry the burden of cost allocation.

Despite the problems in making an equitable allocation of home office expenses, unfortunately many top managers feel that such allocations are important because they draw attention to the total cost of operating the business. Moreover, it is felt that home office cost allocation encourages managers to think in terms of total corporate profitability, not just of the profitability of their own areas. Allocation proponents emphasize that the company as a whole has not earned a profit until all costs, including home office costs, have been covered by revenues. Notwithstanding these alleged benefits, allocation of central corporate expenses is not the best means of achieving them unless division management perceives the allocation system to be fair and equitable. These favorable perceptions probably will not exist if top management uses broad, arbitrary allocation bases, such as total revenues or total profits. As in allocating manufacturing costs, the best results can be achieved only by relating the costs to the cost objectives on a logical cause-and-effect basis. For some home office costs, these bases may not exist.

Even if accurate and equitable allocations can be determined for home office costs, the problem of *imposed services* still should be considered. Frequently, managers feel that the services received from corporate headquarters are not beneficial to their divisions but are imposed by top management, and given the opportunity, they would elect not to buy them at any price. Even if managers believe the services are needed, some would prefer to control the acquisition of the services by purchasing them from sources outside the company. When attitudes like these prevail among a company's managers, probably little is gained from home office cost allocation. Ordinarily, these kinds of negative attitudes are prevalent only in companies where home office costs are allocated to division managers for performance evaluation purposes.

Not-for-Profit Applications

So far we have discussed cost assignment and allocation only in for-profit organizations. Many of the concepts and procedures introduced, however, can be generalized for use in not-for-profit organizations. Historically, not-for-profit accounting has been based on the concept of stewardship (or fund) accounting, which emphasizes the reporting of funds received and their disposition. The use of accounting data to determine the cost of services and to evaluate manager performance has not been widely practiced in not-for-profit organizations.

As we have seen in our discussions of for-profit organizations, the assignment of costs to various cost objectives may be useful in certain circumstances. In not-for-profit organizations, cost allocations may play an even more significant role than in for-profit organizations. Cost allocations may actually reduce the funds available to an agency or operating unit to carry on its programs. For example, the fire department of a small local municipality may have an annual budget of $300,000; however, the cost allocations for general city services to the department may use up $20,000 of the budget, leaving disposable funds of only $280,000. An academic department in a university may have no choice but to obtain computer services from the university's central computer system at a cost substantially higher than comparable services received from outside sources. Charges for these internal services ordinarily are made against the operating funds of the departments.

Because the actual procedures for allocating costs in not-for-profit organizations are essentially the same as those discussed in for-profit organizations, we will not present a detailed discussion. Below is a summary of frequently allocated costs and allocation bases of selected not-for-profit organizations.

Organization	Common Costs	Allocation Base
Hospital	Administration	Patient days
	Cafeteria	Meals served
	Operating room	Actual time used
City government	Municipal building	Space occupied
	Tax assessment and collection	Amount of budget appropriation
	Accounting	Number of transactions processed
University	Classroom costs	Class hours used
	Computer services	Actual or CPU time used
	Academic administration	Student credit hours
Church	Buildings and grounds	Space occupied
	Printing and publicity	Actual services received
	Office and administration	Amount of budget appropriation

SUMMARY

Costs incurred for the benefit of two or more cost objectives (such as products, plants, departments, and territories) are called *common costs*. These costs are often assigned to specific cost objectives through the process of *cost allocation*. Allocation of service department costs to the producing departments allows manufacturing organizations to assign all manufacturing costs to products. Cost allocations are also used for other purposes such as internal reporting and performance evaluation of managers. However, these applications of cost allocation are often accompanied by severe limitations. Managers usually resist being evaluated on the basis of costs over which they have little or no control. When top management uses common cost allocations to evaluate managers, it is important that lower level managers understand and support the allocation system.

The basic cost allocation model consists of three components: cost pools, cost objectives, and allocation bases. Common costs are combined into homogeneous pools of costs to prevent the need for separate allocation of similar costs. The allocation base relates the common costs to the cost objectives, and it provides a logical system for distributing the costs to the various cost objectives. Common costs may be fixed or they may vary with some measure of activity. Fixed common costs are often allocated on the basis of capacity provided, whereas variable costs are allocated according to actual benefits or services received.

Manufacturing organizations ordinarily have producing departments, in which the product is made, and service departments, such as personnel and maintenance, that provide support services to the producing departments. Since service departments are an essential part of the manufacturing process, their costs are usually allocated to the producing departments and included in factory overhead. The direct method allocates all service department costs to the producing departments without any recognition of interdepartmental services between the service departments. Whereas the *step method* gives only partial recognition to interdepartmental services, the *linear algebra method* provides *full recognition* of such services by using linear algebraic equations. Most of the cost allocation procedures discussed for manufacturing service departments can also be applied to nonmanufacturing costs and to common costs in nonmanufacturing organizations, including not-for-profit organizations.

APPENDIX
JOINT PRODUCTS AND BY-PRODUCTS

Joint products are two or more products produced simultaneously by a common manufacturing process. The costs of producing joint products are called **joint costs.** An example of joint products is crude oil products (such as gasoline, diesel, and kerosene) that are produced by a common refining process. Similarly, various chemical products are often produced by a single process. A **by-product** is a product with insignificant value that is produced jointly with one or more other products.

Joint Product Cost Allocation

For product costing purposes it is necessary to allocate joint product costs to the respective joint products. Joint cost allocation occurs at the split-off point in the production process. The **split-off point** is the point in the process where the joint products emerge as separate identifiable products. Any costs incurred in further processing of a joint product after split-off are specific product costs, *not joint costs.*

To illustrate joint cost allocation, assume Aem Enterprises manufactures two automotive fuel additives, Speedo and Econo, from a common manufacturing process. In August 19x3, Aem incurred joint costs of $24,000 in producing 8000 pints of Speedo and 12,000 pints of Econo, as is illustrated below.

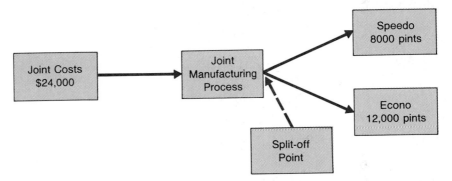

Two methods available for allocating joint costs are the physical quantity method and the sales value method. Under the **physical quantity method,** joint costs are allocated on the basis of relative quantities of a common physical characteristic possessed by the joint products. Physical characteristics used for joint cost allocation include the number of units of product, weight measures, and volume measures. For Aem Enterprises the unit measure (pint) is also a volume measure because 1 physical unit of product consists of 1 pint of volume measure. Under the physical quantity method, using pints of production as the allocation base, the allocated costs, $9600 for Speedo and $14,000 for Econo, are computed as follows:

Product	Quantity (pints)	Relative Quantity		Joint Cost		Allocation
Speedo	8,000	0.40	×	$24,000	=	$ 9,600
Econo	12,000	0.60	×	$24,000	=	14,400
	20,000	1.00				$24,000

Each product has a cost of $1.20 per pint ($9600 ÷ 8000 and $14,400 ÷ 12,000).

If Speedo sells for $3 per pint and Econo sells for $1 per pint, the gross profit for Speedo is $14,400, whereas Econo has a negative $2400 gross profit.

	Speedo	Econo	Total
Unit sales (pints)	8,000	12,000	20,000
Sales price per unit	$3	$1	
Sales	$24,000	$12,000	$36,000
Cost of goods sold	−9,600	−14,400	−24,000
Gross profit	$14,400	$ (2,400)	$12,000

Allocating joint costs on the basis of physical quantities produces a distortion in the gross profit computations any time the selling price per unit of quantity is not the same for all joint products. The reason for this distortion is that the physical quantity method assigns an *equal amount of cost* to each *unit of physical measure* — in this case to each pint — regardless of its selling price. If allocated on the basis of physical quantity, the cost per pint is $1.20 for both Speedo and Econo, but the selling price of Speedo is three times as much as Econo's selling price. Since together the products generate a total gross profit of $12,000, and one product cannot be produced without the other, it is unreasonable to assume that one is produced at a profit and the other is produced at a loss.

If selling prices vary significantly between the joint products, sales value is a more realistic basis for allocating joint costs. Under the **sales value method** each dollar of sales value for all products is assigned an equal amount of cost. The sales value method allocations for Speedo and Econo are as follows:

Product	Sales Value Computation	Amount	Relative Sales Value		Joint Cost		Allocation
Speedo	8,000 × $3 =	$24,000	0.667	×	$24,000	=	$16,000
Econo	12,000 × $1 =	12,000	0.333	×	$24,000	=	8,000
		$36,000	1.000				$24,000

Speedo has a cost of $2 per pint ($16,000 ÷ 8000), and Econo has a cost of $0.667 per pint ($8000 ÷ 12,000).

Using the costs for Speedo and Econo determined by the sales value allocation method, the respective gross profits are $8000 and $4000, as shown in the partial income statements below.

	Speedo	Econo	Total
Unit sales (pints)	8,000	12,000	20,000
Sales price per unit	$3	$1	
Sales	$24,000	$12,000	$36,000
Cost of goods sold	−16,000	− 8,000	−24,000
Gross profit	$ 8,000	$ 4,000	$12,000

Under the sales value method, the gross margin ratio is the same (one third of selling price) for both products; therefore, up to the point of split-off the joint products are considered to be *equally* profitable.

Additional processing may be required after split-off on some joint products. In this case the sales value method must be modified to allocate joint costs on the basis of net realizable value at the point of split-off rather than on the basis of sales value for completed units. Net realizable value is computed as ultimate sales value less additional processing costs incurred beyond the split-off point. For example, if $4000 of additional processing costs were required after split-off before the 8000 pints of Speedo could be sold for $24,000, the joint cost allocation would be made on the basis of relative net realizable values of $20,000 ($24,000 − $4000) for Speedo and $12,000 for Econo.

The decision of whether to continue with additional processing after split-off is unrelated to the cost allocation procedure. Sometimes additional processing is necessary before the product can be sold, in which case further processing ordinarily must be done. In other cases, the product may be sold either at split-off or after additional processing. The decision of whether to continue processing is based entirely on relevant cost analysis. If the additional revenue from processing exceeds the additional cost of processing, the product should be processed further; otherwise, the product should be sold at split-off. These relevant cost issues are discussed and illustrated in Chapter 5.

Accounting for By-products

A by-product is not treated as a joint product and therefore is not allocated costs in the joint cost allocation procedure. Production of by-products is not a major objective of the manufacturing process; it is a result of production of the main products. For example, a furniture factory primarily manufactures furniture, but it produces sawdust (which is saleable) as an inevitable and natural result.

If by-products do not generate revenues, which is the case for many waste by-products, there is no special accounting required other than recording any disposition costs as additional manufacturing expense. If by-products can be sold, and the selling price is insignificant, revenues from the sale of by-products are usually recorded either as other income or as a reduction of joint manufacturing costs. An alternative to this approach is to assign a portion of the joint costs to the by-products equal to the selling price of the by-products. The remaining joint processing costs are then allocated to the joint products by either the physical quantity or sales value method. By costing by-products at selling price, no profit or loss is recognized when they are sold.

Products initially considered to be by-products may later become main products as new uses and applications for them are discovered. When this occurs, the accounting treatment should be revised to reflect a change in assumptions and to begin allocating costs to the products as joint products.

KEY TERMS		
Direct department costs		**Interdepartmental services**
Indirect department costs		**Direct allocation method**
Cost pools		**Step allocation method**
Cost allocation base		**Linear algebra allocation method**
Service department		**Home office expenses**

APPENDIX KEY TERMS		
Joint products		**Split-off point**
Joint costs		**Physical quantity allocation method**
By-product		**Sales value allocation method**

REVIEW QUESTIONS

12–1 What are the primary purposes of cost assignment in a manufacturing organization?

12–2 Explain the difference between the terms cost assignment and cost allocation.

12–3 All costs are directly assignable to a cost objective at some level. Explain this statement.

12–4 Can a cost item be both a direct cost and a common cost at the same time? Explain.

12–5 Which type of cost assignment is more accurate, direct assignment or allocation? Explain.

12–6 Why are cost pools used in allocating common costs?

12–7 Describe two primary considerations in determining how common costs should be pooled.

12–8 What is the primary advantage of allocating fixed and variable common costs separately?

12–9 Give five examples of a cost objective.

12–10 What is the primary consideration in selecting a cost allocation base?

12–11 Identify a likely basis for allocating the following types of common costs: cafeteria costs, utility costs, plant manager's salary, cost of annual employee picnic.

12–12 Indicate the extent of recognition of interdepartmental services under the direct, step, and linear algebra methods of service department cost allocation.

12–13 What is the major limitation of the linear algebra allocation method?

12–14 Allocation of home office expenses on the basis of sales revenue is often characterized as a soak-the-rich approach. Explain.

12–15 Name three common costs that might require allocation if your college or university decided to compute the total cost of offering a section of management accounting.

EXERCISES

12–1 Selecting Cost Allocation Bases

Below is a list of service departments typically found in manufacturing and nonmanufacturing organizations.

Personnel	Payroll
Cafeteria	Building
Electricity	Maintenance
Computer Services	Security
Health Services	General Administration

Required: For each of the above service departments indicate the bases likely to be used to allocate costs to the producing departments.

12–2 Common Cost Allocation Computations

Las Vega Sign Company manufactures hotel signs through a process involving three departments — Molding, Fabrication, and Wiring. The following data were accumulated for 19x9 for these three departments.

	Molding	Fabrication	Wiring
Direct labor hours	10,000	38,000	2,000
Direct labor cost	$70,000	$400,000	$30,000
Number of employees	5	18	2
Square feet occupied	3,000	5,000	2,000

Total indirect costs incurred for the common benefit of all three departments in 19x9 were $150,000.

Required: Determine the common cost allocation for each department on the basis of the following:

1. Direct labor hours.

2. Direct labor cost.

3. Number of employees.

4. Square feet occupied.

12–3 Allocating Service Department Costs: Allocation Basis Alternatives

Clayton Glassworks has two producing departments, P1 and P2, and one service department, S1. Estimated direct overhead costs per month are as follows:

P1	$100,000
P2	200,000
S1	50,000

Other data:

	P1	P2
Number of employees	25	25
Production capacity (units)	50,000	30,000
Space occupied (sq ft)	2,500	7,500
Five-year average percent of S1's service output used	65%	35%

Required: Determine the total estimated overhead cost for P1 and P2 if S1 costs are allocated to the producing departments on each of the following bases:

1. Number of employees.

2. Production capacity in units.

3. Space occupied.

4. Five-year average percentage of S1 services used.

5. Estimated direct overhead costs. (Round your answer to the nearest dollar.)

12–4 Common Cost Allocation: Direct Method

The School of Business Administration of Alpha University consists of three academic departments and three service departments. The Dean of the School has asked you, his assistant, to compute the cost per student credit hour for each of the academic departments. Although the Dean gave no specific instructions on how to make the computations, you have decided that the service department costs should be allocated to the academic departments. You have accumulated the following data for the last school term to be used in the cost computations.

Department	Direct Cost	Allocation Base		
Service:				
Administration	$150,000	Number of faculty		
Student services	75,000	Number of students		
Faculty services	60,000	Number of credit hours		
		Number of Faculty	*Number of Students*	*Number of Credit Hours*
Academic:				
Accounting/Finance	$380,000	20	350	4,500
Management/Marketing	440,000	25	250	3,000
Economics/Quantitative methods	350,000	15	150	1,500

Requirements

a) Prepare a schedule allocating the service department direct costs to the academic departments.

b) Compute the total cost per student credit hour for each academic department.

c) Could the step method have been used with the information provided? Explain.

12–5
Interdepartmental Services: Step Allocation Method

O'Brian's Department Stores allocates the costs of the Personnel and Payroll Departments to three retail sales departments, Housewares, Clothing, and Furniture. In addition to providing services to the operating departments, Personnel and Payroll provide services to each other. O'Brian's allocates Personnel Department costs on the basis of the number of employees, and allocates Payroll Department costs on the basis of gross payroll. Cost and allocation information for June is as follows:

	Personnel	Payroll	Housewares	Clothing	Furniture
Direct department cost	$6,900	$3,200	$11,700	$19,500	$15,250
Number of employees	5	3	8	15	4
Gross payroll	$6,000	$3,300	$11,200	$17,400	$ 8,100

Requirements

a) Determine the percentage of total Personnel Department services that was provided to the Payroll Department.

b) Determine the percentage of total Payroll Department services that was provided to the Personnel Department.

c) Prepare a schedule showing Personnel Department and Payroll Department cost allocations to the operating departments assuming O'Brian's uses the step allocation method. (Round calculations to the nearest dollar.)

12–6 Service Department Cost Allocations: Direct Method

Portland Manufacturing Company has five operating departments, two of which are producing departments (P1 and P2), and three of which are service departments (S1, S2, and S3). All costs of the service departments are allocated to the producing departments. The table below shows the distribution of services from the service departments.

Services Provided from	Services Provided to				
	S1	S2	S3	P1	P2
S1	—	5%	25%	50%	20%
S2	10%	—	5%	45%	40%
S3	15%	5%	—	20%	60%

The direct operating costs of the service departments are as follows:

S1	$42,000
S2	80,000
S3	19,000

Required: Using the direct allocation method, prepare a schedule allocating the service department costs to the producing departments. (Round calculations to the nearest dollar.)

12–7 Service Department Allocations: Step Allocation Method

Refer to the data in Exercise 12–6. Using the step allocation method, prepare a schedule allocating the service department costs to the producing departments. (Round calculations to the nearest dollar.)

12–8 Common Cost Allocation: Determining Total Overhead

Springfield Manufacturing Company has two production departments, Melting and Molding. Common costs incurred for general plant management and for plant security benefit both production departments. Springfield allocates general plant management on the basis of the number of production employees, and plant security on the basis of space occupied by the production department.

In November 19x5, the following costs were recorded.

Melting Department direct overhead	$125,000
Molding Department direct overhead	300,000
General plant management	90,000
Plant security	25,000

Other pertinent data are provided below.

	Melting	Molding
Number of employees	20	40
Space occupied (sq ft)	10,000	40,000

Requirements

a) Prepare a schedule allocating general plant management costs and plant security costs to the Melting and Molding Departments.

b) Determine the total departmental overhead costs for the Melting and Molding Departments.

PROBLEMS

12–9 Service Department Cost Allocation: Predetermined Overhead Rates

The Albany Company applies factory overhead in its two producing departments using a predetermined rate based on budgeted machine hours in the Stamping Department and based on budgeted labor hours in the Fabricating Department. The following data concerning next year's operations have been developed.

	Service Departments		Producing Departments	
	Human	Maintenance		
Budgeted Costs	*Resources*	*and Repairs*	*Stamping*	*Fabricating*
Variable costs:				
Indirect materials	—	$16,000	$200,000	$ 80,000
Indirect labor	$45,000	50,000	140,000	200,000
Miscellaneous	—	—	28,000	30,000
Fixed costs:				
Miscellaneous	20,000	42,000	80,000	120,000
Other data:				
Direct labor hours (capacity)			20,000	30,000
Direct labor hours (budgeted)			14,000	20,000
Machine hours (capacity)			16,000	8000
Machine hours (budgeted)			12,000	6000
Number of employees				
(capacity)			20	30
Number of employees				
(budgeted)			12	18

Fixed Human Resources costs are allocated to the producing departments based on employed capacity and variable costs are allocated based on the budgeted number of employees. Fixed Maintenance and Repairs costs are allocated based on machine hour capacity, and variable costs are allocated based on the budgeted number of machine hours.

Requirements

a) Prepare a schedule showing the allocation of budgeted service department costs to producing departments.

b) Determine the predetermined overhead rate for the producing departments.

12–10 Selecting Cost Allocation Bases

The Minot Company, a new company, has three producing departments, P1, P2, and P3, for which direct department costs are accumulated. In January, the following common costs of operation were incurred.

Plant manager's salary and office expense	$ 4,800
Plant security	1,200
Plant nurse's salary and office expense	1,500
Plant depreciation	2,000
Machine maintenance	2,400
Plant cafeteria cost subsidy	1,200
	$13,100

The following additional data have been collected for the three producing departments:

	P1	P2	P3
Number of employees	10	15	5
Space occupied (sq ft)	2,000	5,000	3,000
Direct labor hours	1,600	4,000	750
Machine hours	4,800	8,000	3,200
Number of nurse office visits	20	45	10

Requirements

a) Group the common cost items into cost pools based on the nature of the costs and their common basis for allocation. Identify the most appropriate allocation basis for each pool and determine the total January costs in the pool. *Hint:* A cost pool may consist of one or more cost items.

b) Allocate the cost pools directly to the three producing departments using the allocation bases selected in requirement (a).

12–11 Common Cost Allocation Bases and Computations

The Cheyenne Company has two service departments, Maintenance and Cafeteria, that serve two producing departments, Mixing and Packaging. The following data have been collected for these departments for the current year.

	Cafeteria	Maintenance	Mixing	Packaging
Direct department costs	$88,000	$112,000	$465,000	$295,000
Number of employees			50	30
Number of meals served			9,000	7,000
Number of maintenance hours used			800	600
Number of maintenance orders			180	170

Requirements

a) Compute the service department cost allocations under the following independent assumptions:

1. Cafeteria costs are allocated based on the number of employees, and Maintenance costs are allocated based on the number of maintenance hours.

2. Cafeteria costs are allocated based on the number of meals served, and Maintenance costs are allocated based on the number of maintenance orders.

b) Comment on the reasonableness of the bases used in the calculations in requirement (a). What considerations should determine which bases to use for allocating Cafeteria and Maintenance costs?

12–12 Direct Method of Service Department Cost Allocation: Determination of Overhead Rates

The Fresno Company, a commercial printer, uses a job-order cost system to compute its product costs. All costs other than direct job costs are accounted for as department overhead in either the producing departments (Office Products and Advertising) or the service departments (Administration and Facilities). Administration and Facilities costs are allocated to the producing departments on the basis of the number of employees and the space occupied, respectively. Overhead is applied to specific jobs on the basis of direct labor hours. The following data were collected for September, 19x8.

	Administration	Facilities	Office Products	Advertising
Direct department costs	$2,500	$1,000	$3,200	$4,800
Number of employees	2	1	4	6
Space occupied (sq ft)	750	—	3,000	2,000
Direct labor hours	—	—	480	640

Requirements

a) Prepare a schedule allocating the service department costs to the producing departments using the direct allocation method.

b) Determine the overhead rate per direct labor hour for each of the producing departments. Round answer to the nearest cent.

c) Job No. 168 required 12 direct labor hours during the month in the Office Products Department. If the direct job cost was $850, how much was the total job cost?

12–13 Cost Allocation and Responsibility Accounting

The Austin Company uses a responsibility accounting system for evaluating its managers. Abbreviated performance reports for the company's three divisions for the month of March are presented below.

	Total	East	Central	West
Income before allocated costs	$165,000	$ 60,000	$ 75,000	$ 30,000
Less allocated costs:				
Computer Services	(60,000)	(20,000)	(20,000)	(20,000)
Personnel	(72,000)	(28,000)	(32,000)	(12,000)
Division income	$ 33,000	$ 12,000	$ 23,000	$(2,000)

The manager of the West Division is very much disturbed over his performance report and rumors that his division may be abolished because of its failure to report a profit in recent periods. He feels that the reported profit figures do not fairly present operating results because he is being unfairly burdened with service department costs. He is particularly concerned over the amount of Computer Services costs charged to his division. He feels that it is inequitable to charge his division with one third of the total cost when it is using only 20 percent of the services. He feels that the Personnel Department's use of the Computer Services Department should also be considered in the cost allocations.

Cost allocations were based on the following distributions of services provided.

		Services Provided to			
Services Provided from	Personnel	Computer Services	East	Central	West
Computer Services	40%	—	20%	20%	20%
Personnel	—	10%	35%	40%	15%

Requirements

a) What method is the company using to allocate Personnel and Computer Service costs?

b) Recompute the cost allocations using the step method. (Round calculations to the nearest dollar.)

c) Revise the performance reports to reflect the cost allocations computed in requirement (b).

d) Comment on the complaint of the manager of the West Division.

12–14 Common Cost Allocation: Predetermined Overhead Rate

The Gervais Company has one plant with two producing departments, Assembly and Testing. All manufacturing overhead costs that are not directly traceable to these departments are accumulated in one cost pool called General Service Department costs. General Service costs are, then, allocated to the producing departments based on direct labor hours. In the process of establishing predetermined overhead rates for 19x5, the chief cost accountant obtained the following data:

	General Service	Assembly	Testing
Budgeted variable overhead costs per direct labor hour	—	$4	$8
Budgeted fixed department overhead	$30,000	$15,000	$30,000

Gervais's operations for 19x5 are budgeted at 6000 direct labor hours in Assembly and 1500 direct labor hours in Testing.

Requirements

a) Prepare a budget of total overhead costs for 19x5 for the producing departments showing both direct department costs and allocated indirect department costs.

b) Determine the predetermined overhead rates for 19x5 for the Assembly and Testing departments.

c) Assuming that Job No. 146 processed in 19x5 required 75 direct labor hours in Assembly and 5 direct labor hours in Testing, determine the amount of factory overhead that should be applied to the job.

12–15 Common Cost Allocations: Linear Algebra Method

Hannibal, Inc. has two service departments (S1 and S2) and two producing departments (P1 and P2). The distribution of services provided by the service departments is as follows:

Services Provided from	Services Provided to			
	S1	S2	P1	P2
S1	—	10%	40%	50%
S2	20%	—	55%	25%

Total department costs for the service and producing departments are as follows:

S1	$ 45,000
S2	30,000
P1	180,000
P2	235,000
Total	$490,000

Requirements

a) Set up algebraic equations expressing the total cost for each department reflecting simultaneous allocation of service department costs to all departments receiving services.

b) Solve the equations in requirement (a) using the substitution method or any other method that you may have learned for simultaneously solving linear equations, including use of a computer. (Round calculations to the nearest dollar if the substitution method is used.)

c) How much cost is allocated between S1 and S2? How much S1 and S2 cost is allocated to P1 and P2?

12–16 Allocation of Common Fixed Costs

The Maintenance Department of Plattsburg Mills provides services to two producing departments, Spinning and Weaving. Maintenance services used are measured by the standard maintenance labor time for the various services provided. The following data are available for the first three months of 19x2 concerning the standard hours for the actual services provided.

	Standard Hours Used	
	Spinning Department	Weaving Department
January	8,000	12,000
February	6,000	12,000
March	4.000	12,000

The Maintenance Department facilities and staff size were established based on expected maintenance needs of 8000 service hours by the Spinning Department and 12,000 hours by the Weaving Department.

Requirements

a) If fixed Maintenance Department costs were $54,000 per month for January through March, how much should be allocated for each month to Spinning and Weaving under the following independent assumptions: (1) that fixed maintenance cost is allocated based on actual service hours; and (2) that fixed maintenance cost is allocated based on the capacity provided?

b) Which method of allocation is most appropriate? Explain.

12–17 Step Allocation: Determination of Cost Reimbursement

Community Clinic is a not-for-profit outpatient facility that provides medical services to both fee paying and low-income government supported patients. Reimbursement from the government is based on total actual costs of services provided, including both direct cost of patient services and indirect operating costs. Patient services are provided through two producing departments, Medical Services and Ancillary Services (includes X-ray, therapy, etc.). In addition to the direct costs of these departments, the clinic incurs common costs accumulated in two service departments, Administration and Facilities. Administration costs are allocated based on the number of full-time employees, and Facilities costs are allocated on the basis of space occupied. Costs, and related data, for the current month are as follows:

	Administration	Facilities	Medical Services	Ancillary Services
Direct costs	$9,000	$2,000	$60,000	$25,000
Number of employees	5	4	12	8
Space occupied (sq ft)	1,500	—	8,000	2,000
Number of patient visits	—	—	4,000	1,500

Requirements

a) Using the step allocation method, prepare a schedule allocating the common service department costs to the producing departments.

b) Determine the amount to be reimbursed from the government for each low-income patient visit. (Round answer to the nearest cent.)

12–18 Common Cost Allocation in a Not-for-Profit Organization

Dunwoody Community Church is organized into four operating divisions: Education, Benevolence, Community Services, and Recreation. Direct costs for each division for the year are as follows:

Education	$ 85,000
Benevolence	230,000
Community Services	125,000
Recreation	50,000
Total	$490,000

Other data pertaining to church operations are as follows:

	Building Space Occupied	Participants Served during Year	Number of Employees
Education	15,000	10,000	8
Benevolence	1,000	2,500	5
Community Services	4,000	7,500	3
Recreation	5,000	5,000	4
Totals	25,000	25,000	20

The common indirect costs of operating the church and the allocation bases are as follows:

	Cost	Allocation Base
Building and utilities	$ 60,000	Space occupied
General administration	45,000	Number of employees
Miscellaneous supplies and costs	25,000	Participants served
Total common costs	$130,000	

Requirements

a) Prepare a schedule allocating each common cost to the operating divisions.

b) Determine the total cost of each operating division broken down into direct and indirect costs.

12–19 Budgeted Service Department Cost Allocation: Pricing a New Product

Trimco Products Company is adding a new diet food concentrate called Body Trim to its line of body building and exercise products. A plant is being built for manufacturing the new product. Management has decided to price the new product based on a 100 percent markup on total manufacturing costs. A direct cost budget for the new plant projects that direct department costs of $2,100,000 will be incurred in producing an expected normal output of 700,000 pounds of finished product. In addition, common costs for Human Resources and Computer Services will be shared by the Body Trim Division with the two exercise products divisions, Commercial Products and Retail Products. Budgeted annual data to be used in making the allocations are summarized below.

	Human Resources	Computer Services	Commercial Products	Retail Products	Body Trim
Number of employees	5	5	50	30	20
Computer time (hrs)	500	—	1,500	1,250	750

Direct costs are budgeted at $80,000 for the Human Resources Department and $120,000 for the Computer Services Department.

Requirements

a) Using the step allocation method determine the total direct and indirect costs of Body Trim.

b) Determine the selling price per pound of Body Trim. (Round calculations to the nearest cent.)

12–20 Joint Cost Allocation: Physical Quantity Method (Appendix)

Chemco, Inc. processes two products, Bugoff and Weedout, used in the control of weeds and pests in lawn care. These products begin from a unique joint refining process in batches of 10,000 liters of mixture. At split-off, one fourth of the mixture emerges as Bugoff and three fourths as Weedout. Both products require further processing after split-off. The following cost and production data for August, 19x1 were determined.

Total joint costs per batch	$15,000
Cost of further processing of Bugoff	5,000
Cost of further processing of Weedout	10,000
Beginning inventories	none

Requirements

a) Determine the joint cost allocation per batch for each product using the physical quantity method.

b) Determine the total cost per liter for each product. (Round answer to the nearest cent.)

c) Assuming that Bugoff and Weedout both sell for $8 per liter, prepare a schedule of gross profit per batch for each product line. Compute the gross profit percentage on each batch. Comment on the appropriateness of the allocation system used.

12–21 Joint Cost Allocation: Physical Quantity and Relative Sales Methods (Appendix)

Hills and Dales Farms is a large poultry producer that processes and sells various grades of packaged chicken to grocery chains. Chickens are grown and accounted for in groups of 1000. At the end of the standard growing period, the chickens are separated and sold by grades. Grades A and B are sold to grocery chains, and grades C and D are sold for other uses. For costing purposes, Hills and Dales treats each batch of newly hatched chicks as a joint product. The following data pertain to the last batch of 1000 chicks.

Grade	Number of Chickens	Average Pounds per Chicken	Selling Price per Pound
A	500	4	$0.50
B	300	3	0.40
C	120	$2\frac{1}{2}$	0.30
D	80	$1\frac{1}{4}$	0.20

Total joint costs for the above batch were $800.

Requirements

a) Determine the cost, gross profit, and gross profit percent per pound for each grade of chickens assuming the physical quantity method of joint cost allocation is used, and the quantity is measured in terms of the number of chickens.

b) Repeat requirement (a) assuming the physical quantity is measured in terms of pounds. (Round calculations to two decimal places.)

c) Repeat requirement (a) assuming the relative sales value method of joint cost allocation is used. (Round calculations to three decimal places.)

12–22 Service Department Cost Allocation: Direct and Step Methods

The Parker Manufacturing Company has two production departments (Fabrication and Assembly) and three service departments (General Factory Administration, Factory Maintenance, and Factory Cafeteria). The costs of the General Factory Administration Department, Factory Maintenance Department, and Factory Cafeteria are allocated to the production departments on the basis of direct labor hours, square footage occupied, and number of employees, respectively. A summary of costs and other data for each department prior to allocation of service department costs for the year ended June 30, 19x3 appears below.

	Fabrication	Assembly	General Factory Administration	Factory Maintenance	Factory Cafeteria
Direct labor costs	$1,950,000	$2,050,000	$90,000	$82,100	$87,000
Direct materials costs	$3,130,000	$950,000	—	$65,000	$91,000
Manufacturing overhead costs	$1,650,000	$1,850,000	$70,000	$56,100	$62,000
Direct labor hours	562,500	437,500	31,000	27,000	42,000
Number of employees	280	200	12	8	20
Square footage occupied	88,000	72,000	1,750	2,000	4,800

Requirements

a) Assuming that Parker elects to distribute service department costs directly to production departments without recognizing interdepartmental services, how much Factory Maintenance Department costs would be allocated to the Fabrication Department?

b) Assuming the same method of allocation as in requirement (a), how much General Factory Administration Department costs would be allocated to the Assembly Department?

c) Assuming that Parker elects to distribute service department costs to other service departments (starting with the service department with the greatest total costs) as well as to the production departments, how much Factory Cafeteria Department costs would be allocated to the Factory Maintenance Department?

d) Assuming the same method of allocation as in requirement (c), how much Factory Maintenance Department costs would be allocated to the Factory Cafeteria?

(CPA Adapted)

12–23 Whether or Not to Allocate: Selecting Bases for Allocation

Bonn Company recently reorganized its computer and data processing activities. The small installations located within the accounting departments at its plants and subsidiaries have been replaced with a centralized data processing department at corporate headquarters responsible for the operations of a newly acquired large-scale computer system. The new department has been in operation for two years and has been regularly producing reliable and timely data for the past twelve months. Because the department has focused its activities on converting applications to the new system and producing reports for the plant and subsidiary managements, little attention has been devoted to the costs of the department. Now that the department's activities are operating relatively smoothly, company management has requested that the departmental manager recommend a cost accumulation system to facilitate cost control and the development of suitable rates to charge users for service. For the past two years, the departmental costs have been recorded in one account. The costs have been allocated to user departments on the basis of computer time used. The schedule below reports the costs and charging rate for 19x5.

(1)	Salaries and benefits	$ 622,600
(2)	Supplies	40,000
(3)	Equipment maintenance contract	15,000
(4)	Insurance	25,000
(5)	Heat and air conditioning	36,000
(6)	Electricity	50,000
(7)	Equipment and furniture depreciation	285,400
(8)	Building improvements depreciation	10,000
(9)	Building occupancy and security	39,300
(10)	Corporate administrative charges	52,700
	Total costs	$1,176,000
	Computer hours for user processing	2,750
	Hourly rate ($1,176,000/2750)	$ 428 (rounded)
	Use of available computer hours:	
	Testing and debugging programs	250
	Set-up of jobs	500
	Processing jobs	2,750
	Downtime for maintenance	750
	Idle time	742
	Total	4,992

The department manager recommends that the department costs be accumulated by five activity centers within the department: System Analysis, Programming, Data Processing, Computer Operations (processing), and Administration. He then suggests that the costs of the Administration activity should be allocated to the other four activity centers before a separate rate for charging users is developed for each of the first four activities. After reviewing the details of the accounts, the manager made the following observations regarding the charges to the several subsidiary accounts within the department.

1. Salaries and benefits — records the salary and benefit costs of all employees in the department.

2. Supplies — records punch card costs, paper costs for printers, and a small amount for miscellaneous other costs.

3. Equipment maintenance contracts — records charges for maintenance contracts; all equipment is covered by maintenance contracts.

4. Insurance — records cost of insurance covering the equipment and furniture.

5. Heat and air conditioning — records a charge from the corporate Heating and Air Conditioning Department estimated to be the incremental costs to meet the special needs of the computer department.

6. Electricity — records the charge for electricity based on a separate meter within the department.

7. Equipment and furniture depreciation — records the depreciation for all owned equipment and furniture within the department.

8. Building improvements depreciation — records amortization of the depreciation of all building improvements required to provide proper environmental control and electrical service for the computer equipment.

9. Building occupancy and security — records the Computer Department's share of the depreciation, maintenance, heat, and security costs of the building; these costs are allocated on the basis of square feet occupied.

10. Corporate administrative charges — records the Computer Department's share of the corporate administrative costs; they are allocated on the basis of the number of employees.

Requirements

a) For each of the ten cost items, state whether or not it should be allocated to the five activity centers, and for each cost item that should be allocated, recommend the basis upon which it should be allocated. Justify your conclusion in each case.

b) Assume that the costs of the Computer Operations (processing) activity will be charged to the user departments on the basis of computer hours. Using the analysis of computer utilization shown above, determine the total number of hours that should be employed to determine the charging rate for Computer Operations (processing). Justify your answer.

(CMA Adapted)

12–24 Joint Cost Allocation: Physical Quantity and Sales Value Methods (Appendix)

Vreeland, Inc. manufactures products X, Y, and Z from a joint process. Joint product costs were $60,000 during the month of September. Additional information is as follows:

Product	Units Produced	Sales Value at Split-Off	Sales Value and Additional Costs if Processed Further	
			Sales Value	Additional Costs
X	6,000	$40,000	$55,000	$9,000
Y	4,000	35,000	45,000	7,000
Z	2,000	25,000	30,000	5,000

Requirements

a) Determine the amount of joint product costs to be allocated to each of the products during September assuming the company uses the physical quantity method of joint cost allocation.

b) Determine the amount of joint product costs to be allocated to each of the products during September assuming the company uses the sales value method of joint cost allocation. (Round calculations to four decimal places.)

(CPA Adapted)

12–25 Joint Cost Allocation: Net Realizable Sales Value Method (Appendix)

Doe Corporation grows, processes, cans, and sells three main pineapple products — sliced pineapple, crushed pineapple, and pineapple juice. The outside skin is cut off in the Cutting Department and processed as animal feed. The skin is treated as a by-product. Doe's production process is as follows:

- Pineapples are first processed in the Cutting Department. The pineapples are washed, and the outside skin is cut away. Then the pineapples are cored and trimmed for slicing. The three main products (sliced, crushed, and juice) and the by-product (animal feed) are recognized after processing in the Cutting Department. Each product is then transferred to a separate department for final processing.

- The trimmed pineapples are forwarded to the Slicing Department, where the pineapples are sliced and canned. Any juice generated during the slicing operation is packed in the cans with the slices.

- The pieces of pineapple trimmed from the fruit are diced and canned in the Crushing Department. Again, the juice generated during this operation is packed in the can with the crushed pineapple.

- The core and surplus pineapple generated from the Cutting Department are pulverized into a liquid in the Juicing Department.

- The outside skin is chopped into animal feed in the Feed Department.

The Doe Corporation uses the relative sales value method (based on net realizable value) to assign costs of the joint process to its main products. The by-product is inventoried at its market value. A total of 270,000 pounds were entered into the Cutting Department during May. The schedule below shows the costs incurred in each department, the proportion by weight transferred to the four final processing departments, and the selling price of each product.

Department	Costs Incurred	Percent of Product by Weight Transferred to Departments	Selling Price per Pound of Final Product
Cutting	$60,000	—	None
Slicing	4,700	35	$0.60
Crushing	10,580	28	0.55
Juicing	3,250	27	0.30
Animal feed	700	10	0.10
Total	$79,230	100	

Requirements

a) Calculate the number of pounds of pineapple that result as output for pineapple slices, crushed pineapple, pineapple juice, and animal feed.

b) Calculate the net realizable value at the split-off point of the three main products.

c) Calculate the amount of the cost of the Cutting Department assigned to each of the three main products and to the by-product in accordance with corporate policy. (Round calculations to four decimal places.)

d) Calculate the gross profits for each of the three main products.

(CMA Adapted)

IV

Selected Topics for Further Study

13

Relevant Costs for Quantitative Models

A **model** is a simplified representation of some real-world phenomenon. Models are used to learn about the related phenomenon and to quickly and inexpensively determine the effect of some proposed action. Children learn by playing with model houses, boats, cars, and horses. Museums and libraries contain educational models of buildings, drilling platforms, spaceships, prehistoric animals, and ecosystems. Airframe manufacturers study the aerodynamics of model planes in wind tunnels. Captains of supertankers learn how to pilot their craft using models in small lakes. These are all examples of **physical models,** scaled down versions or replicas of physical reality.

Managers and other decision makers also use **quantitative models** that are simply a series of algebraic relationships. Quantitative models can be further classified into **descriptive models** that merely specify the relationships between a series of independent and dependent variables and **optimizing models** that suggest a specific choice between decision alternatives. Cost-volume-profit relationships, contribution income statements, and operating budgets are all descriptive models.

The purposes of this chapter are to illustrate the usefulness of optimizing models as decision aids and to discuss the proper use of accounting data in optimizing models. Attention is focused on three models that are widely used by managers and accountants: the economic order quantity, linear programming, and payoff tables. The models introduced in this chapter are not accounting models per se, but they often use accounting data. Consequently, the accuracy and relevance of accounting data is critical to their proper use.

QUANTITATIVE MODELS ARE DECISION AIDS

Quantitative, especially optimizing, models are often criticized as being oversimplistic, unrealistic, and prone to "make" incorrect decisions. It is true that models are a simplified representation of reality, but this is also one of their strengths. The use of a model helps management focus on the few variables that are most critical to a decision. Furthermore, though the assumptions that underlie a model can be specified and evaluated, this is seldom the case for assumptions that underlie a manager's professional judgment.

All quantitative models, descriptive and optimizing, are intended to *assist* managers in decision making. Managers cannot relinquish their decision-making responsibility to models that are merely intended to be decision support systems. In the final analysis, *managers, not models, make decisions.* Managers must carefully evaluate the data used in the model, the assumptions underlying the model, and the output of the model. If everything appears satisfactory, a manager may implement the action suggested by an optimizing model. If a manager suspects faulty data, an oversimplistic assumption, or changed circumstances that invalidate the model, the manager should not implement the suggested action. Instead, the manager should undertake further analysis or make a decision based on professional judgment.

Optimizing models, like many other aspects of a business, should be managed using the principle of exception. When everything is going according to plan, management implements the action suggested by the model. If any invalidating circumstances are suspected, management should intervene. Properly used as decision aids, models increase the speed and quality of management's decisions.

ECONOMIC ORDER QUANTITY

The operating budget (discussed in Chapter 6) specifies the number of units to be purchased or manufactured during a period of time. In merchandising organizations, for example, the number of units to be purchased is computed, for each inventory item, as the total needs for current sales, plus the desired ending inventory, less the expected beginning inventory. The operating budget does not specify the order quantity or the reorder point. The **order quantity** is the quantity of inventory ordered *at one time*, and the **reorder point** is the inventory level at which an order for additional units is placed.

Consider the order quantity. If budgeted 19x4 purchases of inventory item B-25 are 2400 units, management might place one order for 2400 units, three orders for 800 units, 2400 orders for 1 unit, or some other combination of number of orders and order size.

Assume that the demand for item B-25 is constant throughout the year and that new orders are timed to arrive just as the previous order is exhausted. In this case, an order quantity of 800 units might produce the variations in inventory level illustrated in Exhibit 13–1. The maximum inventory level is reached just as a new order is received. Subsequent to the receipt of an order, the inventory level falls at a constant rate per unit of time, and another order is received just as the inventory level falls to zero. With a maximum inventory of 800 units, a minimum inventory of 0 units, and a constant rate of decline per unit of time, the average inventory of item B-25 is 400 units [(800 + 0)/2].

Inventory Costs

There are a variety of costs associated with inventory, including the costs of the units purchased, of ordering inventory, of carrying inventory, and of insufficient inventory. Several costs in each of these categories are listed

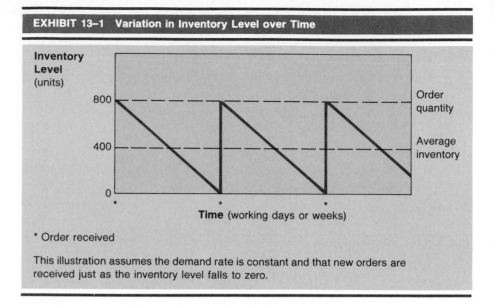

EXHIBIT 13-1   Variation in Inventory Level over Time

* Order received

This illustration assumes the demand rate is constant and that new orders are received just as the inventory level falls to zero.

in Exhibit 13–2. Management's objective is to determine the **economic order quantity** (EOQ), the order quantity that results in the minimum total annual inventory costs. Because only costs that vary with the order quantity are relevant to this decision, each of the cost categories in Exhibit 13–2 is examined to identify the relevant and the irrelevant costs.

In the absence of quantity discounts, the total annual costs of the units purchased vary only with total units purchased, not with the order quantity or the number of orders. Consequently, the total annual costs of the units purchased are irrelevant to determining the order quantity and are excluded from order quantity models.

The total annual costs of ordering inventory are computed as follows:

$$\text{Total annual} \atop \text{ordering costs} = \text{Cost of placing} \atop \text{an order} \times \text{Number of orders} \atop \text{per year.}$$

Because the number of orders per year is computed as the annual demand divided by the order size, the total annual costs of ordering inventory vary with the order size. As the order size increases, the number of orders per year decreases, and the total annual ordering costs decrease. Conversely, as the order size decreases, the number of orders per year increases, and the total annual ordering costs increase.

Assume that the cost of placing an order for part B-25 is $25. If the order quantity is 800 units, the total annual ordering costs are $75 [$25 × (2400/800)]. A decrease in the order size to 600 units would increase the total available ordering costs to $100 [$25 × (2400/600)].

As might be suspected, the costs of carrying inventory also vary with the order size. Increasing the order size increases the average inventory and the total annual costs of carrying inventory. Conversely, decreasing the order size reduces the average inventory and the total annual carrying costs.

Note that the cost of carrying inventory includes an opportunity cost for the money invested in inventory. The interest rate on borrowed money is frequently used to estimate this opportunity cost. However, the rate of return management desires to earn on inventory investments is a better choice. The issues involved in determining this rate are discussed in financial management textbooks; one possible rate is the organization's cost of capital (discussed in Chapter 14).

Carrying costs are often expressed as a percentage of the unit purchase price. Assume the carrying costs for part B-25 are 25 percent of the unit purchase price. If the unit purchase price is $12 and the order size is 800 units, the cost of carrying 1 unit in inventory for 1 year is $3 ($12 $\times$ 0.25), and the total annual carrying costs are $1200 [$3 $\times$ (800/2)].

Operations research textbooks sometimes contain sophisticated models that allow stockouts and backorders to occur. These models then include stockout costs in the determination of the economic order quantity. We shall assume that management does not intentionally allow stockouts to occur. Consequently, the costs of insufficient inventory are irrelevant to the determination of our economic order quantity.

In summary, only the costs of ordering and carrying inventory are

---

EXHIBIT 13–2   Inventory Costs for Purchased Goods Intended for Resale*

Costs of units purchased

Unit price
Transportation-in

Costs of carrying inventory

Insurance
Personal property taxes
Storage-space costs
Deterioration and obsolescence
Opportunity cost of money invested in
  inventory

Costs of ordering inventory

Processing the order
Receiving and inspecting the order
Processing payment for the order

Costs of insufficient inventory

Lost contribution from missed sales
Lost customer goodwill
Cost of special orders
Cost of processing backorders

---

* In the case of manufactured goods, variable manufacturing costs are substituted for the unit price and the cost of ordering inventory includes machine set-up costs. If goods are to be processed further in a subsequent department, the costs of insufficient inventory include the costs of excessive idle time and the costs of expediting production once the goods are available.

relevant to determining the economic order quantity, and these costs vary inversely with each other. As the order size increases, total annual ordering costs decrease and total annual carrying costs increase. As the order size decreases, total annual ordering costs increase and total annual carrying costs decrease. The total relevant costs for determining the economic order quantity are computed as follows:

$$\begin{array}{l} \text{Total annual ordering} \\ \text{and carrying costs} \end{array} = \left(\begin{array}{l} \text{Cost of placing} \\ \text{an order} \end{array} \times \frac{\text{Annual demand}}{\text{Order quantity}} \right)$$

$$+ \left(\begin{array}{l} \text{Unit carrying} \\ \text{costs per year} \end{array} \times \frac{\text{Order quantity}}{2} \right).$$

Determining the Economic Order Quantity

There are two basic approaches to determining the economic order quantity (EOQ): (1) a trial and error tabular approach and (2) a formula approach. Both approaches are based on the following assumptions.

1. The demand rate is known and uniform.
2. There are no quantity discounts.
3. Ordering costs are a known function of the number of orders.
4. Carrying costs are a known function of average inventory.
5. Stockouts are not intentionally permitted.

Though these assumptions are seldom completely valid, the EOQ model is useful because it often produces lower total annual inventory costs than order quantities based on professional judgment.

Trial and Error Approach. Recall that the annual demand for inventory item B-25 is 2400 units, the cost of placing an order is $25, and the cost of carrying 1 unit in inventory for 1 year is $3. If management orders 800 units at a time, the total annual ordering and carrying costs are $1275 (see Exhibit 13–3).

Also tabulated in Exhibit 13–3 are the total annual ordering and carrying costs for several additional order sizes. The information tabulated in Exhibit 13–3 is graphed in Exhibit 13–4. Both exhibits illustrate that *the minimum annual costs occur at the order size where the annual ordering costs equal the annual carrying costs,* 200 units in this example. The essence of the trial and error approach is to find the order size where these two costs are equal by repeated trial and error.

Even though the EOQ model suggests that an order size of exactly 200 units is most economical, management might order in other lot sizes because of quantity discounts, warehouse capacity constraints, limited shelf life of an inventory item, or a variety of other factors. An examination of Exhibit 13–4 reveals that small deviations from the economic order quantity

EXHIBIT 13–3   Relevant Annual Costs for Determining the Economic Order Quantity

Order quantity (units)	20	50	150	200	300	800	1,200	2,400
Number of orders (annual demand ÷ order quantity)	120	48	16	12	8	3	2	1
Average inventory (order quantity divided by two)†	10	25	75	100	150	400	600	1,200
Relevant annual costs:								
Ordering (number of orders × $25)	$3,000	$1,200	$400	$300	$200	$ 75	$ 50	$ 25
Carrying (average inventory × $3)	30	75	225	300	450	1,200	1,800	3,600
Total	$3,030	$1,275	$625	$600*	$650	$1,275	$1,850	$3,625

* Minimum annual ordering and holding costs.

† This assumes that the demand rate is constant and that the inventory level is zero when the new order is received.

are not very costly. The total cost curve is high at both ends but relatively low between 100 and 300 units. The existence of this wide low-cost area near the EOQ, with high costs at order quantities far from the EOQ, is what makes this model so valuable despite its restrictive assumptions. Even if the model is not completely accurate, it helps management get into the low-cost area.

Formula Approach. By setting annual ordering costs equal to annual carrying costs, and solving for the order quantity, the economic order quantity formula is derived.

$$\frac{\textbf{Annual Ordering Costs}}{\text{Cost of placing an order} \times \dfrac{\text{Annual demand}}{\text{Order quantity}}} = \frac{\textbf{Annual Carrying Costs}}{\text{Unit carrying costs per year} \times \dfrac{\text{Order quantity}}{2}}$$

$$\begin{array}{c}\text{Economic} \\ \text{order} \\ \text{quantity}\end{array} = \sqrt{\dfrac{2 \times \begin{array}{c}\text{Annual} \\ \text{demand}\end{array} \times \begin{array}{c}\text{Cost of placing} \\ \text{an order}\end{array}}{\begin{array}{c}\text{Unit carrying} \\ \text{cost per year}\end{array}}}$$

For part B-25, the economic order quantity is once again determined to

EXHIBIT 13–4   Behavior of Inventory Ordering and Carrying Costs

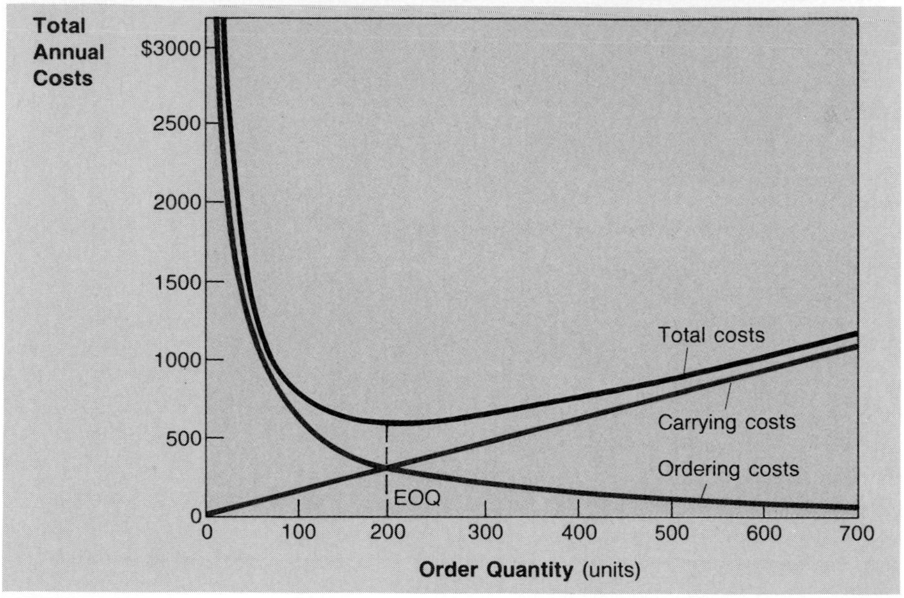

be 200 units:

$$EOQ = \sqrt{\frac{2 \times 2400 \times \$25}{\$3}}$$
$$= 200 \text{ units.}$$

Reorder Point

The reorder point is the inventory level at which an order for additional units is placed. The reorder point must allow sufficient inventory to cover demand during the **lead time,** the time between the placement and the receipt of an order. Assuming demand takes place evenly throughout a year containing n work days, the equation for daily demand is

$$\text{Daily demand} = \text{Annual demand}/n.$$

If the lead time required to fill an order is known and certain, the reorder point that results in a new order arriving just as the previous order is exhausted is computed as

$$\frac{\text{Reorder}}{\text{point}} = \frac{\text{Daily}}{\text{demand}} \times \frac{\text{Lead}}{\text{time.}}$$

Assume the organization using item B-25 operates 240 days per year and that the lead time for this item is 5 days. Under these circumstances the reorder point for B-25 is 50 units:

$$\text{Daily demand} = 2400 \text{ units}/240 \text{ days}$$
$$= 10 \text{ units per day.}$$
$$\text{Reorder point} = 10 \text{ units per day} \times 5 \text{ days}$$
$$= 50 \text{ units.}$$

Management places an order whenever the inventory level falls to 50 units.

Safety Stocks

Safety stocks are extra units of inventory carried to prevent stockouts due to variations in the demand for units during the lead time. Stockouts can occur because of delays in the receipt of an order or increases in the daily demand for an inventory item. If management desires to avoid stockouts, and daily demand or lead time or both are uncertain, they must carry safety stocks.

Safety stocks can be computed as the difference between the maximum lead time demand and the reorder point without safety stocks. Safety stocks do not increase the economic order quantity; they do, however, increase the reorder point. Assume the maximum daily demand for item B-25 is 12 units, and the maximum lead time is 8 days. Under these circumstances, the safety stock for this item would be set at 46 units:

Maximum demand per day	12 units
Maximum lead time	$\times$ 8 days
Maximum lead time demand	96 units
Reorder point without safety stocks	−50 units
Safety stock	46 units

Safety stocks can be viewed as a base inventory. If the safety stocks for item B-25 are never used, they will have an annual carrying cost of $138, computed as the $3 carrying costs per unit per year times 46 units of safety stock.

The economic order quantity for item B-25 will remain at 200 units, but the reorder point will increase to 96 units, computed as the reorder point without safety stocks plus the safety stock. Possible patterns for item B-25's inventory level with safety stocks and variations in lead time demand are illustrated in Exhibit 13–5. Note that the presence of the base inventory layer increases the maximum inventory to 246 units.

The economic order quantity has been discussed in the context of a merchandising firm. However, assuming that production is in batches and no units are available until the batch is complete, the model is also applicable to manufacturing. In this case variable manufacturing costs are substituted for the unit price and the cost of ordering inventory includes machine set-up costs.

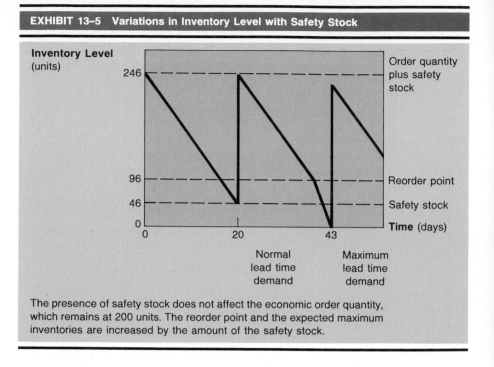

EXHIBIT 13–5   Variations in Inventory Level with Safety Stock

The presence of safety stock does not affect the economic order quantity, which remains at 200 units. The reorder point and the expected maximum inventories are increased by the amount of the safety stock.

LINEAR PROGRAMMING

Linear programming is an optimizing model used to assist managers in making decisions under constrained conditions when linear relationships exist between all variables. This model may be applied to a variety of business decisions, including product mix, raw materials mix, production scheduling, transportation scheduling, and cash management. The objective in linear programming is to determine the action that will maximize profits or minimize costs. The constraints can represent limited resources (such as labor hours, machine hours, raw materials, or money), limited consumer demand, or required physical characteristics of the final product (such as a minimum percentage of protein or a maximum percentage of fat).

Although the concepts underlying linear programming are straightforward, the actual solution to linear programming problems can be extremely complex. Fortunately, the availability of computers and modeling specialists has resulted in situations where the manager need not be concerned about the detailed operation of the solution technique. The manager should, of course, have a general understanding of how the solution is determined (the model's assumptions), and he or she should be able to evaluate both the data used and the suggested solution.

Assumptions and Uses of Accounting Data

As its name implies, the most critical linear programming assumption is that linear relationships exist between all variables. The total contribution from the sale of products X and Y, for example, must be of the form $aX + bY$, where a is the unit contribution of product X, and b is the unit contribution of product Y. Curvilinear relationships, such as $aX - 0.05X^2 + bY - 0.0002bY^3$ are not allowed. Another assumption of linear programming is that fractional production is permitted. The suggested solution to a linear programming problem might, for example, specify the production and sale of 25.2 units of X and 32.7 units of Y.

When these assumptions are not valid, the manager might elect to use other models. Alternatively, if it seems appropriate, the manager might use professional judgment to adjust the suggested linear programming solution; for example, the production of X might be rounded to 25 units, and the production of Y might be rounded to 32 units.

Every linear programming model includes an **objective function,** or goal to be maximized or minimized. Accounting data are often used in the objective function. *If the objective is to maximize profits, the coefficients of the variables in the objective function should be unit contribution margins.* If the objective is to minimize costs, the coefficients should be unit variable costs. The total contribution margin or variable costs of each product will vary in proportion to changes in volume. Profit and cost measures that include an allocation of fixed costs should not be used in the objective function. They do not vary in direct proportion to changes in production; hence their use violates the linearity assumption.

Graphic Analysis of Product Mix Decisions

We will use graphic analysis to illustrate the solution of linear programming problems. Though graphic analysis can be used to solve problems containing only two variables, it provides the general understanding necessary to evaluate more complex problems containing three or more variables. The following steps are involved in graphic analysis.

1. *Develop an equation for the objective function* indicating how each variable affects the profit maximization or cost minimization goal.
2. *Develop an equation for each constraint* indicating how each variable affects the total use of the constraint.
3. *Graph the constraints.*
4. *Identify the feasible solutions* that are bounded by the constraints.
5. *Determine the optimal solution* that maximizes or minimizes the value of the objective function.

Assume the Martin Company produces two products, A and B, in two departments, Assembly and Finishing. Product A has a unit contribution margin of $50, and product B has a unit contribution margin of $40. The demand for each product exceeds Martin's capacity to produce. Production information is as follows:

	Labor Hours per Unit		Total Labor Hours Available per Week
	A	B	
Assembly Department	20	20	600
Finishing Department	20	10	400

Martin can only obtain raw materials sufficient to produce 25 units of B each week. Management desires the product mix that will maximize the weekly contribution of products A and B toward fixed costs and profits. Using the five steps, the problem is solved as follows:

1. *Objective function.* The objective is to maximize the total weekly contribution of products A and B. Given information on the unit contribution margin, Martin's objective function is

$$\text{Maximize } \$50A + \$40B.$$

2. *Constraints.* There are constraints for maximum assembly hours, maximum finishing hours, and maximum production of product B. Because each constraint indicates there is an upper limit on the use of some resource, the symbol $\leq$ for "less than or equal to" is used in each:

$$20A + 20B \leq 600 \text{ Assembly Department hours,}$$

$$20A + 10B \leq 400 \text{ Finishing Department hours,}$$

$$B \leq 25 \text{ units.}$$

The assembly hours constraint indicates that any combination of A and B can be produced, providing it does not require more than 600 assembly hours. The finishing hours constraint indicates that any combination of A and B can be produced, providing it does not require more than 400 finishing hours. Finally, because of raw material limitations, no more than 25 units of B can be produced.

To be technically precise, two more constraints are added to indicate that negative production is prohibited:

$$A \geq 0,$$

$$B \geq 0.$$

The symbol $\geq$ is read "greater than or equal to." Hence the production of A and the production of B must be greater than or equal to zero.

EXHIBIT 13–6 Graphic Approach to Linear Programming

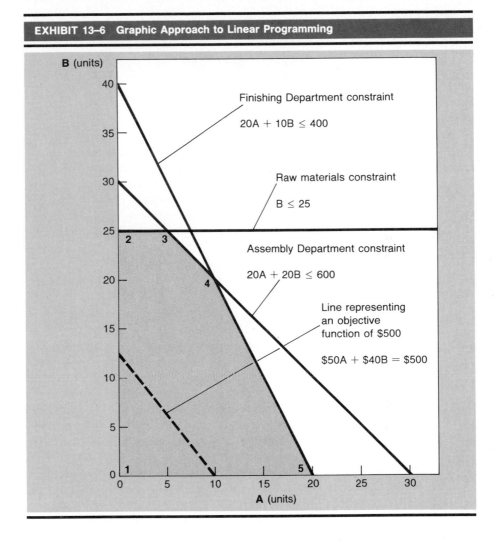

3. *Graph.* One axis must be designated to represent each variable. In Exhibit 13–6, the horizontal axis is labeled Product A, and the vertical axis is labeled Product B. The opposite could also have been done.

The set of all feasible A and B values is determined by solving each constraint for its maximum A and B values, assuming all production was devoted to that product, and drawing lines on graph paper connecting, for each constraint, the maximum value of each product. The maximum values of A and B, for each constraint, are computed as follows:

	Maximum Values	
	Product A	Product B
Assembly hours	600/20 = 30	600/20 = 30
Finishing hours	400/20 = 20	400/10 = 40
Raw materials		25

The lines connecting these maximum values are illustrated in Exhibit 13–6. Because the raw materials constraint affects only Product B, it does not intersect the horizontal axis for Product A. Instead, it is drawn parallel to the horizontal axis. The nonnegativity constraints are represented by the horizontal and vertical axes.

4. *Feasible solutions.* After the lines representing each constraint are drawn, the **feasible region,** representing all possible production volumes and mixes, is depicted by the area between the vertical and horizontal axes and the first set of enclosing lines (the area enclosed by the lines from points 1–2–3–4–5 in Exhibit 13–6). The firm can produce anywhere within the feasible region; however, it is likely that one product mix will provide a higher total contribution than any other mix.

5. *Optimal solution.* In linear programming, the **optimal solution** is the feasible solution that maximizes or minimizes the value of the objective function, depending on management's goal. An important characteristic of linear programming is that *if there is a single optimal solution, it is found at a corner point where the lines representing two or more constraints intersect.* Knowing this, it is only necessary to evaluate the solutions represented by corner points. In Exhibit 13–6, there are five corner points, which, for convenience, are numbered 1 through 5. The value of the objective function at each corner point is computed in Exhibit 13–7. The maximum optimal solution, represented by corner 4, calls for a weekly production of 10 units of Product A and 20 units of Product B. This solution will provide a weekly contribution of $1300. Fixed costs, of course, would be deducted from this amount to determine the weekly profit.

The Corner Solution   The reason that the unique solution is always found at a corner point can be illustrated by drawing a line representing some arbitrary value for the objection function. In the case of the Martin Company, the end points for an objective function with a value of $500 are 10 units of product A and 12.5 units of product B. In general,

$$\text{Desired contribution} \div \text{Unit contribution} = \text{End point}.$$

For A,

$$\$500 \div \$50 = 10 \text{ units}.$$

EXHIBIT 13-7 Evaluation of Alternative Corner Solutions			
	Value of		Value of Objective Function
Corner	A	B	$50A + $40B =
1	0	0	$ —
2	0	25	1000
3	5	25	1250
4	10*	20*	1300
5	20	0	1000

* Optimal solution

For B,

$$\$500 \div \$40 = 12.5 \text{ units.}$$

Drawing this line in Exhibit 13–6, observe that 10 units of A or 12.5 units of B or any combination along this line will provide a weekly contribution of $500. An objective function having a higher value would be drawn farther from the origin, parallel to the first line. To maximize the value of the objective function, additional lines are drawn parallel to the first line, but farther from the origin, until only one point on a line touches the feasible solution. This one unique point will be a corner point; corner 4 in this case. You may draw these additional lines as an exercise.

Simplex Method

Though it is possible to solve two variable problems with the aid of graphic analysis, linear programming problems containing three or more variables must be solved by a mathematical solution technique known as the **simplex method.** The mechanics of the simplex method are far from simple, even though the method arrives at a solution by comparing objective function values at multidimensional corner points, just as was done above with the graphic approach. To solve the Martin Company's product mix problem, the same set of equations would be used as in the above illustration. Most large computers have software packages available to perform the necessary computations.

PAYOFF TABLES

Certainty means the probability of an event's occurring is 100 percent, whereas **uncertainty** means the probability of an event's occurring is less than 100 percent. When the outcome of a decision alternative is uncertain, managers often desire information on the expected value of that alternative. A decision alternative's **expected value** is simply the weighted average of the possible cash flows associated with that alternative. Identifying each possible cash flow as an outcome, the expected value of a decision alternative is computed as follows:

Expected value $= \Sigma$ (Outcome) (Probability of outcome),

where Σ is a summation sign indicating that the product of each cash flow multiplied by its related probability is to be summed.

Assume a particular investment has the following possible outcomes.

Outcome	Net Cash Flow	Probability
1	$2000	0.50
2	5000	0.20
3	8000	0.30
		1.00

This investment has three possible outcomes, and, because one of them will occur, the associated probabilities sum to 1.00, or 100 percent. The expected value of this investment is $4400:

$$\text{Expected value} = (\$2000)(0.50) + (\$5000)(0.20) + (\$8000)(0.30)$$
$$= \$4400.$$

The expected cash flow of $4400 is the weighted average of the possible cash flows of $2000, $5000, and $8000. A cash flow of exactly $4400 will not occur, but this weighted amount is a better *summary measure* of the project's cash flows than any one of the three possible outcomes. The advantages of expected value as a summary measure increase with the number of possible outcomes. With only three possible outcomes the situation is fairly simple, but imagine a situation where there are ten or fifteen possible outcomes; here a summary measure of possible outcomes would be welcome.

Constructing Payoff Tables

Expected value is frequently employed as a decision criterion when a manager must select one of several alternative actions, with the outcomes of each subject to uncertainty. A **payoff table** is often used to enumerate the alternative actions management may take and the possible monetary outcomes of each action. Each monetary outcome results from the joint effect of management's action and an event that can occur. Once the payoff table is constructed the outcome and probability information in it are used to compute each action's expected value. The following example illustrates the relationship between actions, events, and outcomes, as well as the construction and use of payoff tables.

On Saturdays during July and August, Janet Gaines sells hotdogs at a Long Island beach. She acquires the precooked and prepackaged hotdogs for $0.60 each and sells them for $1.00. She must order her hotdogs in lots of 100 on Thursdays. Past daily demand has varied between 200 and 500 units with the following probability distribution.

Event	Probability Distribution
200 units demanded	0.20
300 units demanded	0.30
400 units demanded	0.40
500 units demanded	0.10

Janet wants to know how many hotdogs to order each Thursday to maximize the expected value of hotdog sales. Unsold hotdogs are donated to a local orphanage.

The payoff table for this particular decision is presented in Exhibit 13–8. The decision alternatives are the order sizes listed in the left column. The possible events are the levels of demand listed across the top (along with the related probability of each event). The outcomes, resulting from the joint effect of the order size and the demand, are presented in the center of the table. These outcomes range from a loss of $100 if 500 units are ordered but only 200 are sold to a profit of $200 if 500 units are ordered and sold. Sample computations for other outcomes are presented below the table.

EXHIBIT 13–8 Payoff Table Illustrated

Action	Event				Expected
	Demand (probability)				Value of
Order Size	200 (0.20)	300 (0.30)	400 (0.40)	500 (0.10)	Action
200	$ 80*	$ 80	$ 80	$ 80	$ 80
300	20	120	120	120	100 maximum
400	(40)†	60	160	160	90‡
500	(100)	—	100	200	40

* Example of computation: ($1 × 200) − ($0.60 × 200) = $80.

† Example of computation: ($1 × 200) − ($0.60 × 400) = $(40).

‡ Example of computation: ($ − 40)(0.20) + ($60)(0.30) + ($160)(0.40) + ($160)(0.10) = $90.

The expected values, shown in the right column, are computed for each action as the sum of each outcome times the related probability. The probability of an outcome is the same as the probability of the event that results in that outcome, given an action. In this example, an order size of 300 units has the highest expected value; therefore, using expected value as the decision criterion, Janet Gaines should order 300 hotdogs each Thursday.

Value of Perfect Information

A manager sometimes has an opportunity to acquire additional information before making a decision, but because information is seldom free, the manager should evaluate the potential benefits of the additional information and the cost of obtaining it. The potential benefits are derived from the ability to make decisions that result in increased cost savings or net cash inflows. The cost of information includes the cost of resources used in obtaining it and the cost of delaying a decision. The **value of perfect information** is the maximum amount a manager would be willing to pay for additional information. It is computed as the difference between the expected profits with perfect information and the current expected profits. Though perfect information is seldom available, a manager might still desire to know its value because the value of perfect information serves as an upper limit on the amount he or she would pay for additional information.

If Janet Gaines had perfect information, she would always order the number of hotdogs she could sell. Ordering less would result in lost sales, and ordering more would result in excess costs. A payoff table with perfect information is shown in Exhibit 13–9. The expected value *with* perfect information is $136. This value is computed for the entire set of actions, rather than for each action, because the order size will vary with demand.

EXHIBIT 13–9   Payoff Table for Perfect Information

| Action | Event | | | | Weighted |
| | Demand (probability) | | | | |
Order Size	200 (0.20)	300 (0.30)	400 (0.40)	500 (0.10)	Value
200	$80				$ 16*
300		$120			36
400			$160		64
500				$200	20
Expected value with perfect information					$136

* Example of computation: ($80 × 0.20) = $16.

She will order 200 units 20 percent of the time, 300 units 30 percent of the time, and so forth. The expected value *of* perfect information is $36:

Expected profits with perfect information	$136
Current expected profits	−100
Expected value of perfect information	$ 36

Knowing the expected value of perfect information, Janet is in a better position to bargain with someone who offers her any additional information, perfect or imperfect.

Attitudes toward Risk

The previous discussion assumed that management is completely indifferent toward risk and makes decisions solely on the basis of expected value. Obviously, this is not true. Few managers would be indifferent to the following investment alternatives.

Investment	Outcome	Probability
A	$(10,000)	0.90
	240,000	0.10
B	$ 5,000	0.50
	25,000	0.50

Both investments have an expected value of $15,000.

$$\text{Expected value (A)} = (\${-}10{,}000 \times 0.90) + (\$240{,}000 \times 0.10)$$
$$= \$15{,}000.$$

$$\text{Expected value (B)} = (\$5{,}000 \times 0.50) + (\$25{,}000 \times 0.50)$$
$$= \$15{,}000.$$

Yet investment A has a 90 percent probability of a $10,000 loss, whereas investment B has all positive outcomes. Most decision makers would prefer investment B.

In addition to information on each action's expected value, management should obtain information on the variability of an action's outcome. This information might be the range of possible outcomes, the probability of negative outcomes, or statistical measures such as the standard deviation or the coefficient of variation. Statistical measures are discussed in introductory statistics textbooks. With information on expected values and variability, managers can make whatever trade-offs between return and risk they believe are appropriate.

SUMMARY

A model is a simplified representation of some real-world phenomenon. Managers and other decision makers often use optimizing models, such as the economic order quantity, linear programming, and payoff tables that suggest a specific choice among decision alternatives. These models are decision aids; they do not make decisions. Before implementing a decision suggested by a model, a manager should carefully evaluate the data used in the model, the assumptions underlying the model, and the output of the model. If the manager suspects any problems, the suggested action should not be implemented. Instead, the manager should undertake further analysis or make a decision based on professional judgment. When the outcome of an action is subject to uncertainty, the manager should not act only on the basis of expected value but should obtain information on the outcome's variability and make whatever trade-offs between return and risk he or she believes are appropriate.

APPENDIX
VARIANCE INVESTIGATION DECISIONS

Managers responsible for certain types of processes must often decide whether or not to shut down the process for inspection and adjustment, if necessary. In general, management wants to shut down the process only when it is out-of-adjustment. However, there is no way of knowing for certain whether the process is in-adjustment or out-of-adjustment except by shutting it down and performing an inspection. Obviously, if the process is in-adjustment, no further action is necessary, and if the process is out-of-adjustment, it is necessary to adjust it.

If the managers do not shut the process down for inspection, they may incur excess operating costs if the process is, in fact, out-of-adjustment. Conversely, there will be no excess operating costs if it is in-adjustment.

In summary, there are two possible actions: (1) Inspect and adjust if necessary, and (2) do not inspect. There are also two possible events (or states): (1) The process is in-adjustment, and (2) the process is out-of-adjustment. Payoff tables are often used to summarize the outcomes of these alternative actions and events.

Assume management is trying to determine whether or not to inspect an automatic production process. There is an 80 percent probability that the process is in-adjustment and a 20 percent probability that it is out-of-adjustment. Relevant costs are as follows:

Inspection	$ 200
Adjustment, if necessary	300
Excess operating costs if out-of-adjustment	2000

EXHIBIT 13–10 Payoff Table for Variance Investigation

	Event (probability)		
Action	In-Adjustment (0.80)	Out-of-Adjustment (0.20)	Expected Cost of Action
Inspect and adjust if necessary	$200	$ 500*	$260†
Do not inspect	0	2,000	400‡

* Inspection costs of $200 + adjustment costs of $300

† ($200)(0.80) + ($500)(0.20)

‡ ($0)(0.80) + ($2000)(0.20)

The payoff table for this decision is presented in Exhibit 13–10. Since the objective is to minimize expected costs, the best action here is to inspect and adjust if necessary.

KEY TERMS

Model	Linear programming
Physical model	Objective function
Quantitative model	Feasible region
Descriptive model	Optimal solution
Optimizing model	Simplex method
Order quantity	Certainty
Reorder point	Uncertainty
Economic order quantity	Expected value
Lead time	Payoff table
Safety stocks	Value of perfect information

REVIEW QUESTIONS

13–1 Distinguish between descriptive and optimizing models, and give three examples of each.

13–2 Do optimizing models make decisions? Discuss.

13–3 Once management has decided on the number of units to order during a period of time, what inventory ordering decisions remain?

13–4 What is the relationship between order size, total annual ordering costs, and total annual carrying costs?

13–5 Present a formula to compute the total annual ordering and carrying costs of inventory.

13–6   Identify five assumptions that underlie the economic order quantity model presented in this text.

13–7   Present the economic order quantity formula.

13–8   What adjustments are necessary before the economic order quantity formula can be applied to manufacturing firms?

13–9   What is the objective of linear programming?

13–10   What is the most critical assumption underlying linear programming? What are the implications of this assumption for accounting data used in linear programming?

13–11   Identify the steps involved in solving a linear programming problem with graphic analysis.

13–12   In graphic analysis, if there is a single optimal solution, where is it found?

13–13   How is the expected value of a decision alternative computed?

13–14   For what purpose is a payoff table used? What two factors determine the outcomes included in a payoff table?

13–15   How is the value of perfect information computed?

EXERCISES

13–1 Determining Order Quantity, Reorder Point, and Safety Stock

The annual demand for inventory item Z-10 is 1000 units, the cost of placing an order is $50, and the cost of carrying one unit in inventory for one year is $10.

Requirements

a) Use the economic order quantity formula to determine the optimal order size.

b) Assuming a lead time of 10 days and a work year of 250 days, determine the reorder point.

c) Assuming the maximum lead time is 15 days and the maximum daily demand is 6 units, determine the safety stock required to prevent stockouts.

13–2 Determining Order Quantity, Reorder Point, and Safety Stock

The annual demand for inventory item X-27 is 3000 units, the cost of placing an order is $300, and the cost of carrying one unit in inventory for one year is $20.

Requirements

a) Use the economic order quantity formula to determine the optimal order size.

b) Assuming a lead time of 15 days and a work year of 300 days, determine the reorder point.

c) Assuming the maximum lead time is 20 days and the maximum daily demand is 15 units, determine the safety stock required to prevent stockouts.

13–3 Impact of Deviations from EOQ

Faced with a cash surplus, the Loveday Department Store *increased* the size of several inventory order quantities that had previously been determined using the EOQ model. Use the words "increase," "decrease," or "no change" to indicate the impact of management's decision on each of the following:

1. Average inventory.
2. Number of orders per year.
3. Total annual carrying costs.
4. Total annual ordering costs.
5. Total annual carrying and ordering costs.
6. Cost of goods sold.

13–4 Impact of Deviations from EOQ

Faced with a cash shortage, the Arnold Discount Store *reduced* the size of several inventory order quantities that had previously been determined using the EOQ model. Use the words "increase," "decrease," or "no change" to indicate the impact of management's decision on each of the following:

1. Average inventory.
2. Number of orders per year.
3. Total annual carrying costs.
4. Total annual ordering costs.
5. Total annual carrying and ordering costs.
6. Cost of goods sold.

13–5 Cost Savings with Economic Order Quantity: Shelf Life

The Ridge Way Pharmacy places orders for a particular inventory item in lot sizes of 15 units. Additional information about this inventory item is as follows:

Annual demand	720 units
Ordering costs	$25 per order
Purchase price	$40 per unit

Inventory carrying costs are estimated to be 25 percent of the average inventory investment.

Requirements

a) Determine the economic order quantity.
b) Determine the annual cost savings if Ridge Way changes from an order size of 15 units to the economic order quantity.
c) The shelf life of this item is limited. Assuming that shelf life is based on the number of days it may be used after it is placed in inventory, determine the optimal lot size under each of the following circumstances. Assume a 360 day year.

  1. Shelf life = 60 days.
  2. Shelf life = 20 days.

  Hint: Determine how many days an order will last.

13–6 Cost Savings with Economic Order Quantity: Quantity Discounts

The Holder Company currently purchases a particular item in sizes of 1250 units. Holder's annual use of this item is 6250 units. Ordering costs are $50 per order, and carrying costs are $10 per unit per year.

Requirements

a) Determine the economic order quantity.

b) Determine the amount of the annual cost savings if Holder changes from an order size of 1250 units to the economic order quantity.

c) The supplier offers a discount of $2 per unit if Holder orders in lots of 625 units or more. What action do you recommend? *Hint:* Compare the annual cost savings from the discount to the increased total annual ordering and carrying costs required to qualify for the discount.

13–7 Graphic Analysis

The graph presents a series of maximum production constraints.

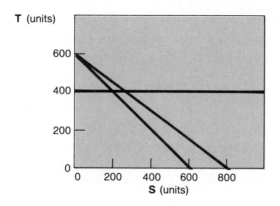

The objective function is:

$$\text{Maximize } \$60S + \$20T.$$

Required: Determine the optimal solution and the corresponding value of the objective function with the aid of graphic analysis.

13–8 Graphic Analysis

Presented are the objective function and the constraints for a linear programming problem:

$$\text{Maximize } \$5M + \$4N$$
$$1M + 2N \leq 12$$
$$1M + 1N \leq 8$$
$$M \leq 6$$
$$M \geq 0$$
$$N \geq 0.$$

Required: Determine the optimal solution and the corresponding value of the objective function with the aid of graphic analysis.

13–9 Linear Programming with Graphic Analysis

The Walker Company produces two products, X and Y, in one department. Product X has a unit contribution margin of $40, and Product Y has a unit contribution margin of $30. The demand for each product exceeds Walker's production capacity, which is limited by available labor and machine hours. Product information follows:

	Hours per Unit		Total Hours
	X	Y	Available per Week
Labor	12	18	180
Machine	6	4	60

Management desires the product mix that will maximize the weekly contribution toward fixed costs and profits.

Requirements

a) Formulate the objective function and constraints necessary to determine the optimal product mix.

b) Determine the optimal solution and the corresponding value of the objective function with the aid of graphic analysis.

13–10 Linear Programming with Graphic Analysis

The Wilmington Desk Company produces two styles of desks, Captain's and Mate's, in two departments, Assembly and Finishing. The Captain's desks have a unit contribution margin of $200, and Mate's desks have a unit contribution margin of $150. The demand for each product exceeds Wilmington's production capacity, which is limited by the available hours in each department. Production information follows:

	Hours per Unit		Total Hours
	Captain	Mate	Available per Month
Assembly Department	10	10	1,500
Finishing Department	40	20	4,000

Management desires the product mix that will maximize the monthly contribution toward fixed costs and profits.

Requirements

a) Formulate the objective function and constraints necessary to determine the optimal product mix.

b) Determine the optimal solution and the corresponding value of the objective function with the aid of graphic analysis.

13–11 Computing Expected Values and Evaluating Risk

Presented is information on the possible outcomes of two investment alternatives.

Investment I		Investment II	
Outcome	Probability	Outcome	Probability
$(20,000)	0.50	$3,000	0.30
0	0.20	5,000	0.40
50,000	0.30	7,000	0.30

Requirements

a) Compute the expected value of each investment.

b) Indicate which you prefer and why you prefer it.

13–12 Computing Expected Values and Evaluating Risk

Presented is information on the possible outcomes of three investment alternatives.

Investment I		Investment II		Investment III	
Outcome	Probability	Outcome	Probability	Outcome	Probability
$10,000	1.00	$10,000	0.30	$−30,000	0.30
		12,000	0.40	0	0.10
		14,000	0.30	10,000	0.20
				47,500	0.40

Requirements

a) Compute the expected value of each investment.

b) Indicate which investment you prefer and why you prefer it.

13–13 Payoff Tables and the Value of Perfect Information

The Black Gold Oil Company prospects for oil in the mountains of Pennsylvania. Currently, the cost of drilling an oil well is $40,000. If oil is found, the well is sold for $800,000. If oil is not found, the well is worthless. At each drilling site, Black Gold has two possible actions: (1) drill, or (2) do not drill. At each drilling site there are two possible states or events: (1) oil is present, or (2) oil is not present. In a particular area of the mountains, the probability of finding oil is 10 percent, and the probability of not finding oil is 90 percent.

Requirements

a) With the aid of a payoff table, determine the expected value of each action for each site.

b) A new testing service can determine in advance whether or not oil will be found at a drilling site. Determine the value of perfect information for each site.

13–14 Payoff Tables and the Value of Perfect Information

The operator of a Westwego newsstand must determine the number of copies of the Bourbon Street Journal to stock each day. The operator buys the Journal for $0.50 per copy and sells it for $0.75 per copy. Unsold papers are worthless at the end of the day. Past daily demand has varied between 150 and 250 copies with the following probabilities.

Event	Probability
150 copies demanded	0.30
200 copies demanded	0.40
250 copies demanded	0.30

Requirements

a) With the aid of a payoff table determine whether the operator should order 150, 200, or 250 copies.

b) Determine the value of perfect information.

13–15 Variance Investigation (Appendix)

The cost of inspection is $500; the cost of adjustment, if necessary, is $800; the excess operating costs if out-of-adjustment equipment is not corrected is $5000. The probability that the equipment is in-adjustment is 90 percent, and the probability that the equipment is out-of-adjustment is 10 percent.

Required: With the aid of a payoff table, determine if the equipment should be inspected and adjusted if necessary.

13–16 Variance Investigation (Appendix)

The cost of inspection is $200; the cost of adjustment, if necessary, is $250; the excess operating cost if out-of-adjustment equipment is not corrected is $4000. The probability that the equipment is in-adjustment is 60 percent, and the probability that the equipment is out-of-adjustment is 40 percent.

Required: With the aid of a payoff table, determine if the equipment should be inspected and adjusted if necessary.

13–17 Variance Investigation (Appendix)

The Bilco Oil Company currently sells three grades of gasoline: regular, premium, and "regular plus," which is a mixture of regular and premium. Regular plus is advertised as being "at least 50 percent premium." Although any mixture containing 50 percent or more premium gas could be sold as "regular plus," it is less costly to use exactly 50 percent. The amount of premium gas in the mixture is determined by one small valve in the blending machine. If the valve is properly adjusted, the machine provides a mixture that is 50 percent premium and 50 percent regular. Assume that if the valve is out-of-adjustment, the machine provides a mixture that is 60 percent premium and 40 percent regular. Once the machine is started it must continue until 100,000 gallons of "regular plus" have been mixed.

Available cost data are as follows:

Cost per gallon:	
Premium	$ 0.64
Regular	$ 0.60
Cost of checking the valve	$80.00
Cost of adjusting the valve	$40.00

Subjective estimates of the probabilities of the valve's condition are estimated to be:

Condition	Probability
Valve in-adjustment	0.70
Valve out-of-adjustment	0.30

Required: With the aid of a payoff table, determine if the valve should be checked, and adjusted if necessary, before each batch of 100,000 gallons of "regular plus" is mixed.

(CMA Adapted)

PROBLEMS

13–18 Economic Order Quantity by Trial and Error and Formula

The Mountain Shop sells 240 Mt. Washington sleeping bags each year. Mt. Washington sleeping bags retail for $175 and wholesale for $100. The Mountain Shop's ordering and carrying costs are as follows:

Cost of placing each order	$50
Annual carrying costs as a percentage of unit cost	15%

Requirements

a) Prepare a table, similar to that in Exhibit 13–3, of the relevant annual costs for determining the economic order quantity. Complete the table for lot sizes of 10, 20, 30, 40, 50, and 60 units. Identify the economic order quantity.

b) Prepare a graph, similar to that in Exhibit 13–4, for the behavior of inventory ordering and carrying costs.

c) Based on requirements (a) and (b), what can be said about ordering and carrying costs at the economic order quantity?

d) Use the economic order quantity formula to determine the optimal order size.

13–19 Economic Lot Size by Trial and Error and Formula

The Designer Phone Company manufactures telephones, in a variety of styles, for residential use. Presented is information about the Classic Touch, one of Designer's models.

Annual sales	500 units
Variable manufacturing costs per unit	$80
Set-up and ordering costs per batch	$50

Carrying costs per year as a percent of variable manufacturing costs are:

Insurance	2.0%
Personal property taxes	0.5
Storage space	3.0
Deterioration and obsolescence	4.5
Opportunity cost of money invested in inventory	15.0
Total	25.0%

Requirements

a) Prepare a table, similar to that in Exhibit 13–3, of the relevant annual costs for determining the economic lot size. Complete the table for lot sizes of 10, 20, 40, 50, 80, and 100 units. Identify the economic lot size.

b) Prepare a graph, similar to that in Exhibit 13–4, for the behavior of inventory ordering and carrying costs.

c) Based on requirements (a) and (b), what can be said about ordering and carrying costs at the economic lot size?

d) Use the economic order quantity formula to determine the optimal lot size.

13–20 Plotting Variations in Inventory Levels with Safety Stocks

An inventory item, with an average daily demand of 5 units and a maximum daily demand of 10 units, has an economic order quantity of 100 units. In the absence of safety stocks, the item's reorder point is 20 units. Safety stocks are set at 30 units.

Requirements

a) Determine each of the following:

   1. Average lead time.

   2. Maximum lead time.

   3. Reorder point with safety stocks.

   4. Maximum inventory level.

b) Graph the variations in inventory level over a period of 50 days. Start on day 1 (time 0) with maximum inventory. Assume inventory is replenished without use of the safety stocks. Continue through a second inventory cycle assuming maximum lead time demand. Clearly identify the maximum inventory, reorder point, and safety stock.

13–21 Economic Order Quantity and Reorder Point: Missing Data

Supply the missing data in each case. Assume that all costs and quantities are optimal, according to the EOQ formula.

	Case 1	Case 2	Case 3	Case 4
Annual demand	250	?	200	?
Economic order quantity	?	?	?	200
Average inventory	?	50	?	?
Orders per year	?	30	5	?
Working days per year	250	?	?	?
Average daily demand	?	12	0.8	?
Lead time in days	10	?	5	8
Reorder point	?	60	?	80
Annual ordering costs	$?	$?	$?	$?
Annual carrying costs	?	1500	?	?
Total	$?	$?	$?	$?
Cost of placing an order	$100	?	$ 20	$ 80
Annual unit carrying costs	$ 20	?	?	$ 10

Hint: For cases 2 and 3, costs are equal at the EOQ; for case 4, work backward from the EOQ.

13–22 Estimating Inventory Ordering and Carrying Costs

Evans, Inc. is a large wholesale distributor that deals exclusively in baby shoes. Because of the substantial costs related to ordering and storing the shoes, the company has decided to employ the economic order quantity (EOQ) model to help determine the optimum quantities of shoes to order from the different manufacturers.

Before Evans, Inc. can employ the EOQ model, it needs to develop values for two of the cost parameters — ordering costs and carrying costs. As a starting point, management has decided to develop the values for the two cost parameters by using cost data from the most recent fiscal year, 19x5.

The company placed 4000 purchase orders during 19x5. The largest number of orders placed during any one month was 400 orders in June, and the smallest number of orders placed was 250 in December. Selected cost data for these two months and the year for the Purchasing, Accounts Payable, and Warehouse departments appear below.

The Purchasing Department is responsible for placing all orders. The costs listed for the Accounts Payable Department relate only to the processing of purchase orders for payment. The Warehouse Department's costs reflect two operations — receiving and shipping. The receiving clerks inspect all incoming shipments and place the orders in storage. The shipping clerks are responsible for processing all sales orders to retailers.

The company leases space in a public warehouse. The rental fee is priced according to the square feet occupied during a month. The annual charges during 19x5 totaled $34,500. Annual insurance and property taxes on the shoes vary with the value of the average monthly inventory. In 19x5 they amounted to $5700 and $7300, respectively. The company's opportunity cost of inventory investments is 20 percent.

	Costs for High Activity Month (June: 400 Orders)	Costs for Low Activity Month (December: 250 Orders)	Annual Costs
Purchasing Department:			
Purchasing manager	$ 1,750	$ 1,750	$ 21,000
Buyers	2,500	1,900	28,500
Clerks	2,000	1,100	20,600
Supplies	275	150	2,500
Accounts Payable Department:			
Clerks	2,000	1,500	21,500
Supplies	125	75	1,100
Data processing	2,600	2,300	30,000
Warehouse Department:			
Supervisor	1,250	1,250	15,000
Receiving clerks	2,300	1,800	23,300
Receiving supplies	50	25	500
Shipping clerks	3,800	3,500	44,000
Shipping supplies	1,350	1,200	15,200
Freight-out	1,600	1,300	16,800
	$21,600	$17,850	$240,000

The inventory balances tend to fluctuate during the year depending upon the demand for baby shoes. The average monthly inventory during 19x5 was $190,000.

The boxes in which the baby shoes are stored are all approximately the same size. Consequently, the shoes all occupy about the same amount of storage space in the warehouse.

Required: Using the 19x5 data, determine estimated values appropriate for (1) the cost of placing an order and (2) the annual carrying costs per dollar of inventory investment.

(CMA Adapted)

13–23 Accounting Inputs to Linear Programming: Graphic Analysis

The Smile Camera Company manufactures two popular cameras, Little Smile and Big Smile. Recent increases in demand have pushed Smile Camera to the limits of their production capacity. The president is a former engineer who knows that linear programming can be used to determine the optimal product mix. However, he needs your assistance in formulating the objective function coefficients and in determining the profit implications of the optimal solution.

The following information is available from the accounting records.

	Little Smile	Big Smile
Unit selling price	$150	$220
Unit manufacturing costs:		
Direct materials	$ 38	$ 54
Direct labor	30	30
Factory overhead	48	80
Total	$116	$164

Production employees are paid $10 per direct labor hour. A total of 450 direct labor hours is available each month. Factory overhead is applied at the rate of $16 per machine hour. Seventy-five percent of the overhead rate is for variable costs, and 25 percent is for fixed costs. A total of 750 machine hours is available each month. The factory overhead rate is based on the full utilization of 750 machine hours each month.

Additional information:

- Because of insufficient raw materials, only 100 Big Smile Cameras can be produced each month.

- Variable selling and administrative expenses are $6 per unit of either product.

- Fixed selling and administrative expenses are $2300 per month.

Requirements

a) Formulate the objective function and constraints necessary to determine the optimal monthly production mix.

b) Determine the optimal solution and the corresponding value of the objective function with the aid of graphic analysis.

c) Determine the Smile Camera Company's expected monthly profit.

13–24 Accounting Inputs to Linear Programming: Graphic Analysis

Kyoto Electric produces two video cassette recorders, a manual model that does not contain an automatic timer, and an automatic model that does. Though demand for the automatic model is only 75 units per month, Kyoto has been unable to satisfy the demand for the lower priced manual model. The following information is available from the accounting records.

	Manual	Automatic
Unit selling price	$200	$329
Unit manufacturing costs:		
Direct materials	$105	$190
Conversion:		
Department 1	24	24
Department 2	45	90
Total	$174	$304

The conversion costs include direct labor, variable overhead, and fixed overhead. In Department 1, conversion costs are assigned at the rate of $20 per hour. Fifty percent is for variable costs, and 50 percent is for fixed costs. A total of 180 hours is available each month in Department 1. In Department 2, conversion costs are assigned at the rate of $30 per hour. Eighty percent is for variable costs, and 20 percent is for fixed costs. A total of 300 hours is available each month in Department 2. The fixed overhead rates, as a portion of total conversion costs, are based on the full utilization of production capacity.

Additional information:

- Variable selling and administrative expenses are $10 per unit of either product.
- Fixed selling and administrative expenses are $1200 per month.

Requirements

a) Formulate the objective function and the constraints necessary to determine the optimal monthly production mix.

b) Determine the optimal solution and the corresponding value of the objective function with the aid of graphic analysis.

c) Determine Kyoto Electric's expected monthly profit.

13–25 Formulating Objective Function and Constraints

Presented is unit information about three products manufactured and sold by Camden Products, Inc.

	Product		
	X	Y	Z
Selling price	$110	$130	$200
Direct materials	35	40	50
Direct labor	32	24	48
Variable factory overhead	25	30	40
Fixed factory overhead	20	24	32
Variable selling and administrative expenses	8	6	10

Additional information:

- Fixed selling and administrative expenses are $60,000 per year.
- The direct labor rate is $16 per hour.
- Variable factory overhead is applied at the rate of $10 per machine hour, and fixed factory overhead is applied at the rate of $8 per machine hour.
- A total of 120,000 direct labor hours and 125,000 machine hours are available each year.
- The fixed overhead rate is based on total available machine hours.
- Management desires to produce a minimum of 10,000 units of Product X and a maximum of 20,000 units of Product Z each year.
- The demand for products X and Y exceeds production capacity.

Requirements

a) Formulate the objective function and the constraints necessary to determine the optimal yearly production mix.

b) Determine the expected annual profit if Camden produces 10,000 units of X, 4000 units of Y, and 20,000 units of Z.

13–26 Formulating Objective Function

A processing department of the East Orange Chemical Company can vary the production mix of two products, Compound B1 and Compound B2. Because of the high demand for these products, a chemical engineer has been requested to determine the optimal monthly volumes of each product. The engineer has formulated all the constraints needed to determine the optimal mix with the aid of linear programming and has asked you to assist in developing the objective function coefficients. The engineer has provided you with the following production information.

	Per Two-Liter Bottle*	
	Compound B1	Compound B2
Raw materials:		
C25	1 liter	2 liters
D80	3 liters	1 liter
MA5	—	1 liter
Bottle	1	1
Direct labor	0.4 hours	0.6 hours

* The difference between total inputs and outputs is due to shrinkage, waste, and evaporation.

You obtain the following information from an analysis of the accounting records.

Selling prices:	
Compound B1	$12.20/bottle
Compound B2	18.00/bottle
Raw materials costs:	
C25	$ 0.80/liter
D80	0.40/liter
MA5	0.65/liter
Bottles	0.50/each
Direct labor rate	$ 9.00/hour
Monthly factory overhead = $20,000 + 0.40 direct labor dollars	
Monthly selling and administrative costs = $15,000 + 0.25 sales revenue	

Required: Formulate the objective function necessary to determine the optimal monthly production in bottles.

13–27 Evaluating and Formulating Objective Function and Constraints

The Elon Co. manufactures two industrial products, X-10, which sells for $90 a unit, and Y-12, which sells for $85 a unit. Each product is processed through both of the company's manufacturing departments. The limited availability of labor, material, and equipment capacity has restricted the ability of the firm to meet the demand for its products. The plant manager believes that linear programming can be used to routinize the production schedule for the two products.

The following data are available to the plant manager.

	Amount Required per Unit	
	X-10	Y-12
Direct materials:		
Weekly supply limited to 1800 pounds at $12 per pound	4 pounds	2 pounds
Direct labor:		
Department 1 — weekly supply limited to 10 people at 40 hours each at an hourly rate of $6	$\frac{2}{3}$ hour	1 hour
Department 2 — weekly supply limited to 15 people at 40 hours each at an hourly rate of $8	$1\frac{1}{4}$ hour	1 hour
Machine time:		
Department 1 — weekly capacity limited to 250 hours	$\frac{1}{2}$ hour	$\frac{1}{2}$ hour
Department 2 — weekly capacity limited to 300 hours	0 hours	1 hour

The overhead costs for Elon are accumulated on a plantwide basis. The overhead is assigned to products on the basis of the number of direct labor hours required to manufacture the product. This base is appropriate for overhead assignment because most of the variable overhead costs vary as a function of labor time. The estimated overhead cost per direct labor hour is as follows:

Variable overhead cost	$ 6
Fixed overhead cost	6
Total overhead cost per direct labor hour	$12

The plant manager formulated the following equations for the linear programming statement of the problem.

A = number of units of X-10 to be produced.
B = number of units of Y-12 to be produced.

Objective function to minimize costs:

Minimize 85A + 62B

Constraints:

Material
$4A + 2B \leq 1800$ pounds
Department 1 labor
$\frac{2}{3}A + 1B \leq 400$ hours
Department 2 labor
$1\frac{1}{4}A + 1B \leq 600$ hours
Nonnegativity
$A \geq 0, \quad B \geq 0.$

Requirements

a) The formulation of the linear programming equations as prepared by the plant manager of Elon Co. is incorrect. Explain what errors have been made in the formulation prepared by the plant manager.

b) Formulate and label the proper equations for the linear programming statement of Elon's production problem.

(CMA Adapted)

13–28 Expected Values for Alternative Actions The Jon Co. has just agreed to supply Arom Chemical, Inc. with a substance critical to one of Arom's manufacturing processes. Because of the critical nature of this substance, Jon Co. has agreed to pay Arom $1000 for any shipment that is not received by Arom on the day it is required.

Arom establishes a production schedule that enables it to notify Jon Co. of the necessary quantity 15 days in advance of the required date. Jon can produce the substance in 5 days. However, capacity is not always readily available, which means that Jon may not be able to produce the substance for several days. There may be occasions when there are only one or two days available to deliver the substance. *When the substance is completed by Jon Co.'s manufacturing department and released to its shipping department, the number of days remaining before Arom Chemical, Inc. needs the substance will be known.*

Jon Co. has undertaken a review of delivery reliability and costs of alternative shipping methods. The results are presented in the following table.

Shipping Method	Costs per Shipment	Probability That the Shipping Will Take This Number of Days					
		1	2	3	4	5	6
Motor freight	$100	—	—	0.10	0.20	0.40	0.30
Air freight	$200	—	0.30	0.60	0.10	—	—
Air express	$400	0.80	0.20	—	—	—	—

Required: Prepare a decision table that can be used by the shipping clerk of Jon Co. to decide which delivery alternative to select. The decision table should specify the shipping method to use as a function of the days, 1 through 6, until the shipment is needed by Arom. Use the expected monetary value decision criterion as the basis for constructing the table. *Hint:* Compute the expected cost of shipping by each method for each alternative number of days until the shipment is needed by Arom.

(CMA Adapted)

14

Capital
Expenditures

Long-term investment and financing decisions are important activities in most organizations. After potentially desirable investments have been identified management must be provided with detailed information relating to each investment's capital demands, cash flows, and financial benefits to the organization. Several models are available to aid in the evaluation of capital budgeting proposals. The purpose of this chapter is to present the most widely used capital budgeting models and to evaluate each model's strengths and weaknesses.

Models relating to long-run decisions are similar to those discussed in Chapter 5 relating to short-run decisions in that both utilize a differential analysis of cash inflows and cash outflows. The major difference is that capital budgeting models (long-run models) involve cash flows over extended periods of time, whereas the short-run models involve only current period cash flows. When cash flows extend over several periods, an adjustment should be made to make the cash flow values comparable. This procedure is referred to as present value analysis.

The appendix at the end of the text discusses the time value of money and its applications to present value analysis as related to this chapter. To simplify the use of the present value concepts, all basic discussions of cash flows are presented in the appendix along with the present value tables. Before continuing this chapter, you should be familiar with present value concepts.

LONG-RANGE PLANNING

Most organizations plan not only for operations in the current period but also for the longer term, perhaps five to ten, or even twenty, years in the future. Most planning beyond the current accounting period is called *long-range planning*. Because it involves projections into the future, long-range planning has more uncertainty than short-range planning. As a result, long-range plans must be formulated in terms of more general objectives and policies than those presented in Chapter 6 with operating budgets. Long-range plans might include efforts to increase a company's share of the market, introduce new products, or expand into a different industry. These types of plans usually result in capital expenditures for plant and equipment or acquisitions of existing businesses.

The variety of factors that affect the long-range plans of most organizations require the formulation of a long-range planning team composed of key individuals within the organization. The management accountant — who is generally expert in data collection, retrieval, and analysis — is normally a part of the long-range planning team. Other team members may be knowledgeable of production techniques, research and development efforts, overall organizational strategy, future marketing activities, and the demands of the organization's stockholders or owners.

When an organization engages in long-range planning, the uncertainties of the future must be carefully considered and the goals and objectives of management fulfilled to the extent possible. The fact that long-range planning involves uncertainties and estimates does not relieve an organization of making decisions that affect future periods. Even if a company does not know exactly what its product demands will be in the future, it still must have facilities with which to manufacture products, sell products, perform research and development, and continue operating. Chapter 13 discussed the basics of uncertainty and probability, some of which can be applied to capital budgeting situations.

This chapter focuses attention on the capital budgeting aspects of long-range planning. Like long-range planning in general, capital budgeting data are subject to considerable uncertainties. Management must make the best decisions it can on the basis of the accounting and financial information available. The techniques and models discussed in this chapter deal with data related to capital budgeting decisions and the evaluation of the outcomes from the various capital budgeting models. **Capital budgeting** involves the allocation of limited financial resources among competing long-term investments.

When using capital budgeting models and making decisions involving long-term investments, an organization evaluates future cash inflows and outflows connected with each investment. Normally, only differential cash flows are evaluated for each investment decision. For example, a new piece of equipment is evaluated on its initial cost (cash outflow) as compared to the future savings or cash inflows it generates for the organization. Every for-profit organization is interested in the returns on its investments and, therefore, very carefully evaluates all alternative uses of funds. Even not-for-profit organizations use capital budgeting to evaluate investments in order to provide services at a minimum cost. Their investment decisions are normally founded on cost minimization objectives, as opposed to profit maximization of for-profit organizations.

Several additional factors must also be considered for capital budgeting decisions. Because most fixed asset investments have a limited life and decline in value over time and with use, consideration should be given to the fact that an investment's return will not continue indefinitely. Another factor is the timing of the returns. Some returns begin immediately, whereas others may take several years to be realized. Cash flows to be received in the future are not worth as much as the cash flows currently being returned to the company. For all long-term capital investments, the time value of money must be considered as an influencing factor. To properly evaluate capital decisions, management should consider all relevant accounting information and any subjective factors such as production quality and employee morale.

CAPITAL BUDGETING TECHNIQUES

When making a capital investment such as a building purchase, management is concerned that the investment returns sufficient funds to recoup the original investment and provides an adequate return for the risks taken. Because the returns are generated over a number of years, the use of discounted cash flow (present value) concepts is desirable. Management must determine for each investment proposal whether the rate of return is smaller than, equal to, or greater than the minimum acceptable rate. The two basic methods for evaluating capital projects using discounted cash flow concepts are (1) the internal rate of return and (2) the net present value. The net present value model may be presented in dollar terms (net present value) or ratio form (the profitability index). Popular nondiscounting models include the payback method and the accounting rate of return.

Because of its simplicity and popularity,[1] the traditional payback method is presented first, followed by the discounted payback method. Next, the payback reciprocal and bail-out factor models are discussed. Important discounting models are then presented: net present value, profitability index, and internal rate of return. The accounting rate of return, a nondiscounting model based on accounting income and book value, is discussed last.

Payback Methods

One of the most often used investment evaluating tools is the payback method. The **payback method** determines the length of time necessary for the cumulative operating cash inflows from a project to equal the initial cash investment for the project. This length of time is called the **payback period.** *The payback method decision rule states that all investment projects should be accepted if the payback is equal to or less than some designated payback period established by management.* The payback method emphasizes the organization's concern with liquidity and the need to minimize risks by stressing the quickest possible recovery of the initial investment.

To compute the payback period, the initial investment amount and the annual estimated operating cash flows are needed. To illustrate, assume

---

[1] A study of 226 large companies by Patrick L. Ramano showed that the payback method was used most often. Eighty-two companies used this method, whereas 68 used internal rate of return, and only 30 listed net present value as a decision tool. *The Controller: Role and Techniques* (New York: National Association of Accountants, 1980).

the Tillman Company is evaluating a project that requires an initial investment of $20,000 that will produce annual operating cash inflows of $5000 for ten years. If the time value of money is ignored and no discount rate is used, the traditional payback period is four years, computed as follows:

$$\text{Payback period} = \frac{\text{Initial investment}}{\text{Annual operating cash flows}}$$

$$= \frac{20,000}{5,000}$$

$$= 4 \text{ years.}$$

When the payback period is computed for an investment that has unequal cash flows, the task is slightly more complicated. For the Alderman Company, an investment of $50,000 results in cash inflows as follows:

Year	Amount
1	$15,000
2	25,000
3	40,000
4	20,000
5	10,000

To compute the payback period, the net unrecovered amount must be determined for each year. In the year of full recovery, the cash flows are assumed to occur evenly and are prorated based on the amount needed to cover the investment increment, in this example $10,000 in year 3.

Year	Amount of Inflow	Unrecovered Investment
0	—	$50,000
1	$15,000	35,000
2	25,000	10,000
3	40,000	—

Therefore, $10,000 of $40,000 is needed in year 3, and this provides a proration of 0.25 ($10,000/$40,000). The payback period is 2 years plus 0.25 of year 3, or 2.25 years. Notice that the amounts of years 4 and 5 are ignored. What if management had decided on a cutoff period of 2 years or less and the above project returned $150,000 in year 4 alone? Would a decision based solely on the payback period be wise? In this situation, the $150,000 would be completely ignored.

When the payback method is adjusted for the time value of money, it is called the **discounted payback method.** It overcomes some of the above weaknesses and provides a perspective that assumes management wants its investments returned with at least a nominal amount of interest. The rate selected for the discount payback method is often a low-risk rate, such as that for current savings accounts or long-term government bonds.

When this method is used, the present values of each of the annual flows must be accumulated and compared to the initial investment. The discounted payback period for the Tillman Company investment is illustrated in Exhibit 14–1. The assumed rate of return is 12 percent. Notice that when discount factors are applied, the present values of the cash inflows are unequal. The payback computation is made similar to that in the Alderman example. An important difference of the discounted payback is that it provides for a payback period longer than the nondiscounted payback period of an identical investment. For the Tillman Company, the payback period increased from 4 to 5.78 years.

Proponents of the payback methods argue that the other investment models place too much emphasis on cash flows that are received over extended periods of time. They argue that many investments increase substantially in risks after three or four years and that the predictability of the cash flows becomes very uncertain. Furthermore, most managers prefer to be evaluated in the short run, and by investing in projects that provide a quick cash return, they tend to receive better performance evaluations. However, the advantages of payback methods are not without some offsetting limitations: They evaluate only the rapidity with which an investment

---

EXHIBIT 14–1 Discount Payback Method

(1)	(2)	(3)	(4) (2 × 3)	(5) (5† − 4)
Year	Amount	12% Present Value Factor	Present Value of Cash Flows	Unrecovered Investment
0				$20,000
1	$5,000	0.893	$4,465	$15,535
2	5,000	0.797	3,985	11,550
3	5,000	0.712	3,560	7,990
4	5,000	0.636	3,180	4,810
5	5,000	0.567	2,835	1,975
6	5,000	0.507	2,535*	—

* $1975/$2535 = 0.78 of period 6. Therefore, the payback period is 5.78 years.

† Prior year unrecovered investment.

will be recovered, they completely ignore the returns after the payback period, and they usually ignore the timing of the cash flows within the payback period. At best, payback methods can be screening devices for the initial evaluation of investment alternatives.

Payback Reciprocal

The **payback reciprocal** is the annual operating cash inflows divided by the initial investment. As indicated by its name, this method is the reciprocal of the traditional payback method. The equation for the payback reciprocal is as follows:

$$\text{Payback reciprocal} = \frac{\text{Annual operating cash flows}}{\text{Initial investment}}, \text{ or } \frac{1}{\text{Payback period}}.$$

The payback reciprocal is often used to estimate the internal rate of return; that is, the discount rate that equates the present value of a project's operating cash inflows with the initial investment. This reciprocal can be an effective estimate when a project has equal annual cash flows and a useful life at least twice as long as the payback period. For the Tillman Company, the payback reciprocal is computed as follows:

$$\text{Payback reciprocal} = \frac{\$5,000}{\$20,000}$$

$$= 0.25, \text{ or } 25 \text{ percent.}$$

The main benefit of this technique is that it provides a starting point when computing the internal rate of return for projects that tend to have long lives. As the life of a project approaches infinity, the payback reciprocal and the internal rate of return become close.

Bail-out Factor

The **bail-out factor** provides management with another quick computation for investment decisions. This model is often used when an investment has a high degree of risk related either to the ability to sell the outputs of the investment or to the technical feasibility of producing the outputs. The **bail-out factor** is defined as the time required to recover the initial investment in a project from any source of funds. Unlike the payback method, which recognizes only the net cash inflows from operations, the bail-out method recognizes cash inflows from either operations or disposal values.

The Brisbane Company is considering a project with an initial investment amount of $50,000. The annual operating cash inflows from the project are estimated to be $10,000 over a useful life of eight years. The salvage value of the investment declines by $10,000 the first year, and $12,000 the second year and all subsequent years, until zero salvage is reached. Under these conditions the bail-out period would be at the end of the first period, while the payback period would be five years. This is shown by the schedule below.

Time Period	Salvage Value	+	Cumulative Operating Cash Inflows	=	Total Recovery
0	$ —		$ —		$50,000
1	40,000		10,000		50,000
2	28,000		20,000		48,000
3	16,000		30,000		46,000
4	4,000		40,000		44,000
5	—		50,000		50,000
6	—		60,000		60,000
7	—		70,000		70,000
8	—		80,000		80,000

The bail-out period simply indicates the ability of the organization to get out of a bad investment. It provides management with a generalized rule of thumb about how long a decision can be postponed until an investment should be stopped. This evaluation tool merely provides a little more information to assist management in making investment decisions.

Net Present Value Method

The **net present value method** compares the initial investment to the present value of all future cash flows, not just those up to the point of payback as with the previous methods. This concept uses a predetermined discount rate established by management. Often the cost of capital (defined later) is used as the minimum acceptable rate. For investments to be acceptable using the net present value concept, they must meet, or exceed, the predetermined rate. If an investment's rate of return is equal to the predetermined rate, the net present value amount will be equal to zero. If an investment's rate exceeds the predetermined rate, there will be a positive net present value amount. Conversely, if an investment's rate does not meet the predetermined rate, the net present value amount will be negative. The net present value amount is computed as follows:

Net present value = Present value of future cash inflows − Initial investment.

As an example of an investment with equal future cash flows, the Carolina Company is considering an investment in a drill press with an expected life of 15 years and an initial cost of $34,055. The drill press is expected to save the company $5000 each year of its expected life. The required rate of return set by management is 12 percent.

The format for solving such problems is shown in Exhibit 14–2. The present value factor at 12 percent for fifteen years is 6.811 (see Table 2

EXHIBIT 14–2 Net Present Value Method with Equal Cash Flows

12 percent return

Present value of future cash flows	
$5000 × 6.811	$34,055
Present value of initial investment	−34,055
Net present value	$ —

14 percent return

Present value of future cash flows	
$5000 × 6.142	$30,710
Present value of initial investment	−34,055
Net present value	$(3,345)

on p. 726). This factor is multiplied by the annual savings of $5000. As is shown in Exhibit 14–2, the present value of $5000 received each year for fifteen years is $34,055. This amount is equal to the initial investment and results in a net present value of zero. Since both amounts are equal, this indicates that the project produces a return of exactly 12 percent.

Suppose, however, that the Carolina Company had demanded a rate of return of 14 percent. From Table 2 the present value factor of an annuity at 14 percent is 6.142. Notice from Exhibit 14–2 that the present value of the cash inflows is $3345 less than the present value of the initial investment. Therefore management would reject the project since the net present value amount is negative.

For projects that have unequal cash flows in future periods, the computations become more complex. To illustrate, consider the Hartwell Company, which is planning to purchase a new machine at a cost of $50,000. The new machine will have net cash inflows of $15,000, $24,000, $30,000 and $10,000 in years 1 through 4, respectively. The company demands a minimum rate on all projects of 14 percent. As shown in Exhibit 14–3 the present value of each unequal cash flow must be determined separately. After the present values of the future cash flows have been totaled, they are then compared to the present value of the initial investment of $50,000. Since the net present value, $7781, is above zero, the project has a return greater than 14 percent and is therefore acceptable to management.

When using the net present value method to compare alternatives with similar investment amounts, the alternative with the highest net present value amount should be selected. However, users of this model must be careful when evaluating investments with substantially different initial investment amounts. For example, an investment of $50,000, with a net pres-

EXHIBIT 14–3   Net Present Value Method with Unequal Cash Flows

		Present Value of Future Cash Flows	
Year	Cash Flow Amount	× Present Value Factor	= Present Value Amount
1	$15,000	0.877	$13,155
2	24,000	0.769	18,456
3	30,000	0.675	20,250
4	10,000	0.592	5,920
Total			$57,781
Present value of initial investment			−50,000
Net present value			$ 7,781

ent value of $10,000, may appear to be a very good investment. However, an alternative investment of $40,000, with a net present value of $9000, may be an even better investment. In such situations, the use of the profitability index may aid in the decision process.

Profitability Index

The **profitability index,** PI, also called the **present value index,** indicates the number of present value dollars generated per dollar of initial investment. It is computed as follows:

$$\text{Profitability index} = \frac{\text{Present value of future cash flows}}{\text{Initial investment}}$$

For the previous example of the Hartwell Company, the equation would be

$$\text{Profitability index} = \frac{\$57,781}{\$50,000}$$

$$= 1.16, \text{ or } 116 \text{ percent.}$$

From the previous illustration of the Carolina Company (see Exhibit 14–2), a profitability index of 1.00 ($34,055/$34,055) indicates a return of 12 percent. If the desired rate was 14 percent, the PI would be 0.90 ($30,710/$34,055). At 12 percent the profitability index of 1.00 indicates a return of exactly 12 percent, whereas any profitability index of less than 1.00 (0.90 at 14 percent) indicates a return below the cutoff rate.

The profitability index provides a standardized measure of the relationship between the present value of a project's future cash flows and the amount of the initial investment. It is often regarded as superior to net present value for the evaluation of alternative projects which have substantially different investment amounts. This index is usually a part of the overall evaluation process and is seldom used alone for making capital investment decisions.

Internal Rate of Return

The **internal rate of return,** often called the **time adjusted rate of return,** is defined as the discount rate that equates the net present value of the cash inflows to the cash outflows. It may also be stated as (1) the maximum interest rate that could be paid for the money invested in a project without incurring a loss or (2) the discount rate that results in a project's net present value equaling zero.

For our first example, equal cash flows are assumed to occur over the life of the project. The Beef Packing Company is considering the purchase of a packing machine that has an expected useful life of fifteen years and an initial cost of $37,400. It will save the company $8000 each year over its expected life.

To compute the internal rate of return for the new machine, it is necessary to find the discount rate that will equate the present value of the cash inflows to the $37,400 initial investment. For projects that have equal flows for their entire life, the investment is divided by the expected annual cash inflows or cash savings. This computation will give a present value factor that can be found in ordinary annuity tables of $1.00.

$$\frac{\text{Initial investment}}{\text{Annual cash flows}} = \text{Discount factor for internal rate of return}$$

This factor (same number as the payback period) can be located in Table 2 to determine the rate of return. For the Beef Packing Company our computation is

$$\frac{\$37,400}{\$8,000} = 4.675.$$

The present value factor that will equate a series of $8000 cash savings for fifteen years with an initial investment of $37,400 is 4.675. Referring to the 15-year row in Table 2, we find that the factor 4.675 is in the 20 percent column.

The next illustration for the internal rate of return method is for an investment with uneven cash flows. Hickory Lumber Company is extending its operations to include the manufacture of pressed boards. A new piece of equipment that has a useful life of three years can be purchased for $73,000. The annual net cash inflows from this new process will be $20,000, $30,000, and $40,000 in years 1, 2, and 3, respectively. The equipment will have zero salvage value at the end of three years.

With unequal cash flow, the trial and error approach is used to determine the internal rate of return. The first step is to select a rate of return estimated to be close to the actual rate of return of the investment. If the resulting present value amounts equal the initial investment, the actual internal rate of return has been selected. However, it is unlikely that the first selected rate will be the exact rate. If the resulting present value amounts are greater than the initial investment, this indicates an actual internal rate of return greater than the initially selected rate. In this case the next step is to select a high rate of return and proceed to determine the present value amounts of the cash inflows. If the present value of the cash inflows is less than the investment, this indicates an internal rate of return less than the second rate selected. Therefore the true rate of return will fall between the first and second rates. If the present value of the cash flows is again greater than the investment amounts, another rate must be selected to determine a range where the actual internal rate of return will fall. This trial and error approach is continued until the actual rate is determined. For the Hickory Manufacturing Company the details of these computations are presented in Exhibit 14–4.

EXHIBIT 14–4 Computation of Internal Rate of Return with Uneven Cash Flows

Selected rate of 12 percent

Future cash flows

Year 1	$20,000 × 0.893 = $17,860	
Year 2	30,000 × 0.797 = 23,910	
Year 3	40,000 × 0.712 = 28,480	$70,250
Initial investment		−$73,000
Net present value		($2,750)

Selected rate of 8 percent

Future cash flows

Year 1	$20,000 × 0.926 = $18,520	
Year 2	30,000 × 0.857 = 25,710	
Year 3	40,000 × 0.794 = 31,760	$75,990
Initial investment		−$73,000
Net present value		$ 2,990

Selected rate of 10 percent

Future cash flows

Year 1	$20,000 × 0.909 = $18,180	
Year 2	30,000 × 0.826 = 24,780	
Year 3	40,000 × 0.751 = 30,040	$73,000
Initial investment		−$73,000
Net present value		$ —

Notice from Exhibit 14–4 that the initial rate selected for the investment resulted in a net present value less than the investment amount. The second rate selected is smaller and thereby increases the present value of the cash inflows. Since the second rate provided a net present value in excess of the initial investment, it is known that the true rate is between 12 and 8 percent. The 10 percent rate is selected for the last trial. Notice that at 10 percent the present value of the cash inflows is equal to the present value of the initial investment amount.

The internal rate of return method provides management with an exact rate of return for each investment alternative. No other model provides information that can be compared directly to the stated cost of capital. It is also an excellent method for ranking projects.

Another advantage of the internal rate of return is that a project's internal rate of return can be computed without knowing the organization's cost of capital. The cost of capital must be known before a project's net present value can be computed. When funds are limited and managers believe all proposed projects are acceptable, the internal rate of return method permits ranking and accepting projects until available funds are exhausted without having to determine the cost of capital. This is one reason why the internal rate of return method is more widely used than the net present value method.

The internal rate of return computation is difficult if manual calculations are required. This problem can be overcome if the company has access to computer programs that can compute the rate. When the annual cash inflows contain a mix of inflows in some years and outflows in others, the internal rate of return can provide more than one rate for a particular project. This method implies that the cash inflows are reinvested at the rate earned by the investment when in fact a given investment may be either above or below the organization's average cost of capital rate.

Accounting Rate of Return

Like the traditional payback method, the **accounting rate of return** is a commonly used capital investment method that ignores the time value of money. As indicated by its title, this method compares the average annual net income associated with an investment to the average investment amount. The computation is as follows:

$$\text{Accounting rate of return} = \frac{\text{Average annual increase in net income}}{\text{Average investment}}.$$

An alternative computation replaces average investment with the initial investment amount. This method is often used for organizations that prefer to evaluate each project based on the accounting income concept.

To illustrate, assume that the Laefitte Company is going to invest in a project that costs $100,000 and has a salvage value of zero. The estimated average accounting income assignable to this project is $11,000. The accounting rate of return is computed as follows:

$$\text{Accounting rate of return} = \frac{\$11,000}{(\$100,000/2)}$$

$$= 22 \text{ percent.}$$

Notice that the average investment is simply the investment divided by two, which averages the amount of the investment from the beginning period to the ending period with an assumed salvage value of zero. If the investment has a salvage value, the average investment is computed as the salvage value plus the average depreciable investment.

While the accounting rate of return gives some recognition to a project's profitability, it does not consider the timing of cash flows. Cash flows and the investment are averaged out over the life of a project.

ADDITIONAL ASPECTS OF CAPITAL BUDGETING

Several aspects of capital budgeting must be considered as we analyze various models available for long-term investment decisions. As an investment concept, *capital budgeting* involves two types of management decisions. First, management must decide on the investment alternatives to be selected. This decision should be separated from the second decision in capital budgeting, that of financing the investment.

The capital budgeting decisions illustrated in this text relate primarily to the typical decisions encountered by most organizations. These decisions include such areas as new equipment purchases, plant expansions, and plant and equipment replacement. For-profit organizations are typically interested in these decisions and how they will increase the profits, either by increasing revenues or by reducing costs, or a combination of both. Not-for-profit organizations are interested in these types of decisions primarily for cost reduction benefits; that is, how they can provide constituents with services at lower costs. For all organizations, capital investment decisions should always be concerned with determining the best alternative uses of scarce resources. These alternatives may include new investments versus current investments, or one new investment versus another new investment.

Cost of Capital

When discounting models such as net present value are used to evaluate capital investment alternatives, management must determine the minimum return acceptable. The **cost of capital** is the average cost, expressed as a percentage, of obtaining the resources necessary to make investments. The cost of capital, which is easy to define but often difficult to measure, may be either (1) the average rate an organization must pay for funds invested in the company or (2) the rate of return for new investment projects that will keep the market value of the company's shares of stock unchanged.

The concept essentially means that a project must generate a return at least equal to the firm's average cost of obtaining its capital. This average cost takes into account such items as interest paid on notes and bonds payable, the effective dividend rate on preferred stock, and the discount rate that equates the present value of the total dividend stream expected over the organization's common stock's life to the current market value of its common stock. If a project earns the average cost of capital, the market value of the company's shares should remain unchanged because the rate of return on capital invested will remain the same. However, if a project has a return in excess of the organization's cost of capital, the market value of the company's shares should increase when the project is undertaken.

The cost of capital is important primarily because it is the minimum rate of return that is acceptable for investment projects. It serves as a cutoff rate for decision purposes. Any project not expected to yield this minimum rate should be rejected, and projects expected to yield equal or higher rates should be accepted.

Because of the difficulties of determining the cost of capital, many organizations adopt a minimum acceptable rate without complicated mathematical analysis. The rate is often called **a target rate of return,** and the firm will use this rate in deciding which projects to accept.

Differential Analysis

Any time that an organization is considering asset replacement decisions, a differential analysis is generally simpler and more straightforward than an analysis of all cash flows. Basically, **differential analysis** focuses on the difference between the cash flows of the current operating conditions and the future alternatives that management is considering. Once these amounts are netted out, the difference can be adjusted for the time value of money. Because current operations may be intertwined with several aspects of the organization, it is often difficult to isolate all the related costs and revenues associated with a given operation. For comparisons of current operating conditions with anticipated changes, management must be very careful to isolate all costs and revenues associated with the project. These items include tax considerations, methods of depreciation, and salvage values of any existing assets. Exhibit 14–5 illustrates the differential approach of evaluating proposals to replace a piece of existing equipment with a piece of new equipment.

EXHIBIT 14-5   Differential Analysis

	Current Equipment	New Equipment	Incremental Cash Flows
Incremental Investment			
New equipment		$180,000	($180,000)
Salvage realized	$ 10,000		10,000
Initial resource commitment			($170,000)
Differential cash flows (*annual*)			
Revenues	$100,000	$140,000	$ 40,000
Labor	25,000	20,000	5,000
Materials	30,000	40,000	(10,000)
Variable overhead	10,000	12,000	(2,000)
Packing expenses	15,000	18,000	(3,000)
Annual net flows favoring new equipment			$ 30,000

A replacement proposal can also be analyzed by using the total cost approach. The **total cost approach** calculates the present value of each project or alternative separately, and the present values of each project are then compared. If the net present value concept is used, the same answer will result whether the incremental approach or the total cost approach is used. Both approaches are very common in capital budgeting applications. The total cost approach is frequently used for new projects with alternatives, whereas the differential approach is commonly used with replacement decisions.

Evaluating Risk

All long-term investments involve considerable uncertainties that occur because of the length of time that is involved. There may be uncertainties about the success of the products, outputs, or activities of the investment, as well as about the amount of cash flows that will be generated from the investment. Though several things can be done to account for the uncertainties in an investment decision, probably the most common adjustment is to increase the desired rate of return for the investment alternative. For example, if the company's cost of capital is 15 percent, an 18 percent minimum rate of return may be required to offset the increased risks involved with the related decisions.

Capital Rationing

When a company has more investment projects than it has available resources to fund the projects, **capital rationing** occurs. This is particularly a problem when there are several investments that can be undertaken and each investment is competing for a set amount of investment dollars.

To maximize the profits of the organization, management must select the best proposals from the set of alternatives that satisfies the minimum cost of capital requirements. Normally this is done by ranking the projects and selecting the acceptable projects from the most favorable to the least favorable until the funds are exhausted. The major difficulty is selecting the criterion by which to rank the projects. To illustrate, assume that a company has four acceptable investments as shown in Exhibit 14–6. Notice from the information given that the initial investment amounts are the same, whereas the estimated useful lives vary.

Using the various investment evaluation models, each of the investments has been ranked as shown in Exhibit 14–7. For each method the projects were ranked from 1, the most favorable, through 4, the least favorable.

EXHIBIT 14–6   Capital Budgeting Alternatives

	Cash Flows			
	Project A	Project B	Project C	Project D
Investment amount	$1000	$1000	$1000	$1000
Period				
1	$ 500	$ 100	$ 100	$ 100
2	400	200	100	200
3	300	300	200	300
4	200	400	800	400
5	100	500	600	400
6				300
7				200
8				100
	$1500	$1500	$1800	$2000

Period	Present value factor at 10 percent	Present Values of Cash Flows			
		Project A	Project B	Project C	Project D
0	1.000	$(1000)	$(1000)	$(1000)	$(1000)
1	0.909	455	91	91	91
2	0.826	331	165	83	165
3	0.751	225	225	150	225
4	0.683	137	273	546	273
5	0.621	62	310	373	248
6	0.565				169
7	0.513				103
8	0.467				47
Cash inflows		1210	1064	1243	1321
Net present value		$ 210	$ 64	$ 243	$ 321

EXHIBIT 14-7   Ranking of Alternatives

Method	Project A	Project B	Project C	Project D
Traditional payback	2.33	4.00	3.75	4.00
Discounted payback	2.95	4.79	4.35	5.00
Net present value	$210	$64	$243	$321
Profitability index	1.21	1.06	1.24	1.32
Internal rate of return	20.30%	12.00%	16.50%	18.00%

	Ranking			
Traditional payback	1	3	2	3
Discounted payback	1	3	2	4
Net present value	3	4	2	1
Profitability index	3	4	2	1
Internal rate of return	1	4	3	2

Of the four projects, not one of them received a 1 ranking from all methods. Though the profitability index and net present value model rank the projects in approximately the same order, they differ substantially with the internal rate of return. Management must decide what objectives are most important for its investment decisions. If a quick return of the initial investment amount is important, weight should be given to the traditional payback period. If management has established minimum rates of return that *must* be met, emphasis should then be given to the internal rate of return or net present value methods. However, the profitability index may be a more efficient measure if alternatives requiring different initial investment are being considered.

In completing an evaluation of the projects, consideration must be given to the differing lives of the projects. Evaluations about what will be done with the returns of investments with short lives to make them equal to the length of the investments with long lives must be made. Can the organization continue with the anticipated rate of return, or will it increase or decrease when the project is over? Should the company evaluate all alternatives based on the expected life of the most short-lived project? These and many other subjective questions should be addressed before a final decision is reached.

Giving the results of all the models may be confusing to management. After some experience, an organization may decide to use only the one or two models that have proved to be most adaptable to the desires of management. Once a set of decision models has been selected, management should continue to track and monitor each investment to ensure that the organizational goals are being met.

SUMMARY

This chapter has presented an analysis of the primary capital investment decision models, including both discounting and nondiscounting techniques. To evaluate capital decisions, management should consider all differential cash flows and subjective factors such as the impact on the quality of products, employees, and operating philosophies.

Discounting models have been emphasized because they consider both profitability and the time value of money. The internal rate of return and net present value approaches are used by most large organizations. When funds are limited and many acceptable investments are available, it is necessary to rank the investments in some manner. While alternative criteria may not provide the same ranking, they do provide management with inputs that emphasize such things as the timing of the cash flows in early years versus later years, the size of comparable alternatives, and the average life between the alternatives. This kind of information generally assists management in making the final decision for capital investment alternatives. The impact of taxes on capital expenditures is an important topic that is considered in Chapter 15.

KEY TERMS

Capital budgeting

Payback method

Payback period

Discounted payback

Net present value method

Profitability index

Present value index

Internal rate of return

Accounting rate of return

Time adjusted rate of return

Payback reciprocal

Bail-out factor

Cost of capital

Target rate of return

Differential analysis

Capital rationing

REVIEW QUESTIONS

14–1   What is the relationship between long-range planning and capital budgeting?

14–2   Why do not-for-profit organizations use capital budgeting?

14–3   How is the payback period computed with equal annual cash flows? With unequal annual cash flows?

14–4   Identify several advantages and disadvantages of the payback method.

14–5   How is the payback reciprocal computed? Why is it used?

14–6   How is a project's net present value computed? How is it used to select from alternatives with similar investment amounts?

14–7   How is the profitability index computed? In what way is this index regarded as superior to net present value when selecting from alternative investments?

14–8   Provide three alternative definitions or descriptions of the internal rate of return.

14–9   What are the primary advantages and disadvantages of the internal rate of return?

14–10   What are two alternative computations of the accounting rate of return?

14–11   Explain two alternative ways of computing the cost of capital. Is it necessary for an organization to know its cost of capital? Explain.

14–12   Distinguish between the differential and the total cost approaches to the analysis of capital expenditure proposals.

14–13   How can risk be accounted for in capital budgeting?

14–14   What capital budgeting techniques are best for ranking investments with different initial investment amounts? Why?

EXERCISES

14–1 Present Value Computations

Using the information and tables in the appendix to the text, determine the answers to the following independent situations.

a) Present value of $1000 to be received in five years at 10 percent.

b) Present value of $1000 to be received at the end of each year for five years at 10 percent.

c) Present value of $1000 to be received at the end of each year for five years at 10 percent beginning two years from today.

14–2 Payback Period and Payback Reciprocal

a) What is the payback period for an investment of $150,000 if annual cash inflows are $50,000 for five years? If annual cash inflows are $30,000 for five years?

b) What are the payback reciprocals for these situations?

14–3 Net Present Value Computations

What is the net present value of an investment of $150,000 with expected annual cash inflows of $50,000 for five years if the company's cost of capital is 18 percent? 20 percent? What is the meaning of the two net present value amounts?

14–4 Profitability Index

What is the profitability index for the following investment alternatives?

a) Investment of $10,000; cash inflows of $2000 per year for fifteen years; and a discount rate of 14 percent.

b) Investment of $40,000; cash inflows of $5000 per year for ten years; and a discount rate of 8 percent.

c) Investment of $4000; cash inflow of $10,000 at end of year 7; and a discount rate of 14 percent.

14–5 Discounted Payback

What is the discounted payback for each of the following?

a) Investment of $10,000; annual cash inflows of $5000 for five years at 18 percent.

b) Investment of $25,000; annual cash inflows of $10,000 for three years at 12 percent.

    c) Investment of $18,000 with cash inflows of $4000 in year 1; $5000 in year 2; $6000 in year 3; $8000 in year 4; and $3000 in year 5; discount rate of 10 percent.

14–6 Internal Rate of Return

a) If an investment of $28,250 earns $5000 at the end of each year for ten years, what is the internal rate of return?

b) If an investment of $2541 earns $1000 in year 1 and $2000 in year 2, what is the internal rate of return?

14–7 Net Present Value

John and Julie want to invest $20,000 in a flower shop. The current owner is making $5000 per year and this should remain constant for seven years. Can John and Julie recoup their investment in seven years if they desire a 12 percent return? Use the net present value approach.

14–8 Present Value Computations for Alternate Decisions

You have just received a sweepstake prize from Publisher's Digest. You can receive a $20,000 lump-sum payment in five years or receive $4000 at the end of each year for the next seven years. If the minimum desired rate of return is 12 percent, which alternative would you prefer?

14–9 Accounting Rate of Return

The Byron Peach Company recently bought a new processing plant for $5,000,000. The plant can produce 1,000,000 cans of peaches a year and has a life of ten years.

Required: If variable operating costs are $1.00 per can and each can sells for $2.00, (1) what (ignoring all other costs) is the annual accounting income? and (2) what is the accounting rate of return on average investment?

14–10 Investment Methods Computation

The Zig Zag Company has the following investment alternatives.

	Investment A	Investment B
Investment amount	$20,000	$25,000
Annual cash inflows	$ 5,000	$ 5,000
Estimated life	9 years	10 years

Required: Compute the following when the cost of capital is 10 percent.

1. Net present value.

2. Internal rate of return (to nearest percent).

3. Payback period.

4. Payback reciprocal.

14–11 Investment Methods Computations

Using the data in Exercise 14–10, compute the following if the cost of capital is 14 percent.

1. Net present value.

2. Internal rate of return (to nearest percent).

3. Payback period.

4. Payback reciprocal.

14–12 Net Present Value

Dallas Company is considering investing $500,000 in equipment that will have an economic life of three years. Scrap recovery is estimated at $20,000 at the end of three years. Annual income from use of the asset has been estimated as follows: Year 1, $250,000; Year 2, $300,000; Year 3, $110,000. Using a rate of return of 10 percent, determine the net present value.

14–13 Investment Methods Computations

Fill in the lettered blanks below.

	Investment A	Investment B	Investment C
Amount of investment	$90,000	$50,000	$250,000
Economic life in years	8	(c)	9
Annual cash inflow	$30,000	$10,000	(e)
Payback period in years	(a)	(d)	(f)
Internal rate of return (nearest percent)	(b)	6%	14%

14–14 Payback Evaluations

Carolina Textiles is evaluating three proposals. In each case the amount of the investment is the same, and the annual cash inflows are uniform. Payback periods and economic lives are as follows:

	Payback	Economic Life
Project A	4.2	10 years
Project B	7.9	16 years
Project C	4.2	4 years

Requirements

Without the use of present value tables, answer the following questions.

a) Which projects, if any, can be rejected without further analysis?

b) What is the approximate rate of return (discounted cash flow) for each project?

c) Which project promises the highest internal rate of return?

PROBLEMS

14–15 Net Present Value with Differential Analysis

Alpha Company is interested in replacing a stamping machine with a new, improved model. The old machine has a salvage value of $10,000 now and zero in six years. The new machine requires an immediate cash outlay of $80,000 and will have a salvage value of $10,000 at the end of six years. The new machine will save the company $20,000 for each of the first three years and $10,000 per year for its remaining life. If the old machine is kept, it must be rebuilt next year at a cost of $20,000.

Required: What is the net present value of the new machine over the old one if the company's cost of capital is 14 percent?

14–16 Net Present Value and Profitability Index of Alternative Decisions

Santee River Sand Company is considering two machines, only one of which can be purchased. Information on the two machines is given below.

	Machine 1	Machine 2
Cost of the machine	$50,000	$150,000
Annual savings in cash operating costs	$20,000	$ 56,000
Life of the machine	5 years	5 years
Salvage value	$10,000	$ 12,000

The cost of capital is 10 percent.

Requirements

a) Compute the net present value of each machine. Based on these data, which machine should be purchased?

b) Compute the profitability index for each machine. Based on the profitability index, which machine should be purchased?

14–17 Net Present Value

The Geiser Company manufactures disco tapes and records. The research department has developed an item that would make a good graduation gift for students. Aggressive and effective effort by the sales personnel has resulted in firm commitments for this product for the next three years. It is expected that the item's value will be exhausted by that time.

In order to produce the quantity demanded, Geiser needs to buy new machinery and obtain an additional 12,500 square meters of space. There are 12,500 square meters of space adjoining the plant that Geiser can rent for three years at $4.50 per square meter per year if it decides to make this product.

The equipment will cost $200,000. It will require $100,000 for modifications, installation, and testing. All the expenditures will be paid for at the time of purchase. The equipment should have a salvage value of about $10,000 at the end of the third year.

The estimates of revenues and expenses for this product are shown below.

	19x1	19x2	19x3
Sales	$1,100,000	$1,500,000	$750,000
Materials, labor, and overhead*	−1,000,000	−1,200,000	−550,000
Net income before rent	$ 100,000	$ 300,000	$200,000

* Excluding depreciation and rent

Requirements

a) If Geiser requires a two-year payback, would this project be accepted?

b) Determine the net present value if the cost of capital is 18 percent.

14–18 Ranking of Investments

Jefferson Company has five investment proposals under consideration. Management wants to know the net present value, profitability index, internal rate of return, and payback period of each. The company's cost of capital is 10 percent.

Proposal	Cash Outlay	Present Value of Cash Inflows	Internal Rate of Return	Payback Period
A	$10,000	$11,000	14%	4
B	12,000	11,000	8%	3
C	8,000	11,000	16%	6
D	16,000	20,000	14%	5
E	15,000	19,000	15%	2

Requirements

a) Rank the investments by each method.

b) Which method is best if Jefferson can make only one investment? Why?

c) If Jefferson has $25,000 to invest, which proposals should be selected? Why?

d) Which methods are best suited for ranking? Explain.

14–19 Profitability Index and Ranking of Investments

Clayton Manufacturing has several investment alternatives that it wants ranked using the profitability index. The relevant data for each alternative are shown below.

	Alternative A	Alternative B	Alternative C
Investment	$10,000	$15,000	$12,000
Useful life	6	6	4
Cash inflows per period:			
1	$ 1,000	$10,000	$ 4,000
2	3,000	8,000	4,000
3	3,000	2,000	4,000
4	4,000	2,000	4,000
5	2,000	2,000	
6	1,000	2,000	

Clayton's cost of capital is 12 percent.

Requirements

a) Determine the profitability index for each alternative.

b) Rank in descending order.

14–20 Investment Methods, Computations, and Rankings

Using the data in Problem 14–19 compute the following and then rank the alternatives with each method, if possible.

Requirements

a) Net present value

b) Discounted payback

c) Profitability index

d) Payback period

14–21 Net Present Value of New Equipment

Harper Manufacturing is planning on purchasing a new machine that costs $45,000. If the new machine is purchased, an old machine will be sold for $5000. The company is convinced that the new machine can produce the following annual cost savings.

Materials and supplies	$7,500
Maintenance	4,500

The new machine will require about $2200 more labor annually to operate than the old machine. It will require an overhaul costing $6000 at the end of six years' use. The new machine will last for eight years, after which time it will have a salvage value of $3000. Harper's cost of capital is 14 percent.

Required: Using net present value, determine if this is a good investment.

14–22 Accounting Rate of Return

Starship Manufacturing is building a new plant for its latest product, Moonride. The total investment will cost $5,000,000 and will have a useful life of seven years. Straight-line depreciation is used.

The following data are available from the planning team.

Annual sales	$8,000,000
Labor costs	1,000,000
Materials	4,000,000
Supplies	1,500,000
Maintenance	200,000
Taxes	200,000

The salvage value of the plant and equipment is expected to be $100,000 at the end of seven years.

Requirements

a) What is the average annual accounting income from the project?

b) What is the accounting rate of return on average investment? (Round your answer to the nearest percent.)

14–23 Differential Versus Total Cost Approach: Keep or Replace Decision

Baker Petroleum is considering the purchase of a new processor. It would cost $120,000. After five years' use the processor could be sold for $12,000. It would provide considerable savings in annual operating costs, as is shown below.

	Old Processor	New Processor
Salaries	$34,000	$44,000
Supplies	6,000	5,000
Utilities	13,000	6,000
Cleaning and maintenance	22,000	5,000
Total annual operating costs	$75,000	$60,000

The old processor will be sold for its salvage value of $30,000. If the new processor is not purchased, the old processor will be used for five more years, then scrapped for a $2000 salvage. The old processor's present book value is $50,000. If kept and used, the old processor would require repairs costing $40,000 in one more year. Baker's cost of capital is 16 percent.

Requirements

a) Use the total cost approach and determine which processor is best.

b) Use the differential cost approach and determine the net present value of the new processor.

14–24 Differential Versus Total Cost Approach: Keep or Replace Decision

Esther's Dating Service must either overhaul its present computer or purchase a new one. Esther has determined the following projections.

	Present Computer	New Computer
Purchase cost new	$40,000	$50,000
Remaining book value	15,000	—
Overhaul needed now	20,000	—
Annual cash operating costs	35,000	20,000
Salvage value (now)	10,000	—
Salvage value (5 years from now)	2,500	10,000

If she keeps the old computer, it will have to be overhauled immediately at the cost shown above. With the overhaul, it will last five more years. If the new computer is purchased, it will be used for five years, after which it will be traded in on another one. All investment projects are evaluated on the basis of a 20 percent rate of return.

Requirements

a) Should Esther's Dating Service keep the old computer or purchase the new one? Use the total cost approach in making your decision.

b) Using the differential cost approach, determine the best decision.

14–25 Purchase Versus Rent

The Gercken Corporation sells computer services to its clients. The company completed a feasibility study and decided to obtain an additional computer on January 1, 19x9. Information regarding the new computer follows:

1. The purchase price of the computer is $230,000. Maintenance, property taxes, and insurance will be $20,000 per year. If the computer is rented, the annual rent will be $85,000 plus 5 percent of annual billings. The rental price includes maintenance.

2. Because of competitive conditions, the company feels it will be necessary to replace the computer at the end of three years with one that is larger and more advanced. It is estimated that the computer will have a resale value of $110,000 at the end of the three years. The computer will be depreciated on a straight-line basis for both financial reporting and income tax purposes.

3. The income tax rate is 50 percent.

4. The estimated annual billings for the services of the new computer will be $220,000 during the first year and $260,000 during each of the second and third years. The estimated annual expense of operating the computer is $80,000 in addition to the expenses mentioned above. An additional $10,000 of start-up expenses will be incurred during the first year.

5. If it decides to purchase the computer, the company will pay cash. If the computer is rented, the $230,000 can be invested at a 14 percent rate of return.

6. If the computer is purchased, the amount of the investment recovered during each of the three years can be reinvested immediately at a 14 percent rate of return. Each year's recovery of investment in the computer will have been reinvested for an average of six months by the end of the year.

Requirements

a) Prepare a schedule comparing the estimated annual income from the new computer under the purchase plan and under the rental plan. The comparison should include a provision for the opportunity cost of the average investment in the computer during each year.

b) Prepare a schedule showing the annual cash flows under the purchase plan and under the rental plan.

c) Prepare a schedule comparing the net present values of the cash flows under the purchase plan and under the rental plan.

d) Comment on the results obtained in requirements (a) and (c). How should the computer be financed? Why?

(CPA Adapted)

14–26 Equipment Replacement

The management of Essen Manufacturing Company is currently evaluating a proposal to purchase a new and innovative drill press as a replacement for a less efficient piece of similar equipment, which would then be sold. The cost of the equipment including delivery and installation is $175,000. If the equipment is purchased, Essen will incur costs of $5000 in removing the present equipment and revamping service facilities. The present equipment has a book value of $100,000 and a remaining useful life of ten years. Because of the new technical improvements that have made the equipment outmoded, it now has a resale value of only $40,000.

Management has provided you with the following comparative manufacturing cost tabulation.

	Present Equipment	New Equipment
Annual production (units)	400,000	400,000
Annual costs:		
Labor	$0.75/unit	$0.05/unit
Operating costs:		
Depreciation (10% of asset book value)	$20,000	$17,500
Other	$48,000	$20,000

Additional information:

- Management believes that if the present equipment is not replaced now, it will have to wait seven years before replacement is justifiable.

- Both pieces of equipment are expected to have a negligible salvage value at the end of ten years.

- If the new equipment is purchased, the management of Essen would require a 14 percent return on the investment before income taxes.

- Management believes that it can sell all it can produce.

Requirements

a) In order to assist the management of Essen in reaching a decision on the proposal, prepare schedules showing the computation of the following:

   1. Net initial outlay before income taxes.

   2. Net present value of investment before income taxes.

b) Would you recommend this investment? Why?

(CPA Adapted)

15

Impact of Taxes on Capital Budgeting and Other Management Decisions

It is important for managers to be able to determine the economic impact of **taxes** on business decisions. Because cash outlays for all expenses adversely affect profitability and liquidity, planning and control measures should apply to all costs, including taxes. A primary consideration of the manager in tax planning is tax avoidance. Unlike *tax evasion* (which is the illegal nonpayment of taxes), **tax avoidance** is the reduction of taxes through legitimate means. For example, failure to report a gain on the sale of assets constitutes tax evasion, whereas planning the disposition of assets through a nontaxable exchange for other assets is a legitimate means of tax avoidance.

In situations where tax avoidance is not an available or feasible option, the manager should consider deferring the payment of taxes. **Tax deferral** refers to the planning and timing of transactions so that the taxpayer qualifies for delays in the payment of taxes. Because of the time value of money, delaying tax payments into the future reduces their present value. Therefore, the objective in tax deferral is to plan transactions within the provisions of the tax law so that the present value of present and future tax payments is minimized.

The purpose of this chapter is to provide an overview of the types of taxes that affect management decisions. The specific effects of taxes on capital budgeting and other management decisions are also discussed. Because of the complexity of this subject, our objective is to expose the reader only to the general significance of taxes in business decision making. For specific applications of tax laws, managers should ordinarily consult the advice of experts in the field of taxation.

TYPES OF TAXES

The types of taxes that affect business enterprises may be classified into four categories: income taxes, property taxes, excise taxes, and foreign taxes.

Income Taxes

An **income tax** is any tax that is based on income. Some examples of income that is taxed are the incomes of individuals, corporations, estates, and trusts. The income of proprietorships or partnerships is not taxed directly; instead, it is passed through to the owners who must pay taxes on the business income based on their individual tax status. The federal government and most states and large cities collect income taxes from individuals and corporations.

Property Taxes

A **property tax** is a tax based on the ownership of property and is usually determined by multiplying a statutory tax rate (often referred to as the tax millage) times the assessed value of the property. The assessed value is usually a specified percentage of estimated fair market value. Tangible property taxes are levied on real property (land and buildings) and tangible personal property (such as equipment and inventories). Intangible personal property taxes are levied on property such as investment securities and receivables. There is no federal property tax, tangible or intangible; however, state and local governments rely heavily on property taxes.

Excise Taxes

An **excise tax** is a tax on an activity performed by, or a privilege granted to, the taxed party. Excise taxes are the broadest form of taxes and include many different types of taxes, such as sales taxes, licenses to do business, cigarette and alcohol taxes, gasoline and other fuel taxes, telephone taxes, import duties, and gift taxes. Excise taxes are levied by government authorities at federal, state, and local levels.

Foreign Taxes

Businesses that operate in foreign countries or conduct transactions with foreign enterprises may be affected by taxes imposed by foreign governments. Most of the types of taxes discussed above can also be found in various foreign countries. In addition, several European countries have adopted a value added tax.

Under a **value added tax,** manufacturers pay taxes based on the value added to goods that they produce during the period. For example, if a manufacturer of electric motors purchases component parts for $25 and sells assembled motors for $45, the value added is $20. The value added tax would be $20 times the tax rate. An appliance manufacturer purchasing the motors for $45, and adding other parts and supplies costing $105, pays value added tax only on the excess of its selling price over $150 ($45 plus $105). Under a value added system, the total value of the final consumable product is taxed as the product moves through the manufacturing and distribution process, but without any duplication of taxes. Several members in the U.S. Congress have advocated the adoption of a value added tax as a partial or total substitute for business income taxes. Many foreign countries, however, have both value added and income taxes.

MEASURING TAXES

For all types of taxes two basic variables determine the amount of taxes owed — the tax base and the tax rate. A **tax base** is a monetary measurement of the conditions or activities subject to taxes. Examples of tax bases are taxable income for income taxes, assessed value of property for property taxes, and total sales for sales taxes. A **tax rate** is a percentage that is multiplied times the tax base to determine total taxes.

For most taxes, the tax base is either provided directly by the taxing authority or is easily determined; however, computing the tax base for income taxes is usually somewhat difficult. Federal and other income taxes are administered under a self-assessment system where the party being taxed has the responsibility of measuring the tax base and computing the taxes due. The general procedure for computing the tax base for corporate income taxes is as follows:

Total revenues earned	$xx	
Less: Nontaxable revenues	xx	
Gross income		$xx
Total expenses and deductions	$xx	
Less: Nondeductible expenses	xx	
Allowable deductions		−xx
Taxable income		$xx

Income tax rates are normally *graduated;* that is, the tax rate increases as taxable income increases. For example, federal income taxes on corporations are computed as follows:

- 15 percent on the first $25,000 of taxable income,
- 18 percent on the next $25,000 of taxable income,
- 30 percent on the next $25,000 of taxable income,
- 40 percent on the next $25,000 of taxable income, and
- 46 percent on all taxable income in excess of $100,000.

Higher tax rates are applied only to *marginal,* or additional, taxable income; therefore, a corporation that has $200,000 of taxable income pays taxes at the 46 percent rate on only the last $100,000 of taxable income. On taxable income of $200,000, total federal income taxes are $71,750, computed as follows:

15% of $25,000	$ 3,750
18% of $25,000	4,500
30% of $25,000	7,500
40% of $25,000	10,000
46% of $100,000	46,000
Total taxes	$71,750

TAXES IN CAPITAL BUDGETING DECISIONS

Capital budgeting was discussed in Chapter 14 as a process for evaluating the desirability of alternative capital expenditure proposals. Using present value techniques, alternative capital investment projects can be reduced to a common basis for making relative comparisons. All future cash outflows and inflows are converted to present value equivalents using a predetermined discount rate. Cash flows from capital expenditures usually affect cash outflows for income taxes.

Cash flows related to capital expenditures may affect taxes in several different ways:

- Operating income[1] generated by capital expenditures increases income taxes.
- Reduced operating costs resulting from capital expenditures increase income taxes.
- Depreciation of capital assets reduces income taxes.
- Investment credit on qualifying asset purchases decreases income taxes.
- A gain on the sale of capital assets increases income taxes, whereas a loss on the sale of capital assets decreases income taxes.

Increased Revenues   A capital expenditure that is expected to generate annual cash flows of $10,000 before taxes will not produce net annual cash flows of $10,000 unless the revenue from the project is nontaxable. Ordinarily, taxes must be paid on a capital project's net revenue, thus reducing the net cash inflow. Assuming a 46 percent tax rate,[2] the annual after-tax cash flow is $5400:

$$\text{After-tax cash flow} = \text{Pretax cash flow} - (\text{Pretax cash flow} \times \text{Tax rate}),$$
$$\text{After-tax cash flow} = \$10,000 - (\$10,000 \times 0.46)$$
$$= \$5,400.$$

Most managers prefer to use the following variation of the above equation:

$$\text{After-tax cash flow} = \text{Pretax cash flow} \times (1 - \text{Tax rate}),$$
$$\text{After-tax cash flow} = \$10,000 \times (1 - 0.46)$$
$$= \$5,400.$$

The after-tax cash flow amount is multiplied times the appropriate discount factor to determine the present value of after-tax cash flows.

Decreased Costs   Many capital outlays have the objective of reducing costs rather than increasing revenues. Cost reduction measures decrease the amount of tax deductible expenses, increase taxable income, and increase income taxes. The after-tax effect of cost reductions can be computed using the equation

---

[1] Operating income equals revenues less the expenses generated by a capital expenditure.

[2] Throughout this chapter unless otherwise stated, the maximum corporate tax rate of 46 percent is used to illustrate the impact of taxes on management decisions.

discussed above. For example, if a capital project is expected to save $8000 per year in costs, the after-tax cost savings, assuming a 46 percent tax rate, are $4320 [$8000 × (1 − 0.46)].

Depreciation

Depreciation is a systematic procedure for allocating the acquisition cost of a capital asset over its useful life. The annual depreciation allocation is not accompanied by a cash outlay; however, it is an expense deduction in computing taxable income. Therefore, depreciation does provide an indirect inflow of cash from the reduction of taxes that it produces. This reduction of income taxes is often referred to as the **depreciation tax shield.** Since the income tax law does not allow capital expenditures to be deducted from income when they are made, it is only logical that depreciation deductions should be allowed.

Under the Economic Recovery Tax Act (ERTA) of 1981, the cost of a capital asset may be depreciated for tax purposes over a period of time shorter than the useful life of the asset. The act created the **Accelerated Cost Recovery System** (ACRS), which allows personal property to be depreciated over three, five, ten, or fifteen years, with most properties qualifying for a five-year write-off. Depreciable real property (primarily buildings) can be depreciated over fifteen years under ACRS. These accelerated write-offs of asset costs result in a higher present value for the depreciation tax shield. In addition, *under ACRS salvage value is ignored* in the computation of depreciation. A company may elect not to adopt ACRS depreciation rates, in which case straight-line depreciation rates based on ACRS asset lives may be used.[3] New businesses operating at a loss in their early years may prefer this option to provide more deductions in later years when higher levels of income are produced.

If straight-line rates are adopted, the *half-year convention* must be used in the acquisition year of an asset. This convention allows the taxpayer to take a full year's depreciation if the asset is acquired during the first half of the year and no depreciation if it is acquired during the last half of the year. When ACRS rates are used, the *full first year's* percentage is allowed regardless of when the asset is purchased during the year.

To illustrate the present value of the depreciation tax shield, assume that machinery purchased in December 19x1 has an ACRS recovery period of five years and a depreciable cost of $15,000. The amount of the annual depreciation tax shield varies depending on whether straight-line or ACRS rates are elected. Under straight-line rates no depreciation is allowed in 19x1; however, beginning with 19x2 the annual depreciation deduction is $3000 per year ($15,000 ÷ 5 years). Assuming a 46 percent tax rate, the

---

[3] When using straight-line rates, the taxpayer may also elect the following longer asset lives: for three-year property, 5 or 12 years; for five-year property, 12 or 25 years; for ten-year property, 25 or 35 years; and for fifteen-year property, 35 or 45 years.

annual depreciation tax shield is $1380 ($3000 $\times$ 0.46) per year for years 2 through 6.

The annual depreciation rates for five-year assets under ACRS are, respectively, 15, 22, 21, 21, and 21 percent. The annual ACRS depreciation deductions and related tax savings are as follows:

	(1)	(2) ACRS Rate	(3) (1) × (2) Annual Depreciation	(4) Tax Rate	(5) (3) × (4) Tax Shield
Year	Cost				
1	$15,000	0.15	$ 2,250	0.46	$1,035
2	15,000	0.22	3,300	0.46	1,518
3	15,000	0.21	3,150	0.46	1,449
4	15,000	0.21	3,150	0.46	1,449
5	15,000	0.21	3,150	0.46	1,449
Total			$15,000		$6,900

Using a 12 percent discount rate, the present values of the depreciation tax shield for straight-line and ACRS depreciation rates are summarized below.

	(1) 12 Percent Present Value Factor	Straight-Line Rates (2) Tax Shield	(3) (1) × (2) Present Value of Tax Shield	ACRS Rates (4) Tax Shield	(5) (1) × (4) Present Value of Tax Shield
Years					
1	0.893	$ —	$ —	$1,035	$ 924
2	0.797	1,380	1,100	1,518	1,210
3	0.712	1,380	983	1,449	1,032
4	0.636	1,380	878	1,449	922
5	0.567	1,380	782	1,449	822
6	0.507	1,380	700	—	—
Total		$6,900	$4,443	$6,900	$4,910

Notice that both depreciation methods produce $6900 of tax shield over the life of the capital project. However, because of the differences in the timing of these reductions, and the time value of money, the present value of the depreciation tax savings is greater for ACRS rates than for straight-line rates. As long as there is taxable income to be absorbed by depreciation, the depreciation method that provides the fastest write-off of capital asset costs also provides the highest present value of the tax shield.

Investment Tax Credit

In addition to depreciation, federal income tax law allows a one-time tax reduction in the year of acquisition for qualifying personal property. This tax reduction is called the **investment tax credit.** Property qualifying for the investment credit includes primarily machinery and equipment, furniture and fixtures, vehicles, and any other tangible personal property used in business activities. Under the provisions of the 1981 Economic Recovery Tax Act, assets that qualify for write-off over three years under ACRS also qualify for a *6 percent investment tax credit,* and all other qualified assets (those depreciated over five, ten, or fifteen years) qualify for a *10 percent investment tax credit.* Ordinarily, buildings and other real property do not qualify for any investment tax credit.

From the standpoint of capital budgeting, the investment tax credit in essence reduces the acquisition cost of the capital asset. For example, if a capital asset costs $10,000 and qualifies for a 10 percent investment tax credit, income taxes in the year of acquisition are reduced by $1000 ($10,000 × 0.10). The $1000 reduction in income taxes is a reduction of cash outlays and has the effect of reducing the asset cost to $9000 ($10,000 − $1000).

Under the Tax Equity and Fiscal Responsibility Act (TEFRA) of 1982, taxpayers are required, for depreciation purposes, to *reduce the asset cost* by *50 percent* of the investment credit claimed on the asset. Consequently, in the example above only $9500 [$10,000 − 0.5 ($1000)] qualifies for depreciation. As an alternative option to making this adjustment to the depreciable cost of the asset, the taxpayer may elect to *reduce the investment credit* by *two percentage points.* If this option were taken in the example above, the total investment tax credit would be $800 [$10,000 × (0.10 − 0.02)] and the full $10,000 of cost would qualify for depreciation. Ordinarily, the value of the additional 2 percent of investment credit is greater than the present value of the depreciation tax shield forfeited as a result of claiming the full investment credit. Consequently, in the examples and problems in this chapter, it is assumed, unless stated otherwise, that the full investment credit allowance is claimed by the taxpayer and that the depreciable cost of the asset is reduced by one half of the total investment credit claimed.

Gain or Loss on Sale of Capital Assets

To determine the total net present value of a capital expenditure, it is necessary to include as cash inflow any expected proceeds from the sale of the asset at the end of its useful life. If a taxable gain is realized on the sale of an asset, the gain increases income taxes, which reduces the net cash generated by the sale. On the other hand, a loss on the sale of an asset is deducted in computing taxable income and, therefore, reduces income taxes. In this case the tax reduction represents additional cash inflow generated by the asset. This cash savings is added to the selling price of the asset to determine the net cash generated by the sale.

To illustrate, assume an asset has a book value (cost less accumulated depreciation) of $5000 at the end of its useful life and is sold for $7000. The sale results in a taxable gain of $2000 ($7000 — $5000). Cash generated directly by the sale is $7000, but the $2000 gain increases taxes by $920 ($2000 × 0.46); therefore, the net cash generated by the sale of the asset is $6080 ($7000 — $920). If the asset sells for only $3000, there is a tax deductible loss of $2000 ($3000 — $5000) that reduces taxes by $920 ($2000 × 0.46). In this case the net cash generated is $3920, the selling price of $3000 plus the tax savings of $920.

The tax effects of gains and losses related to asset dispositions must also be taken into consideration in a capital budgeting decision that involves replacing an asset currently in use. The gain or loss on the sale of the old asset increases or decreases both taxes and the net cash generated by the sale.

Capital Budgeting with Taxes Illustrated

To illustrate how the various effects of income taxes enter into the capital budgeting analysis, assume that Willoughby's Bar and Grill is faced with the problem of its pinball machine becoming obsolete because of the popularity of video computer games. Willoughby's is considering purchasing a video computer game called Challenger that costs $12,000 and is predicted to generate cash revenues of $6000 per year net of operating costs. Challenger's manufacturer predicts that it can be sold for $1000 after five years of use. Willoughby's has a $500 offer from one of its customers for the old pinball machine, which is fully depreciated. Challenger qualifies for a 10 percent investment tax credit and ACRS five-year depreciation. Willoughby's capital investment policy requires new capital expenditures to produce a positive net present value using a 12 percent discount rate. The analysis of the proposal, including tax effects, is presented in Exhibit 15–1 (see page 606).

Exhibit 15–1 shows that Willoughby's can expect a positive net present value of $5187 on the investment after considering all cash flows, including those related to income taxes. Although this alternative might appear to be a desirable investment, Willoughby's should consider all other feasible alternatives before making a decision, including purchasing other games, leasing possibilities, and even the alternative of keeping the old pinball machine. In each case the analysis of cash flows should include the cash flow effects of taxes.

FORMS OF ORGANIZATION AND TAXES

The income tax consequences of management decisions are often affected by the legal form under which a business is organized. The basic forms of business organization are *proprietorships, partnerships,* and *corpora-*

EXHIBIT 15-1   Analysis of Capital Expenditure Including Tax Effects

Cash Flow Item*	Actual Cash Inflows (Outflows)	Year(s) of Cash Flows	12% Present Value Factor	Present Value of Cash Flows
Purchase of Challenger	$(12,000)	0	1.000	$(12,000)
Investment tax credit ($12,000 × 0.10)	1,200	0	1.000	1,200
Sale of pinball machine	500	0	1.000	500
Taxes on gain on pinball machine ($500 × 0.46)	(230)	0	1.000	(230)
Annual operating income generated by Challenger	6,000	1–5	3.605	21,630
Taxes on annual operating income ($6,000 × 0.46)	(2,760)	1–5	3.605	(9,950)
Tax savings on depreciation:†				
Year 1	787	1	0.893	703
Year 2	1,154	2	0.797	920
Year 3	1,101	3	0.712	784
Year 4	1,101	4	0.636	700
Year 5	1,101	5	0.567	624
Sale of Challenger	1,000	5	0.567	567
Taxes on gain on Challenger ($1,000 × 0.46)	(460)	5	0.567	(261)
Net present value of all cash flows				$ 5,187

* All cash flows occur at the end of the year.
† Depreciation cash flow computations:

Year	Cost − 50% of Investment Tax Credit‡		ACRS%		Tax Rate		Cash Savings
1	$11,400	×	0.15	×	0.46	=	$ 787
2	11,400	×	0.22	×	0.46	=	1,154
3	11,400	×	0.21	×	0.46	=	1,101
4	11,400	×	0.21	×	0.46	=	1,101
5	11,400	×	0.21	×	0.46	=	1,101

‡ $12,000 − (50% × $1,200) = $11,400

tions. As discussed earlier, the general model for computing taxes includes a tax base and the appropriate tax rates. To evaluate the differences in taxes for the three alternative business forms, it is necessary to analyze differences in their respective income tax bases and tax rates. The following discussion is limited to federal income tax considerations.

Sole Proprietorships

A **sole proprietorship** is an unincorporated business owned by one individual. Legally, a proprietorship is not a separate entity; therefore, business transactions of a proprietorship are taxed as transactions of the individual taxpayer. All business revenues increase and all business expenses reduce the proprietor's individual income tax base. A proprietor combines business net income with all other types of income (such as salaries, interest, and dividends) in determining total taxable income.

Tax rates for individuals are based on graduated tax tables with rates ranging from 11 percent to 50 percent. Under the Economic Recovery Tax Act of 1981, single individuals, for years after 1983, pay taxes at the 50 percent rate on all taxable income exceeding $81,800. Married individuals filing joint tax returns reach the 50 percent tax bracket at taxable income of $162,400. However, if both spouses are employed, they are allowed a special deduction from taxable income equal to 10 percent of the lesser of (1) $30,000 or (2) the income of the spouse with the lower income. This special deduction effectively reduces the tax rates for some married persons filing jointly.

Partnerships

A **partnership** is an unincorporated business owned by two or more individuals.[4] These businesses are required to report taxable income to the IRS; however, they do not pay taxes on their income. Instead, *the income of partnerships is allocated to the individual partners* who include their pro rata share of partnership income in their individual taxable income. All income of the partnership is allocated to the partners whether or not an equal amount of cash or other assets is distributed to the partners. Consequently, partners may be required to pay taxes on income that they actually have not received during the period. Partnership income is taxed to the individual partners at rates applicable to the partners' income, that is, at a maximum rate of 50 percent for individuals and 46 percent for corporations.

Corporations

A **corporation** is a legally recognized entity created by an act of the state and empowered to conduct business activities within the provisions of a corporate charter issued by the government of the state of incorporation. As a separate legal entity, a corporation is not dependent on its owners for legal recognition. It can conduct in its own name almost any transaction that an individual can conduct.

Unlike proprietorships and partnerships, a corporation is a separate taxable entity that must pay taxes on its taxable income. In addition, any dividends distributed by a corporation to its owners (shareholders) must be included in the income tax base of the individual owners. Consequently, *dividend income received by corporate stockholders is subject to double taxation*—corporate taxes and individual taxes. To illustrate the potential

---

[4] Although partners are ordinarily individuals, other entities may also form a partnership. For example, the partners of a partnership may consist of a combination of individuals, corporations, trusts, and even other partnerships.

impact of double taxation, assume that a corporation distributes a $54,000 dividend, representing the amount remaining after subtracting corporate taxes at 46 percent on $100,000 of earnings. Assuming the stockholders receiving the dividends are in the 50 percent tax bracket, they pay $27,000 taxes on the dividends received. The income available to the stockholders after taxes is only $27,000 ($54,000 less $27,000 taxes). As shown below, of the $100,000 in corporate taxable income, corporate taxes of $46,000 and individual taxes of $27,000 are paid for a total of $73,000, leaving only $27,000 to the stockholders after the payment of corporate and individual income taxes.

Corporate income providing dividends	$100,000
Less: Corporate income taxes (46%)	− 46,000
Total dividend distributed	$ 54,000
Less: Individual income taxes (50%)	− 27,000
Income to stockholders after corporate and individual income taxes	$ 27,000

Salaries paid to corporate employees who are also stockholders are deductible business expenses of the corporation in computing taxable income. The income used to pay salaries to stockholders, therefore, avoids corporate taxes and is taxed only to the stockholders. In the example above, if the $100,000 of corporate income that provided the dividends had been distributed as salaries, no corporate income taxes would have been paid. The employee-stockholders would have received the full $100,000 as salaries and would have paid $50,000 ($100,000 × 0.50) in individual taxes, leaving them $50,000 after taxes. By paying salaries instead of dividends, total taxes decrease from $73,000 to $50,000, and total after-tax income available to the employee-shareholders increases from $27,000 to $50,000. Distributions to shareholders cannot be arbitrarily designated as salaries to avoid double taxation. According to the federal tax law, salary payments must be commensurate with services provided by the stockholders to the corporation. Otherwise, the Internal Revenue Service will disallow the salary deduction to the corporation and treat the distribution as a dividend.

Subchapter S Corporations

A **subchapter S corporation** is a business that is legally organized as a corporation, but has opted under a special provision of the tax law to be taxed as a partnership. A subchapter S corporation enjoys the legal advantages of incorporation (such as limited liability and unlimited life), without the disadvantages of corporate taxation. Like a partnership, the income of a subchapter S corporation is allocated to the owners and included in their taxable income whether or not it is actually distributed to them. The corporate income is allocated in proportion to the ownership percentages of the stockholders.

To qualify for subchapter S tax treatment, a corporation must (1) have no more than thirty-five stockholders; (2) have only one class of stock; (3) have no stockholders other than individuals, estates, and trusts; (4) have the approval of all stockholders for the tax option treatment; and (5) receive no more than 25 percent of its gross receipts from passive sources such as dividends, interest, rents, royalties, and gains on stocks or other securities.

SELECTING A TAX ENTITY

Selection of an organizational form and tax entity is an easy decision for most large business enterprises. Clearly, the majority of all large organizations find it advantageous and necessary to operate and be taxed as *corporations*. The advantages of incorporation for large businesses are related to the following points.

- The ease with which capital funds can be generated through the issuance of publicly traded securities.
- The ease with which ownership can be readily transferred through the sale of shares of stock.
- The limitation of liability for owners of corporate stock to the amounts of their investments.
- The unlimited life of corporate organizations.

Although examples are not as numerous, some very large businesses operate as partnerships. For example, most public accounting firms are organized as partnerships; several of them have more than 1000 partners and generate more than $1 billion in revenues annually. The relatively small number of owners and the low turnover of ownership make the partnership alternative feasible for these organizations. Most large corporations, however, have thousands (in some cases millions) of different owners, and changes in ownership occur daily as shares of capital stock are purchased and sold. The corporate form is the only feasible alternative for these organizations.

Organizations that are not constrained by their large size to operate as corporations may base the organizational decision to a large extent on tax considerations. Although there are no clear-cut rules for determining which organizational form and tax entity should be adopted, there are several tax related variables discussed below that should be considered.

Utilization of Income

Business income can be either distributed to the owners or reinvested into the business for operating or expansion purposes. If the owners anticipate distribution of profits, incorporation poses the potential problem of double taxation. However, if earnings are not distributed, incorporation probably produces the lowest taxes since the maximum corporate rate is lower than the maximum individual rate (46 percent versus 50 percent), and individual rates increase more rapidly than corporate rates with increasing taxable income.

Utilization of Operating Losses

If a business has a negative taxable income (that is, expenses exceed revenues), the result is an **operating loss.** Obviously, in this situation no income taxes are due on current business operations; however, in some cases the taxpayer may be able to offset current business losses against profits or gains from other sources, or even against the organization's profits from other years. From the standpoint of operating losses, it is generally desirable to use the losses to offset profits from other sources. For example, if an individual has two businesses and one has taxable income of $10,000, whereas the other has an operating loss of $10,000, the taxpayer would prefer not to pay any taxes since the combined net income is zero. Operating losses of one business can be offset against profits of another business owned by the taxpayer only if the businesses are organized as proprietorships, partnerships, or subchapter S corporations. The income or loss of a regular corporation ordinarily cannot be combined with that of another corporation, except for corporations that qualify for consolidated tax reporting.

All types of tax entities are permitted to apply operating losses to reduce taxable income for the previous three years and the following fifteen years. When losses are used to reduce taxable income of previous years, the taxes that were paid in those years are refunded. Losses applied to future periods merely reduce taxable income and taxes due for those years. When applying current operating losses to other years, the losses must first be carried back to the third preceding year. If all the loss is not absorbed by the income of that year, the remainder is applied to the second preceding year, then to the first preceding year, and then to the fifteen years following the current period. With the carryback and carryover provisions, most operating losses are usually eventually used, but it may take as long as fifteen years to realize the total tax benefits from the current period's losses.

Employee Benefits

As explained earlier, a stockholder of a corporation may be an employee of the company and receive salary payments that are deductible as expenses by the corporation in computing its taxable income. The concept of owner-employee does not apply to proprietorships and partnerships because these businesses are inseparable from their owners. If a proprietorship or partnership deducts payments to its owners as salaries, these deductions are offset by the salaries received, which are included in the owners' taxable incomes.

All businesses are allowed under the tax law to deduct the cost of qualified fringe benefits provided for their employees, including medical insurance, certain death benefits, certain meals and lodging, recreation, and deferred compensation benefits. These expense deductions are available even for benefits paid to employees who are also stockholders of the corporations. Because proprietors and partners cannot be employees of their own companies, these tax deductible employee benefits are not available to proprietorships or partnerships. However, the tax laws allow individuals who are proprietors or partners to take a personal deduction for certain contributions to qualified retirement plans. There is no provision for individuals to deduct costs associated with the other employee benefits named above.

Dividends Received Deduction

A *dividends received deduction* is a deduction from gross income granted to *corporations* based on a percentage of dividends received from investments in other corporations. Corporations are permitted to deduct 85 percent of the dividends received from other domestic corporations, thus paying taxes on only 15 percent of the dividends. Proprietorships and partnerships are not allowed this deduction. Individuals are granted a minimal dividends received deduction (for example, $200 per year for married couples filing jointly). No dividends received deduction is available to subchapter S corporations.

If a business receives dividends that are expected to be reinvested in the business, the corporate dividends deduction may be a significant advantage related to the corporate form. However, if the dividends received are distributed, the owner-stockholders are required to include them in their taxable incomes.

Capital Gains and Losses

A **capital asset** is generally defined for tax purposes as an asset held for investment gain; it, therefore, excludes assets such as inventory, accounts receivables, and assets used in the business such as land, buildings, and equipment. A gain or loss on the sale of a capital asset is called a **capital gain or loss.** The excess of capital gains over capital losses is a net capital gain. Conversely, the excess of capital losses over capital gains is a net capital loss. Capital gains and losses are long term if the capital asset was held for more than one year; otherwise, they are short term.

Net Long-Term Gains and Losses. Corporations are required to include net long-term capital gains in taxable income; however, a special alternative tax rate of 28 percent is available for net long-term capital gains *for corporations.* The alternative rate produces a tax savings for a corporation only if its marginal tax rate on other taxable income is more than 28 percent, that is, on taxable income above $50,000. *Individuals* are allowed to deduct 60 percent of their net long-term capital gains, thereby paying taxes on only 40 percent. There is no special long-term gain tax rate for individuals; however, the maximum rate is, effectively, only 20 percent (maximum tax rate of 50 percent times the taxable gain portion of 40 percent). Therefore, the effective tax rate on net long-term capital gains favors individuals slightly (20 percent compared to 28 percent).

Corporations are not permitted to deduct net long-term capital losses from other taxable income. Net capital losses by corporations can be carried back three years and forward five years and used to reduce capital gains for those years. Individuals are permitted to deduct 50 percent of net long-term losses in the current year from other taxable income up to an annual limit of $3000 with any excess carried forward indefinitely to reduce future capital gains or to be deducted against future taxable income subject to the same 50 percent/$3000 limitation.

Net Short-Term Gains and Losses. Both *corporations* and *individuals* are required to include net short-term capital gains in taxable income as ordinary income without any special deduction or any reduction in tax rates. A net short-term capital loss by a *corporation* may only be carried back three years and forward five years to offset capital gains for those years; none of it may be used to directly reduce taxable income. *Individuals* may deduct 100 percent of net short-term capital losses in the current year from taxable income up to an annual limit of $3000 (including short-term and long-term capital losses) with any excess carried forward indefinitely to reduce future capital gains or to be deducted against future taxable income. Exhibit 15–2 illustrates the basic tax provisions related to the sale of capital assets for various combinations of capital gains and losses. This part of the tax law is very complicated and requires more coverage than is provided here to be fully understood. However, from this cursory review it should be apparent that, overall, the tax provisions for capital asset transactions favor slightly the noncorporate organizational form over the corporate form.

Terminating a Business

When planning the sale of a business as a going concern or the sale of all of its individual assets, it is usually advantageous to be able to treat the disposition as a sale of a *capital asset* if a *gain resulted,* and as a sale of a *noncapital asset* if a *loss resulted.* Ordinarily, it is easier to treat the disposition as a sale of a capital asset if the business was incorporated. When an unincorporated business is sold, the transaction is treated for tax purposes as a sale of the individual parts of the business, most of which are not capital assets. However, when a corporation is sold, the sale of the business is usually viewed as a sale of an equity investment (shares of capital stock), which is a capital asset.

From the above discussion it is obvious that there is no clear answer to the question of which organizational form provides the greatest tax advantage. On certain points incorporation is preferred, whereas on other points a noncorporate form (proprietorship or partnership) is more desirable. Exhibit 15–3 summarizes the factors to consider in selecting a tax entity

EXHIBIT 15–2 The Tax Treatment of Selected Combinations of Capital Gains and Losses

Net Short-Term Gain (*Loss*)	Net Long-Term Gain (*Loss*)	Total Capital Gain (*Loss*)	Tax Treatment	
			To an Individual	To a Corporation
$5,000	$ —	$5,000	$5,000 is taxed at regular rates.	$5,000 is taxed at regular rates.
—	7,000	7,000	$4,200 (60%) long-term deduction is applicable. $2,800 is included in taxable income.	$7,000 is taxed at maximum rate of 28%.
8,000	(2,000)	6,000	$6,000 is taxed at regular rates.	$6,000 is taxed at regular rates.
(2,000)	8,000	6,000	$3,600 (60%) long-term deduction is applicable. $2,400 is included in taxable income.	$6,000 is taxed at maximum rate of 28%.
1,000	(9,000)	(8,000)	$4,000 (50%) is deductible subject to maximum $3,000 limit. $1,000 may be carried forward to future periods.	$8,000 may be carried back three years and forward five years.
(5,000)	1,000	(4,000)	$4,000 is deductible subject to maximum $3,000 deduction. $1,000 may be carried forward to future periods.	$4,000 may be carried back three years and forward five years.
4,000	3,000	7,000	$5,200 is taxed at regular rates, $7,000 minus $1,800 (60%) long-term gain deduction.	$4,000 is taxed at regular rates, and $3,000 is taxed at maximum rate of 28%.
(5,000)	(4,000)	(9,000)	$7,000 is deductible ($5,000 + $\frac{1}{2}$ of $4,000) subject to $3,000 limit. $4,000 may be carried forward to future periods.	$9,000 may be carried back three years and forward five years.

EXHIBIT 15–3 Factors in Selecting a Tax Entity — Corporate Versus Noncorporate Forms of Organization

Factor	Organizational Form Favored	
	Corporate	Noncorporate (Proprietorship and Partnership)
1. Utilization of income:		
(a) Earnings distributed		x
(b) Earnings not distributed	x	
2. Operating loss provisions		x
3. Owner–employee benefits	x	
4. Dividends received deduction	x	
5. Capital gains and losses		x
6. Terminating the business	x	

and the relative benefits of incorporation as opposed to selecting a noncorporate form of organization.

OTHER TAX CONSIDERATIONS
FOR MANAGEMENT

In tax accounting, just as in financial accounting, there are several areas where alternative methods and treatments are available for measuring taxable revenues and deductible expenses. In most cases the alternative selected for financial accounting purposes does not necessarily have to be the same method chosen for tax purposes. The alternative chosen for *financial accounting purposes* should be dictated by the company's particular circumstances and management's desire to present fairly the company's financial picture. For *tax purposes* the choice among alternative treatments is a management decision that should be aimed at minimizing taxes and maximizing the net present value of future cash flows. Economically, the tax alternative decision is similar to a product pricing decision or a capital budgeting decision. Several tax-related areas where management decisions are often required are discussed below.

**Depreciation
Alternatives**

Before the Economic Recovery Tax Act of 1981, the costs of assets used in a trade or business were recoverable, for tax purposes, through depreciation using straight-line, sum-of-years-digits, or declining balance depreciation. The laws restricted the applicability of these methods based on the types of assets in use and their expected useful lives.

The Economic Recovery Tax Act of 1981 replaced traditional depreciation methods (sum-of-the-years-digits and declining balance) with the *Accelerated Cost Recovery System*. The ACRS provides for the recovery of asset costs over shortened time periods using statutory depreciation rates that approximate declining balance depreciation during the earlier years and sum-of-years-digits depreciation during the remainder of the recovery period. The alternative of using straight-line depreciation and longer asset lives is also available under the 1981 law.

All depreciation methods provide an absolute tax shield equal to the cost of the depreciable asset times the tax rate. However, as observed in the capital budgeting discussion, *because of variations in the timing of the tax shield, accelerated depreciation rates produce the greatest present value of the future tax benefits from depreciation*. Unfortunately, the depreciation decision is not as simple as it seems at first glance because the method chosen may also affect the taxability of any gain realized on the ultimate sale of the asset. Generally, the use of accelerated depreciation disqualifies part or all of any gain on the sale of the asset from capital gain treatment. Consequently, the gain is taxed as ordinary income with no long-term capital gain deduction or lower alternative tax rates allowed. This does not pose a problem if an asset is expected to be substantially worthless at the time of its retirement from service with little or no gain realized.

Inventory Costing Alternatives

Whenever a company has inventory on hand at the end of the year, the total cost of goods available for sale during the year must be allocated between goods that were sold during the year and goods that are on hand at the end of the year. In some cases it is appropriate to determine by specific identification the costs of units sold and units still on hand. In many cases it is necessary for organizations to use an arbitrary cost flow method in making the allocation. Even if specific costs can be determined, it may be advantageous to use a cost flow method to gain maximum benefit from the provisions in the tax law. For tax purposes a company may use either a specific cost or a cost flow method based on a first-in first-out (FIFO), last-in first-out (LIFO), or average cost assumption. FIFO assigns the cost of the earliest acquired units to cost of goods sold, and the cost of the latest acquired units to ending inventory. LIFO assigns the cost of the latest acquired units to cost of goods sold, and the cost of the earliest acquired units to ending inventory. The average method assigns the average cost of all units available during the period to both units sold and units in ending inventory.

During *inflationary periods* FIFO produces the lowest cost of goods sold, the highest taxable income, and the highest taxes, whereas LIFO results in the highest cost of goods sold, the lowest taxable income, and the lowest taxes. The average cost method results in amounts for cost of goods sold, taxable income, and taxes between the two extremes of FIFO and LIFO. The net economic difference between FIFO and LIFO during an inflationary period is illustrated in Exhibit 15–4. For each of the three years, there are 200 units in both beginning and ending inventory, and 800 units are both purchased and sold. At the beginning of the first year, inventory is valued at $1 per unit, and the purchase price of inventory is $2 in the first year, $3 in the second year, and $4 in the third year. Goods are sold at twice the current purchase price.

Notice in Exhibit 15–4 that under FIFO, ending inventory is $200 greater than beginning inventory for each of the three years, whereas under LIFO, beginning and ending inventory are the same. The number of units in beginning and ending inventory is the same for each period; therefore, LIFO is charging all costs of purchases to cost of goods sold. Since the purchase price of units increased by $1 per unit each year, FIFO charges $200 ($1 times 200 units) more to ending inventory each period than for the previous period. Consequently, cost of goods sold is $200 less each year for FIFO than for LIFO, FIFO taxable income for each period is $200 more than LIFO taxable income, and taxes are $92 ($200 × 0.46) more for FIFO than LIFO each year. The obvious conclusion is that *as long as prices are increasing, LIFO costing minimizes taxable income and taxes.*

Revenue Recognition Alternatives

For financial accounting purposes, revenues generally may be reported either as cash is collected (*cash basis*) or as the right to receive the cash is realized (*accrual basis*). Ordinarily, a company must report income for tax purposes on the same basis used for financial reporting purposes. If

EXHIBIT 15–4   Comparison of Tax Effects of FIFO and LIFO Inventory Costing Methods

	Year 1		Year 2		Year 3	
FIFO inventory method	*Units*	*Cost*	*Units*	*Cost*	*Units*	*Cost*
Beginning inventory	200 at $1	$ 200	200 at $2	$ 400	200 at $3	$ 600
Purchases	800 at 2	1,600	800 at 3	2,400	800 at 4	3,200
Goods available for sale	1,000	$1,800	1,000	$2,800	1,000	$3,800
Ending inventory	− 200 at $2	− 400	− 200 at $3	− 600	− 200 at $4	− 800
Goods sold	800	$1,400	800	$2,200	800	$3,000
Sales	800 at $4	$3,200	800 at $6	$4,800	800 at $8	$6,400
Cost of goods sold		−1,400		−2,200		−3,000
Taxable income		$1,800		$2,600		$3,400
Taxes (at 46%)		$ 828		$1,196		$1,564
LIFO inventory method	*Units*	*Cost*	*Units*	*Cost*	*Units*	*Cost*
Beginning inventory	200 at $1	$ 200	200 at $1	$ 200	200 at $1	$ 200
Purchases	800 at 2	1,600	800 at 3	2,400	800 at 4	3,200
Goods available for sale	1,000	$1,800	1,000	$2,600	1,000	$3,400
Ending inventory	− 200 at $1	− 200	− 200 at $1	− 200	− 200 at $1	− 200
Goods sold	800	$1,600	800	$2,400	800	$3,200
Sales	800 at $4	$3,200	800 at $6	$4,800	800 at $8	$6,400
Cost of goods sold		−1,600		−2,400		−3,200
Taxable income		$1,600		$2,400		$3,200
Taxes (at 46%)		$ 736		$1,104		$1,472
LIFO tax savings						
Excess of taxes under FIFO over taxes under LIFO		$ 92		$ 92		$ 92

inventory transactions represent a significant part of a company's operations, sales and cost of goods sold are required for tax and financial accounting purposes to be reported on the accrual basis. An exception to this general rule is available for reporting installment sales for tax purposes. Although most sales made on installment are fully recognized as revenues in the financial statements at the time the sales are made, for tax purposes revenue recognition may be deferred until the cash payments are collected.

To illustrate the *installment sales method,* assume that in 19x4 a company sells $100,000 of merchandise that was purchased for $65,000. The $100,000 is to be collected in five equal annual payments. The total gross profit on the sale is $35,000, or 35 percent of sales. Under the accrual basis the full $35,000 of gross profit is recognized in 19x4; however, under the installment method only the gross profit on the portion of the revenues collected, that is, $7000 ($20,000 × 35%), is included in taxable income in 19x4. The taxable income and taxes due in 19x4 under the accrual and installment methods are summarized below. Operating expenses are assumed to be $5000 for the year.

Accrual Method		Installment Method	
Sales	$100,000	Installment collections	$20,000
Cost of goods sold	− 65,000	Gross profit on collections	
Gross profit (35%)	$ 35,000	($20,000 ×35%)	$ 7,000
Operating expenses	− 5,000	Operating expenses	− 5,000
Taxable income	$ 30,000	Taxable income	$ 2,000
Taxes ($30,000 × 0.46)	$ 13,800	Taxes ($2,000 × 0.46)	$ 920

The current tax savings from electing the installment method was $12,880 ($13,800 − $920). In reality this is not a tax savings but rather a tax deferral. The company still has $28,000 of unreported gross profit ($35,000 − $7000). As the $80,000 balance in unpaid installments is collected, $28,000 ($80,000 × 0.35) of additional gross profit will be reported as taxable income resulting in taxes of $12,880 ($28,000 × 0.46).

The primary benefit in adopting the installment method is related to the time value of the deferred tax payment. By investing the $12,880 tax deferral, a substantial amount of additional income can be earned. This income is the economic benefit resulting from the tax deferral. Another potential benefit for smaller companies, whose marginal tax rates are near or below the maximum tax rate, is that by spreading gross profit over several years the marginal tax rate may be lowered resulting in a direct tax savings. This benefit is in addition to the time value benefit realized on the deferral of the tax payment.

Capital Funding Alternatives

As previously stated, corporations are not permitted to deduct dividends paid on equity capital in computing taxable income. Interest expense on borrowed capital, however, is a deductible expense. *Because of the interest expense deduction, debt capital may be less expensive to a company than equity capital.* To illustrate, assume that a company plans to acquire a new building costing $1,000,000 and that the funds can be obtained either by selling 12 percent long-term bonds (debt capital) or by selling 12 percent preferred stock (equity capital). In both cases the annual outlay to service the capital funds is $120,000 ($1,000,000 × 0.12). However, since interest payments are deductible, the annual after-tax cost of the bonds is only $64,800 [$120,000 × (1 − 0.46)], and the annual cost of the bonds after taxes as a percent of the funds obtained is 6.48 percent ($64,800 ÷ $1,000,000), compared to 12 percent for the preferred stock.

Investment Alternatives

When evaluating alternatives for investing excess funds, two important tax considerations are (1) the taxability of the income received on the investment and (2) the taxability of the gain or loss on the sale of the investment. Most assets held for investment purposes qualify for favorable capital asset treatment. However, the tax treatment of periodic income is not the same for all investments. Corporations are allowed an 85 percent special deduction on dividends received from investments in other corporations. Another tax break on investment income available to all taxpayers (corporate and noncorporate) involves interest received on *municipal bonds* issued by government agencies other than the federal government. The federal constitution prohibits the IRS from taxing income on municipal bonds; therefore, the after-tax return for these bonds is the same as the stated interest rate. Taxpayers in the 46 percent tax bracket investing in 10 percent municipal bonds pay no taxes on the interest received, and their after-tax yield on the investment is 10 percent. In contrast, if these taxpayers invest in 12 percent corporate bonds, the interest is taxable and the after-tax yield is only 6.48 percent [0.12 × (1 − 0.46)]. In this case, taking taxes into consideration, the municipal bonds offer a higher return to the investor. Ordinarily, the interest rate on municipal bonds is considerably lower than that on comparable corporate bonds; however, for a taxpayer in a high tax bracket the return on municipal bonds is often higher than the after-tax return on corporate bonds.

SUMMARY

The effects of taxes on business enterprises represent one of the most important considerations in management decision making. Effective management of resources requires that efforts be undertaken to avoid taxes where possible through legally available means. Probably the most important category of taxes is income taxes; however, most businesses must also contend with property and excise taxes. Taxes are exacted against businesses by the federal government as well as by state, local, and even foreign governments.

Understanding taxes is particularly important in capital budgeting. Taxes affect capital budgeting decisions through (1) the reduction of operating profits, (2) the depreciation tax shield, (3) the investment tax credit, and (4) the tax on the sale of assets. Income taxes also play an important role in the selection of the organizational form for a business. Sole proprietorships and partnerships merely serve as conduits through which profits flow into the tax returns of the business owners. Corporations, however, are separate taxable entities whose profits are taxed directly. Corporate profits that provide dividends suffer a double tax burden; they are taxed first to the corporation and then to the stockholders.

The income tax laws provide numerous choices in reporting various types of revenues and expenses for tax purposes. Through careful planning and the effective utilization of alternative tax treatments, management can minimize the adverse effect of taxes on the firm.

KEY TERMS

Tax avoidance	Investment tax credit
Tax deferral	Sole proprietorship
Income tax	Partnership
Property tax	Corporation
Excise tax	Subchapter S corporation
Value added tax	Operating loss
Tax base	Capital asset
Tax rate	Capital gain
Depreciation tax shield	Capital loss
Accelerated Cost Recovery System (ACRS)	

REVIEW QUESTIONS

15–1 Define and differentiate the following three types of taxes: income taxes, property taxes, and excise taxes.

15–2 Many European countries have a value added tax. Explain how a value added tax works.

15–3 What are the two basic components in determining the amount of any tax?

15–4 Assuming the entire pretax cash flow is subject to taxes, complete the following equation:

After-tax cash flow = $\underline{\ ?\ } \times (1 - \underline{\ ?\ })$.

15–5   Explain the concept of depreciation as an income tax shield.

15–6   What is the absolute amount of the depreciation income tax shield provided by an asset costing $10,000 if the tax rate is 46%? Explain.

15–7   Why does ACRS depreciation usually provide a greater tax shield in real terms than straight-line depreciation?

15–8   Describe the investment tax credit. How does it affect capital asset costs?

15–9   Describe generally how the following tax entities are treated for income tax purposes under the federal income tax law: proprietorships, partnerships, and corporations.

15–10 One of the major disadvantages of corporations is the problem of double taxation of dividends paid to shareholders. Explain.

15–11 What is an operating loss? How are operating losses treated for tax purposes?

15–12 Compare the tax treatment of net long-term capital gains between corporations and individuals.

15–13 During a period of rising prices, which inventory method minimizes the present value of present and future taxes? Explain.

15–14 The installment sales method of revenue recognition provides for tax deferral, not tax avoidance. Explain the difference.

15–15 How can lower interest municipal bonds sometimes produce a higher after-tax return to the investor than higher interest corporate bonds?

EXERCISES

15–1 Corporate Tax Computation: Marginal Tax Rate

Ajax Corporation reported taxable income of $82,000 in 19x5.

Requirements

a) Using the federal corporate tax rates given in the chapter, compute the total tax liability for Ajax Company for 19x5.

b) What was Ajax's marginal tax rate?

15–2 Computation of After-Tax Cash Flows

Rustin Company has an opportunity to purchase a machine that will generate annual pretax cash inflows and additional taxable income of $50,000. Rustin has a marginal tax rate of 46 percent.

Required: Compute Rustin's predicted after-tax net cash flows from the purchase of the machine. Ignore depreciation.

15–3 Depreciation Tax Shield

The Statesboro Company purchased a new machine costing $20,000 at the beginning of 19x1. For tax purposes the machine can be depreciated over five years on a straight-line basis, or it can be depreciated under ACRS over five years using the following rates.

Year	Percent
1	15
2	22
3	21
4	21
5	21

Statesboro's marginal tax rate is 46 percent.

Requirements

a) Compute the absolute amount of the total tax shield over the life of the machine under both depreciation alternatives.

b) Compute the real amount of the total tax shield under both depreciation alternatives using a present value rate of 12 percent. (Round calculations to the nearest dollar.)

15–4 Capital Budgeting Cash Flows

Douglas Company is considering purchasing a new machine that has a cost of $35,000. The machine qualifies for ten-year ACRS depreciation and a 10 percent investment tax credit. Management predicts that the new machine would increase revenues by $5000 per year for fifteen years and would reduce operating costs by $2500 per year. At the end of its useful life it can be sold for $2500.

Required: Prepare a list of the cash flow items that are relevant to Douglas Company's capital budgeting decision concerning the purchase of the machine. Do not attempt to compute the amount of each cash flow item.

15–5 Capital Funding Alternatives

Jordan Company, a soft drink producer, is engaged in negotiations for the acquisition of a company that manufactures aluminum cans. Jordan's management believes that the company can be purchased for $10 million and paid for by issuing either 15 percent long-term bonds or 15 percent preferred stock. Jordan Company has a marginal tax rate of 46 percent.

Requirements

a) Compute the annual after-tax cost of the funds used to acquire the can company assuming long-term bonds are issued.

b) Compute the annual after-tax cost of the funds used to acquire the can company assuming preferred stock is issued.

15–6 Taxability of Investment Income

To help finance future expansion, the Baldwin Company is investing a substantial portion of its excess cash resources in an expansion fund consisting of low-risk securities. At the end of 19x5 the corporate treasurer was instructed to purchase another $100,000 of securities for the fund. The following securities are being considered.

- Acme Corporation common stock, expected to pay annual dividends of $10,000 with no significant market appreciation over the next five years.

- Bilkko Corporation bonds, bearing interest at the rate of 10 percent per year, maturing in five years.

- Central County municipal bonds, bearing interest at the rate of 7 percent per year, maturing in five years.

Requirements

a) Compute the annual after-tax income from each of the securities under consideration assuming the full $100,000 is invested in the same security and the company is in a 46 percent tax bracket.

b) Repeat requirement (a) assuming the company is in a 30 percent tax bracket.

15–7 Electing an Investment Tax Credit Alternative

Freeman's Tours purchased a new touring bus in 19x3 for a total cost of $120,000. The bus qualifies for three-year cost recovery and 6 percent investment tax credit under ACRS. The ACRS depreciation rates are 25 percent for year 1, 38 percent for year 2, and 37 percent for year 3. Freeman's is in the 46 percent tax bracket and has an average cost of capital of 12 percent.

Requirements

a) Compute the present value of the depreciation tax shield forfeited if Freeman's elects to claim the full 6 percent of investment tax credit (instead of reducing it by 2 percent). (Round calculations to the nearest dollar.)

b) Compute the present value of the investment tax credit lost if Freeman's elects to depreciate the full cost of the bus and reduce the investment tax credit rate by 2 percent.

c) Should Freeman's elect to claim the full investment credit or reduce the investment credit by 2 percent?

15–8 Carryback and Carryover of Operating Losses

Because of poor weather conditions, Bob Moore's Ski Shop had a 19x5 operating loss of $30,000. The company earned an operating profit of $5000 in 19x4, $15,000 in 19x3, and $6000 in 19x2.

Requirements

a) Explain specifically how Bob Moore may use the 19x5 operating loss to reduce taxes in other years if his store is operated as a proprietorship.

b) How may Bob Moore use the 19x5 operating loss if his business is incorporated?

15–9 Selecting an Organizational Form

Sharon and Janice plan to open a new gifts and antiques shop in a mountain resort location. They have sought your advice on whether they should organize their business as a partnership or as a corporation. Sharon's other taxable income places her in a 40 percent tax bracket already, but Janice has no other income. Sharon will be working half time in the shop, and Janice will be working full time refinishing furniture and managing the shop. The anticipated profits of $50,000 per year will be divided as follows:

	Sharon	Janice	Total
Remuneration for services	$10,000	$20,000	$30,000
Division of remaining profits	10,000	10,000	20,000
Totals	$20,000	$30,000	$50,000

Requirements

a) Identify and explain the issues involved in the selection of a tax entity for this new business.

b) Which alternative tax entity do you recommend for this business based on the limited information available to you? Explain the reasons for your recommendation.

PROBLEMS

15–10 Capital Budgeting Decisions with Tax Considerations

J. R.'s Painting Company, a residential and commercial paint contractor, is considering expanding into industrial painting and related services, including sandblasting. This expansion would require purchasing sandblasting equipment costing about $50,000. The equipment would last an estimated ten years, but it could be depreciated under ACRS over five years. It would also qualify for the 10 percent investment tax credit. After ten years, J. R.'s expects to be able to sell the equipment for about $1200. Predicted income and expenses related to sandblasting services are as follows:

	Year 1	Year 2	Year 3	Years 4–10 (per year)
Revenues	$20,000	$30,000	$40,000	$50,000
Expenses:				
Labor	$18,000	$18,000	$18,000	$18,000
Sand	5,000	7,500	10,000	12,500
Repairs	500	1,000	1,500	2,000
Total	−23,500	−26,500	−29,500	−32,500
Income before depreciation	$ (3,500)	$ 3,500	$10,500	$17,500

J. R.'s tax rate is 46 percent, and the required return on new investments is 16 percent.

Required: Compute the net present value of the investment in the sandblasting equipment. Assume J. R. takes the full investment tax credit. Should J. R.'s purchase the equipment? (Round calculations to the nearest dollar.)

15–11 Capital Budgeting with Tax Considerations

Jones, Jones, and Jones, a medium-sized law firm, currently has five secretaries employed in its secretarial pool. An office equipment salesperson recently told the Joneses that a word processing system would improve the efficiency and effectiveness of their clerical department and should save the cost of one secretary's salary each year. The proposed system would cost $15,000 and has an estimated useful life of seven years, after which it can be sold for an estimated $1000. By adding word processing, the attorneys believe that only four secretaries will be needed — three doing conventional typing and one operating the word processor. The total cost of employing a secretary is $15,000 per year; however, word processing secretaries usually earn about 20 percent more than conventional secretaries. The annual maintenance contract on the word processing equipment would be $1000. The equipment qualifies for five-year ACRS depreciation and a 10 percent investment tax credit. The company has a 46 percent marginal tax rate.

Requirements

a) Compute the net present value of the investment in the word processing equipment assuming a present value rate of 14 percent. Assume the Joneses take the full investment tax credit. (Round calculations to the nearest dollar.)

b) Was the salesperson correct in claiming that the word processing system would save the cost of one secretary?

15–12 Selection of Organizational Form

Bob Allen and Joyce Baker, two college professors specializing in environmental science, own a consulting firm to which they devote time during their evenings, weekends, and vacations. The firm also employs four other full-time professionals. Currently, Allen and Baker are each in a 50 percent marginal tax bracket, not including their consulting business income. In 19x6, the business had net income before owners' salaries and income taxes of $80,000. Allen and Baker believe that the time they put into their firm would justify an annual salary of $25,000 each if the business were operated as a corporation.

Requirements

a) How would the $80,000 of business income be taxed if the business operated as a partnership? How much total taxes would be paid by the partners on the business income?

b) How would the $80,000 of business income be taxed if the business operated as a regular corporation and only normal salaries were distributed to the owners? How much total taxes would be paid on the business income by the corporation and the owners?

c) Repeat requirement (b) assuming the remainder of the business income after taxes is distributed to the owners as dividends.

d) How would the $80,000 of business income be taxed if the business operated as a subchapter S corporation? How much total taxes would be paid by the corporation and the owners on the business income?

15–13 Taxability of Capital Gains and Losses

Don Rowe owns two tracts of investment land, tract A and tract B, both of which he intends to sell during the next three months. He anticipates no other capital asset transactions during the year. Tract A has been held for three years and tract B for six months. Consider the following eight alternative capital gain and loss possibilities for the sale of the two tracts of land.

	Tract A	Tract B	Net Capital Gain (Loss)
1.	$5,000 gain	$3,000 gain	$ 8,000
2.	5,000 loss	3,000 loss	(8,000)
3.	5,000 gain	3,000 loss	2,000
4.	5,000 loss	3,000 gain	(2,000)
5.	3,000 gain	5,000 gain	8,000
6.	3,000 loss	5,000 loss	(8,000)
7.	3,000 gain	5,000 loss	(2,000)
8.	3,000 loss	5,000 gain	2,000

Requirements

a) Indicate how the net capital gain or loss will be treated for the eight alternatives listed above, assuming Don Rowe is an individual.

b) Repeat requirement (a) assuming that Don Rowe is a corporation.

15–14 Impact of Inventory Costing Methods on Taxes

Marco Company, a regional distributor of a new microcomputer called Comp-10, has just completed its third year of operations. Purchases and sales data for each of the first three years are given below.

	Year 1	Year 2	Year 3
Purchases (units)	1,500	2,750	4,000
Cost per unit	$120	$100	$ 90
Sales (units)	1,450	2,720	3,980
Selling price per unit	$300	$250	$225
Tax rate	46%	46%	46%
Operating expenses (as a percent of gross profit)	50%	50%	50%

Requirements

a) Compute total income taxes for each year assuming FIFO inventory costing is used.

b) Repeat requirement (a) assuming LIFO inventory costing is used.

c) Comment on the tax effects of inventory costing methods (FIFO versus LIFO) in times of (1) falling prices and (2) rising prices.

15–15 Deferred Income Taxes: Installment Sales

Druid Corporation is selling some of its excess land that is no longer needed in operations. The land was purchased fifteen years ago for $25,000 and now is worth $100,000. Since the land is a capital asset, any gain on its sale will be taxed at a maximum tax rate of 28 percent. A prospective buyer has offered to purchase the land with a $25,000 down payment and three payments of $25,000 at the end of each of the next three years.

Requirements

a) Compute the total amount of income taxes that will be paid on the sale of the land assuming it is reported for tax purposes all in the year of sale.

b) Repeat requirement (a) assuming the sale is reported on the installment basis.

c) Which method of tax reporting is preferred? Explain.

d) If the company had the option of a cash sale for $100,000, should it be rejected in order to qualify the sale for the installment sales method?

15–16 Timing the Payment of Taxes

The Burdock Company's transactions are summarized below for 19x5, its first year of operations. Recognizing the company's critical shortage of cash, the president instructed the controller (who is also the tax manager) to consider all options in the tax law that might reduce tax payments for the current year.

1. Purchased equipment in September at a cost of $20,000. The equipment qualifies for five-year cost recovery under ACRS.

2. A total of 400 units of product were sold during the year. The following purchases of inventory were made during the year.

   50 units at $40
   200 units at $45
   200 units at $50
   50 units at $55

3. The 400 units were sold (all on installment accounts) for a total of $50,000. During the year, $20,000 was collected on the accounts.

4. Operating expenses paid during the year totaled $9000. An additional $4000 of expenses was accrued but unpaid at the end of the year. The only other expense was depreciation on the equipment.

Requirements

a) For each of the four items listed above, indicate the alternative tax treatments that are available to the Burdock Company.

b) Assuming there were no other transactions during the year, compute the minimum tax liability for the company for 19x5. Burdock Company is organized as a regular (not subchapter S) corporation.

15–17 Effect of Inventory Alternatives on Taxes

The management of Stark Products Company has asked its accounting department to describe the effect on income taxes of accounting for inventories on the LIFO rather than the FIFO basis during 19x4 and 19x5. The accounting department is to assume that the change to LIFO would have been effective on January 1, 19x4, and that the initial LIFO inventory was the ending 19x3 FIFO inventory.

Presented below are selected data for the years 19x4 and 19x5 during which the FIFO method was employed.

	12/31/x3	12/31/x4	12/31/x5
Inventory	$69,000	$ 75,000	$ 84,000
Sales		$540,000	$617,500
Less: Cost of goods sold		$294,000	$355,000
Other expenses		135,000	154,000
Total		−429,000	−509,000
Net income before income taxes		$111,000	$108,500
Less: Income taxes (46%)		−51,060	−49,910
Net income		$ 59,940	$ 58,590

Additional information:

- Inventory on hand at 12/31/x3 consisted of 30,000 units valued at $2.30 each.
- Sales (all units sold at the same price throughout the year):

  19x4 — 120,000 units at $4.50 each
  19x5 — 130,000 units at $4.75 each

- Purchases (all units purchased at the same price throughout the year):

  19x4 — 120,000 units at $2.50 each
  19x5 — 130,000 units at $2.80 each

- Income taxes at the effective rate of 46 percent are paid on December 31 each year.

Required: If inventories had been valued using LIFO, determine the values for 19x4 and 19x5 for ending inventories, net income before income taxes, income taxes, and net income.

(CMA Adapted)

15–18 Capital Budgeting and Funding Alternatives

LeToy Company produces a wide variety of children's toys, most of which are manufactured from stamped parts. The Production Department recommended that a new stamping machine be acquired. The Production Department further recommended that the company consider using the new stamping machine for only five years. Top management concurs with the recommendation and has assigned Ann Mitchum of the Budget and Planning Department to supervise the acquisition and analyze the alternative financing available. After careful analysis and review, Mitchum has narrowed the financing of the project to the two following alternatives.

1. The first alternative is a lease agreement with the manufacturer of the stamping machine. The manufacturer is willing to lease the equipment to LeToy for five years even though it has an economically useful life of ten years. The lease agreement calls for LeToy to make annual payments of $62,000 at the beginning of each year. The manufacturer (lessor) retains the title to the machine, and there is no purchase option at the end of five years. Investment credit is claimed by the lessor and does not flow through to LeToy (lessee). The lease payments would be deductible as operating expense for tax purposes.

2. The second alternative would be for LeToy to purchase the equipment outright from the manufacturer for $240,000. LeToy can claim an investment tax credit of 10 percent and recover the cost under ACRS over five years. The asset would be sold for $45,000 at the end of five years, all taxable as ordinary income.

All maintenance, taxes, and insurance are the same under both alternatives and are paid by LeToy. LeToy has an average cost of capital of 12 percent and is in a 46 percent tax bracket.

Requirements

a) Calculate the net-of-tax present value cost of acquiring the stamping machine through the leasing alternative. (Round computations to the nearest dollar.)

b) Calculate the net-of-tax present value cost of acquiring the stamping machine through the purchase alternative. Assume LeToy will take the full investment tax credit. (Round computations to the nearest dollar.)

(CMA Adapted)

15–19 Tax Considerations in Using Payback, Accounting Rate of Return, and Net Present Value

The Baxter Company manufactures toys and other short-lived faddish items. The Research and Development Department came up with an item that would make a good promotional gift for office equipment dealers. Aggressive and effective effort by Baxter's sales personnel has resulted in almost firm commitments for this product for the next three years. It is expected that the product's appeal will be exhausted by that time. In order to produce the quantity demanded, Baxter will need to buy additional machinery and rent some additional space. It appears that about 25,000 square feet will be needed; 12,500 square feet of presently unused, but leased, space is available now. (Baxter's present lease with ten years to run costs $3 a square foot.) There is another 12,500 square feet adjoining the Baxter facility, which Baxter will rent for three years at $4 per square foot per year if it decides to make this product. The equipment will be purchased for $900,000. It will require $30,000 in modifications, $60,000 for installation, and $90,000 for testing; all these activities will be done by a firm of engineers hired by Baxter. All the expenditures will be paid for on January 1, 19x3. The equipment will be depreciated over three years under ACRS (25 percent in 19x3, 38 percent in 19x4, and 37 percent in 19x5) and will qualify for a 6 percent investment tax credit. At the end of the three years, the asset is expected to be sold for $180,000. The following estimates of revenues and expenses for this product for the three years have been developed.

	19x3	19x4	19x5
Sales	$1,000,000	$1,600,000	$800,000
Materials, labor, and overhead outlays	$ 400,000	$ 750,000	$350,000
Allocated general overhead	40,000	75,000	35,000
Rent	87,500	87,500	87,500
Depreciation	270,000	410,400	399,600
Total expenses	− 797,500	−1,322,900	−872,100
Income before taxes	$ 202,500	$ 277,100	$ (72,100)
Income taxes (46%)	− 93,150	− 127,466	—
Net income (loss)	$ 109,350	$ 149,634	$ (72,100)

Requirements

a) Prepare a schedule that shows the incremental after-tax cash flows for this project. *Hint:* Baxter did not take the full 6 percent investment tax credit.

b) If the company requires a two-year payback period for its investment, would this project be undertaken?

c) Calculate the after-tax accounting rate of return on initial investment for the project. (Round answer to three decimal places.)

d) A newly hired business school graduate recommends that the company consider the use of the net present value method to study this project. If the company sets a required rate of return of 20 percent after taxes, will this project be accepted? (Round calculations to the nearest dollar.)

(CMA Adapted)

15–20 Selecting Tax Alternatives to Minimize Taxes

The Janeski Service Corporation has just completed its first year of operations. The income statement (on an accrual basis) for the year prepared by the bookkeeping department is as follows:

Sales	$325,000
Gain on sale of land	32,000
Interest income	1,000
Total revenues	$358,000
Materials and supplies	$128,000
Wages and benefits	43,000
Depreciation (straight-line)	7,000
Bad debts	500
Interest	5,500
Administrative services	11,000
Other expenses	5,000
Total expenses	−200,000
Net income	$158,000

Mr. Janeski has made the following preliminary calculation of his tax liability.

Tax on first $25,000 at 15%	$ 3,750
Tax on next $25,000 at 18%	4,500
Tax on next $25,000 at 30%	7,500
Tax on next $25,000 at 40%	10,000
Tax on next $26,000 at 46%	11,960
Tax on $32,000 capital gain at 28%	8,960
Total taxes	$46,670

You have just been hired by Janeski as an accountant, and he indicates that the company is in a "cash-squeeze" position. As your first task, he asks you to review the tax computation to determine if this year's tax liability might be reduced. In reviewing the firm's records, you assemble the following information.

1. There are no ending inventories.

2. Accounts receivable at year end amount to $18,000, and accounts payable and other current payables are $4000.

3. New equipment costing $60,000 was purchased early in the year. In the book-keeper's depreciation calculation, salvage value was estimated to be $4000, and the useful life of the equipment was estimated at eight years. You determined that the equipment qualified for five-year ACRS write-off and investment tax credit.

4. A tract of land, acquired in January as a building site at a cost of $12,000 was sold in November when a new shopping plaza was constructed on adjoining land. The land was sold for $44,000, of which $33,000 will be received in future years.

Required: Present a revised determination of taxable income and total taxes that takes advantage of all available means (discussed in this chapter) to reduce this year's taxes. Explain any items where your presentation differs from the income statement given above.

(CMA Adapted)

16

Financial Statement Analysis and the Statement of Changes in Financial Position

General purpose financial statements are designed to provide information to a large and diverse group of users, including stockholders, creditors, and managers. Because of the broad objectives of financial statements, they do not include certain financial measures needed by specific user groups. Through financial analysis, however, individual users are able to generate a considerable amount of additional useful information from the statements.

Financial statement analysis is the process of interpreting and evaluating financial statements by using data contained in them to produce additional financial measures. Financial statement analysis involves comparing financial statements for the current period with those of previous periods, studying the internal composition of the financial statements, and studying relationships within and between the financial statements.

The purpose of financial statement analysis is to give the user an understanding of the firm and its operations beyond that provided by merely reading the statements. Financial statements have not been used to their fullest potential until they have undergone financial analysis. Through analysis a large amount of useful information is tapped that otherwise is not immediately obvious to the user. For example, creditors can evaluate the likelihood that the company will make its interest and principal payments on time, stockholders can evaluate the profitability of the firm's assets and the return on investment to various equity holders, and managers can evaluate their own effectiveness in using the resources entrusted to them by creditors and stockholders.

The primary purpose of this chapter is to discuss the benefits of financial analysis to managers and to illustrate several analytical measures that provide information useful to managers. The second part of this chapter discusses the statement of changes in financial position. This statement and the income statement and balance sheet together comprise the basic financial statement package. To gain maximum benefit from financial statements, all three statements should be utilized.

FINANCIAL STATEMENT ANALYSIS
BY MANAGERS

One of the most important reasons for managers to analyze their firm's financial statements is to evaluate the overall performance of the firm. Managers should be aware of total company performance, not just the performance of their particular areas of responsibility. By analyzing the financial statements for the company as a whole, managers gain a perspective on how the organization is performing.

General purpose financial statements provide the only overall measure of the firm's performance available to some managers. The internal reporting system is often limited to reporting component performances, with no report of overall performance provided to managers below the top levels.

By evaluating the overall performance of the organization, managers are able to compare their firm with similar firms and identify potential weaknesses that may be worthy of management attention. For example, if a firm has a return on equity of 8 percent while the industry norm is 15 percent, this comparison might signal an existing problem requiring management attention. In fact, there may be good reasons for the below average return; without financial analysis, however, management may not even be aware of the deficiency, or the conditions causing it. Since internal reports of other companies are not available, the only basis for making comparisons with those companies is through their external financial statements and other published materials.

Financial analysis is also necessary for managers whose firms have lending agreements that impose financial restrictions on the organization. Analysis of the financial statements is often necessary to determine if restrictions are being met. For example, an agreement may require the debt-to-equity ratio to be maintained at a specified level. Failure to comply could result in a call for immediate liquidation of the debt and could damage the firm's credit rating and its ability to obtain borrowed capital in the future.

A more subtle, but no less important, reason for managers to analyze financial statements is to see their firm as outsiders see it. The financial statements are, in effect, the only window through which outsiders may view the firm. By evaluating the firm's financial statements, managers may better understand the behavior and attitudes of outsiders toward the firm and may develop a more realistic view of the firm themselves.

THE NEED FOR EVALUATIVE STANDARDS

Information obtained directly from the financial statements, and analytical measures derived from the statements, have little usefulness standing alone. To be interpreted effectively, this information must be evaluated against some *standard*. Depending on managers' objectives, several different standards may be used. The most common financial analysis standards are (1) the firm's financial measures for previous periods, (2) financial measures for other firms and industry averages, and (3) budgeted measures for the firm for the period under evaluation.

An important aspect of financial analysis is tracking the firm's progress over time, which is done by comparing the firm's performance for the current period with several previous periods. To get an indication of future performances, it is useful for managers to compare the firm's current performance to its past performances. This comparison, however, should not be the only standard used because it tends to encourage mediocrity if the only objective is to improve on previous periods' performances.

Evaluating financial measures against comparable measures for other firms in the same industry is also beneficial to managers, especially in heavily competitive industries. Several financial information organizations (including Dun and Bradstreet, Standard and Poors, and Moody's) publish averages for commonly used financial measures for all major industries. Failure to perform close to industry norms could signal difficulties in competing with other firms in the future.

When comparing a firm's financial measures with those of other firms, it is necessary to consider any material differences that might exist between the firms. For example, if one firm is located farther from major suppliers than other firms in the industry, higher freight costs and possibly lower profits may occur. Differences in accounting practices must also be taken into account in comparing firms; for example, allowances must be made in comparing two firms that use different methods of inventory valuation. Although there are limitations in making intercompany comparisons, looking at other firms' performances is a useful indicator of relative performance.

From management's perspective, probably the most realistic standard of performance is the firm's budgeted performance. Chapter 6 discussed operating budgets and pro forma financial statements, which represent management's most realistic expectations for the period. Analytical measures taken from these statements should be compared with the same measures derived from the actual financial statements for the period. For performance evaluation purposes, this comparison is likely to provide managers the most useful evaluation of current financial statements.

PROCEDURES FOR FINANCIAL STATEMENT ANALYSIS

Financial statement analysis measures may be divided into two groups: measures of *solvency* of the firm and measures of *performance*. The 19x4 and 19x3 balance sheets and income statements for Dunfield's, Inc. are provided in Exhibit 16–1 as a basis for illustrating these two groups of analytical measures. Financial statements for two successive periods are presented because several of the ratios require averages to be computed for the period. To obtain average information, the beginning and ending balances are summed and divided by 2. Normally, averages computed from

EXHIBIT 16–1 Comparative Financial Statements

Dunfield's, Inc.
Comparative Income Statements
For the years ended December 31, 19x4 and 19x3
(*in thousands*)

	19x4	19x3
Sales	$9,734	$8,028
Cost of goods sold	−6,085	−4,843
Gross profit	$3,649	$3,185
Operating expenses:		
Selling	$1,030	$ 891
General and administrative	602	527
Total	−1,632	−1,418
Operating income	$2,017	$1,767
Other revenues and expenses:		
Interest income	$ 90	$ 84
Interest expense	(345)	(314)
Total	− 255	− 230
Income before income taxes	$1,762	$1,537
Provision for income taxes (46%)	− 811	− 707
Net income	$ 951	$ 830
Earnings per share	$ 2.35	$ 2.05

Dunfield's, Inc.
Comparative Balance Sheets
December 31, 19x4 and 19x3
(*in thousands*)

Assets	19x4	19x3
Current assets:		
Cash	$1,335	$1,341
Marketable securities	250	200
Accounts receivable	1,678	1,386
Inventories	1,703	1,439
Other current assets	280	156
Total current assets	$5,246	$4,522
Property, plant, and equipment	$6,861	$6,041
Less: Accumulated depreciation	−3,426	−3,080
Net	3,435	2,961
Other assets	73	72
Total assets	$8,754	$7,555

EXHIBIT 16-1 (*cont.*)

Liabilities and Stockholders' Equity

Current liabilities:		
Accounts payable	$1,564	$1,228
Taxes payable	482	336
Other current liabilities	202	178
Total current liabilities	$2,248	$1,742
Long-term debt	1,208	1,192
Deferred taxes payable	271	230
Total liabilities	$3,727	$3,164
Stockholders' equity:		
Common stock ($1 par, 404,000 shares outstanding)	$ 404	$ 404
Premium on common stock	270	270
Retained earnings	4,353	3,717
Total stockholders' equity	5,027	4,391
Total liabilities and stockholders' equity	$8,754	$7,555

values for only two points during the year (beginning and ending) should be used only if monthly or quarterly data are not available. In the following discussion, each analytical measure is presented in general form along with an example of the measure for Dunfield's for 19x4.

Measures of Solvency

Solvency refers to the ability of a firm to pay its debts as they become due. The primary measures of *short-term solvency* are the current ratio, acid test ratio, inventory turnover, and number of days receivables outstanding. The debt-to-equity ratio and the times-interest-earned measure are useful in assessing *long-term solvency*.

Current Ratio. The **current ratio** measures the relationship between current assets and current liabilities. The general equation for the current ratio and the computation for Dunfield's are as follows:

General equation: $\text{Current ratio} = \dfrac{\text{Current assets}}{\text{Current liabilities}}$

Example: $= \dfrac{\$5,246}{\$2,248}$

$= 2.33$

Current assets represent cash and other assets that will be converted into cash (either directly or indirectly) through operations within a reasonably short period of time. Under normal operating conditions, cash is generated by sales of inventory and collection of accounts receivable. Current liabilities are financial obligations that will become due within a relatively short period of time and will be paid from cash currently on hand and from the pool of cash generated from current assets. Therefore comparing current assets to current liabilities indicates the extent to which current assets are available to cover current liabilities. Dunfield's current ratio of 2.33 implies that the company has $2.33 of current assets for each $1 of current liabilities.

There is no universal guideline for evaluating the current ratio. Although a current ratio of 2.0 is often considered to be the norm, using an artificial guideline like this may lead to erroneous conclusions. For example, a current ratio of 2.0 is inadequate for a firm that has 90 percent of its total current assets tied up in obsolete or slow-moving inventory, while most of its current liabilities are due in the near term. The adequacy of a particular current ratio depends on (1) the composition of the current assets and how quickly they will convert to cash and (2) how soon current liabilities must be paid.

The current asset and current liability accounts are often referred to as *current operating,* or *current working,* accounts because assets and liabilities related to operating revenues and expenses normally flow in and out of the balance sheet through these accounts. The difference between current assets and current liabilities may be viewed as the net amount of working funds available in the short run. This fund is referred to as **working capital.** Dunfield's working capital is computed as follows:

$$\text{Current assets} - \text{Current liabilities} = \text{Working capital,}$$

$$\$5{,}246 \quad - \quad \$2{,}248 \quad = \quad \$2{,}998.$$

The concept of working capital as a pool of operating funds is discussed in greater detail later in this chapter.

Acid Test Ratio. Current liabilities are usually paid with cash, not with other current assets. The **acid test ratio** is more specific than the current ratio as a test of short-term solvency. It measures the availability of cash, and other current monetary assets that can be quickly converted into cash, to pay current liabilities. *Current monetary assets* include cash, marketable securities, and current receivables. The general equation for the acid test ratio and the computation for Dunfield's are as follows:

$$\text{General equation:} \quad \text{Acid test ratio} = \frac{\text{Cash} + \begin{array}{c}\text{Marketable}\\\text{securities}\end{array} + \begin{array}{c}\text{Current}\\\text{receivables}\end{array}}{\text{Current liabilities}}$$

$$\text{Example:} \quad = \frac{\$1,335 + \$250 + \$1,678}{\$2,248}$$

$$= 1.45$$

Dunfield's acid test ratio indicates that it has $1.45 of current monetary assets for each $1 of current liabilities. This ratio is also referred to as the **quick ratio** because it shows the amount of cash that can be obtained relatively quickly for each $1 of current liabilities outstanding. Many analysts consider an acid test ratio of 1.0 to be adequate for most businesses; however, as stated earlier in discussing the current ratio, the composition of the ratio components must be considered before deciding what is an adequate ratio. When evaluating the current and acid test ratios, the manager must consider other factors, such as seasonal characteristics of the business, the availability of short-term credit lines, the collection terms for accounts receivables, and the payment terms of accounts payable.

As a follow-up to the current ratio and the acid test ratio, most analysts evaluate the liquidity of the primary assets in the cash flow stream — namely, inventory and accounts receivable. The inventory turnover and days receivables outstanding are the measures ordinarily used for this purpose.

Inventory Turnover. **Inventory turnover** indicates the approximate number of times the average stock of inventory was sold and replenished during the year. Inventory turnover is computed as the total cost of the inventory sold during the year divided by the average inventory on hand during the year.

$$\text{General equation:} \quad \text{Inventory turnover} = \frac{\text{Cost of goods sold}}{\text{Average inventory}}$$

$$\text{Example:} \quad = \frac{\$6,085}{(\$1,703 + \$1,439)/2}$$

$$= 3.87 \text{ times}$$

During 19x4, Dunfield's sold inventory costing $6085, and the average inventory for the year was $1571 [($1703 + $1439)/2]; therefore, the average stock of inventory was sold and replenished 3.87 times during the year. Assuming a 365-day year, the average number of days required for each turnover of inventory was 94.3 days (365 days ÷ 3.87). That is, during the year the average inventory on hand was sufficient to meet the average sales needs for 94.3 days. Since ending inventory is somewhat higher than the average inventory for the year, inventory at year-end is sufficient to supply somewhat more than 94.3 days' average sales.

What constitutes an appropriate inventory turnover ratio varies from industry to industry. Obviously, a fast food restaurant should have a high inventory turnover, whereas a jewelry store ordinarily has a low inventory turnover. The nature of the firm's supply sources, the use of inventory display in selling merchandise, the quickness with which inventory must be delivered to customers, and information on industry norms all should be considered in interpreting the inventory turnover ratio.

Days Receivables Outstanding. Next to cash and marketable securities, receivables are the most liquid assets. They are converted directly into cash in the normal course of business. The **days receivables outstanding** ratio measures the number of days, on the average, it took to generate the sales uncollected at the year end. It is computed as ending receivables divided by average daily sales.

$$\text{Days receivables outstanding} = \frac{\text{Ending receivables}}{\text{Average daily sales}}$$

General equation:

Example:

$$= \frac{\$1,678}{\$9,734/365}$$

$$= 62.9 \text{ days}$$

At the end of the year, Dunfield's had receivables on hand equal to the average sales for 62.9 days. In evaluating this measure, management should consider the terms under which credit sales are made. For example, if Dunfield's sells goods and services on 30-day credit terms, a ratio of 62.9 days probably indicates serious receivables collection problems. This ratio, which is a broad average, is a reliable indicator only if the amount of daily sales was fairly even throughout the year. For more precise information, management should conduct a detailed aging analysis of year-end receivables to determine their ages and probable collection periods.

Long-term solvency is a separate matter from that of short-term solvency. Obviously, all long-term debts must eventually be paid in some future current period; however, solvency is a matter that should be monitored both for the near term and the extended future. The debt-to-equity ratio and the times-interest-earned measure are useful in analyzing long-term solvency.

Debt-to-Equity Ratio. Most business enterprises have two basic sources of capital — *debt* and *equity*. The balance between the amounts of capital provided by creditors and owners is important in evaluating the long-term solvency of a business. Creditors regard equity as a cushion against future operating losses and bankruptcy. The larger the percentage of total assets financed by equity capital, the more secure are the creditors. Aggressive, growth-oriented organizations tend to rely more heavily on debt than equity, whereas stable, conservative organizations tend to have a larger proportion of equity. The **debt-to-equity ratio** is computed as total liabilities divided by total stockholders' equity.

$$\text{General equation:} \quad \text{Debt-to-equity ratio} = \frac{\text{Total liabilities}}{\text{Total stockholders' equity}}$$

$$\text{Example:} \qquad\qquad\qquad = \frac{\$3,727}{\$5,027}$$

$$= 0.74$$

Dunfield's debt-to-equity ratio of 0.74 indicates that the creditors have provided $0.74 of capital for each $1 provided by the stockholders. Stated another way, for each $1.74 of asset book values, the company could suffer a $1 loss and still have total assets on the books equal to total liabilities. In evaluating the debt-to-equity ratio, it is necessary to recognize the possible understatement or overstatement of assets and owners' equity. For example, if a company purchased land for $1 million that has a fair market value of $10 million, the company in effect has $9 million of unrecorded assets and owners' equity. Although the debt-to-equity ratio is useful as a general indicator of the adequacy of long-term solvency, the amount of long-term debt that a company can justify is primarily related to its ability to repay the funds plus interest.

Times Interest Earned. Because a financially sound business pays interest obligations out of current earnings, creditors are interested in the adequacy of earnings to provide payment of interest charges. **Times interest earned,**

a measure of interest paying ability, shows the relationship between earnings available to pay interest and total interest expense.

General equation:	$\text{Times interest earned} = \dfrac{\underset{\text{income}}{\text{Net}} + \underset{\text{expense}}{\text{Interest}} + \underset{\text{taxes}}{\text{Income}}}{\text{Interest expense}}$
Example:	$= \dfrac{\$951 + \$345 + \$811}{\$345}$
	$= 6.11 \text{ times}$

In the numerator, interest expense and income taxes are added to net income to determine the pool of earnings from which interest expense is paid. Since interest expense is deducted in computing taxable income, the earnings pool from which interest is paid is income before deductions for interest and taxes. For Dunfield's this pool of earnings for 19x4 is 6.11 times the amount of the current year's interest charge on debt, indicating that earnings are more than adequate to cover the interest requirements.

Measures of Performance

Operating performance is related to the broad objective of profitability. The basic activities that characterize a typical for-profit organization are as follows:

- Generating capital (equity and debt).
- Acquiring assets with capital.
- Using assets to generate sales and profits.
- Using profits to pay the cost of capital.

The measures discussed below assist managers in evaluating their performance of these activities.

Asset Turnover. The **asset turnover** ratio measures the ability of the firm to use its assets to generate sales. It is computed as sales divided by average total assets.

General equation:	$\text{Asset turnover} = \dfrac{\text{Sales}}{\text{Average total assets}}$
Example:	$= \dfrac{\$9,734}{(\$8,754 + \$7,555)/2}$
	$= 1.19 \text{ times}$

For Dunfield's, the asset turnover of 1.19 times indicates that on the average each $1 of assets generated $1.19 of sales during the year. The interpretation of this measure depends largely on the nature of the business. Organizations that are capital intensive, such as utilities or heavily automated manufacturers, typically have a lower asset turnover than organizations that are primarily dependent on labor, such as a garment manufacturer. Also, firms that generate a small amount of sales with each dollar of assets usually have a higher percentage of profit in each sales dollar than firms that produce a high amount of sales with each invested asset dollar.

Return on Sales. The ability of a firm to generate sales with available assets is important; to be profitable, however, these sales must exceed the cost of generating them. **Return on sales** is a measure of the ability of the firm to generate profits from sales produced by the firm's assets; it is computed by dividing the sum of net income plus net-of-tax interest expense by sales.

$$\textit{General equation:} \quad \text{Return on sales} = \frac{\text{Net income} + \begin{matrix} \text{Net-of-tax} \\ \text{interest expense} \end{matrix}}{\text{Sales}}$$

$$\textit{Example:} \quad = \frac{\$951 + \$345\,(1 - 0.46)}{\$9,734}$$

$$= 0.117, \text{ or } 11.7\%$$

Interest expense is added to net income because it is not considered an expense of using assets, but rather a cost of providing the capital invested in assets. Since interest expense reduces taxes, it is adjusted for taxes at the current tax rate of 46 percent. On the average, 11.7 percent of each $1 of Dunfield's sales remained as profit after covering all expenses other than interest.

Return on Assets. The **return on assets** ratio combines the asset turnover and return on sales ratios to measure directly the ability of the firm to use its assets to generate profits. The return on assets computation is derived from the asset turnover and return on sales ratios as follows:

$$\text{Return on assets} = \text{Asset turnover} \times \text{Return on sales}$$

$$= \frac{\text{Sales}}{\text{Average total assets}} \times \frac{\text{Net income} + \text{Net-of-tax interest expense}}{\text{Sales}}$$

General equation:
$$= \frac{\text{Net income} + \text{Net-of-tax interest expense}}{\text{Average total assets}}$$

Example:
$$= \frac{\$951 + \$345 \, (1 - 0.46)}{(\$8,754 + \$7,555)/2}$$

$$= 0.139, \text{ or } 13.9\%$$

The return on assets for Dunfield's may also be determined by multiplying the asset turnover of 1.19 times the return on sales of 11.7 percent. From the previous analyses it can be concluded that on the average each dollar of assets generated $1.19 of sales and $0.139 of income, and each dollar of sales resulted in $0.117 of income. Return on assets is an important indicator of the overall performance of management because it measures management's effectiveness in using the total capital entrusted to them by both the creditors and the stockholders. A variation of this ratio (return on investment), discussed in Chapter 9, is commonly used for evaluating the performance of divisions in decentralized organizations.

The return on assets ratio measures profitability before deducting capital costs (interest and dividends); therefore, the adequacy of the profitability indicated by this ratio depends on the cost of debt and the return expected by the stockholders on their investments.

Return on Equity. **Return on equity** measures the profits attributable to the shareholders as a percentage of their equity in the firm. This measure is more specific than the return on assets ratio in measuring performance because it focuses only on *stockholders'* profits and investment. The profits available to stockholders consist of net income after deducting all costs and expenses, including interest expense. Return on equity is computed as net income divided by average stockholders' equity.[1]

---

[1] If there is more than one class of capital stock outstanding, the return on equity is computed as the return on common equity. In computing return on equity, net income must be reduced by the amount of annual dividends on preferred stock, and stockholders' equity must be reduced by the book value of preferred stock.

General equation: $\text{Return on equity} = \dfrac{\text{Net income}}{\text{Average stockholders' equity}}$

Example: $= \dfrac{\$951}{(\$5{,}027 + \$4{,}391)/2}$

$= 0.202, \text{ or } 20.2\%$

The return attributable to Dunfield's shareholders was 20.2 percent, compared to a return on assets of 13.9 percent. The return to the shareholders is higher than the return on assets as a result of financial leverage. **Financial leverage** refers to the use of capital that has a fixed interest or dividend rate. Any time capital can be acquired at a fixed rate,[2] and the return on assets is higher than that fixed rate, the return to the common shareholders is increased through *favorable financial leverage.* Conversely, if the fixed cost of capital is greater than the return it generates, the shareholders are subsidizing the cost of debt or other fixed rate capital, and there is *unfavorable financial leverage.* For Dunfield's, favorable financial leverage resulted because the return on assets was 13.9 percent, whereas the interest rate as a percent of average total liabilities was only 10 percent, computed as follows:

$$\text{Average interest rate} = \dfrac{\text{Interest expense}}{\text{Average total liabilities}}$$

$$= \dfrac{\$345}{(\$3{,}727 + \$3{,}164)/2}$$

$$= 0.10, \text{ or } 10.0\%.$$

The total debt required a return of only $345 (or 10 percent); therefore the return above 10 percent on the assets acquired with debt increased the return to the shareholders to 20.2 percent.

Earnings per Share. For external reporting purposes, earnings per share amounts are disclosed on the face of the income statement. If a company has gains or losses from extraordinary sources such as a natural disaster, or from other unusual and infrequent events, income and earnings per share figures must be presented separately for income before extraordinary items and for net income. Notice on Dunfield's income statement in Exhibit

---

[2] In an unstable money market the actual interest rate on a loan may change from period to period as the prime rate changes. These are called *variable rate loans.* Even in these situations the interest rate is fixed for a short period of time, and management's ability to generate favorable leverage varies inversely with changes in the applicable interest rate.

16–1 that reported earnings per share are $2.35 in 19x4 and $2.05 in 19x3. Since there were no extraordinary items, only earnings per share amounts for net income were presented.

Earnings per share for companies with simple capital structures is computed as net income divided by the average number of shares outstanding for the period. A simple capital structure is one consisting only of common stock. The computations are more difficult for companies with more complex capital structures that include preferred stock, convertible bonds, or other types of equity securities. Since financial statements already include earnings per share figures, the manager does not have to compute these figures.

Earnings per share measures are used extensively by investors as a basis for evaluating the overall profitability of the firm. The advantage of the earnings per share measure is that it is reported on the same basis as capital stock prices — that is, on an individual share basis. Investors often use the **price earnings ratio,** which compares earnings per share with the current market price of the stock, to arrive at a multiple of earnings represented by the selling price.

Managers also may use earnings per share as a broad measure of overall performance; however, it should not be relied on too heavily, nor should it be substituted for other more detailed profitability ratios. Changes in the capital structure during the year make it more difficult to compare earnings per share from year to year. The other profitability measures discussed above are likely to be more beneficial to managers in evaluating overall management performance. Another reason why managers should monitor earnings per share figures is to be familiar with the measure used extensively by investors in making decisions about the company's capital stock.

STATEMENT OF CHANGES IN FINANCIAL POSITION

The **balance sheet** presents a picture of an organization's financial position at a specific point in time. It summarizes all resources (assets) owned by an organization and the sources of those resources, which include investments by creditors and stockholders as well as earnings retained in the business. The only reason a company's balance sheet changes is that the company engages in transactions involving resource inflows and outflows. Otherwise the balance sheet would be static.

Revenue and expense transactions summarized on the *income statement* constitute a major portion of all resource flows. By definition, revenues represent the inflow of resources generated from the sale of goods and services, and expenses represent the outflow of resources necessary to generate revenues. As illustrated in the first part of this chapter, many significant decisions of investors, creditors, and managers are based on information obtained from the income statement.

In addition to resource flows reported on the income statement, many other significant transactions generate and use resources. Information about these transactions is also important for decision making. This information — which relates primarily to questions about debt and equity increases and decreases and major asset acquisitions and dispositions — has significant long-run implications on the firm's operations.

The **statement of changes in financial position** presents an overall summary of all major transactions that cause the balance sheet to change between two balance sheet dates. This statement includes *operating* (revenue and expense), *financing* (capital producing), and *investing* (capital investment) transactions. The balance sheet changes because of resource inflows and outflows; consequently, the statement of changes in financial position could be called a statement of resource inflows and outflows. Though the format of the statement is not uniform for all companies, it invariably provides information about all significant inflows and outflows of resources and the net change in resources.

The Basis for Measuring Resource Inflows and Outflows

There are several different ways to measure resources and their inflows and outflows. Resources are received by a business in a variety of forms, such as cash, receivables, equipment, and other assets. Likewise, resources flow out in a variety of forms, such as cash, inventory, and other assets.

Because a substantial amount of resource flows are in the form of cash, many companies find it useful to summarize resource inflows and outflows in terms of *cash*. When this approach is used, the primary objective of the statement of changes in financial position is to summarize all transactions that generated and used cash, with the difference being the net change in cash. Since many important resource inflows and outflows do not affect cash, a statement of changes in financial position prepared on the basis of cash must be supplemented by additional information about noncash transactions.

Another common approach for preparing the statement of changes in financial position is the *working capital* basis. Earlier in this chapter we defined working capital as current assets minus current liabilities. Working capital may be viewed as a pool of funds through which most resources flow in and out of the business. In this sense, current liabilities are viewed as negative working capital rather than as debt, and working capital represents a pool of funds consisting of total current assets less total current liabilities.

Many resource inflows increase working capital even though they do not increase cash. An example is rendering services on account. In this transaction working capital is increased by an increase in accounts receivable, but cash is not immediately affected. This sale is treated as a resource inflow on the working capital basis but not on the cash basis. Similarly, many resource outflows, such as the consumption of supplies, decrease working capital even though they do not decrease cash.

When the working capital basis is used for preparing the statement of changes in financial position, all increases in working capital are recognized as resource inflows, and all decreases in working capital are recognized as resource outflows. If there are significant resource changes not affecting working capital, information about these transactions is also disclosed in the working capital basis statement of changes in financial position. An example of a transaction of this type is the purchase of equipment by the issuance of a long-term note payable. The preparation of the statement of changes in financial position on the cash basis and the working capital basis is illustrated below. Most companies currently use the working capital basis for external financial reporting, although many managers prefer the cash basis.

STATEMENT OF CHANGES IN FINANCIAL POSITION — WORKING CAPITAL BASIS

Under the working capital basis, the primary objective in preparing the statement of changes in financial position is to identify all transactions that increased or decreased working capital during the period. The basic accounting (or balance sheet) equation can be used to illustrate the types of transactions that increase and decrease working capital. By modifying the equation to show working capital isolated on the left side, the types of transactions that increase and decrease working capital can be readily identified:

$$\overbrace{\underset{\text{assets}}{\text{Current}} - \underset{\text{liabilities}}{\text{Current}}}^{\text{Working capital}} = \underset{\text{liabilities}}{\text{Long-term}} + \underset{\text{equity}}{\text{Owners'}} - \underset{\text{assets}}{\text{Noncurrent}}.$$

The left side of the equation represents working capital; therefore only transactions that increase the net amount of the left side of the equation increase working capital, and only transactions that decrease the net amount of the left side of the equation decrease working capital. Since the equation must balance, working capital is increased or decreased only by transactions that affect both sides of the equation. If a transaction affects only the left side of the equation, there are offsetting changes in the working capital accounts but no change in total working capital. Examples of transactions affecting only the left side of the equation are (1) paying a $200 account payable with cash, (2) purchasing $500 of supplies with cash, (3) purchasing $750 of inventory on account, and (4) paying a $400 account payable by issuing a six-month note payable.

If a company has total current assets of $5000 and total current liabilities of $2100 before completing the four transactions above, its total working capital is $2900 both before and after the transactions. The calculations are illustrated below.

	Current assets	−	Current liabilities	=	Working capital
Beginning balances	$5,000		$2,100		$2,900
(1) Paid $200 account payable with cash	(200)		(200)		—
Balances	$4,800		$1,900		$2,900
(2) Purchased $500 of supplies with cash	500*				
	(500)		—		—
Balances	$4,800		$1,900		$2,900
(3) Purchased $750 of inventory on account	750		750		—
Balances	$5,550		$2,650		$2,900
(4) Paid $400 account payable by issuing a six-month note payable	—		(400)†		—
			400		
Ending balances	$5,550		$2,650		$2,900

* Increased one current asset and decreased another

† Increased one current liability and decreased another

From the analysis above it is apparent that any transaction affecting only working capital accounts does not change the total amount of working capital. These transactions, therefore, do not constitute sources or uses of working capital. *For working capital to be increased or decreased there must be changes in the nonworking capital components of the balance sheet equation;* that is, there must be a change in long-term liabilities, owners' equity, or noncurrent assets. The most common changes in these components can be summarized as follows:

Component	Type of Change in Component	Effect on Working Capital	Common Sources (*Increases*) and Uses (*Decreases*) of Working Capital
Long-term liabilities	Increase	Increase	Borrowing on long-term debt
	Decrease	Decrease	Repayment of long-term debt
Owners' equity	Increase	Increase	Sale of capital stock Operating at a profit
	Decrease	Decrease	Purchase of treasury stock Operating at a loss Payment of dividends
Noncurrent assets	Increase	Decrease	Purchase of noncurrent assets
	Decrease	Increase	Sale of noncurrent assets

Net Income and Working Capital

One of the most important sources of working capital for a well-managed company is its normal operating activities. These activities generate revenues, expenses, and the resulting net income, all of which are reported on the income statement. Since normal operations are expected to be a major source of working capital, this source is usually reported first on the statement of changes in financial position. To measure the effects of operations on working capital, it is usually necessary to make one or more adjustments to net income. Seldom is net income, as reported on the accrual basis income statement, equal to the change in working capital caused by operating transactions.

Although most revenues and expenses on the income statement reduce working capital, some revenues and expenses have no effect on working capital. Consequently, to determine the effects of operations on working capital, it is necessary to convert net income as computed on the income statement to a working capital basis. This conversion involves making adjustments to net income to remove any items reflected in net income that have no effect on working capital. The adjustment for depreciation expense is the one most often required. Depreciation is recorded in the accounting records by the following journal entry.

Journal entry

Depreciation Expense	xx	
Accumulated Depreciation		xx

The effect of the debit in this entry is to decrease net income, and the effect of the credit is to decrease noncurrent assets. Depreciation Expense and Accumulated Depreciation are both nonworking capital accounts; therefore this entry does not increase or decrease working capital. To adjust net income to reflect only expenses that decreased working capital, depreciation expense must be removed from the net income computation as follows:

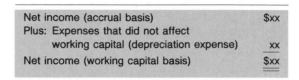

Net income (accrual basis)	$xx
Plus: Expenses that did not affect working capital (depreciation expense)	xx
Net income (working capital basis)	$xx

Other examples of transactions that require adjustments to net income are listed below:

- Amortization of intangible assets.
- Depletion of natural resources.
- Amortization of premium or discount on long-term debt.
- Amortization of premium or discount on long-term investments.
- Increases or decreases in deferred (long-term) tax liabilities.

This list includes the most common income statement items that do not affect working capital. The general rule is that any revenue or expense that is recorded without an offsetting increase or decrease in a working capital account will necessitate an adjustment to net income to determine the amount of working capital generated by operations.

Illustration of Statement of Changes in Financial Position — Working Capital Basis

The comparative balance sheets for Omega Corporation presented in Exhibit 16–2 are used to illustrate the statement of changes in financial position under the working capital basis. Because changes in financial position are always accompanied by changes in nonworking capital accounts, *the procedure for identifying transactions that cause changes in working capital involves analyzing the nonworking capital accounts to identify changes in them that increased or decreased total working capital.* This procedure is much easier than the alternative of analyzing every transaction in each working capital account. The majority of the transactions recorded in the working capital accounts usually have no effect on total working capital. Therefore, examining the mass of transactions recorded in the working capital accounts to identify transactions that affected total working capital would ordinarily be an enormous task and an inefficient method of identifying them.

The information obtained by analyzing the transactions entered in the nonworking capital accounts for Omega Corporation, including an indica-

---

EXHIBIT 16–2 Comparative Balance Sheets

Omega Corporation
Comparative Balance Sheets
December 31, 19x5 and 19x4

Assets	19x5	19x4
Current assets:		
Cash	$ 700	$ 800
Accounts receivable (net)	5,055	2,100
Inventory	6,800	7,500
Prepaid insurance	150	450
Total	$12,705	$10,850
Land	25,000	15,000
Building	40,000	40,000
Accumulated depreciation (building)	(9,000)	(8,000)
Equipment	18,000	18,000
Accumulated depreciation (equipment)	(7,700)	(6,500)
Total assets	$79,005	$69,350
Liabilities and Stockholders' Equity		
Current liabilities:		
Accounts payable	$ 2,400	$ 3,600
Notes payable	—	5,000
Dividends payable	1,000	—
Total	$ 3,400	$ 8,600
Mortgage note payable	34,250	35,000
Total liabilities	$37,650	$43,600
Stockholders' equity:		
Common stock	$25,000	$10,000
Premium on common stock	2,200	2,000
Retained earnings	14,155	13,750
Total stockholders' equity	41,355	25,750
Total liabilities and stockholders' equity	$79,005	$69,350

---

tion of how each change affected working capital and cash, is summarized below. Later we will use the information pertaining to changes in cash to prepare a cash basis statement of changes in financial position.

Land. The increase in land was caused by the issuance of Omega common stock in exchange for five acres of land to be used for plant expansion. This represented an inflow of new resources that had no effect on either working capital or cash.

Building. No transactions.

Accumulated Depreciation — Building. Depreciation expense of $1000 was recorded on the building. This transaction decreased net income but had no effect on working capital or cash. This $1000 will be added to net income in determining the effect of operations on working capital.

Equipment. No transactions.

Accumulated Depreciation — Equipment. Depreciation expense of $1200 was recorded on the equipment. This transaction decreased net income but had no effect on working capital or cash. This $1200 will be added to net income in determining the effect of operations on working capital.

Mortgage Note Payable. A $6000 payment was made on the note. Of this amount, $5250 was applied to interest expense, and $750 reduced the principal amount of the note. The effect of the interest expense was to decrease net income, working capital, and cash. The payment of principal reduced both working capital and cash by $750.

Common Stock. Two transactions were recorded in the common stock account. First, 10,000 shares of common stock were issued at par value in exchange for land. (See the above explanation for land for the effects on working capital and cash.) Second, 5000 shares were issued for $5200 cash, including $200 in excess of par value. This transaction increased both working capital and cash by $5200.

Premium on Common Stock. See previous explanation.

Retained Earnings. This account was increased by net income of $1405 and decreased by a dividend declaration of $1000. Net income of $1405 must be adjusted for nonworking capital expenses (depreciation on building and equipment) to determine the effect of operations on working capital. The dividend declaration was recorded by a debit to Retained Earnings and a credit to Dividends Payable, a current liability account. This transaction decreased working capital by $1000 but had no effect on cash.

Notice that this analysis of working capital accounts is in the same order in which the accounts are presented in the balance sheet. This approach provides an orderly procedure for gathering the data for preparing the statement of changes in financial position. The changes in working capital explained above are summarized in the statement of changes in financial position in Exhibit 16–3.

EXHIBIT 16–3 Statement of Changes in Financial Position — Working Capital Basis

Omega Corporation
Statement of Changes in Financial Position
For the year ended December 31, 19x5

Sources and Uses of Working Capital

Sources of working capital:		
Operations:		
Net income (accrual basis)	$1,405	
Plus expenses that did not decrease		
working capital:		
Depreciation expense	2,200	
Working capital provided by		
operations		$ 3,605
Sale of common stock		5,200
Total sources of working capital		$ 8,805
Uses of working capital:		
Payment of mortgage note principal	$ 750	
Declaration of cash dividend	1,000	
Total uses of working capital		−1,750
Increase in working capital		$ 7,055

Other Resources Received and Used Not Affecting Working Capital

Issued 1000 shares of common stock at	
par value in exchange for 5 acres of land	$10,000

Schedule of Changes in Working Capital

	December 31 19x5	December 31 19x4	Working Capital Increase (Decrease)
Working Capital Accounts:			
Cash	$ 700	$ 800	$ (100)
Accounts Receivable (net)	5,055	2,100	2,955
Inventory	6,800	7,500	(700)
Prepaid Insurance	150	450	(300)
Accounts Payable	(2,400)	(3,600)	1,200
Notes Payable	—	(5,000)	5,000
Dividends Payable	(1,000)	—	(1,000)
Total	$ 9,305	$ 2,250	$ 7,055

Notice in Exhibit 16–3 that although net income is $1405 before adjustment, $3605 of working capital is provided by operations. Included on the income statement was one expense item (depreciation expense) that did not reduce working capital. To show the effects of operations on working capital, this item had to be removed from the computation of net income. Because most revenue and expense items produce a direct effect on total working capital, ordinarily very few of these adjustments are required.

All significant inflows and outflows of resources should be included in the statement of changes in financial position, including those not affecting working capital. Working capital was not affected by the issuance of 1000 shares of common stock by Omega Corporation in exchange for five acres of land; however, this transaction involved significant resource flows affecting the financial position of the firm. It is therefore included on the statement as an additional item presented below the computation of the increase in working capital. Several different formats are used in practice for disclosing these additional resource inflows and outflows. Some accountants merely list these resource flows in a footnote to the statement of changes, whereas others show the sources and uses of them as separate items on the statement, for example, the land acquisition in exchange for stock could have been presented as follows:

Sources of resources not increasing working capital:	
Issuance of common stock (in exchange for land)	$10,000
Uses of resources not decreasing working capital:	
Acquisition of land (by issuing common stock)	$10,000

This presentation emphasizes that the issuance of common stock represented an inflow of resources and that the acquisition of land represented a use of equity resources.

A schedule is also ordinarily included at the bottom of the statement of changes that shows the specific working capital account changes that make up the total change in working capital. For Omega Corporation the $7055 net increase in working capital was reflected in the working capital accounts by a $100 decrease in cash, a $2955 net increase in accounts receivable, and so forth. The changes shown in the schedule of changes in working capital resulted from the sources and uses of working capital summarized in the statement. These account changes also reflect transactions that affected only working capital accounts.

STATEMENT OF CHANGES IN FINANCIAL POSITION — CASH BASIS

Under the cash basis, the primary focus of the statement of changes in financial position is on transactions that increased or decreased cash during the period. One way to identify these transactions is to conduct a detailed analysis of each of the many cash receipts and disbursements recorded during the period. A more efficient approach, however, is to analyze the accounts other than Cash, since every debit or credit to Cash must be offset by a debit or credit to some other account.

Adjusting Net Income to Cash Basis

To determine the effects of operations on cash, it is necessary to adjust net income as reported on the income statement to the cash basis. Two types of adjustments are required: (1) revenues and expenses that did not affect working capital accounts and (2) changes in working capital accounts other than cash. For the first group the same adjustments made to net income under the working capital basis are required under the cash basis. If a revenue or expense item does not affect a working capital account, it obviously does not affect cash either, since cash is part of working capital.

The adjustments in the second group are necessary to eliminate from net income the effects of increases and decreases in the current accrual accounts. If a company were using a strict cash basis of accounting for net income, revenues and expenses would be recognized only upon the receipt and payment of cash. Therefore Accounts Receivable, Inventory, and Prepaid Expenses would not be recognized in the accounts.[3] Similarly, there would be no recognition of liabilities for Accounts Payable and Accrued Expenses Payable. *Increases and decreases in these working capital accounts result entirely from applying accrual concepts in measuring net income.* The types of adjustments required to convert accrual net income to a cash basis are described below. These adjustments for changes in working capital accounts are in addition to the nonworking capital revenue and expense adjustments (such as depreciation) made under the working capital basis.

Accounts Receivable. Under accrual accounting, Accounts Receivable increases if sales exceed collections during the period, and it decreases if cash collections exceed sales. Under the cash basis, revenues are equal to cash collections during the period. Therefore, accrual basis revenues exceed cash basis revenues if Accounts Receivable increased during the period,

---

[3] Even on a strict cash basis, a business would, of course, need to keep records outside the formal ledger accounts on its receivables and payables.

and cash basis revenues exceed accrual basis revenues if Accounts Receivable decreased during the period. To convert net income to a cash basis, increases in Accounts Receivable are subtracted from accrual net income, and decreases are added to accrual net income.

Inventory. Under the accrual basis of measuring net income, inventory is recognized as an asset when purchased, and it is recorded as an expense when sold. Under the cash basis, inventory purchases are recorded immediately as expenses. On the accrual basis, if the balance in Inventory increases during the period, this indicates that the cost of inventory sold is less than the amount purchased. To adjust to the cash basis, it is necessary to deduct the increase in Inventory from net income. Conversely, if Inventory decreases, cost of inventory sold exceeds inventory purchases, and this decrease is added to net income to adjust to the cash basis.

Prepaid Expenses. Under accrual accounting, prepayments for supplies, insurance, rent, and other expenses are recognized as assets and deducted as expenses when the items are consumed; on the cash basis, however, these items are expensed when cash payments are made. Increases in prepaid expense accounts during the period indicate that payments for these items exceeded the amounts deducted on the income statement. This increase is subtracted from net income to adjust to the cash basis. Conversely, decreases in prepaid expense accounts represent excess expenses over cash payments and are added back to net income to adjust to the cash basis.

Accounts Payable and Accrued Payables. The balances in Accounts Payable and Accrued Payables for salaries, taxes, or other expenses, represent liabilities for inventory purchases and other expenses that have been incurred but not paid. If either Accounts Payable or Accrued Payables increases during the period, the expense deduction on the income statement is greater than the amount paid during the year for the related expenses. These increases are added to net income to adjust to the cash basis. Conversely, net income must be reduced by the amount of any decreases in Accounts Payable or Accrued Payables, since these decreases represent cash payments made during the period that were not recorded as expenses.

To summarize, in adjusting accrual net income to the cash basis, it is necessary to make the following adjustments to net income.

1. Adjustments for revenues and expenses not affecting working capital:
   - Subtract revenues that were not accompanied by increases in working capital accounts.
   - Add expenses (such as depreciation) that were not accompanied by decreases in working capital accounts.

2. Adjustments for changes in working capital accounts other than cash:

- Subtract increases in current accrual asset accounts, such as Accounts Receivable, Inventory, and Prepaid Expenses.

- Add decreases in current accrual asset accounts, such as Accounts Receivable, Inventory, and Prepaid Expenses.

- Add increases in current accrual liability accounts, such as Accounts Payable and Accrued Payables.

- Subtract decreases in current accrual liability accounts, such as Accounts Payable and Accrued Payables.

The adjustments to net income in the first group are required under both the working capital basis and the cash basis, whereas the second group of adjustments is required only under the cash basis.

After determining the amount of cash generated by operations, all other sources and uses of cash are determined by analyzing the nonworking capital accounts and any working capital accounts (such as short-term notes payable) that were not analyzed in making the adjustments to net income. The presentation of the cash basis statement of changes in financial position is very similar to the statement presented on the working capital basis. Omega Corporation's statement of changes in financial position prepared on the cash basis is presented in Exhibit 16–4.

Comparison of Exhibits 16–3 and 16–4 reveals some interesting differences between the working capital and cash basis statements. Omega reported $1405 in *net income* on its income statement prepared in accordance with accrual accounting concepts. *Working capital* provided by operations was $3605, and *cash* provided by operations was $405. Although the company reported a $7055 *increase* in working capital, it had a $100 *decrease* in cash. On the working capital basis, the declared dividend entered into the primary computation of resource changes, but on the cash basis it was reported as a supplementary item. The reason for this difference is that the dividend declaration decreased working capital but had no effect on cash. The decrease in cash for the dividend will be shown as a use of cash in the period when the dividend is paid.

In Exhibit 16–4 the amount of cash generated by operations was determined by adjusting accrual net income to remove items not increasing or decreasing cash. A more direct approach is to adjust each item on the income statement to produce a cash basis income statement. Although this is ordinarily not done on the statement of changes in financial position, it may be useful for managers and other financial statement users to receive a complete cash basis income statement, which would show not only cash net income but also how each component of the income statement increased or decreased cash. Exhibit 16–5 illustrates the conversion of the

EXHIBIT 16–4   Statement of Changes in Financial Position — Cash Basis

Omega Corporation
Statement of Changes in Financial Position
For the year ended December 31, 19x5

Sources and Uses of Cash

Sources of cash:		
Operations:		
Net income (accrual basis)	$ 1,405	
Plus expenses not decreasing working capital:		
Depreciation expense	2,200	
Accrual adjustments:		
Increase in Accounts Receivable	(2,955)	
Decrease in Inventory	700	
Decrease in Prepaid Insurance	300	
Decrease in Accounts Payable	(1,200)	
Cash provided by operations		$ 405
Sale of common stock		5,200
Total sources of cash		$ 5,650
Uses of cash:		
Payment of short-term note payable principal	$ 5,000	
Payment of mortgage note payable principal	750	
Total uses of cash		−5,750
Increase (decrease) in cash		$ (100)

Other Resources Received and Used Not Affecting Cash

Dividends declared but not paid		$ 1,000
Issued 1000 shares of common stock at par value in exchange for 5 acres of land		$10,000

complete income statement for Omega Corporation from the accrual basis to the cash basis.

INTERPRETING THE STATEMENT OF CHANGES IN FINANCIAL POSITION

Techniques like those illustrated earlier in this chapter for analyzing the balance sheet and income statement are not available for analyzing the statement of changes in financial position. There are no widely used ratios

EXHIBIT 16–5   Conversion of Income Statement from Accrual Basis to Cash Basis

Omega Corporation
Accrual and Cash Basis Income Statements
For the year ended December 31, 19x5

	Accrual Basis	Increase	Decrease	Cash Basis
Sales	$58,000		$2,955*	$55,045
Cost of goods sold:				
Beginning inventory	$ 7,500			
Plus purchases	31,300			
Less ending inventory	(6,800)			
Total	−32,000	1,200†	700‡	−32,500
Gross profit	$26,000			$22,545
Operating expenses:				
Salaries expense	$12,000			$12,000
Bad debts expense	545			545
Insurance expense	300		300§	—
Depreciation expense	2,200		2,200#	—
Interest expense	5,750			5,750
Other expenses	3,800			3,800
Total	−24,595			−22,095
Net income	$ 1,405			$ 450

* To remove sales related to the increase in Accounts Receivable that increased Sales but did not affect cash

† To include in Cost of Goods Sold the decrease in Accounts Payable paid in cash during the current period

‡ To remove from Cost of Goods Sold the decrease in Inventory acquired in a previous period that had no effect on cash in the current period

§ To remove the decrease in Prepaid Insurance expensed in the current period but paid for in the previous period

\# To remove Depreciation Expense that did not affect cash

for examining this statement and its relationship to the other financial statements. Despite the lack of uniform analytical procedures, the statement of changes in financial position is important in communicating useful financial information. Whether the working capital or cash basis is used, this statement often provides the best available report of the company's overall performance. Unlike the income statement, which reports primarily operating activities, the statement of changes in financial position summarizes management's financing, investing, and operating activities for the period. It tells where capital came from, where capital was invested, and how profitable past company investments were during the period.

Many important questions that investors, creditors, and managers have about a company can be answered with information obtained from the statement of changes in financial position. Some of these questions are listed below.

- Were capital investments compatible with the sources of capital?
- Did management use short-term capital to finance long-term investments?
- Was the decision to raise dividends consistent with the level of resources generated by operations?
- Why did short-term liquidity deteriorate even though earnings increased?
- Were the increases in working capital (or cash) generated primarily by operations or by long-term capital sources?
- How much was invested in new capital assets during the year?
- What happened to funds generated by the sale of common stock or long-term bonds, or generated by the disposition of a division or other segment of the business?

Managers should give close attention to the statement of changes because it often portrays a different picture of management's performance than that revealed in the income statement and balance sheet. For example, if long-term financial stability were sacrificed during the period for current liquidity and profitability, this development would probably be apparent in the statement of changes in financial position. The assessment of a company's overall performance is not completed until the manager, or other user, has read and interpreted all financial statements, including the income statement, the balance sheet, and the statement of changes in financial position.

SUMMARY

Financial statement analysis is the process of using financial statement data to generate additional financial information. Investors and creditors, as well as managers, can benefit from financial analysis. In this chapter the primary focus was on analytical measures that benefit managers.

Measures for analyzing financial statements can be classified into solvency and performance measures. For evaluating short-term solvency, the current ratio and acid test ratio are used to determine the sufficiency of current assets to satisfy current liabilities. Other short-term solvency measures aimed at evaluating the liquidity of current assets are inventory turnover and the number of days receivables outstanding. Long-term solvency can be evaluated by computing the debt-to-equity ratio and the times interest earned multiple. These measures indicate the overall riskiness of the creditors' investment in the firm and the ability of the firm to meet its continuing interest requirements.

To evaluate current performance, several measures are available that focus both on the ability of the assets to generate sales and profits and on the profit returns attributable to creditors and stockholders. The productivity of the firm's assets is measured by the asset turnover multiple, the return on sales ratio, and the return on assets ratio. The profitability of the shareholders' investment is measured by the return on equity ratio. The favorable or unfavorable use of financial leverage can be determined by comparing return on assets with return on equity. Favorable leverage exists when the return on equity exceeds the return on assets; unfavorable leverage exists when the return on equity is less than the return on assets. Earnings per share may be helpful in assessing overall company performance, although it should be used with caution.

Historically, the income statement and the balance sheet have been the primary financial statements used to evaluate a company. The statement of changes in financial position, however, contains a substantial amount of useful information not found in these other statements. Though the income statement summarizes changes in the balance sheet related to operating transactions, the statement of changes in financial position reports all material changes in the balance sheet. Complete information about financing and investing transactions is found only in the statement of changes in financial position.

The statement of changes in financial position summarizes balance sheet changes in terms of resource inflows and outflows. Two methods for measuring resource flows are the working capital basis and the cash basis. Although most companies use the working capital basis in their published financial statements, managers often find cash basis statements more useful.

KEY TERMS

Financial statement analysis

Solvency

Current ratio

Working capital

Acid test ratio

Quick ratio

Inventory turnover

Days receivables outstanding

Debt-to-equity ratio

Times interest earned

Asset turnover

Return on sales

Return on assets

Return on equity

Financial leverage

Earnings per share

Price earnings ratio

Statement of changes in financial position

REVIEW QUESTIONS

16–1 Explain why general purpose financial statements must be analyzed for them to provide maximum benefit to specific users.

16–2 Name three reasons managers should analyze their firm's financial statements.

16–3 What is the purpose of evaluation standards in financial analysis?

16–4 What types of standards are probably most relevant for financial analysis by managers?

16–5 Explain and differentiate the terms "solvency evaluation" and "performance evaluation."

16–6 Explain the difference between the current ratio and the acid test ratio.

16–7 Why is it useful to compute the inventory turnover and the days receivables outstanding? How is each of these measures computed?

16–8 What are the primary measures of long-term solvency? How are they computed?

16–9 Which analysis measure provides information concerning the sales output produced by a firm's assets?

16–10 Why is interest expense added in the numerator in computing return on assets?

16–11 Explain the concept of financial leverage. What causes leverage to be favorable? Unfavorable?

16–12 What is the purpose of the statement of changes in financial position? What is its relationship to the income statement and the balance sheet?

16–13 Why is depreciation expense added to net income in measuring resources generated by operations on the working capital basis? On the cash basis?

16–14 Name three major sources and three major uses of working capital.

16–15 How would net income be adjusted for the following account changes in preparing a statement of changes in financial position on the cash basis: increase in Accounts Receivable, decrease in Inventory, increase in Prepaid Insurance, and increase in Accounts Payable?

EXERCISES

16–1 Short-Term Solvency Ratios

Windover, Inc. had the following current assets and current liabilities in its financial statements for 19x1 and 19x0.

Current Assets	19x1	19x0
Cash	$ 1,500	$ 1,700
Accounts receivable	16,200	6,900
Marketable securities	2,000	2,500
Inventory	8,300	7,400
Total	$ 28,000	$ 18,500

Current Liabilities		
Accounts payable	$ 5,600	$ 3,700
Notes payable	1,000	1,000
Accrued expenses payable	5,400	4,300
Total	$ 12,000	$ 9,000

Additional data:

	19x1	19x0
Sales	$220,000	$195,000
Cost of goods sold	158,000	132,000
Inventory, beginning of 19x0		6,800

Required: Compute the following ratios for 19x1 and 19x0. (Round calculations to two decimal places.)

1. Current ratio

2. Acid test ratio

3. Inventory turnover

4. Days receivables outstanding

16–2 Short-Term Solvency Ratios

The following items (listed alphabetically) were taken from the 19x7 year end financial statements of Monteray Corporation.

Accounts payable	$ 27,500
Accounts receivable	32,000
Cash	4,800
Cost of goods sold	195,000
Inventory, beginning	80,000
Inventory, ending	65,000
Marketable securities	15,750
Other current payables	8,200
Sales	325,000

Required: Compute the following ratios. (Round calculations to two decimal places.)

1. Current ratio

2. Acid test ratio

3. Inventory turnover

4. Days receivables outstanding

16–3 Long-Term Solvency Ratios

Selected financial statement data for 19x5 are given below for Vail Construction Company.

Income taxes	$ 36,018
Interest expense	3,834
Net income	48,178
Total assets	340,595
Total liabilities	133,121

Requirements

a) Compute the debt-to-equity ratio. (Round calculations to two decimal places.)

b) Compute the ratio of times interest earned. (Round calculations to two decimal places.)

16–4 Short-Term Solvency Ratios

The financial data given below were obtained from the end-of-year financial statements of York Company for 19x2, 19x1, and 19x0.

	19x2	*19x1*	*19x0*
Accounts receivable	$ 153,000	$ 165,000	$ 150,000
Cost of goods sold	1,680,000	1,450,000	1,600,000
Current assets	750,000	600,000	675,000
Current liabilities	525,000	450,000	500,000
Inventory	375,000	275,000	325,000
Sales	1,850,000	2,000,000	1,750,000

Requirements

a) Compute the following financial ratios for 19x2 and 19x1. (Round calculations to two decimal places.)

1. Current ratio

2. Acid test ratio

3. Inventory turnover

4. Days receivables outstanding

b) Comment on the short-term solvency of York Company for 19x1 and 19x2. Did the company's short-term solvency improve or deteriorate during 19x2? Explain.

16–5 Long-Term Solvency Ratios

Summaries of the end-of-year financial statements of Palo Alto Company for 19x6 are given below.

Income statement:

Sales		$5,854,325
Less: Cost of goods sold	$3,425,000	
Selling expenses	625,000	
Administrative expenses	525,000	
Interest expense	1,475,300	
Income tax expense	50,250	−6,100,550
Net income		$ (246,225)

Balance sheet:

Total assets	$850,000	Total liabilities	$600,000
		Stockholders' equity	250,000
		Total	$850,000

Requirements

a) Compute the ratio of times interest earned. (Round computations to two decimal places.)

b) Compute the debt-to-equity ratio.

16–6 Effects of Financing Decisions

Provo, Inc. has total assets of $2,500,000 and total liabilities of $2,000,000. Provo is considering two alternatives for acquiring additional warehouse space. Under the first alternative the building would be purchased for $300,000 and financed by issuing long-term bonds. Under the other alternative the building would be rented on an annual lease of $30,000 per year.

Requirements

a) Compute the current debt-to-equity ratio.

b) What effect will the addition of the warehouse space have on the debt-to-equity ratio (1) assuming the building is purchased by issuing bonds and (2) assuming the building is rented on an annual lease?

16–7 Ratio Analysis: Measures of Performance

The following selected data were obtained from the end-of-year financial statements of Nelox Corporation for 19x9 and 19x8.

	19x9	19x8
Total assets	$7,349,000	$6,553,000
Interest expense	115,000	102,000
Long-term liabilities	1,239,000	1,220,000
Net income	619,000	563,000
Sales	8,196,000	6,996,000
Stockholders' equity	3,624,000	3,221,000

Requirements

a) Compute the following performance measurement ratios for 19x9. (Round computations to three decimal places. Ignore income taxes.)

1. Asset turnover

2. Return on sales

3. Return on assets

4. Return on equity

b) Is Nelox Company using financial leverage? If so, is the leverage positive or negative? Explain.

16–8 Schedule of Changes in Working Capital

Roswell Company's current assets and current liabilities at the end of 19x6 and 19x5 are as follows:

	19x6	19x5
Current assets:		
Cash	$ 8,500	$ 6,400
Accounts receivable	17,000	20,200
Inventory	41,000	44,000
Prepaid expenses	800	950
Total	$67,300	$71,550
Current liabilities:		
Accounts payable	$15,500	$17,200
Notes payable	10,000	7,500
Taxes payable	1,500	1,250
Total	$27,000	$25,950

Required: Prepare a schedule of changes in working capital for 19x6.

16–9 Effects of Operations on Working Capital

Bob's Big Pizza Restaurant had the following income statement for 19x9.

Bob's Big Pizza Restaurant
Income Statement
For the year 19x9

Sales		$88,000
Less costs and expenses:		
Cost of food	$25,000	
Wages	21,000	
Utilities	6,000	
Rent	18,000	
Depreciation	1,000	
Miscellaneous	3,500	−74,500
Net income		$13,500

Requirements

a) Indicate for each item on the income statement which working capital accounts were most likely affected by the revenue or expense transaction and whether total working capital was increased or decreased.

b) Adjust net income from the accrual basis to the working capital basis.

16–10 Changes in Working Capital

Below is a list of typical financing, investing, and operating transactions.

1. Sold capital stock for cash.
2. Purchased a building for cash.
3. Declared cash dividends.
4. Retired long-term bonds payable.
5. Recorded a net loss for the period.
6. Purchased a building site by issuing long-term bonds.
7. Sold equipment with a five-year remaining life for an amount equal to book value.
8. Acquired treasury stock for cash.
9. Borrowed cash on a long-term note.
10. Sold a fully depreciated piece of equipment.

Required: For each of the above transactions indicate whether working capital increased, decreased, or was not affected. Also indicate whether the change in working capital was accompanied by a change in noncurrent assets, long-term liabilities, or owners' equity.

16–11 Effects of Transactions on Working Capital

Fastdata, Inc. had the following account balances at June 30, 19x1.

Accounts Payable	$ 7,500
Accounts Receivable	12,600
Cash	2,500
Inventory	18,000
Notes Payable	3,000
Supplies	300
Wages Payable	1,325

In July the following transactions were recorded.

- Collected $7500 of accounts receivable.
- Paid the balance of wages payable.
- Paid $4250 on accounts payable.
- Negotiated a six-month extension on a $2000 account payable, and issued a note payable for that amount.
- Purchased $2500 of inventory for cash and $6300 on account.

Requirements

a) Compute working capital at June 30, 19x1.

b) Prepare a schedule showing the effect of each of the July transactions on working capital and showing the July 31 working capital. Compute the net change in working capital during July.

16–12 Effects of Transactions on Working Capital

Hendrix Company reported current assets of $45,000 and current liabilities of $31,500 on its December 31, 19x5 balance sheet. During January, 19x6 the following transactions were recorded.

- Purchased $3000 in inventory on account.

- Purchased land for $15,000 paying a $2500 cash down payment and issuing a long-term note for the balance.

- Sold merchandise costing $5000 for $9250.

- Paid $4500 on accounts payable.

- Paid cash expenses of $1800.

- Purchased supplies for $250 cash.

Requirements

a) Compute Hendrix Company's working capital at December 31, 19x5.

b) Prepare a schedule showing the effect of each of the January transactions on working capital and showing the January 31 working capital.

PROBLEMS

16–13 Financial Leverage

The following data have been determined for McClellan Company and McDonough Company for 19x5.

	McClellan	McDonough
Net income	$ 270,000	$ 405,000
Interest expense	112,500	120,000
Total assets, beginning of 19x5	3,750,000	6,375,000
Total assets, end of 19x5	4,042,500	6,847,500
Stockholders' equity, beginning of 19x5	1,594,500	3,703,500
Stockholders' equity, end of 19x5	1,689,000	3,832,500

Requirements

a) Compute the following ratios for McClellan and McDonough Companies at the end of 19x5. (Ignore taxes and round calculations to three decimal places.)

1. Return on assets

2. Return on equity

b) Comment on the use of financial leverage by these two companies. Which company is the most highly leveraged? Which company's stockholders are benefiting the most from the use of leverage?

16–14 Comprehensive Ratio Analysis   Rocky Mountain Company's financial statements are presented below.

Rocky Mountain Company
Comparative Balance Sheets
December 31, 19x4 and 19x3

Assets	19x4	19x3
Cash	$ 243,000	$ 270,000
Accounts receivable	1,147,000	1,120,000
Inventory	637,000	556,000
Total current assets	$2,027,000	$1,946,000
Property, plant, and equipment (net)	7,587,000	6,952,000
Total assets	$9,614,000	$ 8,898,000

Liabilities and Stockholders' Equity	19x4	19x3
Accounts payable	$ 297,000	$ 256,000
Accrued expenses payable	607,000	594,000
Total current liabilities	$ 904,000	$ 850,000
Long-term debt	1,350,000	1,282,000
Total liabilities	$2,254,000	$2,132,000
Common stock	$5,200,000	$ 5,200,000
Retained earnings	2,160,000	1,566,000
Total stockholders' equity	7,360,000	6,766,000
Total liabilities and stockholders' equity	$9,614,000	$ 8,898,000

Rocky Mountain Company
Income Statement
For the year ended December 31, 19x4

Sales		$11,677,000
Cost of goods sold		− 6,513,000
Gross profit		$ 5,164,000
Less operating expenses:		
Depreciation	$ 567,000	
Other expenses	2,882,000	− 3,449,000
Income from operations		$ 1,715,000
Less interest expense		− 94,000
Income before income taxes		$ 1,621,000
Less income taxes		− 486,000
Net income		$ 1,135,000

Requirements

a) Prepare a short-term solvency ratio analysis for Rocky Mountain Company for 19x4. (Round all calculations to three decimal places.)

b) Prepare a long-term solvency ratio analysis for 19x4.

c) Prepare a performance ratio analysis for 19x4.

16–15 Comprehensive Financial Analysis

Comparative income statements and balance sheets for Seneca Company are presented below for 19x9 and 19x8.

Seneca Company
Comparative Income Statements
For the years ended December 31, 19x9 and 19x8

	19x9	19x8
Sales	$11,778,070	$11,241,498
Cost of goods sold	− 6,615,148	− 6,395,466
Gross profit	$ 5,162,922	$ 4,846,032
Less selling and administrative expenses	− 3,565,750	− 3,363,722
Operating income	$ 1,597,172	$ 1,482,310
Other revenues and expenses:		
Interest revenue	141,264	80,198
Interest expense	(76,698)	(70,204)
Other expenses	(47,230)	(18,850)
Income before income taxes	$ 1,614,508	$ 1,473,454
Income taxes	− 720,368	− 660,818
Net income	$ 894,140	$ 812,636

Seneca Company
Comparative Balance Sheets
December 31, 19x9 and 19x8

Assets	19x9	19x8
Cash	$ 241,816	$ 259,370
Marketable securities	437,268	202,802
Accounts receivable	966,982	1,046,246
Inventory	1,501,438	1,620,470
Prepaid expenses	124,988	115,618
Total current assets	$ 3,272,492	$ 3,244,506
Investments and other assets	774,836	604,368
Property, plant, and equipment (net)	2,818,912	2,681,680
Trademarks and other intangibles	263,322	281,362
Total assets	$ 7,129,562	$ 6,811,916

Liabilities and Stockholders' Equity		
Notes payable	$ 179,294	$ 175,174
Current maturities of long-term debt	10,030	15,056
Accounts payable and accrued expenses	1,822,326	1,932,930
Total current liabilities	$ 2,011,650	$ 2,123,160
Long-term debt	556,368	539,280
Total liabilities	$ 2,568,018	$ 2,662,440
Common stock	$ 124,778	$ 124,744
Additional paid-in capital	228,388	226,344
Retained earnings	4,208,378	3,798,388
Total stockholders' equity	4,561,544	4,149,476
Total liabilities and stockholders' equity	$ 7,129,562	$ 6,811,916

Requirements

a) Prepare a comprehensive financial analysis of Seneca, Inc. for 19x9, including (1) short-term solvency ratios, (2) long-term solvency ratios, and (3) performance measurement ratios. (Round all calculations to three decimal places.)

b) Comment on the financial condition of Seneca, Inc. with respect to short-term solvency, long-term solvency, and performance.

16–16 Adjustment of Net Income for Working Capital Basis and Cash Basis Statements of Changes in Financial Position

The current assets and current liabilities for Macon Company are summarized below for 19x1 and 19x0.

Current Assets	19x1	19x0
Cash	$ 230,000	$ 147,000
Accounts receivable	523,000	435,000
Inventory	810,000	670,000
Prepaid expenses	58,000	52,000
Total	$ 1,621,000	$ 1,304,000
Current Liabilities		
Accounts payable	$ 733,000	$ 577,000
Notes payable	88,000	104,000
Accrued expenses	164,000	199,000
Current portion of long-term debt	8,000	4,000
Total	$ 993,000	$ 884,000

Additional information:

- Net income for 19x1 was $422,000.
- Depreciation expense for 19x1 was $134,000.
- Amortization expense on intangible assets for 19x1 was $38,000.

Requirements

a) Compute the amount of working capital provided by operations.

b) Compute the amount of cash provided by operations.

16–17 Conversion of Net Income: Working Capital Basis and Cash Basis

Ferguson Company has the following changes in selected current asset, current liability, and other accounts during 19x4.

1. Decrease in Accounts Receivable—$15,000
2. Increase in Accumulated Depreciation—$10,000
3. Increase in Accumulated Amortization on Intangible Assets—$3000
4. Decrease in Wages Payable—$3500
5. Decrease in Prepaid Expenses—$1250
6. Increase in Inventory—$4500
7. Decrease in Accounts Payable—$75
8. Decrease in Discount on Bonds Payable—$400
9. Decrease in Interest Payable—$350
10. Increase in Cash—$5250

Additional information:

- Net income for 19x4 was $45,250.
- There were no acquisitions or dispositions of fixed or intangible assets during the year.
- Bonds payable were not issued or retired during the year.

Requirements

a) Prepare a schedule showing the adjustment to net income (increase or decrease) for each of the ten items above in computing the amount of working capital provided by operations.

b) Prepare a schedule showing the adjustment to net income (increase or decrease) for each of the ten items above in computing the amount of cash provided by operations.

16–18 Statement of Changes in Financial Position: Working Capital Basis

Comparative balance sheets for Arnold's Computer Repair, Inc. for 19x7 and 19x6 are given below.

Arnold's Computer Repair, Inc.
Comparative Balance Sheets
December 31, 19x7 and 19x6

Assets	19x7	19x6
Cash	$ 1,200	$1,550
Supplies	850	600
Prepaid insurance	450	375
Total current assets	$ 2,500	$2,525
Land	$15,000	$ —
Tools and testing equipment	8,750	8,750
Less accumulated depreciation	(4,375)	(3,500)
Total fixed assets	19,375	5,250
Total assets	$21,875	$7,775
Liabilities and Owners' Equity		
Accounts payable	$ 650	$ 488
Interest payable	563	—
Total current liabilities	$ 1,213	$ 488
Notes payable (equipment)	$ 4,000	$5,000
Notes payable (land)	15,000	—
Total long-term liabilities	$19,000	$5,000
Common stock	$ 1,000	$1,000
Retained earnings	662	1,287
Total stockholders' equity	1,662	2,287
Total liabilities and stockholders' equity	$21,875	$7,775

Additional information:

- Net income was $21,850.
- Land was acquired by issuing a ten-year note payable.
- Dividends were paid during the year to Arnold, the company's only stockholder.

Requirements

a) Prepare a statement of changes in financial position under the working capital basis showing all significant changes in resources.

b) Prepare a schedule of changes in working capital.

16–19 Statement of Changes in Financial Position: Cash Basis

Using the information provided in Problem 16–18, prepare a statement of changes in financial position under the cash basis for Arnold's Computer Repair, Inc. for 19x7.

16–20 Statement of Changes in Financial Position: Working Capital Basis

Financial statements for Instaprint Corporation are given below.

Instaprint Corporation
Comparative Balance Sheets
December 31, 19x9 and 19x8

Assets	19x9	19x8
Cash	$ 530,000	$ 192,000
Accounts receivable	606,000	578,000
Inventories	792,000	822,000
Prepaid expenses	108,000	152,000
Total current assets	$2,036,000	$1,744,000
Land, buildings, and equipment	$1,606,000	$1,500,000
Less accumulated depreciation	(852,000)	(756,000)
Total fixed assets	754,000	744,000
Patents	100,000	—
Total assets	$2,890,000	$2,488,000

Liabilities and Stockholders' Equity		
Accounts payable	$ 342,000	$ 382,000
Accrued expenses payable	112,000	70,000
Short-term notes payable	146,000	200,000
Total current liabilities	600,000	$ 652,000
Long-term debt	248,000	—
Total liabilities	$ 848,000	$ 652,000
Common stock and paid-in capital	$ 410,000	$ 310,000
Retained earnings	1,632,000	1,526,000
Total stockholders' equity	2,042,000	1,836,000
Total liabilities and stockholders' equity	$2,890,000	$2,488,000

Instaprint Corporation
Income Statement
For the year ended December 31,19x9

Sales	$2,902,000
Cost of goods sold	−1,662,000
Gross profit	$1,240,000
Less operating expenses	− 968,000
Operating income	$ 272,000
Other income (interest and gain on sale of land)	50,000
Other expense (interest)	(34,000)
Income before taxes	$ 288,000
Income taxes	− 118,000
Net income	$ 170,000

Additional information:

- Depreciation expense for the year was $96,000.
- Cash dividends of $64,000 were declared and paid during the year.
- Land acquired for $20,000 ten years ago was sold during the year for $50,000.
- Equipment costing $126,000 was acquired during the year.
- A patent was acquired in 19x9 in exchange for common stock.

Requirements

a) Prepare a statement of changes in financial position for 19x9 under the working capital basis.

b) Prepare a schedule of changes in working capital.

16–21 Statement of Changes in Financial Position: Cash Basis

Using the financial statements and other information on the Instaprint Corporation provided in Problem 16–20, prepare a statement of changes in financial position for 19x9 under the cash basis.

16–22 Working Capital and Cash Provided by Operations: Cash Basis Income Statement

Parks Company's income statement for 19x5 is given below.

Parks Company Income Statement For the year ended December 31, 19x5		
Sales		$98,000
Cost of goods sold:		
Beginning inventory	$18,000	
Plus purchases	62,000	
Less ending inventory	(23,500)	−56,500
Gross profit		$41,500
Operating expenses:		
Salaries	$14,000	
Insurance	500	
Depreciation	1,250	
Interest	900	
Supplies	450	
Other	2,500	−19,600
Net income		$21,900

Current assets and current liabilities for Parks Company at the end of 19x5 and 19x4 were as follows:

Current Assets	19x5	19x4
Cash	$ 1,200	$ 800
Accounts receivable	4,900	6,000
Inventory	23,500	18,000
Prepaid insurance	525	500
Supplies	750	1,100
Total current assets	$30,875	$26,400
Current Liabilities		
Accounts payable	$ 8,200	$ 8,500
Wages payable	1,150	950
Interest payable	325	400
Total current liabilities	$ 9,675	$ 9,850

Requirements

a) Compute the amount of working capital provided by operations.

b) Compute the amount of cash provided by operations.

c) Prepare a schedule converting Parks Company's income statement from the accrual basis to the cash basis. *Hint:* Use format in Exhibit 16–5.

16–23 Ratio Analysis   Presented below are the 19x1 balance sheet and income statement for MND Corporation.

MND Corporation
Balance Sheet
As of December 31, 19x1

Assets		
Cash		$ 8,000,000
Accounts receivable		12,000,000
Inventory		9,000,000
Property, plant, and equipment	$48,400,000	
Less: Accumulated depreciation	−11,900,000	36,500,000
Total assets		$65,500,000
Liabilities and Stockholders' Equity		
Accounts payable		$10,700,000
Notes payable (short term)		5,300,000
Mortgage bonds (due in 19x4)		9,500,000
Common stock ($10 par value, 4,500,000 shares authorized, 2,500,000 shares issued and outstanding)		25,000,000
Paid in capital in excess of par value		5,000,000
Retained earnings		10,000,000
Total liabilities and stockholders' equity		$65,500,000

MND Corporation
Income Statement
For the year ended December 31, 19x1

Cash sales		$10,000,000
Credit sales		60,000,000
Total sales		$70,000,000
Cost of goods sold:		
Beginning inventory of finished goods	$ 4,000,000	
Cost of goods manufactured	50,000,000	
Goods available	$54,000,000	
Ending inventory of finished goods	− 5,000,000	−49,000,000
Gross profit		$21,000,000
Operating expenses:		
Selling	$ 3,000,000	
General	10,800,000	−13,800,000
Operating income		$ 7,200,000
Interest expense		− 1,200,000
Income before income taxes		$ 6,000,000
Income taxes (40%)		− 2,400,000
Net income		$ 3,600,000

Requirements

a) Compute the following solvency ratios for MND Corporation for the fiscal year 19x1. (Round calculations to three decimal places.)

    1. Current ratio

    2. Acid test ratio

    3. Days receivables outstanding (based on credit sales)

    4. Finished goods inventory turnover

    5. Debt-to-equity

    6. Times interest earned

b) Compute the following performance ratios. (Round calculations to three decimal places.)

    1. Asset turnover

    2. Return on sales

    3. Return on assets

    4. Return on equity

(CMA Adapted)

16–24 Interpreting Financial Analysis Ratios

Thorpe Company is a wholesale distributor of professional equipment and supplies. The company's sales have averaged about $900,000 annually for the three-year period 19x3–19x5. The firm's total assets at the end of 19x5 amounted to $850,000. The president of Thorpe Company has asked the controller to prepare a report that summarizes the financial aspects of the company's operations for the past three years. This report will be presented to the Board of Directors at their next meeting. In addition to comparative financial statements, the controller has decided to present a number of relevant financial ratios to assist in the identification and interpretation of trends. At the request of the controller, the accounting staff has calculated the following ratios for the three-year period 19x3–19x5.

	19x3	19x4	19x5
Current ratio	2.00	2.13	2.18
Acid test ratio	1.20	1.10	0.97
Days receivables outstanding	37.60	42.60	51.20
Inventory turnover	5.25	4.80	3.80
Debt-to-equity ratio	0.79	0.69	0.61
Asset turnover	1.75	1.88	1.99
Sales as a percent of 19x3 sales	1.00	1.03	1.06
Gross profit percent	40.00	38.60	38.50
Return on sales	7.8%	7.8%	8.0%
Return on assets	8.5%	8.6%	8.7%
Return on equity	15.1%	14.6%	14.1%

In the preparation of his report, the controller has decided first to examine the financial ratios independently of any other data to determine if the ratios themselves reveal any significant trends over the three-year period.

Requirements

Answer the following questions. Indicate in each case which ratio(s) you used in arriving at your conclusion.

a) The current ratio is increasing, whereas the acid test ratio is decreasing. Using the ratios provided, identify and explain the contributing factor(s) for this apparently divergent trend.

b) In terms of the ratios provided, what conclusion(s) can be drawn regarding the company's use of financial leverage during the 19x3–19x5 period?

c) Using the ratios provided, what conclusion(s) can be drawn regarding the company's ability to generate sales and profits from the assets available to management?

(CMA Adapted)

16–25 Statement of Changes in Financial Position: Cash Basis

The schedule shown below presents the net changes in the balance sheet accounts as of December 31, 19x2, as compared to December 31, 19x1, for the Lock Company. Lock's statement of changes in financial position has not yet been prepared for the year ended December 31, 19x2. Additional information regarding Lock's operations during 19x2 follows the schedule.

Debit Balance Accounts	Net Change Increase (Decrease)
Cash	$ (340,000)
Accounts Receivable	1,040,000
Inventories	580,000
Property, Plant, and Equipment	1,800,000
Total	$3,080,000
Credit Balance Accounts	
Allowance for Bad Debts	$ 600,000
Accumulated Depreciation	950,000
Accounts Payable	1,250,000
Notes Payable (current)	(150,000)
Bonds Payable	(2,000,000)
Common Stock, $10 par value	9,000,000
Paid in Capital in Excess of Par Value	1,300,000
Retained Earnings	(7,870,000)
Total	$3,080,000

Additional information:

1. Lock Company incurred a net after-tax loss from regular operations of $500,000 for the year. In addition, Lock had an extraordinary gain from the sale of condemned land of $1,400,000 net of $600,000 taxes. The condemned land had a book value of $2,500,000.

2. Accounts receivable of $650,000 were written off during 19x2 by debiting Allowance for Bad Debts. The provision for bad debts expense for the year was $1,250,000.

3. Machinery acquired five years earlier at a cost of $2,000,000 was sold for $550,000 during 19x2. The machinery had a book value of $350,000 at the date of sale.

4. A new parcel of land with a market value of $6,300,000 was purchased in April, 19x2 and was paid for with cash of $1,500,000 plus 400,000 shares of Lock's common stock.

5. Two million dollars of bonds issued at par value ten years ago were retired during 19x2.

6. A 5 percent stock dividend was declared on January 15, 19x2 on 10,000,000 shares of Lock common stock. The market value of the stock on that date was $11 per share.

7. A cash dividend of $0.30 per share of common stock was declared on December 31, 19x2 payable on January 15, 19x3.

Requirements

a) Prepare a statement of changes in financial position for Lock Company for the year ended December 31, 19x2. Prepare the statement on the cash basis but include all significant resource flows in the statement.

b) Prepare a schedule of changes in working capital.

(CMA Adapted)

16–26 Financial Statement Analysis: Cash Basis Statement of Changes in Financial Position

You have been assigned by the acquisitions committee of Control Group, Inc. to examine a potential acquisition, Retailers, Inc. This company is a merchandising firm that appears to be available because of the death of its founder and principal shareholder. Recent financial statements of Retailers, Inc. are shown below.

Retailers, Inc.
Comparative Balance Sheets
December 31, 19x1 and 19x2

	19x1	19x2
Cash	$ 120,000	$ 130,000
Accounts receivable	370,000	430,000
Inventory	400,000	400,000
Property, plant, and equipment	800,000	900,000
Less: Accumulated depreciation	(250,000)	(325,000)
Total assets	$1,440,000	$1,535,000
Accounts payable	$ 260,000	$ 300,000
Long-term note payable	280,000	280,000
Common stock	690,000	690,000
Retained earnings	210,000	265,000
Total equities	$1,440,000	$1,535,000

Retailers, Inc.
Income Statement
For the year ended December 31, 19x2

Sales	$2,943,000
Less expenses:	
Cost of goods sold	$2,200,000
Wages expense	350,000
Supplies expense	42,600
Depreciation expense	100,000
Interest expense	22,400
Loss on sale of fixed assets	75,000
Total	−2,790,000
Net income before taxes	$ 153,000
Income taxes	− 68,000
Net income	$ 85,000

Retailers, Inc.
Statement of Changes in Financial Position
For the year ended December 31, 19x2

Sources of working capital:
  From operations:
    Net income .... $ 85,000
    Plus: Depreciation expense 100,000
        Nonoperating loss on sale
          of equipment 75,000
      Working capital from operations .... $ 260,000
  From sale of equipment 50,000
      Total sources of working capital .... $ 310,000
Uses of working capital:
  To purchase property, plant, and equipment ... $ 250,000
  To pay dividends 30,000
      Total uses of working capital .... − 280,000
Increase in working capital .... $ 30,000

Requirements

a) Calculate the following ratios for 19x2. (Round calculations to three decimal places.)

1. Current ratio
2. Acid test
3. Inventory turnover
4. Days receivables outstanding
5. Debt-to-equity
6. Times interest earned
7. Asset turnover
8. Return on sales
9. Return on assets
10. Return on equity

b) Prepare a statement of changes in financial position for 19x2 on the cash basis.

c) Explain why working capital was generated by the sale of equipment, even though there was a loss on the sale.

d) What is your recommendation regarding the acquisition of Retailers, Inc?

(CMA Adapted)

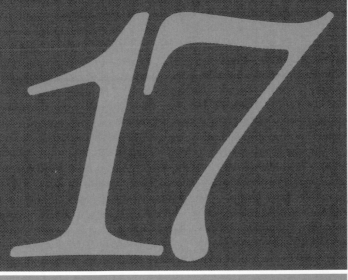

The Impact of Changing Prices

A **price index** is a standardized measure of the amount of money needed to purchase a standard package or basket of goods and services. In the United States, the **Consumer Price Index** (CPI), prepared by the U.S. Department of Commerce, Bureau of Labor Statistics, is a widely used measure of the cost of living for the typical consumer household. The CPI, for a particular time period, is computed by comparing the cost of a standard package of goods and services during that period with the cost during some base period. The base period, currently 1967, is assigned an index of 100 and the index of any other period is expressed as a multiple of 100. The 1983 index of 299.3 indicates that the cost of the standard package increased 199.3 percent between 1967 and 1983, when $299.30 was required to buy what $100 would buy in 1967.

The purchasing power of money varies inversely with prices. During periods of **inflation,** the purchasing power of money declines as prices rise. Conversely, during periods of **deflation,** the purchasing power of money increases as prices fall. Inflation and deflation cause dollar measurements to become a rubber meterstick that expands and contracts over time. The dollars spent to purchase land in 19x5 have a different purchasing power than the dollars spent to purchase inventory in 19x8. Yet, dollars spent in both years are treated as identical measures in traditional accounting reports. This variability creates problems for managers who use accounting data to plan and control activities. The severity of the problem depends on the rate of inflation or deflation and the length of management's planning period. During the late 1970s and early 1980s, when annual inflation exceeded 10 percent in the United States and many other nations, ignoring inflation was folly. Even a small rate of inflation can have a significant impact on the evaluation of multiyear capital expenditure proposals. A recent study sponsored by the National Association of Accountants reported that managers of leading corporations have responded to inflation in a variety of ways, including those listed below.

- Using replacement costs rather than historical costs in pricing decisions.
- Building an allowance for inflation into budgets.
- Updating standard costs more frequently.
- Adjusting performance reports to separately identify variances caused by inflation.
- Increasing the hurdle or discount rates used for capital budgeting.
- Adjusting financial ratio analysis for inflation.
- Placing increased emphasis on the funds statement (statement of changes in financial position).[1]

---

[1] Allen H. Seed, III, *The Impact of Inflation on Internal Planning and Control* (New York: National Association of Accountants, 1981). This report describes how inflation has affected internal planning and control practices in leading corporations.

The purpose of this chapter is to indicate how the usefulness of management accounting data and reports can be enhanced by adjusting them for changing prices. To provide a framework for the discussion of management accounting applications, we begin with an illustration of how general purpose financial statements are adjusted for changes in the general price level. Next we consider the uses and limitations of general price level adjusted financial statements and identify some alternative approaches that might be used to prepare financial statements during periods of changing prices. Finally, we focus on price level adjustments to management accounting data and reports.

CONSTANT DOLLAR FINANCIAL INFORMATION

Nominal dollars are the dollar amounts actually recorded in historical cost accounting records and presented in traditional financial statements. The nominal dollar amounts assigned to assets acquired in different years may not represent dollars of uniform purchasing power. **Constant dollars** are dollars of uniform purchasing power. **Constant dollar accounting** involves restating the nominal dollar amounts presented in financial statements into dollars of uniform purchasing power. This is accomplished by multiplying the nominal dollars actually paid for an asset by a conversion ratio computed as

$$\text{Conversion ratio} = \frac{\text{Price index on the date being adjusted to}}{\text{Price index on the date being adjusted from}}.$$

Assume land was purchased for $50,000 in 19x3, when the price index was 120. If management is preparing constant dollar financial statements as of December 31, 19x5, when the price index was 150, the constant dollar amount paid for the land is computed as follows:

Constant dollars = Nominal dollars × Conversion ratio,
Constant dollars = $50,000 × (150/120)
= $62,500.

In terms of *general* purchasing power, $62,500 is required on 12/31/x5 to have the same buying power as $50,000 in 19x3. The price index is based on the overall cost of a specific package of goods and services. Changes in the index represent changes in the overall cost of the package. The prices of individual items in the package and the prices of items not included in the package may change at different rates. Consequently, if an organization were to buy or sell this *specific* asset on 12/31/x5, its actual price would likely be something other than $62,500.

Following Securities and Exchange Commission and Financial Accounting Standards Board guidelines, many large corporations prepare constant dollar financial information to *supplement* traditional financial statements that use nominal dollars. The constant dollar data are expressed either in terms of uniform purchasing power as of the financial statement date or in terms of the average purchasing power for the reporting period, using the Consumer Price Index.

In preparing constant dollar financial statements, an important distinction is made between monetary and nonmonetary items. **Monetary items** are assets and liabilities whose values are fixed in terms of nominal dollars, for example, cash, accounts receivable, accounts payable, and bonds payable. Cash represents current purchasing power. The number of dollars a firm will receive to settle its accounts receivable or pay to settle its liabilities is not affected by changes in the price level. **Nonmonetary items** are assets and equities whose values are not fixed in terms of nominal dollars, for example, inventory, land, buildings, equipment, and total stockholders' equity. The number of dollars land can be sold for is likely to be affected by changes in the price level.

EXHIBIT 17–1   Historical Cost Balance Sheet

Custard Park Lodge
Balance Sheet
December 31, 19x6

Assets

Cash		$ 14,400
Accounts receivable		1,000
Inventories		4,500
Property, plant, and equipment	$250,000	
Less: Accumulated depreciation	−60,000	190,000
Total assets		$209,900

Liabilities and Stockholders' Equity

Liabilities:		
Accounts payable	$ 2,500	
Long-term debt	100,000	$102,500
Stockholders' equity:		
Common stock ($5 par; 10,000 shares outstanding)	$ 50,000	
Premium on common stock	35,400	
Retained earnings	22,000	107,400
Total liabilities and stockholders' equity		$209,900

Constant Dollar Balance Sheet

Assume that the December 31, 19x6 historical cost balance sheet of Custard Park Lodge, presented in Exhibit 17–1, is to be restated in terms of the December 31, 19x6 price level. Because the dollar amounts assigned monetary assets and liabilities represent December 31, 19x6 purchasing power, they are not restated. The amounts assigned the nonmonetary assets represent purchasing power as of the date each asset was acquired. Accordingly, to prepare a constant dollar balance sheet in terms of the December 31, 19x6 price level, the nonmonetary assets must be restated using the appropriate conversion ratios.

Although it is possible to restate all the elements of stockholders' equity in terms of December 31, 19x6 purchasing power, this would require a complex analysis of all the increments to retained earnings. Instead, total stockholders' equity is computed as the residual amount, that is, total constant dollar assets minus total constant dollar liabilities.[2]

To prepare constant dollar financial statements, information is needed regarding (1) the current price index, (2) the price index when all currently owned nonmonetary assets were acquired, and (3) the average price index of all periods included in the statements. Presented below is all the price level information needed to prepare constant dollar financial statements for Custard Park Lodge.

Date or Period	Price Index
1/1/x3	120
8/1/x5	145
1/1/x6	150
5/1/x6	157
Average 19x6	160
12/31/x6	165

Only three of these indexes are used in preparing Custard Park Lodge's constant dollar balance sheet. The ending inventory was acquired on 5/1/x6 when the price index was 157. The plant, property, and equipment was acquired on 1/1/x3 when the price index was 120. The 12/31/x6 price index is 165. The remaining indexes will be used to prepare a constant dollar income statement. Custard Park Lodge's constant dollar balance sheet is presented in Exhibit 17–2.

Comparing the nominal amounts with the constant dollar amounts, we see that the use of constant dollars (rather than nominal dollars) can have a significant impact on financial statement analysis. The debt-to-equity

---

[2] If Custard Park Lodge had preferred stock outstanding, it would normally be treated as a monetary liability.

EXHIBIT 17–2   Nominal and Constant Dollar Balance Sheets

Custard Park Lodge
Nominal and Constant Dollar Balance Sheets
December 31, 19x6

	(1) Nominal Dollars	(2) Conversion Ratio	(3) Constant Dollars
Cash	$ 14,400	M	$ 14,400
Accounts receivable	1,000	M	1,000
Inventories*	4,500 ×	165/157 =	4,729
Property, plant, and equipment†	250,000 ×	165/120 =	343,750
Less: Accumulated depreciation†	(60,000) ×	165/120 =	(82,500)
Total assets	$209,900		$281,379
Accounts payable	$ 2,500	M	$ 2,500
Long-term debt	100,000	M	100,000
Stockholders' equity	107,400	R	178,879
Total liabilities and stockholders' equity	$209,900		$281,379

M = Monetary item, already stated in terms of 12/31/x6 dollars
R = Residual interest of stockholders, computed as total constant dollar assets less total liabilities
* The ending inventories were acquired on 5/1/x6 when the price level was 157.
† The property, plant, and equipment was acquired on 1/1/x3 when the price level was 120.

ratio (computed as total liabilities divided by total stockholders' equity), for example, changes from 0.95 under nominal dollars to 0.57 under constant dollars:

$$\frac{\text{Nominal dollar}}{\text{debt-to-equity ratio}} = \frac{\$100,000 + \$2,500}{\$107,400}$$

$$= 0.95,$$

$$\frac{\text{Constant dollar}}{\text{debt-to-equity ratio}} = \frac{\$100,000 + \$2,500}{\$178,879}$$

$$= 0.57.$$

The constant dollar ratio indicates that creditors have provided a significantly smaller portion of capital than the nominal dollar ratio would suggest. The firm's financial position appears stronger using constant dollars.

Constant Dollar Income Statement

Assume Custard Park Lodge's nominal dollar income statement for the year ended December 31, 19x6 (presented in column (1) of Exhibit 17–3) is to be restated in terms of the December 31, 19x6 price index. It is necessary to restate all transactions in terms of the December 31, 19x6 price index. To simplify computations assume all transactions, except those pertaining to inventory and fixed asset acquisition, occurred evenly throughout 19x6 at an average price index of 160. The costs assigned to supplies expense include costs of supplies acquired on 8/1/x5 when the price index was 145 and on 5/1/x6 when the price index was 157. The depreciation assigned to 19x6 is for assets acquired on 1/1/x3 when the price index was 120.

Each of the nominal dollar amounts in column (1) of Exhibit 17–3 is multiplied by a conversion ratio in column (2) to obtain the constant dollar amount presented in column (3). Again, the use of constant dollars, rather than nominal dollars, can have a significant impact on financial statement analysis. The income tax rate, for example, is 49.01 percent under constant dollars ($15,572/$31,776), but it is only 39.84 percent under nominal dollars

---

EXHIBIT 17–3 Nominal and Constant Dollar Income Statements

Custard Park Lodge
Nominal and Constant Dollar Income Statements
For the year ended December 31, 19x6

	(1) Nominal Dollars	(2) Conversion Ratio	(3) Constant Dollars
Sales*	$170,000	165/160	$175,313
Less expenses:			
Supplies (FIFO):			
Purchased 8/1/x5	$ 3,600	165/145	$ 4,097
Purchased 5/1/x6	2,500	165/157	2,627
Salaries*	90,000	165/160	92,813
Depreciation	20,000	165/120	27,500
Miscellaneous*	4,000	165/160	4,125
Total	−120,100		−131,162
Operating income	$ 49,900		$ 44,151
Less: Interest expense*	− 12,000	165/160	− 12,375
Income before income taxes	$ 37,900		$ 31,776
Provision for income taxes*	− 15,100	165/160	− 15,572
Net income	$ 22,800		$ 16,204

* These items occur evenly throughout 19x6 at an average price level of 160.

($15,100/$37,900). Many people point to constant dollar financial statements and ratios to argue that profits are not as large as they appear, and effective tax rates are higher than they appear.

Return on sales (computed as net income plus net-of-tax interest expense divided by sales) also changes, from 17.66 percent under nominal dollars to 12.84 percent under constant dollars:

$$\frac{\text{Nominal dollar}}{\text{return on sales}} = \frac{\$22,800 + \$12,000\,(1 - 0.3984)}{\$170,000}$$

$$= 0.1766, \text{ or } 17.66\%;$$

$$\frac{\text{Constant dollar}}{\text{return on sales}} = \frac{\$16,204 + \$12,375\,(1 - 0.4901)}{\$175,313}$$

$$= 0.1284, \text{ or } 12.84\%.$$

The constant dollar percent indicates that expenses other than interest absorb a higher portion of revenues than the nominal dollar percent suggests.

Purchasing Power Gains and Losses

Holding monetary assets produces losses as purchasing power falls during inflationary periods and gains as purchasing power rises during deflationary periods. Conversely, owing monetary liabilities produces gains during inflationary periods and losses during deflationary periods. These gains and losses, due entirely to changes in the purchasing power of money, are called **purchasing power gains and losses.** Because inflation is more common than deflation, the effects of holding monetary assets and owing monetary liabilities during inflationary periods are the ones emphasized in this chapter.

Assume Thomas Lee held $10,000 in cash throughout 19y4, as the price index rose from 200 to 240. Because the $10,000 declined in purchasing power, he sustained a loss, the amount of which can be computed in terms of the price level at the beginning of the year, the end of the year, or any other time. Managers are likely to prefer that amounts be stated in terms of the more current end-of-year dollars. The general approach is to restate the nominal dollars held at the beginning of the year, and any nominal dollar changes that took place during the year, into constant end-of-year dollars. The number of constant end-of-year dollars needed to avoid a loss is then computed as the beginning balance in constant dollars, plus any increases in constant dollars, or minus any decreases in constant dollars. If fewer nominal dollars are actually held at the end of the year, the difference is a purchasing power loss. If more nominal dollars are held, the difference is a purchasing power gain. Thomas Lee's loss from holding cash is computed as follows:

	Nominal Dollars	Conversion Ratio	Constant Dollars
Cash balance, 1/1/y4	$10,000	240/200	$12,000
Change	—		—
Cash balance, 12/31/y4	$10,000		$12,000
Purchasing power loss (L)	$ 2,000 L		

A total of 12,000 end-of-year dollars are required to have the same purchasing power as 10,000 beginning-of-year dollars. Thomas Lee lost $2000 in purchasing power by holding $10,000 in cash throughout 19y4.

If Thomas Lee owed a $20,000 note throughout 19y4, he would have had a purchasing power gain. The dollars owed at the end of the period were cheaper than the dollars owed at the beginning. The purchasing power gain, in terms of constant end-of-year dollars, is $4000:

	Nominal Dollars	Conversion Ratio	Constant Dollars
Note payable, 1/1/y4	$20,000	240/200	$24,000
Change	—		—
Note payable, 12/31/y4	$20,000		$24,000
Purchasing power gain (G)	$ 4,000 G		

These examples illustrate why, other things being equal, debtors prefer inflation and creditors prefer price stability or deflation. However, other things are seldom equal. The gains from owing monetary liabilities and the losses from holding monetary assets can be reduced or eliminated by abnormally high interest rates. Treasurers must take inflationary expectations and interest rates into consideration when planning their organizations' mix of monetary assets and liabilities. Information on purchasing power gains and losses can be useful in evaluating the success of these plans.

It is customary to disclose purchasing power gains and losses in constant dollar financial statements. To do this for Custard Park Lodge, the following additional information is needed regarding the beginning and ending balances, and changes, in monetary accounts.

	19x6		
	Beginning Balance	Change	Ending Balance
Cash	$ 4,000	$+10,400	$ 14,400
Accounts Receivable	2,000	−1,000	1,000
Accounts Payable	5,000	−2,500	2,500
Notes Payable	100,000	—	100,000

The purchasing power gains and losses for each monetary item are computed in Exhibit 17–4. For simplicity, assume all changes took place evenly throughout the year at an average price level of 160. The gain or loss on each item is computed as the difference between expected constant dollars and actual nominal dollars at the end of 19x6. Custard Park Lodge had a net purchasing power gain of $9528 during 19x6.

EXHIBIT 17–4   Purchasing Power Gains and Losses on Monetary Items

Custard Park Lodge
Schedule of Purchasing Power Gains and Losses
For the year ended December 31, 19x6

	Nominal Dollars	Conversion Ratio	Constant Dollars	Gain (G) or Loss (L)
Cash:				
Beginning, 1/1/x6	$ 4,000	165/150	$ 4,400	
Change	10,400	165/160	10,725	
Ending, 12/31/x6	$ 14,400		$ 15,125*	$ 725 L
Accounts receivable:				
Beginning, 1/1/x6	$ 2,000	165/150	$ 2,200	
Change	− 1,000	165/160	− 1,031	
Ending, 12/31/x6	$ 1,000		$ 1,169*	169 L
Accounts payable:				
Beginning, 1/1/x6	$ 5,000	165/150	$ 5,500	
Change	− 2,500	165/160	− 2,578	
Ending, 12/31/x6	$ 2,500		$ 2,922*	422 G
Notes payable:				
Beginning, 1/1/x6	$100,000	165/150	$110,000	
Change	—	165/160	—	
Ending, 12/31/x6	$100,000		$110,000*	10,000 G
Purchasing power gain				$ 9,528 G

* This is the expected account balance in the absence of purchasing power gains or losses.

Selecting the Price Index

Once the mechanics are mastered, the preparation of constant dollar financial statements is straightforward. More troublesome are the selection of an appropriate price index and the interpretation of the resulting financial statements.

The Consumer Price Index is the most widely known index, and it is prescribed by the Financial Accounting Standards Board as the index to use in preparing any required constant dollar financial information. The CPI is based on the cost of food, clothing, shelter, fuel, transportation, doctors' services, and other items that a typical consumer household buys for day-to-day living. The exact manner in which the prices of specific items enter into the determination of the CPI and the scope of the CPI are subject to criticism. Individual consumers are affected by the cost of the items they buy rather than the cost of the items included in the index. Before the elements of the index were changed in 1982, for example, it was based on the assumption that individual consumers participated in the purchase of a new house every month. Many managers also argue that the CPI is so oriented to consumers that it does not adequately capture the changing costs of items their organizations purchase in their daily operations.

Although some businesses must use the CPI in preparing certain constant dollar financial information distributed to outsiders, they are free to select another price index for internal use. The use of such an index would have to be justified on the basis of costs and benefits. Possible alternatives include the Gross National Product Implicit Price Deflator and a variety of specific industry and firm indexes.

The **Gross National Product Implicit Price Deflator,** published by the U.S. Department of Commerce, is a broad-based index that encompasses the entire U.S. economy. Because it is more comprehensive, many managers prefer it to the CPI. However, it is prepared quarterly, whereas the CPI is prepared monthly. During periods of high inflation, managers may prefer the more frequently available CPI.

A specific price index might be prepared to track the cost of items of particular interest to an industry or firm. Inland Steel, for example, prepares an internal construction cost index for use in long-range planning.[3] Specific indexes are useful for valuing specific assets, and for internal planning and control, but they are not useful for evaluating changes in general purchasing power.

Alternative Approaches to Price Level Adjustments

The two basic approaches to adjusting for changes in the price level are constant dollar accounting and current cost accounting. Constant dollar accounting does not involve a new basis for accountability. Historical dollars

---

[3] See Seed, pp. 117–121.

are still accounted for using standard accounting procedures; however, the resulting financial data are adjusted for changes in general purchasing power. Constant dollar costs are not intended to measure the replacement cost or the sales value of nonmonetary assets, such as inventory, land, buildings, and equipment. Managers interested in these amounts often request current cost information.

Current cost accounting updates balance sheet asset items to their current value and then adjusts the income statement to reflect these changes. Current cost accounting involves a departure from historical dollars and standard accounting procedures. Alternative approaches to current cost accounting are based on replacement costs (sometimes called entry values or input values) and sales values (sometimes called liquidation values, exit values, or output values). A **replacement cost** is the current cost to purchase or reproduce an asset or its productive capacity. Replacement cost information is useful in pricing decisions, in which managers try to price products so that their selling prices exceed their purchase or current reproduction costs. Replacement cost information might be developed using current labor rates and materials costs, price lists for used or new equipment, engineering studies, and specific price indexes, such as Inland Steel's internal construction cost index. Sales values for fixed assets can be developed in a similar manner. Sales value information would be particularly relevant to a decision to continue or discontinue some aspect of operations. If a plant's net sales value exceeds the present value of its future operating cash flows, management should consider selling the plant.

PRICE LEVEL ADJUSTMENTS FOR MANAGEMENT ACTION

In the preceding sections we mentioned or illustrated how management might use price level adjusted information for ratio analysis, financial planning and performance evaluation, product pricing, and the decision to continue or discontinue some aspect of operations. In this section we will focus on some additional uses of price level adjusted information, namely, cost behavior analysis, budgeting, performance evaluation, and capital budgeting.

Cost Behavior Analysis

Changes in prices reduce the comparability of costs incurred in different time periods, making it more difficult to analyze cost behavior. In Chapter 3 we suggested that one response to this problem is to use something other than cost as the dependent variable. Direct labor hours might be substituted for labor dollars, kilowatt hours might be substituted for the cost of electricity, and so forth. In budgeting, the use of these variables could be predicted and then multiplied by their predicted unit cost. One disadvantage of this approach is that it is necessary to implement it on a very disaggregated basis. An alternative approach, if an appropriate price index is available or can be developed, is to analyze cost behavior in constant, rather than nominal, dollars. Consider the following data:

Observation	Unit Volume	Total Cost (Nominal Dollars)
Y1	500	$2450
Y2	300	2000
Y3	400	2700
Y4	200	2000

Plotting these data on a scatter diagram (see Exhibit 17–5a) does not reveal an obvious cost behavior pattern. There are at least three possible explanations: (1) There is no distinct relationship between unit volume and total cost, (2) there have been technological changes in the product or the production process, or (3) there have been changes in the price level. Perhaps management believes there should be a positive relationship between volume and costs, and that technology is constant. This leaves changes in the price level as the most logical explanation of the lack of a relationship.

EXHIBIT 17–5   Cost Estimation with Changing Prices

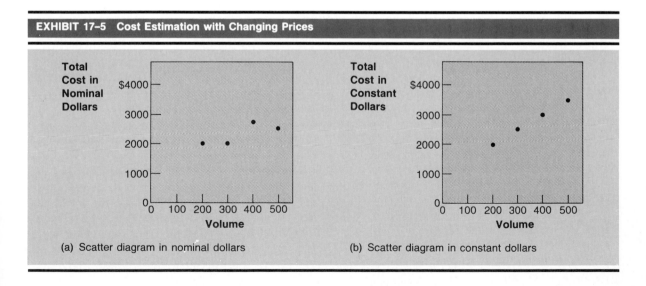

(a) Scatter diagram in nominal dollars

(b) Scatter diagram in constant dollars

Assume that an industry price index is available and management is able to obtain the following information:

Observation	Price Index
Y1	154
Y2	176
Y3	198
Y4	220

All costs can now be restated in terms of the price index at observation Y4:

Observation	Unit Volume	Total Cost (Nominal Dollars)		Conversion Ratio		Total Cost (Constant Dollars)
Y1	500	$2450	×	220/154	=	$3500
Y2	300	2000	×	220/176	=	2500
Y3	400	2700	×	220/198	=	3000
Y4	200	2000	×	220/220	=	2000

Plotting the constant dollars in Exhibit 17–5(b) reveals a cost behavior pattern with a high positive correlation between unit volume and total costs. Based on this information, an equation can be developed for total costs using any of the methods discussed in Chapter 3. The cost estimation equation will, of course, only be valid for the price level at observation Y4. If the price level is expected to increase to 230, the cost estimating equation should be adjusted using a conversion ratio of 230/220 before cost predictions are made.

Budgeting

The accuracy of predictions for revenues and expenditures is affected by price changes. If such changes can be predicted with reasonable certainty, they should be incorporated into the budget. If price changes are uncertain, but potentially large, budget forecasts can be prepared for the lowest possible, the most likely, and the highest possible price changes. These three-tiered budgets are useful in alerting management to the potential problems and opportunities that accompany varying levels of inflation.

If price level changes occur that are not allowed for in the budget, it may be desirable to revise the budget and any related standard costs. The need for such revisions might be signaled by an investigation of cost and revenue variances.

In attempting to budget future revenues and expenses in nominal dollars (dollars to be actually recorded in the accounting records), it is important to recognize that the effects of inflation will vary. Different price indexes and predictions (subjective and analytic) might be used for different budget items, as management deems appropriate. Furthermore, the budgeted nominal dollar depreciation on fixed assets acquired in prior periods will not be affected by subsequent price changes.[4] No future cash flows are associated with sunk costs.

Performance Evaluation

Theoretically, standard costs should be continually updated to reflect current prices. If this were done, performance reports would always be based on the prices in effect during the evaluation period, and it would not be necessary to make explicit adjustments for changing prices in performance reports.

Because of the time and cost of updating standard costs, especially when they are used for inventory valuation, many firms prefer to update standards only once a year, or once every six months. Under these circumstances, if significant price changes occur, it is desirable to make a special allowance for price changes in performance reports. Two frequently mentioned approaches to making such allowances involve the use of (1) planned variances or (2) price level adjusted flexible budgets.

Under the planned variance approach, standard costs for each input are based on the average prices predicted for the coming year, or other budget period. If management expects costs to rise throughout the year, they will plan on favorable variances during the early portions of the year and unfavorable variances during the later portions of the year. Though inventory could then be valued on the basis of the unadjusted standard costs, budgets for the year and performance reports prepared during the year would also reflect the planned variances.

A price level adjusted flexible budget[5] is prepared by adjusting a regular flexible budget for changes in the price level that were not allowed for in the standard costs. The adjustment is for changes in the *price level* rather than changes in the *costs of specific inputs* acquired. The appropriate managers may still be held responsible for any additional deviations between the price level adjusted cost of inputs and the actual cost of inputs. In subsequent analysis these additional deviations would be included in

---

[4] If management were attempting to price products to provide for the replacement of fixed assets, they should consider the replacement cost rather than the historical cost of the asset. This is an example of the use of different costs for different purposes.

[5] Seed, pp. 86–87. D. I. MacGibbon, "Why Not Price Adjust Your Budget?" *The Australian Accountant,* November 1979, pp. 686–687.

the materials price variance, the labor rate variance, the variable overhead spending variance, and the fixed overhead budget variance.

Capital Budgeting

The profitability of long-term investments in plant and equipment is significantly affected by changes in the price level, even if the annual price level changes are quite small. An annual inflation rate of 5 percent, for example, will amount to a 63 percent increase in prices when compounded annually over ten years. If inflation might affect future cash receipts and disbursements to this extent, management most certainly should consider it in evaluating capital expenditure proposals. Two methods are used to allow for inflation in such evaluations:

1. Predict future cash receipts and disbursements in constant dollars that reflect the current price level, and evaluate these constant dollar cash flows using a discount rate that does not include an allowance for inflation.

2. Predict cash receipts and disbursements in nominal dollars that reflect expected changes in the price level, and evaluate these nominal dollar cash flows using a discount rate that includes an allowance for inflation.

In the first method inflation is eliminated from the predicted cash flows by using constant dollars at the current price level, rather than expected, actual, nominal dollars. An advantage of this method is that many managers find it easier to think in terms of constant, current prices. Projections of large future nominal dollar cash flows may be as confusing as they are enlightening. A problem with this method is the determination of a discount rate that excludes an allowance for inflation. If financial markets reflect inflationary expectations, the cost of capital will include an allowance for inflation that must be estimated and deducted to determine the discount rate.

When taxes are an important consideration, the first method also requires an adjustment of the depreciation tax shield from nominal dollars to constant dollars. The depreciation tax savings, realized in periods subsequent to acquisition, are based on the unadjusted historical cost of an asset. Because inflation causes purchasing power to fall, these future tax savings have less purchasing power than current dollars. Accordingly, when the first method is used, the depreciation tax savings must be adjusted from nominal dollars to constant dollars.

In the second method inflation is incorporated into the predicted cash flows by using nominal dollars, which are the expected, actual, cash receipts and disbursements. These nominal dollars are often predicted on the basis of current prices adjusted for expected future changes in the price level. The inflation adjusted present value of $1 to be received in n periods is a function of both the unadjusted time value of money and the rate of inflation. It is computed as

$$iapv\ \$1 = \frac{1}{(1+r)^n} \times \frac{1}{(1+i)^n},$$

where $iapv\ \$1$ = inflation adjusted present value of $1,
r = unadjusted discount rate,
i = rate of inflation,
n = number of periods.

If the unadjusted discount rate is 12 percent and the expected rate of inflation is 8 percent, the present value of $1 to be received in one year is computed, using factors found in Table 1 (see p. 726), to be $0.827:

$$pv\ \$1 = (0.893)\ (0.926)$$
$$= 0.827.$$

An organization's cost of capital may already include an allowance for expected inflation. If this is so, management might use the cost of capital percent as the adjusted discount rate.

To illustrate the first method, assume the Downtown Hotel is evaluating a proposal to install vending machines in an empty storage room. The machines cost $12,000 and have an estimated life of six years. In current dollars, management believes the machines will produce $4000 in annual operating cash inflows and $1000 in salvage value. The hotel's discount rate of 12 percent does not include an allowance for inflation. The hotel's marginal tax rate is 46 percent. The machines qualify for a 10 percent investment tax credit and five-year accelerated cost recovery system (ACRS) depreciation. Downtown Hotel intends to take the entire $1200 investment tax credit ($12,000 × 0.10) and reduce the depreciable cost of the asset for tax purposes by one half of this amount. Tax savings, rounded to the nearest dollar, with the use of ACRS depreciation are as follows:

Year	Cost		ACRS Rate		Annual Depreciation		Tax Rate		Tax Shield
1	$11,400	×	0.15	=	$ 1,710	×	0.46	=	$ 787
2	11,400	×	0.22	=	2,508	×	0.46	=	1,154
3	11,400	×	0.21	=	2,394	×	0.46	=	1,101
4	11,400	×	0.21	=	2,394	×	0.46	=	1,101
5	11,400	×	0.21	=	2,394	×	0.46	=	1,101
					$11,400				$5,244

Exhibit 17–6 presents the computation of the project's net present value using constant dollars and a 12 percent discount rate that excludes an

EXHIBIT 17–6 **Capital Budgeting with Constant Dollars and a Discount Rate That Excludes Inflation**

Cash Flow Item:	Predicted Cash Inflows (Outflows)	Year(s) of Cash Flow	12 Percent Present Value Factor	Present Value of Cash Flows
Acquisition cost	$(12,000)	0	1.000	$(12,000)
Investment tax credit ($12,000 × 0.10)	1,200	0	1.000	1,200
Annual operating cash inflow	4,000	1–6	4.111	16,444
Taxes on annual cash inflow ($4000 × 0.46)	(1,840)	1–6	4.111	(7,564)
Tax savings on depreciation:*				
Year 1	729	1	0.893	651
Year 2	989	2	0.797	788
Year 3	874	3	0.712	622
Year 4	809	4	0.636	515
Year 5	749	5	0.567	425
Disposal value	1,000	6	0.507	507
Taxes on gain on disposal ($1000 × 0.46)	(460)	6	0.507	(233)
Net present value of all cash flows				$ 1,355

* Tax savings on depreciation:

	Year 1	Year 2	Year 3	Year 4	Year 5
Tax savings in nominal dollars	$ 787	$1,154	$1,101	$1,101	$1,101
Conversion to constant dollars	÷1.08	÷ 1.08^2	÷ 1.08^3	÷ 1.08^4	÷ 1.08^5
Tax savings in constant dollars	$ 729	$ 989	$ 874	$ 809	$ 749

allowance for inflation. To conserve space, a separate schedule converting the annual tax savings from nominal to constant dollars, assuming an expected annual inflation rate of 8 percent, is presented at the bottom of the exhibit. The project's net present value is $1355.

To illustrate the second method, assume management believes annual inflation will be 8 percent over the life of the project. The project is reevaluated in Exhibit 17–7 using nominal dollars and inflation adjusted discount factors, which are computed at the bottom of the exhibit. Annual after-

EXHIBIT 17-7   Capital Budgeting with Nominal Dollars and a Discount Rate That Includes Inflation

Cash Flow Item:	Predicted Cash Inflows (Outflows)	Year(s) of Cash Flow	Adjusted Present Value Factor†	Present Value of Cash Flows
Acquisition cost	$(12,000)	0	1.000	$(12,000)
Investment tax credit				
($12,000 × 0.10)	1,200	0	1.000	1,200
Annual after-tax cash inflows*				
Year 1	3,120	1	0.827	2,580
Year 2	3,674	2	0.683	2,509
Year 3	3,822	3	0.565	2,159
Year 4	4,040	4	0.467	1,887
Year 5	4,275	5	0.386	1,650
Year 6	3,427	6	0.319	1,093
Disposal value				
($1000 × 1.08⁶)	1,587	6	0.319	506
Taxes on gain on disposal				
($1587 × 0.46)	(730)	6	0.319	(233)
Net present value of all cash flows				$ 1,351

* Schedule of annual after-tax nominal dollar cash inflows:

	Year 1	Year 2	Year 3	Year 4	Year 5	Year
Constant dollar operating cash inflows	$4,000	$4,000	$4,000	$4,000	$4,000	$4,000
Conversion to nominal dollars	× 1.08	× 1.08²	× 1.08³	× 1.08⁴	× 1.08⁵	× 1.08⁶
Nominal dollar operating cash inflows	$4,320	$4,666	$5,039	$5,442	$5,877	$6,347
Income taxes at 46%	− 1,987	− 2,146	− 2,318	− 2,503	− 2,703	− 2,920
After-tax cash flow without tax shield	$2,333	$2,520	$2,721	$2,939	$3,174	$3,427
Tax savings on depreciation	787	1,154	1,101	1,101	1,101	—
Annual after-tax nominal dollar cash inflows	$ 3,120	$ 3,674	$ 3,822	$ 4,040	$ 4,275	$ 3,427

† Computation of inflation adjusted present value factors:

	Year 1	Year 2	Year 3	Year 4	Year 5	Year 6
Unadjusted factor for 12% discount rate	0.893	0.797	0.712	0.636	0.567	0.507
Factor for 8% rate of inflation	×0.926	×0.857	×0.794	×0.735	×0.681	×0.630
Adjusted present value factor	0.827	0.683	0.565	0.467	0.386	0.319

tax nominal dollar cash flows, also computed at the bottom of Exhibit 17–7, assume operating cash inflows will increase at the inflation rate of 8 percent each year. The nominal dollars are the expected actual cash flows, subject to taxes at 46 percent. The tax savings from depreciation, based on the unadjusted historical cost of the vending machines, are stated in nominal dollars and do not require additional adjustments. The second method indicates the project's net present value is $1351. The difference between the net present values using the first and second methods is due to rounding errors. The choice of the method to use is a matter of personal preference.

SUMMARY

The purchasing power of money varies inversely with prices. During periods of inflation, the purchasing power of money declines as prices rise. Conversely, during periods of deflation, the purchasing power of money increases as prices fall. This variability creates problems for investors as they attempt to interpret accounting data presented in general purpose financial statements, and for managers who use accounting data to plan and control firm activities.

In an attempt to make general purpose financial statements more useful, many large corporations prepare constant dollar financial data to supplement traditional financial statements that use nominal dollars. The managers of leading corporations have responded to price level changes by using replacement costs rather than historical costs in pricing decisions, building an allowance for inflation into budgets, updating standards more frequently, adjusting performance reports to separately identify variances caused by inflation, increasing the hurdle or discount rates used for capital budgeting, adjusting ratio analysis for inflation, and placing increased emphasis on the statement of changes in financial position.

Managers often ignore the impact of changing prices during periods of relative price level stability. However, the profitability of long-term investments in plant and equipment is significantly affected by changes in the price level, even if the annual price level changes are quite small. Two methods of allowing for inflation in the evaluation of capital expenditure proposals were presented in this chapter. With the first method, future cash receipts and disbursements are predicted in constant dollars that reflect the current price level, and these constant dollar cash flows are then evaluated using a discount rate that does not include an allowance for inflation. With the second method, future cash receipts and disbursements are predicted in nominal dollars that reflect expected price level changes, and these nominal dollar cash flows are then evaluated using a discount rate that includes an allowance for inflation.

KEY TERMS

Price index

Consumer Price Index

Inflation

Deflation

Nominal dollars

Constant dollars

Constant dollar accounting

Monetary items

Nonmonetary items

Purchasing power gains and losses

Gross National Product Implicit
  Price Deflator

Current cost accounting

Replacement cost

**REVIEW
QUESTIONS**

17–1 How is the Consumer Price Index computed for a particular time period?

17–2 What is the relationship between prices and purchasing power?

17–3 Identify some of the ways managers respond to inflation.

17–4 A ratio is used to convert nominal dollars to constant dollars. How is this conversion ratio computed?

17–5 Provide examples of monetary items and nonmonetary items.

17–6 How can an organization have a purchasing power loss during an inflationary period? How can it have a purchasing power gain during an inflationary period?

17–7 Why do managers sometimes criticize the Consumer Price Index?

17–8 Identify and distinguish between the two basic approaches to adjusting for changes in the price level.

17–9 Give two examples of decisions for which managers might prefer current cost information to constant dollar information.

17–10 In budgeting, how might management evaluate the potential impact of uncertain, but potentially large, price changes?

17–11 When might management use a price level adjusted flexible budget?

17–12 When a price level adjusted flexible budget is used for performance evaluation, are managers relieved of all responsibility for variations in input costs?

17–13 Why are even low rates of inflation important in capital budgeting?

17–14 Briefly describe two alternative approaches to allowing for inflation in the evaluation of capital expenditure proposals.

17–15 Why isn't the depreciation tax-shield affected by changes in the price level?

EXERCISES

**17–1 Constructing a
Price Index**

Presented at the top of the next page is information on the total cost of a standard package of goods during each of five years.

Year	Cost
19x2	$304
19x3	320
19x4	368
19x5	400
19x6	560

Required: Treating the 19x3 price level as the base period, develop a price index for each year. *Hint:* The base year price level is assigned an index of 100. Determine the cost in other years as a ratio of the base year cost and multiply this ratio by 100.

17–2 Constructing a Price Index

A manufacturer that produces a variety of goods from three raw materials has asked you to construct a materials price index. The index is to be based on the sum of the unit prices of each material. Presented is cost information for each of five years.

Year	Unit Price of Material			Total Cost of Standard Package
	1	*2*	*3*	
19y4	$135	$245	$208	$588
19y5	150	250	200	600
19y6	168	275	217	660
19y7	180	295	233	708
19y8	210	325	245	780

Requirements

a) Treating the 19y5 price level as the base period, develop a price index for each year. *Hint:* The base year price level is assigned an index of 100. Determine the cost in other years as a ratio of the base year cost and multiply this ratio by 100.

b) Determine if the price index computed in requirement (a) is equally useful in tracking the cost of each material. Present supporting calculations. *Hint:* One approach is to construct a price index for each material.

17–3 Price Level Adjusted Salary

Eleanor Frost studied hard in school and worked hard at her job. She was pleased with her annual salary increases, regarding them as both a reward and an incentive. Yet, her money did not seem to go as far as when she started working. Information on Eleanor's salary and the price level follows:

	19x1	19x2	19x3	19x4	19x5
Salary	$24,000	$26,400	$31,000	$33,200	$36,000
Price index	120	135	150	170	190

Required: Evaluate Eleanor's salary in constant 19x5 dollars. Round calculations to the nearest dollar.

17–4 Price Level Adjusted Sales

Harold "Hot" Aire, the sales manager of Burpo Beverage, was on his way to an executive committee meeting to argue for a salary increase. He brought the following sales data as justification for the increase.

	19y2	19y3	19y4	19y5	19y6
Sales revenue	$325,000	$420,000	$465,000	$500,000	$550,000

Though Mr. Burpo, the president of Burpo Beverage, was impressed with the sales figures, he asked you to perform some additional analysis of Burpo's sales record. You obtain the following price level information.

	19y2	19y3	19y4	19y5	19y6
Price index	120	160	180	200	240

Required: Evaluate Burpo Beverage's sales revenue in constant 19y6 dollars.

17–5 Constant Dollar Balance Sheet Items

Presented is information taken from the nominal dollar balance sheet of the Brantford Machine Shop, as of December 31, 19x9.

Cash	$ 7,500
Inventory	18,000
Buildings, net of accumulated depreciation	120,000
Land	90,000
Bonds payable	250,000

The price indexes on the dates of transactions affecting these items are as follows:

Transaction	Price Index
Acquired land, 2/1/x2	150
Issued bonds, 1/15/x3	160
Completed construction of building, 6/1/x4	175
Acquired current inventory, 9/15/x9	300

The price index as of December 31, 19x9, was 280.

Required: Determine the amount of each item in constant dollars as of December 31, 19x9.

17-6 Constant Dollar Balance Sheet

Presented is the nominal dollar balance sheet of the Rapid City Supply Company, as of December 31, 19x7.

Rapid City Supply Company
Balance Sheet
December 31, 19x7

Assets

Cash		$ 27,000
Accounts receivable		30,000
Inventories (FIFO)		45,000
Property, plant, and equipment	$240,000	
Less: Accumulated depreciation	−60,000	180,000
Total assets		$282,000

Liabilities and Stockholders' Equity

Liabilities:		
Accounts payable	$ 25,000	
Notes payable	140,000	$165,000
Stockholders' equity:		
Common stock ($1 par; 30,000 shares outstanding)	$ 30,000	
Premium on common stock	25,000	
Retained earnings	62,000	117,000
Total liabilities and stockholders' equity		$282,000

The price indexes on the dates of significant transactions affecting these items are as follows:

Transaction	Price Index
Issued common stock, 1/15/x1	127
Acquired property, plant, and equipment, 6/1/x4	140
Issued notes payable, 6/1/x4	140
Acquired ending inventory, 10/1/x7	200

Required: Prepare a constant dollar balance sheet as of December 31, 19x7. The December 31, 19x7, price index is 210.

17-7 Constant Dollar Income Statement

Presented is the Jones Company's nominal dollar income statement for the year ended December 31, 19x7.

Jones Company
Income Statement
For the year ended December 31, 19x7

Sales		$600,000
Cost of goods sold:		
From beginning inventory	$ 56,000	
From current purchases	240,000	−296,000
Gross profit		$304,000
Other expenses:		
Salaries	$180,000	
Depreciation	21,000	
Miscellaneous	30,000	−231,000
Income before income taxes		$ 73,000
Provision for income taxes		− 24,000
Net income		$ 49,000

The beginning inventory was acquired when the price index was 280. The fixed assets were acquired when the price index was 240. All other acquisitions, revenues, and expenditures took place evenly throughout 19x7 at an average price index of 300. The December 31, 19x7 price index is 320.

Required: Prepare a constant dollar income statement.

17–8 Constant Dollar Income Statement

Presented is the Williams Company's nominal dollar income statement for the year ended December 31, 19y5.

Williams Company
Income Statement
For the year ended December 31, 19y5

Sales		$480,000
Cost of goods sold:		
From beginning inventory	$ 20,000	
From current purchases	210,000	−230,000
Gross profit		$250,000
Other expenses:		
Salaries	$120,000	
Depreciation	90,000	
Miscellaneous	24,000	−234,000
Income before income taxes		$ 16,000
Provision for income taxes		− 4,500
Net income		$ 11,500

The beginning inventory was acquired when the price index was 160. The fixed assets were acquired when the price index was 80. All other acquisitions, revenues, and expenditures took place evenly throughout 19y5 at an average price index of 180. The December 31, 19y5 price index is 210.

Required: Prepare a constant dollar income statement.

17–9 Purchasing Power Gains and Losses

Presented is information regarding two monetary accounts.

Account	Balance 1/1/x7	Change 19x7	Balance 12/31/x7	Change 19x8	Balance 12/31/x8
Accounts Receivable	$45,000	$9,000	$54,000	−$12,000	$42,000
Taxes Payable	30,000	−8,100	21,900	6,000	27,900

Additional information:

Date	Price Index
1/1/x7	240
Average 19x7	288
12/31/x7	320
Average 19x8	300
12/31/x8	280

All changes in account balances took place evenly throughout each year at the year's average price index.

Requirements

a) Determine the 19x7 purchasing power gain or loss for each item. Present your answer in terms of the 12/31/x7 price level.

b) Determine the 19x8 purchasing power gain or loss for each item. Present your answer in terms of the 12/31/x8 price level.

c) Explain your answers to requirements (a) and (b).

17–10 Purchasing Power Gains and Losses

Presented is information regarding two monetary accounts.

Account	Balance 1/1/y3	Change 19y3	Balance 12/31/y3	Change 19y4	Balance 12/31/y4
Cash	$28,000	$8,000	$36,000	−$11,000	$25,000
Accounts Payable	16,380	−1,380	15,000	8,800	23,800

Additional information:

Date	Price Index
1/1/y3	210
Average 19y3	200
12/31/y3	180
Average 19y4	220
12/31/y4	240

All changes in account balances took place evenly throughout each year at the year's average price index.

Requirements

a) Determine the 19y3 purchasing power gain or loss for each item. Present your answer in terms of the 12/31/y3 price level.

b) Determine the 19y4 purchasing power gain or loss for each item. Present your answer in terms of the 12/31/y4 price level.

c) Explain your answers to requirements (a) and (b).

PROBLEMS

17–11 Price Level Adjusted Flexible Budget

The Lee Company's budgeted monthly production costs are as follows:

Direct materials	$ 8 per unit
Direct labor	10 per unit
Variable overhead	6 per unit
Fixed overhead:	
Depreciation	$22,000 per month
Other	40,000 per month

During May, 19y3, Lee produced 22,000 units and incurred the following production costs.

Direct materials	$196,000
Direct labor	250,000
Variable overhead	148,500
Fixed overhead:	
Depreciation	22,000
Other	46,000

All materials and other supplies are purchased and paid for in the month of use. Except for depreciation, the budgeted costs are based on a price index of 160. Depreciation is based on a price index of 80. The price index during May was 180.

Requirements

a) Prepare a traditional (nominal dollar) performance report based on a budget drawn up for the actual level of activity.

b) Prepare a price level adjusted performance report in constant May 19y3 dollars. This performance report should also be based on the actual level of activity. *Hint:* Actual depreciation must be restated.

17–12 Price Level Adjusted Flexible Budget

Presented is the April 19x2 performance report for the production department of the Kiger Company.

**Kiger Company
Production Department Performance Report
For the month of April, 19x2**

	Actual	Budget	Variance
Volume	12,000	10,000	
Manufacturing costs:			
Direct materials	$ 63,000	$ 50,000	$13,000 U
Direct labor	74,000	60,000	14,000 U
Variable overhead	52,000	40,000	12,000 U
Fixed overhead:			
Depreciation	20,000	20,000	—
Other	31,000	30,000	1,000 U
Total	$240,000	$200,000	$40,000 U

All materials and other supplies are purchased and paid for in the month of use. Except for depreciation, the original budget was based on a price index of 120. Depreciation is based on a price index of 100. The average price index during April 19x2 was 126.

Requirements

a) Prepare a traditional (nominal dollar) performance report based on a budget drawn up for the actual level of activity.

b) Prepare a price level adjusted performance report in constant April 19x2 dollars. This performance report should also be based on the actual level of activity. *Hint:* Actual depreciation must be restated.

17–13 Price Level Adjusted Cost Estimation and Cost Prediction

The following information is available concerning unit production volume, materials costs, and a specific price index for materials costs.

Observation	Unit Volume	Materials Cost	Price Index
19x1	25,000	$594,000	220
19x2	15,000	405,000	250

Requirements

a) Develop a cost estimating equation in terms of the 19x2 price index. Use the high-low method.

b) Management expects to produce 24,000 units in 19x3. The predicted 19x3 price index is 275. Adjust the equation developed in requirement (a), and then use it to predict the 19x3 materials costs.

c) Compare the equation developed in requirement (a) to one developed using nominal dollars. What cost prediction error would likely occur if an equation based on nominal dollars were used to predict 19x3 materials costs?

17–14 Price Level Adjusted Cost Estimation and Cost Prediction

The following information is available concerning unit production volume and maintenance costs.

Year	Unit Volume	Maintenance Costs
19x2	5,000	$54,250
19x3	3,500	42,400
19x4	4,000	51,625
19x5	3,000	47,500
19x6	4,500	67,000

Management has asked you to assist in developing an equation to predict 19x7 maintenance costs.

Requirements

a) Plot the volume and cost data on a scatter diagram. Does there appear to be a high correlation between volume and maintenance costs?

b) Assume the Accounting Department has developed the following specific price index for maintenance costs.

	19x2	19x3	19x4	19x5	19x6
Price index	310	320	350	380	400

Restate all maintenance costs in terms of the 19x6 price index, and plot the adjusted volume and cost data on a scatter diagram. Does there appear to be a high correlation between volume and maintenance costs?

c) Use the high-low method to develop a cost estimating equation at the 19x6 price level.

d) The predicted 19x7 production volume and price index are 4200 units and 410, respectively. Predict the 19x7 maintenance costs in 19x7 nominal dollars.

17–15 Trend Analysis of Constant Dollar Income Statements

Presented are comparative nominal dollar income statements for Ontario Computer Services for the years ending December 31, 19x1 through 19x5.

Ontario Computer Services
Comparative Income Statements
For the years ending December 31, 19x1 through 19x5

	19x1	19x2	19x3	19x4	19x5
Sales	$200,000	$250,000	$275,000	$350,000	$400,000
Less expenses:					
Salaries	$150,000	$160,000	$180,000	$210,000	$240,000
Depreciation	30,000	30,000	30,000	30,000	30,000
Other	6,000	7,200	7,500	9,000	11,000
Total	−186,000	−197,200	−217,500	−249,000	−281,000
Income before income taxes	$ 14,000	$ 52,800	$ 57,500	$101,000	$119,000
Provision for income taxes	− 5,600	− 21,100	− 23,000	− 41,000	− 48,000
Net income	$ 8,400	$ 31,700	$ 34,500	$ 60,000	$ 71,000

Ontario Computer Services began operations on April 1, 19x1 by acquiring property, plant, and equipment costing $250,000. Sales and profits have increased every year since then. In late 19x5, Ontario's management offered to sell the firm to Canadian Computing, Ltd. for $500,000. This price is relatively low given Ontario's earnings record and projected earnings growth. The primary reason for the sale is a need for cash to replace old computer equipment.

As part of its evaluation procedures, Canadian Computing has asked you to prepare comparative constant dollar income statements as of December 31, 19x5. You have acquired the following information.

	Price Index
April 1, 19x1	100
Average, 19x1	120
Average, 19x2	140
Average, 19x3	150
Average, 19x4	180
Average, 19x5	175
Average, 19x6	200
December 31, 19x6	210

Requirements

a) Prepare comparative constant dollar income statements in terms of the December 31, 19x6 price index.

b) Evaluate Ontario Computer Services' constant dollars earnings record.

17–16 Price Level Adjusted Capital Budgeting: No Taxes

Megabucks Incorporated's management became increasingly concerned about the impact of inflation on the profitability of capital expenditures. In response to this concern, the capital budgeting committee passed a resolution stating that inflation was to be given explicit consideration in the evaluation of all capital expenditures, by increasing the discount rate from 12 to 20 percent, to allow for expected annual inflation. No other adjustments were recommended, and projected cash flows continued to be stated in current dollars.

Following adoption of the resolution, the profitability of accepted projects increased, but Megabucks found itself with a large amount of excess cash to invest in short-term securities. Of more concern was that the overall profitability and stock prices were actually falling, whereas liquid assets were increasing. Megabucks was becoming a prime candidate for a corporate takeover.

Requirements

a) Explain how management's attempt to cope with inflation may have contributed to Megabucks' problems.

b) Suggest two alternative methods of allowing for inflation in the evaluation of capital expenditure proposals.

c) Determine the present value of the following project with the inflation adjusting approach used by Megabucks and each of the methods suggested in requirement (b).

Initial investment	$2,800,000
Life	4 years
Salvage value	none
Annual operating cash inflow	$1,000,000

(Round calculations to the nearest dollar. Ignore taxes.)

17–17 Price Level Adjusted Capital Budgeting: No Taxes

Tiger Package Company is evaluating the desirability of purchasing a small delivery truck for $13,000. Use of the truck would save Tiger $5000 in operating expenses during each of the next four years. The truck has a salvage value of $1500 at the end of its four-year life. All dollar amounts are stated at the current price level. Tiger's discount rate of 10 percent does not include an allowance for inflation.

Requirements

a) Determine the truck's net present value using constant dollars and the unadjusted discount rate.

b) Assume management expects inflation of 6 percent during each of the next three years. Determine the truck's net present value using nominal dollars and an inflation adjusted discount rate. (Round calculations to the nearest dollar.)

17–18 Price Level Adjusted Capital Budgeting with Taxes

Refer to Problem 17–17. Assume management expects inflation of 6 percent during each of the next three years. Also assume that Tiger Package Company has a marginal tax rate of 46 percent and that the delivery truck qualifies for a 6 percent investment tax credit of $780 ($13,000 × 0.06) and a three-year accelerated cost recovery system depreciation. The depreciable cost of the asset is reduced by one half of the total investment credit, which provides the following tax savings.

Year	Cost		ACRS%		Tax Rate		Tax Savings
1	$12,610	×	0.25	×	0.46	=	$1450
2	12,610	×	0.38	×	0.46	=	2204
3	12,610	×	0.37	×	0.46	=	2146

Requirements

a) Determine the truck's net present value using constant dollars and the unadjusted discount rate.

b) Determine the truck's net present value using nominal dollars and an inflation adjusted discount rate. (Round calculations to the nearest dollar.)

17–19 Price Level Adjusted Capital Budgeting: No Taxes

Kwick Kopies is evaluating the desirability of opening a new photocopy service center on College Avenue. Kwick Kopies would sign a seven-year nonrenewable lease and invest $100,000 in the building and photocopy equipment. Management expects the center to provide operating cash inflows of $25,000 during each year. The photocopy equipment has an expected salvage value of $10,000 at the end of seven years. All dollar amounts are stated at the current price level. Kwick Kopies' discount rate of 12 percent does not include an allowance for inflation.

Requirements

a) Determine the project's net present value using constant dollars and the unadjusted discount rate.

b) Assume management expects inflation of 8 percent during each of the next seven years. Determine the project's net present value using nominal dollars and an inflation adjusted discount rate. (Round all calculations to the nearest dollar.)

17–20 Price Level Adjusted Capital Budgeting with Taxes

Refer to Problem 17–19. Assume management expects inflation of 8 percent during each of the next seven years. Also assume that Kwick Kopies has a marginal tax rate of 46 percent and that the project qualifies for a 10 percent investment tax credit of $10,000 ($100,000 × 0.10) and a five-year accelerated cost recovery system depreciation. The depreciable cost of the asset is reduced by one half of the total investment credit, which produces the following tax savings.

Year	Cost		ACRS%		Tax Rate		Tax Savings
1	$95,000	×	0.15	×	0.46	=	$6,555
2	95,000	×	0.22	×	0.46	=	9,614
3	95,000	×	0.21	×	0.46	=	9,177
4	95,000	×	0.21	×	0.46	=	9,177
5	95,000	×	0.21	×	0.46	=	9,177

Requirements

a) Determine the project's net present value using constant dollars and the unadjusted discount rate.

b) Determine the project's net present value using nominal dollars and an inflation adjusted discount rate. (Round calculations to the nearest dollar.)

Appendix:
Time Value
of Money

The concept of time value of money explains why an amount of money received today is worth more than the same amount received at some future date. Because money can be invested to earn interest, a given amount of money today will accumulate to a greater amount in the future. Stated another way, for a given value one must have more money in the future than today to maintain the same value. Conversely, a sum of money to be received in the future is worth less in the present.

Future value is the amount a current sum of money earning a stated rate of interest will accumulate to at the end of a future period. Suppose you deposit $500 in a savings account at a financial institution that pays interest at the rate of 10 percent per year. At the end of the first year the original deposit of $500 will have grown to $550 ($500 × 1.10). If you leave the $550 for another year, the amount will grow to $605 ($550 × 1.10). It can be stated that $500 today has a future value in one year of $550, or conversely, that $550 one year from today has a present value of $500. Notice that interest of $55 ($605–$550) was earned in the second year, whereas interest of only $50 was earned in the first year. The reason for the increased amount is that interest during the second year has been earned on the principal plus interest from the first year ($550). When periodic interest is computed on principal plus prior period's accumulated interest, the interest is said to be compounded.

To determine future values at the end of each period, multiply the beginning amount by 1 plus the interest rate. Where multiple periods are involved, the future value is determined by repeatedly multiplying the beginning amount times 1 plus the interest rate for each period. When $500 is invested for two years at an interest rate of 10 percent per year, its future value is computed as $500 × 1.10 × 1.10. In general,

$$fv = pv(1 + r)^n,$$

where fv = future value amount,
pv = present value amount,
r = interest rate per period,
n = number of periods.

For the above situation the equation becomes

$$fv \text{ of } \$500 = pv (1 + r)^n$$
$$= \$500 (1 + 0.10)^2$$
$$= \$605.$$

From the general future value equation the compound amount, or future value, of $1.00 can be derived any time the interest rate and number of periods is known. Once the future value for $1.00 is determined, this amount may be multiplied by any present value amount to determine its future value.

Present value is the current worth of a specified amount of money to be received at some future date at some interest rate. Present value, then, is the inverse of future value. Solving for pv in the future value equation, the new pv equation can be determined as

$$fv = pv \, (1 + r)^n$$

$$pv = \frac{fv}{(1 + r)^n}.$$

The present value equation is often expressed as the future value amount times the present value of $1.00:

$$pv = fv \times \frac{\$1}{(1 + r)^n}.$$

Using the first equation, the present value of $8800 to be received in one year, discounted at 10 percent, is computed as follows:

$$pv \text{ of } \$8800 = \frac{\$8800}{(1 + 0.10)^1}$$

$$= \frac{\$8800}{1.10}$$

$$= \$8000.$$

This amount can also be computed by multiplying $8800 times the present value of $1.00:

$$pv \text{ of } \$8800 = \$8800 \times \frac{1}{(1 + 0.10)^1}$$

$$= \$8800 \times 0.909$$

$$= \$8000.$$

Thus when the time value of money is 10 percent, the present value of $8800 to be received one period from now is $8000.

The present value of $8800 two periods from now is $7273 [$8800/ $(1.10)^2$]. The computation can also be expressed as $8800 $\times 1/(1.10)^2$. Although these factors can be computed by hand, this approach is quite time-consuming for multiperiod problems. Tables providing the present value of $1.00 have been prepared for various interest rates and time periods to facilitate computations. Table 1 in this appendix can be used to determine the present values of future amounts. Using the factors in Table 1 (see p. 726) for the present value of $1.00, the present values of any future amount can be determined. For example, with an interest rate of 10 percent, the present value of the following future amounts to be received in one period are as shown below.

Future Value Amount		Present Value Factor of $1.00		Present Value
$ 100	×	0.909	=	$ 90.90
628	×	0.909	=	570.85
4285	×	0.909	=	3895.07
9900	×	0.909	=	9000.00

To further illustrate the use of Table 1, consider the following application. Alert Company wants to invest its surplus cash at 12 percent in order to have $10,000 to pay off a long-term note due at the end of five years. Examining Table 1 we see that the present value factor for $1.00, discounted at 12 percent per year for five years, is 0.567. Multiplying $10,000 by 0.567, the present value is determined to be $5670:

$$pv \text{ of } \$10,000 = fv \times pv \text{ of } \$1 \text{ factor}$$
$$= \$10,000 \times 0.567$$
$$= \$5670.$$

Therefore, if Alert invests $5670 today, it will have $10,000 available to pay off its note in five years.

Present value tables are also used to make investment decisions. Assume that the Monroe Company can make an investment that will provide a cash flow of $12,000 at the end of eight years. If the company demands a rate of return of 14 percent per year, what is the most it will be willing to pay for this investment? From Table 1 we find that the present value factor for $1.00, discounted at 14 percent per year for eight years, is 0.351:

$$pv \text{ of } \$12,000 = fv \times pv \text{ of } \$1 \text{ factor}$$
$$= \$12,000 \times 0.351$$
$$= \$4212.$$

If the company demands an annual 14 percent return, the most it would be willing to invest today is $4212.

ANNUITIES

Not all investments provide a single sum of money. Many investments provide periodic cash flows called annuities. An **annuity** is a series of equal cash flows received or paid over equal intervals of time. Suppose that $100 will be received at the end of each of the next three years. If the time value of money is 10 percent, the present value of this annuity can be determined by summing the present value of each receipt:

$$\text{Year 1} \quad \$100 \times \frac{1}{(1 + 0.10)^1} = \$\ 90.90$$

$$\text{Year 2} \quad \$100 \times \frac{1}{(1 + 0.10)^2} = \quad 82.65$$

$$\text{Year 3} \quad \$100 \times \frac{1}{(1 + 0.10)^3} = \quad \underline{75.13}$$

$$\text{Total} \qquad\qquad\qquad\qquad\qquad \$248.68$$

Alternatively, the following equation can be used to compute the present value:

$$pva = \frac{a}{r}\left(1 - \frac{1}{(1 + r)^n}\right),$$

where pva = present value of an annuity of $1.00 (also called the annuity factor),

r = prevailing rate per period,
n = number of periods,
a = annuity amount.

This equation is used to compute the factors presented in Table 2. The present value of an annuity of $1.00 per period for three periods, discounted at 10 percent per period, is as follows:

$$pva \text{ of } \$1 = \frac{\$1}{0.10}\left(1 - \frac{1}{1 + 0.10)^3}\right)$$

$$= 2.4868.$$

Using this factor, the present value of a $100 annuity can be computed by multiplying $100 × 2.4868, which yields $248.68. To determine the present value of an annuity of any amount, the annuity factor of $1.00 can be multipled by the annuity amount:

$$pva = a \times (pva \text{ of } \$1).$$

As an additional illustration of the use of Table 2, assume that the Red Kite Company is considering an investment in a piece of equipment that will produce net cash inflows of $2000 at the end of each year for five years. If the company's desired rate of return is 12 percent, an investment of $7210 will provide such a return:

$$pva \text{ of } \$2000 = \$2000 \times (pva \text{ of } \$1)$$
$$= \$2000 \times 3.605$$
$$= \$7210.$$

Here the $2000 annuity is multiplied by 3.605, the factor for an annuity of $1.00 for five periods, discounted at 12 percent per period. This factor is found in Table 2.

Another use of Table 2 is to determine the amount that must be received annually to provide a desired rate of return on an investment. Assume the Burnsville Company invests $33,550 and desires a return of the investment plus interest of 8 percent in equal payments at the end of each year for ten years. The minimum amount that must be received each year is determined by solving the equation for the present value of an annuity:

$$pva = a \times (pva \text{ of } \$1)$$
$$a = pva/(pva \text{ of } \$1).$$

From Table 2 we see that the 8 percent factor for ten periods is 6.710. When this is divided by the investment of $33,550, the required annuity is computed to be $5000:

$$a = \$33,550/6.710$$
$$= \$5000.$$

UNEQUAL FLOWS

Many investment situations do not produce equal periodic cash flows. When this occurs, the present value for each cash flow has to be determined independently because the annuity table can be used only for equal periodic cash flows. Table 1 is used to determine the present value of each future amount separately. To illustrate, assume the Atlantic Sabres wishes to acquire the contract of a popular baseball player who is known to attract large crowds. Management believes this player will return incremental cash flows to the team at the end of each of the next three years in the amounts of $25,000, $40,000, and $15,000. After three years, the player anticipates retiring. If the team's owners require a minimum return on their investment of 14 percent, how much would they be willing to pay for the player's contract?

To solve this problem, it is necessary to determine the present value of the expected future cash flows. Here we use Table 1 to find the $1.00 present value factors at 14 percent for periods 1, 2, and 3. These factors are then multiplied by the related cash flows:

Year	Present Value at 14 Percent		Annual Cash Flow		Present Value Amount
1	0.877	×	$25,000	=	$21,925
2	0.769	×	$40,000	=	30,760
3	0.675	×	$15,000	=	10,125
Total					$62,810

The total present value of the cash flows for the three years, $62,810, represents the maximum amount the team would be willing to pay for the player's contract.

DEFERRED RETURNS

Many times organizations make investments for which no cash is received until several periods have passed. The present value of an investment discounted at 12 percent per year, which has a $2000 return only at the end of years 4, 5, and 6, can be determined as follows:

Year	Amount		Present Value at 12 Percent		Present Value Amount
1	$ —	×	0.877	=	$ —
2	—	×	0.769	=	—
3	—	×	0.675	=	—
4	2000	×	0.636	=	1272
5	2000	×	0.567	=	1134
6	2000	×	0.507	=	1014
Total					$3420

Computation of the present value of the deferred annuity can also be performed using the annuity tables if the cash flow amounts are equal for each period. The present value of an annuity for six years, minus the present value of an annuity for three years, yields the present value of an annuity for years 4 through 6:

Present value of an annuity for six years at 12 percent:	4.111 × $2000 =	$8222
Present value of an annuity for three years at 12 percent:	2.402 × $2000 =	−4804
Present value of the deferred annuity		$3418*

* The difference between the $3420 above and the $3418 is caused by rounding error.

TABLE 1   Present Value of $1.00

Present value of $1.00 $= \dfrac{1}{(1+r)^n}$.

Periods	6%	8%	10%	12%	14%	16%	18%	20%	22%	24%	26%	28%	30%
1	0.943	0.926	0.909	0.893	0.877	0.862	0.847	0.833	0.820	0.806	0.794	0.781	0.769
2	0.890	0.857	0.826	0.797	0.769	0.743	0.718	0.694	0.672	0.650	0.630	0.610	0.592
3	0.840	0.794	0.751	0.712	0.675	0.641	0.609	0.579	0.551	0.524	0.500	0.477	0.455
4	0.792	0.735	0.683	0.636	0.592	0.552	0.516	0.482	0.451	0.423	0.397	0.373	0.350
5	0.747	0.681	0.621	0.567	0.519	0.476	0.437	0.402	0.370	0.341	0.315	0.291	0.269
6	0.705	0.630	0.564	0.507	0.456	0.410	0.370	0.335	0.303	0.275	0.250	0.227	0.207
7	0.665	0.583	0.513	0.452	0.400	0.354	0.314	0.279	0.249	0.222	0.198	0.178	0.159
8	0.627	0.540	0.467	0.404	0.351	0.305	0.266	0.233	0.204	0.179	0.157	0.139	0.123
9	0.592	0.500	0.424	0.361	0.308	0.263	0.225	0.194	0.167	0.144	0.125	0.108	0.094
10	0.558	0.463	0.386	0.322	0.270	0.227	0.191	0.162	0.137	0.116	0.099	0.085	0.073
11	0.527	0.429	0.350	0.287	0.237	0.195	0.162	0.135	0.112	0.094	0.079	0.066	0.056
12	0.497	0.397	0.319	0.257	0.208	0.168	0.137	0.112	0.092	0.076	0.062	0.052	0.043
13	0.469	0.368	0.290	0.229	0.182	0.145	0.116	0.093	0.075	0.061	0.050	0.040	0.033
14	0.442	0.340	0.263	0.205	0.160	0.125	0.099	0.078	0.062	0.049	0.039	0.032	0.025
15	0.417	0.315	0.239	0.183	0.140	0.108	0.084	0.065	0.051	0.040	0.031	0.025	0.020
16	0.394	0.292	0.218	0.163	0.123	0.093	0.071	0.054	0.042	0.032	0.025	0.019	0.015
17	0.371	0.270	0.198	0.146	0.108	0.080	0.060	0.045	0.034	0.026	0.020	0.015	0.012
18	0.350	0.250	0.180	0.130	0.095	0.069	0.051	0.038	0.028	0.021	0.016	0.012	0.009
19	0.331	0.232	0.164	0.116	0.083	0.060	0.043	0.031	0.023	0.017	0.012	0.009	0.007
20	0.312	0.215	0.149	0.104	0.073	0.051	0.037	0.026	0.019	0.014	0.010	0.007	0.005

TABLE 2   Present Value of an Annuity of $1.00

Present value of an annuity of $1.00 = \dfrac{1}{r}\left(1 - \dfrac{1}{(1+r)^n}\right)$.

Periods	6%	8%	10%	12%	14%	16%	18%	20%	22%	24%	25%	26%	28%	30%
1	0.943	0.926	0.909	0.893	0.877	0.862	0.847	0.833	0.820	0.806	0.800	0.794	0.781	0.769
2	1.833	1.783	1.736	1.690	1.647	1.605	1.566	1.528	1.492	1.457	1.440	1.424	1.392	1.361
3	2.673	2.577	2.487	2.402	2.322	2.246	2.174	2.106	2.042	1.981	1.952	1.923	1.868	1.816
4	3.465	3.312	3.170	3.037	2.914	2.798	2.690	2.589	2.494	2.404	2.362	2.320	2.241	2.166
5	4.212	3.993	3.791	3.605	3.433	3.274	3.127	2.991	2.864	2.745	2.689	2.635	2.532	2.436
6	4.917	4.623	4.355	4.111	3.889	3.685	3.498	3.326	3.167	3.020	2.951	2.885	2.759	2.643
7	5.582	5.206	4.868	4.564	4.288	4.039	3.812	3.605	3.416	3.242	3.161	3.083	2.937	2.802
8	6.210	5.747	5.335	4.968	4.639	4.344	4.078	3.837	3.619	3.421	3.329	3.241	3.076	2.925
9	6.802	6.247	5.759	5.328	4.946	4.607	4.303	4.031	3.786	3.566	3.463	3.366	3.184	3.019
10	7.360	6.710	6.145	5.650	5.216	4.833	4.494	4.192	3.923	3.682	3.571	3.465	3.269	3.092
11	7.887	7.139	6.495	5.938	5.453	5.029	4.656	4.327	4.035	3.776	3.656	3.544	3.335	3.147
12	8.384	7.536	6.814	6.194	5.660	5.197	4.793	4.439	4.127	3.851	3.725	3.606	3.387	3.190
13	8.853	7.904	7.103	6.424	5.842	5.342	4.910	4.533	4.203	3.912	3.780	3.656	3.427	3.223
14	9.295	8.244	7.367	6.628	6.002	5.468	5.008	4.611	4.265	3.962	3.824	3.695	3.459	3.249
15	9.712	8.559	7.606	6.811	6.142	5.575	5.092	4.675	4.315	4.001	3.859	3.726	3.483	3.268
16	10.106	8.851	7.824	6.974	6.265	5.669	5.162	4.730	4.357	4.033	3.887	3.751	3.503	3.283
17	10.477	9.122	8.022	7.120	6.373	5.749	5.222	4.775	4.391	4.059	3.910	3.771	3.518	3.295
18	10.828	9.372	8.201	7.250	6.467	5.818	5.273	4.812	4.419	4.080	3.928	3.786	3.529	3.304
19	11.158	9.604	8.365	7.366	6.550	5.877	5.361	4.844	4.442	4.097	3.942	3.799	3.539	3.311
20	11.470	9.818	8.514	7.469	6.623	5.929	5.353	4.870	4.460	4.110	3.954	3.808	3.546	3.316

Glossary

The number enclosed in parenthesis after each term refers to the chapter where the term is first defined.

Absorption Cost Basis of External Reporting   (2) A method of external reporting under which all manufacturing costs are product costs and all selling and administrative costs are period costs.

Absorption Costing   (10) A product costing procedure where all manufacturing costs (fixed and variable) are assigned to products and inventoried (also called **Full Costing**).

Accelerated Cost Recovery System (ACRS)   (15) An asset depreciation method created by the Economic Recovery Tax Act of 1981 that allows personal property to be depreciated for tax purposes over three, five, ten, or fifteen years, with most properties qualifying for a five-year write-off. Under ACRS depreciable real property can be depreciated over fifteen years, and salvage value is ignored in the computation of depreciation.

Accounting Rate of Return   (14) A method used to evaluate capital expenditures that ignores the time value of money. It is computed as the average annual net income associated with an investment divided by the average investment amount.

Acid Test Ratio (16) A measure of the availability of cash and other current monetary assets to pay current liabilities. It is computed as the sum of cash, current receivables, and marketable securities divided by current liabilities.

Allocation Basis (12) The factor or characteristic common to cost objectives that is used to determine how much of a cost (or cost pool) is assigned to each objective.

Annuity (Appendix) A series of equal cash flows received or paid over equal intervals of time.

Appropriation Budgets (6) Budgets used in not-for-profit organizations to provide the authorization for expenditures during a specified period.

Asset Turnover (16) A ratio that measures the ability of an organization to use its assets to generate sales. It is computed as sales divided by average total assets.

Bail-Out Factor (14) The time required to recover the initial investment in a capital project from any source of funds.

Bottom-Up Approach to Budgeting (6) See **Participation Budget.**

Break-Even Point (4) The unit or dollar sales volume where total revenues equal total costs.

Budget (1) A formal plan of action expressed in monetary terms.

Budgetary Slack (6) Occurs when managers intentionally request more funds in the budgets for their departments than they need to support the anticipated level of operations.

Budget Committee (6) A group responsible for supervising budget preparation that also serves as a review board for evaluating requests for discretionary funds and new projects.

By-Product (12) A product with relatively insignificant value produced jointly with one or more other products.

Capacity Costs (3) Fixed costs that are related to capacity.

Capital Asset (15) Generally defined for tax purposes as an asset held for investment gain.

Capital Budgeting (14) The allocation of limited financial resources among competing investments.

Capital Gain (15) A gain on the sale of a capital asset.

Capital Loss (15) A loss on the sale of a capital asset.

Capital Rationing (14) The process of selecting the most desirable project(s) from a group of alternative investments.

Cash Budget (6) A summary of all cash receipts and disbursements expected to occur during the budget period.

Centralization (9) The retention of decision-making authority by top management.

Certainty (13) A condition that exists when the probability of an event's occurrence is 100 percent.

Certificate in Management Accounting (CMA) (1) A designation intended to recognize professional competence and educational attainment in the field of management accounting.

Certified Public Accountant (CPA) (1) A designation intended to recognize professional competence and educational attainment in the field of public accounting.

Chartered Accountant (CA) (1) A designation similar to the CPA. It is used in Canada and several other countries for people who perform independent evaluations of public organizations and the other activities normally associated with being a CPA in the United States.

Chief Financial Executive (1) A position that often combines the duties of the controller and the treasurer.

Coefficient of Determination (3) A measure of the percent of variation in the independent variable that is explained by the cost estimating equation; it indicates how good the equation fits the historical data.

Committed Fixed Costs (3) Costs required to maintain the current service or production capacity.

Common Segment Costs (10) Costs related to more than one segment of an organization and not directly traceable to any particular segment (also called **Indirect Segment Costs**).

Constant Dollar Accounting (17) A method of restating the nominal dollar amounts presented in financial statements into dollars of uniform purchasing power.

Constant Dollars (17) Dollars of uniform purchasing power.

Consumer Price Index (CPI) (17) A widely used measure of the cost of living for the typical consumer household prepared by the U.S. Department of Commerce, Bureau of Labor Statistics.

Continuous Budgeting (6) A budget based on a moving fixed time frame that constantly extends over the same fixed period.

Contribution Income Statement (4) A type of income statement in which costs are classified according to behavior. All variable expenses are grouped together and subtracted from revenues to produce contribution margin. All fixed costs are subtracted from contribution margin to produce net income.

Contribution Margin (4) The difference between revenues and variable costs.

Contribution Margin Ratio (4) The ratio of contribution margin to sales revenue. It indicates the portion of each sales dollar available for fixed costs and profits.

Controller (1) The chief accountant of an organization.

Controlling (1) The process of ensuring that results agree with plans.

Conversion Costs (2) Direct labor and factory overhead costs incurred to convert raw materials into finished goods.

Corporation (15) A legal entity recognized by an act of the state and empowered to conduct business activities.

Correlation Coefficient (3) A standardized measure of the degree to which two variables move together.

Cost (2) A monetary measure of the economic sacrifice made to obtain some product or service.

Cost Behavior Analysis (3) The study of how costs respond to changes in the volume of an activity.

Cost Center (7) A responsibility center held accountable only for the incurrence of costs. It does not have a revenue responsibility.

Cost Elements (2) The detailed categories of costs assignable to a cost objective.

Cost Estimation (3) The determination of previous or current relationships between cost and activity.

Costing Purpose (2) The basic reason a cost concept is used and a cost measurement is made.

Cost Objectives (2) Objects, such as departments, jobs, and products, to which costs are assigned.

Cost of Capital (14) The average cost, expressed as a percentage, of obtaining the resources necessary to make investments.

Cost of Goods Manufactured (2) Total costs assigned to products completed during a period of time.

Cost of Production Report (11) A summary of the unit and cost data of each department in a process cost system. It includes the summary of units worked on, the computation of unit costs, the total costs to be accounted for, and the total costs accounted for.

Cost Pool (2, 12) A group of related costs, such as factory overhead and service departments costs, that are allocated together to other cost objectives.

Cost Prediction (3) The process of forecasting the future relationships between cost and activity.

Cost Prediction Error (5) The difference between a predicted future cost and the actual amount of the cost when, and if, it is incurred.

Cost Reduction Proposal (5) A proposed action or investment intended to reduce the cost of an activity that the organization is committed to keeping.

Cost Techniques (2) The procedures used to assign cost elements to cost objectives.

Cost-Volume-Profit Analysis (4) A technique used to examine the relationships between volume, total costs, total revenues, and profit.

Cost-Volume-Profit Graph (4) Illustrates the relationship between volume, total revenues, total costs, and profit.

Current Cost Accounting (17) The updating of balance sheet items to their current value and then adjusting the income statement to reflect the changes.

Current Manufacturing Costs (2) Total additions to Work-in-Process inventory during a given period.

Current Ratio (16) A measure of short-term solvency. It is computed as current assets divided by current liabilities.

Cycle Budgeting (6) A budget method based on the life cycle of a project.

Days Receivables Outstanding (16) The number of days, on the average, required to generate the sales uncollected at year end.

Debt-to-Equity Ratio (16) A measure of long-term solvency. It is computed as total liabilities divided by total stockholders' equity.

Decentralization (9) The delegation of decision-making authority to successively lower management levels in an organization.

Decision Package (6) Identifies activities, departments, or agencies in budget planning. They may be related to goods, services, geographic areas, capital projects, or any other activity as related to an organization's goals and objectives.

Deflation (17) The purchasing power of money increases as prices fall.

Denominator Variance (8) See **Volume Variance.**

Depreciation Tax Shield (15) The reduction in taxes due to the deductibility of depreciation from taxable revenues.

Descriptive Model (13) A type of quantitative model that specifies the relationships between a series of independent and dependent variables.

Differential Analysis (5, 14) The determination of the difference between the cash flows of competing alternative actions that management is considering.

Direct Allocation Method (12) A procedure whereby all service department costs are allocated directly to the producing departments without any recognition of interdepartmental activities.

Direct Costing (10) See **Variable Costing.**

Direct Departmental Costs (12) The department to which costs are assigned at the time of their incurrence.

Direct Labor (2) Wages earned for the time workers actually spent on a particular product or process.

Direct Labor Ticket (11) A document used in product costing systems to record direct labor hours and cost.

Direct Materials (2) The cost of primary raw materials that are converted into finished goods.

Direct Product Costs (2) Direct materials costs plus direct labor costs.

Direct Segment Costs (10) Costs that are directly identifiable with a segment and avoidable if the segment is discontinued.

Discounted Payback Method (14) The payback method adjusted for the time value of money.

Discretionary Cost Center (7) A cost center that does not have clearly defined relationships between effort and accomplishment.

Discretionary Fixed Costs (3) Costs that are set at a fixed amount each year at the discretion of management (also called **Managed Fixed Costs**).

Divisional Segment Margin (10) The difference between a division's contribution margin and all direct fixed expenses identifiable with the division.

Earnings per Share (EPS) (16) A measure of profitability. It is computed as net income divided by the average number of shares of stock outstanding during a given period.

Economic Order Quantity (EOQ) (13) The order quantity that results in the minimum annual costs of ordering and carrying inventory.

Effectiveness (7) The concept of getting the job done.

Efficiency (7) Operating with the lowest use of resources possible under the circumstances.

Electronic Data Processing (EDP) (1) The storage, manipulation, retrieval, and communication of data by electronic means.

Employee Fringe Benefits (2) The additional labor costs paid by the employer on behalf of employees.

Equivalent Completed Units (11) The number of completed units that is equal (in terms of manufacturing effort) to a given number of partially completed units.

Excise Tax (15) A tax on an activity performed by, or a privilege granted to, a taxed party.

Expected Value (13) The weighted average of the possible cash flows associated with a decision alternative.

Expired Costs (2) Expenses that are deducted from revenues on the income statement.

Factory Overhead (2) Manufacturing costs other than direct materials and direct labor (also called **Indirect Product Costs**).

Favorable Variances (1) The resulting difference when actual costs are less than allowed costs.

Feasible Region (13) In a linear programming problem, the area that represents all possible production volumes and mixes. It is depicted by the area between the vertical axis, and horizontal axis, and the first set of enclosing lines in a graphic analysis of product mix.

FIFO (First-in First-out) Inventory Method (11) An approach to process costing in which beginning inventory units each period are costed as a separate group consisting of the portion processed during the previous period plus the additional processing required to complete them during the current period.

Financial Accounting (1) A segment of accounting concerned with providing financial information to persons outside the firm, especially investors, labor unions, and creditors.

Financial Leverage (16) The use of capital funds from debt or equity that have a fixed interest or dividend rate.

Financial Statement Analysis (16) The process of interpreting and evaluating financial statements by using data contained in them to produce additional ratios and statistics.

Finished Goods Inventory (2) The manufactured products held for sale outside the organization.

Finished Goods Inventory Record (11) A document maintained for each completed product indicating the number of units produced, sold, and on hand, as well as the related product costs.

Fixed Cost (3) A cost that does not respond to changes in the volume of activity within a given period.

Fixed Overhead Budget Variance (8) The difference between budgeted and actual fixed overhead cost.

Flexible Budgets (7) Based on cost-volume-profit or cost-volume relationships, they are used to determine what costs should be at the actual level of production.

For-Profit Organizations (1) Organizations that have profit as a primary goal.

Full Costing (10) See **Absorption Costing.**

Full Costs (5) Costs that include all fixed and variable product costs and all period costs.

Functional Income Statement (4) A type of income statement in which costs are classified according to function, such as manufacturing, selling, and administrative.

Future Value (Appendix) The amount a current sum of money earning a stated rate of interest will accumulate to at a future period.

General and Administrative Expense Budget (6) A schedule that presents the expected costs and disbursements for the overall administration of the organization.

Gross National Product Implicit Price Deflator (17) A broad-based price index published by the U.S. Department of Commerce encompassing the entire U.S. economy.

High-Low Method of Cost Estimation (3) An approach that uses two observations to estimate the variable and fixed elements of a mixed cost.

Idle Time (2) The time employees are not working on the product or performing other production-related tasks.

Imposed Budget (6) An approach to budgeting whereby top management decides on the goals and objectives of the organization and communicates these to lower management levels (also called **Top-Down Approach**).

Income Tax (15) A tax based on the income of individuals, corporations, estates, or trusts.

Incremental Approach to Budgeting (6) A method that budgets cost for a coming period as a dollar or percentage change from the amount budgeted for (or spent during) a prior period.

Indirect Department Cost (12) A cost reassigned to a department from another cost objective to which it was directly assigned.

Indirect Labor (2) The salaries and wages earned by production employees for the time they spend performing tasks not directly related to production.

Indirect Materials (2) Low-cost materials that are difficult to associate with specific units of a final product.

Indirect Product Costs (2) See **Factory Overhead.**

Indirect Segment Costs (11) See **Common Segment Costs.**

Inflation (17) Purchasing power of money declines as prices rise.

Input-Output Approach to Budgeting (6) A method of budgeting physical inputs and costs based on a planned activity level.

Interdepartmental Services (9) Support activities that one service department provides to another service department within the same organization.

Internal Auditing (1) An accounting function intended to ensure that management's operating policies are being followed and that the organization's assets are properly safeguarded.

Internal Rate of Return (IRR) (14) The discount rate that equates the net present value of a project's cash inflows with the initial investment in the project (also called the **Time-Adjusted Rate of Return**).

Inventory Turnover (16) A measure of the number of times the average stock of inventory was sold and replenished during the period. It is computed as cost of goods sold divided by average inventory amount.

Investment Center (7) A responsibility center held accountable for the relationship between its profits and total assets.

Investment Tax Credit (15) A one-time tax reduction in the year of acquisition for qualifying personal property.

Job Cost Sheets (11) A record used to accumulate the costs for specific jobs in a job cost system.

Joint Costs (5, 12) The costs of producing joint products that are incurred prior to the split-off point for joint products.

Joint Products (5, 12) Two or more products simultaneously produced from common inputs by a single process or common manufacturing activity.

Labor Rate Variance (8) The difference between the actual cost of the actual labor hours and the standard cost of the actual labor hours.

Lead Time (13) The amount of time between the placement and the receipt of an order.

Least-Squares Method of Cost Estimation (3) An approach that uses the mathematical criteria of least-squares to estimate the variable and fixed elements of a mixed cost.

Linear Algebra Allocation Method (12) A procedure whereby all service department costs are allocated simultaneously both interdepartmentally and to producing departments.

Linear Programming (13) An optimizing model used to assist managers in making decisions under constrained conditions when linear relationships can be assumed.

Line Item Budget (6) A type of budget in which revenues and expenditures are assigned to specific categories and items of responsibility, often used in not-for-profit organizations.

Lump Sum Budget (6) A type of budget that is very popular with not-for-profit organizations in which only general areas are allocated revenue and expenditures.

Managed Fixed Costs (3) See **Discretionary Fixed Costs.**

Management Accounting (1) A segment of accounting concerned with providing financial information to managers and other persons inside specific organizations.

Management by Exception (1) A concept where managers focus their attention on those aspects of operations that are not operating as planned, rather than constantly monitoring all activities.

Management by Objectives (1) A concept where the head of an agency or department and the immediate superior agree to a set of short-run nonmonetary objectives, which are subsequently used as a basis of performance evaluation for the agency or department head.

Manufacturing Budget (6) A budget used to plan materials, labor and factory overhead requirements, and costs for a future period.

Manufacturing Cost Markup (5) Used for pricing, it is computed as the total predicted selling and administrative costs plus the desired profit divided by the predicted manufacturing costs.

Manufacturing Margin (10) Segment sales minus direct manufacturing costs.

Manufacturing Organizations (2) Organizations that process raw materials into finished products for sale to others.

Marginal Cost (3, 5) The varying increment in total costs required to produce and sell an additional unit.

Marginal Revenue (5) The varying increment in total revenue derived from the sale of an additional unit.

Margin of Safety (4) The excess of actual or budgeted sales over break-even sales. It indicates the amount that sales could decline before the organization would show a loss.

Materials Price Variance (8) The difference between the actual cost of the actual materials inputs and the standard cost of the actual materials inputs (also see **Materials Purchased Price Variance**).

Materials Purchased Price Variance (8) The actual cost of materials purchased minus the standard cost of materials purchased (also see **Materials Price Variance.**

Materials Quantity Variance (8) The difference between the standard cost of actual materials inputs and the standard cost of material inputs allowed for the actual outputs.

Materials Requisition Form (11) A record used to record transfers of direct materials from raw materials to work-in-process.

Merchandising Organizations (3) Organizations that buy and sell goods; included in this category are most retail organizations.

Minimum Level Approach to Budgeting (6) An approach to budgeting in which a base amount for all budget items is established and an explanation or justification is required for all amounts in excess of the base.

Mixed Costs (3) Costs that contain both a fixed and a variable cost element (also called **Semivariable Costs**).

Model (1, 13) A simplified representation of some real-world phenomenon.

Monetary Items (17) Assets and liabilities whose values are fixed in terms of nominal dollars.

Net Present Value Method (14) A method used to evaluate capital expenditures that compares the initial investment to the present value of all future cash flows using a predetermined discount rate.

Net Sales Volume Variance (7) Indicates the impact of a change in sales volume on the contribution margin, given the budgeted selling price and the budgeted variable costs.

Nominal Dollars (17) Amounts actually recorded in historical cost accounting records and presented in traditional financial statements.

Nonmonetary Items (17) Assets and liabilities whose values are not fixed in terms of nominal dollars.

Normal Equations (3) Equations used to compute the constant term and the slope that best meets the least-squares criteria.

Normal Factory Overhead Accounting (12) A method of accounting for factory overhead that uses a multiyear overhead and eliminates the need to close the balance in Factory Overhead at the end of each year.

Not-for-Profit Organizations (1) Organizations that do not have profit as a goal.

Objective Function (13) In linear programming, this is the goal to be maximized or minimized.

Operating Activities (6) Activities performed in conducting the daily affairs of an organization. They include such things as purchasing, production, and sales.

Operating Budget (6) A formal financial document that indicates planned revenues and expenses and other activities for a future period.

Operating Loss (15) The excess of operating expenses over operating revenues that ordinarily may be carried back three years and carried forward fifteen years.

Opportunity Cost (2) The net cash inflow that could be obtained if the resources committed to one action were used in the most desirable other alternative action.

Optimal Solution (13) In linear programming, this is the feasible solution that maximizes or minimizes the value of the objective function.

Optimizing Models (13) A type of quantitative model that suggests a specific choice between decision alternatives.

Order Filling Costs (7) Costs incurred to place finished goods in the hands of the purchasers.

Order Getting Costs (7) Costs incurred to obtain a customer's order.

Order Quantity (13) The amount of inventory ordered at a particular time.

Organization (1) A group of people united to achieve a common goal.

Organization Chart (1) An illustration of the formal relationships that exist among the elements of an organization.

Organizing (1) The process of making the organization into a well-ordered whole.

Outlay Costs (5) Future costs that require future expenditures of cash or other resources.

Overtime Premiums (2) Bonus wages in excess of the regular hourly rate paid to production employees who are working more than the regular number of hours.

Participation Budget (6) An approach to budgeting in which managers at all levels, and in some cases even nonmanagers, become involved in budget preparation. Because this budget approach often starts at the lowest levels of management, it is sometimes called **Bottom-Up Budgeting.**

Partnership (15) An unincorporated business ordinarily owned by two or more individuals.

Payback Method (14) An approach to evaluating capital expenditures on the basis of their payback period.

Payback Period (14) The length of time necessary for the cumulative operating cash inflows from a project to equal the initial cash investment for the project.

Payback Reciprocal (14) The ratio that results when the annual operating cash flows of an investment are divided by the initial investment amount.

Payoff Table (13) A table used to enumerate the alternative actions management may take and the possible monetary outcomes of each.

Performance Reports (1) Reports provided to management during and after the budget period that compare actual results with plans.

Period Costs (2) Expired nonproduct costs; they are always an expense.

Physical Models (13) Scaled-down versions or replicas of physical reality.

Physical Quantity Method (12) A method of allocating joint costs on the basis of relative quantities of specific common physical characteristics possessed by the various joint products.

Planning (1) The formulation of a scheme or program for the accomplishment of a specific purpose or goal.

Planning, Programming, and Budgeting Systems (PPBS) (6) A concept that emphasizes outputs, rather than inputs, of an organization in programmed areas.

Predetermined Factory Overhead Rate (2) An overhead rate determined at the start of the year by dividing the predicted overhead costs for the year by the predicted activity level.

Present Value (Appendix) The current worth of a specified amount of money to be received at some future date at some discount rate.

Present Value Index (14) The number of present value dollars generated per dollar of initial investment (also called the **Profitability Index**).

Price Earnings Ratio (16) The current market price of a firm's stock divided by its earnings per share of stock.

Price Index (17) A standardized measure of the amount of money needed to purchase a standardized package or basket of goods and services.

Price Variance (8) The actual costs of actual inputs minus the standard cost of actual inputs.

Prime Product Costs (2) Direct materials costs plus direct labor costs.

Product Costing (2) The process of assigning costs to inventories as they are converted from raw materials to finished goods.

Product Costing System (11) A system used to assign manufacturing costs to products consisting of the records of manufacturing inventories, activities, and costs.

Product Costs (2) Costs assigned to products as they are produced that are expensed when the products are sold.

Production Budget (6) A budget indicating the number of units of product an organization plans to produce in a coming period. It is based on predicted sales, adjusted for beginning inventory and desired ending inventory.

Product Margin (10) Product sales revenue less direct product costs.

Product Reporting (10) A type of reporting in which revenues and expenses are presented for product lines of an organization.

Profitability Index (PI) (14) See **Present Value Index.**

Profit Center (7) A responsibility center held accountable for both revenues and costs and evaluated on their differences.

Profit-Volume-Graph (4) A graph used to illustrate the relationship between volume and profits.

Pro Forma Financial Statements (6) Hypothetical financial statements that reflect the "as if" effects of budgeted activity on the financial position of a firm.

Property Tax (15) A tax based on the ownership of property. It is usually determined by multiplying a statutory tax rate (referred to as a tax millage) times the assessed value of the property.

Purchasing Power Gains and Losses (17) Gains and losses that result from changes in the purchasing power of money during a given period.

Quantitative Models (13) A series of algebraic relationships intended to represent some real-world relationships.

Quantity Variance (8) The standard cost of actual inputs minus the standard cost of inputs allowed for the outputs produced.

Quick Ratio (16) See **Acid Test Ratio.**

Raw Materials Inventories (2) The physically existing items that are to be converted into a finished product.

Raw Materials Inventory Record (11) A record used to record increases and decreases in the available balance for each type of raw material.

Relevant Costs (2) Costs that differ among competing alternatives.

Relevant Range (3) The area of operation, within which a linear cost function is a good approximation of the economists' curvilinear cost function.

Reorder Point (13) The inventory level at which an order for additional units is placed.

Replacement Cost (17) The current cost to purchase or reproduce an asset or its productive capacity.

Residual Income (9) The excess of investment center income over the minimum return set by the company.

Residual Income Ratio (9) The residual income divided by the investment base.

Responsibility Accounting (7) The structuring of performance reports addressed to individual or group members of an organization in a manner that emphasizes factors controllable by them.

Responsibility Center (7) A person or organizational unit that has been assigned certain responsibilities. Examples are investment centers, profit centers, revenue centers, and cost centers.

Return on Assets (16) A measure of the ability of the firm to profitably use its assets. It is computed as net income plus net-of-tax interest expense divided by average total assets.

Return on Equity (16) A measure of the profits attributable to the shareholders as a percentage of their equity in the firm. It is computed as net income divided by average stockholder's equity.

Return on Investment (9) A measure of the earnings per dollar of investment. It is computed by dividing the income of the investment center by its asset base.

Return on Sales (16) A measure of the ability of the firm to generate profits from sales. It is computed as net income plus net-of-tax interest expense divided by sales.

Revenue Budgets (6) Budgets that establish the amount expected to be collected from each revenue source during the upcoming period.

Revenue Center   (7) A responsibility center held accountable for generating sales revenue.

Robinson–Patman Act   (5) A law of the United States that prohibits firms from charging purchasers different prices when the purchasers compete with each other in the sale of their products.

Safety Stocks   (13) The actual units of inventory carried to prevent stockouts due to variations in the demand for units during the lead time.

Sales Budget   (6) A forecast of unit and dollar sales volume. It may also contain a forecast of sales collections.

Sales Mix   (4) The relative portion of unit or dollar sales that is derived from each product or service.

Sales Price Variance   (7) The total difference in revenues for the actual sales volume resulting from a change in the selling price from the budgeted price.

Sales Value Method   (12) A method of allocating joint costs based on the relative sales values of the joint products.

Sales Volume Variance   (7) The impact on revenues of a change in sales volume, assuming no change in selling price.

Scatter Diagram   (3) A graph of actual volume and cost data.

Segment Margin   (10) The amount that a segment contributes toward the common (indirect) costs of an organization and toward profit of the organization.

Segment Reports   (10) Income statements that show operating results for some portion or segment of a business.

Selling Expense Budget   (6) A schedule of the costs and disbursements the organization plans to incur in connection with budgeted sales and distribution.

Semivariable Costs   (3) See **Mixed Costs.**

Sensitivity Analysis   (4) The study of the responsiveness of a model's dependent variable(s) to changes in one or more of the model's independent variables.

Service Costing   (2) The process of assigning costs to units of service.

Service Department   (12) A department that provides support functions for one or more production departments.

Service Organizations   (2) Nonmanufacturing firms that perform work for others. Included in this category are banks, hospitals, and real estate agencies.

Simplex Method   (13) A mathematical technique used to solve linear programming problems.

Slope   (3) The responsiveness of cost to changes in volume in a cost-volume relationship (also see **Variable Cost**).

Sole Proprietorship   (15) An unincorporated business owned by one individual.

Solvency   (16) The ability of a firm to pay its debts as they come due.

Split-Off Point   (5, 12) The point in a process where the joint products emerge as separately identifiable products or units.

Standard Cost (7) A budget for one unit of product. It indicates what it should cost to produce one unit of product under efficient operating conditions.

Standard Cost Center (7) A cost center that has clearly defined relationships between effort and accomplishment and uses a standard cost system.

Standard Cost Variance Analysis (8) The process of analyzing flexible budget variances.

Standard Error of the Estimate (3) A measure of the variability of actual costs around the cost estimating equation. It is used to construct probability intervals for cost estimates.

Statement of Changes in Financial Position (16) An overall summary of all major transactions that cause changes in the balance sheet (statement of financial position) between two statement dates.

Statement of Cost of Goods Manufactured (2) A financial summary of the activity in the Work-in-Process inventory accounts. It may also summarize activity in the Raw Materials inventory account.

Statement of Cost of Goods Manufactured and Sold (2) A financial summary of the activity in all major inventory accounts.

Static Budget (7) A budget based on a prior prediction of expected sales and production.

Step Allocation Method (12) A procedure whereby service department costs are allocated in a manner that gives partial recognition to interdepartmental services among the service departments.

Step Costs (3) Costs that are constant within a range of activity, but different between ranges of activity.

Subchapter S Corporation (15) A business legally organized as a corporation, that has opted under a special provision of the tax law to be taxed as a partnership with income flowing directly to the individuals holding the shares of stock.

Sunk Costs (2) Historical costs that result from past decisions that management no longer has control over.

Target Rate of Return (14) The minimum acceptable rate used by firms to decide which projects to accept.

Tax Avoidance (15) The reduction of taxes by legitimate means.

Tax Base (15) A monetary measurement of the conditions or activities subject to taxes, such as taxable income and assessed value.

Tax Deferral (15) The planning and timing of transactions to cause legal delays in the payment of taxes.

Tax Rate (15) A percentage that is multiplied times the tax base to determine total taxes.

Territory Margin (10) The contribution margin of the territory less the related direct fixed expenses associated with a given market area.

Time Adjusted Rate of Return (14) See **Internal Rate of Return.**

Times Interest Earned   (16) A measure of interest paying ability, computed as the earnings available to pay interest divided by the total interest expense.

Top-Down Approach to Budgeting   (6) See **Imposed Budget.**

Transfer Price   (9) The internal value assigned a product or service one division provides to another.

Transferred-In Costs   (11) Costs assigned to units transferred in from a previous department.

Treasurer   (1) The officer responsible for money management in an organization.

Uncertainty   (16) A condition that exists when the probability of an event's occurring is less than 100 percent.

Unexpired Costs   (2) Incurred costs recorded as assets on the statement of financial position.

Unfavorable Variances   (1) Variances that result when actual costs exceed allowed costs.

Unit Contribution Margin   (4) The difference between unit selling price and unit variable costs.

Value Added Tax   (15) A tax based on the value added to the goods produced during a period.

Value of Perfect Information   (13) The maximum amount a manager would be willing to pay for additional information.

Variable Cost   (3) The uniform incremental cost of each additional unit.

Variable Costing   (10) A product costing procedure whereby only variable manufacturing costs are assigned to products (also called **Direct Costing**).

Variable Cost Markup   (5) Used for product pricing, it is computed as the total of the predicted fixed costs plus targeted profit divided by the predicted variable costs.

Variable Cost Ratio   (4) The ratio of variable costs to sales revenue. It indicates the portion of each sales dollar that is used to cover variable costs.

Variable Overhead Efficiency Variance   (8) The difference between the standard variable overhead cost for the actual activity and the standard variable overhead cost of the activity allowed for the actual outputs.

Variable Overhead Spending Variance   (8) Difference between the actual variable overhead cost incurred and the standard variable overhead cost for the actual activity base inputs.

Variance   (1) The difference between actual and allowed costs.

Variance Analysis   (8) The process of analyzing the difference between the actual cost and the standard cost allowed by the flexible budget for manufacturing a product or providing a service.

Volume Variance   (8) The difference between the total budgeted fixed overhead and the total standard fixed overhead assigned to production.

Weighted Average Inventory Method (11) In process costing, an inventory valuation procedure where all equivalent units in process are assigned the same average cost.

Working Capital (16) The difference between current assets and current liabilities.

Work-in-Process Inventories (2) The raw materials that are in the process of being converted into a finished product.

Zero Base Budgeting (6) An approach to budgeting based on the premise that every dollar of a budget expenditure must be justified.

Index